Food and Morality
Proceedings of the Oxford Symposium on Food and Cookery 2007

Food
and
Morality

Proceedings of the Oxford Symposium on Food and Cookery 2007

Edited by Susan R. Friedland

Prospect Books
2008

First published in Great Britain in 2008 by Prospect Books, Allaleigh House, Blackawton, Totnes, Devon, TQ9 7DL.

ISBN 978-1-903018-59-0

The illustration on the cover is courtesy of Charles Foster-Hall.

Design and typesetting in Gill Sans and Adobe Garamond by Tom Jaine.
Printed and bound in Great Britain by The Cromwell Press, Trowbridge.

Contents

5

7

Food in a Time of War:
Food Rationing in Britain during World War II

Joan P. Alcock

Before the War

Before World War II, the British government had had experience of enforcing a rationing policy and had also determined that this should be on nutritional principles. During World War I a Ministry of Food had been created to ensure that certain foodstuffs were rationed and that a policy of fair shares was ensured, which on the whole was successful and would act as a precedent. The war also revealed that a nutritional policy was necessary as many poor people were ill fed, and the Depression exacerbated their condition. The studies of Broadley and Crawford (1937) and John Boyd Orr (1934; 1936; 1940) revealed many people had diets deficient in vitamins and low in calories. Based on these studies, on information by other writers, such as George Orwell's *The Road to Wigan Pier* (1937) and on his own researches, the government's Scientific Advisor to the Ministry of Food, Jack Drummond, produced a wartime diet based on sound nutritional principles (Fergusson 2007), paying special attention to vulnerable groups and devising a system of vitamin classification (Drummond 1947). In this way the government indicated that it was prepared to take moral judgments based on moral issues inevitably connected with food supply and demand.

The Beginning of War

The British government had been aware since 1936 that war was inevitable, and took a decision that food controls should be imposed once war broke out. (Hammond 1962). The Italian invasion of Abyssinia (1936) resulted in the Committee of Imperial Defence setting up a Food Supply Committee. This consulted Sir William Beveridge, Director of the London School of Economics, a former official of the Ministry of Food. Beveridge advised that an administrative system was needed so the government established a Food (Defence Plans) Department.

Ration books were printed by August 1939; in September they were ready for distribution to the total population. Britain was divided into regions. Each region had a Food Controller, who supervised local Food Offices, one in each town or rural district. Essential supplies of tea, butter, and frozen meat were identified and made ready to be moved from vulnerable port sites if necessary. Certain commodities had been stockpiled. In fact, the British government had almost caused a crisis in 1938 by buying the total supply of whale oil from Norway, the whole grain supply from Romania, and most of the Caribbean sugar crop.

War was declared on 3 September 1939. On 8 September the Ministry of Food was formally established with W.S. Morrison as its first Minister. In March 1940 Lord Woolton, who managed the Ministry with great efficiency for the next three years, succeeded Morrison. Orders were issued that any available land – lawns, gardens, roadside verges – were to be used to produce food. 'Dig for Victory' was the patriotic slogan, so that after 1940 arable land increased by over 60 per cent. Even Lord's Cricket Ground was not spared and the Tower of London moat was cultivated for vegetables (Davies 1993).

In order to make sure that food was not wasted and that its nutritional value would be appreciated, the Ministry of Food produced reams of advice including leaflets called 'Food Facts' and short films, which were flashed on local cinema screens. Although today their advice might be considered patronising, they indicated the moral tone gradually being adopted by the government. 'Eat up your greens'; 'Experiment with your meals, it gives variety and does you good'; 'Avoid fried foods, they are seldom fully digested'; 'Waste not, want not'; 'Dry cubes of bread in the oven to eat as breakfast cereal.' Potato Pete posters were a great hit: 'Potatoes are the goods'; 'Cook potatoes in their jackets and eat the jacket.'

The British Broadcasting Corporation (BBC) programme 'The Kitchen Front' every morning provided hints on the preparation of food and how to make nutritious meals from leftovers and meagre portions. Experts such as Marguerite Patten provided numerous recipes to make palatable a variety of foods including many 'mock ones' (Patten, 1985). Popular cartoon strips urged people to try different recipes. Prohibitions against hoarding were numerous. The *Daily Telegraph* (22 July 1939) emphasised the difference between hoarding and storing. The latter was intelligent storing and maintenance of an extra reserve supply of perishable goods.

In 1940 Lord Woolton announced that tea would be rationed to two ounces per head and expounded his moral views (*Daily Telegraph* 9 July 1940). After stating that 20 to 25 cups of tea could be made from two ounces, he said, 'I am stopping luxurious feeding.' The time had come for people to undertake hard living conditions. It would become a criminal offence to waste food. The hotel trade was told that it must stop all luxury feeding, cutting cut out the meat or the fish course. Later, hotels and restaurants were ordered to keep the price of meals to five shillings (25p) but they could add a 'house charge,' a 'dance band charge' and other charges, and it was obvious that austerity eating was not going to be shared by all the population.

Rationing

The Ministry avoided using the term rationing, preferring to speak of allowances. The policy was that, if commodities were available, the public shared in them. Thus possession of a ration book guaranteed or allowed a share in what was available. The public was not fooled. It spoke of rationing and knew what was implied. When the expected air raids did not arrive, the government hesitated about rationing. But when imports of butter and bacon from Denmark ceased in January 1940, rationing began. On 8 January the Ministry 'allowed' four ounces of bacon and four ounces of butter weekly. The public responded by hoarding food, especially sugar, so the Ministry quickly responded by 'allowing' the public eight ounces of sugar a week. Rationing of other foods followed. In July rationing of chocolates and sweets began, and children under five were not allowed a tea ration.

Ration books

Rationing was not to be by price control, because this would allow the richer part of the population to obtain more food. A ration book entitled a person to obtain an essential supply of commodities (*Your Food in Wartime*. Public Information Leaflet, No. 4, July 1939). Adults' books were a buff colour; adolescents' had a blue cover; babies had a green book; children under six (later five) and the armed forces had differently coloured books. In addition, coupons for sweets and 'points' varied each month. These were used to buy tinned goods such as soup, fish and meat, dried fruit, pulses, breakfast cereals, and biscuits.

At first the retailer sent coupons, cut from books, to the supplier, via the Food Office. Inspectors made spot checks, but the millions of tiny squares overwhelmed the system. In 1941, the retailer was ordered to cancel squares with a blue pencil. Later, instead of each commodity having a single page, each was placed in date order so that a single stroke cancelled a week's rations. Each book had a counterfoil that was handed to the retailer in order to register and also an application for a new book.

11

Registration

The key to the whole policy was registration. Each person was tied to a retailer who issued the requisite allowance. Most people registered with one shop, as it was easier. The retailer registered with a supplier, who issued goods according to the number of people registered and on the authority of a permit issued by the Ministry of Food. The morality of tying consumer to retailer to supplier reduced the risk of fraud and the misuse of ration books. If a ration book was stolen, in theory it could not be used by anyone else for basic commodities, though the sweet coupons and the points could be cut out. It is not certain how many illegal ration books were issued but policing their use depended on the integrity of the retailer. If ration books were genuinely destroyed, as for example in an air raid, new books were immediately issued. Great trust was placed on the individual, which for the most part, was honoured.

Food rations

The government's aim was to ensure a fair distribution of food and an allowance or ration that was morally acceptable to the public and provided a reasonably nutritious diet. The amount of food which the Ministry deemed adequate varied weekly. Rationing continued until 1954 and some of the smallest amounts of food were

12

RATIONS FOR ONE WEEK IN 1941

1 EGG

4 oz BUTTER

2oz LARD

2oz MARGARINE

2 oz CHEESE

2 oz BACON

2oz TEA

8 oz SUGAR

4oz SWEETS

2 PINTS OF MILK

2 CHOPS

2 SAUSAGES

2 SLICES OF CORNED BEEF

The average weekly rations for one person

issued in 1946 and 1947 when Britain was struggling to pay her war debts and the weather was harsh. (A list of foods and their quantities is given in Appendix A.) Meat, as in World War I, was rationed by value and not by price, and folk memory has to recall what could be obtained for 1s 1d. Extra rations were issued at Christmas and a special allowance was made in June 1953 to enable people to celebrate the coronation of Queen Elizabeth II. Bread was not rationed during the war years but for a two-year period beginning in July 1946. Male factory workers had 15 ounces per week and female workers 11 ounces. People were expected to fill up with potatoes.

Allowances and a welfare policy

One of the most remarkable facts about the whole organisation was how carefully the Ministry of Food decided allowances, basing their judgement on what it thought the public would accept. Government propaganda was utilized to make people accept changes in rations, and the Ministry of Food was given total control of rations. The basic ration of bacon for example changed 35 times in fourteen years. The quantity was more regular during the wartime years than afterwards. It remained at four ounces from 10 June 1940 to 23 July 1944, but in 1950 the variations were as follows: 29 January 5 oz; 23 April 4 oz; 18 June 3 oz; 8 October 4 oz; 22 October 3 oz; 17 December 5 oz; and 24 December 3 oz. This painstaking attempt to be fair, the calculation of stocks which would allow such precise alterations, and the courting of unpopularity by announcing the reducing of the ration on Christmas Eve fill one with a sense of awe.

13

A sugar allowance of eight ounces a week seems generous, but at the time the British heaped sugar into tea. The ration also provided for all baking, preserving and jam-making. The obtaining of other sweeteners such as honey and treacle was controlled by the points system. A mixed morality underlay this, for the government hoped that this would reduce the population's dependency on sugar, not merely for health reasons, but also to reduce imports from overseas.

Vegetables and potatoes were not rationed but their availability depended on production and storage methods, which were not always efficient. In 1940, for example, carrot and onion crops were so abundant that they could not be distributed quickly and much was ploughed into the land. The Ministry planned to distribute the 1941 crop more quickly, but unfortunately the 1941 summer was wet and cold. Much of the onion crop failed, few sacks were available to bag the remainder, and reports sent in by growers reached the food offices when many officials were on holiday. Although the onion crop rotted in the ground, the carrot crop had a second bumper year, but nothing was done to move it or to sell it locally. People went into the fields to pick what they could.

Vegetables and fruits were sold locally though sales were often erratic being organised by local retailers. Often bush telegraph resulted in a queue forming quickly and it was up to the conscience of the shop keeper whether to serve anyone or keep goods 'under the counter' for loyal customers. To ensure supplies, dried eggs replaced fresh eggs, milk by National Dried Milk, and vegetables by dehydrated vegetables. Many households preserved eggs by placing them in isinglass or pickling hard-boiled eggs, a favourite food in Northern England.

A welfare policy with strong moral overtones was developed during the war, often in subtle ways, although this was not the first concern of the Ministry, which felt that its primary duty had to be the control of regular food supplies and prices, and ensure equality in the event of shortages. But the Ministry had to check the effect of food allowances and thus was forced to initiate a health policy. For example, the almost complete lack of citrus fruits meant children and expectant mothers received vitamin C in bottles of blackcurrant or rose-hip syrup and from concentrated orange juice, shipped from the United States, a policy devised by Drummond.

Vitamin A came in cod liver oil often blended with groundnut (peanut) oil. Later this was reinforced with synthetic calciferol to provide vitamin D. An aggressive advertising campaign ensured that children and expectant mothers took these products. The result was an improvement in infant and children's health and a decline in the infant mortality rate. Bread was fortified with synthetic vitamin B, dried milk and margarine with vitamin A and D. Vitamin supplements were available for expectant mothers and the elderly. The National Wholemeal Loaf, though disliked thanks to our preference for white bread, provided the public with more dietary fibre than they were used to eating.

14

Exceptions to the normal rations

The government showed the same careful consideration of fair allowance and was careful to avoid controversy when food could not be eaten for religious or moral reasons. In October 1939, for example, it announced that Jewish people would be allowed extra butter or margarine in lieu of bacon. The next month, however, the *Jewish Chronicle* wrote that as rationing affected only butter, bacon, and ham there was no need for Jews to be granted extra butter. Its editorial added, somewhat warily, that if extra rations were granted this might result in an outbreak of anti-Semitism.

By October 1941 this stance had lessened. The Ministry of Food announced special concessions to Orthodox Jews. They could apply to their Local Food Office to have cooking fats coupons in ration books marked vegetarian-kosher margarine. To obtain this concession they would have to surrender their bacon coupons, which as the Ministry pointed out, no Orthodox Jew needed.

In February 1943 the Ministry went further, granting an extra two ounces of vegetarian margarine per week, but as supplies of vegetarian cooking fats were now available, the option of allowing them to take their cooking fats in the form of vegetarian margarine was to be withdrawn. When new ration books were issued in June 1944 Jews had to visit their local Food Office to ensure that bacon coupons were cancelled and vegetarian margarine coupons issued instead. They had to tell their grocer of this change and he had to pass on the applications in bulk to the food office. How far these regulations were followed by the Jewish population is unclear, but given the problems that had been endured by Jews fleeing Germany in the 1930s, most felt they must adhere to the system.

Vegetarians were treated with equal respect. They were also allowed extra cheese, mainly 12 ounces a week, and vegetarian margarine. Nut-butter might be supplied in place of butter or cooking fats. A new page of coupons had to be inserted in a ration book for the extra cheese ration. In their case ration books had to contain unused cooking fats, meat and bacon coupons for three months before they could claim special ration allowances. Applicants had to apply to their local Food Office with their ration book. They had to fill in a 'Form of Declaration' and send it to the Secretary of the Vegetarian Society to be countersigned.

To ensure vegetarians had enough protein the cheese ration was carefully maintained. In April 1944, for example, the Ministry of Food announced that although the cheese ration was to be reduced to two ounces the rations for vegetarians would be unchanged at 12 ounces. It is also clear that unofficial bartering also occurred. Families that disliked cheese exchanged their ration with vegetarians who could supply them with other food (although not meat and bacon as vegetarians had surrendered their meat and bacon coupons). Fresh fruit and vegetables were not rationed, but as in the case of the rest of the population, it often depended where a person lived as to whether supplies were easily obtained. The Vegetarian Society urged its members to buy as much as they could at local health food shops to ensure that the largest repeat supplies of commodities could be available. The BBC included vegetarian recipes in 'The Kitchen Front' broadcasts and these also helped other people to supplement their normal diet.

During the war the Vegetarian Society continued to cooperate with the Ministry of Food to ensure that alternative foods, such as dried fruits and nuts, were available.

This liaison was so successful that in 1944 the society wrote that the Ministry had 'received the Committee of Vegetarian Interests appeals and protests with courtesy and understanding and vegetarians have little to complain about in the matter of retailing' (*Vegetarian Messenger and Health Review*, 41.4. 1944, 232).

Results of rationing

During fourteen years the British public was compelled to change its eating habits and in doing so the health of the nation improved. Infant and maternal mortality dropped and anaemia declined. Fifty years later a series of articles, TV programmes, and books praised the diet forced on the public between 1940 and 1954 especially the reduction in the consumption of fats and sugar. The Ministry of Food, following Drummond's advice, evolved a low cholesterol, high fibre diet which, together with a reduction in the amount of food consumed, provided a diet that nutritionists are advising the general public to adopt today. The public, whether it liked it or not, was being bullied into a healthier lifestyle. This was not appreciated at the time because of the lack of variety of food, the monotony of having to prepare meals with the same ingredients, and the inability to substitute one item for another.

Lack of meat meant increased consumption of vegetables and potatoes. Because fruit was scarce, it was appreciated much more. The public moaned that it had no treats such as cream but it was the better for not having them. The bitterest complaint was deprivation in sweets, chocolate, and sugar, but this ensured a cutting down in sweet products. The notorious British sweet tooth either accommodated itself to saccharine and its unpleasant metallic taste or did without. Consequently the amount of dental caries was reduced.

Although the lack of fats and protein might be debilitating to part of the population, on the whole the more vulnerable sections obtained more protein and vitamins and a much healthier diet than that they had had formerly They also received a fairer share of the food supply especially as prices were kept as low as possible. Meat prices, for example, were not increased dramatically until 1949.

The government had a moral purpose to ensure that food was not wasted and that the nation should eat as healthily as possible. The public also was censorious where food was concerned. People found to be hoarding or wasting food, such as throwing away unused bread or scraps that might go to feed pigs were very sharply told to stop this by watchful neighbours. A Bethnal Green Food Officer, making a surprise visit to a house, found over 70 mouldy loaves, together with spoiled jam and margarine. A magistrate sentenced the woman to two months imprisonment and criticised her sharply, saying that this was a very serious case: 'In these days when men are giving their lives on the high seas in order to bring food, you are wasting enough food to feed many families' (*Military Illustrated*, March 2007, 23).

Enforcement officers checked food that needed a permit such as eggs. Anyone who kept over 25 hens had to sell the eggs to a licensed buyer or packer and not to an individual or a local café. Disobeying this meant the egg supplier was fined, as happened in Congleton, Cheshire, where a café proprietor was fined £9 (almost three weeks' wages) for obtaining fresh eggs from an unlicensed individual and not keeping a daily record of meals and beverages served (*Congleton Chronicle*, 15 January 1949). Outrage was expressed when people obtained rations to which they were not entitled. Congleton Food Control Committee was told of a woman who obtained extra oranges by erasing the lead pencil marks in the ration book and going back for more. She had then 'bragged about this' (*Congleton Chronicle*, 29 October 1943).

Nevertheless, many people were willing to obtain goods on the black market (Smithies 1982). The government played down the extent of this and Lord Woolton, thought that the tough penalties for infringement of food regulations meant that few were willing to ignore them. In this he was totally wrong and although over 130,000 people were fined or imprisoned, the black market thrived. On a minor scale bakers would exchange products with milkmen, and butchers would keep something 'under the counter' for favoured customers (Chamberlain 1972, 75). People bartered one food for another: cheese for tea, sweet coupons for sugar. On a major scale goods were sold openly in local markets. Stolen goods from the docks found their way onto market stalls. In the East End of London farmers from East Anglia brought food to markets at Romford and in Petticoat Lane where it was eagerly snapped up by the local population as well as West End restaurateurs (*Military Illustrated*, March 2007, 18). Prosecutions were few and fines proved no deterrent.

Industrial canteens and schools provided communal feeding. British restaurants, run by local authorities, introduced the public to the concept of self-service and provided an adequately balanced two-course meal at reasonable prices. Winston Churchill, the British Prime Minister, ordered that these should not be called Communal Feeding Centres in case they deterred people from using them. Organisations such as the WVS (Women's Voluntary Service) and the Salvation Army regarded it as a moral duty that they should provide mobile canteens to feed people in bomb-damaged areas. Often, after a bombing raid, cauldrons of soup were cooked on open fires in the streets.

Larger families pooled rations, especially if there were small children because they received the equivalent of adult rations apart from meat. The two groups who suffered the most were single persons and adolescent boys who always seemed to be hungry. School meals and canteen meals helped, but many boys did not feel their hunger was satisfied until they were conscripted into the armed forces. Members of the armed forces were given ration cards when they came home on leave so that their families did use their own rations to feed them. People going on holiday or staying in hotels handed over ration books to the establishment so that they could be used to obtain rations. The sense of a puritan morality of fairness that no one should be deprived or suffer a shortage was obvious.

17

End of rationing

Had rationing ceased in 1945 more would have given approval to the system. But rationing continued; possibly, as has been suggested, as part of the Labour Government's policy to impose a collective utopia on Britain by encouraging a moral purpose of fair shares for all (Zweiniger-Bargielowskar 2000). Food supplies from the United States and other countries were diverted to help a starving Europe and there was a world food shortage especially in cereal crops, which meant bread and flour were rationed in July 1946; bread units (BUs) were issued, each one representing a given weight of bread. The winter of 1946–47 was particularly severe when snow fell steadily until the end of March. Rations were then at their lowest level, cheese, butter, and tea being reduced to two ounces per week, bacon to two ounces per fortnight and meat to one shilling a week; vegetables and potatoes were in short supply.

When rationing ended in July 1954 there was a burning of ration books, which accounts for the fact that these have became a rare commodity. Before that, certain foods had already been derationed: bread in 1948, tea in 1952, sweets and chocolate in 1953. By then people were tired of rationing and the restraints that it put on them. The public might have wanted things to be fair, but as far as they were concerned the war was over and restrictions should be removed.

No amount of government propaganda alleviated the resentment felt by hair-dressers who were prosecuted for giving clients a cup of tea and a biscuit. Food hints became more bizarre: 'For a nourishing meal for all the family, hare is recommended. Small families may enjoy wood pigeon.' The government in 1948 had imported ten million tons of snoek from South Africa. Nothing urged by the then Minister of Food, John Strachey, saying that 'it is good and palatable' would persuade the public to buy it. They were proved right in 1950 when the minister admitted that it was the dullest fish he had ever eaten. It is rumoured that eventually it was used in tins of cat food. The cats' reaction is not recorded, but the public also recoiled in horror from eating horsemeat and whale meat.

It cannot be denied that there were often shortages, that the system was not totally fair, and that the imposition of state control over food supplies was resented, as was the fact that richer people managed to eat well. Producing meals was a boring and wearisome task and recipes issued to the public were greeted with suspicion. Food parcels, sent from America and Australia, helped to relieve monotony. Probably only half the nation fully accepted the necessity of rationing. Rationing is essentially ineq-uitable in that it provides the same quantities of food for each person without any consideration of his or her needs and eating habits. But the alternative is to consider what would have happened without rationing and whether the public would have been fed so successfully. Even in 1943 when German U-boat attacks were at their most ferocious and Winston Churchill feared that Britain had only three week's food supplies, the nation was reasonably well fed and relatively healthy. The moral verdict must be that during World War II, the government produced, possibly without realis-ing it, one of the fairest and healthiest eating policies of the twentieth century.

APPENDIX

Weekly basic food rations during World War II
(Information taken from official records of the detailed items per week issued by Defence Emergencies and Crop Improvement Division, Ministry of Food, 1940–1954.)

Bacon and ham: 2 oz to 4 oz. End of rationing: 3 July 1953.
Cheese: 1 oz to 6 oz. End of rationing: 8 May 1954.
Cooking fats: 1 oz to 3 oz. End of rationing 8 May 1954.
Butter and margarine: alternated between 4 oz for butter and 8 oz for margarine. End of rationing: 8 May 1954.

Sugar: 8 oz per week. This also had to cover cake and biscuit baking, and jam making and preservatives.

Tea: usually 2 oz. End of rationing: 5 October 1952.

Meat was rationed by value, usually 1s 2d a week, which would buy a small joint or some chops. End of rationing: 3 July 1954.

Corned beef when available was 2 oz per week.

Milk: 2 pints.

Eggs: 1 per week plus 1 packet dried egg per 4 weeks.

Sweets: 12 oz per 4 weeks.

Tinned food, biscuits, dried fruit and certain pulses were allotted points. Tinned salmon, particularly appreciated for Sunday tea in the north of England, was rated at 16 points in December 1941 and a horrendous 32 points by March 1942.

Bread and flour were rationed between July 1946 and July 1948. Flour was bought in sealed tins.

Sir Jack Drummond (Fergusson, 2007, 48) estimated an ideal weekly ration as bacon and ham: 4 oz; butter: 2 oz; Cheese: 2 oz; margarine: 4 oz; cooking fat: 4 oz; sugar: 8 oz; tea: 2 oz; sweets: 12 oz; milk: 3 pints and 1 packet of dried skimmed milk; preserves: 1 lb every 2 months; eggs: 1 shell egg and 1 packet of dried egg per month.

Bibliography

Boyd Orr, J., *National Food Supply and its Influence on National Health* (London: Macmillan, 1934).

Boyd Orr, J., *Food, Health and Income* (London: Macmillan, 1936).

Boyd Orr, J. and Lubbock, D., *Feeding the People in Wartime* (London: Methuen, 1940).

Broadley, H. and Crawford, W., *The People's Food* (Kingswood: Windmill Press, 1938).

Chamberlain, E. R., *Life in Wartime Britain* (London: Batsford, 1972).

Davies, J., *The Wartime Kitchen and Garden* (London: BBC Publications, 1993).

Drummond, J., 'Scientific Approaches to Food Problems during the War' (*Nutrition, Dietetics, Catering*, I 1947, 47).

Fergusson, J., 'A Menu for Murder,' *The Guardian Weekly*, May 19, 2007.

Hammond, R. J., *Food*, History of the Second World War, Volume III. (London: HMSO. and Longmans Green, 1962).

H. M. S. O. 'How Britain was Fed in Wartime,' *Food Control 1939–45* (London: HMSO, 1946).

Orwell, G., *The Road to Wigan Pier* (London: Gollancz, 1937).

Patten, M., *We'll Eat Again* (London: Hamlyn, 1985).

Smithies, E., *Crime in Wartime* (London: George Allen and Unwin, 1982).

Zweiniger-Bargielowska, I., *Austerity in Britain: Rationing, Controls and Consumption, 1939–1954* (Oxford: Oxford University Press, 2000).

The archives of the Imperial War Museum, London, contain information on rationing and the museum often has excellent exhibitions relating to the 1939–1954 food policy.

I am grateful to Professor Bryan Reuben for help in obtaining information on Jewish rations, to Su Taylor, Press Officer of the Vegetarian Society, and to organisations, relatives, and friends for memories of wartime food.

The Moral Economy of Red Meat in Australia

Rachel A. Ankeny

Since the middle of the twentieth century when the Australian government began keeping statistics on food consumption, annual individual consumption of meat has not changed dramatically, ranging from a low of 90 kilograms to a high of 120 kilograms, with an average consumption of around 111 kilograms per person as of 1999 (the last year for which government statistics are available).[1] A recent nutritional survey found that over 65 per cent of respondents had moderate meat consumption (eating red meat between one and four times per week) and close to 11 per cent had high meat consumption (eating red meat daily or almost daily).[2] Until recently, the bulk of consumption has been of red meats, but chicken consumption has risen significantly to around 33 kilograms per person annually, one of the highest rates in the world, with beef consumption dropping to around 37 kilograms.[3] There has been a recognised general trend toward decreasing red meat consumption since the 1970s.[4] Pork consumption has risen slightly, but lamb and mutton consumption also are declining though not as dramatically as beef.[5]

These trends are somewhat surprising in a country well recognised for its red meat consumption; in 1897, Dr Philip Muskett infamously and ironically described meat eating as 'almost a religion' for Australians.[6] Throughout much of its history, Australians have been among the world's biggest eaters of red meat per capita. The attraction of fresh meat was used as an enticement to migrants in early 1800s, as it was not commonly available to the working classes in England. The slogan 'Meat Three Times a Day' was used in 1847 to promote the improved lifestyle one could have in the colonies, where meat was cheap and sometimes even cheaper than bread on a pound-for-pound basis.[7]

Scholars trace the changes in modern consumption rates to a range of factors including new culinary interests particularly the increasing popularity of international or ethnic cuisines, changing lifestyles including less time available for food purchasing and preparation, the rise of health consciousness, and the development of new food products including different cuts of meats that are faster to cook or pre-cut for easy preparation.[8] In addition, beef has fared much less well than chicken in recent surveys of consumer perceptions; for instance in a 2002 survey, chicken outscored beef on all criteria including taste, versatility, ease of preparation, consistency, and perhaps most importantly, being nutritious and healthy.[9] Similarly a national nutrition survey conducted in 2000 showed that the primary reason reported for drops in both men and women's meat consumption was that red meat is perceived as being 'fattening,' even though the fat contained by lean Australian red meat is approximately equal to that of chicken with its skin removed, according to some estimates.[10]

Hence against this backdrop of declining red meat consumption and negative consumer perceptions of beef at least in comparison to chicken, Meat & Livestock Australia (MLA), the main organisation that markets red meat, has been facing a serious challenge to reverse these trends. MLA describes its aims as: 'promot[ing] the high quality of Australian red meat to both the domestic and international markets – its versatility and enjoyment, and value for money, with a particular focus on the important nutritional role red meat has in a healthy diet'.[11] In recent years, MLA has run a series of campaigns designed to promote beef and lamb consumption. This paper examines two of these campaigns with particular focus on the campaigns' uses of moralizing content. It shows how these campaigns have reversed the logic often utilized by vegetarians, animal rights advocates, and environmentalists relating to the immorality of eating meat by developing explicit arguments that encourage consumers to eat red meat, and moreover, to view eating it as a moral duty for a variety of reasons. It is argued that the moral imperatives expressed in these campaigns are compelling because they echo current notions of personal identity as well as Australian cultural and national identity, and because they play into people's underlying attitudes toward red meat and their relationship to it.

'We Love Our Lamb'

In 2004, MLA enlisted Sam Kekovich, a former Australian rules football player turned politically-incorrect comedian, to promote the virtues of lamb. This campaign was a continuation of a strategy that began in 1999 to promote lamb in conjunction with Australia Day, in an attempt to position lamb as the 'national meat,' particularly for barbeques that are popularly associated with this end-of-summer holiday.[12] It had previously employed such controversial techniques as using a modified version of the national anthem, 'Advance Australia Fair,' with lyrics relating to lamb chops, among other strategies.[13] However, there is some evidence that these campaigns worked, as within a year of their commencement, the number of lamb servings had increased by 1.2 million per week.[14] Overall, sales of lamb grew from 1.1 billion Australian dollars in 1999 to 1.7 billion in 2005.[15]

The current campaign is clearly tongue-in-cheek, with advertisements for instance featuring Kekovich seated in front of the Australian flag with the national anthem playing (now without lyrics) in the background.[16] In one set of advertisements, he appears to be making a political address to the nation in his trademark monotone; he accuses vegetarians (as well as hippies, backpackers, and other 'dole-bludging types') of being part of a trend toward un-Australianism that is 'eroding our great traditions, like serving lamb on Australia Day.' He derides such fancy habits as wearing patterned flip-flops, and makes derogatory comments about various foreign habits. 'A balanced Australia Day diet,' he claims, 'should consist of a few nice juicy lamb chops and some beer, and perhaps a bit of pavlova for those with a sweet tooth.' The link to patriotism is explicit: 'do you think the diggers in the trenches were thinking of tofu sausages? No! They were thinking of grabbing a lamb chop off the barbie with their bare fingers.' Portions of the ad were reproduced in butchers shops, with warnings about getting caught eating anything but lamb on Australia Day; these feature informal, tabloid-style photographs of 'un-Australian' types buying pizza, fast-food chicken, and 'number 42 with rice' (a comment aimed at Asian takeaway-food) on Australia Day.

A second television ad is explicitly cast as a political promotion for the 'Australia Day Party' (fictional, but no more absurd than the names of many minor political parties in Australia) and shows other instances of un-Australianism such as having too many 'greens' (every political pun intended) in comparison to lamb chops. A third, simpler ad uses a stark graph to note the dramatic decrease in un-Australianism in direct correlation to the increase in lamb consumption.

The television ad that was broadcast on Australia Day in January 2006 explicitly connected 'un-Australian behaviour' to the Cronulla beach riots that occurred in December 2005, noting that 'you can't bash someone with a cutlet.' It also attributed the loss of the Ashes to Australian cricket players sending text messages to 'English trollops' rather than eating lamb. The threat (loaded with xenophobic overtones) is clear: 'as mishaps spread throughout the land like bird flu through a Chinese chicken coop, what [are] we doing about it?...it's time to remind ourselves of what lies at the core of our national identity: lamb chops on a barbie.' Kekovich's version of multiculturalism suggests that you should 'invite everyone over; if you can't pronounce their name, just call them 'mate' and celebrate living in the best bloody country on earth.' All of the advertisements conclude with the slogan: 'Serve lamb on Australia Day. You know it makes sense.'

Red meat as a 'Foundation Food'

The 'Foundation Food' campaign, featuring the actor Sam Neill, began in March 2006 and built on a previous campaign called 'Red Meat. Feel Good', which starred a group of dancing butchers. Instead of portraying meat as fun, as in the previous advertisements, the new campaign began utilizing scientific and nutritional evidence particularly to sell beef to a specific market, mothers. As described by the MLA, 'It has also gone a long way in repositioning red meat as a central part of the family's diet – mums are now seeing why it's so important to serve up red meat 3–4 times a week. Red meat is making its way back to the top of the shopping list.'[17] MLA reportedly spent close to $5 million on the launch alone, making this its largest-ever marketing campaign.[18]

The 'Foundation Food' campaign has had three stages thus far: the first stage, 'Evolution,' was aimed at convincing consumers, particularly mothers, that humans were 'meant' to eat red meat. Though it is unclear where this slogan originated, it is notable that a scholarly survey done in the early 2000s about perceptions with regard to vegetarianism asked respondents to consider the statement 'I think humans are meant to eat meat.' Overall 44 per cent agreed with the statement; however, agreement was correlated with gender, with women expressing lower agreement than men (39 per cent as compared to 49 per cent) and with age (only 33 per cent of those 40–55 years of age agreed, whereas 57 per cent of those 56–91 years of age agreed).[19] Hence, probably not coincidentally, this campaign targets women and those in the middle-aged and younger generations, though a few elderly women appear in one of the advertisements.

In the 'Evolution' advertisements, Neill explains the role that red meat plays in brain development: 'If our ancestors hadn't eaten red meat, our brains wouldn't be the size they are today!' The advertisements designed for glossy magazines and other print media include a dramatic vista of a rough, misty jungle, presumably where humans might have first hunted for red meat, or a timeline tracing the period from when apes jumped out of trees to when they ate meat (and became humans?), followed closely thereafter by the invention of everything from language, fire, and beer. The print advertisements also feature references to academic journal articles to substantiate their claims about brain development and function, such as 'the proteins and essential nutrients in red meat helped our brains to grow…feeding your children lean red meat 3–4 times a week can help their bodies and their brains. After all, look what it did for mankind.' The television advertisement is much more playful, but uses familiar scientific imagery such as Darwin's ascent of man from ape to humanoid (in this case, Neill is represented as the culmination of humankind).

The second commercial, 'Library,' takes Neill to a library full of attentive children quietly studying, their palpable intelligence coming from their consumption of meat. A small girl makes faces at Neill's claim that our ancestors were *Homo habilus,* and corrects him after looking up the correct answer in a thick book. As the MLA description of this commercial notes: 'Sam taught mums that protein and essential nutrients in red meat are vital for brain development – something every mum wants for a growing family.'

The latest stage of the campaign, 'Instinct,' again starring Neill, was launched in February 2007 and makes claims that craving red meat is an instinctive behaviour that humans have had for millions of years: The ad centres around a classic backyard barbeque showing how just the aroma of red meat on the barbeque arouses instinctive desires. Smaller print advertisements for magazines and display in butchers' shops emphasize that 'healthy eating has looked the same for millions of years' (accompanied by a photograph of a woman biting into a beef kebab) and 'give in to your two million year old cravings' (featuring a photo of a man biting into a steak that he is holding with his fingers, for added primitive imagery).

Some vegetarians have publicly stated that the MLA should be sued for calling meat essential or fundamental, and complaints have been filed with the Advertising Standards Bureau, but the campaign has continued to run.[20]

Discussion

The marketing of red meat in Australia appears, in a sense, to be preaching to the converted: a survey examining barriers to vegetarianism reported the main perceived barrier to adopting a vegetarian diet was 'enjoying red meat,' according to 78 per cent of respondents.[21] A study of Australians' attitudes toward red meat found that even provision of authoritative, scientific information about the potential nutritional deficiencies of red meat did not alter attitudes toward red meat among so-called high meat identifiers for whom the symbolic meanings associated with red meat are central.[22]

The Australia Day lamb campaigns, though obviously well-crafted and clever satire, play to current-day Australian fears including xenophobia and the so-called tall poppy syndrome, a negative, levelling attitude toward anyone who tries to strive higher socially, economically, or otherwise. Hence many personal qualities that are different, foreign, or 'fancy' are derided as un-Australian. The moral imperative of the Australia Day advertisements is clear: any 'good' Australian has a moral duty for love of country to consume lamb. The direct symbolic link to patriotism is left unarticulated, despite being invoked implicitly throughout the campaign; it is clear that the marketers assume that humour is more likely to be effective than an explicit, prescriptive moral message.

These advertisements also draw on a theme that was implicit in the earlier 'Feed the Man Meat!' campaign from the 1970s, namely that eating meat (and lamb in particular) is a type of moral right that one has by virtue of being Australian. This idea arises in part out of the early settler history detailed above, where eating meat in relatively large quantities was an expectation, and hence meat became a sort of cultural superfood, that is, a staple that because of its dietary prominence has special cultural or even supernatural properties.[23] This idea parallels more general trends noted by various anthropologists and sociologists that meat is the most highly prized and culturally significant of all foods in Western society, so critical to us that lack of meat is described as a 'meat hunger…a food habit that is a feature of society and is integrated into a structure of social values that may have nothing to do with the principles of nutrition.'[24]

As a group of Australian researchers has noted, those who identify themselves closely with meat are likely motivated to eat meat because 'via its symbolism [meat] allows them to maintain, enhance and express their self-concepts and human values.'[25] One of these concepts relating to identity is one's association with the nation. A study of vegetarian beliefs among Australians found that so-called cognitive vegetarians, those who are not themselves vegetarians but who hold similar beliefs about diet as vegetarians, were less likely than omnivores to identify themselves as Anglo–Australian or to have been born in Australia.[26] To be Australian in part means to eat meat, particularly red meat, with everything that entails including identifying oneself as a red meat eater. Rather than experiencing a cringe about how Australia does not measure up culturally and otherwise to other countries (particularly England), these advertisements contend that Australians should pride themselves on their traditions, be they flip-flops, barbeques, beer, or pavlova. But they particularly should celebrate the joy of being Australian by eating lamb, the national icon of the pastoral tradition associated with the early settlers. It is unclear whether this vision of the good life is open to non-Anglo Australians, those whose names can't be pronounced, but it is implied that they too can be converted to Australian ways around a lamb barbeque.

Though also drawing on humour, the Foundation Food campaign combines two more serious (and subtle) strategies: an assertion of the scientific validity of the instinct to eat meat, and an emphasis on women's moral responsibilities as mothers to provide proper nutrition for their children.

The targeting of women's moral responsibilities as mothers is an interesting twist on an old theme in Australian red meat marketing: some classic campaigns by the MLA's predecessor, the Australian Meat & Livestock Corporation, were lauded for being among the first advertising campaigns explicitly to recognize working women. As one industry observer described it, they focused on selling beef as a 'modern food-stuff relevant to working women and two-income households.'[27] This campaign also sought to overcome traditional assumptions of beef as a fatty, masculine product, which had been promoted in such early campaign slogans as 'Feed the Man Meat!' The current Foundation Food campaign shares the underlying assumption with this previous one that meat is basic, fundamental, and meant for everyday consumption.[28] However, it steers clear of the recognised association between attitudes toward meat and the traditional domination of men over women, steering clear of the so-called sexual politics of meat.[29] Instead, women are now portrayed as responsible, knowledgeable consumers who should be able to make the right choices for their families, not because of male preferences or taste, or because of the pressures of their working lives, but for scientific and nutritional reasons.

In addition, this campaign inverts a key theme associated with the symbolism of red meat, namely that it is more powerful than other foodstuffs. Such power is typically associated with humans' 'animal nature,' which includes qualities such as strength, aggression, passion, and sexuality.[30] Although the Foundation Food campaign does toy with the idea of meat consumption as instinctual, in its more serious moments it emphasizes humans as having higher cognitive abilities than other non-human animals, stressing that 'Hunting forced us to think. We learnt to work together, shape tools and communicate. The pursuit of red meat was literally making us smarter.' The scientific claims connected with these claims are extremely dubious, however. For example one scientific article that is cited describes brain size as inversely related to gut size, and increased consumption of 'high quality' food (including, but not limited to, animal products) as leading to smaller gut size; therefore due to reduced nutritional needs elsewhere in the body combined with long-term evolutionary processes, brain size increased.[31] Instead of being presented in this manner, the

25

campaign reinterprets this claim as a simple and direct causal one: eating red meat made humans brains bigger. Hence our bigger brains give us certain rights and need, which include the right and need to consume red meat.

The Foundation Food campaign also plays on a documented cultural theme previously noted by Nick Fiddes and others (in advertising, among other types of historic source materials) that meat represents domination of, among other things, humans over animals and nature.[32] The domination is implicit, as the advertisements merely claim that humans are distinct from and more advanced than other animals, particularly with regard to cognitive abilities. This claim of course is not factually controversial; what is debatable (and frequently disputed by a range of parties including animal rights activists, feminists, and vegetarians) is whether this implies a moral claim to superiority and therefore dominion of humans over non-human animals.

It is obvious that these advertising campaigns are meant to be humorous and to entertain, goals that, in my opinion, they successfully achieve. But at the same time, these advertisements also clearly are aimed at changing attitudes and particularly at changing consumer food behaviours. In so doing, they employ a complex network of cultural, historical, and social beliefs connected with red meat. But most importantly, they implicitly exploit a series of moral imperatives that are related to such deeply held beliefs as the desire to be a good mother and to be loyal to country, and thus are likely to be compelling to many viewers.

26

Bibliography

Adams, Carol J., *The Sexual Politics of Meat: A Feminist-vegetarian Critical Theory*. New York: Continuum, 1990.

Aiello, Leslie C. and Wheeler, Peter, 'The expensive-tissue hypothesis: the brain and the digestive system in human and primate evolution' in *Current Anthropology*, vol. 36 (1995), pp. 199–221.

Allen, Michael W. and Ng, Sik Hung, 'Human values, utilitarian benefits and identification: the case of meat' in *European Journal of Social Psychology*, vol. 33 (2003), pp. 37–56.

Anonymous, 'Singing red meat's praises,' *The Daily Telegraph* (15 February 2002).

Anonymous, 'Meat and Livestock Australia: Marketing strategies' in *B&T*, (17 January 2005), http://www.bandt.com.au/news/07/0c02c007.asp, last accessed 4 July 2007.

Anonymous, 'Beauty and the beef,' *MSN Bulletin*, (2006), http://bulletin.ninemsn.com.au, last accessed 7 April 2007.

Anonymous, 'Ad campaign pushes beefy nutrition message,' *ABC Premium News*, (11 March 2006).

Australian Bureau of Statistics, *Apparent consumption of foodstuffs (4306.0)* (Canberra: AGPS, 1998–99).

Baghurst, Katrine, Record, Sally and Leppard, Phil, 'Red meat consumption in Australia: Intakes, nutrient contribution and changes over time' in *Australian Journal of Nutrition and Dietetics*, vol. 57 (2000), pp. S3–S36.

Fairbrother, Jeffory G. and The Australian Chicken Meat Federation, *Submission to Parliamentary Joint Committee of Public Accounts and Audit on review of Australia's quarantine function* (North Sydney, NSW: Australian Chicken Meat Federation, 2002).

Fiddes, Nick, *Meat: A Natural Symbol*. New York: Routledge, 1991.

Gatfield, Terry, 'Australia's gone chicken! An examination of consumer behaviour and trends related to chicken and beef meats in Australia' in *Journal of Food Products Marketing*, vol. 12 (2006), pp. 29–42.

Le Gros Clark, F., 'Food habits as a practical nutrition problem' in *World Review of Nutrition and Dietetics*, vol. 9 (1968), pp. 56–84.

Lea, Emma and Worsley, Anthony, 'The cognitive contexts of beliefs about the healthiness of meat' in *Public Health Nutrition*, vol. 5 (2002), pp. 37–45.

Lea, Emma and Worsley, Anthony, 'Benefits and barriers to the consumption of a vegetarian diet in Australia' in *Public Health Nutrition*, vol. 6 (2003), pp. 505–11.

Lea, Emma and Worsley, Anthony, 'What proportion of South Australian adult non-vegetarians hold similar beliefs to vegetarians?' in *Nutrition & Dietetics*, vol. 61 (2004), pp. 1–21.

Meat & Livestock Australia, *Red meat in the Australian diet: findings from the national nutrition survey.* (Sydney: Meat & Livestock Australia, 2000).

Meat & Livestock Australia, 'Marketing red meat', (no date), http://www.mla.com.au/TopicHierarchy/ Marketing/default.htm, last accessed 13 July 2007.

Santich, Barbara, 'Feed the man meat!' in *Staple foods: Oxford Symposium on Food and Cookery 1989 proceedings,* ed. Harlan Walker (London: Prospect Books, 1990), pp. 224–7.

Santich, Barbara, 'Wear it or eat it!' in *Wool in the Australian imagination,* ed. Shelley Neller (Sydney: Historic Houses Trust NSW, 1994), pp. 32–41.

Santich, Barbara, *What The Doctors Ordered: 150 years of dietary advice in Australia.* South Melbourne: Hyland House, 1995.

Shoebridge, Neil, column in *Business Review Weekly* (1 April 1999), p. 90.

Twigg, Julia, 'Vegetarianism and the meanings in meat in *The sociology of food and eating: essays on the sociological significance of food,* ed. Anne Murcott. Aldershot: Gower, 1983, pp. 18–30.

Notes

1. Australian Bureau of Statistics.
2. Lea and Worsley (2003) p. 507.
3. Fairbrother p. 6.
4. Baghurst, Record, and Lepperd.
5. Australian Bureau of Statistics.
6. Santich (1995).
7. Santich (1994).
8. Gatfield p. 30.
9. Gatfield p. 34.
10. Gatfield p. 35.
11. Meat and Livestock Australia (n.d.).
12. Anonymous (2005).
13. Anonymous (2002).
14. Anonymous (2006).
15. Anonymous (2005).
16. Meat and Livestock Australia (n.d.).
17. Meat and Livestock Australia (n.d.).
18. Anonymous (2006).
19. Lea and Worsley (2003).
20. Anonymous (2006).
21. Lea and Worsley (2003).
22. Allen and Ng p. 53.
23. Santich (1990) p. 226.
24. Le Gros Clark p. 69.

25. Allen and Ng p. 54.
26. Lea and Worsley (2004) p. 20.
27. Shoebridge.
28. Santich (1990) p. 224.
29. Adams.
30. Twigg p. 22.
31. Aiello and Wheeler p. 270.
32. Fiddes.

The Civility of Eating

Robert Appelbaum

The Western world has a bad conscience about its 'civility.' Civilisation is a character of the past; it has risen and fallen and now it is both everywhere (unfortunately) and nowhere (thankfully); it is a whole system whose means and ends we have come to despise; it was and is a tool of oppression. From the time of Rousseau and Kant we have learned to distinguish between 'civilisation,' which is at best ceremonial, and 'culture' (the German *Kultur*), which is where real meaning, value, and sustenance lie. The Rousseauvian idea is that civilisation corrupts; humanity is naturally good and free, but everywhere in the world there is viciousness, and everyone is in chains. The Kantian idea is only slightly more lenient. We have made all sorts of progress in manners, in civility, Kant argues; but we have made little in morality. Through culture rather than through civilisation, through the cultivation our moral instincts and our sense of justice, we may make some real progress. But civilisation by itself won't get us there. It may make us wealthier in possessions, and more successful in interpersonal relations, but it will not make us richer in our souls; it will not even, according to Kant, make us more free.[1]

The point is nearly universally acknowledged. We have all learned from Walter Benjamin that there is no document of civilisation that is not also a document of barbarism. But the problem is that even so, we must cling to our civility, our active participation in this thing we call civilisation. We cannot do without it. And those of us who take a special interest in food are thus faced with a challenge. For eating well is a function of civility. We may well be sympathetic to the Rousseauvian and Kantian point of view, and prefer culture and morality and freedom to the siren call of civilisation; we may well hearken to Benjamin's angel of history, and be wary of the barbarism and violence underlying the Western way of life. But good food is a product of civilisation; it is an expression of it, as well as a tool of it; it is a vital means of civility and an end of civility, a goal toward which civility aims. As Brillat-Savarin puts it: 'Gourmandism is the common bond which unites the nations of the world'; by which the gastronome indicates that the production, distribution, and consumption of good food is both a thing that makes civilisation civil, and an end toward which a civilised world must tend.[2] But Brillat-Savarin's vision of the gourmand's civility is in sharp conflict with the critique of civility embedded in the concept of *Kultur*, or what today might be called concept of the ethics of eating. And what then?

The problem is literally ancient. Civilisation – the Romans mainly called it *humanitas* – was necessary, gratifying, noble; it tamed the beast in us, it united different peoples, it made learning rather than instinct the ruling principle of social life, it brought comfort and plenty to the world. But civilisation was also selfish, excessive, decadent, and destructive; it couldn't tame the beast without also violating nature, it couldn't unite people without violent conquest, it couldn't extol learning without overvaluing eloquence at the expense of wisdom. And if comfort and plenty, including good food, was a means and end of civilisation, then there was a problem. Who really needed all the things that civilisation provided, and indeed provided as if a matter of necessity? Who could be content with what it required us to require? In this Age of Iron, we had pushed ourselves away from nature too far, demanded too much, and gotten things confused. We built empires by having taught ourselves to need what we don't need, to indulge in what isn't good for us, to take pleasure in that which isn't, inherently, pleasant. We plundered the sea, we scorched the earth, we humiliated fellow nations, we caused peoples to be enslaved, we made the whole world rather mad, and all for the sake of a kind of pathological egotism, a need for things that aren't needed. The 'Lucrine oysters' that Horace famously eschews in his Second Epode to his patron Maecenas, along with the 'wrasse or turbot' brought ashore from thundering Eastern waves, the 'African fowl, the Ionian partridge' – these are the things that empire encourages us to crave. But who needs them? Home grown olives, sorrel, and mallows for a salad, a lamb that one has raised and sacrificed in the proper way, or 'a kid saved from the wolves,' will more than suffice.[3]

By the time we get to modern Europe, the idea of the madness of civilisation and its practices of food consumption is commonplace. Here, for example, is an early modern rendition, by Huguenot poet Guillaume du Bartas:

> O gasping gullets! O bottomless bellies!
> All the exquisite living things of a thousand worlds
> Dreamed up by the Abderos cannot satisfy you.
> For you, greedy stomachs, to the Moluccas
> For fine spices we have to journey,
> To Crete for wine, to the Canaries for sugar.
> To gratify your gluttonous appetites we have to plow
> The sacred breast of the blue Thetis sea.
> We have to depopulate the air. The phoenix alone
> Can scarcely escape your ravenous maws.[5]

The problem is manifold. First is the sheer emptiness of the epicurean desire motivating the spread of civilisation. It is never satisfied. It is bottomless and greedy. A second problem is the civilising appetite's rapaciousness toward nature. Everything is fair game, and nature is at risk; as the allusion to the phoenix suggests, epicurean civilisation is dangerous to the point where it almost threatens nature with extinction. A third problem is imperialism. Desire makes us masters of the world, putting us on our endless journeys, colonizing and trading from one corner of the globe to another. And to what end? As the poem goes on to say, this aggressive, empty, ruthless appetite actually debilitates us. The word du Bartas uses is effeminacy. The demand for luxury effeminises the hearts of warriors, and threatens the security and integrity of a nation. The proof of this is in the story du Bartas is telling. The occasion for the poet's rail against gluttony is the banquet that the Assyrian general Holofernes is throwing in honour of a guest from a Jewish village he has been besieging, a widow he is hoping to seduce. Holofernes eats and drinks too much, and while he lies in a stupor, in his bed, the widow Judith takes up Holofernes's own sword and cuts off the general's head.

Let us take another example, this time from Rousseau himself. 'We go to dine in an opulent home,' Rousseau recounts, in his book *Émile*, where he imagines himself in the role of tutor to his eponymous character.

> We find the preparation for a feast – many people, many lackeys, many dishes, an elegant and fine table service. All this apparatus of pleasure and festivity has something intoxicating about it that goes to the head when one is not accustomed to it. I have a presentiment of the effect of all this on my young pupil. While the meal continues, while the courses follow one another, while much boisterous conversation reigns at the table, I lean toward his ear and say, 'Through how many hands would you estimate that all you see on this table has passed before getting here?'

The effect on Émile is monumental. 'While the philosophers, cheered by the wine, and perhaps by the ladies next to them, prate and act like children,' Rousseau says, Émile 'is all alone philosophizing for himself in his corner.'[6] Though the philosophers are taken in by the delights of civility, Émile is caused to reflect on his world in the anti-social, mindful spirit of *Kultur*.

In a sense, Rousseau is merely reviving the ancient discourse on luxury and gluttony, just as du Bartas had done 150 years earlier. But Rousseau adds some details that bring us closer to home. Rousseau's feast is a modern dinner party. There is something intoxicating about it. People sit around the table. They joke, they flirt, they get drunk, they regale in both the elegance and the festivity of the moment; they are being served, they are having a good time. And this is just what Rousseau wants his *Émile* to be thoughtfully distraught about.

> With a healthy judgment that nothing has been able to corrupt, what will [Émile] think of this luxury when he finds that every region of the world has been made to contribute; that perhaps twenty million hands have worked for a long time; that it has cost the lives of perhaps thousands of men, and all this to present to him with pomp at noon what he is going to deposit in his toilet at night?[7]

The image is not Rousseau's invention; the stoic Seneca had used it much earlier. But it is decisive. Not only is the civility of the table rapacious, it is cloacal. Civilisation is shit. And the main defence of the individual is to be aware of this; it is to take an uncivil turn away from the fopperies of civility, and spend one's energies on philosophical mindfulness. Rousseau has his Émile leave the table, refuse the con-

31

viviality, and think with some distress, in a frame of high-minded seriousness, about the unpalatability of it all.

Of course there have always been countervailing discourses. For every rejection of the pleasure of the table, there has been at least one enthusiastic embrace. The ancients and early moderns alike understood food as being central to happiness: the happiness of health, of conviviality, of social stability. And civility, as readers of Norbert Elias know, for all the difficulties associated with it, is the name of a process through which the Western way of life expanded from its capitals to its provinces, from the rich to the poor, from the educated to the uneducated. It was nearly identical to what we call progress. But happiness, health, social stability, progress – what are any of these things in the face of the moral imperatives? The moral imperatives of mindfulness, of kindness toward others, of distributive justice, of stewardship toward nature, seem to preclude that healthy happiness experienced by the diners at Rousseau's elegant dinner party. Indeed, the Rousseauvian position denies that the dinner party is really happy, or really healthy; it wants to expose the pleasure of the dinner party as empty, its conviviality as a charade, an insincere performance of sociality motivated by naked self-interest.

What we need instead of this phony civility, according to humanist tradition, is something more authentic. We need to content ourselves with what the ancients called the *vita parva*, the simple life, where real needs are satisfied, and false needs rejected. And we need to reject 'society' in favour of 'community.' Instead of performing sociality out of self-interest, we need to aim toward a genuine absorption in the world of others: an idea imbued with spiritual significance among Christian writers, for whom a shared table is always potentially a recollection of holy communion, and with a romantic or nostalgic significance among post-Christian writers like Rousseau.[8]

So, civility is suspect according to humanist tradition. It continues to be suspect today in our post-humanist age. Take for example how contemporary Anglophone sociology responds to that most civilised of dining customs, the restaurant meal. Joanne Finkelstein argues that restaurant dining is a form of bad faith; it is artificial, unequal, unfair; indeed, it so false, that it amounts to what Finkelstein calls incivility (which she defines idiosyncratically) detracting from the practices of the examined life, and the pursuit of social equality.[9] Alan Warde and Lydia Martens grant that eating is a source of pleasure, concerning which a great deal of social consensus can be documented, but they define it from the outset as something novel, foreign, and threatening.[10] Eating *out*, that's how our sociologists think of it. The very idea implies the moral precedence of an eating *in*, at hearth and home, site of primitive familiarity. And indeed, one of the issues that most excites the interest of English-speaking sociologists of food is the apparent unfamiliarity of restaurants. Fast food, ethnic food, exotic food, in unusual surroundings, frequently designed in unusual ways, according to themes, and loaded with ethnic and geographical references, in keeping with far flown and invented rather than local and authentic traditions: the modern restaurant in Britain and Australia strikes the Rousseauvian sociologist as just so much shit, or at best, as an interesting distraction from more important things in life, like self-awareness and class solidarity. But civility, as I have suggested, cannot be dispensed with, not in food and not in many other areas of material life. Our civility is (among other things) gastronomic, and gastronomy unites the nations of the world.

We often think of civility merely as good manners, to be sure, and especially as good manners toward strangers. Since Elias, however, we have had to take a broader view of the phenomenon. In Elias's hands, civility becomes an economy of the body and a medium for social life. It not only expresses attitudes and beliefs; it even produces them. A structure of convivial behaviour, of what the French call the *vivre-ensemble*, civility constitutes us as subjects in the social world. And so it is not merely a way of doing things; it is also a value assigned to things done. Eventually it comes to signify 'the self-consciousness of the West' and indeed the consciousness of its own 'superiority' with regard to non-Western peoples.[11] But it also signifies science, trade, technology, political values, and for that matter moral values too: the knowledge, the infrastructure, the convictions, and the imperatives of living in the world of the West. From good manners, or rather a certain fashion of good manners, civility unfolds as a system of modern life: for better or worse, the Western way of life.

Today, although the idea of civilisation is at its lowest repute ever, we still speak of 'civil society,' and we still speak of the imperatives of civility and the material life it organises. In current usage, civil society is a form of collective action, voluntarily entered into by individuals concerned for supporting social welfare. Its sphere of interest is distinguished from those of other essential institutions like the family, the marketplace, or the state; civil society is concerned with the infrastructure of social welfare that unites those things. Doctors, nurses, and engineers are the heroes of 'civil society': they cure bodies, they build roads, they make healthy material life available, even in the absence of effective markets, government agencies, and family structures.[12] In fact, and I will get back to this, the Slow Food movement that originated in Italy is in large part an organ of civil society in the technical sense; it is a non-governmental agency assisting the development of the infrastructure of common material life.

As for the imperatives of civility, this related idea finds its most elaborate development in work based on philosopher Jurgen Habermas's theory of communicative action. The Belgian philosopher Jean-Marc Ferry, a student of Habermas, thus discusses the general 'civility' of social life in the modern world as necessary medium of behaviour in public. Civility is imperative in the sense that it is indispensable to conduct in the public sphere; it is the very medium of conduct there, and necessary for the development of economies, political alliances, and 'culture.' Ferry is thinking of manners in the broadest sense, of how people live together outside the confines of immediate community, but below the level of political association, the state and the law. He is thinking of 'conviviality' and the '*vivre-ensemble*' – those are the words he uses – outside of familiar habitats, and so of interaction among strangers in cosmopolitan spaces. Civility allows modern society to subsist in 'a spirit of conviviality without immediacy,' he writes. We live together; we live together peacefully and col-laboratively, even if we are strangers, and even if we know ourselves by our differences from one another, because we are civil among ourselves.[13]

A main point of reference for Ferry is the postmodern city. Civility in the city is a form of mediation, allowing us to live together and pursue individual but common interests in an urban context, among fellow strangers. If you take it away, if you suf-fer a 'loss of civility,' you take away both our ability to live together outside of our immediate communities and our connection to all those things that civility encour-ages: economic activity, political alliance, cultural production. Civility, moreover, has a value over and above its utility; for civility according to Ferry 'is a principle of socialisation mediated by the recognition of individual differences, that is to say by a generalised form of respect.'[14] We have civility rather than some other form of sociality precisely because we live in a world of differences, and precisely because, in a modern society of difference, we require from ourselves an ethos of 'respect.' I give way to the stranger on the pavement as he approaches on the right not because he is a member of my community, and holds a certain rank in it to which I defer, and not because it is the law that I must give way, as it would be on a motorway, but because I am being civil. I am showing the passer-by not love, not solidarity, not political pas-sion or legality, but respect. And so we live together.

This civility cannot be taken for granted. It has to be taught; it even has to be engineered. One of the paradoxes of the postmodern world is that we have discovered that the promotion of civility requires a considerable expenditure of resources, from the design of pavements in city centres to the establishment of laws governing con-gregation. We can be civil to one another because we have planned it that way. The great leisure zones of towns like London are examples of this: Leicester Square, the Chinatown Gerrard Street plaza. These are the spaces that Rousseauvian social think-ers like to criticise precisely for their artificiality: manufactured sites for the satisfac-tion of manufactured desires, importing as their meaning a pastiche of stereotypical images from the past, these civic spaces are examples of what is sometimes called the 'fantasy city.'[15] Where once a real city thrived, we now have pleasure zones for visi-tors, serving up phony pleasures. And the Rousseauvian thinkers have a point. But what the civil society of towns like London has created in places like Leicester Square and the Chinatown plaza is a structure of conviviality, a conglomerate of sites where crowds of strangers can live together and enjoy material pleasures together, including the pleasure of congregating.

Food practices in the postmodern world are obviously a major part of this convivial civility. It is not just that more and more people are 'eating out'; it is also that more and more are 'eating with,' if not in communion with one another at least in civic harmony. And it is not just that more and more products are being gathered from the four corners of the earth to provide Londoners with strawberries in the winter and a steady supply of prawns, if not Lucrine oysters, year round. It is that more and more people are united in the harvest and distribution of foodstuffs across the globe – united, again, not in community, and not in political affiliation, but in the civility of civil society. There are problems with the internationalisation of the food supply in the modern world – inequality, exploitation, ecological devastation – and they need to be solved, but there are also lines of 'communicative action' embedded in it. Prawns from Thailand and apples from South Africa, imported to a nation like Britain, which ought to have prawns and apples of its own, means that more and more people are involved in supplying material life to one another in more and more interconnected places.

Nevertheless, even our best champions of good eating commonly adopt the language of *Kultur* when they try to influence opinion. This civic 'eating with' is not enough. It doesn't make eating *ethical* enough: mindful, caring, nurturing, decent. Consider the case of Alice Waters, owner of the famous restaurant Chez Panisse in Berkeley, California. She insists that she is teaching us to care for the environment, urging us to establish communities of farmers and consumers, or even, as she has put it recently, to 'save the world.'[16] What she and many others have constructed is a valorisation of good eating that far exceeds the claims of civility, or even of gourmandism and gastronomy, for what good eating does, it turns out, in spite of all the evidence to the contrary, is promote a kind of religious community without religion.

In what has been mythologised, beginning with Waters herself, as a kind of founding moment of what would eventually be called California cuisine, Waters reports on an early experience in rural Brittany, which has all the trappings, and all the contradictions, of a conversion experience. This was the meal where her jaded French companions finally united in praising a restaurant unreservedly. 'They applauded the chef and cried, "*C'est fantastique!*".' Waters writes:

> I've remembered this dinner a thousand times: the old stone house, the stairs leading up to the small dining room, which seated no more than twelve at the pink cloth-covered tables and from which one could look though the windows to the stream running beside the house and the garden in back. The chef, a woman, announced the menu: cured ham and melon, trout with almonds, and raspberry tart. The trout had just come from the stream and the raspberries from the garden. It was this immediacy that made those dishes so special.[17]

In Waters's mind this was an experience without mediation. Rousseau might well have approved. It is rapturously romantic. But the vision just doesn't hold. Where did almonds come from? Most likely from Provence, or Spain, or northern Africa. What about the cured ham? Not at all an 'immediate' product, it was very likely from somewhere like Bayonne or Parma, and it had taken half a year or more to make. Where did the tablecloths come from? Where did the diners come from? Where did they get their money? Where did they get their leisure? Where did they acquire their habit of taking leisure in institutions run by strangers for profit? The answer, I am afraid, is civilisation.

If we think of good eating as a function of civility rather than of culture, we come much closer to the Brillat-Savarin's view of gastronomy. Certainly we lose associations with good eating that we may find comforting, like community. And if we asked, is civility enough? We would have to answer no. Civility cannot replace morality, or religion, or philosophical self-awareness. Why should it? Civility cannot teach us to be kind to other people. It can only teach us to respect them. The same goes for other areas where the question of the ethics of food may lead us. Civility probably has nothing to tell us about cruelty to animals, for example. But the ethic of civility has much to be said for it on the subject of good eating. Civility is the basis of the modern restaurant and the modern dinner party. It is a principle of gastronomic leisure in the postmodern world. It is the necessary condition of material life so far as it requires contact and collaboration between people above the level of family and community and below the level of the state.

And though one can find fault with eating in the modern world from all sorts of moral and political positions, the position based on the ethos of civility has something to offer as well. Take the case of fast food. Our moral, political, and economic instincts give us plenty of energy for decrying things like the low wages of the employees fast food restaurants, or protesting against what is done to the earth in order for it to yield Big Macs and golden fries. But from the point of view of civility we can ask still another pertinent question: do fast food restaurants promote the kind of civility we want to require of ourselves? The answer is probably no. In fact, it is just this idea about failures in civility that will make urban planners and community activists object to establishing too many fast food restaurants in civic spaces. Fast food may be convenient, and according to the rules of free trade it has as much right as any other kind of convenience to be offered for sale in commercial zones. But in certain conditions it may be uncivil, or promote incivility, or the wrong kind of civility, and in the fragile civic spaces of the postmodern city it can be a nuisance that society has an obligation to defend itself against. It is clear that we now need to defend our *vivre-ensemble* against the encroachments of what sociologist Stephen Mennell calls 'de-civilisation,' and excluding fast food from fragile urban spaces may be a tool in that defence.[18]

In any case, to encourage good eating we do not need to appeal to the moral high ground occupied by *Kultur*. Civility is enough. In fact, civility is required. And arguments that depend on appeals to the moral high ground can be distracting, counterproductive, and false.

I mentioned Slow Food, with which Waters is also associated. Slow Food, again, is an association at the level of civil society, but if you look at the statements of Carlo Petrini and his associates you find a curious mixture of appeals to civility on the one hand and our *Kultur* on the other. Massimo Montanari, the great food historian, is very good with culture, his latest book even being called *Food Is Culture*, but he is somewhat uncomfortable with civilisation.[19] Carlo Petrini, the leader of Slow Food, for his part vacillates between *Kultur* and civilisation. His instincts are to support the former. The local, the familial, the communal, the authentic, the maternal and the primitive, besieged as all these aspects of *Kultur* are by the vapid rapidity of late modernity, are the mainspring of the value system behind Slow Food. What do you like to eat, he is asked:

> I have simple tastes. For example, I like pasta with tomato sauce. Still there are some dishes that in our experience represent our mothers, and our grandmothers: dishes that transmitted their love for their children and grandchildren. The food I consumed at the house of my grandmother Caterina was the authentic cuisine of the Piedmont lowlands; I was brought up with it. I cannot recall eating a packaged snack, but I do remember *some d'aj*, which is a slice of bread brushed with garlic, and a little olive oil and salt. When I was a kid, I had that as a snack. [20]

So Petrini's Slow Food is based on the values of *Kultur*, in a mode that resembles the thought of Horace and Rousseau: local products and simple pleasures, taken independently from the buzz of the business of empire, and enjoyed while mindful of the ancient truth of *terroir* become for Slow Food the bedrock of an old/new ethic of production and consumption. But Petrini also espouses civilisation, in quite another frame of mind. He cites Brillat-Savarin quite often. He has built up a civil society uniting the nations, forming networks of exchange and communication, of markets and distribution lines, all on the rationale with what he openly calls a gastronomic 'science.' The 'convivial' of Slow Food protect local products; but they also put the products in contact with a world of buyers and sellers. And when Petrini gets away from that primitive nostalgia that has so often caused thoughtful people to turn away from society and its material pleasures, he expresses the kind of ethic that Jean-Marc Ferry is promoting: 'Food is most important to me as a way of relating to others', he says. But not as *community*, exactly, and not as *culture*; if you look at what Petrini actually says in this light, it turns out that he embraces fine dining rather as a civil sort of vivre-ensemble, among strangers.

> Even when I happen to eat by myself in a restaurant, which is rare, I feel I am sharing my meal with the environment that surrounds me. I look around, I observe people's attitudes and listen to the discussions at other tables with curiosity. That way I feel I am an integral part of social life. Sharing food is one of the highest elements of civilisation. [21]

The point is clear enough, even if it is expressed with some ambivalence. There is a cultural morality of food, a *Kultur* of food, and apparently we need to encourage traditional food practices. But once you reach past the bounds of traditional and immediate community, once you find yourself eating in the real world, in a condition vis-à-vis other people not of friendship and familiarity but of convivial respect, you are eating well or ill within a context of 'civilisation.'

Notes and sources

1. Jean-Jacques Rousseau, *Discourse on Inequality*, trans. Maurice Cranston (Harmondsworth: Penguin, 1984); Immanuel Kant, 'Ideas for a Universal History with a Cosmopolitan Purpose', in *Political Writings*, ed. Hans Reiss, trans. H.B. Nisbet (Cambridge: Cambridge University Press, 1991); Norbert Elias, *The Civilizing Process*, trans. Edmund Jephcott (Oxford: Blackwell, 1994), pp. 1–28. And see Stephen Mennell, *Norbert Elias: Civilization and the Human Self-Image* (Oxford: Basil Blackwell, 1989), especially pp. 35–36; also see Robert Appelbaum, *Aguecheek's Beef, Belch's Hiccup, and Other Gastronomic Interjections: Literature, Culture and Food Among the Early Moderns* (Chicago: University of Chicago Press, 2006), chapter six.

2. Jean Anthelme Brillat-Savarin, *The Physiology of Taste*, trans. Anne Drayton (Harmondsworth: Penguin, 1994), p. 133.

3. Horace, *Odes and Epodes*, ed. Niall Rudd (Cambridge, MA: Harvard University Press, 2004).

5. Guillaume du Bartas, *La Judit*, ed. André Bâche (Toulouse: Association des publications de la Faculté des lettres et sciences humaines, 1971), 6.7–17.

6. Jean-Jacques Rousseau, *Emile, or, On Education*, trans. Allan Bloom (Basic: 1979), p. 190. I discuss this passage and the Rousseauvian position at length in *Aguecheek's Beef*, chapter eight.

7. Ibid., 190–91.

8. An especially pertinent example of the shared meal as communion is *The Godly Feast* in Desiderius Erasmus, *The Colloquies of Erasmus*, trans. Craig R. Thompson (Chicago: University of Chicago Press, 1965).

9. Joanne Finkelstein, *Dining Out: A Sociology of Modern Manners* (Cambridge: Polity Press, 1989).

10. Alan Warde and Lydia Martens, *Eating Out: Social Differentiation, Consumption, and Pleasure* (Cambridge: Cambridge University Press, 2000). But see also David Bell and Gill Valentine, *Consuming Geographies: We Are Where We Eat* (London: Routledge, 1997), who provide an interesting contrast between the 'community' and the 'city' as sites of dining.

11. *The Civilising Process*, 3, 41.

12. 'Civil society refers to the arena of uncoerced collective action around shared interests, purposes and values'. Centre for Civil Society, London School of Economics, http://www.lse.ac.uk/collections/CCS/introduction.htm (15 June, 2007).

13. Jean-Marc Ferry, *De la civilisation: civilité, légalité, publicité* (Paris: Editions de Cerf, 2001), 21. Also see Hélène Merlin-Kajman, 'Civilité: une certain modality du vivre-ensemble', in *Civilization in French and Francophone Literature*. French Literature Series, 33. Ed. Buford Norman and James Day (Amsterdam and New York: Rodopi, 2006), 205–19.

14. Ferry, p. 58.

15. John Hannigan, *Fantasy City: Pleasure and Profit in the Postmodern Metropolis* (London: Routledge, 1998).

16. Alice Waters, The Delicious Revolution, January, 2005. http://www.chezpanisse.com/pgdrevolution.html

17. Alice Waters, *The Chez Panisse Menu Cookbook* (New York: Random House, 1982), p. x. And see David Kamp, *The United States of Arugula: How We Became a Gourmet Nation* (New York: Broadway, 2006), pp. 231–266.

18. Stephen Mennell, 'L'Envers de la medaille: les processes de décivilisation,' in *Norbert Elias: La politique et l'histoire*, ed. Alain Garrigou and Bernard Lacroix (Paris: La Découverte, 1997).

19. Massimo Montanari, *Food Is Culture*, trans. Albert Sonnenfeld (New York: Columbia University Press, 2004), 139–40.

20. Carlo Petrini and Gigi Padovani, *Slow Food Revolution: A New Culture for Eating and Living* (New York: Rizzoli, 2006), pp. 179–80. Also see Carlo Petrini, *Slow Food: The Case for Taste*, trans. William McCuaig (New York: Columbia University Press, 2004).

21. *Slow Food Revolution*, p. 179.

From Rules to Principles:
The Transformation of a Jewish Agricultural Ethic

Travis Berg

Are monotheistic religions essentially anthropocentric and utilitarian concerning the land and the food produced from it? Can Judaism produce its own ecological principles with regard to food production laws, or is philosophy needed to purify and correct religion's ethical failings? Modern ecologists have found the Judeo-Christian tradition to be anthropocentric, domineering, and exploitive. The classic paper that defined this view was 'The Historical Roots of Our Ecologic Crisis' by Lynn T. White Jr. White claimed that Christianity 'not only established a dualism of man and nature but also insisted that it is God's will that man exploit nature for his proper ends.'[1] By indicting Christianity through Old Testament passages from Genesis, White condemns Judaism as being as utilitarian in its food production philosophy as Christianity.

Academics like White are not the only critics of Judaism's supposed anthropocentric worldview, however. Lawrence Troster, a rabbi in New Jersey, also makes the assumption that Judaism has 'an anthropocentric view of the world, [in] its relation to humanity and to God.[2] In order to 'purify' the Jewish faith, Troster proposes a synthesis of Judaism and the Gaia theory. The Gaia theory was proposed by the British chemist James Lovelock and states that the world is one living organism.[3] I suspect this synthesis is comparable to Aquinas' blending of Aristotelian philosophy and Christian theology in the Middle Ages. Unfortunately, Troster's need for a synthesis merely proves that Judaism is inherently exploitive and that philosophy is needed to 'correct' this flaw. Troster forgets about the development of a whole other tradition within Judaism itself, Kabbalism, which is much more ecologically sensitive to food production. This paper charts the historical development of the Kabbalist tradition and its relevance to contemporary ecological questions.

In order to see the historical development of the ecologically friendly Kabbalist tradition, one must start at the foundation of the Jewish faith. Judaism's foundation rests on the Tanakh, which consists of the Torah (the Law), Nevi'im (the Prophets), and Kethuvim (the Writings). A section of the Torah, which include the first five books traditionally attributed to Moses, are the focus of this paper. The majority of the verses used in this paper come from Leviticus. The verses that this paper discusses are as follows: 'But in the seventh year shall be a Sabbath of solemn rest for the land…thou shalt neither sow thy field, nor prune thy vineyard,'[4] 'Thou shalt not wholly reap the corner of thy field…thou shalt leave them for the poor and for the stranger,'[5] and 'Thou shalt not let thy cattle gender with a diverse kind.'[6] A passage from Deuteronomy is also used in this paper: 'Thou shalt not plow with an ox and an ass together.'[7]

Old Testament scholars are divided on the historicity of the Pentateuch. While there are many different scholarly opinions, this paper will present the traditional, documentary hypothesis, and a modern reinvestigation of the documentary hypothesis. According to Julius Wellhausen in his seminal *Prolegomena zur Geschichte Israels*, Leviticus belonged to the so-called Priestly source, since it was mainly concerned with cultic interests. Wellhausen's thesis argues that Leviticus was created after sources J, E, and D. Wellhausen argues that J and E sources both argue for a multiplicity of altars, while D source argues for a highly centralized cult in Jerusalem. P source seems to presuppose centralization, and writes its history accordingly through the tabernacle narrative.[8] This puts Leviticus at a post-seventh century date, but pre-exilic as well.[9] Pekka Pitkanen's dissertation, *Central Sanctuary and Centralization of Worship in Ancient Israel*, suggests otherwise. Pitkanen claims that the Priestly material that constitutes Leviticus was written earlier than the disaster at Aphek and the rejection of Shiloh as the central sanctuary around 1050 BCE.[10]

Scholarly opinion regarding Deuteronomy is no less debated. Proposed by Wellhausen in his *Prolegomena*, the documentary hypothesis considered Deuteronomy to be a later development in Jewish religion. Deuteronomy was a seventh-century manuscript that was written to increase the authority of Jerusalem during the reign of King Josiah. This hypothesis was proposed because many of the religious measures done during the reign of Josiah in 2 Kings parallel the commands of Deuteronomy.[11] Pitkanen disagrees with Wellhausen. Pitkanen claims that the core of Deuteronomy was written before the loss of the ark to the Philistines around 1050 BCE.[12] Now that the historical and biblical foundation of food production laws has been established, one must see how the Jewish community interpreted these laws in the Mishnah.

The Mishnah is a principle component of the Judaic canon and is foundational for other works, such as the Talmud. It was compiled at the end of the second century CE by Judah the Patriarch, who was the head of the Jewish community of Palestine. It has been described as a list of judicial rulings, a school manual, and a program for consecration.[13] One could say that the rulings of the Mishnah are a practical, human response of reconciling the Torah's commands to commonplace circumstance. The Mishnah is divided into six orders describing agricultural rules, appointed seasons, property transfers, civil and criminal law, ritualistic laws concerning the Temple, and purity laws.[14] The order on agricultural rules, the *Zeraim*, is the main focus of investigation.

Lev. 19:9-10 is discussed in the tractate 'Peah,' which translates as 'corner.' This verse only says that the poor should be left the corners of a crop. This leaves a lot of room for interpretation because the command is very ambiguous. For example, when can the poor collect the leftovers? While this question does not seem important, it had a great impact on the farmer and on the poor that collected the leftovers. There needed to be a balance between the rights of the farmer and the poor. If the poor came too many times during the day, they would interfere with the harvest. If the farmer's rights were favored, he might impose too many limits on the collection of leftovers. Here one sees the Mishnah's practical tradition in establishing agricultural halakhah (judicial rulings). The anonymous ruling, which was the view of the majority, says that the poor should come three times a day: morning, midday and afternoon.[15] This is not the end of the debate, however. Two of the great sages, Rn. Gamaliel II and R. Akiba, debated whether these three trips were the maximum or the minimum number of times the poor should come.[16] The practicality of these rulings is evident, and no allegorical interpretation of the Torah is put forward.

Deut. 22:10 and Lev. 19:19 are discussed in the tractate 'Kilayim,'which translates as 'mixtures.' The mixtures referred to in this tractate are the forbidden mixtures of unlike kinds. Questions immediately arose for the Jewish people: to what extent can diverse animals interact with one another without violating this prohibition? The Mishnah only considers the case of cattle, unlike Lev. 19:19. The Mishnah states: 'Mixtures of cattle are permitted to be reared and matured except they are prohibited from copulating…[and from ploughing] with one another.'[17] Brewer finds this curious, since this ruling, Kil. 8.1., may have acted as an introduction to the tractate. The formulation also has no universal prohibition of heterogeneous animals ploughing or copulating together.[18] However, the prohibition for mixing other animals is universalized in Kil. 1:6. This ruling states that even though animals, like dogs and wolves or a mule and a donkey, may be 'similar to one another, they are [considered] diverse kinds with one another.'[19]

Lev. 25:4 is discussed in the tractate 'Shebiit,' which translates as 'Sabbath Year.' The Sabbath Year was a command that at best inconvenienced the Jewish people, and at worst threatened the poorer part of the population with starvation. Since the Torah forbade the cultivation of the land, one can certainly see that food shortages became a major issue, especially when the law prohibited storing of uneaten food during this year by Lev. 25:6. In order for the Jewish people to survive this agricultural dilemma, rabbis needed to come up with guidelines that allowed farmers to follow the Sabbath Year halakhah without severely harming the next year's harvest or creating extreme hardship for the poor. The definition of the word 'cultivation' was an important issue for Jewish farmers. What could one do to ready one's field for next year without breaking the Sabbath Year ethic? The majority ruling on the issue was that a field cleared of thorns during a Sabbatical Year could be sown, but a field that was improved by stone removal or by transhumance could not be sown the next year.[20] This ruling raised further questions, however. A clear example is the actual violation of the cultivation law. Could one consume the produce of a field that was cultivated during a Sabbatical Year? The House of Hillel prohibited the consumption of such produce, but the House of Shammai thought that a person could eat the produce only as a gift.[21]

It is evident that the Mishnah's conception and expansion of the agricultural ethic was relentlessly literal. In all of the sections of the order *Zeraim*, there is not one mystical or allegorical interpretation. This should not be surprising. The basis for the agricultural rulings of the Mishnah, if not the very formulations themselves, date back before the destruction of the Temple in 70 CE.[22] This means that the agricultural halakhah was still applicable to Jewish farmers in the land of Israel.

Having looked at the Mishnah's exposition of the Jewish agricultural ethic, one needs to observe the later development of agriculture in the religious life in Judaism. This necessarily leads us to the Talmud, which was complied around 400 CE. The Talmud is a further codification of the Mishnah's legal discussions about one's biblical duties, but it is much more than that. The Talmud also includes *aggadic* (legend) collections, *beraytot* (traditions that claim to date from Mishnaic times but are not preserved in the Mishnah), and had been added to, complied, and edited by some of the greatest rabbinic minds of the Amoraim period. The best way to describe the function of the Talmud is that it fulfils the positive religious duty of studying the Torah. There were two Talmuds that were created during the Amoraim period: the Balvi (Babylonian) Talmud, and the Yerushalmi (Palestinian) Talmud.

The Palestinian Talmud occupies the period of transition between the actual practice of the second Temple era and the obsolete position agricultural halakhah took in the Babylonian Talmud. Since the sages that codified the Palestinian Talmud still lived in Holy Land, the agricultural ethic was still relevant to many of the scholars there. This is evident because the Palestinian Talmud discusses all of the tractates of the *Zeraim* order.[23] Even though the Palestinian Talmud kept the agricultural ethic relevant to its readers, this last hurrah of the literal view of ethical farming would never become popularized among the Jews of the Diaspora. By the fourth century CE, the Jewish population of Palestine began to emigrate due to heavy taxation and persecution from the new, official religion of the empire: Christianity.[24] Because of all these outside pressures, the Palestinian Talmud was never properly edited, and was compiled too quickly and imprecisely. The Palestinian Talmud also lacks *aggadah,* which was so popular among the common people.[25] Because of these factors, the Palestinian Talmud never rose in popularity nor did it hold the same authority as the Balvi Talmud.[26]

The Balvi Talmud shows the increasingly obsolete position the agricultural laws had begun to take. The Babylonian Talmud, by far the most popular and prominent of the two, almost completely ignores the halakhah of Israel's agriculture.[27] In fact, the only tractate discussed in the Babylonian academies was 'Berakhot,' which deals with benedictions and prayers and not with agriculture.[28] This was not surprising, since the Balvi Talmud ignores other orders of the Mishnah that lacked practicality in Babylon. Most of *Toharot* (purification) order was also left out of the Balvi Talmud because of its lack of importance.[29]

It seems that rabbinic Judaism had forgotten its agricultural ethic due to its lack of application on their traditional land. This posed a significant problem for halakhah in general; how can one simply ignore an ethic just because one cannot fulfill it due to external circumstances? Ironically, this problem was completely avoided by descendents of the Babylonian Talmudists: the Spanish Kabbalists.

Kabbalism was significantly important to the history of Judaism. While many Jews were turning to extreme Aristotelian rationalism (Maimonides), some rabbinic Jews took a more mystical route. This movement cannot be stressed enough. Gershom Scholem argues that Kabbalism was the foundation for the Sabbatian heresy, which engulfed the Jewish nation from the Ukraine to the Levant, and captured the imaginations of many distinguished figures of the rabbinic elite. Scholem has also drawn a relationship between the Sabbatian movement and Reform Judaism, the Hebrew Enlightenment, and Jewish participants in the French Revolution.[30] It is within the pages of the Zohar, the seminal text of Kabbalism, that one sees the transformation of the Jewish food production ethic from a normative set of rules to a set of principles.

The Zohar was written by Moses ben Shemtob de Leon in thirteenth-century Castile, Spain. Composed in the style of a mystical novel, the Zohar records the sublime discourses and adventures of R. Simeon ben Yohai and his disciples as they travel through Palestine.[31] Though it is purported to be the authentic teachings of Mishnic rabbis, the Zohar was almost certainly a production of medieval Kabbalism. The principle exegetical fact that needs to be kept in mind while reading the Zohar is this: the literal narrative and commands of the Zohar are only part of the divine mystery. Nothing can say this better than the text itself: 'Woe unto those who see in the Law nothing but simple narratives and ordinary words…The narratives of the Law are but the raiment in which it is swathed.'[32]

Unfortunately, the Zohar does not interpret Lev. 19:9-10, which is the basis for the tractate 'Peah.' Fortunately, it does include a story that illustrates the principled nature of Kabbalism. R. Jose and R. Hiya were traveling together and they observe a man give all of his food to a starving beggar. Shortly after, the man who had given all of his food away becomes faint and falls asleep under a tree. As he is sleeping, a fiery adder stands guard over the man and protects him from danger.[33] The story shows the Zoharic tendency to universalize normative rules into principles. If one feeds the poor in any way, one restores the primeval communion with the land and with nature that Adam enjoyed.

Even though the biblical ethic of Deut. 22:10 and Lev. 19:19 could be literally observed even to the present day, the Zohar transforms this ethic into a metaphysical symbol of Divine order. According to Kabbalism, everything has its distinct and natural place in the world, even the tiniest herb. To mix heterogeneous species together was to cause disorder and chaos in the celestial household. The exegesis behind this reasoning was that the word *kilaim* (diverse kinds) connected with the word *kele* (prison). *Kele* can also mean prevention, which indicates that one who mixes forbidden animals together prevents celestial powers from carrying out their natural duties.[34] This ethic also became a symbol of religious differences between the Jewish people and the gentile nations. The donkey in verse 22:10 is considered to come from the left or severe emanation of the Deity, while the ox is believed to come from the right or merciful emanation of the Deity. The donkey corresponds to the gentile nations, who did not receive the Torah. The ox, on the other hand, corresponds to the Jewish nation, who has received the innumerable blessings of the Torah. One cannot mingle the two together under the plough, 'lest the junction should harm the world, whereas he who keeps them separate benefits the world.'[35]

The Zohar no longer deals with the Sabbatical year as a religious obligation of abstinence from cultivation every seventh year. Rather, this ethic becomes a beatific vision of complete harmony between all of the opposing powers of the universe. The conflicting divine forces of Judgment (*geburah*) and Mercy (*hesed*) are reconciled by the evening sacrifices of Israel, and Israel herself ascends to join the Deity in perfect unity.[36] According to the Zohar, this was the situation of the Jewish people when they had first entered the Land of Israel. The Jewish people had destroyed the unification of the divine by their sins, however. Having been exiled for their transgressions, the Zohar offered the Jews a message of hope: through their prayers, Israel could hasten the unification of the Divine Name, destroy the gentile nations, and the earth itself would be renewed.[37] Kabbalism seems to view this verse as a reminder of the paradise they had lost through sin, but also as a promise for a paradise regained through virtue.

Is the Zohar relevant to contemporary discussions on food production? What would it have to say about genetically modified crops, for example? At first glance, the Zohar would seem to be firmly against any idea of tampering with the genetic make-up of crops. The prohibition against mixing unlike creatures found in Deut. 22:10 seems absolute. Looking closer at the Zoharic text however, one sees that in certain situations mixing unlike things is beneficial to the cosmic order. According to the Zohar, the high priest would enter the Sanctuary with wool and flax garments together. This would normally be forbidden by the *kilaim* laws of the Mishnah. However, the Sanctuary is a place where 'all the different celestial species were found together in harmony,' so it did not matter if the high priest 'mixed' unlike kinds.[38] It seems that if one is cautious and reverent to the celestial hierarchy, one may safely mix unlike kinds like, for example, genetically modified crops. If one does not respect the divine scheme of the universe, however, disastrous consequences follow.

The Zohar's view of the earth answers the condemnation of critics who denounce Judaism as merely utilitarian in its view of food production and separate from the land that it labors over. A prime example is found in the creation story in Genesis. This creation myth became more than a simple act of creation by the fiat of God. For the Zohar, the land came to symbolize the eternal movements that occur within and outside of the Godhead itself. The verses, 'And God said, Let there be a firmament... Let the dry land appear' from Gen. 1:6, 9 have to do with the Tetragrammaton, the

44

divine name YHVH. The י signified the most recondite point of the tree of life, which is known as *kether*. This was found in the word, *reshith*, or the beginning. This is the first word of the book of Genesis. The first ה corresponds to the phrase 'Let there be a firmament.' This has to do with the upper realm, or heaven. The last ה corresponds to the verse, 'Let the dry land appear.' This ה has to do with the lower realm, or earth, which is the opposite of the previous ה. The oppositional ה 's, the higher and lower realms are connected by the letter ו, which corresponds to the phrase 'under the firmament' in Gen. 1:9. It is only when these oppositional, primeval letters are united into the divine name that 'the earth put forth grass, herb yielding seed, etc.'[39] God Himself is made manifest in creation. He is not the distant watchmaker of the deists, but immanent in nature. To treat nature as an object of gratification is to treat the Deity in the same manner.

The Zohar also teaches that humanity's actions are inseparable from the land. The story of Noah is a prime example of this. The earth itself was corrupted by the sins of men because 'mankind constitute[s] the essence of the earth.'[40] Humanity's corruption of the earth even led to a division of the Godhead, because the corruption did not allow the upper ה and the lower ה to meet, thereby splitting up the divine name. Even the earth itself was punished as a human sinner would be in Jewish society. Deut. 25:3 states that 'Forty stripes he may give him, he shall not exceed.' This corresponds to the forty days of flooding that killed every living thing, according to Genesis' account. The actions of humanity corrupted the earth, but righteous actions can also make it plentiful. Noah was a righteous man, and through his righteousness the world was properly settled: 'The world was in a state of poverty and misery from the time Adam transgressed the command of the Almighty until Noah came and offered up a sacrifice, when its prosperity returned.'[41] As one can see, the land's prosperity depends on the purity of the Community of Israel. This is not a master/slave relationship; the land and humanity are so intertwined that as one suffers, the other suffers.

The evolution of the Jewish food-production ethic from normative laws to a set of prescriptive principles in part answers critics like White and Troster who claim that the Judeo-Christian tradition is in essence only exploitive and anthropocentric. This paper is also a reminder to people within the Judeo-Christian tradition. Unfortunately, the rise of historical criticism has fostered the development of fundamentalist factions with wooden, literalist hermeneutics. Many people within the Judeo-Christian tradition have forgotten the rich, vibrant exegesis of the past. As we turn to religious texts for moral guidance, we should not forget the works of men like Philo, Isaac Luria, and Moses de Leon.

Bibliography

Instone-Brewer, David, *Traditions of The Rabbis From the Era of the New Testament: Vol. 1: Prayer and Agriculture*. Cambridge: William B. Eerdmans Publishing Co., 2004.

The Mishnah, trans. Jacob Neusner. London: Yale University Press, 1988.

Pitkanen, Pekka, *Central Sanctuary and Centralization of Worship in Ancient Israel*. Piscataway: Gorgias Press, 2003.

Scholem, Gershom, *Major Trends in Jewish Mysticism*, New York: Schocken Books, 1974.

Steinsaltz, Adin, *The Essential Talmud*, trans. Chaya Galai. New York: Basic Books, 1976.

The Holy Scriptures: According to the Masoretic Text. Philadelphia: The Jewish Publication Society of America, 1965.

The Zohar: Vol. I, trans. Maurice Simon and Harry Sperling. New York: Soncino Press, 1978.

The Zohar: Vol. V, trans. Maurice Simon and Harry Sperling. New York: Soncino Press, 1978.

Troster, Lawrence, 'Created in the Image of God: Humanity and Divinity in an Age of Environmentalism,' *Environmental Ethics*, ed. Susan J. Armstrong and Richard G. Botzler, Third Ed. Boston: McGraw-Hill, 2004.

Wellhausen, Julius, *Prolegomena to the History of Israel*, trans. J. Sutherland Black, M.A., and Allan Menzies, B.D. 11th Ed. (Project Gutenberg, Dec. 2003).

White Jr., Lynn T., 'The Historical Roots of Our Ecologic Crisis,' *Environmental Ethics*, Third Ed. (Boston: McGraw-Hill, 2004).

Notes

1. White p. 221.
2. Troster p. 226.
3. Troster p. 226-227.
4. Holy Scriptures, Lev. 25:4.
5. Holy Scriptures, Lev. 19:9-10.
6. Holy Scriptures, Lev. 19:19.
7. Holy Scriptures, Deut. 22:10.
8. Wellhausen, I.II.1–I.III.1.
9. Pitkanen p. 49.
10. Pitkanen p. 276.
11. Wellhausen, Introduction II.
12. Pitkanen p. 276.
13. *Mishnah* p. xiv, xv.
14. *Mishnah* p. xv.
15. *ishnah* p. 21.
16. *Mishnah* p. 21.
17. *Mishnah* p. 64.
18. Brewer p. 211.
19. *Mishnah* p. 50.
20. *Mishnah* p. 76.
21. *Mishnah* p. 76–77.
22. Brewer p. 1.
23. Steinsaltz p. 93.
24. Steinsaltz p. 53.
25. Steinsaltz p. 54.
26. Steinsaltz p. 55.
27. Steinsaltz p. 54.
28. Steinsaltz p. 279.
29. Steinsaltz p. 282–283.
30. Scholem p. xix, xx.
31. Scholem p. 157.
32. *Zohar* Vol. I, p. viii, ix.
33. *Zohar* Vol. V, p. 149.
34. *Zohar* Vol. V, p. 102.
35. *Zohar* Vol. V, p. 103.
36. *Zohar* Vol. V, p. 146.
37. *Zohar* Vol. I, p. 100–101, Vol. V, p. 330.
38. *Zohar* Vol. V, p. 103.
39. *Zohar* Vol. I, p. 77–78.
40. *Zohar* Vol. I, p. 201.
41. *Zohar* Vol. I, p. 207.

'Torah On the Table': A Sensual Morality

Jonathan Brumberg-Kraus

'Is the pleasure we derive from eating morally valuable?' This paper answers an emphatic 'Yes!' Since Plato's *Symposium*, the sensual pleasures of eating have been employed to provoke intellectual conversation and moral action. Early rabbinic tradition and subsequent Jewish interpretations and applications of it adopted this convention of Greco-Roman symposia in such institutions as Pharisaic table fellowship associations (*havurot*), the Passover *seder* rite, and the *Derekh Eretz* literature concerned with table etiquette.[1] Rabbenu Bahya ben Asher the thirteenth–fourteenth century Spanish Jewish preacher, Biblical exegete, and kabbalist, summarized, synthesized, and re-interpreted these streams of rabbinic sympotic traditions about table talk and table ethics – 'torah on the table' – in an elegant little handbook, *Shulhan Shel Arba* ['*The Four-Legged Table*']. In it, he laid the foundation for a sort of theological gastronomy, which idealized the fusion of the physical pleasures of eating and the spiritual pleasures of conversation and religious insight as the highest form of service to God. Rabbenu Bahya thus offers us a noteworthy example of a religious case for the moral value of the pleasures of the table. While my paper focuses primarily on Rabbenu Bahya's case for the moral value of the pleasures of dining, I will also show how his ideas are similar to those in more modern, humanistic texts of gastronomy, indeed to such iconic gastronomic works as Jean Anthelme Brillat-Savarin's *Physiology of Taste*, Isak Dinesen's 'Babette's Feast,' as well as Michael Pollan's currently influential book *The Omnivore's Dilemma*. Perhaps it is not totally coincidental, since they too are the heirs of the same Greco-Roman heritage of sympotic conviviality, albeit through a different chain of tradition.

While these four gastronomes share the view that the sensual pleasures of the table have moral value and that the conversations at the table play a crucial role in connect-ing the experiences to moral action, they have been chosen for the variety of views they assumed their audiences had about the relationship between pleasure and moral-ity. I remember when the topic of 'Food and Morality' was announced, there was a palpable groan among some participants whom I suspect were certain that surest way to kill the pleasures of the table was to moralize. Rabbenu Bahya ben Asher had no such qualms. As a mystic and Aristotelian, he was quite certain that the pleasures of the table were a gift of God and part of our natural human constitution, and therefore must be consistent with the moral and theological purpose, *telos*, for which human beings were created. Later, Brillat-Savarin, a product of the French Enlightenment, had little need to reconcile the physical pleasures of the table with religious morality, since in his day traditional religion had fallen into disfavor; the religion of reason ruled. On the other hand, 'Babette's Feast,' which Karen Blixen as Isak Dinesen first published in the *Ladies Home Journal* in 1950, played with the assumption that pious religious morality and the sensual pleasures of the gourmet table were diametrically opposed.[2] But the moral of her story is that true gastronomic artistry can reconcile the two. Finally, Michael Pollan represents a contemporary perspective akin to those seeking alternatives to traditional organized religions and what is perceived as their authoritarian morality. In the *Omnivore's Dilemma* Pollan tries to persuade his readers to do what is morally right – producing and consuming food that is ecologically and economically sustainable – because it tastes better![3] The sensual pleasures of the sustainable table themselves sustain a non-authoritarian morality, the ethical dimension of new secular alternatives to organized religion – e.g., the environmentalist, 'Slow Food,' local food, and organic food movements. But as different as their audiences' assumptions about the compatibility of food and morality may be, all suggest that moral awareness is conveyed in the stories we tell about matters of the table at the table. Thus, I will show how Rabbenu Bahya's medieval religious Jewish handbook on eating anticipates the more modern secular expressions of the idea that *stories and talk about dinner over the dinner table* ('Torah on the table' as the rabbis put it) not only enhance our sensual enjoyment of the meal, but also connect and channel those pleasurable experiences into an impetus to moral action.[4]

Let me first make clear what I mean by 'pleasure.' Since we are referring here primarily to the pleasures of the dinner table, it makes sense to turn to a definition and important distinction made by the father of modern Western gastronomy, Jean Anthelme Brillat-Savarin. In *The Physiology of Taste*, he distinguishes 'the pleasures of the table...from the pleasure of eating, *their necessary antecedent*,' as follows:

48

The pleasure of eating is the actual and direct sensation of satisfying a need.

The pleasures of the table are a reflective sensation which is born from the various circumstances of place, time, things, and people who make up the surroundings of the meal.

The pleasure of eating is one we share with animals; it depends solely on hunger and what is needed to satisfy it.

The pleasures of the table are known only to the human race; they depend on careful preparations for the serving of the meal, on the choice of place, and the thoughtful assembling of the guests.

The pleasure of eating demands appetite, if not actual hunger; the pleasures of the table are most often independent of either one or the other...

During the first course, and at the beginning of the feast, everyone eats hungrily, without talking, without paying any attention to what may be going on about him, and no matter what his position or rank may be he ignores everything in order to devote himself to the great task at hand. But as these needs are satisfied, the intellect rouses itself, conversation begins, a new order of behavior asserts itself, and the man who was no more than an eater until then becomes a more or less pleasant companion, according to his natural ability.[5]

I will focus primarily on the moral value of the second type, 'the pleasures of the table,' though it is quite clear that the pleasures of the table are impossible without the pleasure of eating, and that they naturally follow after it, as the last paragraph of this definition suggests. The pleasures of the table inextricably combine physical and spiritual experiences. As Brillat-Savarin goes on to say,

[A]t the end of a well-savored meal both soul and body enjoy a special well-being. Physically, at the same time that a diner's brain awakens, his face grows animated, his color heightens, his eyes shine, and a gentle warmth creeps over his whole body. Morally, his spirit grows more perceptive, and clever phrases fly to his lips.[6]

This underlines two more crucial points. First, the pleasures of the table start from the sensual experience of the meal: the tastes, smells, sights, touches, and sounds one has in the company of their table companions. Secondly, it is *the talk* over the table prompted by those experiences that rouses the intellect and connects the sensory pleasures of the table to a moral sensibility. All of the savants of the dinner table I discuss here emphasize both of these points in one way or another.

This conceit of words about the table over the table was something with which Rabbenu Bahya ben Asher was quite taken. His wit, psychological insight, and high estimation of the pleasures of the table tempt me to describe him as a sort of medieval Jewish Brillat-Savarin (though his handbook of mystical eating etiquette, *Shulhan Shel Arba*, is more a theology than a physiology of taste) He knew it in the form of one my favorite passages in the classic text of rabbinic Judaism, the Talmud:

Rabbi Simeon said: If three have eaten at one table and have not spoken over it words of the Torah, it is as though they had eaten of the sacrifices of the dead, for it is written (Isaiah 28:8) 'For all tables are full of vomit, no place is without filthiness.' But if three have eaten at one table and have spoken over it words of the Torah, it is as if they had eaten from the table of God, for it is written (Ezekiel 41.22) 'He said to me, "This is the table which is before the LORD".' (m. Avot 3:3)

Rabbenu Bahya took this earlier tradition to mean that his circle of fellow mystics and rabbinic scholars should pepper their conversations at the dinner table with certain key passages from the Torah that talked directly or indirectly about eating, i.e., the pleasures of the table.[7] With his little handbook by their side at the table to provide talking points, Rabbenu Bahya advised his companions (and many other

49

Jews in subsequent generations) literally to speak 'words of Torah on – that is, about, the table – on, that is, physically over the table.[8] Why? Because in Rabbenu Bahya's view, the pleasures of the meal, eaten with the proper intent, that is by saying 'right words' can become the occasion of an ecstatic divine revelation, a visionary experience, equivalent to the visionary experience of the elders of the Israelites at Mount Sinai, who according to scripture, 'saw God and they ate and drank' (Ex 24:11) – the authentic 'real eating' about which I spoke at the 2005 Oxford Symposium.[9]

The moral significance of the this-worldly and otherworldly pleasures of Rabbenu Bahya's 'four-legged table' is that they are the cause, means, and reward for human beings to be what they were created for, to perform God's will that He revealed in the Torah. He says,

> the choicest of enjoyments, the pleasures of food were created only for the sake of the Torah, and for this reason they said in the Chapters of the Fathers: 'If there is no choice flour, there is no Torah, and if no Torah, no choice flour' (m. Avot 3:17), that is to say, there would be no pleasures of food.[10]

Rabbenu Bahya means several things by this. First, as Brillat-Savarin later concurs, the spiritual pleasures of the table cannot occur until your physical hunger for food is satisfied; you cannot be engaged in Torah, at least not on a regular basis, on an empty stomach. In that sense, *kemah*, which I translated as 'choice flour' is just a synonym for food in general. But *kemah's* literal meaning as finely ground flour, suggest that it's not just any food, but only the finest, more delicate foods, e.g., 'wine and fragrant foods,' and small poultry, that sharpen and purify the intellect 'for the soul to be lifted up and develop the aptitude to receive the Torah,' rather than beef, barley, and onions, 'coarse foods' typical of the diet of those with a coarseness of intellect.'[11] Joel Hecker aptly called the former 'brain foods' in his discussion of similar ideas in the Zohar.[12] Thirdly, Rabbenu Bahya interprets the converse, 'no choice flour, if no Torah,' to mean that the quantities, types, and occasions to eat foods that the Torah prescribes become occasions to know God better, since they indicate how God sustains the world.[13] It's precisely the knowledge of Torah that enables a person to turn even 'coarse' food like beef into something finer, that is, through the process of digestion only a Torah scholar can raise the animal soul of the beef he eats to a higher status nearer to God, through a sort of gastronomic metempsychosis.[14] The *words of Torah* about the table over the table direct the Torah scholars' minds to divine origin and messianic perfection of the foods they are presently eating (and the joys they are experiencing as they eat). This in effect transforms both themselves and their food (via the combustion-like process of their digestion) into something like the sacrificial fires on the altar of the ancient Temple in Jerusalem, which raise their material forms into something more ethereal and closer to God in heaven, 'a pleasing odor before the Lord.'[15] This process underlies the final point Rabbenu Bahya makes about the parallelism of the phrase in m. Avot 3:17, namely, if there is no food for the body (flour) there is no food for the soul (Torah), and if no food for the soul (Torah), no food for the body (flour) – *both* must have their due. Real eating is a fusion of body and soul pleasures toward their moral end, for 'the powers of the soul are invisible and are actualized only through the body.'[16] This is why Rabbenu Bahya is so insistent in the 4th Gate of his book that the messianic banquet reserved for the righteous in the world to come will be a real material meal of the flesh of Leviathan, Behemoth, and Bar Yochnai, and not a just a metaphor as some of the medieval philosophers took the rabbinic descriptions of this eschatological banquet to be. Even at the end of time, the soul can be perfected enough to have the capacity to see God only after the body is restored by this meal to its original immortal, perfect stature.[17] Thus Rabbenu Bahya asserts that eating and its concomitant, fused corporeal and psychic pleasures has moral value as the highest form of worship of God:

> See how one's eating is considered a perfect act of worship like one of the forms of the divine sacrifices, as the quintessential commandment. And this is the point of having the right intention at a meal at the table – that the body be nourished by it and take its bodily portion from the bodily eating, and the soul by this act of thought *is filled, fed, and satisfied as if from the choicest parts of real eating* of the ways of Ha-Shem and His *pleasantness*, and regarding this it is said, 'Your table is laid out with rich food.' (Job 36:16)[18]

51

This understanding of pleasure may also help clear up a significant modern misconception about religious faith. Many assume that religious faith is non-empirically based, but primarily on 'things unseen.' Therefore, it can be easily dismissed as irrational. Not so Jewish faith (and most others I suspect as well). Rabbenu Bahya employs a wonderful metaphor to make this point. Interpreting a peculiar Talmudic phrase, the 'three-legged table,' he asks, why a three-legged table when people ordinarily eat on a table of four legs? Because it hints at the fourth leg, which is invisible – the divine Reality behind the tangible ones we know through our senses.[19] Hence, the title of Rabbenu Bahya's book, '*The Four-Legged Table.*' What's striking is the proportion of the visible to the invisible, 3:1! True faith is firmly rooted in the empirical experiences of our senses, which the sensual pleasures of the table exemplify, and point to the graciousness and wisdom of God, and our moral obligation of gratitude.

Now we leave the medieval world of the Jewish mystics and turn to our examples of more modern, secular gourmands and gastronomes, and their views on the moral value of the pleasures of the table. First we return to Jean Anthelme Brillat-Savarin, who in *The Physiology of Taste* (1826) reiterates the importance of conversation for mediating the moral benefits of the pleasures of the table, in particular for encouraging harmonious social relations:

Gourmandism is one of the most important influences in our social life; it gradually spreads that spirit of conviviality which brings together from day to day differing kinds of people, melts them into a whole, animates their conversation, and softens the sharp corners of the conventional inequalities of position and breeding.

It is gourmandism, too, which motivates the effort any host must make to take good care of his guests, as well as their own gratitude when they perceive that he has employed all his knowledge and tact to please them; and it is fitting at this very place to point out with scorn those stupid diners who gulp down in disgraceful indifference the most nobly prepared dishes, or who inhale with impious inattention the bouquet of a limpid nectar.

General rule. Any preparation which springs from a high intelligence demands explicit praise, and a tactful expression of appreciation must always be made whenever it is plain that there is any attempt to please.[20]

Here, Brillat-Savarin's humanistic Enlightenment perspective comes to the fore, since pleasure encourages gratitude to one's fellow human beings, rather than God. Gourmandism not only promotes excellent social values, but does so in the form of appropriate speech by intelligent appreciative people at the dinner table.

Brillat-Savarin appreciated the importance of the pleasures of table talk as glue that holds society together.[21] If in his ideal table conversations, you didn't 'see God,' as Rabbenu Bahya' promised in his, Brillat-Savarin believed you could truly see one another and appreciated their company, his humanistic equivalent to the experience of divine revelation.

In Isak Dinesen's classic of gastronomic fiction, and the basis for the movie of the same name, *Babette's Feast*, we have a more explicit claim that the sensual pleasures of the table at a truly great meal enables its participants to 'see God,' despite pious fears to the contrary.[22] Particularly striking is the contrast the story sets up between silence and speech at the table of 'Babette's feast.' The elder members of the community, torn between their horror that the sensual pleasures of the sumptuous meal Babette prepared for them would drive them straight to hell, and their gratitude for all she had done for them in their soup kitchen, and now for them on the occasion of the hundredth anniversary of the preacher who founded their community,

[they] promised one another that... they would, on the great day, be silent upon all matters of food and drink. Nothing that might be set before them, be it frogs or snails, should wring a word from their lips.

'Even so,' said a white-bearded Brother, 'The tongue is a little member and boasteth great things. The tongue can no man tame; it is an unruly evil, full of deadly poison. On the day of our master we will cleanse our tongues of all taste and purify them of all delight or disgust of the senses, keeping and preserving them for the higher things of praise and thanksgiving.[23]

But the meal had quite a different effect on the tongue of the one guest who had not been a party to their covenant, General Loewenhielm, a sort of prodigal son figure who, now a real man of the world, at long last had returned home to the small village of his birth. As the unaccustomed wine was served to his solemn, silent table companions and him,

> General Loewenhielm, took a sip of it, startled, raised the glass first to his nose and then to his eyes, and sat down bewildered. 'This is very strange!' he thought. 'Amontillado! And the finest Amontillado that I have ever tasted.' After a moment, in order to test his senses, he took a small spoonful of his soup, took a second spoonful and laid down his spoon. 'This is exceedingly strange!' he said to himself. 'For surely I am eating turtle soup – and what turtle soup!' He was seized by a queer kind of panic and emptied his glass.
>
> Usually in Berlevaag people did not speak much while they were eating. But somehow this evening tongues had been loosened. An old brother told the story of his first meeting with the Dean. Another went through that sermon which sixty years ago had brought about his conversion. An aged woman, the to one whom Martine had first confided her distress [about the meal], reminded her friends how in all afflictions, any Brother or Sister was ready to share the burden of any other.[24]

And so the conversation went, until it culminated in a marvelous speech by the General, pointing to this meal as a striking manifestation of grace, beginning and ending with the beautiful image of harmony and reconciliation in an allusion to Psalm 85 in Scripture: 'Mercy and Truth, my friends, have met together...Righteousness and Bliss shall kiss one another.' Though his table companions didn't understand everything he said, the effect of 'his collected and inspired face and *the sound of well-known and cherished words had seized and moved all hearts.*'[25] Here, the combination of inspired food, inspired speech, and a long, complex shared history of the meal's participants seemed to have turned Babette's feast into a joyously moral lesson about the power of grace. The pleasures of Babette's feast repaired all the broken pieces of the world of the characters of Dinesen's story: the quarreling members of the community, the unrequited love between the pious sisters and their frustrated, more worldly suitors, the artists denied by fate the chance to practice their art, the living separated from their sorely missed dead, the presumably insurmountable chasm between the pleasures of the body and the pleasures of the soul. The talk prompted by Babette's remarkable feast reconnected its participants to one another and to the complex world.

Finally, we turn to Michael Pollan's observation about the power of words and the experience of grace that he makes at the end of *The Omnivore's Dilemma* on the occasion of the 'sustainable' banquet he holds for the friends who helped him bring it about:

53

[As] the conversation at the table unfurled like a sail amid the happy clatter of silver, tacking from stories of hunting to motherlodes of mushrooms to abalone adventures, I realized that in this particular case words of grace were unnecessary…

As you might expect from this crowd and occasion, the talk at the table was mainly about food. Yet this was not the usual food talk you hear nowadays; less about recipes and restaurants, it revolved around specific plants and animals and fungi, the places where they lived. The stories told by this little band of foragers ventured a long way from the table, the words (the tastes, too) recalling us to an oak forest in Sonoma, to a pine burn in the Sierra Nevada, to the stinky salt flats of San Francisco Bay, to slippery boulders on the Pacific coast, and to a backyard in Berkeley. The stories, like the food that fed them, cast lines of relation to all these places and the creatures living (and dying) in them, drawing them all together on this table, on these plates, in what to me began to feel a little like a ceremony. And there's sense in which the meal had become just that, a thanksgiving or a secular seder, for every item on our plates pointed somewhere else, almost sacramentally, tell a little story about nature or community or even the sacred, for mystery was very often the theme. Such storied food can feed us both body and soul, the threads of narrative knitting us together as a group, and knitting the group into the larger fabric of the given world.[26]

The stories he and his guests tell link the food part to the whole, cosmic, ecological picture. Good food and good conversation made Michael Pollan's meal a 'sacred,' 'sacramental' or 'mysterious' experience. The moral value of the pleasures of the table is precisely in the power of

storied food [to] feed us both body and soul, the threads of narrative knitting us together as a group, and knitting the group into the larger fabric of the given world.[27]

Pollan's 'words' and 'the tastes, too,' Dinesen's 'sound of well-known and cherished words' at Babette's feast, and Brillat-Savarin's 'spirit of conviviality which brings together … differing kinds of people, melts them into a whole, [and] animates their conversation' are not so far from Rabbenu Bahya's call for 'words about the table over the table.' All unite the pleasures of the table into a single experience that is both sensual and intellectual, enabling diners to both feel and know their connectedness to the people and natural world around them – seen and unseen. So we need both 'the table and the words of Torah over the table,' because as the Zohar says, 'Blessing does not rest on an empty place.'[28] Thus Rabbenu Bahya recommended the practice not only to say blessings over food before eating, but also to keep crumbs of food on table after eating for grace after meals, to draw down blessing. For only God creates something from nothing: we must create something from something.[29] There has to be something there, to which we are attached body and soul, some thing so good for us we can taste it, if we are to be moved to moral action. That is why the demonstrative is so important in our rituals of dinner. It 'cast[s] lines of relation' from what we are enjoying directly to the broader web of human and natural connections in our stories that demand a moral response – *this* is table of the Lord; *this* is my body, my blood; *this* is the wine and quail I tasted so many years ago in Paris before the war; *these* are the truffles we gathered ourselves, and the boar I hunted and caught: *these* eggs were from free-range chickens fed only on organic foods without growth hormones; *this* soup and salad is from the greens we planted and picked ourselves at our local CSA. Can the pleasures of good eating and good company get us to do the moral good? Speech-cued, mindful acts of eating, which, according to all four of our gastronomes, fuse the pleasures of the body and soul, indeed seem to give us the impetus to act morally.

Acknowledgements

I thank Zoe Brumberg-Kraus for her careful reading of this paper and thoughtful editorial suggestions, my research assistant Lindsay Van Clief, and Wheaton College for supporting my attendance at the 2007 Oxford Symposium with a Mellon Summer Faculty Research Stipend.

Notes

1. Daniel Sperber, *A Commentary on Derech Erez Zuta. [2], Chapters Five to Eight* (Ramat-Gan, Israel: Bar-Ilan University Press, 1990); Siegfried Stein, 'The Influence of Symposia Literature on the Literary Form of the Pesah Haggadah,' *Journal of Jewish Studies* 8:1–2 (1957), 13-44; Ze'ev Gries, *Sifrut Ha-Hanhagot: Toldoteha u-Mekomah be-Haye Haside R. Yisrael Ba'Al Shem-Tov* (Yerushalayim: Mosad Byalik, 1989), 18–22; Jonathan Brumberg-Kraus, 'Meals as Midrash: A Survey of Ancient Meals in Jewish Studies Scholarship' in *Food and Judaism*, eds. Leonard J. Greenspoon, Ronald Simkins and Gerald Shapiro, Vol. 15 (Omaha, NE; Lincoln, NE: Creighton University Press; distributed by the University of Nebraska Press, 2005), 300–302.
2. Jean Schuler, 'Kierkegaard at Babette's Feast: The Return to the Finite,' *Journal of Religion and Film* 1, no. 2 (1997): par. 2, http://www.unomaha.edu/jrf/kierkega.htm.
3. See especially now his new book *In Defense of Food: An Eater's Manifesto* (New York: Penguin Press, 2008).
4. Bahya ben Asher ben Hlava, 'Shulhan Shel Arba', in *Kitve Rabenu Bahya*, ed. Charles Ber Chavel, 1969), 453–514; Jean Anthelme Brillat-Savarin, *The Physiology of Taste, Or, Meditations on Transcendental Gastronomy* , trans. M.F.K. Fisher (Washington, D.C: Counterpoint Press, 1999); Isak Dinesen, 'Babette's Feast', in *Anecdotes of Destiny ; and, Ehrengard* (New York: Vintage Books, 1993), 21–59; Michael Pollan, *The Omnivore's Dilemma: A Natural History of Four Meals* (New York: Penguin Press, 2006), 450.; Jonathan Brumberg-Kraus, 'Meat-Eating and Jewish Identity; Ritualization of the Priestly Torah of Beast and Fowl (Lev 11:46) in Rabbinic Judaism and Medieval Kabbalah,' *AJS Review*

24, no. 2 (1999), 227–262; 'The Ritualization of Scripture in Rabbenu Bahya's *Shulhan Shel Arba*,' *World Congress of Jewish Studies* 13 (2001): 1–17; '"Real Eating": A Medieval Spanish Jewish View of Gastronomic Authenticity' in *Authenticity in the Kitchen : Proceedings of the Oxford Symposium on Food and Cookery*, ed. Richard Hosking (Totnes: Prospect Books, 2006), 119–131.

5. Ibid., 182. Kass, *The Hungry Soul*, 134, cites this passage favorably to emphasize that there is a uniquely human way of satisfying our natural hunger, which distinguishes us from other animals.

6. Brillat-Savarin, *Physiology of Taste*, 183.

7. Bahya ben Asher ben Hlava, *Shulhan Shel Arba*', 474.

8. Ibid., 460. The Hebrew word '*al*' in the expression '*divre Torah al ha-shulhan*' from m. Avot 3:3 can have this double meaning, especially in the playful way the rabbis interpreted their texts.

9. Ibid., 492–3; Brumberg-Kraus, 'Real Eating,' 119–131. The relatively numerous extant manuscripts and printed editions of *Shulhan Shel Arba* attest to its popularity, especially among Eastern European Hasidim, well beyond Rabbenu Bahya's elite circle of Spanish kabbalists. See Chavel's introductory comments in Bahya ben Asher ben Hlava, *Kitve Rabenu Bahya*, ed. Charles Ber Chavel (Yerushalayim: Mosad ha-Rav Kuk, 1969), 456.

10. Bahya ben Asher ben Hlava, *Shulhan Shel Arba*', 496.

11. Ibid., 496.

12. Joel Hecker, *Mystical Bodies, Mystical Meals: Eating and Embodiment in Medieval Kabbalah* (Detroit: Wayne State University Press, 2005), 282.

13. Bahya ben Asher ben Hlava, *Shulhan Shel Arba*', 496–7.

14. Ibid., 496.

15. This interpretation turns on the similarity of Hebrew words for man (*ish*), fire (*esh*), and 'My sacrificial fire' or 'My sacrificial fire offering' (*ishi*):

> And from this understand the matter of the sacrifices, which are the hidden things of the Torah, about which it is written: 'to My [offering by] fire, my pleasing odor' [Nu 28:2]. The power of the higher soul increases and is added to by the fire offerings in the eating of the sacrifices, and so our rabbis said;16 'My sacrifice, My bread, to My [offering by] fire.' ... to My fire you give it, i.e., 'My man,' the Torah scholar, ibid., 492.

17. Ibid., 492.

18. Ibid., 504. According to rabbinic tradition, Adam and Eve's original physical stature in the Garden of Eden was dramatically diminished as a consequence of their eating of the forbidden fruit, ibid., 458.

19. Ibid., 497.

20. Ibid., 461.

21. Brillat-Savarin, *The Physiology of Taste*, 153.

22. Ibid.

23. Dinesen, *Babette's Feast*, 21–59; *Babette's Feast*, directed by Gabriel Axel (New York, N.Y.: Orion Home Video, 1989).

24. Dinesen, *Babette's Feast*, 41.

25. Ibid., 48–49.

26. Ibid., 53.

27. Pollan, *The Omnivore's Dilemma*, 406–408.

28. Ibid., 408.

29. Hecker, *Mystical Bodies, Mystical Meals*, 145–146.

30. Bahya ben Asher ben Hlava, *Shulhan Shel Arba*', 477; Hecker, *Mystical Bodies, Mystical Meals*, 148–149.

From Necessity to Virtue:
The Secondary Uses of Bread in Italian Cookery

Anthony F. Buccini

Introduction.[1]

In the early to mid twentieth century and to some degree beyond, among southern Italians both in Italy and in emigrant communities outside of Italy, there was a widespread and strong feeling of respect for and even reverence toward bread, an attitude which was intimately connected to the belief that it was in a real sense a sin to waste bread. Insofar as most southern Italians in that period were themselves either poor or of relatively limited means or at the least were in one way or another not far removed from such circumstances, it is not surprising that they generally shared a deep appreciation of frugality in the kitchen and an overarching abhorrence for the wasting of food of any kind. And yet, beside or beyond such general culinary ethics stood the particular attitude toward bread, the seriousness of which was manifested in some of the customs surrounding its treatment. For example, a whole or partial loaf had to be set down properly, oriented with top and bottom as they had been in the oven, and if, for some reason, a loaf was not standing as it should, a watchful elder would soon rectify the situation; even in the large bins of a busy bakery, each loaf would have to be arranged properly. More striking still is the custom attached to the accidental dropping of a piece of bread: the bread had to be retrieved immediately, blown on to remove any dust it had picked up, and then, according to what I take to be the mainstream and older tradition, the bread was kissed and eaten; for some, the kiss was or could be replaced by the making of the sign of the cross and, when and where hygiene came to take precedence over sustenance, the bread could be thrown out, but only after the proper gestures expressing respect, regret and contrition.

Southern Italians were not unique in having a special regard for bread, for, without doubt, similar strong feelings and even reverence toward bread have been and are parts of many cultures: one might, for example, be reminded here of the special place of bread in Greek Orthodox belief and custom or of the 'bread and salt' traditions of eastern Europe. And, indeed, though I do not know exactly how widespread the custom of respectfully kissing and then eating or saving for later a fallen piece of bread was in European cultures, I know it was still recently practiced to a degree at least in some Roman Catholic countries other than Italy, such as Portugal.

Basic foodstuffs take on a symbolic value in all cultures and such is the case with the 'holy trinity' of the Mediterranean area: wine, olive oil and, above all, bread. In the products of both high and popular culture, bread stands symbolically not just for food in general but for other forms of sustenance as well. This symbolic value of bread grew out of its fundamental position in the diet of most elements of society in the past and to the degree that bread has lost that fundamental status, its symbolic value has become more an historical artifact and less a psychological reality. But up to the recent past, growing out of the necessity of the poor to use every crumb they had, there was a strong moral feeling about 'the staff of life,' a feeling that clearly transcended mere issues of necessity and compelled people to treat bread with the particular measure of respect described above: to waste bread was not just an act of economic irresponsibility but one of moral transgression.

In this paper, we consider the development of moral feelings regarding the use of bread and examine the place of bread in the cuisine of Italy generally and southern Italy in particular and discuss the many ways in which stale bread – which on account of economic, moral and aesthetic needs was regularly on hand – came to be a basic and esteemed ingredient in traditional cookery. In concluding, we briefly consider how the central place of bread in the diet of some communities has been lost and with it many of the uses of stale bread, along with the moral sentiment toward it.

The principal place of bread

The great regional diversity of Italian cuisine has become axiomatic among students of food history and cookery and also increasingly among the ever-expanding body of non-professional food enthusiasts around the world. Whereas not long ago most non-Italians may only have been vaguely aware of some general and basic differences between so-called northern Italian cuisine and so-called southern Italian cuisine, nowadays one observes a rapidly growing interest in and appreciation of genuinely regional food products and dishes, as reflected in the subjects of cookbooks and television cooking shows, as well as in the offerings of grocery shops and restaurants.

This regional culinary diversity in Italy can be traced from the present day back through the twentieth and nineteenth centuries to a remarkable degree and further back to the early modern period to a more limited degree. Yet, a great many of the regional cuisines and traditional food-ways of Italy that we admire and enjoy today were perhaps admired but not widely enjoyed by the bulk of the Italian population; rather, much of what we think of today as basic and staple elements of the regional cuisines were enjoyed regularly only by the upper and middle classes and by the lower classes and especially the peasantry either not at all or only on the rare and special occasion.

This last point draws attention to a commonly ignored or underappreciated fact about Italian culinary culture, namely, that regional diversity, especially at the level of the official and historical regions (*regioni*) such as Liguria or Tuscany or Calabria, is but one parameter of variation in the nation's patterns of alimentation. For within each of the historical regions and operating across the regional borders are further important parameters of variation, such as that of socio-economic class, to which we just alluded, and basic contrasts, that correspond to significant divisions in culinary habits; that is, in addition to the oppositions of class such as rich vs. poor or bourgeois vs. working, there are other significant oppositions, such as urban vs. rural, coastal vs. interior, plains vs. mountains. To be sure, these oppositions are of steadily diminishing significance at the present time but as one looks at progressively earlier periods, they correspond to increasingly noteworthy differences in diet and foodways.

The complex intersection of cultural historic, socio-economic, and climatic-geographical factors has produced over time the remarkable culinary diversity of Italy but within the complexity one can detect some basic principles around which several of the aforementioned oppositions tend to cluster. To be specific, both diversity of ingredients and overall nutritional quality of ingredients has tended, not surprisingly, to be higher in the diet of the rich than in that of the poor, but aligning themselves in a general way here are also the oppositions of urban vs. rural and coastal vs. interior. Of course, this kind of gross generalisation has the weakness of ignoring all sorts of extremely important exceptions and interesting wrinkles but it does bring to light the fundamental historical division in the culinary culture of Italy, which is not northern vs. southern but rather, in the first place, coastal vs. mountain, and allied to that, bourgeois vs. peasant. Though this claim may seem at first blush unsurprising or even trivial, it is not, at least insofar as much of what is today thought of as fundamental to Italian cuisine in a general sense and assumed to have had that status throughout time, was in fact largely only marginally present in the diets of large portions of the Italian population. Specifically, pasta, seafood and olive oil, though perhaps always more or less universally appreciated and desired, were rarely consumed by the peasants of the non-coastal areas of Italy. And if one considers the geography of the country and its socio-economic history, one realises that before the early to mid twentieth century, the diet of many Italians was in some very basic ways quite different from what it is today. The late twentieth and early twenty-first century notion of the Mediterranean Diet, especially as the term is romanticised in advertising copy and bandied about in mass media, is something of an abstraction and idealisation with an ultimately real but surprisingly qualified foundation in reality.

That an accomplished student of Italian culinary traditions can write – with justification – that [today] 'the main Italian staple made of wheat flour is certainly pasta (Parasecoli 2004: 47) attests to the degree to which the basic eating habits of Italy have changed over the past hundred years and in particular how they have become progressively more bourgeois. Into the early twentieth century, bread was without question the main staple in the Italian diet, for it not only appeared at virtually every meal for the general population but for many Italians it typically did so as the primary element of most of those meals. Though wheat has been divided between use for bread and use for noodles, as well as pastries and such, from the Roman days of 'bread and circuses,' its undisputed primary use was for the making of bread.

Now, in saying that it is only a fairly recent development that one might conceive of pasta as the 'main Italian staple made from wheat flour' and not bread, we are most certainly not claiming that pasta is either a more or less recent development in the history of alimentation in Italy nor that it has been an unimportant element in Italian culinary tradition; on the contrary, pasta has long been an important and genuinely beloved part of the culinary repertoire of almost all the regions of Italy but the frequency with which it appeared on tables was by all accounts far less than it is in current times. In fact, in general it tended to be in a sense a luxury item and thus was until recently a rare treat for the poorest elements of society and something that only relatively well-off people could enjoy on ordinary occasions. Rice had a similar status in most of the country. Indeed, in rural Italy, for a couple of hundred years before the twentieth century, maize and potatoes seem generally to have been a far more significant element in terms of nutrition of the broader population's diet than either pasta or rice, even if these last two foods have generally held a higher place in Italian culinary imagination and aesthetics than the two starchy imports from the Americas.

What determines the diet of the poorer classes has historically been more a question of availability than choice and so it was with the staple foods for the bulk of the rural population of Italy before the current period of vastly increased prosperity.[2] Most important is the fact that the high value of wheat assured that the tenant farmers, sharecroppers and day-labourers who worked to produce Italy's wheat got to eat precious little of it, with most of the produce being shipped to market and destined for urban and well-off consumers. Throughout the modern period up to the twentieth century, the limited access to wheat and especially to highly refined kinds of flour meant not only that pasta was a luxury food for much of the Italian population but, in fact, so too was bread made wholly from wheat. Indeed, there existed a whole range of bread types, depending on the quality and kinds of ingredients used to make them, which closely reflected the economic circumstances of the consumer and which were conceptually linked to the relative station and worth of the social groups that ate them.

At the two extremes of this range of basic bread types were *pane bianco*, 'white bread,' which was made of refined wheat flour, and *pane nero*, 'black bread,' which was made of a combination of ingredients. The former was, of course, expensive and sufficiently so for the general populace in Calabria that in that region the phrase *donna di pane bianco*, 'lady of white bread,' came to be equivalent to the term *signora* (Helstosky 2004: 14). Even if made with less refined grades of flour, bread made solely from wheat was, depending on region and sometimes also time of year, often an extreme luxury and, again, in Calabria, the habit of reserving such *pane di grano* – that is, 'bread from wheat grain' – for people in ill health and especially those on their death-bed, gave rise to a popular turn of phrase: to say that someone *è a pane de ranu* meant that he is close to death (Storchi 1985: 156; cf. Teti 1998: 80).

At the other end of the spectrum was the black bread, which varied considerably across space and time in its exact constitution but which always involved the presence of substantial amounts of non-wheat flour, typically alongside some more or less limited amount of coarsely milled wheat flour. The non-wheat ingredients could include spelt, rye, buckwheat, oats, barley, millet, chick-pea, fava, chestnut, the potentially toxic chickling vetch and, after the diffusion of New World products, maize and potato. Given such a wide variety of possible ingredients, it seems safe to say that these peasant breads varied greatly in their flavour, their nutritional value, etc., and in certain times and places, the product could surely be quite good. Compared to *pane bianco*, *pane nero* was, of course, not only darker in colour but also often rather more coarse and dry in texture and heavy in consistency. When circumstances rendered the better grains unavailable and only the other kinds of ingredients were at hand in any appreciable amounts, the peasants' black breads could apparently be quite unpalatable with regard both to flavour and texture and of very limited nutritional value (Teti 1998: 79).

Whether the peasants' black bread was good or bad, it had to be eaten, for the other elements of their diet – the legumes in the winter, the greens and garden vegetables in the spring and summer, and the typically meagre quantities of fish and animal products – were pretty much all to be viewed as *companatici*, that is, as accompaniments to bread. Under such circumstances, it is by no means difficult to imagine how the reverence for bread, however old it was in origin, had come about and been maintained, especially with the psychological reinforcement it received from the sacral role of bread in the Universal Church. The means of physical survival, associated with the body of Christ and spiritual salvation through Catholicism's central sacrament, bread was literally and figuratively life and any disrespect toward it or wasting of it could not help but be viewed as sinful.

The secondary uses of bread

In general, there is an interplay between technological, agricultural and economic necessities and limitations surrounding food production and preparation and the nutritional and aesthetic needs and desires of consumers; out of that interplay arises the cuisine of those consumers. In the case of the rural poor of Italy in the eighteenth, nineteenth and early twentieth centuries, the opposing influences or forces were clearly out of balance and these people's inability to overcome the externally imposed limitations and satisfy their nutritional needs and aesthetic desires was keenly felt. With specific regard to the place of bread in their cuisine, we have already noted above how the expense of wheat and, to various degrees at various times and places, the dearth of other, better, ingredients for bread forced people to eat loaves that were both nutritionally and aesthetically unsatisfying.

But beyond the basic issues of the quantity and quality of bread available, there was a further crucial limiting factor: their access to the ovens and fuel needed to bake their bread. The very poorest of the rural and urban poor did not have ovens of their own, nor did many of the less desperately poor. For these people, communal or professional ovens had to be used and they could bake bread only occassionally, because the expense of heating an oven demanded, a large quantity had to be made to amortize the cost. The consequence of this occasional ability to bake – perhaps once a week or every other week or even in some circumstances only at much greater intervals – was that the loaves tended to be large and were necessarily consumed in varying states of desiccation and staleness.

Bearing the above in mind, namely, that the basic bread of the poor was in effect not intended to be eaten fresh out of the oven and for the most part was expected still to be the main form of sustenance when dry and stale, the reference to the uses of bread to be discussed here as secondary betrays the modern perspective of a time when freshness in bread is expected and stale bread is generally unwanted and routinely thrown in the trash.

Yet, between the world of the rural poor of eighteenth or nineteenth century Italy, in which giant loaves of homemade bread, baked once every now and again, represented the main food for entire families, and the modern consumerist world in which factory made bread is expected to be available fresh any day and time, there exists a middle place where the exigencies of grinding poverty no longer demand that one consume little more than *pane nero* at every meal and yet the feelings of reverence toward bread have remained alive and along with them a strong sense that one must not waste bread under any circumstances.

I grew up, among the descendants of people who had escaped the poverty of southern Italy by emigrating to the United States and it is primarily from that particular perspective that I discuss the secondary uses of bread, though I draw connections to parallels elsewhere in Italian culinary traditions and beyond.

Se non è zuppa è pan bagnato. The problem of what to do with stale bread and more specifically, how to make it less of a challenge to tooth and jaw, is surely as old as bread itself and so too is the prime solution, namely, to soak or cook the bread in water or broth. And indeed, this practice is known to have been used already in the ancient Near East where, for example, there is attested in Hittite a word – borrowed from Luwian – for bread soup.[3] Indeed, the word *soup* almost certainly Germanic in origin and probably originally referring to the bathed bread rather than the bath itself, long ago became an international word with cognate or borrowed forms in all the languages of western Europe. In traditional parlance, Italian *zuppe* have remained true to the old sense of the word and involved the bringing together of the liquid element with bread, as reflected in the Italian expression analogous to the English 'six of one, half dozen of the other,' which is *se non è zuppa è pan bagnato*: 'if it's not soup, it's soaked bread.'

While Italian *zuppe* traditionally include bread of one sort or another, either in the form of slices of relatively fresh or toasted bread, fried slices or croutons, or slices or chunks of stale bread, there are throughout Italy a number of other terms that are also used to refer to the union of liquids and bread. Probably the best known of these outside of Italy is *pancotto* or *panecotto*, literally, 'cooked bread,' which in some places is thought of in terms of more or less set combinations of locally favoured ingredients but from a broader perspective implies little more than the idea of a dish comprised of a cooked liquid or broth that is used at once to flavour and soften stale bread. Whether it is possible to offer neatly contrasting definitions for *zuppa* on the one hand and *pancotto* on the other seems to me unlikely, though for what it's worth it is my feeling that there is a difference in emphasis and in relative quantities: in a *zuppa*, the bread complements the chief ingredients of the soup and in the sorts of dishes that typically sport the name *pancotto*, the central ingredient is the bread. In my experience, the liquid element of *pancotto* tends to be thin and watery in consistency; soups can be more or less watery but tend toward having a thicker consistency.

Other names for generally similar combinations of soupy preparations and bread – usually stale – are *panata* or *panada*, *pan bollito*, 'boiled bread', and *acqua cotta*, 'cooked water.' More regionally bound names of dishes of this sort from the south are *licurda*, featuring fresh favas and bread, and *licurdia*, an onion based soup with bread, both from Calabria, and *cialdedda*, which in Lucania denotes a soupy dish with tomatoes and bread.[4]

While the subject of this paper is secondary uses of bread in Italian cookery and thus features the uses of stale bread, a special kind of baked product that is perhaps not immediately thought of as bread in the usual sense very much deserves to be treated here, namely, the breads that are twice baked – *biscotti* or *pane biscottati* – in order that they can easily be preserved for long term use without becoming stale. It seems highly likely too that this product was conceived of as a further way to maximise every bit of energy generated in the heating of the oven for a large-scale 'bake.' In the cookery of Campania and more generally of southern Italy, there are two forms of biscuit used in ways analogous to the ways that stale bread is used, namely, *biscuotti*, often made by baking a second time a (partially or wholly) sliced loaf of just baked bread, or *freselle*, which are made by making small ring-shaped or doughnut shaped breads, baking them and then slicing each one horizontally to leave two rings, which are then baked a second time.

These biscuits can serve as the core ingredient in many of the preparations in which stale bread is used but also have their own traditional applications. In my own experience, a favourite use of *biscuotti* involves soaking them in a spicy tomato sauce and serving them alongside shrimp or mussels or other kinds of seafood that have been cooked and dressed in that same sauce. For *freselle*, two common and quite different preparations spring immediately to mind. The one is of a soupy nature and involves the soaking of pieces of *freselle* in what is known as 'bean water' (*acqua di fagioli*), which is to say the water left over from the cooking of dry (usually *cannelini*) beans, which can be augmented with some of the beans themselves, and dressed with olive oil, oregano or parsley, and black pepper; the simplicity of this dish belies its

63

deliciousness.[5] Another common way to eat *freselle* is in a dish known in continental southern Italy as *caponata* which is not to be confused with the Sicilian eggplant dish that bears the same name. Southern Italian *caponata* is in essence a salad in which the most substantial component is the desiccated bread. Pieces of *freselle* are softened by being dunked in water and then are dressed with slices of tomato, olive oil, salt, garlic and oregano, optionally also celery, black olives and capers.

A couple of further observations about *biscuotti* and *freselle* deserve mention here. One point is that while versions of these items made with refined white flour exist, whole-wheat versions seem to have always been more popular and in that way perhaps reflect a peasant or poor person's tradition in which the bread was necessarily not 'white.' Another point to be mentioned is the degree to which the southern Italian biscuits resemble in form and use the traditional biscuits of Crete and mainland Greece, the *paximadia*, though in Crete and Greece these remain even closer to an older tradition in that they are most often made with mixtures of wheat and other grains, especially barley.

These dishes that feature softened dry or stale bread are clearly not especially in vogue, either in Italy or in emigrant communities of Italians, much less with the many non-Italians who appreciate the cuisines of Italy; consequently, they are not especially well known outside of their traditional settings. To this there is, however, perhaps one major exception: With the remarkable popularity of Tuscany as a tourist destination and of its cuisine as an important cultural aspect of a region that bears a definite cachet, it seems the Tuscan analogues of these bread-based dishes have gained some popularity and their own measure of cachet among cognoscenti. Among the soupy preparations, Tuscany's *ribollita* is surely known to a degree outside of its native region and outside Italy as well and in the class of bread-based salads, which includes the aforementioned southern Italian *caponata*, the Tuscan *panzanella* is also well known outside its home region and is, for example, appearing now regularly in the foodie-mass media of the United States. A further traditional Tuscan dish that uses old bread is *pappa al pomodoro*, a thick sort of a soup made with cubes of stale bread, garlic, tomatoes and basil or sage. As in the other cases, the Tuscan dish has some close analogues in other regional traditions of Italy and among southern Italians, a dish that is essentially identical to the Tuscan *pappa al pomodoro* in ingredients but slightly different in method of preparation exists: whereas in Tuscany the cubed bread is typically fried in the pan to which are then added the tomatoes, the versions I know involve the making of a simple tomato sauce in which slices of stale bread are subsequently cooked. In this style of dish is *'u pesce fujjute* ('the escaped fish') from Termoli, Molise, which features slices of stale bread standing in for the fish that fled, cooked atop a base made with olive oil, onion, tomato, sweet and hot peppers along with some water.

'Cause meatballs like you don't bounce. We proceed now from the group of dishes described above, in which bread features as the primary or one of the primary ingre-

dients, to one in which bread is a major element but, especially from the modern standpoint, is conceptually of secondary importance.

First among these dishes are the myriad of variants on the meatloaf or meatball theme (*polpettone, polpette*). Though these preparations are certainly enjoyed by rich and poor alike, they are widely recognised as being an especially handy way for those who have little or no access to high quality cuts of meat to get the most out of what is on hand. In many parts of Italy and especially in the rural south, muscle meat was rarely available for much of the population and when it was, it was often the very tough meat from the carcass of a working animal that was too old or ill to be useful.[6] The toughness of the meat could be overcome through grinding and the overall quantity could be stretched through the inclusion of stale bread. But whereas one may be inclined to think of the bread element of meatballs as filler, it actually can also serve to render the texture of the meatball lighter, more tender and juicy. For the bread to serve in this way, there must be a sufficient quantity of it and it must be in the right form. In my experience, the quantity of bread used by the most accomplished and traditional cooks is quite substantial, in the range of 40 per cent of the quantity of the meat used, and the form of the bread employed should be the crumb from a stale loaf which is then soaked. As Schwartz (1998: 271) has noted, the greater availability of meat for Italian immigrants in the United States has not necessarily had a good effect on the production of meatballs, for the tendency is for many cooks to decrease the bread filler and to use dry breadcrumbs instead of the soaked stale crumb, yielding meatballs that are dense and heavy and quite unlike the traditional version.

Also to be mentioned here is the traditional use of the soaked crumb from a stale loaf as the principal component of stuffings for vegetables, especially in instances where the cavity to be filled is fairly large, as in the case of bell peppers.

Pangrattato and Mollica. In Italian, a distinction is made between two forms of bread that can both be referred to as 'breadcrumbs' in English. *Pangrattato*, literally 'grated bread,' is indeed made by grating thoroughly desiccated or stale bread and thus corresponds to the substance most commonly called 'breadcrumbs.' *Mollica* in Italian corresponds to the term 'crumb' – as opposed to the crust – in talking of bread but then is also used to refer to this substance as used in dishes, where it can be toasted or fried and end up resembling dry breadcrumbs.[7] Be that as it may, it seems that in the modern kitchen, it is increasingly the case that the one very well-known use for stale bread is the production of breadcrumbs (*pangrattato*), which continue to be used in a wide variety of ways: as coating for all kinds of foods that are to be fried, as toppings for baked dishes, as fillings for vegetables and, as mentioned above, as 'filler' in preparations featuring minced or chopped meat or fish, including in the stuffings used in such pasta as ravioli and tortellini.

Further uses of breadcrumbs in Italian cooking – both *pangrattato* and *mollica* – is their use as a dressing or topping in pasta dishes. Of these, the most widely known examples outside of Italy are probably ones which have their origins in the traditional regional cooking of Sicily: *pasta con le sarde*, pasta with sardines, and the no less delicious *pasta con i broccoli arriminati*, pasta with cauliflower, both highly seasoned dishes that include anchovy and saffron, as well as a number of other ingredients. Toasted breadcrumbs are an integral part of the dish with sardines and a very common addition to that with the cauliflower. Toasted or fried breadcrumbs are a traditional topping for pasta in the southern part of the mainland and in Lucania (the modern region of Basilicata). One of the most famous dishes combines homemade long noodles made with the aid of a thin metal spoke (*maccherone al ferro*, also known as *ferretti* or, in dialect, *firzuli*) with a dressing of garlic, ground red chile and breadcrumbs, all of which is fried in olive oil or lard (Palazzo, Chapter 5). Analogues to this supremely simple dish are known in many other parts of Italy, from Sicily all the way to Tuscany (Bugialli 1988: 54).

Reasons for using breadcrumbs as toppings on pasta dishes surely include both their positive contributions in taste and texture and also their availability to people unable to afford much cheese, but it should also be noted that in using breadcrumbs and not using cheese, many of these dishes get a boost in taste and texture while remaining completely free of animal products and thus are appropriate for consumption on Catholic fast days according to the old, conservative rules.

Noodles and Dumplings. One last category deserves at least brief mention in this review, though for the most part the dishes that belong here are from outside the southern Italian regions that have been our central focus. The use of bread and breadcrumbs to form noodles and dumplings seems to be a practice that is far more a part of northern Italian traditions and, moreover, can be seen as one of a number of culinary features that are shared between the northern regions of Italy and southern Germany and Austria and further on in neighbouring Slavic lands. Given that, it's not surprising that some of the most famous examples of this use of bread from Italy come from the German-speaking region of Trentino, namely *canederli* (German *Knödel*) and the local bread-based dumpling that goes under the name *strangolapreti* ('priest-strangler'), a name that is used for various kinds of noodles or dumplings elsewhere in Italy.

At some distance from the German-speaking areas there are bread-based noodles and dumplings from various places in northern and north-central Italy and it appears likely that this tradition was once more widespread than it is today. A dumpling made with bread that cannot be overlooked here are the *pisarei* of Monferrato in Piemonte, which are made with flour, breadcrumbs and water and are dressed with beans and a sauce featuring tomatoes, aromatic vegetables and pancetta. According to Bugialli (1988: 190), virtually the same dish is traditionally made in the relatively far-off Piacenza, in Emilia-Romagna. More widespread in this last region, as well as in neighbouring Tuscany and Le Marche, are the bread-based noodles known generally as *passatelli*. These noodles always include as their basis breadcrumbs, eggs and parmesan cheese and are cooked in and eaten with broth (Bugialli 1988: 321–3).

That analogous dishes were once made in the south of Italy seems quite possible but certainly there are no widespread or well-known counterparts to the *passatelli* of the north. I know, however, of one dish that is from a practical standpoint a bread based form of pasta, namely, the dumplings known as *scescille* from Molise. Much like *passatelli*, these are made from breadcrumbs, eggs and grated cheese but, rather than being cooked in broth, they are cooked in a sauce of olive oil, tomato and onion. Conceptually, these dumplings seem to stand halfway between the classic dumplings of Italian cookery, *gnocchi*, and meatless meatballs, which are or at least once were a widely known treat of the *cucina povera* of southern Italy.

Death of a tradition

I once wrote in reference to *panecotto* and more generally to the use of stale bread that 'what for many would seem like something barely worthy of eating, would be turned into a treat that you would find yourself longing for.' Sophia Loren (1998: 24) wrote in the context of recalling the appearance of dishes featuring stale bread on the family table that 'in absolute childhood innocence, I'd wish those hard times would come upon us more often.' Perhaps there is a bit of bourgeois sentimentality behind such statements, romanticizing of things that seem much better in memory and at a certain distance. To be sure, the tendency has been for Italians both in Italy and elsewhere to reduce the centrality of bread in their diet, with pasta taking an ever larger role. And among Italians outside of Italy, assimilation to non-Italian culinary culture has resulted in many cases to an almost complete loss of any special reverence or feeling toward bread and with that an equally large-scale reduction in the secondary use of bread in their cookery.

The loss of the sense of reverence for bread and of the concomitant sense of a need to use every bit of it one has is the loss of a fundamental cultural principle that signals a change in the entire cuisine itself, even if, at the surface, many or most dishes continue to be made in the same ways as always. To make an analogy to language, individual dishes are like individual words but an ethical belief such as that concerning bread forms part of the grammar of a cuisine, and a fundamental change of the grammar is significant not only in the short term but increasingly so in the long term.

Perhaps those who are inclined to sing the virtues of the uses of stale bread are guilty of foolish sentimentality but for some of us, the moral compulsion to save and use every scrap of bread is too strong to give up and, in fact, the dishes made with that old bread too delicious to abandon.

References.

Buccini, Anthony F., 'Western Mediterranean Vegetable Stews and the Integration of Culinary Exotica' in *Authenticity in the Kitchen: Proceedings of the Oxford Symposium on Food and Cookery 2005*, ed. Richard Hosking (Totnes: Prospect Books, 2006), pp. 132–45.

——, 'On *Spaghetti alla Carbonara* and Related Dishes of Central and Southern Italy' in *Eggs in Cookery: Proceedings of the Oxford Symposium on Food and Cookery 2006*, ed. Richard Hosking (Totnes: Prospect Books, 2007) 36–47.

Bugialli, Giuliano, *Bugialli on Pasta* (New York: Simon & Schuster, 1988).

Capatti, Alberto, and Massimo Montanari, *Italian Cuisine: A Cultural History*, trans. Aine O'Healy (New York: Columbia University Press, 2003).

Helstosky, Carol, *Garlic and Oil* (Oxford: Berg, 2004).

Lambertini, Egano, Enrico Volpe and Antonio Guizzaro, *Miseria e nobiltà nella storia della cucina napoletana* (Napoli: Tempo Lungo, 1999).

Loren, Sophia, *Recipes & Memories* (New York: GT Publishing, 1998).

Melchert, H. Craig, 'Prehistory' in *The Luwians*, ed. H. Craig Melchert (Leiden: Brill, 2003), pp. 8–26.

Palazzo, Isabella, *Il pane quotidiano: l'alimentazione lucana dall'Unità ad oggi* (Calice Editore; online: http://www.starttel.it/palazzo/1_copertina.html).

Parasecoli, Fabio, *Food culture in Italy* (Westport, CT: Greenwood Press, 2004).

Schwartz, Arthur, *Naples at Table* (New York: HarperCollins, 1998).

Simeti, Mary Taylor, *Pomp and Sustenance: Twenty-five Centuries of Sicilian Food* (New York: Henry Holt, 1991).

Storchi, Mario R., 'L'alimentazione nel Regno di Napoli attraverso i dati della statistica murattiana' in *Studi sul Regno di Napoli nel Decennio francese (1806–1815)*, ed. Aurelio Lepre (Napoli: Liguori, 1985). pp. 145–61.

Taddei, Francesca, 'Il cibo nell'Italia mezzadrile fra Ottocento e Novecento' in *Storia d'Italia, Annali 13, L'alimentazione*, ed. Alberto Capatti, Alberto De Bernardi and Angelo Varni (Torino: Giulio Einaudi, 1998), pp. 23–61.

Teti, Vito, 'Le culture alimentari nel Mezzogiorno continentale in età contemporanea' in *Storia d'Italia, Annali 13, L'alimentazione*, ed. Alberto Capatti, Alberto De Bernardi and Angelo Varni (Torino: Giulio Einaudi, 1998), pp. 65–165.

Notes

1. This paper is dedicated to my friends, the Masi brothers, Frank, Joe and Sam, at the Italian Superior Bakery, Chicago. It is part of an on-going series of studies on the culinary ethno-history of the Mediterranean area and has been preceded by Buccini (2005) and Buccini (2006). As always, I owe a considerable debt of gratitude to Amy Dahlstrom for the various ways in which she helped me with this paper. I also thank Frank Masi, for all that he has taught me not only about the traditions of his family and neighbourhood, but also about the making of various traditional Italian breads: *mille grazie al mio maestro*.

2. For a discussion of the diet and food-ways of the rural population in north-central Italy in the eighteenth and nineteenth centuries, see Taddei 1998, and regarding bread, especially p. 30ff. Treatment of the diet of the rural population in the south of Italy can be found in Teti 1998, with a discussion of bread on pp. 76ff. Broader overviews of social history and food in Italy can be found in the relevant chapters of Capatti & Montanari 2003, Helstosky 2004 and Parasecoli 2004.

3. Melchert (2003: 17–8): 'The inflection of NINDA *harzazun* - *harzazut* – 'bread-soup, ribollita' shows that it is also a Luwian loanword [into Hittite].'

4. In Puglia, however, the name *cialdedda* or *cialedda* often refers to a drier dish, more like the

Neapolitan *caponata* discussed below, with the stale bread being just moistened with water before being dressed with oil, tomatoes, etc.

5. According to Lambertini et al. (1999: 159), between the world wars, it was often joked about that many Neapolitan working class families would subsist all during the week on nothing but soupy beans and bread and then splurge on Sundays with a grand dinner of maccheroni and meat.

6. See, for example, Storchi 1985 on the availability of meat in various parts of the south in the early nineteenth century and the reliance on sick or dead work animals as the main source of meat in the poorest regions.

7. Cf. Bugialli's (1988: 53) discussion of the distinction between *mollica* and *pangrattato*; a slightly different formulation is offered by Simeti 1991: 12.

Food, Morality, and Politics:
The Spectacle of Dog-Eating Igorots
at the 1904 St Louis World Fair

Bel S. Castro

About the time the World's Fair city is waking at early morning, one hundred bare-limbed Igorot often sacrifice and eat a dog on the Philippine Reservation. At the same hour, scarcely two hundred yards away, a bugle sounds reveille, and four hundred well-trained soldiers in the blue of the United States Army hustle from their tents. The yells of the dog-dance have scarcely ceased before the blue line is formed for roll call, and the Philippine soldiers stand beneath an American flag, while the Philippine band plays an American air. All of these people live on the same island in the Philippines. The Igorot represent the wildest race of savages, the scouts stand for the results of American rule – extremes of the social order in the islands.

Promotional Brochure, Philippine Exposition 1904 St Louis World Fair[1]

In 1904, a World Fair of unprecedented proportions was assembled in St Louis, Missouri to commemorate the centennial of the Louisiana Purchase – an event in American history said to rank second in importance only to the Declaration of Independence. No exposition prior to or since then, has ever matched the St Louis World's Fair in scale or grandeur. Several years in the making and built at the cost of $50 million – ironically, over three times the amount the US paid for the Louisiana Territory – the Exposition was an immense undertaking. Covering over 516 hectares of land, over 1,576 buildings were built for the exhibits of over 50 foreign countries and 43 of the 45 US states that existed at the time.[2]

Central to the fair was the 47-acre Philippine Exhibit, dubbed 'the Philippine Reservation.' Assembled at a cost of $2 million, it was the largest and costliest of the foreign exhibits and included a series of villages populated by over 1,100 Filipinos, including Moros, Visayans, Negritos, and Igorots, among others.[3] Heavily publicized, it easily became the most popular, most visited, and most lucrative exhibit at the fair. Of the estimated 20 million visitors who went to the St Louis Fair, 99 per cent of them paid the nickel entrance fee to view the Philippine Reservation.[4]

In the many months leading up to the World's Fair, many Filipinos bitterly opposed the Philippine Reservation in St Louis. It was felt that the Reservation would unfairly present all Filipinos as primitives, and – despite declarations by US representatives to the contrary – would be a cog in a deliberate campaign to establish the 'white man's burden' of the United States to 'civilize' the Filipinos, give the 'pacification' of the Filipino people a moral imperative and thus rally flagging domestic support for the 'benevolent assimilation' of the Philippines. History tells us how successful this campaign was. As Filipino nationalists had feared, by the time the fair closed on 1 December, 1904, the most vivid and dominant image that millions of visitors retained was the image of the 'savage' and 'barbaric' dog-eating Igorots. By extension, this image came to apply to all Filipinos, regardless of region, history, or origin. This damaging view of the Filipino as savage and primitive, and thus incapable of self-government, persisted long after the fair ended.

The dog-eating spectacle and the image it constructed powerfully demonstrates the defining nature of food and how our food preferences and aversions can relate to issues of moral superiority, racial prejudice, and even to wholesale denigration.

In this paper, I examine the spectacle of dog-eating Igorots at the 1904 World Fair and attempt to show how the spectacle helped fabricate and project a national identity that was false, and as a propaganda tool, helped forward a political agenda. I also examine a bitter legacy of the Fair; the ethnic slur 'dog-eater,' which has since been extended to apply to all Filipinos.

Setting the stage

Any investigation of the 1904 St Louis Fair has to be viewed against the backdrop of the Philippine-American War as well as the antecedent conflict, the Spanish-American War.

The Spanish-American War, which ended with the Treaty of Paris of 1898, effectively gave the United States control over Spain's remaining overseas territories: Cuba, Puerto Rico, Guam, the Caroline Islands, and the Philippines. The Spanish-American War is significant in American history as the Treaty effectively expanded American dominion outside its continental borders and thus marked the birth of the United States as a colonial power. [5]

A critical element in bringing a quick end to the Spanish-American War was the alliance forged between US forces and the Filipino revolutionaries led by General Emilio Aguinaldo. As the US Navy neutralized the Spanish naval forces at sea, Filipino forces – as de facto allies of the United States – engaged the Spanish on land. After a few months of fighting, Aguinaldo's forces gained control of Manila and much of Luzon and on 12 June, 1898, issued a Declaration of Independence. Recognizing that defeat was imminent, but not wanting to submit to Philippine authority, Spain negotiated a separate agreement with the United States and surrendered to US forces on 13 August, 1898. In what would spark the ugliest chapter in Philippine-American relations, the Philippines was summarily annexed by the United States. The betrayal of the United States and the subsequent refusal of the US to recognize the new independent Republic of the Philippines triggered the start of the Philippine-American War which lasted until 1913. [6]

The annexation of the Philippines by the United States had not happened without domestic opposition in the United States, with the debate polarizing Americans into expansionist and anti-imperialist camps. Anti-imperialists, who numbered among them the great writer Mark Twain, argued that the forced annexation of other countries betrayed the nationalist doctrines and core democratic principles enshrined in the US Declaration of Independence. From their perspective, it was a matter of honor for every freedom-loving American to oppose annexation.[7] Fervent imperialists like Indiana Senator Albert Beveridge saw it differently and opposed the tenet that 'we ought not to govern a people without their consent.' For him and those like him, Americans had 'world duties,' a moral obligation to go beyond their borders, as 'a people imperial by virtue of their power, by right of their institutions, by authority of their Heaven-directed purposes.'[8]

Ultimately, the expansionists ruled the day and with the Treaty of Paris ratified, the United States took its place as an imperial power. In an oft-related anecdote, US President William McKinley, after supposedly praying for several days, made his famous statement on the assimilation of the Philippines: '…there was nothing left for us to do but take them all, and educate the Filipinos and uplift them and civilize and Christianize them.'[9]

At its core, the 1904 World's Fair was to celebrate the centennial of the Louisiana Purchase of 1803, which had doubled the size of the United States and thus, had the celebration of US domestic expansionism as its ideological focus. But coming so soon after the ratification of the Treaty of Paris, the American federal government immediately saw that the fair presented an opportunity to make the Philippine annexation seem like a natural progression in America's linear history of nationalist expansionism, and thus convey to the American people that the new US role as a colonial power was a positive one. By controlling the messages of the fair – by manipulating the impressions that fairgoers would get from encounters with the Philippine exhibits at the fair – the US government could pursue its objectives of drumming up domestic support while at the same time, quelling anti-imperialist opposition for its continued administration of its newly acquired overseas territories. In all the world's fairs before it, the expositions promoted the superiority of the Caucasian race by celebrating its commercial, technological, and cultural achievements. Philippine colonial officials, War Department officials, and the 1904 St Louis Fair exhibition planners were well aware of, and drew on, these traditions.[10]

So the stage was set. On November 11, 1902, the politically appointed Philippine Commission passed Act 514 authorizing the Philippines to participate in the St Louis World's Fair. Among the act's stated objectives were to show off the Philippines: its civilization, culture, and economy; promote its products and natural resources and attract traders, buyers, and investors; pacify and improve the Filipino condition; and '…make Americans realize what its new colony holds in promise in a way of potential wealth, opportunity for service, and exotic wonders'.[11]

The Philippine exhibit was unique in that the United States government was involved from the outset.[12] Act 514 may have been framed in cultural, economic, and educational contexts, but because of the involvement of the US federal government, the fair also had to take on a political agenda: to establish Filipino incapacity for political sovereignty and reinforce the necessity of American colonial rule. In addition, it became the mandate of the Philippine Exposition Board to convince skeptics that all Philippine resistance against American rule had ended and that the US government had the benevolent intention of civilizing its 'little brown brothers'.[13] The clashing political, commercial, educational, and scientific agendas would play out time and again throughout the course of the fair.

The 'savaging' of the Filipino

To portray the image of the Filipino incapable of self-rule, the Philippine Exposition Board fell back to old tactics. In the late nineteenth century, the display of 'savage' peoples had become the staple of anthropological displays at Euro-American expositions and the 1904 St Louis Fair merely continued in this pattern.

As early as 1902, it was decided that a battalion of American-trained martial troops would have a model camp on the exposition grounds to be contrasted against a backdrop of exotic and backward native peoples. From David R. Francis, president of the Louisiana Purchase Exposition, came the idea of sending the Philippine Scouts, and from the Philippine Exposition Board came the suggestion to send the Philippine Constabulary Band. And it was Director of Exhibits, Dr Gustavo Niederlein, who, in the name of 'scientific service' selected the Igorots, among others, to form the living anthropological exhibits of the fair.[14]

Underpinned by then popular Darwinist theories, a major theme at fairs was the idea that all peoples of the world could be hierarchically ordered according to their racial characteristics, and hence according to their stage of cultural and social development. A dominant belief at the time was that the evolution of mankind from savagery-to-barbarism-to-civilization was also an evolution of the races with Anglo-Saxons at the top of the ladder, and beneath them, an array of 'lesser races' down to the darkest, and thereby the most savage, peoples.[15]

This manner of thinking was fully exploited at the fair where the juxtaposition of the 'head-hunting,' 'half-naked,' 'dog-eating' Igorot and the American-trained 'civilized' Philippine Scout would become a symbolic and iconic display of the Filipino's capacity to become successfully pacified and civilized with American intervention.[16]

The campaign of the Philippine Exposition to elevate the Philippine Scouts while bashing the Igorot was well-planned, well-calculated, and well-funded. Two departments were tasked to heavily advertise the Philippine exhibit: the publicity department and the exploitation department. The efforts of these two departments were supported by the Louisiana Purchase Exposition's own Department of Exploitation. In a massive publicity campaign that could rival any today, six newspapers printed daily articles about the fair for three years, beginning many months before the fair opened; nearly four million pieces of publicity material in multiple languages were distributed in the first six months of the fair; more than four hundred newspapers were provided with up to 20,000 words of releases daily. Photographs were taken and shown, hundreds of thousands of handbills were distributed, and hundreds of tickets were given away.[17]

Initial publicity on the Igorots focused on their nudity, propensity for violence (i.e. head-hunting), and exotic practices (gong banging, dancing, and dog-eating) to best communicate ideas of savagery and barbarity. The scandalous impact of the displays on fairgoers was not only predicted, it was calculated, with near-nakedness and the taking of human heads expected to be the most offensive, touching on taboos of sexuality and the crime of murder. Yet it was the most quotidian of activities, eating, that proved to be the most successful in capturing public attention.

Decoding the dog-eating ritual in Igorot culture

The Igorots well-advertised fondness for eating dogs – the 'Bow-Wow Feast' as it was called – snowballed from an exotic curiosity to the fair's most dominant human spectacle, and brought the Igorots great notoriety. Because of the sheer volume of press coverage on the dog-eating ritual of the Igorots, we can speculate that many of the visitors to the fair came with a pre-conceived, if inaccurate view of the ceremonial use of dogs by the Igorots.

In contrast, it is with great certainty that we can assume that the Philippine Exposition Commission could not have been ignorant of the true nature of Igorot rituals, as it had appointed no less than Dr Albert E. Jenks as Chief of the Department of Ethnology at the Philippine Exposition. No doubt, Dr Jenks was awarded the position in great part because of his having just completed a comprehensive ethnological survey of the Bontoc Igorots in the year prior to the St Louis Fair.[18]

In his 1903 survey, Jenks had determined that the ritual of dog-killing and eating was a rare event and that the dog was the ritual sacrificial animal of last resort. 'In Bontoc society, the use of dogs as a ritual sacrifice is held sacred…the last animal to be butchered (from the usual chickens and pigs) after a successful headhunt (*namaka*) by the warriors of the village. The dog is offered to perform the ritual called *sumang*, believed to drive away the spirits of the dead enemies. Spirits of people who just died are still lingering on earth, and to drive them away, the dogs are butchered. This is to counter the bad omen so as to evade the ill effects. The dog is also used as a medium to heal people possessed by bad spirits or afflicted with illnesses.'[19]

Recent field research conducted by Salvador confirms the persisting ritual status of the dog among the native Cordillerans. Among the Benguet Igorots, the cleansing ritual known as *tomo* or *temmo* is performed for the warriors who had directly or indirectly participated in inter-village conflicts (*faroknit*). The ritual animal has to be the dog, based on the belief that its barks can drive away haunting spirits.[20]

In 1904, it was reported that 'the dog teeth were carefully preserved and these would be polished and sold as souvenirs.' This is curious as dog teeth to the Igorots are not trinkets but also have ritual purpose. A *sa-ong* or a dogtooth necklace is thought to protect the wearer from snakebites and lightning and is still worn today by the Igorots in Bontoc. Among Ifugao Igorot warriors, it was believed that the inscribing of *ahu* or dog tattoos on arms and chests could also invoke the power of the dog to be a protector or guardian spirit.[21]

In all cases, the sacrificial dog was associated with head-hunting, illness, or misfortune. For rituals surrounding life or agricultural cycles, chickens were the most common animal offered to the gods, followed by the pig and occasionally the carabao or water buffalo. As it seems then, the word 'dog-feast' as is it was used during the 1904 World's Fair, is actually a misnomer as the rituals that require a dog sacrifice are more closely associated with death than with life.

Even nowadays, dog sacrifice connotes bad luck, tragedy, or death. If a family killed a dog – the family dog and not just any dog acquired in another way – it indicated that the family was not celebrating but was either mourning, in extreme pain, or involved in some other activity connected with death. In what is probably a carryover from this belief, even among Christian Filipinos, it's a common superstitious belief that if a family dog takes ill and dies, it is because the dog sacrificed itself to appease the gods, thus 'saving' a member of the family from sickness or death.

For contemporary Igorots in the Cordilleras, dog-eating at home still takes place in the context of ceremonial and healing rituals, and only rarely, as a cheaper access to meat. The contexts that involve dog or dog eating tend to revolve, not around gastronomic whim, but around needs to be satisfied, risks to be reduced, and problems to be resolved, and are performed at appropriate times and places.'[22] Dog sacrifice for such religious purposes remains permitted under the Philippine Animal Welfare Act.[23]

The controversy surrounding the present-day illegal trade of dogs involves the non-ritual slaughter and consumption of dog meat as a delicacy and has no relationship with the ritual beliefs and practices of the Igorot. Igorots are the first to profess that dogs do not form part of their regular day-to-day diet and Igorot families would much prefer to avoid the circumstances that might lead them to sacrifice their family dog.[24]

At the 1904 World Fair, there is some indication that the initial dog sacrifices were associated with ritual. Deaths at the fair, protection from the cold, the need to appease gods, and save members of the group from illness may have prompted the first dog killings. But later on, the situations that commanded dog sacrifice were no longer present and divorced from their meaning, dog-killing became mere performance. Ultimately, the simulation of the 'dog-feasting ritual' became scripted and routinized by fair officials. Repeated monotonously, the only purpose of the performances was to satisfy the voyeuristic and morbid curiosities of the nickel-paying visitors to the Philippine Reservation.[25]

That the Igorots were ignorant and passive participants to this display is to take a lot for granted. Even in 1904, the Igorots were known for being shrewd and clever traders, with a well-developed sense of commerce and the value of currency.[26] However shortsighted it may have been at the time, it seems that some Igorots willingly participated in the selling of the fiction of their day-to-day life for profit.

Most manuscripts on the participation of Filipinos in the 1904 World's Fair do not include the Igorot point-of-view and work done by Afable, Buangan, and Salvador help to fill the gaps.[27] Some sources indicate that the Igorots were aware that the dog-killings were a 'show' for the audience, meant to satisfy a hunger for the 'exotic.' Some Igorots agreed to these performances, for pay, transforming the once 'sacred ritual' to a 'circus act' for entertainment, even as Salvador determined that 'it was a mutual obligation that did not equally extend to all the Igorot participants'.[28]

In interviews with descendants and surviving participants, if there were any feelings of exploitation, there was no mention of it. The Igorots who had been to the World's Fair became known as *Nikimalika*, or those 'who went to *Amerika/Malika*' and Amelika or Amerika was simply 'where the Igorot goes to find work.'[29]

When asked what they remembered from the fair, they related that they found the Americans kind, indulgent, if somewhat gullible. The average salary of each person in the native villages was supposed to be about ten dollars a month. Apparently, the moneys were not distributed equally. 'We were cheated, for we were paid only five pesos in salary, even [though] at the end of the day, we saw men dragging sacks full of coins from our village…' To augment their income, the Igorots willingly performed for the American visitors, dancing for coins that they divided among themselves at the end of each day. Young men took turns pretending to be 'chiefs.' As 'they [Americans] would buy anything offered them for sale,' roughly made spears, and even such invented items as 'Igorot' bracelets were hastily manufactured to be sold as souvenirs. 'We made extra money by weaving bamboo rings. We fooled the Americans, telling them they were ethnic wedding rings. They bought a lot.'[30] And as for the dog-eating ritual, the Igorots grew tired of the *'milika ahu'* (American dogs) and finding them *'nalangsi* and fatty' would kill the dogs, and not eat them but bury them at the edge of the reservation.[31]

Subject to further examination, one can only speculate how the Igorots were able to reconcile the corruption of a sacred ritual involving what they considered a sacred animal with their animist beliefs. Perhaps it was because the dogs were merely provided to them, and having no attachment to them, had no fear of divine or supernatural consequences. Maybe they felt that they could assign the spirits of the dogs to the living members of their group. Perhaps it mattered that the dogs were 'American' and therefore foreign. It may no longer be possible to know. No one from the original group remains to give us a first-hand account.

Social scientists have long posited that it's the culture that invests a practice or situation with meaning. Dog-eating to the 1904 Igorot was sacred and did not become savage and barbaric until the active viewers to the dog-eating display at the fair, ignorant of Igorot culture, decided that it was. And in an ironic twist, the moment the Igorots began to slaughter the dogs for no reasons other than commerce and entertainment was when the performance became truly barbaric.

The bitter legacy

At the conclusion of the fair, it was clear that the Philippine Exposition was a failure on many fronts. Of the $2 million spent on the exhibits, only half a million dollars was recouped. The promised trade contracts had failed to materialize. The ambition of the nascent science of anthropology to find legitimacy was thwarted. But on the political front, the Philippine Exposition was an unqualified success.

Long before the participating Filipinos stepped on the first boats to Louisiana, the Filipino elite was vocal in its opposition to the way Filipinos were to be represented at the fair. In an editorial in the independent newspaper, *El Renacimeinto*, on the inclusion of Igorots, Negritos, and Moros, writer Lauro Mataas wrote that, 'Only we, by some strange privilege…take advantage of as many occasions as are offered us to be represented before the civilized world by the most uncultured that inhabit our soil.' Expositions, he added, were mounted to compete for honors, to attract capital and seek markets, and to present 'before the eyes of the world the advances and progresses that the country has realized.' Mataas warned that the participation of the native peoples would obscure all the successes of Filipino artists and industrialists, and present the Filipino people to the world 'not as cultured, progressive beings, deserving of wide political concessions' but rather as 'perfectly characterized savages for whom the quantity of 'self-government' granted in the Philippine Bill was too much.'[32] His words were prescient.

By the close of the Louisiana Purchase Exposition, it can be deduced from the numerous letters, diary entries, and other accounts that, of the many memorable impressions retained by the majority of the visitors to the Philippine Reservation, chief among them was the vision of the Igorot's simmering pot of dog stew.[33] This image, together with the display of backward village life, in sharp contrast with the obedient, disciplined cadre of Philippine Scouts under American command bolstered the impression of the Filipinos as a people ripe for reform but in need of imperialist guidance and support.

Of the many messages of the fair – the Filipino's incapacity for self-government – was a message that was also directed to Filipinos as well as the American people. Together with crippling defeats at home, the immense show of power by the United Stated helped to undermine Filipino base support for the revolutionary struggle for independence. And then there were the federalists, consisting of the educated and cosmopolitan Filipino elite, who, instead of seeking independence, believed that the path to Philippine progress lay in statehood. The futility of their efforts became painfully clear when the federalists traveled to the St Louis Exposition. Horrified at the racism they witnessed, Honorary Commissioner Vicente Nepumoceno declared, 'The damage had been done…the impression had gone abroad that we are barbarians; that we eat dog and all sorts of thing, and no matter how long we stay here we cannot convince the public to the contrary.' The visit to the fair, along with the refusal of the American Congress to 'incorporate' the Philippines, compelled these elites to accept their fate. The movement for statehood lost support and was eventually defeated.[34]

In the tug-of-war between commercial and political agendas on one hand and ethnographic and educational purposes on the other, the racist messages from the fair could have been corrected. Surely, as the volume of publicity materials released during the fair proves, the fair organizers had the means to achieve that end. However, the mandate of the Philippine Exposition had been made clear from the start. And so it was, that the racist bashing of the Filipino was institutionalized and Igorot ritual of dog-eating and its association with barbarity not corrected, but repeatedly reinforced, to great effect.

As for the Igorots, the stereotype 'Igorots as dog-eaters' has dogged them for more than a century and the role that the Nikimalika may have played in the creation of that 'constructed reality' is a dark spot in their history. It is also significant to note that the Nikimalika, upon returning home from the fair, failed to elevate their status in the community. Neither did they acquire the same prestige that went to members of that generation who stayed behind, continued their education, and went on to become to fluent English-speaking workers, teachers, and civil servants for the next two decades.[35] Some Nikimalika even felt cursed; 'punished' by their ancestors.[36]

In a book published by the Cordillera Schools Group, Inc., *Ethnography of the Major Ethnolinguistic Groups in the Cordillera*, conspicuous in its absence is any detailed account of dog killing and eating rituals. This definitive volume, which covers the religious beliefs and rituals of the major ethno linguistic groups in the Cordilleras, devotes more space to rituals involving chickens and pigs with scarce mention of sacrificial dogs.[37] Indeed, some modern-day Igorots now choose to deny their past, refuse to self-identify as dog-eaters, and reject dog killing and eating as part of, or ever having been part of their culture.[38]

For Filipinos at large, such was the phenomenal success of the 1904 World's Fair in defining a national Filipino identity for the American people – albeit a false one – that, even today, Filipinos traveling abroad still have to field innocent questions from well-meaning individuals like, 'Do Filipinos use spoons and forks to eat?' 'Do Filipinos still live in trees?' and 'Do all Filipinos eat dog?'

Conclusion

In this paper, I have attempted to bring a critical perspective to the dog-eating spectacle the 1904 World's Fair. How food and meaning can relate to issues of morality, national identity, and ultimately, race, politics, and the shaping of a nation.

Food and drink have long been used in racial and ethnic slurs. A few familiar ones come to mind: frog-eater = Frenchman; kraut or krauthead = German; cabbage-eater = German or Russian; potato-head, potato-eater = Irishman. This is what Allan and Burridge refer to as 'Gastronomic Xenophobia,' where, given the symbolic values we attach to foodstuffs and foodways it is not surprising to find that food can 'have a significant role to play in the language of nationalism and race.'[39]

This paper puts forward the thesis that the dog-eating spectacle of the Igorots in the 1904 World's Fair stands apart as a unique situation in history where food, disgust, identity, and power collided and decades later, continues to resonate and exert influence. It is a rare case where a ritual of eating and dining became a tool for vilification and was instrumental in pushing forward a political agenda. To paraphrase Looy, this paper is an initial attempt to define the context, identify the major issues, raise questions, and is an invitation to scholars with expertise in other related fields to respond.

Acknowledgements

This paper was inspired by 'Bark from the Pan: Decoding the Spectacle of Dog-Meat Eating in the 1904 St Louis Fair and in the Cordillera.' by Analyn Ikin V. Salvador, a paper presented at the Doreen Gamboa Fernandez Food Symposium 2005: Vanishing Food in the Philippines, Filipinas Heritage Library, Makati City on August 27, 2005. This acknowledges the research assistance of Jennifer Y. Dee, Margarita A. Ramos and Sharra L. Vostral and also thanks Jess Macasaet, Martha Goebel, Allan Roi Roño and Erwin Lizarondo for their assistance in reading drafts and developing the ideas in this paper.

Notes

1. Newell, Alfred C.
2. Ibid.
3. St Louis Convention & Visitors Commission, *Louisiana Purchase Exposition (1904 Worlds Fair) Fact Sheet*, http://www.explorestlouis.com/factSheets/fact_worldsFair.asp?PageType = 4.
4. Delmendo, Sharon 2005, p. 51; Fermin, Jose D. 2004, p. 17.
5. For lack of space, Philippine historical events antecedent to the 1904 World Fair are referred to very briefly. For more detailed information, see Renato Constantino 1975. Also, Paul A. Kramer 2006. For a brief overview of the Spanish-American War of 1898, and how it relates to the history of US Imperialism, see and how it relates to the history of US Imperialism, see *Monthly Review*, 'Kipling, the 'White Man's Burden,' and US Imperialism'.
6. On July 4, 1902, US President Theodore Roosevelt issued a proclamation declaring the Philippine-American War officially over, even as armed conflict continued for over a decade. Nationalist Filipino historians tend to view these skirmishes as a continuation of the war and peg the war's end to 1913. See Samuel K. Tan 2002.
7. It was at the height of the expansionism debate that Rudyard Kipling published the now famous poem, 'White Man's Burden,' subtitled 'The United States and the Philippine Islands,' in *McClure's Magazine* in February 1899, exhorting the United States to perform its moral duty 'to rule lesser races and encourage them in their development, until they can take their rightful place in the world'. The poem came out as the debate over the ratification of the Treaty of Paris was still raging, and while the anti-imperialist movement in the United States was trying to gain ground. Opponents to the anti-imperialists latched on to Kipling's poem as an anthem for colonialism, justifying, as it did,

the proposed annexation by giving it a moral and noble dimension.
8. For complete text of the speech see, Albert Beveridge, *The March of the Flag 1898*.
9. Delmendo, p. 47.
10. Kramer, p. 238–39.
11. Rydell quoted in Fermin, p. 37.
12. Delmendo, p. 51.
13. Fermin, p. 38.
14. Ibid., p. 45.
15. Go, Julian, 2003; Vostral, Sharra L., 1993, 23.
16. Delmondo, p. 53.
17. Fermin, pp. 8–10.
18. Ibid., p. 4.
19. Jenks, Albert Ernest.
20. Salvador, Analyn Ikin V.
21. Ibid.
22. Ibid.
23. *Philippine Laws.*
24. Dawang, Bing A.
25. Fermin, p. 3–4; Kramer, p. 266; Salvador.
26. Jenks, p. 151–157.
27. Afable, Patricia O., 2004; Buangan, 2004.
28. Salvador.
29. Afable, Patricia O. and Cherubim A. Quizon, 2004, p. 441.
30. Fermin, p. 140–4; Afable, p. 462–63.
31. Salvador.
32. Kramer, p. 249–50.
33. Vostral, p. 19, 23.
34. Go.
35. Afable, p.463.
36. Salvador.
37. Cordillera Schools Group.
38. Dawang.
39. Allan, Keith and Kate Burridge.

Bibliography

Afable, Patricia O., 'Journeys from Bontoc to the Western Fairs, 1904–1915: The 'Nikimalika' and Their Interpreters,' *Philippine Studies* 52, no. 4 (2004),

Afable, Patricia O. and Cherubim A. Quizon, 'Rethinking Displays of Filipinos at St Louis: Embracing Heartbreak and Irony,' *Philippine Studies* 52, no. 4 (2004).

Allan, Keith and Kate Burridge, 'Forbidden Words: Taboo and the Censoring of Language,' (2005), p. 148. [E-Book]. http://www.arts.monash.edu.au/linguistics/staff/kallan-forbidden-words.pdf.

Benedict, Burton, 'International Exhibitions and National Identity.' *Anthropology Today* 7, no. 3 (1991): 5–9.

Beveridge, Albert, '*The March of the Flag 1898*', *Internet Modern History Sourcebook* Fordham University 1997, http://www.fordham.edu/halsall/mod/1898beveridge.html.

Buangan, Antonio S., 'The Suyoc People Who Went to St Louis 100 Years Ago: The Search for My Ancestors.' *Philippine Studies* 52, no. 4 (2004): 474–98.

Constantino, Renato, *The Philippines: A Past Revisited (Pre-Spanish-1941)*. 2 vols. Vol. 1. Quezon City: Renato Constantino, 1975. 19th reprint.

Cordillera Schools Group Inc., *Ethnography of the Major Ethnolinguistic Groups in the Cordillera* (Quezon City: New Day Publishers, 2003).

Dawang, Bing A., 'Dog-Eating and My Culture' *K9 Perspective Online,* Issue 16, p. 3, [Online Magazine], http://www.k9magazinefree.com/k9_perspective/iss16p3.shtml.

Delmendo, Sharon, *The Star-Entangled Banner: One Hundred Years of America in the Philippines.* Quezon City: The University of the Philippines Press, 2005.

Fermin, Jose D., *1904 World's Fair : The Filipino Experience.* Diliman, Quezon City: University of the Philippines Press, 2004.

Go, Julian, 'Modes of Rule in America's Overseas Empire: The Philippines, Puerto Rico, Guam, and Samoa.' (Paper presented at the Louisiana Purchase Conference, Austin, Texas, February 20–23, 2003).

Jenks, Albert Ernest, *The Bontoc Igorot.* Gutenberg Project: 2005 [E-Book]. http://www.gutenberg.net.

Kramer, Paul A., *The Blood of Government: Race, Empire, the United States and the Philippines.* Philippine Edition (Quezon City: Ateneo de Manila University Press, 2006).

Looy, Heather, 'Disgust, Morality, and Human Identity: A Neurobiological, Psychosocial and Theological Investigation', *The Global Spiral,* Dec. 3, 2001 [Online Magazine]. http://www.metanexus.net/magazine/ArticleDetail/tabid/68/id/4978/Default.aspx.

Monthly Review, 'Kipling, the 'White Man's Burden,' and US Imperialism', Vol. 55, no. 6 (2003) [Online Magazine] http://monthlyreview.org/1103editors.htm.

Newell, Alfred C., editor. *Philippine Exposition World's Fair St Louis, 1904*: Department of Exploitation, 1904. Promotional Brochure (Igorot Cover).

Philippine Laws, Statutes and Codes: Republic Act No. 8485 (Chan Robles Publishing Company, 2006) [Virtual Law Library]. Available from http://www.chanrobles.com/republicactno8485.htm.

Rydell, Robert W., All the World's a Fair: Visions of Empire at American International Expositions, 1876–1919. Chicago: University of Chicago Press, 1984.

Salvador, Analyn Ikin V., 'Bark from the Pan: Decoding the Spectacle of Dog-Meat Eating in the 1904 St Louis Fair and in the Cordillera.' (Paper presented at the The Doreen Gamboa Fernandez Food Symposium 2005: Vanishing Food in the Philippines,, Filipinas Heritage Library, Makati City, August 27, 2005).

St Louis Convention & Visitors Commission, *Louisiana Purchase Exposition (1904 Worlds Fair) Fact Sheet*. http://www.explorestlouis.com/factSheets/fact_worldsFair.asp?PageType = 4.

Tan, Samuel K., *The Filipino-American War, 1899–1913.* Quezon City: Cavite Historical Society and the University of the Philippines Press, 2002.

Vostral, Sharra L., 'Imperialism on Display: The Philippine Exhibition at the 1904 World's Fair.' *Gateway Heritage* Spring 1993 (1993): 18–31.

Les Halles and the Moral Market:
Frigophobia Strikes in the Belly of Paris

Kyri Watson Claflin

Sociologist Claude Fischler writes that conservatism in food matters, which he calls 'le néophobie,' could be fundamental in human societies perpetuating habits and tastes to the exclusion of new trends. However, Fischler adds that there may be 'a tendency to overestimate the perennial character of our foodways.'[1] Just how deeply embedded food practices are in any culture is a question that continues to benefit from on-going study. In the example of refrigeration and the moral market in France we see that economic and political factors had a considerable influence on what we customarily think of as food preferences that are embedded in culinary culture and cultural identity.

The legendary Paris central market for fresh food, Les Halles in the city's 1st arrondissement, was torn down in 1969 after centuries on that location. The move was a long-overdue step in modernizing the French food chain, but it was controversial. Historian Louis Chevalier said that Les Halles was not only the belly of Paris, but also its heart. He called the bureaucrats who ripped the market out of the center of Paris 'assassins.' He was not alone in his condemnation.

For many people, the lasting image of Les Halles was the one that Emperor Napoleon III (1852–1870) and the novelist Émile Zola fixed in the collective consciousness in the nineteenth century. So many aspects of Paris were mythical in the nineteenth century, especially after Haussmannization. Les Halles was certainly in the top rank. Once Victor Baltard's great iron and glass pavilions were erected, this was the moment when Les Halles was finally completely modern and sufficiently spacious. More than before, it was the most prestigious market in France, attracting sellers and seducing buyers. Writers found it endlessly fascinating. Literary descriptions perpetuated the myth of Les Halles long into the twentieth century, arresting this place in time during its finest hour. Les Halles at the center of Paris was richly symbolic of Paris as the center of the gastronomic universe.

Les Halles was also the Parisian pantry, the 'great meal that Paris devours each day,' as Balzac wrote. The nature of this 'pantry' was that it could never be big enough for the varied and opulent alimentary demands of the capital of the nation that invented haute cuisine. Only fifteen years after opening, even before the Second Empire fell in 1870, the Imperial Les Halles was overcrowded with merchants, customers, and food.[2] By the 1880s, members of the Paris Municipal Council were alarmed that the population of the city was over 2.2 million, an increase of more than 700,000 since the new Les Halles was built.[3] There was not enough room for all the food the city now required. In 1883, City Council member Henri Mathé exclaimed that,

> at this moment, all the emplacements are occupied: the sidewalks, the street, the covered passages, disappear under all kinds of merchandise, and there is not a small corner around Les Halles that has not been invaded by merchants. If you add to this the stopped vehicles that serve to unload and load merchandise, standing in the adjacent streets, one wonders how transactions take place.[4]

Inside the pavilions, the physical impediments to business, the profusion of shipping boxes, containers, baskets, bags, and crowding were just as bad. Mathé declared that the best thing for the provisioning of Paris was to have more sellers, more producers and middlemen sending foodstuffs. Everyone would profit, although he despaired that the city could not provide more space to accommodate the additional people and food.[5]

In the 1890s, the population of Paris increased by another 400,000. During a government investigation in 1891, the city's official middlemen, called *mandataires* – the only sellers authorized to conduct business at Les Halles – invited the Deputies of the Seine and members of the Municipal Council to visit the market. In the words of one *mandataire*:

> There you will see the accumulation of merchandise, to the great detriment of its freshness and conservation, and for the greatest inconvenience of the buyers, that is to say, when the merchandise is not simply exposed on the sidewalk, in the middle of the street, or under the feet of passersby and in horse urine.[6]

83

Reconstruction of the great market, particularly enlargement, was called for regularly after 1875, but approval and funding never materialized. By 1902, 190 million kilograms of foodstuffs came into the central market, nearly double the volume the space was designed to hold.[7] In 1912, a Parisian newspaper reported that the physical situation at the market was 'a shameful spectacle,' and described 'masses of vegetables of all kinds, fruits and the baby vegetables, the most delicate products of French and colonial growers, piled on the ground, with the mud and garbage.'[8] On the eve of World War I in 1914, this was the material reality of belly of Paris, the most prestigious market to which a producer could send his finest merchandise, and where a simple gust of wind and a little rain 'could come along to partially ruin, or even destroy in an instant the fruits of his labors.'[9]

The physical condition of Les Halles was even more central to reform discussions when the cost of living, the biggest part of which was the cost of food, started going up precipitously in the early years of the twentieth century. Before World War I, and most especially during the war, food prices in Paris skyrocketed. Many people believed that modernizing the central market was a vital weapon in the struggle against the intractable cost-of-living problem, and the installation of refrigerators for the safe and hygienic storage of excess foodstuffs was considered a core component in any effective reorganization of the market.

In 1914, there were for all intents and purposes, no refrigerators at Les Halles. What is more, it was against market regulations for *mandataires* (brokers) to put aside unsold food in any kind of storage facility and then reintroduce it for sale on the next market day. As long as this was the case, refrigeration was hardly considered to be worth a substantial investment of municipal funds. The restrictions on food storage bring us to the subject of the moral market and the philosophy behind the design of the Paris market and French urban provisioning.[10]

The moral market

For centuries, the principal rationale behind Paris provisioning was to ensure that consumers had access to an abundance of fresh food at the lowest prices. This goal dictated how business was conducted at Les Halles, which in turn supplied the fundamental model of Parisian food commerce. The eighteenth-century police commissioner Nicolas Delamare, who literally wrote the book on the policing of provisioning in Paris, explained the philosophy behind the central market:

> ...one must create markets...to gather as much as is possible, in the same place,
> of all the merchandise of the same kind, because this abundance is known to
> produce low prices or at least a considerable drop in price.[11]

This was the philosophy of 'procuring abundance' to assure 'just' prices, which could only be guaranteed in a moral marketplace. In France, the concept of the 'moral economy,' or an honest and just marketplace, persisted because the structures of modern food commerce were still underpinned with the belief that the law of supply and demand could only work fairly if all parties in a transaction abided by rules that minimized opportunities for sellers to cheat.[12] Well into the twentieth century, Les Halles market regulations still derived from what Pierre du Maroussem referred to as the 'goal of political economy found at every turn in the French tradition, which derives from the formula in Delamare's admirable *Traité de la Police*.'[13]

Making Les Halles a moral marketplace required that all of the fresh food that came into the central Paris market in the morning was to be put out on display and sold on the same day between the opening and closing market bells. This model of commerce in the market accomplished four goals. First, each buyer literally saw all that was on offer and each could judge for himself the state of the supply of any product. A buyer therefore made his bids based on complete transparency of information – nothing was put in a back room or hidden from view to distort his knowledge of the supply. Second, the need to sell everything by the end of each day's market meant that high prices in the early hours would necessarily begin to fall as time drew nearer to the closing bell. This mechanism enabled diverse types of buyers with different means and needs to find their provisions at the central market. Third, with the market emptied each day, every morning a new supply of fresh foodstuffs arrived to fill it up again, which assured the farmers who sent their goods to the *mandataires* that they would have an equal opportunity to have their produce displayed and sold under the best circumstances possible. Last, these three precepts made possible a fourth: continued incentive for the provinces to send their best foodstuffs to the Paris market, the most important market in France, where they were likely to get the best return.

This philosophy of procuring abundance by means of a moral marketplace was incompatible with any practice that obscured the transparency of market transactions. Food kept out of the buyer's sight, stored in any way, constituted 'reserves,' as they were called. The very term in French, *la resserre* contained the 'profane idea' of hiding (*'l'idée de serrer, de cacher'*) and implied that the *mandataires* were speculating in unsold merchandise, falsifying supplies and rigging prices.[14] A report to the Commission Supérieure des Halles noted that the word *resserre* had a psychological impact on buyers: Its meaning in the public mind symbolized speculation, and did not indicate a simple truth that occasionally or even regularly not all merchandise found buyers.[15]

Why all of this theorizing to run a food market? Food in France has not traditionally been considered a commodity like any other, and French authorities in the Old Regime believed that only a regulated and policed official market could assure citizens that transactions were honest and prices were fair; the word the authorities used was 'moral.'[16] France in modern times, that is to say from the eighteenth century, wrestled with ideas about alimentary justice and the proper role of the state. Some historians and economists have insisted that in food commerce before World War I, free market forces alone carried the day, and that the only legal role for state intervention was policing fraud. Others have argued that enforcing sanitary regulations in food production and commerce was the only preoccupation of the public authorities.

However, provisioning Paris in the late nineteenth and early twentieth centuries involved more than these standard arguments allow. Paris provisioning required creating systems that balanced free trade and state regulation of food markets in order to achieve two goals of post-Revolutionary French society: to promote individual wealth and liberty while also adhering to practices meant to safeguard consumer rights and the social peace in the best interest of the collectivity.[17] Even many economic liberals argued in favor of some intervention, acknowledging 'the state should manage public works and cause (private enterprise) to work in complete harmony.' In 1914, Minister of Commerce Étienne Clémentel described the distinctly French philosophy of the market by saying that it was necessary for the state to allow liberty of commerce while simultaneously preventing and punishing the excesses of human greed. He insisted that such constraints on markets were 'in no way incompatible with the principles of the Revolution.'[18]

This persistence of paternalist and mercantilist values accounts, in part, for the striking constancy in the regulation and operation of Paris provisioning from the Old Regime down to the Third Republic (1870–1940). People at all levels of French government and society believed in a code of marketplace behavior that legitimized some degree of state intervention to regulate food commerce to assure a level playing field for buyers and sellers.[19] The French accepted, even while constantly negotiating, a political economy of food provisioning. The phenomenon that historian E.P. Thompson labeled the 'moral economy' of the eighteenth-century English marketplace had indeed receded as a relic of Britain's pre-industrial past, as Thompson argues. But, it is a mistake to believe because the moral economy gave way to laissez-faire in the English marketplace that the same transformation took place in France.[20]

What is immoral about a refrigerator?

There was substantial opposition to modernizing the market with refrigeration for two reasons. First, officials and the public believed that putting refrigerators in Les Halles to make storage of food more hygienic would encourage *mandataires* to abuse reserves in order to manipulate prices in the market and cheat consumers and the producers who sent their foodstuffs to be sold in Paris. *Mandataires* were public 'agents of confidence' in the market, not businessmen, and their integrity had to be guaranteed by the authorities. Second, there was widespread prejudice against refrigeration *tout court* among consumers, as well as many public authorities and private merchants. Many French people believed that eating cold-stored foods was a dangerous health hazard. In the professional press, the pre-war phenomenon of seemingly irrational rejection of the development of the refrigeration industry and installation of cold storage systems throughout commercial food circuits was called *frigophobie,* or fear of refrigerators.

Not only was Les Halles Centrales filled and emptied each day, but also the fundamental premise of the Parisian way of shopping and eating was that people bought food often during the week, even daily. Parisians had fresh foods regularly and did not need to stock foods in their tiny apartments and kitchens. And of course, homes and even fine restaurants did not have refrigerators. A few food shops, such as Félix Potin and Damoy, put in refrigeration around the turn of the century, but this was not the norm. Alphonse Marguery, president of the Comité de l'Alimentation Parisienne and himself a restaurateur, presented a report to the Paris Chamber of Commerce in 1899 in which he identified the French habit of *alimentation journalière* as the central question in the high price of food.[21]

Given the organization of Paris provisioning, it was unavoidable that there would be, on occasion, leftover unsold foods at Les Halles, which would be put away in less than ideal conditions because no provision had been made for food storage. The reserves would be inspected the next day, and some of it would be found unsanitary and need to be destroyed. The normal amount was perhaps two to three per cent and a little higher in summertime. Many believed that refrigerated conservation of food, especially meat, would be a powerful weapon in reducing food waste and battling the high cost of living. Moreover, foods could be put aside when they were plentiful in the market to protect consumers from the ups and downs of the agricultural cycle. However, since daily provisioning was built into many of the structures of French food commerce, as well as the Parisian life style, change at Les Halles would entail changes throughout the system.

When World War I broke out in August of 1914, the havoc that mobilization caused with train schedules, arrivals of perishable foods, uncertain quantities and prices, and excessive food waste forced questions about hygienic food storage and about refrigeration into the daily public discourse. The war made any food waste obscene, and especially when market inspectors seized and destroyed large quantities of chicken, pork, and other meats that had spoiled for want of buyers at high prices or because some merchants at Les Halles secreted food in reserves to wait for prices to go up – these were the allegations, although *mandataires* denied the charges. Reporters feasted on stories of rotten eggs, vegetables, and fruit found in the market, claiming was that as much as six to eight per cent of the perishable food did not sell because the prices were too high, was then put aside in unsanitary conditions, and went off before it could be put out for sale again. Seine Council member and market reformer Ambroise Rendu reported in 1915 on the excessive food loss due to spoilage saying that, 'Every loss of foodstuffs is a veritable public calamity.'[22]

One of the leading proponents of provisioning reform, City Councillor Henri Sellier said in 1916 that Les Halles was a market that conformed to life and commerce in another era of Paris history. The problems of the day demanded a new approach to provisioning Paris: excessive food waste would be remedied by the installation of refrigerators in the central market where sellers could store their unsold food until the next market was held, and changes in the regulations on reserves could be successful in avoiding speculation. The same year, Minister of the Interior Louis Malvy spent an hour touring Les Halles where *mandataires* tried to convince him that to permit a change of regulations to allow reserves would produce lower prices. Malvy responded, 'That's paradoxical, no?'[23] The question was how could the authorities design a central market that was both moral and modern at the same time? The complexity of any reform process in Paris provisioning is well illustrated by the on-going debates on refrigeration and its place in French life. It is an example of the strong pull of traditional values as well as the difficulty of reaching consensus on changing entrenched habits and ways of thinking.

87

Frigophobia and other food fears

Frenchman Charles Tellier invented the process of refrigeration in the nineteenth century. The innovation was soon popular in other countries. There were proponents of artificial cold storage of foods from the turn of the twentieth century in France, but the industry made very slow progress. Commercial firms in Le Havre and Marseille, cities highly dependent on maritime trade, were among the first to experiment with refrigerated ships and installations at the ports in order to encourage more trade in frozen and chilled meat from South America. But the efforts failed for lack of interest from the public and bad word-of-mouth in the press. The story goes that Tellier died in his homeland, unappreciated and destitute.

The Premier Congrès International du Froid took place in Paris in October 1908. The reports from the meeting indicate that there was little interest on the part of the public authorities throughout France to promote and fund this technology, but in the United States, Great Britain, Germany, and Argentina there was a great deal of enthusiasm for using refrigeration. Entrepreneurs and governments in these other countries invested in continued improvements in the technology and successfully overcame any initial consumer mistrust. In France, there was no organized support for the widespread use of refrigeration in food preservation and commerce. The delegation from Lyon at the 1908 Congrès wrote that,

> at the moment of the organization of this large Congrès des Industries du Froid in Paris, where all the countries of the world will be represented, we have been astonished to see the extent to which the French refrigeration industry has been ignored by the general public.[24]

When, in 1911, there were riots in various parts of France over the high cost of living, the trade press of retail and wholesale butchers and the refrigeration industry was filled with articles about refrigerators, frozen meat, packing plants in the colonies (especially Madagascar), dire price predictions, and endless debate about whether frozen meat was 'normal' or full of deadly toxins.[25] Persistent technical problems with refrigerators provoked complaints from merchants that they could not obtain good results with conservation in a refrigerator. A common refrain in Paris was that refrigerated meat was not 'to French tastes' although there were on-going efforts by scientists to prove and publicize the superior hygiene and good taste of refrigerated foods.

There was financial resistance to building refrigerated storage in the centers of agricultural production. Such a facility must be in constant use to be cost-effective, which may have been possible in a few large centers of consumption, but not widely on any scale in the provinces. Paris was provisioned from different provinces on a rolling schedule according to the season and produce, and Les Halles functioned as a clearinghouse redistributing foods out again to smaller markets in other regions. The design of the system for supplying Paris assured this constant flow because the producing regions got rid of their fresh fruits, vegetables, cheeses, and other perishable foods as soon as the harvest was over or the production process completed. Agricultural credit systems were also based on this premise.[26]

There was as well a good deal of semantic confusion because the terms for frozen meat (*congelée*) and chilled meat (*frigorifiée* or, rarely, *réfrigerée*) were used inter-changeably and indiscriminately. Especially during the wartime experiments with cold-stored meat, sometimes the author or speaker specified the precise temperature, but normally the references were vague. It was the same with refrigerators and freez-ers, all typically falling under the general terms 'installations froid,' or simply 'frigos.' Occasionally, the writer resorted to the English 'freezer' and 'frozen,' or sometimes it came out 'froozen' or 'chillée.' It would, in fact, be decades before refrigeration found a comfortable linguistic place in French.

With all these obstacles to overcome before major change could happen in French urban provisioning, what would it take to reach the tipping point in favor of reform? To make a long story short, during World War I, at the persistent urging of the City Council, the city of Paris contracted for refrigeration to be installed at Les Halles. We have seen that the material defects of Les Halles went beyond a wartime problem, but the war made the consequences of having an outmoded market more keenly felt. By the end of 1915, regardless of the *mandataires*' protests of innocence, a casual observer in the market could see that at the end of many days there was unsold mer-chandise without the expected reduction in prices.[27] A 1916 headline in *Le Matin* asked, 'When is it coming, this refrigerator we await so impatiently?' A reporter for the newspaper *La Liberté* wrote,

> The public authorities should have concerned themselves long ago with resolv-ing this urgent problem. Now, during the war, they only know how to apply measures that are completely ineffective, like the creation of official prices of which we have indicated the inconveniences, and sales to the public in the fish and poultry pavilions, which have not had the hoped-for results. Yes, they cre-ated commissions! But foodstuffs rot just the same.[28]

The refrigeration project at Les Halles at last got underway in 1917. The principal refrigerator was to go under the meat pavillion, and another smaller one under the fish pavillion. The initial cost to the city was estimated at 2.2 million francs. But construction could not be completed until after the war was over. By this time, the projected cost of the refrigerators had gone up to 4 million francs.[29] Meanwhile, the regulations prohibiting legal reserves were not changed and the debate on the place of reserves in the moral marketplace continued apace.

Conclusion: culture and compromise

One part of the refrigeration project went into operation in August 1920, the so-called Part C under the fish pavilion, and *mandataires* were permitted to pay for the use of space. Part of the space was reserved for private merchants in the neighborhood, some of whom had previously used the refrigerator under the Bourse du Commerce. In April 1922, less than three-quarters of the refrigeration at Les Halles was being used by anyone working in the market.[30] By the mid-twenties 'les grands frigorifiques,' as they were called, in Dunkerque, Le Harvre, Saint-Nazaire, La Pallice, Bordeaux, and Marseille, built during the war at a total cost of more than 50 million francs and representing 100,000 cubic meters, were closed or only partially in use. While the French railroad companies had supplied train stations with refrigerated storage areas during the war, once frozen imports were no longer coming into France, the companies found these units were usually empty as long as there was a plentiful supply of fresh domestic foodstuffs riding the rails.[31] Certainly, refrigeration could have been a solution to the high cost of food only if merchants and consumers actually used it.

By 1926, the Les Halles refrigeration project begun in 1917 was finally completed.[32] But, in a move designed to discourage *mandataires* from abusing the refrigerators for keeping reserves to make illicit profits, the Prefect of Police in conjunction with the Commission Supérieure des Halles decided to impose new taxes for each day that the same merchandise stayed in reserves.[33] Also in the Paris central market, as elsewhere, when there were sanitary problems with food that had been stored in the new refrigerators, the technology often took the blame for making the food inedible when the *mandataires* had stored the merchandise after it had already begun to spoil.[34] Few people seemed to understand that it was essential that food going into refrigerated storage be unadulterated by bacteria or other agents of putrefaction. Food reform advocate Maurice Piettre writes that good refrigeration at Les Halles would have been the greatest source of positive propaganda against the resistance of butchers, charcutiers, tripiers, and other professionals who had the most to gain from its use; however, 'judicious regulation' would have to make sure that commercial refrigerators did not continue to be habitually abused.

Within a few years, Piettre noted that both refrigerators in Les Halles and the old one in the Bourse de Commerce were too damp (as they were in the basements) and humid, with condensation on the walls and ceilings. Worse, so many people passed in and out that on some days, 'the doors stay open 17 and even 18 hours out of 24.'[35] Piettre went on to describe the refrigerated *sous-sol* of Les Halles in an eerie echo of Émile Zola's revolting description of the same area when he wrote his literary observations in the 1880s.[36] Piettre tells of huge masses of diverse foodstuffs piled up against the walls, the separating grills, and even touching the floor; 'fresh meats rotting, prepared foods in an advanced state of decomposition, putrefied offal, game that has been forgotten for months and is completely mummified.'[37]

The war was not, as it turns out, a tipping point. Accepting significant change in traditional concepts appears to have been a near-impossibility at official levels for reasons even beyond the deeply-entrenched belief that reserves had no place in a moral market. Food adulteration and fraud, only having been legislated against in 1905, were vivid in recent memory. Consumers, especially working class Parisians, were very suspicious of being victims of dishonest merchants. Refrigerators allowed one more layer of complexity, and one more opportunity to tamper with the people's food. Municipal authorities, as well as the French medical community, remained divided on the question of both the safety of refrigerated foods and the good sense of allowing reserves, and few politicians and bureaucrats were willing to advocate bold action to promote the technology when the risk of failure was so high. In France, while war demanded temporary changes and expedient solutions, the philosophy of Parisian provisioning and the institutions and ideas that supported it had taken shape over a long period of time. Reforms adopted in a moment of crisis did not result in permanent change, at least in the short run.

Notes

1. Claude Fischler, *L'homnivore* (Paris: Éditions Odile Jacob, 1990), 155–59.
2. Maxime du Camp, 'L'Alimentation de Paris,' Pt 2, *Revue des Deux Mondes*, 15 June 1868: 906.
3. Archives de la Préfecture de Police (APP) DB/344, Henri Sellier, Note sur la cherté de la vie et la réorganisation du Marché central des denrées alimentaires dans l'agglomération parisienne, Conseil Général de la Seine, 1916.
4. Quoted in Sellier, Note sur la cherté de la vie et la réorganisation du Marché central.
5. Ibid.
6. Ibid.
7. Claude Prudhomme, *La Questions des halles et le problème actuel du ravitaillement de Paris* (Paris: Librairie Générale de Droit et de Jurisprudence, 1927), 126.
8. Quoted in Sellier, Note sur la cherté de la vie et la réorganisation du Marché central.
9. Ibid.
10. For a detailed discussion of the philosophical and physical design of Les Halles and how this institution fit into the Paris provisioning machine, see my doctoral dissertation, 'Culture, Politics, and Modernization in Paris Provisioning 1880–1920,' (Ph.D. Diss., Boston University, 2006).
11. Quoted in Pierre Du Maroussem and Camille Guérie, *La Question ouvrière*, vol. 4, *Halles Centrales de Paris*, (Paris: Librairie Nouvelle de Droit et de Jurisprudence, 1894), 7.
12. Archives Nationales (AN) F/11/2679, Commission Supérieure des Halles, Note sur l'administration des marchés et des Halles Centrales et sur le régime des ventes en gros, Préfecture du Département de la Seine, 19 March 1873. Rapport présenté à M. le Ministre de l'Intérieur par la Commission chargée d'examiner les conditions d'après lesquelles devra être réglée définitivement l'organisation du service des Halles et Marchés de la Ville de Paris, 14 May 1877.
13. Du Maroussem and Guérie, *La Question ouvrière*, vol. 4, *Halles Centrales de Paris*, 7.
14. Archives de Paris (AP) 1338W 1144, Rapport présente par M. Bouche à la Commission Supérieure des Halles, n.d.
15. Ibid.
16. AN F/11/2679, Commission Supérieure des Halles, séance 20 November 1911. 'M. Audiffred constate que le nouveau texte tend à 'moraliser' le commerce des Halles: il peut affirmer en sa qualité de rapporteur de la loi de 1896 que cette 'moralisation' fut le but poursuivi par le législateur; il ne peut donc que s'associer à toute proposition tendant à cette fin. '
17. AN F/11/2679, Rapport sommaire sur Halles centrales, n. 693, M. le Baron de Ladoucette, 19 June 1890.
18. Étienne Clémentel, *Un Drame Économique* (Paris: Pierre Lafitte & Cie., 1914), 62–63.
19. See, among other studies, Judith A. Miller, *Mastering the Market: The State and the Grain Trade in Northern France, 1700–1860* (Cambridge: Cambridge University Press, 1999).
20. E.P. Thompson, *Customs in Common: Studies in Traditional Popular Culture*, Chapter 4, 'The Moral Economy of the English Crowd in the Eighteenth Century.' New York: The New Press, 1993.

21. Archives Chambre du Commerce de Paris (ACCP) V–4.50 (3), Rapport par M. Marguery, Abrogation des articles 30 et 31 de la loi des 19 et 22 juillet 1791 sur la taxe du pain et de la viande de boucherie, 30 octobre, 1899.

22. APP DB/345, Ambroise Rendu, Rapport au nom du Bureau 1, sur l'organisation de l'Office départemental d'approvisionnement, n. 14, Conseil Général de la Seine, 1915.

23. AP DR7/106, *L'Événement*, 27 May 1916.

24. Premier Congrès International du Froid, *État actuel et desiderata de l'industrie du froid en France* (Paris: Secrétariat Général, 1908), 13–16.

25. 'La Vie chère: prix de la viande,' *La Boucherie en Gros de Paris*, 23 September 1910; 'Le Rôle du froid dans la crise de la vie chère,' *La Revue Générale du Froid* 3 (October 1911); 'Les boeufs au Maroc,' *Journal du Syndicat de la Boucherie de Paris*, 8 January 1911; 'Rapport sur la cherté de la viande,' *Journal du Syndicat de la Boucherie de Paris*, 25 June 1911; 'La crise alimentaire et l'industrie frigorifique,' *Journal du Syndicat de la Boucherie de Paris*, 17 March 1912; 'Contre la viande chère,' *Gargantua* 1 (1), 1912; 'La Question de mieux-vivre: le développement de l'industrie frigorifique,' *La Ligue Nationale* (Organe de la Ligue nationale de défense du commerce de l'alimentation, de l'industrie et de la production agricole), 28 November 1912. My gratitude to Susanne Freidberg for sharing her research on these sources with me.

26. Robert Deutère, 'Contribution à l'étude des marchés alimentaires d'une grande ville,' (Mémoire de Fin d'Études, Institut d'Urbanisme de l'Université de Paris, 1942), 189–191. My thanks to Mary and Philip Hyman for sharing this unpublished manuscript with me.

27. 'Le Marché des Halles,' *Le Temps*, 14 December 1915.

28. 'Aux Halles: Resserres trop abondantes – denrées perdues – l'inertie de l'Administration,' *La Liberté*, 8 August 1916.

29. AP 1338W1144, Letters regarding La Société d'Entrepôts Frigorifiques des Halles de Paris, 16 November 1921, 8 February 1922, 17 March 1922, 11 April 1922.

30. AP 1338W 1144, Letter to M. Robin, Inspecteur général adjoint des services de la Préfecture de la Seine from the Chef du bureau administrative de l'Approvisionnement, 11 April 1922.

31. Ibid., 216–217.

32. Prudhomme, *La Question des halles et le problème actuel du ravitaillement de Paris*, 76.

33. AP 1338W 1144, Commission Supérieure des Halles Centrales de Paris, Séance du 24 July 1924.

34. Maurice Piettre, *Introduction aux diverses techniques de conservation des denrées périssables* (Paris: Librairie de l'Enseignement Technique, 1934), 216.

35. Ibid., 149.

36. See Émile Zola, *Carnets d'enquêtes: Une ethnographie inédite de la France* (Paris: Librairie Plon, 1986), 402.

37. Piettre, *Introduction aux diverses techniques de conservation*, 149–150.

Virtuous Food:
'Conscientious Production' as Moral Imperative

Michaela DeSoucey & Gary Alan Fine

In March, 2007, there were reports in the media on celebrity chef Wolfgang Puck's press release announcing his new culinary philosophy. Promoted as part of Spago's twenty-fifth anniversary celebration, Puck voiced concerns about the need to educate the broader public about healthy eating. Interviewed by *The New York Times*, he said, 'we decided ... to be much more socially responsible; our conscience feels better' (Severson 2007). Puck's restaurants will promote the use of certified organic ingredients, no longer serve foie gras, eggs from battery-caged hens, pork from gestation-crated pigs, veal from confinement crates; serve only sustainable seafood, all-natural or organic chicken and turkey, and expand vegetarian menu options. Importantly, his announcement followed a targeted campaign against him and his 'egregious practices,' organized by animal rights groups, including Farm Sanctuary and the Humane Society of the United States.

Wolfgang Puck's venture (and pressure) into 'conscientious food' offers a lens through which to examine frames being used to redefine what we know about our food's qualities and origins. Advocates of what Michael Pollan, author of *The Omnivore's Dilemma*, has called an 'alternative food future – slow, organic, local,' are reacting to ideas that our industrial food system is 'unsustainable,' making food an ideological battleground for the network of activists and organizations urging diners to identify as moral actors (2006). They aim to legitimize movements popularizing *conscientious production* as the moral way to resist the consolidated systems that produce, distribute, and market food in the Western world.

Consumers in advanced societies have many culinary options, and often consider qualities of their food choices beyond simple availability (Halweil 2004). In recent years, increasing numbers of consumers in post-industrial societies have altered their eating habits because of concerns about health, animal welfare, and the food industry's impact on the environment (Singer 1995; Allen 1993). Recasting food as a battleground of ethical consumption contributes to literature on food's symbolic and cultural significance in creating and maintaining boundaries around identity, nation, and class (see for e.g. Beardsworth and Keil 1997; Bourdieu 1984; Mennell 1985). Consumers are frequently told they have the opportunity to make a political statement every time they eat, and that 'eating is an agricultural act' (Berry 2002). Pollan's 'alternative food future,' injects ideas about one's civic duty to consider qualities in food choices beyond cost and even taste. The overall goal of conscientious production is to add virtue, as well as value, to the system of food production and, thus, civil society.

We address the ideological work of individuals and organizations who serve as present-day moral entrepreneurs, examining how they use narratives, images. and symbols – the fabric of cultural sociology – to make claims about what constitutes virtuous food, and what does not. Our analysis draws on data representing several virtuous food movements in the United States – organic food, local food, Slow Food, and the grass-fed beef movement – to argue that the concept of *conscientious production* reflects how these frameworks create new markets and respond to increased public attention. Our cases possess overlapping and contradictory features of what is considered virtuous: local production, pesticide free, humane conditions, environmental friendliness, protection for small farmers, land stewardship, and renewed community engagement. Together, a locally grown, non-organic apple sold at a local farmers market can be virtuous, as can an organic apple grown overseas and sold at Whole Foods.

Our goal for this paper is to address challenges and questions raised by the growing market for conscientious production, in order to open up understandings of power within the cultural system of food production and its compatibility with market processes (Counihan 2002). Our case is the United States; however, concepts and discussions are transferable to other Western countries struggling with similar issues of food production and morality.

94

What is conscientious production?

Scholars of consumption recognize that consumer culture establishes moral-political relationships among lived culture, material goods, and social resources as mediated through markets (Cross 2000; Zukin 2004). The consumer in this scenario is the *purchaser* who stimulates the economy with her purchases and who develops a social identity around the consumption of goods and methods of consuming (Fournier 1998).

Consumption cannot happen without production. As such, consumer-based morality movements are not only about changing behaviors and educating new audiences; they are also about buying and selling. The marketplace must be utilized for these foods to gain public visibility and appeal because they are literally and necessarily consumable objects. Social movement rhetoric is necessarily merged with language more typical of the mainstream marketplace. The emergence of industries around organic food, Fair Trade labeling, and anti-sweatshop campaigns, signals two important and related concepts: first, a contemporary desire for morally responsible *production* and, second, the institutionalization of these values (for example, by certification) over time (Zhouri 2004; Raynolds, Murray, and Heller 2007). Conscientious production engages these facets of industries to humanize unknown producers in order to 1) create awareness of industrialized and globalized production methods, 2) generate a sympathetic consumer response, and 3) add moral value to the consumption transaction.

'Conscientious production' is historically situated. Social problems associated with the Industrial Revolution (child labor, sanitary conditions, housing, etc.) permeated public knowledge about what was happening inside the sites of production (McKendrick, Brewer, and Plumb 1982). Exposés such as Upton Sinclair's *The Jungle* (2002[1906]) caused public outcry over business practices considered disreputable, stimulating governmental regulation, including the passage of the Pure Food and Drug Act of 1906. Today, issues such as environmental damage and the poor treatment of workers have contributed to pressure on companies to operate in socially and environmentally-friendly ways (Vogel 2005), affecting marketing, branding, and structuring of consumer choices (Thompson 2004). Likewise, demands on governments to regulate business practices have grown out of claims that information about the ways in which things are produced matters for the informed consumer (Pines and Meyer 2005). This focus on the *how* of production engages organizations possessing interests and agendas mobilized to influence meaning-making within a generalized moral framework (Haveman and Rao 1997).

Public attention is frequently paid to morality issues promoted by those with ideologies linked to both privileged consumption practices (Fourcade-Gourinchas and Healy 2007). Resistance to mass and popular culture is often a marker of, but is not necessarily specific to, upper-middle class professional lifestyles (Gans 1974). Privileged claims makers have the ability, as well, to use law to institute their ideas of 'human values' or 'civilized values' (Elias 1978) in policy and legislation, although not without challenge. Elite and exclusive objects that fit these settings are valorized as desirable signals of status, but combating the food and agriculture industries means challenging the second largest US industry after defense.

Relatively few products have become as recently politicized as food. Consumer-based trends in eating, food scares resulting from contamination, and impending health crises resulting from poor nutrition and growing obesity rates are part of the public discourse (Saguy and Riley 2005). The media help to mainstream the concept of conscientious production and to encourage consumers to seek out virtuous food from producers who are likewise under a public microscope (Kalaitzandonakes, Marks, and Vickner 2004). The effectiveness of these arbiters in creating moral boundaries around virtuous food production reflects shifts in the classification and categorization of cultural aesthetics (Fine 1992) to include the importance of the production methods (the *how)* as well as physical qualities, such as ingredients or shelf-life (the *what*).

Data and methods

Based on data collected from 2003 to 2007, this research examines the concept of virtuous food through a multi-method approach of 60 interviews with producers, chefs, and others in the food industry; observations at field sites in which these foods – and the discourse about them – are available to consumers (including local farmers markets, area farms, events, and three conferences on alternative agriculture); and content analysis of articles from national and local newspaper and magazines, industry-specific publications, websites, Internet blogs, menus, cookbooks, and newsletters. We examined the process by which food, through its production and distribution locations, is constructed as virtuous in order to understand the issues that these food producers and advocates face. We examine cultural codes and micro-level processes at the level of meaning-making, marketing, and understanding, looking directly at 'how the content of culture is influenced by the milieu in which it is created, distributed, evaluated, taught and preserved' (Peterson 1994, p. 165).

Identifying virtue

Variation in conscientious production is evident in the complexity that accompanies the wide range of imagery and narrative used to make these movements more enticing, to the extent where the act of purchase becomes a sought-after experience in and of itself (Fournier 1998). Each domain of virtuous food draws from reference points in both social movement and market ideal types, yet all emphasize the importance of *trust in the production method as ethical*. In an important respect, the foods are themselves the basis for advocating social change. We identify the ideal type characteristics of 'virtuous food' as: connecting nature with culture through the language of authenticity; building relationships of trust with producers; justifying environmental support and stewardship; and considering the social implications of consumer choice. These categories illustrate how promoters use social movement rhetoric to describe the production process as well as how those schemas become redefined by marketplace demands.

Connecting nature with culture

Even though the majority of contemporary farming and farmers in the United States has ceased to fit the model of small, family-based production, the independent farmer has long been idealized in cultural history (Browne et al. 1992). Small-scale producers who participate in direct-selling relationships with their customers (through farmers markets or community-supported agricultural groups) claimed that they are not just selling food; they are selling *themselves* and *their experiences* as meaningful, giving these foods storied connections to person and place. This traceability is used to mark the food as real, genuine, and authentic, and venerates the grower's experience in the production itself. One farmer explained, 'I used to bring pictures of the farm to the farmers markets. People would come up, look at the photos, and say "you're living our dream." They don't think we're crazy at all. Some other people ask me, "Are you still having fun?" Fun is not a word here. Farming isn't 'fun.' That's a very urban kind of notion, not a farmer's notion.' Another echoed this sentiment: 'People are so

96

romantic about farming. They think it is a wonderful life; they have pastoral visions. It's really sweat, blood, and tears.' So although farmers dispute the urban romanticism of rural life, they also use it as a marketing tool by drawing upon cultural narratives conceptualizing authenticity and commitment, drawing moral boundaries around themselves and their products.

Cultural gatekeepers in the worlds of food media and restaurants also rely on this idea that the connections with place and relationships with the growers are salient to the symbolic value of virtuous food. Within the past ten years, the names of the farms that supply top restaurants in urban areas have appeared as acknowledgements on menus, linking the foods' status with their own. Farmers are regularly interviewed on National Public Radio talking about their asparagus, and 'meet the grower' human-interest stories have appeared with increasing frequency in local and regional news outlets each year (fieldnotes). Media outlets have power to shape the images of farmers as producers of culture and meaning, as well as of food. The story of the farm and farmer is suggested in the space of such exchanges, whether or not it is readily accessible in practice.

Moral solutions to social problems

Moral entrepreneurs' subjective experience of moral virtue and value congruity is based on values encoded in the framework of conscientious production to which they subscribe. When comparing their practices to others, producers attempt to 'trigger moral indignation' (Gamson 1995) in marketing themselves, their organizational ties, and the 'conscience' found in their offerings. They experience their commitment as congruent with personal values and social morality (Fourcade-Gourinchas and Healy 2007), that they are 'doing the right thing,' juxtaposed against conventional agriculture. One grass-fed rancher drew this symbolic boundary by lamenting, 'Have you been to a feedlot? Those animals require fresh air, and they stand there all day long taking in nothing but toxic and fecal dust and they are so sick…e.coli, that is feedlot beef. ' Another characterized the conventional system as 'against nature to me. It didn't seem like the right thing to do for the animals. I didn't like the chemical fertilizers and pesticides on our land.'

Connecting social problems about land usage, environmental degradation, rural communities, and human health with moral solutions confirms the concept of *trust* as implicit in marketing conscientious production. From this, how does one know if something is consciously produced or not, if they do not see the production first-hand? In part, this is an organizational problem of disseminating information; brands and labels serve as mechanisms to inform and instruct consumers as to who did the production and the conditions under which the products were produced (Prasad et al. 2004). They are typically viewed as essential in the larger marketplace for ensuring that the product stands up to its moral claims.

The USDA's organic labeling program, instituted in 2002, marks the most distinct of these symbolic boundaries. This label attempts to reconcile food business with consumer interest in social and environmental practices. Through this labeling, companies such as the Body Shop, Tom's of Maine, and Ben and Jerry's ice cream have straddled a blurry middle ground between traditional distribution chains and small, independent food producers. The paradox is that as the market expands for ethically produced products, it simultaneously has the potential to dilute or undermine the company or movement's original goals. The Body Shop is now owned by L'Oreal, Tom's of Maine by Colgate-Palmolive, and Ben and Jerry's by Unilever. Wal-Mart is currently the largest distributor of organic food in the world, raising eyebrows among those who equate organic with virtue. Organic producers, especially, face challenges in reconciling their narratives of virtue with market imperatives, as they continue to enter mainstream consumer culture (Fromartz 2007).

Here, institutional power can operate to prevent cultural production as well as to enable it. One farm, which grows organically without being USDA certified due to the cost and resources necessary for certification, feels it 'doesn't matter for their customers, many of whom they've developed multi-year relationships with.' Several interviewees spoke of their disdain for Whole Foods, a national chain of specialty grocery stores which carries many organic foods and food products, and their refusal to ask Whole Foods to carry their products. By selling to a national chain, authenticity (from the producers' point of view) can easily be lost, indicating the drawing of symbolic boundaries between different types of virtuous food and the moral status that each possesses in the greater food marketplace. This demonstrates both the high costs of monitoring labeling and certification practices and the limitations to different markets for virtuous foods.

Does conscientious production work?

Following Carlo Petrini (2001), founder of Slow Food, we note that rising market demand for 'conscientious production' demonstrates that virtues associated with food choices are not attained through consuming alone. Though many people claim concern for the moral, health and safety implications of food production systems, fewer act on these beliefs when it comes to their grocery budgets (Kendall, Lobao, and Sharp 2006). Price has long been the main impetus of food purchasing choices. However, sales of different types of virtuous food, each with their own political agenda and set of public concerns, are increasing. For instance, Fair Trade coffee sales have tripled since 1999 (Raynolds 2002), farmers markets around the US have grown enormously in number and size (United States Department of Agriculture 2006); and, the international Slow Food movement recently hosted its second Terra Madre conference in Italy. Support from local governments and media further helps conscientious production gain popular support.

Conscientious production methods are sustainable in the long-term, however, only if virtue pays off. Many of the moral entrepreneurs in our sample, however, encourage moral, rather than monetary, criteria, placing primacy on personal relationships, trust, taste, and stewardship of land and environment (however, economic success is necessary to continue, and this was repeatedly emphasized.) These entrepreneurs define social responsibility as something that consumers will seek out, and as such, will attract further sales and enhanced reputation (fieldnotes). All categories of virtuous food producers regard their reputations as crucial to their success. Accordingly, many have decided it is in their interest to coordinate and cooperate with other producers, for example forming cooperatives, selling side-by-side at farmers markets, and hosting events as fundraisers and public awareness initiatives.

At present, virtuous foods are understood as a niche rather than a generalized market strategy; it makes sense for *some* producers and *some* consumers under *some* circumstances. If virtue was the main variable in individuals' decisions about what and where to buy their food, the market for virtuous food would work efficiently, and all food producers would possess incentives to change their practices. For some, the moral choice is price; many consumers still frequently wish (or need) to be price sensitive, demonstrated by success of stores like Wal-Mart, CostCo, and others. Virtuous food often remains an option of the well-heeled.

To understand food consumption, we must recognize that interrelated public and private forces, including corporate industries, governmental and regulatory bodies, food stores, and restaurants mediate what we do or do not eat, as well as what is available to be consumed. The marketing of production practices deemed 'authentic,' 'socially responsible,' and 'ethical' as a form of consumer resistance has actually helped to reinvigorate consumer capitalism by offering *more* choices to consumers (Frank 1997; Heath and Potter 2004; Beverland 2005). Advocates and marketers have responded to discontent generated by the food industry by giving 'conscientious consumers' more consumption outlets from which to choose. Likewise, watchdogs of corporate and industry citizenship are mainly found among individuals and organizations with a strong activist commitment, resources, and the political opportunities to act at an institutional level (Thompson 2004). Although 'alternative' foods pose no immediate competitive threat to the food industry, we argue that their very existence raises hard questions about the practices and power of agribusiness.

The market for conscientious production thus works imperfectly; gaps between industry codes and actual production methods remain significant, often due to problems with self-monitoring or uneven compliance with regulatory codes (Vos 2000). Labels, like the USDA's organic certification label, help because some consumers do choose to pay more for such foods. Though the market for Fair Trade coffee, for example, remains small (only about 5 per cent of coffee sold in the US in 2004), it is growing and has received the majority of its support from Starbucks, currently the largest roaster and retailer of Fair Trade coffee in the US Starbucks increased its purchases from Fair Trade cooperatives from 653,000 to 2 million pounds between 2001 and 2004, further mainstreaming the arena of conscientious production (Vogel 2005).

Conclusion

The domain of virtuous food is much different than it was just ten years ago. Changes include the strengthened emergence of local food movements, the increased involvement of community groups and environmental organizations working on farm and agricultural issues, interest from the public health community in countering both obesity and the impact of food antibiotics and pesticides on human health, and the willingness of large corporations, such as Starbucks, Whole Foods, and even Wal-Mart, to embrace portions of these movements. These combined forces have played a large role in this transformation by educating consumers, building organizational ties with industry, and in questioning the practices of food companies and producers, often by naming (and shaming) them into change, viewing consumers as their silent partners (Kozinets and Handelman 2003).

Cultural sociology, with its sensitivity to objects, narratives, and symbols, offers the scholar of food studies a key advantage in this regard. Virtuous food, as a meaning system, speaks to the contextual moral conditions of cultural production. It joins material resources and cultural frames in reaching out to morally-concerned consumer-citizens (Thompson 2004; Raynolds 2002). The market exchange of cultural goods (especially in large, globalizing markets) influences the process of cultural production, encouraging the emergence of new forms and methods of dealing with exchange partners (Fourcade-Gourinchas and Healy 2007), further complicating what gets counted as a virtue. It is similarly crucial not to downplay the cultural forces that occur outside the immediate context of production, for example the salience of health providers, media outlets, and especially the role of the Internet.

Shopping at the farmers market and voting are not mutually exclusive acts, yet conscientious production encourages people to identify as consumers, where purchasing power is used to demonstrate concern for a particular moral issue. Fears that a consumerist approach to conscientious production and virtuous food will detach such products from concerns with the problematic operation of markets reveals the complexities of what it means to market morality in today's culinary environment. Just ask Wolfgang Puck.

100

Bibliography

Allen, Patricia. 'Connecting the Social and the Ecological in Sustainable Agriculture', *Food for the Future: Conditions and Contradictions of Sustainability*. Ed. Patricia Allen. New York: John Wiley & Sons, Inc., 1993.

Beardsworth, Alan, and Teresa Keil. *Sociology on the Menu: An Invitation to the Study of Food and Society*. London; New York: Routledge, 1997.

Berry, Wendell. 'Death of the American Family Farm', from *The Progressive*. 2002. [http://www.organic-consumers.org/corp/familyfarm042202.cfm].

Beverland, Michael B. 'Crafting Brand Authenticity: The Case of Luxury Wines.' *Journal of Management Studies* 42.5 (2005): 1003–29.

Bourdieu, Pierre. *Distinction: A Social Critique of the Judgement of Taste*. Trans. Richard Nice. Cambridge, MA: Harvard University Press, 1984.

Browne, W., et al. *Sacred Cows and Hot Potatoes: Agrarian Myths in Agriculture Policy*. Boulder, CO: Westview Press, 1992.

Counihan, Carole. *Food in the USA: A Reader*. New York: Routledge, 2002.

Cross, Gary S. *An All-Consuming Century: Why Commercialism Won in Modern America*. New York: Columbia University Press, 2000.

Elias, Norbert. *The Civilizing Process*. Trans. Edmund Jephcott. 2 vols. New York: Urizen Books, 1978.

Fine, Gary Alan. 'The Culture of Production: Aesthetic Choices and Constraints in Culinary Work.' *American Journal of Sociology* 97.5 (1992): 1268–94.

Fourcade-Gourinchas, Marion, and Kieran Healy. 'Moral Views of Market Society.' *Annual Review of Sociology* 33 (2007).

Fournier, Susan. 'Consumers and Their Brands: Developing Relationship Theory in Consumer Research.' *Journal of Consumer Research* 24.March 1998.

Frank, Thomas. *The Conquest of Cool: Business Culture, Counterculture, and the Rise of Hip Consumerism*. Chicago: University of Chicago Press, 1997.

Fromartz, Samuel. *Organic, Inc.: Natural Foods and How They Grew*. New York: Harvest Books, 2007.

Gamson, William A. 'Constructing Social Protest.' *Social Movements and Culture*. Eds. Hank Johnston and Bert Klandermans. Vol. 4. Social Movements, Protest, and Contention. Minneapolis: University of Minnesota Press, 1995.

Gans, Herbert J. *Popular Culture and High Culture: An Analysis and Evaluation of Taste*. New York: Basic Books, 1974.

Halweil, Brian. *Eat Here: Reclaiming Homegrown Pleasures in a Global Supermarket*. 1st ed. New York: W.W. Norton, 2004.

Haveman, Heather, and Hayagreeva Rao. 'Structuring a Theory of Moral Sentiments: Institutional and Organizational Coevolution in the Early Thrift Industry.' *American Journal of Sociology* 102.6 (1997): 1606–46.

Heath, Joseph, and Andrew Potter. *Nation of Rebels: Why Counterculture Became Consumer Culture*. New York: HarperBusiness, Harper Collins, 2004.

Kalaitzandonakes, N., L. A. Marks, and S. S. Vickner. 'Media Coverage of Biotech Foods and Influence on Consumer Choice.' *American Journal of Agricultural Economics* 86.5 (2004): 1238–46.

Kendall, Holli A., Linda M. Lobao, and Jeff S. Sharp. 'Public Concern with Animal Well-Being: Place, Social Structural Location, and Individual Experience.' *Rural Sociology* 71 (2006): 399–428.

Kozinets, Robert, and Jay M. Handelman. 'Adversaries of Consumption: Consumer Movements, Activism and Ideology.' *Journal of Consumer Research* (2003).

McKendrick, Neil, John Brewer, and J.H. Plumb. *The Birth of a Consumer Society: The Commercialization of Eighteenth-Century England*. Bloomington: Indiana University Press, 1982.

Mennell, Stephen. *All Manners of Food: Eating and Taste in England and France from the Middle Ages to the Present*. New York: Basil Blackwell, 1985.

Peterson, Richard A., ed. *Culture Studies through the Production Perspective: Progress and Prospects.* Oxford; Cambridge, Massachusetts: Blackwell, 1994.

Petrini, Carlo, ed. *Slow Food: Collected Thoughts on Taste, Tradition, and the Honest Pleasures of Food.* White River Junction, Vermont: Chelsea Green Publishing, 2001.

Pines, Gina L., and David G. Meyer. 'Stopping the Exploitation of Workers: An Analysis of the Effective Application of Consumer or Socio-Political Pressure.' *Journal of Business Ethics* 59.1 (2005): 155–62.

Pollan, Michael. *The Omnivore's Dilemma.* New York: Penguin, 2006.

Prasad, Monica, et al. 'Consumers of the World Unite: A Market-Based Response to Sweatshops.' *Labor Studies Journal* 29.3 (2004).

Raynolds, Laura T. 'Consumer/Producer Links in Fair Trade Coffee Networks.' *Sociologia Ruralis* 42.4 (2002): 404–24.

Raynolds, Laura T., Douglas Murray, and Andrew Heller. 'Regulating Sustainability in the Coffee Sector: A Comparative Analysis of Third-Party Environmental and Social Certification Initiatives.' *Agriculture and Human Values* 24.2 (2007): 147–63.

Saguy, Abigail C., and Kevin W. Riley. 'Weighing Both Sides: Morality, Mortality, and Framing Contests over Obesity.' *Journal of Health Politics, Policy & Law* 30.5 (2005): 869.

Severson, Kim. 'Celebrity Chef Announces Strict Animal-Welfare Policy.' *New York Times* March 22, 2007.

Sinclair, Upton. *The Jungle.* Modern Library Classics. Modern Library pbk. ed. New York: Modern Library, 2002[1906].

Singer, Peter. *How Are We to Live?: Ethics in an Age of Self-Interest.* Amherst, N.Y.: Prometheus Books, 1995.

Thompson, Craig J. 'Marketplace Mythology and Discourses of Power.' *Journal of Consumer Research* 31 June 2004.

United States Department of Agriculture. 'Farmers Market Facts'. 2006. http://www.ams.usda.gov/farmersmarkets/facts.htm.

Vogel, David. *The Market for Virtue: The Potential and Limits of Corporate Social Responsibility.* Washington, D.C.: Brookings Institution Press, 2005.

Vos, Timothy. 'Visions of the Middle Landscape: Organic Farming and the Politics of Nature.' *Agriculture and Human Values* 17 (2000): 245–56.

Zhouri, Andréa. 'Global-Local Amazon Politics: Conflicting Paradigms in the Rainforest Campaign.' *Theory, Culture & Society* 21.2 (2004): 69–89.

Zukin, Sharon. *Point of Purchase: How Shopping Changed American Culture.* New York: Routledge, 2004.

Eat Like There's No Tomorrow and Other Lessons Learned from Last Meals

Doug Duda

A growing interest in food and morality is bound up in new discoveries – and with them, new speculation – regarding the power of individual food choice to affect the wider well being of families, communities, nations, and the planet as a whole. In this context, the phenomenon of the last meal represents something increasingly rare: the prospect of a meal without a morning after.

At first glance, the final food choices made by prisoners on death row, the terminally ill, religious martyrs, and suicide victims seem hopelessly idiosyncratic and ultimately marginal to the ongoing struggle most of us have with applying knowledge and principle to appetites that often resist such meddling. However, dining without possibility of ongoing reflection or recrimination, precisely because it is inherently disconnected from future-focused, consequence-oriented, and science-inspired food ethics, appears to offer unique lessons about the world of food choice we face today.

Lesson 1: Have it your way

In January 2007, on the occasion of the thirtieth anniversary of the reinstatement of the death penalty in the United States, Amnesty International noted that 1,059 men and women had been executed during this time, with the state of Texas representing over a third of this total.[1] As a result, for capital-punishment researchers, many roads lead to Texas, including those focused on the last-meal requests of the condemned. Records kept by Brian Price, a former inmate in the Huntsville, Texas prison who prepared nearly 200 of these final meals, indicate that the most frequently requested entrée is the cheeseburger and the most frequently requested side dish is French fries, although the following last-meal request by David Allen Castillo illustrates a not uncommon desire to order such items with 'the works': [2]

Twenty-four soft shell tacos
Six enchiladas
Six tostadas (chalupas)
Two whole onions
Five jalapenos
Two cheeseburgers
One chocolate milk shake

One quart of milk
One pack of Marlboro cigarettes.[3]

In American sports, particularly football and basketball, the phrase 'garbage time,' refers to the last few minutes left to play in a game that the loser has little hope of winning, where the now-or-never imperative for the loser is to take all remotely possible shots, without self-censorship.

This presumption of having already lost, not present in the optimistic and forward-looking ethical food-chooser, threatens to transform the last meal of death row inmates like Castillo into a last binge. However, this gastronomic finale is also similar to the last few minutes of a fireworks display, not so much indiscriminate as determinedly in the moment.

Viewed in this context, such a menu is not simply another brick in the great wall of inappropriate food choices that stand between us and our ideal weight, spiritual state, or conscious selves. Rather the menu becomes more purely about the food itself, no longer an instrument hurtling toward a goal, now somehow more clearly visible for hanging suspended, stripped of direction and velocity.

And in this context, it is possible to understand why those faced with a final choice between steak and hamburger so often choose hamburger. The likely greater experience with the humbler cut, the hamburger as icon of the appetites and freedom of youth, the evocation of family, friends, and better times – all are embodied in this most popular of last-meal requests. Last meals typically provide comfort beyond their chemistries. They are context foods, a last taste of the present and past.

The Texas last-meal request list, whose core is the generally familiar cheeseburgers and fries, steak and eggs, and ice-cream and Coca-Cola, is also embroidered with more personal memories:

Catfish and hush puppies
Chicken and dumplings
Iced tea with real sugar
Baked potato with sour cream and jalapenos
Half a pound of chitterlings
Wild game
Honey buns with melted butter on the side.[4]

Importantly, the desire to use the last meal to embrace important life memories is not limited to prison inmates. Former US senator and would-be presidential candidate, Fred Thompson, would like a last bite of his mother's fresh coconut cake with fluffy white frosting for his last meal. Professional golfer, Greg Norman, would eat one more Australian meat pie. New Orleans musician, Dr John, would have a last sip of Barq's root beer. There are exceptions that prove the rule, but the majority of last requests are food choices that summon not our better selves, but our truer selves.

Eat drink and be merry, for tomorrow we die

The last meal was not and is not always a solitary act. Socrates' cup of hemlock evokes rituals of suicide with honor in ancient Greece and Rome that were particularly public acts conducted in the midst of friends and family. The roughly contemporaneous last meal of Buddha, surrounded by his followers, indicates that the concept of a communal last meal is firmly rooted in the East as well.[5] In fact, even last meals on death row today can be social. Deadmaneating.com, the official website devoted to last meals, reports that condemned killer Larry Eugene Hutcherson forsook a final meal request in favor of a family meal with all members eating from the visitor room's vending machine, and it is easy to imagine similar meals in the many other instances meals where the condemned make no formal last request.[6]

None of these are examples of particularly merry meals, however, at least not for the guests. Socrates and Buddha are both famous for their attempts to keep up the spirits of their companions. In an infamous experiment with widening the last-meal ritual to include family, the state of Indiana allowed the mother of convicted murderer Gerald Blivins to cook his favorite meal, chicken and dumplings, in the prison with him and eat it together, only to find that the experience prompted her to attempt suicide when she returned to her hotel that evening.[7]

While *De, bibe, lude – post mortem nulla voluptas* (eat, drink, be merry, after death there are no such pleasures) is a deeply rooted sentiment expressed in various sources, from Isaiah to Ecclesiastes to the Rubaiyat, it's enjoinment to merriment feels today approximately equal to such sentiments as, 'in heaven there is no beer, that's why we drink it here.' While underscoring the temporal nature of sensual pleasure, including the pleasures of the table as distinct from those of the food itself, one might not connect it to the ritual of last meals.

Nonetheless, the history of societies and their efforts to reconcile the general population to the use of power by the state – including the death penalty – is a history of social rituals aimed at congeniality at least. In recent centuries the last meal has evolved into a gesture by the condemned that he or she accepts the verdict, affirms the correctness of the punishment and absolves the executioner and the community as a whole of responsibility.

In eighteenth-century Germany,[8] where religious conversion of malefactors was a common goal of the state, the condemned might enjoy food richer than any they had ever had before in their lives as a reward for accepting their sins during the three-day pre-execution period set aside for intensive lobbying by family and clergy. On the morning of the hanging, an executioner was apt to visit the condemned for a ritual drink called the *Johannessegen* in memory of the blessing John the Baptist is believed to have conferred upon his executioners. Following all was a ritual known as *Henkersmahlzeit* (Hangman's Meal) where officials, judges, condemned, and executioner ate a rich feast together, before the gallows march through town where inn-keepers under state contract offered the prisoner additional drinks to further insure congenial acceptance of the ultimate fate.

A food ethicist concerned about the consequences of thoughtless consumption might question the wisdom of offering an elaborate ritual of food choice to an offender whose actions have robbed others of all their choices – including food.

Whether fattening up victims before a Mayan sacrifice or walking a condemned seventeenth-century Englishman from prison to brothel to pub to gallows, the last meal as social act teaches us to acknowledge a power that the condemned have that transcends individual food choice in the ordinary sense, and that elevates such choices to public catharsis.

You can't always get what you want

While the last meal may function as an acceptance of society's judgment, there is at the same time a sense that it signals a release from taboo. Reviewing records of denied requests for a last cigarette (most prisons no longer allow smoking, for health reasons) or a last drink (most rituals of a last short one with the warden have similarly disappeared) simply emphasizes the obvious lack of options for the forbidden at prisons. Perhaps more instructive are instances among the terminally ill.

When they are out of reasons for denying themselves the experience, the termi-nally ill are more apt and often better equipped than the prisoner to reach for the ultimate food taboo: poison.[9] The fact that such lethal last meals are often taken with friends and family[10] suggests that the taboo is breaking down, and a 2004 Gallup survey in the United States indicating that a majority of Americans now find physi-cian-assisted suicide morally acceptable suggests that baby boomers have found a new phase of their lives to obsessively control.

Behind prison walls, the last-meal ritual is able to not only preserve its taboos but invent new ways to make sure that you can't always get what you want. According to CNN, in May 2007, Philip Workman's last-meal request was a pizza, to be delivered to a homeless man. While the request was denied on the grounds it exceeded the rule limiting last meal costs to $20, it appears that the taboo was really the crossing of the line governing what the public will and will not pay for on the prisoner's behalf. Taxpayers will feed a condemned prisoner, but won't provide a charitable donation of equal value to a designated charity.

Although the response to Workman's failed request took place after he was execut-ed, the many posthumously donated pizzas distributed to homeless throughout the city stand as proof that while you can't always get what you want, if you try sometime, you do get what you need.[11]

The Devil made me do it

Nutrition studies with inmate populations support the idea that bad behavior arises from bad diet. Castillo's 24-taco last-meal request isn't just the end of the road, it is the road.

In recent years a number of studies have looked at the correlation between what prisoners eat and the behavior that landed them in prison to begin with.[12]

In a series of institutional settings, from schools to prisons, research results indicate that the population is less prone to violence and serious anti-social behavior when vitamin-mineral supplements met the current dietary recommendations.

In fact, incidents of violence reportedly decreased by as much as one-third,[13] as measured by a reduction in the number of disciplinary offenses when studied in a prison setting. There is finally hard evidence that the so-called Twinkie defense, in which an attorney argued that junk food addled an accused murderer, might have been something more than a late-night talk-show punch line.

Yet, all of this points to a circular dimension to the relationship between the quality of choices one makes about food and the ability to act on those choices. If the devil made me eat the devil's food, and the devil's food made me do it, what compromised our food choices? How much is the notion of food choice itself simply a light hum hovering above the grinding machinery of food necessity set in motion by choices made long ago, as often as not made by others on our behalf, about what we should eat?

107

Conclusion: Eat like there's no tomorrow

Timothy McVeigh, the infamous Oklahoma City bomber, murdered 168 men, women and children, and ordered two pints of mint chocolate-chip ice-cream for a last meal. As his execution approached McVeigh was lobbied by PETA to go out with a vegan meal.

If the specter of organizations billboarding the last meals of famous prisoners raises the question whether the next stone in this road is an organic grocer providing a check to the condemned – the surviving family can use it – for the right to sponsor the last meal, then you are grasping the tsunami just as it's about to crest. Why is this somehow imaginable in a way that the official athletic shoe of the condemned ('Dead Man – Running!') is so clearly not?

The phrase is 'eat like there's no tomorrow,' and not 'dress like there's no tomorrow' illustrates the unique role of food choice in defining who we are, where we've been, and where we're going. Whether our food choices are statements of what we are and have been, an act of reconciliation between the state and the individual, a cathartic challenge of taboo, or a foregone conclusion based on deteriorated nutrition, there is an urgency to dispatching meals that will never attach to wearing shirts since, for starters, you can wear a shirt more than once.

Notes

1. Amnesty International, *'United States of America: The experiment that failed, a reflection on 30 years of executions'* (16 January, 2007), pp. 6–7.
2. Price, pp. 13, 244–5.
3. Black, pp. 60–3. This includes a photograph of the requested last meal.
4. Price, pp. 25–394.
5. Dillon, Matthew, 'Dialogues with Death: The Last Days of Socrates and the Buddha' in *Philosophy East and West*, vol 50, no. 4, pp. 525–558.
6. Price, pp. 259–260
7. Sharp, pp. 86–7.
8. Evans, pp. 66–75. See particularly pp. 67–8, for a Hangman's Meal menu of fried sausages, beef, baked carp, larded vropast veal, soup, cabbage, bread, a sweet and a 1748 wine.
9. Delury, pp. 172–7.
10. Quill, pp. 169–170.
11. Fantz, Ashley, 'Killer orders pizza for homeless as last meal' on cnn.com, 2007.
12. Eves, Anita and C. Bernard Gesch. 'Food provision and the nutritional implications of food choices made by young adult males, in a young offenders' institution' in *The British Dietetic Association Ltd/ Human Nutrition and Dietetics*, 2003, pp. 167–179.
13. Gesch, C. Bernard, Sean M, Hammond, Sarah W. Hampson, Anita Eve, and Martin Crowder, 'Influence of supplementary vitamins, minerals and essential fatty acids on the anti-social behaviour of young adult prisoners' in *British Journal of Psychiatry*, 2 (2002), pp. 22–8.

Bibliography

Black, Jacquelyn C. . . . *last meal*. Monroe: Common Courage Press, 2003.

Delury, George E. *But What If She Wants To Die? A Husband's Diary*. New York: Birch Lane Press/Carol Publishing Group, 1997.

Dickerson, James L. *Last Suppers: If The World Ended Tomorrow, What Would Be Your Last Meal?* New York: Citadel Press, 2003.

Evans, Richard J. *Rituals of Retribution: Capital Punishment in Germany 1600–1987*. Oxford: Oxford University Press, 1996.

Price, Brian. *Meals To Die For*. San Antonio: Dyna-Paige Corporation, 2004.

Quill, Timothy E. *A Midwife Through The Dying Process: Stories of Healing and Hard Choices at the End of Life*. Baltimore: The John Hopkins University Press, 1996.

Sharp, Susan F. *Hidden Victims: The Effects of the Death Penalty on Families of the Accused*. New Brunswick: Rutgers University Press, 2005.

Scientists and Food – Moral, Immoral or Amoral?

Len Fisher

Scientists have had a lot to do with food over the centuries. Their role goes back at least to the Romans, and to the discovery of some scientifically-minded but misguided genius that wine tasted sweeter when drunk from pewter goblets. Of course it did. The acid in the wine dissolved the lead to produce sweet-tasting, but poisonous lead acetate.

The Romans soon learned by experiment that they could do even better by adding a syrup made of unfermented grape juice that had been boiled down in lead-lined pots, not realising that this would be at the expense of their health, and would contribute (according to some historians) to the collapse of their empire. The ambivalent relationship between science and gastronomy continues in the present day, with science being used in 'molecular gastronomy' to widen our food experience, but also being used to produce uniform, monotonous (but cheaper) foods that are often full of additives. Here I investigate the ethics of the scientist's role in gastronomy and how that role has changed throughout history, asking the question 'When you sup with a scientist, should you use a long spoon?' Have scientists been responsible for damaging and devaluing our eating experience, or have they contributed to it and enhanced it?

A convenient starting point for my investigation is 1820, because this was the year when the German chemist Frederick Accum published *A Treatise on Adulteration of Food, and Culinary Poisons*. Its title page bore a picture of a skull and a biblical quotation 'there is death in the pot.' There certainly was in 1820, because some of the additives that food producers were using to 'improve' their products weren't exactly guaranteed to improve the health of the consumer. Here are just a few:

- Used tea leaves were recycled by being boiled with copperas (ferrous sulphate) and sheep's dung, then coloured with Prussian blue (ferric ferrocyanide) and verdigris (basic copper acetate).
- Strychnine was used to enhance the bitter taste of beer (and save on the cost of hops).
- Concentrated sulphuric acid was added to beer to darken its colour, and added to vinegar to 'sharpen' it.
- Red cheese was coloured with red lead (lead oxide) or vermilion (mercuric sulphide).
- Pickles were coloured with green copper salts.
- Sweets were sometimes coloured with any of the above, and also with 'Emerald green' (copper arsenite).

Accum used the methods of analytical chemistry to expose these practices. Unfortunately for his future career, he also published the names and addresses of the people who used them. He often used the library at London's Royal Institution, where some of these people were members, and they conspired to accuse him of tearing pages out of the Institution's library books for his own use. Instead of being praised for his whistle-blowing activities, he was hounded out of England with his reputation in ruins.

Accum's work laid the foundations for the whole field of food analysis. The use of scientific techniques to detect the presence of adulterants has now reached very refined levels. The adulterant needn't be deliberately added. It could be something like ergot alkaloids on rye or aflatoxins on peanuts. The latter are highly carcinogenic compounds produced by a fungus, and detectable in minute quantities because they fluoresce under ultraviolet light. It is interesting that they occur in much higher concentrations in the 'natural' peanut butters sold by health-food shops than they do in peanut butter produced by more 'technological' methods.

Food analysis reveals the presence of such contaminants, and helps to protect us from them. Surely this makes food analysis morally praiseworthy at best, or at least morally innocuous. But is it? The same techniques that are used to detect the presence of adulterants can also be used to analyse the constituents of the foods themselves, especially those that contribute to taste and flavour. Most of these can be synthesised in the laboratory, some very cheaply. They are identical to the natural product. But what is the morality of the food analyst who goes looking for them so that they can be added to prepared foods to enhance their flavour? To give one example, it is rare today to find Earl Grey tea whose flavour is not enhanced with cheaper synthetic aromas rather than the more expensive natural bergamot oil.

Does it matter? Some would argue that the answer depends on whether the addition is declared openly, or concealed. It seems obvious (at least at first glance) that there is no major ethical problem with adding synthetic flavours and flavour enhancers to a dish if the consumer knows about this and can use the information to accept or reject the dish. It seems equally obvious that trying to fool the consumer about the quality by adding synthetic flavours is ethically reprehensible. But appearances can be deceptive.

For a start there is Gresham's Law of Gastronomy. In economics, Gresham's Law states that 'Bad money drives out good money'. I believe that a similar law applies to our food, and that too often bad food drives out good food. It can be argued, for example, that the availability of cheap but relatively tasteless convenience foods, using synthetic flavours and other additives (listed on the packet) to ensure stability and long life, has debased our communal palates to the point where it is not worth the food producer's while to produce better foods. Our choice of options is thus increasingly narrowed. Fast food has driven out slow food. Bad food has driven out good food.

There are plenty of examples to support this argument, such as the lamentable quality of 'century eggs' that are now produced rapidly by immersing the eggs in caustic soda, instead of slowly by using the traditional and gentler wood ash. I am not convinced that it is the scientists' fault for making the process available, so much as that of manufacturers in search of a quick profit. I will return to this question later, but there is another, more subtle argument which suggests that concealing the presence of additives (synthetic or natural) is not always a bad thing.

We know by experience, and more recently by scientific experiment, that our perception of flavour is strongly influenced by expectation. We taste with our brains, not just with our tongues and noses. An added aroma can lead us to expect a better dish, and we will not be disappointed – unless some spoilsport tells us that the flavour was added, and not naturally present. Heston Blumenthal, for example, makes a beetroot jelly to which he adds some tartaric acid, which makes the jelly taste 'tart,' and which, combined with the colour, can lead the taster to believe that the jelly is really blackcurrant. When he was developing this dish, he tried it out on a taster who thoroughly enjoyed it until he was told that it was beetroot, not blackcurrant. The taster immediately rejected it as unpalatable until Heston, interested to see what the effect would be, told him that it was okay, it was really blackcurrant. The taster then went right back to enjoying it.

The moral of this little story is that a person's eating pleasure can be enhanced if the presence of a flavour-changing additive is concealed, and spoiled if its presence is admitted. So perhaps it is morally better under some circumstances to conceal rather than reveal. This would certainly fit with the philosophy of Epicurus, who proposed as a touchstone for moral judgments that pleasure is the ultimate goal and that 'The highest good is pleasure.' He even had this motto carved on the gate to the garden where he taught his students, way back in 300 BCE. According to Epicurean philosophy, science is good if it increases our eating pleasure, and bad if it spoils our eating pleasure.

This begs the question, though, of what we mean by 'eating pleasure.' Epicurus himself had a rather ascetic definition. He believed that pleasure reaches a maximum as soon as desire is satisfied. He did leave room for manoeuvre, however, because he admitted that the *type* of pleasure could still be varied subsequently. So if you pop in to the Hind's Head pub in Bray for a meal of Heston Blumenthal's excellent fish and chips, sufficient to satisfy your hunger, and then carry on to the Fat Duck to work your way through his tasting menu, you are following the true Epicurean tradition.

Epicureanism seems to be a rather simplistic moral framework within which to make ethical judgments, but it is surprisingly difficult to find a different framework that does not also have serious flaws. Some modern philosophers have simply given up the search and returned to the ancient Aristotelian concept of '*virtue ethics*', where the individual relies on personal intuition to tell him or her what is right or wrong.

Most of us use 'virtue ethics' to make everyday judgments concerning food. I use it myself when I express my loathing for tomatoes where genetic selection has been used to increase physical toughness at the expense of flavour. The Nobel Prize-winning scientist Peter Medawar was using it when he described a modern loaf of sliced white bread as a 'pre-sliced, pre-digested, pre-packed parallelepiped in a polythene shroud.' 'Virtue ethics' might also be described as 'gut feeling' – an appropriate phrase when it comes to judging the contribution of science to food and gastronomy. The gut feeling of many people is that granary bread is good, while white bread is bad; 'organic' foods are good, but foods that have been treated with pesticides are bad; foods without preservatives are good, while foods that contain preservatives are bad.

But gut feelings need to be tempered by an awareness of consequences. This applies especially to preservatives in food. Would you prefer your soft drinks to contain sodium benzoate, which kills bacteria and is flushed rapidly out of the body in the urine, or would you prefer the bacteria themselves. Would you prefer chlorine in your water, or cholera? Would you prefer peanuts that have been treated with fungicides, or peanuts covered with aflatoxin-producing, cancer-causing fungi?

The obvious philosophical framework within which to answer such questions is *utilitarianism*, whose central premise is that the morality of actions depends entirely on their consequences, and especially on the balance of pleasure over pain. It sounds like an ideal framework within which to judge the impact of science on food and gastronomy. It even subsumes the Epicurean concept of pleasure. There is only one problem. It doesn't work, because in most cases it is just too difficult to predict the consequences of scientific discoveries, or even to predict the consequences of applying known science to provide technological solutions to problems.

Take the example of genetically modified foods. Man has been genetically modifying foods by selection for millennia. That is why we have modern wheat, corn, and a host of other food basics that we take for granted. But our efforts to understand how living organisms develop and function, which culminated in the 1950s with the discovery of the structure and role of DNA, unpredictably resulted in a technology that provided a much wider range of genetic options, over a much shorter time scale. We can now use biotechnology to produce crops with improved nutritional or flavour qualities, faster growth, and immunity to plant viruses. None of this was predictable when the original scientific discovery was made. Now that the discovery has been made, and we have worked out how to apply it (to modify food crops, for example), we can predict the short-term consequences (cheaper or better food, at least for some nations) but predicting the long-term consequences (such as environmental damage) is a much trickier business. In fact, I believe that it is virtually impossible to predict the long-term consequences of genetic modification, for good or for evil, and hence virtually impossible to make reasoned moral judgments that are based on those consequences.

So where does that leave us? Scientists are in the position of Aladdin, rubbing a magic lamp to see what comes out. But who should take responsibility for the consequences when a genie emerges – the one who releases the genie, or the one who then asks for three wishes to be granted?

My personal view is that the one who asks for a wish to be granted holds the primary responsibility, whether that wish is for a richer food experience, a cheaper food experience or a more profitable food experience. This does not absolve the scientist from responsibility, especially if he or she suggests the question in the first place on the basis of his or her special knowledge. But making moral judgments about that responsibility can be a very tricky business, as I hope this talk has shown. Perhaps the best that we can do, after all, is to go back to Epicurus and accept that, so far as the serious foodie is concerned, if science enhances our food experience, it's good. If it spoils it, it's bad.

Notes

Lead acetate is sometimes called 'sugar of lead' because of its sweet taste. Robert Boyle coined this name for it in 'The Sceptical Chymist,' published in 1661. It was believed by the Romans to be an aphrodisiac, but that's another story.

Frederick Accum was born in Germany in 1769, and migrated to England in 1793. He was the first chemist to make his living by teaching the subject, but chemistry was not all that he was known for. The architectural historian Sir John Summerson described him thus: 'German by birth, and cosmopolitan by nature, he was singularly versatile. Besides being a bookseller and publisher, he was a successful coach designer, ran an art school, sold artist's materials and fancy goods, and organized help for refugees from Napoleonic oppression.' He was also a pioneer in the use of gas lighting. Quite a man.

'there is death in the pot'. II Kings chap.4, verse 40.

Hounded out of England with his reputation in ruins See Noel G. Coley 'The Fight Against Food Adulteration' (*Education in Chemistry*, March 2005).

Aflatoxin in peanut butter An article in *Environmental Nutrition* (Februray 1995) quotes a Consumer's Union survey which revealed that fresh-ground peanut butter sold in health food stores can contain up to ten times the concentration of aflatoxins found in 'name' brands.

Epicurus was very much a forerunner of science in the modern sense. He was an 'atomic materialist' who believed, like Democritus before him, that the Universe consisted of indivisible atoms flying through empty space, and that everything that occurs is the result of the atoms colliding, rebounding, and becoming entangled with one another, with no purpose or plan behind their motions. He is a key figure in the development of science and the scientific method because of his insistence that nothing should be believed except that which was tested through direct observation and logical deduction.

Epicurean philosophy. One interesting factoid about Epicurean philosophy is that it was the subject of Karl Marx's doctoral dissertation, submitted to University of Jena in 1841.

Some modern philosophers have ... returned to the ancient Aristotelian concept of 'virtue ethics'. A trend that was started by James Martineau.

GM foods. For an excellent summary of the debate from both sides, see http://www.food.gov.uk/gmdebate/?view=GM+Microsite).

it is virtually impossible to predict the long-term consequences of genetic modification, for good or for evil, and hence virtually impossible to make reasoned moral judgments that are based on those consequences. Does this mean that we should stop doing science, or concentrate only on science where we *can* predict the consequences? Of course not, although that is what Government laboratories such as the food laboratory where I used to work are often asked to do. To quote the famous physicist J.J. Thomson, though: 'If Government laboratories had existed in the stone age, we would have wonderful stone

113

axes, but no-one would have discovered metals.' We can't stop making discoveries, or looking for ways to apply them for our benefit, because of fear of what the consequences of our knowledge might be.

Acknowledgements

I thank the many colleagues who have offered suggestions and contributed to the formation of my ideas. In particular I thank Peter Barham, who introduced me to the field, Tony Blake, who has always been willing to share his vast knowledge and experience, Heston Blumenthal, who has taken the role of science in gastronomy to new levels, and (in alphabetical order) Fritz Blank, Shirley Corriher, Harold McGee and Elizabeth Thomas for their perceptive and helpful comments. A further list of those who have informed and encouraged me would probably run into hundreds. I thank them all, and apologise profusely if I have inadvertently failed to name some whose contributions have been really major, as I am almost sure to have done.

Smell and Morality in the Dining Environment

Charles Foster-Hall

The smell of food cooking is often compelling; meat roasting in the oven, the aroma of onions being fried in butter, fresh bread from the oven or of garlic cooking. As these olfactory stimuli reach the brain, the appetite awakes, calling us to the table.

Smell can influence several forms of behaviour, most notably attraction and repulsion and the evocation of memories and emotions. The attractive and repulsive powers of smell are sometimes dramatic, but smell's evocative power is often the most surprising, especially when seemingly unconnected memories and their associated feelings come flooding back on the merest hint of a particular smell. As described in *Remembrance of Things Past* by Marcel Proust, the taste of a madeleine dipped in tea plunged the writer into the world of his childhood.[1] The sensations he felt were dramatic, triggered by the memory of his Aunt Leonie giving him a piece of madeleine dipped in tea when he was a child; this event took him back to 'the immense edifice of memory' surrounding that time and place.[2]

How we respond to olfactory influences in the dining environment is constrained by our conscious and conditioned acceptance of social mores; to do otherwise would be considered impolite or even immoral. The inherent conflict is that an odour may instinctively direct behaviour in one direction, while awareness of social constraints directs it the other way. This conflict is the essence of drama, whose stage is set once companions are seated at the dinner table.

Dining is ostensibly concerned with the biological function of eating and nourishment; however the ritualising of behaviour in the form of table etiquette paradoxically distances the diner from the primary biological task of feeding. The focus turns to the company at table and the social interactions that ensue. In the theatre, this is known as 'suspension of disbelief' and allows participants to experience the full emotional force of the represented reality without concerning themselves about the fact that they are sitting in a theatre or acting on a stage.

That smell and taste are inextricably linked becomes evident when eating without a sense of smell; if we have a bad cold for example or the way a child holds his or her nose when taking an unpleasant medicine. The way smells are perceived in the air is known as orthonasal olfaction; the air carrying the odour is inhaled through the nostrils, over the olfactory receptors at the top of the nasal cavity, and from there signals are sent to the brain. As food is chewed in the mouth it releases odorants, or volatile smell molecules, which, as we exhale through the nose, pass over the olfactory receptors giving rise to retronasal olfaction. Food eaten without a functioning sense of smell loses much of its 'taste.'[3]

According to research done by Susan Schiffman, 80 per cent of flavour is dependent on smell.[4] Certainly, for anyone with an interest in gustatory pleasures, a sense of smell takes on great importance.

In the French societies of ortolan eaters, both orthonasal and retronasal olfaction are used to extract as much pleasure as possible from the diminutive birds. These clandestine societies gather to eat ortolan, a small song bird that is a protected species. Even though it is illegal in France to kill and eat these birds, their appeal has drawn many French notables, including the late President Mitterrand into their circles. The birds have to be prepared in a particular manner, which includes drowning them in Armagnac. Once served on the plate, there follows a peculiar ritual. The diners cover their heads, plate, and bird with a cloth and inhale the reputedly delicious smell for a while, before placing the whole bird in their mouths and chewing head, bones, and all for as long as fifteen minutes.

Of all the senses, smell has had a particularly chequered history; Plato thought that we could gain little useful knowledge about the world from smells since they are only distinguished as being painful or pleasant.[5] Aristotle noted 'the close links between the act of smelling and human emotions. The fact that the perception of any odour is necessarily accompanied by some feeling of pain or pleasure reveals a sense organ incapable of transcending its physical matrix.'

These observations put the sense of smell in an ambiguous situation; we cannot deny the power that smell can hold over us, and yet at the same time the intellect finds it hard to rationalise the information gained from olfaction. Throughout history attitudes to smell have varied greatly on account of this ambiguity; some, like the early Christians considered any kind of olfactory adornment a moral excess to be avoided and a distraction from the paths of sanctity. There may also have been economic factors at play due to the price of imported frankincense. Later, Michel de Montaigne enjoyed pleasant smells as he 'sought to achieve a balance between sensual pleasure and spiritual delight.' Although he felt the senses should be governed by reason, 'they are our masters ... Knowledge begins through them and is resolved into them.'[6]

The divergence of opinions continued between rationalists and religionists, romanticists and sanitation reformers, until the later part of the nineteenth century when the work of Darwin placed olfactory communication in the lower evolutionary orders, and the work of Freud sent olfactory pleasures to the regions of infantile neuroses.[7]

Evolutionarily, smell is considered the primary sense; the first of the five senses to develop. It is also known as a chemical sense since its main function is to situate an organism in its chemical environment. This is best illustrated by imagining an organism waking up in the primal soup at the dawn of evolution. In order to feed the organism will need to recognize food by its 'smell' or the chemicals diffusing from it, and then climb the concentration gradient towards its prey. The same goes for reproduction; the organism locates and is attracted to a suitably receptive mate by smell, again climbing the concentration gradient towards the object of its desire. Two points should be noted: first, it is the smell that attracts the organism; and second, it is the change in the intensity of the smell that directs the organism's behaviour. In the case of danger or the presence of predators, the pattern is reversed and the organism will descend the concentration gradient of the predator's olfactory signal, thus escaping.

Over time other senses develop, a sensitivity to light becomes sight; to heat and pressure, touch; to vibrations, hearing and the less complex but more robust chemical sense of taste.

With increasing complexity as organisms evolve, behaviour memory develops; the organism will start to recall the smells not only of particularly good foods and receptive mates or terrifying predators, but also very minor differences to the usual olfactory signals. Humans are immediately on their guard if a food smells even slightly different from what is expected, signalling that the food may be potentially dangerous. Often we may not even be able to put the perceived change into words, apart from saying that the food smells 'off.' It would seem that smell has certain behavioural imperatives that are necessary for survival.

The world we live in today, however, has become largely odor-sanitized, ambient smells are banished wherever possible. We tend to avoid smells and complain when they inconvenience us, even ones generally considered pleasant. Traveling to France for the first time some years ago, I was struck on arrival by the all-pervasive smell of Gauloise cigarettes and garlic; more recently, I noticed on stepping out of the Eurostar train in Paris that those smells are no longer there.

Although the disappearance of evocative smells leaves a twinge of nostalgia, earlier descriptions of the French olfactory environment are much more dramatic. Norbert Elias, in *The Civilizing Process* quotes from a letter written by the Duchess of Orléans:

> The smell of the mire is horrible. Paris is a dreadful place. The streets smell so badly that you cannot go out. The extreme heat is causing large quantities of meat and fish to rot in them, and this, coupled to the multitude of people who… in the street, produces a smell so detestable that it cannot be endured.[8]

Judging from the duchess's description, we have much to be thankful for, but the question arises, have we gone too far? Have we thrown the baby out with the bath water and does this sanitization process give us an understanding of the moral implications of smell?

In the nineteenth century, scientific advances, through the work of Pasteur in particular, gave a clearer understanding of the microbial causes of disease and the need for public sanitation.[9] Previously, it was thought on occasion that the presence of filth, excrement, and foul smells were a factor in keeping people healthy. As Corbin recounts in *The Foul and the Fragrant,* 'During the reign of Charles II the authorities in London ordered that all the cesspools in the city be opened in order to conquer the plague by means of unpleasant odor.'[10] The lower classes in France were resistant to the removal of odors as they considered them part of their identity and even virility; once the bourgeoisie came to consider unpleasant smells and mephitic miasmas as socially undesirable in the eighteenth and nineteenth centuries, the move for public sanitation then became a class issue, the working people using smell as a defining barrier between themselves and the well-to-do.[11]

On a more metaphysical level, smell was considered to be part of a person's essence that would mingle with that of another person when they were in close proximity. Later, in the nineteenth century, the idea of a person's essence as represented by smell and its evocative power, found expression in literature.[12,13,14] The subsequent work of Freud in conjunction with the ideas of Darwin, then further relegated the place of smell to infantile anality, evolutionary regression, and fetishism.[15,16]

Back at the dinner table, social etiquette had been developing first in courtly circles and subsequently amongst the bourgeoisie, notably following publication of a treatise by Erasmus of Rotterdam, *De civilitate morum puerilium* (On civility in boys), which appeared in 1530.[17] In the medieval courts, men at arms would hunt and the quarry would be butchered, cooked, and eaten; this was a hands-on affair demanding action and no doubt offering significant olfactory stimulation. With the development of table etiquette, much of the gore was dispensed with along with the ensuing odors. These included personal odors, less for reasons of hygiene, than for civility. The concepts of hygiene were generally applied to these customs at a later date and are now used to justify habits of etiquette that would have found their origins elsewhere.[18]

The development of table manners had the effect of creating a barrier between people, as described by Elias:

> What was lacking in this *courtois* world, or at least had not been developed to the same degree, was the invisible wall of affects which seems now to rise between one human body and another, repelling and separating, the wall that is often perceptible today at the mere approach of something that has been in contact with the mouth or hands of someone else, and that manifests itself as embarrassment at the mere sight of many bodily functions of others, and often at the mere mention, or as a feeling of shame when one's own functions are exposed to the gaze of others, and by no means only then.'[19]

As the intermingling of personal odours became unacceptable, the olfactory pleasure of food was replaced by the visual, as in the *pièces montées* food sculptures of late eighteenth century Europe.

As Elias summarised: 'Here we see one of the interconnections through which a different sense organ, the eye, has taken on a very specific significance in civilized society. In a similar way to the ear, and perhaps even more so, it has become the mediator of pleasure, precisely because the direct satisfaction of the desire for pleasure has been hemmed in by a multitude of barriers and prohibitions.'[20] Dining had transformed from direct action to spectatorship.

Recent scientific studies, however, are starting to shed light on some intriguing areas of olfaction.

Although we are consciously aware of odours, they also affect us in an unconscious manner. The olfactory system is structured in such a way that information from the olfactory receptors in the nose is distributed to several areas of the brain concurrently.[21] In addition to the frontal cortex area of the brain that is associated with consciousness and the stimuli that we are aware of, olfactory information is also sent directly to the part of the brain controlling the visceral systems (a particular smell may, for example, raise the heart rate, or make us feel sick) and the limbic system, which is associated with the emotions. Unlike visual stimuli, where we need to identify the source of the stimulus before an emotional response is elicited, we know whether a smell is pleasant or not often before we can identify it. This limits conscious control of behaviour brought about by olfactory stimuli. It is as though the body does not trust consciousness to do the right thing when responding to certain olfactory stimuli. For this reason, smell, unlike the other four senses, is not subject to a complete conscious analysis. Depending on where we focus our attention, we can be 100 per cent conscious of stimuli received by the senses of touch, taste, hearing, and sight, but with smell we can not always be so sure.

119

The fickleness of smells that has contributed to their unreliable reputation has its scientific basis in the organism's need to monitor the change in odour intensity, which necessitates ignoring ambient smells. Humans start to lose awareness of an unchanging smell after about eighty seconds, after five minutes many smells are no longer perceived consciously, although this does not mean that they no longer have an effect on other areas of the brain.

Studies by Köster et al. have shown that the capacity to respond verbally to a particular smell actually slows reaction time, presumably indicating that olfactory neural pathways developed before verbal areas of the brain.[22] This allows us to react to a particular smell before we can say what it is, unlike the senses of sight and hearing where the stimulus needs to be identified rationally and a conscious decision informs the reaction.

Perhaps the most far-reaching implications of scientific research in this area relate to pheromones and the vomeronasal organ. Pheromones are chemicals emitted by one animal that have a behavioural effect on other animals of the same species, usually at a hormonal level. One particular example is the swine sex pheromone produced by pigs that induces mating. A close analogue to this chemical is found in black truffles, which is why pigs can locate the fungus up to a meter underground. The question arises as to whether the ascribed aphrodisiac properties of black truffles for humans bears any relation to the presence of this chemical.

Whether pheromones exist in humans has long been debated and the physiology is as yet unclear. The effects of what may be human pheromones are however becoming clearer. Martha McClintock's work on menstrual synchrony at the University of Chicago in 1971 led this area of research, while more recently Claus Wedekind at the University of Berne found that like mice, humans tended to select mates whose personal smell indicated a widely differing immune profile from their own, thus conferring on their offspring a much broader immune profile.[23, 24]

In order to observe the effects of smell in the dining environment we are confronted with a vastly more complex situation than can be created in the laboratory, and it would be counterproductive to even try to limit the variables; the more variables, the better the meal, and although theatre may be a good paradigm in which to see the dinner, it would again be pointless to impose any roles on diners; this is a theatre of improvisation, where what we are looking for are the impulses created by smell and the point at which moral constraints are approached or even over-ridden. The thought process of logical analysis is less appropriate for this study, as much as anything because the observed is also the observer. The alternative to logical analysis is pattern recognition or selectionism, a more creative but less quantifiable form of thought based on value judgments and associations of memories.[25] Meaning is arrived at by identifying patterns that hold personal significance that correspond to a particular event.

When one begins to consider the implications of smell in the dining environment, its dramatic potential becomes great. On the one hand 'the invisible wall of affects which seems now to rise between one human body and another' to quote Elias (one has only to think of the moral opprobrium attached to farting at the dinner table for example), and on the other hand there is the likelihood that we choose our mates by their smell (amongst other factors).

In order to discover more about the implications of smell in the dining environment and how it affects our accepted moral boundaries it may be necessary to emphasise the inherent conflict and drama between instinctively smell-induced behaviour and socially constrained behaviour.

Attempts were made during the early twentieth century by the Italian Futurist movement to incorporate smell more fully into the dining environment by bursting balloons filled with scent above the dinner table.[26] However, the scent organ described by Aldous Huxley in *Brave New World* would create a more comprehensive enhanced olfactory environment in which a symphony of smells are presented to diners:

> The scent organ was playing a delightfully refreshing Herbal Capriccio – rippling arpeggios of thyme and lavender, of rosemary, basil, myrtle, tarragon; a series of daring modulations through the spice keys into ambergris; and a slow return through sandalwood, camphor, cedar and new mown hay (with

occasional subtle touches of discord – a whiff of kidney pudding, the faintest suspicion of pig's dung) back to the simple aromatics with which the piece began. The final blast of thyme died away; there was a round of applause; the lights went up.[27]

The technology for Huxley's scent organ may yet be some way off but attempts have been made to use enhanced olfactory environments for entertainment. AromaRama and Smell-O-Vision were both developed for cinema audiences in response to the perceived threat of television in the late 1950s, neither with great success.[28] Currently some museums such as the historic kitchens at Hampton Court Palace near London use artificial smells to recreate more fully the environments that they represent but these are generally single odors.

In parts of the world where the Western degree of odor sanitation has not yet been attained, olfactory cues can take on surprisingly different meanings.

A personal anecdote:

I had arrived in Kathmandu, the capital of Nepal after a long journey by train and bus from New Delhi in India. The voyage had involved an evening stop at the India-Nepal border where it was necessary to wait for visas. The smell of grilling meat suffused the warm evening air and we ate kebabs at a street side restaurant. Going to visit the Pashparpartinath Temple on the outskirts of Kathmandu a few weeks later, I was once again met by the delicious smell of grilling meat and quite naturally I began to feel hungry. It was only on stepping over the threshold of the temple that I remembered that Hindus tended to be vegetarian and kebab sellers were unlikely to be found within the temple precincts. After a few steps inside the temple all became clear as I was confronted by a funeral pyre; the body being cremated was so charred as to be completely inedible.

121

In the end we are left with our own emotional responses to smells; these would tend to be highly personal. Research has also shown that the range of responses not only varies between different individuals, but also for the same individual at different times, a fact that can confound the best planned experiment. Constantin Stanislavski noted that an actor's best performance occurred when they are emotionally alive.[29] Might it then not be possible and effective to use the lexicon of smells in the dining environment as tokens of our own personal memories and emotions at the theatre of the table?

Notes

1. Proust, Marcel, *Swann's Way,* in *Remembrance of Things Past,* New York: Random House, 1913, pp. 50–51.
2. Ibid.
3. Pelchat, Marcia L. and Blank, Fritz, 'Learning by Mouth: Edible Aids to Literacy', *Proceedings of the Oxford Symposium on Food and Cookery 2000,* Prospect Books, 2001, p. 192.
4. Schiffman, S.S., and Gatlin C., 'A Clinical Physiology of Taste and Smell,' *Annual Review of Nutrition,* vol. 13: 405–436 (Volume publication date July 1993).
5. Plato, 'Timaeus' in *The Collected Dialogues,* Princeton University Press 1961, p. 1190.
6. Michel de Montaigne, 'Essays,' in *Complete Works of Montaigne,* Palo Alto: Stanford University Press, 1957.
7. Freud, S., *Civilization and its Discontents,* London: The Hogarth Press, 1963, chapter 4.
8. Elias, Norbert, *The Civilizing Process: Sociogenetic and Psychogenetic Investigations,* rev. ed., trans. by Edmund Jephcott, Oxford: Blackwell Publishers, 1994, p. 108.
9. Debré, P., *Louis Pasteur,* Baltimore: Johns Hopkins University Press, 1998.
10. Corbin, Alain, *The Foul and The Fragrant, Odor and the French Social Imagination,* trans. by L. Kochan, R. Porter and C. Prendergast, Oxford: Berg Publishers, 1986, p. 212.
11. Corbin, p. 214.
12. Proust, *Swann's Way* in *Remembrance of Things Past.*
13. Flaubert, *Selected Letters 1830–57,* p. 50 (Aug 8, 1846), p. 53 (Aug 9, 1846), p. 64 (Aug 15, 1846); *Letters of Flaubert to Louise Colet,* trans. F. Steegmuller, Cambridge: Belknap/Harvard University Press, 1980.
14. Corbin, p. 207.
15. Freud, S., chapter 4.
16. Freud, S. 'Notes upon a Case of Obsessional Neurosis (The Rat Man)', *Case Histories* II, vol. 9, London: Penguin Books, 1979, pp. 36–128.
17. Elias, p. 43.
18. Elias, p. 93.
19. Elias, p. 56.
20. Elias, p. 166.
21. Öngür, D., Price, J.L., *Cerebral Cortex,* vol. 10, no. 3, 206–219, Oxford: Oxford University Press, March 2000.
22. Köster, E.P., 'Does Olfactory Memory Depend on Remembering Odors?' *Chemical Senses,* vol. 30 suppl 1, Oxford: Oxford University Press, 2005.
23. McClintock, Martha K., 'Menstrual Synchrony and Suppression', *Nature,* 229: 244–45, 1971.
24. Claus Wedekind, Thomas Seebeck, Florence Bettens, Alexander J. Paepke, 'MHC-Dependent Mate Preferences in Humans', *Proceedings: Biological Sciences,* vol. 260, no. 1359 (22 June, 1995), pp. 245–249.
25. Edelman, G. M., *Wider than the sky, A Revolutionary View of Consciousness,* New York: Penguin Books, 2005, pp. 146–7.
26. Marinetti, F.T., *The Futurist Cookbook,* trans. Suzanne Brill, Bedford Arts, USA, 1989.
27. Huxley, A., *Brave New World,* 1932, ch. 11.
28. Kaye, J.N., Thesis on Symbolic Olfactory Display, M.I.T. 1999.
29. Stanislavski, C., *An Actor Prepares,* New York: Routledge, 1989, p. 163.

Bibliography.

Blake, Anthony, 'Amarcord: the Flavour of Buried Memories,' *Proceedings of the Oxford Symposium on Food and Cookery 2000*, Prospect Books, 2001, p. 49.

Darwin, C., *The Descent of Man,* Princeton, NJ: Princeton University Press, 1981.

Buck, Linda B., 'Unraveling the Sense of Smell', Nobel Lecture, December 8, 2004.

Young, Carolin C., *Apples of Gold in Settings of Silver*, New York: Simon and Schuster, 2002.

Hirsch, Alan R., 'Exploring the Potentials of Human Olfaction, An Interview with Alan R. Hirsch, M.D., F.A.C.P.,' *The Official Journal of The Society of Integrative Medicine*, vol. 11, no. 3, June 2005.

123

The Foie Gras Fracas:
Sumptuary Law as Animal Welfare?

Cathy K. Kaufman

No foodstuff has provoked angrier debate than the extraordinarily fattened livers of certain breeds of geese and ducks known by the French label *foie gras*. Animal rights activists, farmers, scientists, veterinarians, ethicists, legislators, chefs, and the general public all have opined on the appropriateness of raising these waterfowl in controlled conditions to produce an expensive delicacy enjoyed by only a tiny fraction of the world's diners. The main, but not sole, objection to the rearing of animals for foie gras is the gavage technique that takes place during the last nine days to three weeks of the animal's life, by which a tube is inserted down the animal's esophagus and a mixture of corn mush, fat, and water is pumped into the animal's gullet. The high carbohydrate mix allows the animal to gain weight rapidly, with the fat stored primarily in the liver, although other parts of the animal are similarly fattier than their non-gavage feed counterparts and yield other specialized products such as magret, the meaty, tender breast that is often prepared like steak, and plump legs that form the bistro favorite, confit.[1] Much of the public's repulsion comes from the idea of gavage and its gag-inducing reflex in humans: opponents often call the technique by the tortuous-sounding label 'force (or forced) feeding,' while those tolerant of gavage suggest 'tube feeding.'[2]

Farm Sanctuary, an animal rights organization and major opponent of foie gras production, pulls no punches in decrying foie gras produced by gavage as immoral:

> Nobody needs foie gras. It's only eaten by a few people, and its production and consumption represent egregious, gratuitous cruelty. Prohibiting the sale of this inhumane product reflects and upholds our society's values. It is sadly ironic that in the face of vast hunger around our globe, foie gras producers force-feed animals until the brink of death to produce an expensive delicacy for the few who can afford it.[3]

Others have echoed this sentiment, calling foie gras a 'frivolity,' the 'delicacy of despair,' 'food for sadists,' and other emotionally and morally-charged epithets.[4] Legislation has been enacted or proposed in many jurisdictions, including the European Union, Israel, and various locales within the United States, to limit or ban the rearing, sale, or consumption of foie gras on the sole ground of cruelty. As an enthusiastic foie gras cook and conscientious eater who lives in New York, where a ban is pending, the ethics of foie gras consumption is of personal and practical interest.

This paper starts from the premise that killing animals for food is morally acceptable provided that animals not suffer unnecessarily in their rearing or slaughtering. Defining 'unnecessary suffering' is, of course, the crux of the issue and implicates questions of animal welfare. Animal welfare has no single definition, but experts suggest assessing the subjective experience of the animal, the biological functioning of the animal, and the extent to which the animal can express its natural, instinctive behaviors.[5] Putting aside the utopian dream of animal husbandry where all food animals are happy, healthy, and live completely natural lives and then die instantly and painlessly a moment before their life expectancy, some impairment of animal welfare inevitably occurs. The animals' mental and physical state and quality of life, however, need to come into play in assessing whether the welfare of geese and ducks raised for foie gras is so compromised as to constitute unnecessary suffering. Contrary to the conclusory declarations of the animal rights activists, the fact that foie gras is an expensive, elitist luxury alone does not render it morally objectionable. Nor is there any intellectual justification why the techniques used to raise the birds for this rarified delicacy should be scrutinized more rigorously than those used for any other food animals.

Traditional husbandry: the origins of foie gras

Gavage may be the oldest agricultural technique designed specifically to fatten animals for the diner's gourmet pleasure. The preference for unctuous foods has continued, uninterrupted, since early history. Egyptian tomb paintings from 2500

BCE clearly illustrate workers hand-cramming geese and waterfowl; it is believed that the practice resulted from the observation that geese in the wild would gorge themselves before migrating. Egyptians are credited with this first interference with natural eating patterns to obtain fattier birds. The written and artistic record is silent about whether the Egyptians consumed the livers, but it stretches credulity that only the fatty meat was consumed and that the rich organ was overlooked. Excerpts from Athenaeus's *Deipnosophists* refer to fatted geese and even to 'sumptuous goose livers.'[6] Roman agricultural treatises offered detailed instruction for cramming geese and hens by pushing moist barley mash into the mouths of the birds, or, alternatively, using chopped dried figs as the food.[7] The French word for liver, *foie*, derives from the Latin *ficus*, or fig, and the Latin phrase *iecur ficatum*, literally liver stuffed with figs, is a lasting memorial to the Romans' preferred fattening agent and linguistically reflects the historic practice. Jewish slaves within the Roman Empire are thought to have performed much of the cramming of geese for wealthy Roman tables.[8] Martial, Juvenal, Horace, and Statius all lampooned fatted liver in ways that suggested the gourmands' depravity.[9]

The historical record becomes skimpy after the fall of the Roman West. It is possible that an unrecorded cottage industry continued in Frankish Gaul and medieval France, particularly in the south-west, which claims foie gras as a particular item of its culinary patrimony. The best written evidence for the medieval production of foie gras – and its ambiguous moral status – is found among the writings of the Ashkenazi Jews who spread throughout Europe. Rabbi Rashi (1040–1105) spent most of his life in Troyes, France, save for a brief sojourn in Germany. His Talmudic commentaries warned that those who crammed geese and made them suffer would have to answer to God: to this day, gavaged birds have their esophagi examined to check for any damage before the birds can be certified as kosher. This is to meet the dual requirements of avoiding unnecessary cruelty and avoiding torn, and thus defiled, flesh. The fourteenth century urban Jewish writer, Eleazar of Mainz, disdained foie gras on the grounds of gluttony, but cramming nonetheless was practiced in European Jewish communities, especially rural farmers, through the nineteenth century to provide a source of cooking fat in place of always *treyf,* pig lard or butter, which could never be used with meat.[10]

By the sixteenth century, foie gras spread from the ghetto and shtetl to the elite tables of France, Germany, and Italy. The French especially brought foie gras into the pantheon of ingredients necessary to the emerging haute cuisine; indeed, well before the La Varenne's 1651 *Le Cuisinier françois,* with its first French recipes for foie gras, agricultural treatises such as Charles Estienne's *L'Agriculture et la maison rustique* (1564) and Olivier de Serre's *Le Théâtre d'agriculture* (1600) gave instructions for fattening geese, although it is believed that the livers would not have reached the size, color, and consistency of modern foie gras. The process took two months to fatten the birds, and did not involve gavage, but instead encouraged the birds to eat freely but copiously. The husbandry included instructions to blind the birds, and later, to nail their feet in place to minimize their movement. These directions leave modern farmers mystified, as both techniques would likely have induced high levels of stress in the birds and a disinclination to eat. Both recommendations fell from favor in the early nineteenth century.[11] At that time, the modern gavage technique was invented in Alsace, by which funnels were used to cram the birds' gullets with specific instructions to use 'smoothly welded [funnels] to prevent any harmful chafing to the animal.'[12] The task of cramming the geese generally was relegated to farm wives, helping to create the image of foie gras as a traditional, artisanal food of France.[13] Gavage-by-funnel has been the basis of foie gras cultivation ever since.

The industrialization of foie gras

The mid-twentieth century brought several significant changes in foie gras production. Historically, various fowl had been fattened, although two strains of geese were most frequently chosen, the *oie du Gers* and the *oie grise du sud-ouest* because of their outstanding ability to produce fatty livers. Although generally believed to produce the most succulent livers, the geese had two drawbacks for large-scale production: they were susceptible to disease and took longer and more frequent feedings to reach optimum weight. In the 1950s, French farmers began using the mule (also known as mulard) duck, the sterile offspring of a Muscovy drake and Pekin duck. The mules are relatively disease-resistant, have large, resilient esophagi and livers that fatten easily. They reach slaughter-size faster and with fewer daily feedings (two or three for ducks versus four for geese), making them superior candidates for industrial production. Because of significant sexual dimorphism in the mules, only much-larger males are reared for foie gras.[14] Their livers grow larger and contain fewer veins than those of females; the veins are considered a minor defect by chefs preparing elegant dishes. Nowadays, well over 90 per cent of foie gras is made from ducks, with only a small and super-elite market in goose liver.

127

Depending on the facility, the foie gras mule's quality of life varies. Surreptitiously-shot footage from unidentified factories in France has been posted on several animal rights websites[15] and detailed descriptions of rearing practices on American farms have been widely disseminated by both proponents and opponents of gavage. There is little disagreement over the first three months of the young duck's life, which even critics in some of the films and other literature concede is bucolic by the standards of modern farming practices.[16] Ducklings have access to sunlight, adequate water and food, and grassy slopes on which to waddle to strengthen their legs for the rapid weight gain that comes with gavage. Feeding is divided into four phases. For the first six to nine weeks, the ducklings are allowed to eat whenever they want and in whatever quantity (*ad libitum*). Grass is usually included in the diet to help expand the esophagus, which is very flexible (witness the ability of ducks to swallow fish whole, with the fish visibly distending the esophagus on its way down). For the second phase, the next three to five weeks, the ducks are fed on a restricted schedule using one of two techniques: either large amounts of food are offered for limited periods of time, or food is more frequently available, but in lesser quantities. The third phase, the pre-gavage period, lasts from three to ten days. Food is offered more frequently or in increasing quantities so that the birds, which 'have a spontaneous tendency to over-feed,' naturally exceed expected *ad libitum* levels. The carefully crafted feeding regimen is designed to set the stage for gavage by (1) increasing the bird's underdeveloped crop,[17] the area in which food is held before passing to the stomach for digestion; (2) stimulating digestive secretions, and (3) starting hepatic steatosis, or absorption of fat in the liver.[18] More on steatosis later, one of the most controversial points in determining the welfare of the fowl.

Gavage is the last, critical stage in the cultivation of foie gras. According to regulations promulgated by the French government and generally agreed to by the American producers, Sonoma Valley Foie Gras (California), Hudson Valley Foie Gras (New York), and Au Bon Canard (Minnesota), there can be no true foie gras without gavage. Four thousand years elapsed from the initial hand cramming of birds to simple manual funnel feeding, aided by a stick to push the grain mass down the funnel's neck; over the last sixty years, as foie gras moved from artisanal to factory production, gavage technology quickly evolved to permit fewer feeders to cram larger flocks. Starting in the 1950s, a manual screw was added to the funnels to speed the delivery of the corn mash; soon thereafter, the screw was motorized, and delivery of the mash would take between thirty and sixty seconds. By the 1980s, pneumatic and hydraulic pumps with computerized dosing were introduced in some facilities, requiring only two to three seconds to dispense the mash.

Depending on the size and location of the operation, the birds are housed differently. In the largest French factories, the birds are confined to small, individual cages that severely restrict their movement, minimizing caloric loss and allowing the pneumatic or hydraulic feeding to take place with a small number of human feeders moving the dispenser from bird to bird. In smaller operations in France and at the three foie gras farms in the United States, the birds are placed in a series of pens that allow them some ability to walk around, preen, and engage in social behavior, although certainly not to the extent they would in the wild. The feeder enters the pen, takes hold of each bird individually, and performs the gavage, using motorized, but not pneumatic, pumps. After feeding the birds drink water from troughs located just outside the pens, although they never see the outdoors again. At the largest American foie gras producer, Hudson Valley Foie Gras, the feedings are claimed to be calibrated for the expressed purpose of minimizing stress to the birds: initial gavage introduces only an ounce of food, increasing after a day or two as the birds become acclimated to the procedure to reach large quantities of mash for the last few days of the gavage cycle.[19] Depending on the exact technique used and the producer's standards, gavage can last anywhere from nine days to three weeks for mule ducks.

Evaluating animal welfare and abuse: what the birds think, how their physical condition compares, and how they behave

Opponents of foie gras have a relatively easy time whipping up public opinion, as both specialists and non-specialists tend to define animal welfare through anthropomorphism.[20] Well-meaning letters to the editors of major newspapers assume that because humans don't want to be force fed, neither should waterfowl.[21] Defenders of foie gras production cite scientific studies that are claimed to show that the birds are treated humanely, or at least non-cruelly, although most acknowledge that the studies have yet to address every issue involved in foie gras husbandry.

Advocates on both sides of the debate cite the 1998 European Union Scientific Committee on Animal Welfare and Animal Health Report on Foie Gras ('SCAHAW Report'). While refusing to recommend the banning of foie gras production outright, the money quote for opponents of gavage is that 'force feeding, as currently practised, is detrimental to the welfare of the birds.'[22] The committee was composed of thirteen scientists and veterinarians from various EU countries; one dissented from the report and concluded that foie gras production as currently practiced should be banned.[23] The committee viewed animal welfare as a continuum in which 'poor welfare should be minimized and very poor welfare avoided.' The committee also urged that decisions be based on 'good scientific evidence,' taking into account the frequency, duration, and severity of the poor welfare.[24] Among the specific recommendations of the committee were:

129

(1)   No feeding procedure should be used that causes substantial discomfort to the birds, as evidenced by aversion to the feeding; automatic feeding devices need to be proven safe, and

(2)   Individual cages for feeding should be eliminated to allow birds to walk, preen, and engage in other social behaviors.[25]

This latter recommendation has been implemented in a 1999 resolution of the European Council banning the introduction of new individual cages after December 31, 2004, and requiring that individual cages be eliminated by December 31, 2010.[26]

As part of the SCAHAW Report, a group of European scientists, including one member of the SCAHAW Report committee, performed controlled experiments to determine whether ducks and geese exhibited aversion to force feeding. The purpose was 'to understand how the force feeding procedure *is perceived by the animal* to evaluate the welfare aspects of the process' (emphasis added).[27] The experimenters kept separate groups of mule ducks and geese in pens, one for general rearing, and an adjacent pen eight meters away solely for feeding. The birds were herded back and forth between the pens for some days in a 'training period', during which time they ate *ad libitum* from troughs in the feeding pen, in an attempt to acclimate them to voluntarily moving into the feeding pen. To the experimenters' surprise and frustration, the ducks never fully mastered the movement during the training period, unlike the geese, who entered the feeding pen with little hesitation by the end of the training period. At the end of the training period, some groups of birds of each species were force fed, while others continued to eat from troughs in amounts comparable to the force fed birds.

A separate experiment by the same group measured the ducks' tendency to avoid the force feeder. Ducks were held in cramped individual cages like those used in industrial production. They were force fed by the same individual twice a day for two weeks. Between feedings, on days 3, 7, 9, and 11, the force feeder and a stranger separately walked by the ducks, and the amount of withdrawal of the ducks was measured.

Building on previous studies that had shown that animals are frightened by places where they suffer pain and by the people who inflict it, the scientists hypothesized that if the birds found force feeding painful, they would not voluntarily enter the feeding pens and would withdraw from the force feeders. The study found that (1) while some ducks avoided the feeding pens where gavage took place, other force fed ducks did not, and that a more important and consistent factor in the ducks' avoidance was the presence of a stranger in the pen; (2) geese exhibited no avoidance of the pens where gavage took place; and (3) ducks withdrew from strangers more than from the force feeders, although the avoidance lessened as the ducks began to recognize the stranger. The scientists concluded that 'ducks do not perceive the force feeder as inflicting pain.'[28]

Another study measured corticosterone levels in mule ducks before and after force feeding. Corticosterones are released in response to adrenalin, so that elevated levels would indicate stress. Ducks were force fed standard (i.e., *ad libitum*) and larger amounts of food (comparable to the later stages of gavage). There were no significant variations in corticosterone levels or other blood indicators of stress, leading to the conclusion that the ducks did not perceive the experience as stressful.[29]

Critics dismiss these scientists as flacks for the foie gras industry and claim that gavage is, by definition, cruel. The debate reached American shores in 2004, when the American Veterinary Medical Association formally considered whether officially to oppose force feeding. Based on a review of the scientific literature, the AMVA's Animal Welfare Committee recommended opposing gavage, but tabled the vote for lack of direct information. In July 2005, two veterinarians active in the AVMA visited Hudson Valley Foie Gras. Their report was unexpected: according to one,

> We've all seen the pictures. Seeing with your own eyes and penetrating the issue is worth a thousand pictures. After being on the premises, my position changed dramatically. I did not see animals I would consider distressed, and I didn't see pain and suffering.[30]

The other veterinarian was less impressed, but from the viewpoint that gavage induced disease (he considered hepatic steatosis to be a disease) and that the cultivation of foie gras was 'not a good use of these animals.' His observations of the birds were that they did not seem distressed, that their conditions were better than most battery-raised broiler chickens, and that they seemed generally well cared for.[31] These first-hand observations led to the defeat of the AVMA resolution opposing foie gras and to an anti-scientific backlash among some of the members. Specialists in animal pain complained that 'clinical investigations and scientific committees will not help us here ... [as] science is irrelevant,' while others saw crass caving to 'big industry.'[32] Scientists claiming science is irrelevant is food for thought, as is the thought that the $17.5 million American foie gras industry is 'big.'[33]

The disease paradigm identified by the concerned AVMA veterinarian is the second arrow in the animal welfare quiver of foie gras opponents and raises concerns about first, the physical welfare of the ducks and second, the physical welfare of diners who eat foie gras. Opponents of foie gras claim that foie gras is a diseased organ and thus unwholesome to eat, playing on fears and prejudices; it is simply a scare tactic, designed to inflame.

The question of whether gavage induces disease is more serious. Everyone agrees that chemical changes take place during the final stage of gavage, in which hepatic steatosis, or 'fatty liver,' develops. Although the medical term sounds ominous, the AVMA was split as to whether hepatic steatosis actually is a disease.[34] The SCAHAW Report similarly concluded that, as long as the gavage did not continue beyond traditional time frames, there was insignificant impact on the birds' health. Hepatic steatosis occurs normally in waterfowl preparing to migrate, albeit to a lesser degree. Although blood circulation within the liver decreased, the livers functioned adequately to process foods. Prolonging force feeding eventually would be lethal, but producers were careful (admittedly in their economic self-interest) not to over-gorge the birds. Finally, hepatic steatosis was found to be reversible; once gavage stopped, the livers returned to normal size, leaving the question open as to whether this indicated pathology.[35] The SCAHAW Report found that gavaged birds had other physical impairments, including panting, skeletal lesions, semi-liquid feces, and foot injuries, although none of these were particular areas of concern. In particular, they were not able to draw any conclusions about esophageal pain resulting from gavage, other than that the bird feeders endeavored to avoid injuring the esophagus.[36] Other scientists have indicated that at least some of these conditions occur naturally and without any animal abuse.[37]

The last aspect of animal welfare, the birds' ability to engage in species-appropriate behavior, was compromised for the period of gavage, especially when birds were kept in individual cages. Because this led to a conclusion of poor welfare, the SCAHAW Report advocated abolition of cages. For the three months prior to gavage, the birds were generally reared in flocks with free access to the outdoors. The report found no welfare problems other than a possible lack of a swimming pool.[38]

131

Alternative techniques for foie gras cultivation

Scientists and farmers have attempted to develop alternative husbandry techniques that will eliminate gavage. In France, scientists have injected birds with dopamine to alter the brains' chemical balance and have zapped the medio-ventral nucleus of the bird's hypothalamus to encourage gorging; while the birds ate more than unaltered birds, it was not enough to produce livers comparable to gavage and would likely have raised new objections among critics.[39]

Farmers in Spain and the United States have very recently unveiled fatted livers obtained without gavage, although it is unclear how these livers compare with the traditional product. Patería de Sousa won the 2006 Coup de Coeur for innovation at the Paris International Food Salon for its canned goose liver pâté that was made from free-ranging geese who fed *ad libitum*. The birds were slaughtered just prior to their instinctive migration time, and the company can thus only have one crop per year.[40] A similar approach has been independently hit upon by the Schlitz Goose Farm in South Dakota. Owner Jim Schlitz noticed in the early 1990s that geese slaughtered later had differently-colored livers, and that the color, size, and consistency could be affected by changing the feed.[41] The farm does not claim that its product is precisely equivalent to foie gras, but rather that it is humane and delicious. The liver and resulting pâtés are tan, rather than creamy beige, and differed in flavor and texture from traditional foie gras, making them an imperfect substitute.[42] These livers may be similar to those produced before the nineteenth century's introduction of the gavage funnel.

132

Is the foie gras battle an effort to impose a modern sumptuary law?

Sumptuary laws have historically been means of ordering societies to maintain social distinctions (laws in medieval and Renaissance Europe limited wearing certain colors, fabrics, furs and the like to members of identifiable social classes) or to limit conspicuous consumption (Roman and various medieval and Renaissance laws limited the number of dishes that could be served at banquets). They typically have a moral component.[43] While foie gras opponents view its consumption as immoral, even among the most fervent supporters of foie gras, the notion of sin lurks. Foie gras is called 'the guilty pleasure,' with food critics waxing rhapsodically that each bite of foie gras was 'a little bit of sin.'[44] To be fair, these food writers were describing the high fat content of foie gras in fat-phobic times, rather than animal welfare, but others see the gavage process as 'contribut[ing] to the blasphemy of consuming it.'[45]

Banning foie gras is an inversion of the normal, class-reinforcing function of sumptuary laws. Outside of France, the only country where foie gras is eaten by a substantial part of the populace, foie gras is eaten only by a tiny minority of wealthy diners. Banning foie gras in the guise of animal welfare is thus no sacrifice to all but affluent gourmets who love its incomparable flavor and texture.

Activists exploit its elitist connotations and lack of familiarity. Farm Sanctuary hired Zogby International to poll Americans in different states in support of a foie gras ban. Not surprisingly, majorities of respondents in each of the states polled had never even heard of foie gras when the polling started in March 2005, including 51 per cent of New Yorkers. Regardless of previous familiarity, respondents were asked the following leading question:

> Foie gras is an expensive food item served in some upscale restaurants. It is produced by force-feeding geese and ducks large quantities of food, causing the animals' livers to swell up to ten times their normal size. A long metal pipe is inserted into the animal's esophagus several times a day. Often, this process causes the animals' internal organs to rupture. Several European countries and the state of California have outlawed this practice as cruel. Do you agree or disagree that force feeding geese and ducks to produce foie gras should be banned by law in New York?

Given that the question focused on elitism, cruelty, and illegality, a remarkable 15 per cent of the respondents disagreed that foie gras should be banned, and another 7 per cent were unsure.[46] The poll was repeated in May 2006; although New Yorkers' awareness of foie gras had increased substantially (only 34 per cent claimed never to have heard of the product), presumably from the tremendous amounts of publicity that the California and Chicago bans had received, the percentages declining to ban foie gras held firm at 22 per cent.[47] These numbers are consistent with survey results from other jurisdictions, regardless of whether there is a local foie gras industry.

Animal rights activists view foie gras as the wedge issue that will allow them to reach out to other perceived instances of animal abuse in the food chain. Although the public face of certain animal rights organizations asserts that the ban on foie gras is not part of an effort to delegitimize meat consumption, at least some factions in the animal rights movement admit that this is precisely the agenda. In the words of one activist, it is attainable 'baby steps' towards the ultimate goal of imposing veganism or vegetarianism.[48] In this sense, the foie gras ban may be viewed as a sumptuary law, whereby those morally opposed to eating animals will use the law to reshape society to their utopian vision.

133

Notes

1. Critics of gavage do not lobby against magret or confit de canard, even though they can only be prepared as a by-product of gavage; there is something deeply symbolic about eating oversized livers, rather than breast or leg, that grabs the public's attention, reminiscent of pagan sacrifice or more distasteful because of the generally low esteem in which organ meats are held. The unforgettable line from the cannibal, Hannibal Lechter in the motion picture 'Silence of the Lambs' is that he ate his victim's liver with fava beans and a nice Chianti, exploiting the American popular aversion to organ meats.
2. Kahler, p. 689.
3. www.nofoiegras.org/FGabout.htm, accessed July 10, 2007.
4. Jack Markowitz, 'Foie gras ban is one the protesters get right,' *Pittsburgh Tribune-Review*, 8/20/06; www.pittsburghlive.com/x/pittsburghtrib/business/columnists/markowitz/s_466854.html.
5. Blandford, p. 2.
6. Athenaeus, *Deipnosophists.* IX:384b.
7. Cato, *On Farming,* 89; Columella, *On Agriculture* 8.7.5.
8. Guémené and Guy (2004), p. 211.
9. Ginor, pp. 5–7.
10. Ginor, pp. 11–12.
11. Ginor, pp. 15–16; 26.
12. Quoted in Ginor, p. 27.
13. Jeanne Strang, 'Foie Gras as Seen from Southwest France,' *Gastronomica* 7(1):64–69 (Winter 2006) at 67; Isabelle Téchoueyres, 'Development, Terroir and Welfare: A Case Study of Farm-produced Foie Gras in South West France,' *Anthropology of Food*, S2, Mars 2007, http://aof.revues.org/documents510.html. Accessed June 20, 2007.
14. Female mules apparently are raised for their meat, although certain animal rights organizations claim that they are mutilated and suffocated after hatching. This would seem to be against the farmers' economic interest, especially in light of the greater demand for duck meat in Europe in the 1990s, after the incidence of BSE. SCAHAW Foie Gras Report 16; Guémené and Guy (2004) p. 213.
15. http://www.nofoiegras.org/discover-foie-gras.wmv; http://www.banfoiegras.org.uk/
16. McKenna, p. 14.
17. In comparison to other birds, foie gras waterfowl have very poorly developed or non-existent crops, although there is some broadening of the esophagus at the entrance to the stomach. There is no evidence whether expansion of this proto-crop causes any pain to the birds. SCAHAW Report, p. 46.
18. SCAHAW Report, p. 19; Guémené and Guy (2004), p. 214; Ginor, p. 78.
19. SCAHAW Report, pp. 19–20; Guémené and Guy (2004), pp. 213–14; Ginor, p. 78–9.
20. *Journal of the American Veterinary Medical Association*, 227:1402 (Yost letter) (November 1, 2005).
21. Blandford, p. 6; New York Times,www.nytimes.com/2007/05/02/dining/02lett.html
22. SCAHAW Report, p. 65.
23. SCAHAW Report, p. 69.
24. SCAHAW Report, pp. 1, 5.
25. SCAHAW Report, pp. 67–8.
26. Cited in Guémené and Guy (2004), p. 219.
27. Faure (2001), p. 158.
28. Faure (2001), p. 163.
29. Guémené (2001), p. 655.
30. Kahler, p. 689.
31. Kahler, p. 689.
32. *Journal of the American Veterinary Medical Association*, 227:1402, 1404 (Yost and Hansen/Bowden letters) (November 1, 2005).

33. http://www.shepstone.net/economicreport.pdf
34. Kahler, p. 689.
35. SCAHAW Report, pp. 38–44; 48; 61. www.animalagalliance.org/images/ag_insert/20060505_Foie_Gras.pdf, pp. 17–21.
36. SCAHAW Report, p. 63.
37. SCAHAW Report, pp. 45–6; http://www.artisanfarmers.org/images/Dr._Bartholf_Letter_to_Chicago_City_Council.pdf
38. SCAHAW Report, pp. 63–4.
39. SCAHAW Report, p. 57; McKenna, p. 22
40. Glass, p. 1.
41. http://foieblog.blogspot/2007/03/interview-with-jim-schlitz-developer-of.html
42. Glass, p. 2.
43. Hunt, Alan, *Governance of Consuming Passions: A History of Sumptuary Law*, London: MacMillan Press, 1996, pp. 5–7.
44. Ginor, pp. 73–4.
45. Davis, Mitchell, *Love 'er or Liver – Foie Gras, an Unlikely Delicacy Gains F(l)avor in America* www.nyu.edu/classes/bkg/foie, p. 5, accessed April 20, 2007.
46. http://www.nofoiegras.org/Zogby_NY.pdf; http://www.nofoiegras.org/zogby.htm
47. http://www.nofoiegras.org/Zogby_NY5-06.pdf
48. www.nofoiegras.org; Stephen Hanson, 'Utilitarianism, Animals, and the Problem of Numbers,' *Animal Liberation Philosophy and Policy Journal*, 2:1–16 (2004), 6 ('The eventual aim of all animal liberation efforts is a world in which animals are not treated as food. . ..'); Marshall Sella, 'Does a Duck Have a Soul? How Foie Gras Became the New Fur,' *New York Magazine*, 6/27/05; http://nymag.com/nymetro/food/features/12071/

Bibliography

Blandford, David, Jean-Christophe Bureau, Linda Fulponi, and Spencer Henson, 'Potential Implications of Animal Welfare Concerns and Public Policies in Industrialized Countries for International Trade,' in *Global Food Trade and Consumer Demand for Quality* (Barry Krissoff, Mary Bohman, and Julie A. Casswell, eds.), International Agricultural Trade Research Consortium, Regional Research Project Ne-165, Kluwer Academic Publishers, 2002.

EU Scientific Committee on Animal Health and Animal Welfare, *Report on the Welfare Aspects of the Production of Foie Gras in Ducks and Geese*, 1998, http://ec.europa.eu/food/fs/sc/scah/out17_en.pdf ('SCAHAW Report')

Faure, Jean-Michel, Daniel Guémené and Gérard Guy, 'Is There Avoidance of the Force Feeding Procedure in Ducks and Geese?,' *Animal Research* 50(2):157–64 (2001).

Ginor, Michael A., Mitchell Davis, Andrew Coe, and Jane Ziegelman, *Foie Gras: A Passion*, New York: John Wiley & Sons, 1999.

Glass, Juliet, 'Foie Gras Makers Struggle to Please Critics and Chefs,' *New York Times,* April 25, 2007; www.nytimes.com/2007/04/25/dining/25foie.html

Guémené, Daniel and G. Guy, 'The Past, Present and Future of Force-Feeding and 'Foie Gras' Production,' *World's Poultry Science Journal*, 60:210–222 (June 2004).

Guémené, Daniel, G. Guy, J. Noirault, M. Garreau-Mills, P. Gouraud, and J.M. Faure, 'Force-Feeding Procedure and Physiological Indicators of Stress in Male Mule Ducks, '*British Poultry Science*, 42:650–7 (2001).

Kahler, Susan C., 'Farm Visit Influences Foie Gras Vote,' *Journal of the American Veterinary Medical Association*, 227:688–9 (Sept. 1, 2005).

Lang, Christopher D., Matthew D. Lang, Maciej Witkos, and Michelle Uttaburanont, 'Foie Gras: the Two Faces of Janus', *Journal of the American Veterinary Medicine Association*, 230: 1624–1627 (June 1, 2007).

McKenna, Carol, *Forced Feeding: An Inquiry into the Welfare of Ducks and Geese Kept for the Production of Foie Gras*, Edinburgh and London: Advocates for Animals and World Society for the Protection of Animals, 2000.

SELECTED WEBSITES (ALL ACCESSIBLE AS OF JULY 13, 2007):
Pro foie gras:
http://www.artisanfarmers.org/home.html
http://foieblog.blogspot.com
http://www.hometownsource.com/2005/october/20business.html
Anti foie gras:
http://www.farmsanctuary.org/
http://www.peta.org/mc/factsheet_display.asp?ID=97
http://www.avmahurtsanimals.com/foieGras.asp
http://www.banfoiegras.org.uk/
Alternatives to foie gras:
http://www.roastgoose.com/products/fatty_goose_liver.htm

Why not Eat Pets?

Bruce Kraig

Any discussion by humans who consume meat and are concerned about the ethics of eating, anyone worried about the environmental effects of modern food-producing systems, a person intent on locally sourced foods, inasmuch as it is possible, must consider the possibility of a food supply that meets all ethical criteria: companion animals, or pets. To reject this idea violates all pragmatic approaches to the problems mentioned here and constitutes carnivore hypocrisy.

In April of 2007 the great terror swept across the United States. It was not 'terrorism' in the usual sense of the word – bomb-bearing fanatics – but something worse: fifteen pet cats and at least one dog, had died and thousands more were sickened by tainted pet food.[1] The substance, melamine, came from wheat gluten that had been produced in China, sold to a Las Vegas, Nevada company, and then resold to Master Foods, a pet food manufacturer in Canada.[2] This wasn't the first such recall: a year before a corn aflatoxin had killed perhaps one hundred dogs.[3] Nevertheless, the latest news brought floods of public commentary ranging from outright xenophobia, to new concerns about food safety in general. The last was reinforced by widely publicized revelations about contaminated food from China. The fact that 70–80 per cent of the US fish supply originates in Asia, much of it farm-raised under unsanitary conditions in China, has shocked Americans whether of nativist sympathies or not.

In a small piece of irony, about a week after the dreadful story appeared as lead-item news everywhere, one of the hosts of a morning national television talk show devoted to mainly women's issues, declared that during the same period as the sixteen pet deaths, sixteen US soldiers had been killed in Iraq. That news, from a far away place, the host observed, was relegated to back pages and 20-second sound bites. The host was replaced soon thereafter.

The deaths of beloved dogs and cats made Americans think about unclean food from distant lands, or produced by people from alien places (Mexico, mainly), reinforced by deepening fears about climate change and loss of whole species, to say nothing of unending war.

The pet-poisoning scare pustulated greater concerns that broke out in the popular national media.[4] Conservative newspapers such as the *Chicago Tribune*, have discovered the many serious assaults by human activity on the natural world, from climate change, to catastrophic fishing practices, now approvingly report on sustainable farming, harvesting, and on local production. Perhaps only pets could have brought forth such a torrent of interest in clean, wholesome, ecologically sound, food practices. If followed through to a logical conclusion, then pets, principally dogs and cats, might be more important to our food supply than they could know.

Rationale

In 1885 Vincent M. Holt published a small tract entitled, *Why Not Eat Insects?* In it he asks his fellow Englishmen to consider consuming wholesome insects for a variety of reasons:

> One of the constant questions of the day is, How can the farmer most success-fully battle with the insect devourers of his crops? I suggest that these insect devourers should be collected by the poor as food. Why not? [5]

Holt's argument makes sound ecological sense: eat locally available foods, and eat as low on the food chain as possible, though with the understanding that in our industrialized food world complete local food sourcing is difficult.[6] Good Victorian that he was, Holt implied a higher moral value to his proposal, feeding the poor and conserving resources. In Holt's day, and in rural economies today, entomophagy is more than reasonable. In our modern urban setting, when (as of 2007) a majority of the world's population is urban or suburban, other foods often eschewed as inedible are at hand, companion animals. In a word if one is a carnivore no meat should be rejected.

138

At first blush one might think of pets as parasites. We certainly spend a great many resources on them. Seventy-one million US households have pets, among them 38.4 cats (about 10 million in the UK) and 44.8 dogs (almost 7 million in the UK). American spending on pets in 2007 will be more than $40 billion, with $16.1 billion going to food. That amounts to $192.00 annually per pet for food, or 52¢ each day. In a world where 854 million human beings suffer from acute hunger and almost 1 billion people live on less than one dollar a day one might wonder about the ethics, much less the moral basis, of feeding pets rather than needy human beings.[7]

Horrifying as the image of starving children may be, the view that pet food is made, bought, sold and consumed at the expense of the world's poor is naive. In fact, there is more than enough food available to adequately feed all the planet's human population. Hunger has other causes, mainly political and having to do with market economies.[8] The ethical reasons for consuming pets, companion non-human animals, are deeper than human hunger that can and should be alleviated by other means.

Why are some companion animals privileged?

In July 2007 the State of Illinois closed down the last horse knackering plant in the state. Although the meat was for Europe, killing horses offended the delicate sensibilities of the governor and a number of the state's citizens.[9] Sixty thousand horses are slaughtered in the United States each year, much for human consumption, some for pet food. That dogs can eat horseflesh bothers some, but not to the extent that human consumption does.[10] Why?

How dogs, cats, horses and other animals came to be pets and subject to informal eating taboos in Western societies has been widely discussed and need not be chewed over at length.[11] The arguments can be categorized as follows: narcissistic; pragmatic; affective; and higher-level ethics.

The first category is obvious. Pets can satisfy their keepers' emotional needs. Many of the 400 AKC recognized dog breeds were created to gratify human whims.[12] What else accounts for the Papillon (unless as an hors d'oeuvre), Cockapoo, Shitzubichon or any other such Dr Moreau-like creations except that they are shaped to human desires. Cats seem to be mostly immune to such changes, as a recent genetic study shows.[13] Of recent historical vintage such ideas make the thought of dog or cat eating akin to human cannibalism, among some, even worse. This critique does not mean that one should not love their companion animals; most are as cute as can be.

Pragmatism has many meanings, not the least being an argument to eat companion animals. However, Marvin Harris's well-known Cultural Materialist theories about aversion to eating animals critical to an economy applies not just to cows in India but to dogs. They are not consumed in areas where they are used for hunting or herding but are eaten as luxury or medicinal treatments in regions where hunting and herding are not important.[14] Working dogs, then, might be exempt from the dinner table. However, as will be shown, this is an even better reason not to exclude them. And, consider eating useful dogs among Native Americans, a meat so delectable that Meriwether Lewis, reporting on the adventures of the Corps of Discovery between 1803 and 1806, preferred it to all others (his partner, William Clark did not).[15]

Affective reasons combine emotional responses and pragmatism. Domestic animals have been imbued with admirable human qualities in every facet of popular culture. From Lassie to Skippy the Bush Kangaroo, charming non-human animals have been admired for their resourcefulness, adaptability, loyalty, and intelligence (hard to accept for a kangaroo).

Anthropomorphism is yet another way to manipulate animal species to match human ideals and to make the alien familiar. Creatures other than dogs and cats have been afforded such preferred treatment, if not love. Babe the pig, Charlotte the spider, penguins, and even rats. Water Rat in *The Wind in the Willows* and as in the foodie film *Ratatouille*, are heroes (each would be rare test subjects at the University of Georgia's Animal Cognition Laboratory where rats are 'stars').[16] Rarely have other companion animals such as cockroaches been so appreciated, Archy of *Archy and Mehitabel* one exception. Most of the anthropomorphized animals have been either working (Lassie) or wild (even if in zoos, such as in the animated film *The Wild*) or extinct (the 'Ice Age' films). As Harris would have it, of all such animals, only dogs have been privileged in Western culture, perhaps horses now in the United States.[16]

Cruelty is another element in this category. No one can read about 'traditional' Korean dog slaughter practices without shuddering. Similar sentiments are filtering down to other food animals, even to lobsters, as evidenced by the debate over how to kill them painlessly. Ordinary human sentiment works here, but there is pragmatic, indeed moral, side: if we are indifferent to inflicting pain on living things, then will we care about pain in related species and will we be sensitive to the environmental, social problems involved with the food production system, or just human suffering?

Finally, there are higher-level arguments against dining upon our pets. Since the publication of Peter Singer's *Animal Liberation* a considerable discussion about non-human animal rights has ensued. While many of the arguments have been among philosophers, ranging from Kantian to Utilitarian and Pragmatic approaches, these have filtered down into popular consciousness. The very word, coined by Singer, 'speciesism' fires the blood of those sensitive to issues of human (and animal) rights. Tom Regan's arguments for equal rights of mammals is also compelling. Some in the ecological community think of caring for the natural world as a prime ethical consideration and, of course, simple compassion for the suffering of any living thing is at work in the argument. (The latter two are both Utilitarian and Pragmatic in effect, if not necessarily in their original forms.) Related to the last is on ongoing debate about animal consciousness: are mammals sentient beings with consciousness of self? As is well known, pigs are not only much smarter and more charming than dogs but they are not nearly as sycophantic. So why slaughter pigs and not dogs?[17]

140

Why eat companion animals (pets)?

My stepmother ate her cat. Two of them, twenty years apart. The first time, as a small child, was during the wars of the Russian Revolution, the horrors of which are vividly depicted in Isaac Babel's *Red Cavalry*. Starving while fleeing fighting, the family resorted to eating their little daughter's pet cat. Twenty years later, while escaping from the Soviet Union during World War II in deep winter with no food or possessions, they again stewed and ate their pet cat. My stepmother, with the clinical detachment that went with her training as a physician, said that it tasted much like rabbit. They would not have done so except in the extremity of hunger, but to her mind, this was survival of the fittest, or the most powerful.

The argument from extremity has many implications, the simplest being that non-working pet – dogs and cats in particular – consume food resources that could go to needy people. As mentioned above, there is more than enough food in the world to feed everyone somewhere in the range of four-plus pounds each day, or more than 4,000 calories. Maldistribution of income and food itself is the problem.

We could argue that the $192 spent on pet food each year should be donated to buying food for the world's hungry. The United States government contributes about 60 per cent of the world's food aid to the tune of about $1.2 billion, but only a fraction of that is food.[18] In this sense, there are very good arguments for encouraging and supporting local production of food, and donations to NGOs that do this are helpful. Spending one's pet food budget on that would be a wonderful charitable act, but most middle class households can match that sum, that is, support both. Considering that the United States government spends officially $12 billion each on the war in Iraq and Afghanistan, private pet food allocations are small. Still, the spectacle of pampered artificially miniature dogs, delectable morsels that they are, in the face of dire poverty is troubling.[19]

More compelling arguments for companion animal consumption are ecological. If an ethical goal is for people to eat as economically as possible, then the closer to the sources of production, the lower on the food chain, the better.[20] This is hard for carnivores, since most studies show that it takes on average eleven pounds of food to produce one pound of edible meat (more for beef, less for poultry). Dog and cat feeding is cheap, relatively speaking, and well within the means of most conscientious pet owners. Though some think otherwise, dogs are omnivores, and can eat a wide range of even low protein foods, while cats are 'obligate carnivore[s] and requires at least 41 essential nutrients for healthy body.'[21]

Premium commercial-grade dog food might contain lamb, chicken, turkey or beef meal; brewers rice, corn, oats, rice, barley, wheat, sorghum, soybean hulls, wheat bran, beet pulp, rice bran, oat bran, pea fiber, lots of chemicals, not necessarily in this order.[22] At $250 per ton for high-protein corn meal (60 per cent protein), meat and bone meal at $145 a ton, and brewer's rice selling for $10.75 a hundredweight, dry dog food is cheap to make.[23] A pound of dry dog food equals about 1,400 calories and most domestic dogs need roughly 30 calories per pound of body weight.[24] Cat food is similar in content but with more protein in canned varieties. Both dog and cat canned foods are composed, among other things, of animal parts considered unusable by humans,[25] unless one were making really old-fashioned sausages or haggis.

141

Despite the fact that most pet foods are produced by industrialized farming and processing, with all of their costs, pets are certainly feeding efficiently. If dogs and cats were allowed to feed naturally, costs would be lower. Again, dogs are omnivores whose olfactory sensibilities (and taste?) pleasures differ from our own. They like carrion, are coprophages, will scavenge all kinds of garbage, and even eat human leftovers. Cats, if allowed to hunt, are scourges of bird and rodent populations. Therefore ecological considerations, food efficiency, suggest that eating ones' pets would be an ethical act, assuming that one is an omnivore. In fact, such eating would be closer to humanity's hunting-gathering and early horticultural roots. No doubt, the earliest domesticated dogs and cats descended from wild varieties (cats still hardly domesticated) that lived symbiotically with humans, as scavengers and emergency food sources.

Eating pets addresses questions not only about ecological soundness, but ethical concerns. These are not factory farmed creatures, subjected to all the attendant cruelties. One need only see monstrous places such as a factory pig plant or chicken factories to appreciate the differences between the lives of pets and food animals. Those who are distressed at the very thought of dining upon a pet should consider what qualities differentiate a food animal, such as a pig, from a dog or cat. In the case of pigs it cannot be cognition, for pigs are smarter than either, and a sweet-faced Jersey or Swiss Brown cow is certainly more attractive than, say, a grotesque bulldog. If one argues, as do some, that the very existence of many farm animals depends on them serving as human food in a more symbiotic way than just scavenging around human settlements, then pets are surely the paradigm of the breed. [26] Other peoples have kept pets and used them as food, some still do, e.g. ancient Hawaiians and modern Peruvians with their beloved *cuy*.

To obviate apprehension about cruelty to animals, whether sentient or not, one solution arises. Why not eat, or at the least send off for processing in other animal food one's deceased pets. What we celebrate in Kobe beef – Wagyu cattle – is that they are allowed to live a long time, closer to full lives than most food cattle, massaged and treated with care. The same could be said for dogs and perhaps cats, only pet keepers could wait until natural death is near or occurs. Of course, as in the case of a food emergency as my stepmother encountered, there is always ready protein at hand. The US government estimates that 33 million Americans are 'food insecure' (a neologism for 'hungry' and the number is actually higher), yet hardly any would consider their companion animals as food.

And why stop at cats and dogs when thinking about companion animals? We have many others from which to choose. Rodents abound, from mice (caught by a cat, perhaps) to squirrels in the attic, all can be good food sources. And then there are many insects....

Notes

1. Ember, Lois, 'Pet food recall: Aminoprotein, a rodent-killing compound, is found in samples of pet food', *Chemical & Engineering News* 85.14 (April 2, 2007): 11(1). Expanded Academic ASAP. Thomson Gale. Roosevelt University Library. 3 June, 2007 is an early notice in a science journal; an avalanche of mass-media accounts soon followed. By the end of April, 2007, the US Food and Drug Administration had received 17,000 complaints with some 1950 cat deaths and 2200 dog fatalities (see: http://www.fda.gov/consumer/updates/petfoodrecallup.html). The PetConnection site's survey puts total fatalities at 4,867 (http://www.petconnection.com/recall/).

2. See David Barboza and Alexei Barrionuevo, 'Filler in Animal Feed Is Open Secret in China', *The New York Times* (April 30, 2007); Judi McLeod, 'How pet food makers get their supplies a tawdry tale', http://www.canadafreepress.com/2007/cover040607.htm (April 6, 2007); Lisa Wade McCormick, 'China Opens Investigation into Pet Food Contaminant', http://wwww.consumeraffairs.com/news04/2007/04/pet_food_recall17.html (April 7, 2007).

3. Sarah Muirhead, 'Pet food varieties recalled. (Food and Drug Administration and state feed regulatory agencies' investigation of dog deaths)', *Feedstuffs* 78.3 (Jan 16, 2006), p. 3. Expanded Academic ASAP. Thomson Gale. Roosevelt University Library. 3 June, 2007.

4. Perhaps the best-known commentator on these matters is Lou Dobbs broadcasting weeknightly on the CNN cable network (see: http://www.cnn.com/CNN/Programs/lou.dobbs.tonight/).

5. Vincent M. Holt, *Why Not Eat Insects?* (repr. with intro. by Laurence Mound, London: British Museum, 1988 [1885]), pp. 14–15.

6. See Michael Pollan's *The Omnivore's Dilemma: A Natural History of Four Meals*, New York: Penguin Press (2006), for a cogent argument about this.

7. State of Food Insecurity in the World 2006. Food and Agriculture Organization of the United Nations. 2006. (ftp://ftp.fao.org/docrep/fao/009/a0750e/a0750e02.pdf) and World Development Indicators 2007. The World Bank. March 2007 (http://web.worldbank.org/WEBSITE/EXTERNAL/DATASTATISTICS/0,,contentMDK:21298138~pagePK:64133150~piPK:64133175~theSitePK:239419,00.html). See also 'Hunger Facts: International - World Hunger and Poverty: How They Fit Together', http://bread.org (http://www.bread.org/learn/hunger-basics/hunger-facts-international.html).

8. See Frances Moore Lappe, Joseph Collins, Peter Rosset, Luis Esparza, *World Hunger: Twelve Myths*, New York: Grove Press, 1998, and Institute for Food and Development Policy, '12 Myths About Hunger.' Summer 1998 (http://www.foodfirst.org/pubs/backgrdrs/1998/s98v5n3.html).

9. Dan Strumpf, 'Judge dismisses challenges from Illinois horse slaughter plant', *Chicago Tribune* (July 5, 2007); see also Dahleen Glanton, 'Program lets prisoners care for thoroughbreds headed for slaughter', *Chicago Tribune* (June 11, 2007).

10. Outrage at human equinophagy can be found at http://www.equineprotectionnetwork.com/slaughter/faq.htm, though the USDA permits its use in dog food: http://a257.g.akamaitech.net/7/257/2422/14mar20010800/edocket.access.gpo.gov/cfr_2003/pdf/9CFR355.29.pdf.

11. See Keith Thomas, *Man in the Natural World*, New York: Pantheon Books, 1983; and this writer's modest effort, Bruce Kraig, 'Cynophagy: A Western Taboo', *Proceedings of the Oxford Symposium 1984 & 1985* (London: Prospect Books, 1986).

12. See Catherine C. Greer, *Pets in America*, Chapel Hill, NC: University of North Carolina Press, 2006; Angela G. Ray and Harold E. Gulley, 'The place of the dog: AKC breeds in American culture', *Journal of Cultural Geography*, 08873631, Fall/Winter 1996, vol. 16, issue 1. Academic Search Premier.

13. Carlos A. Driscoll, et al., 'The Near Eastern Origin of Cat Domestication', *Science* 28 June 2007. Science Express Reports.

14. Marvin Harris, *Cows, Pigs, Wars, and Witches: The Riddles of Culture*, New York: Vintage Books, 1975; Marvin Harris, *Good to Eat: Riddles of Food and Culture*, New York: Waveland Press, 1998 [1986].

15. Raymond D. Burroughs, ed., *The Natural History of the Lewis and Clark Expedition*, new ed. East Lansing: Michigan State University Press, 1995.

16. See http://www.uga.edu/animal-cognition-lab/.

17. Peter Singer, *Animal Liberation: A New Ethics for Our Treatment of Animals*, New York: Random House, 1975; and Peter Singer and Jim Mason, *The Way We Eat, Why Our Food Choices Matter*, New York: Rodale Books, 2006, especially Chapter 17. Tom Regan, *The Case for Animal Rights*, Berkeley: University of California Press, 1983; and *Defending Animal Rights*, Urbana and Champaign: University of Illinois Press, 2001. See also the discussion of animal cognition in: Animal Cognition, http://cognition.icapb.ed.ac.uk/; M.K. Holder, 'Smart Puzzle #3 Pig', Center for the Integrative Study of Animal Behaviors, Indiana University, 1999 in http://www.peta.org/mc/factsheet_display.asp?ID=11; an account of Cambridge University's Professor Donald Broom, on pig intelligence in 'The Millennium List,' *The Times* (London), 9 Jan. 2000 in http://www.goveg.com/f-hiddenlivespigs_experts.asp. An excellent summary of most of the ethical arguments is Julian H. Franklin, *Animal Rights and Moral Philosophy*, New York: Columbia University Press, 2005.

18. See http://observer.guardian.co.uk/foodmonthly/story/0,,2086227,00.html.

19. The pioneering work on this and other dog unpleasantries: Iris Nowell, *The Dog Crisis*, New York: St. Martin's Press, 1978. Also see a report saying that worldwide spending on pet care products in 2007 will be about $92 billion, $22 billion in the US: Professor Philip M. Parker, Ph.D. 'The 2006–2011 World Outlook for Pet Food and Pet Care Products', www.icongrouponline.com.

20. See Singer and Mason in addition to many other sources.

21. www.pfma.org.uk.

143

22. http://www.purina.com/dogs/food/FactsAboutFeeding.aspx
23. http://www.ams.usda.gov
24. http://www.phouka.com/dogs/dog_amount.html.
25. 'Cow brains. Sheep guts. Chicken heads. Road kill. Rancid grain. These are a few of the so-called nutritionally balanced ingredients found in the commercial pet food served to companion animals every day. More than 95 per cent of US companion animals derive their nutritional needs from a single source: processed pet food. When people think of pet food, many envision whole chickens, choice cuts of beef, fresh grains, and all the nutrition that a dog or cat may ever need – images that pet food manufacturers promote in their advertisements.' Tina Perry, 'The Truth About Commercial Pet Food', reprinted from *The Animals' Agenda* (Nov/Dec 1996). http://www.preciouspets.org/truth.htm. Actual sales of animal products for pet food in the United States for 2007 are $107 million. Professor Philip M. Parker, Ph.D. 'The 2006–2011 World Outlook for Animals.' www.icongroupon-line.com.
26. See Pollan for an extended discussion of Joel Salatin; a critique in Singer and Mason, pp. 255–256.

How Clean Is Your Plate?

Steven Kramer

Faced with finicky eaters, parents often admonish their children to clean their plates because people in other parts of the world go hungry. Hence, we are given an early lesson in the moral significance of food and eating. Contemporary ethicists have broadened this discussion by pointing out that our food choices implicate us in a wide variety of immoral practices, from the exploitation of farm laborers and the economies of developing countries, to cruelty towards animals and environmental destruction on a broad scale. In addition, money spent on fine dining and such culinary staples as saffron, imported olive oils and French sea salt all seem like selfish indulgences in a world where childhood malnutrition rates in some regions reach upwards of 50 per cent. Even this symposium itself can, somewhat paradoxically given our topic, be viewed with moral suspicion when we take into account the combined expenses of attending this conference and the very real environmental impacts associated with the extensive travel required to bring us all together. In this paper I will argue that these are serious issues that deserve far more attention than they typically receive and those of us who view food as an important area of both inquiry and practice ought to encourage this discourse. However, I shall also argue that focusing too much attention on them raises an equally significant concern. Cooking and eating become such morally-laden enterprises that we lose sight of the role of the enjoyment, delight and pleasure that we find in these activities and thus miss much of what is of value in food and the important role it plays in our lives. Recognizing this danger leads to a re-examination of our childhood lesson in order to explore the question: how clean does my plate have to be?

The re-emergence of food ethics

In the United States, the growing concern over the moral implications of food is evidenced by the popularity of such books as Barbara Kingsolver's *Animal, Vegetable, Miracle* and Michael Pollan's *The Omnivore's Dilemma*, as well as the expanding markets in organic, fair trade, and local foods. Nevertheless, it would be an overstatement to see these as symbolizing anything more than a beginning. I suspect that, for most Americans at least, their daily habits of eating are simply not viewed as a matter of ethics. In fact, it has been my experience that one can run into a great deal of hostility when one even tries to raise the subject. Specific concerns, such as that over the welfare of animals in concentrated animal feeding operations, are frequently dismissed out-of-hand as some kind of political correctness run amok.

It is healthy, therefore, to interject a little historical perspective at this point and remind ourselves that this is not a new subject.. In fact, the conceptual categories of food and eating may require a moral component in order to distinguish them from, say, forage and feeding. Furthermore, the communal approach to the hunting and gathering of food and the adaptive advantage this gave our ancestors may well be the source for the evolutionary development of the capacity for moral reasoning itself.[1] So, we ought to recognize that however silent we have been on the subject of late, the questions concerning food and morality represent the re-emergence of a very old conversation, and not an entirely new field of inquiry.

I suspect that much of the common dismissal of concerns about food ethics is, in part, due to a kind of defensive posture. We simply do not like to subject ourselves to such moral scrutiny, especially when the result is likely to call our behavior into question. This is particularly true in the rural agricultural area in which I live. The corn/soybean complex that dominates the landscape in the Midwestern United States represents the heart of industrial agriculture. If, as Michael Pollan argues, the dominance of corn in the American food supply has led to a 'national eating disorder'[2] my region has largely been responsible. The changes that Pollan and others are calling for represent a wholesale transformation of the economy of this region, and many people are simply unwilling to consider this possibility.

There is, however another source for this reluctance to consider the ethical implications of food and that is the disassociation from and trivialization of food that is the result of the modern food industry. As Eric Schlosser notes in his exposé *Fast Food Nation,* 'what we eat has changed more in the past forty years than in the previous forty thousand.'[3] Food has, to a large extent, been removed from its central place in people's experience and has been reduced to a commodity that requires little thought or effort on our part to consume. The result, as Wendell Berry points out is that 'industrial eating has become a degraded, poor, and paltry thing.'[4] In short, food just does not seem important enough to worry much about.

It would, however, be wrong to lay the complete blame for this on industrial capitalism. While modern agribusiness may have provided the mechanism, philosophy had long ago sown the seeds of justification for this denigration of food. Plato, for instance, simply dismissed food and cooking as subjects unworthy of philosophical concern, centered as they were on supplying mere nutrition or bodily pleasures. Following in kind, Aristotle pointed out that the nutritive aspect of humans is something that they shared with all living things, and therefore not informative for answering the basic question of what the good of a human being is.

A number of contemporary moral theorists have challenged this traditional philosophical dismissal of food by arguing that food is an important subject of analysis because, at least in the context of global industrial agriculture, our food choices implicate us in a wide variety of immoral practices involved in the production of these foods. These practices range from the exploitation of farm laborers, the creation of hunger in lesser-developed countries, the fostering of an epidemic of obesity, the systematic cruelty towards animals in factory farming, to environmental destruction on a global scale. The complexity of the issues here is often matched only by our degree of ignorance of them. For instance, the seemingly simple question of whether to order the shrimp cocktail off the appetizer menu at the restaurant last night is moved beyond the level of taste and appetite when one realizes that the reason shrimp is so ubiquitous on menus these days is because it is relatively inexpensive. The drastic drop in the cost of shrimp over the last decade is due to the fact that the vast majority of it is coming from aquaculture facilities in the developing world. The resource requirements of such facilities have meant that they are usually placed along the coast, primarily in mangrove swamps. The physical destruction of these swamps caused by the building of these facilities has been magnified by the pollution of the effluents of this intensive form of aquaculture. This has resulted in devastating impacts not only to these ecosystems, but also to traditional fisheries and the people who depend upon them. The organic soup created in the tanks has led to the use of powerful and often dangerous pesticides and antibiotics that have serious implications for workers and consumers alike.[5] Okay, at this point you might be thinking just to order the salad. But even an organic salad is likely to have come from a large industrial farming operation dependent on migrant labor and intensive use of scarce water resources... I think you get the picture, and we haven't even gotten to the entrée yet.

The collective force of the concerns just outlined are summed up in the title of Peter Singer and Jim Mason's recent book, *The Way We Eat: Why Our Food Choices Matter.* They matter because they too often support not only unwise, but immoral practices. To the extent such choices are made in ignorance, and all too often a seemingly willed ignorance, the authenticity of our lives is undermined. We simply fail to recognize or take responsibility for the true costs of our actions. Also, the extent of the immorality involved in the practices of producing the foods we consume, even if such choices were adequately informed, would hardly make such behavior a model for leading the good life. What these authors are calling for is a wholesale re-examination of our eating habits in order to bring them more in line with defensible moral principles.

While one might think at this point that the traditional philosophical dismissal of food that we have inherited from Plato has been defeated, I think that such a conclusion would be premature. We should note that in the *Phaedo* what Socrates is dismissing are the 'so-called pleasures connected with food and drink,' lumping them together with such concerns as having 'smart clothes and shoes and other bodily ornaments.' The true philosopher we are told 'despises them...free[ing] his soul from association with the body, so far as is possible, to a greater extent than other men.'[6] Note the subject regards the 'pleasures' associated with these things and the caveat about distancing oneself from the concerns of the body 'so far as is possible.' I think that a charitable reading of these passages does not indicate an outright dismissal of the topic of food altogether. In fact, Schlosser's critique of the food industry in *Fast Food Nation* and the implications of this diet depicted in the film *Supersize Me* seem

147

to me to be perfect examples of the tyrannical state and soul outlined in the *Republic*. And while Deane Curtin is right in pointing out that in the just state Plato outlines, food is relegated to the artisan class, which must 'get the meal on the table somehow,'[7] it should not be overlooked that the wealth and property resided in this class, and their needs were met. This is certainly a far cry from the plight of agriculture and food industry workers today, whether in the United States or the developing world. The point that Plato seems to be making is that, to a philosopher, food has no real intrinsic interest. Whatever interest it might have is merely extrinsic to food itself. And this is a view that the aforementioned critiques do not impact. Food choices are simply being recognized as another in a long list of consumable products that implicate us in a wide variety of immoral practices – whether it is the shrimp I eat, the Nike shoes I put on my feet, or the diamond ring I wear.

However commendable and convincing I find many, though certainly not all, of these moral critiques of our food habits, I do have a broader worry about the general perspective as I have outlined it. The fear I have is that without a more direct challenge to the underlying philosophical assumptions about food, these moral theorists may well have set us on a course that will salvage morality, but do so at the expense of food. It is this worry that will be the focus of the next section of this paper.

Cleaning up our plates

The lesson from our discussion so far seems to be that we should have listened to our parents more and taken their admonishment to 'clean up our plate' to heart. And this is all well and good, to a point. The question we need to turn to now is: how far are we to take this point? What exactly is the nature of the moral lesson being imparted in the situation described at the beginning of this paper?

At first glance, the parents seem to be pointing out a basic moral lesson about being thankful for what one has, as well as highlighting the wrongness of wasting food in a world where people routinely go without. I take it that few would find reason to quibble with these principles. There is, in addition, a deeper message here about the weight of moral principles. The fact that the child does not like the food placed before her – children rarely need to be admonished to eat food they like – seems to bear little weight when confronted with the prohibition against wasting food. And here again, the recognition that moral prescriptions may call on us to override our personal desires and inclinations is something that only the most thoroughgoing egoist would generally question. The question that I want to raise, however, is not whether the dictates of morality *may* override our desires and inclinations, but rather, *must* this be so? It is this stronger interpretation that a number of moral philosophers have endorsed, Peter Singer among them. And, as Susan Wolf points out, even those that do not explicitly endorse such a principle are nevertheless pushed in that direction by an unquestioned metaethical commitment to the view 'that one ought to be as morally good as possible.'[8] But, should we be so?

If, for instance, we apply this stronger principle to the recognition that many people in the world suffer from a lack of adequate food, we quickly see that the moral implications go way beyond simply eating everything on our plate. Not wasting food may indeed be better than wasting it because such wastage seems to represent an attitude of indifference about a grave situation. We do have to recognize, however, that it does nothing to alleviate that suffering. Maybe instead of eating everything on our plate, we should in fact reduce what is on our plate and use the money we would otherwise spend to help those in need. This is exactly the line of reasoning that Singer has used to argue that in the face of such suffering, we should give up everything we have until we are at the point of sacrificing things of 'comparable moral significance.'[9]

Taking a look at my own situation, it is not hard to see the dramatic impacts this would have on my cooking and eating habits. Though I generally do not lead a lavish or overly consumptive lifestyle, I do take cooking and eating seriously and subsequently have a well-stocked but not extravagant pantry. It is, however, hard to see what would remain if I really took Singer's principle to heart. Certainly out would go the *fleur de sel* along with the bottles of imported olive oils, balsamic vinegars and the like. Equally, the rack of spices and herbs would have to go, apart from those things that I have managed to gather or grow myself. While these things do indeed enhance the variety and quality of the food I serve, it would stretch credulity to count them as having moral significance. In the end, in fact, I am not sure what would remain besides a few staples such as flour. At this point it is important to note that we have already cleaned out my cupboard and we have not even addressed many of the moral concerns noted in the previous section. While many of us would balk at such a demanding morality as this, it is very hard to see exactly where the reasoning falters that leads us to this conclusion and how such unwillingness is not simply an unjustified indulgence of our own selfish desires.

Susan Wolf, however, points us to the ideal of moral sainthood as the possible source of the problem here. A moral saint, she notes, is 'a person whose every action is as morally good as possible.'[10] Someone who exhibits these virtues is bound to eliminate most of things in life that many of us find meaningful. Speaking specifically of food she states:

> An interest in something like gourmet cooking will be…difficult for a moral saint to rest easy with. For it seems to me that no plausible argument can justify the use of human resources involved in producing a *pâté de canard en croûte* against possible alternative beneficent ends to which these resources might be put. If there is a justification for the institution of haute cuisine, it is one which rests on the decision *not* to justify every activity against morally beneficial alternatives, and this is a decision a moral saint will never make.[11]

Given such a fact, Wolf questions whether the ideal of moral sainthood is really an ideal that we should aspire to. And it is precisely this tension, between a drive for moral purity and the pleasures of food, which is at the center of Isak Dinesen's remarkable short story, 'Babette's Feast.' A brief examination of the literary thought experiment that Dinesen poses will thus be particularly useful for our present deliberations.

Messing up our plates

'Babette's Feast' takes us into the lives of a small, pious Lutheran community in Norway. In language reminiscent of Plato's discussion of the Forms, we are informed that the members of the sect 'renounced the pleasures of this world, for the earth and all that it held to them was but a kind of illusion, and the true reality was the New Jerusalem toward which they were longing.'[12] Prominent among these was a renunciation of the pleasures of food and eating. Their diet was sustaining but bland, largely consisting of salted cod and bread soup. The community, however, is set on a path that will challenge these commitments when the two daughters of the sect's patriarch are confronted with the presence of a French refugee on their doorstep, Babette. Untrusting of the notoriously exotic appetites of the French, the sisters nevertheless answer their Christian duty and give Babette shelter, taking her on as a cook.

Though always remaining somewhat of a mysterious presence, Babette works herself into the fabric of the community. Through her hands, the foods they had always eaten seemed to regain the healing and restorative powers that prayer alone was not supplying. The story's climax, however, comes as the result of a stroke of luck. An old lottery ticket pays off and Babette finds herself the recipient of a sudden windfall. Seizing the opportunity of the hundredth anniversary of the deceased patriarch's birth, Babette convinces the sisters to allow her to return their kindness by cooking a French meal for the community. Their reluctant agreement, however, evolves into trepidation when provisions for the feast start arriving. Bottles of wine, unknown substances, and even the monstrous figure of a live sea turtle make the sisters worry that they have unwittingly entered into a pact with the devil. Nevertheless, they are bound by their word to honor Babette's request. The community, however, steels itself for the encounter by making a solemn pact to endure the meal yet avoid temptation by cleansing their 'tongues of all taste and purify them of all delight or disgust of the senses.'[13]

The meal laid before them, though, proves too much for their resolve. Babette, as it turns out, was a celebrated chef and the sumptuous pleasures of the food and drink she presents makes it impossible to simply eat without tasting. As the meal goes on their somber natures lighten, and the fear and petty grievances that had worked into the group over the years start to melt away. What started out to be a somber observance ends up as a celebration and a reminder of the true nature of the spiritual quest that initially brought them all together.

In her analysis of 'Babette's Feast,' Carolyn Korsmeyer notes the following:

Dinesen's dislike of the pious, bourgeois Christianity of her youth in Denmark is well known and this triumph of Babette's presents her own choice of a life in which the senses are honored, along with their pleasures. As with the feast, intense sense experience is not accurately described simply as bodily indulgence; it is a means by which spiritual, perhaps even mystical truths about life's transience and splendor are realized.[14]

But the critique here goes beyond bourgeois Christianity to philosophy itself. In fact, the hymn the dinner-group sings before the feast contains lines that could have come directly out of the *Phaedo*; 'Take not thought for food or raiment / careful one, so anxiously …'[15] The challenge that Dinesen poses is not to set up a test between the life of the spirit with its focus on morality, and the life of the body and its sensual pleasures, rather it is a test between a life that integrates both these elements and a life where one is divorced from the other. This is made clear in the closing passages of the story, where Babette not only reveals to the sisters her past as a celebrated chef, but reveals to the reader that the patrons of her restaurant, who were in a far better position to fully appreciate her talents, included those who had murdered her husband and son, causing her to flee in the first place.

Dinesen's story powerfully illustrates the criticism that Wolf makes against the ideal of moral sainthood. The moral saint must lead 'a life strangely barren,'[16] absent the development of many of the non-moral virtues that can objectively be identified as providing important components of a rich and meaningful life, 'Babette's Feast' stands as a testimony for counting the rich pleasures associated with food and cooking in that category. The concern I raised at the end of the previous section is that this is precisely the component that philosophical moralists like Singer are missing in their analysis. The only answer they propose for why our food choices matter is that they carry moral implications. What Dinesen's thought experiment shows us is not that this answer is wrong, so much as it is incomplete. Without a richer analysis of the value of food and its attendant pleasures, these aspects of our lives will simply be overwhelmed by the very real moral issues we face. Those of us who choose to continue to indulge ourselves in this manner are left looking as self-centered as the child who will not clean her plate.

What Dinesen seems to be pointing us toward is not just the need to strike a balance between the enjoyment of sensual pleasures and the supposedly loftier demands of morality, but to see that they can exhibit a kind of harmony – that is, if we take each seriously. What is so striking about the way she presents this is how it raises a cautionary tale for so much of what we focus on in discussing food and morality today. After all, the lifestyle of the villagers seems to exhibit all the hallmarks of consuming less, living simply, and eating organically, locally and sustainably. The feast, on the other hand, raises a host of moral concerns, from eating exotic foods of unknown origins that are shipped long distances, to lavish consumption and even eating rare, sentient creatures. As the moralists are telling us to clean up our plates, Dinesen seems to be urging us to mess them up a bit.

How clean should it be?

So, in the final analysis, how clean should our plates be? That is the question Dinesen leaves us with, and I am not sure that I know the answer to it. In fact, I am somewhat pessimistic about being able to come up with a theoretical perspective on the correct balance of the moral and non-moral aspects of our lives that such an answer would rest on. I suspect, it is simply a matter that requires continuous reflective practice. However, I do think we can frame the answer to the question within some broad parameters – undoubtedly a whole lot cleaner than they are, but definitely not spotless.

Notes

1. Hauser, pp. 211–53.
2. Pollan, pp. 1–123.
3. Schlosser, p. 7.
4. Berry, p. 375.
5. For a good introduction to the issues surrounding consumption of shrimp see Barry Easterbrook, 'Do I Dare to Eat a Shrimp?' That such articles are showing up in the pages of leading food magazines such as *Gourmet* shows that there is some progress being made on clearing up our collective ignorance, but there is still a long way to go.
6. Plato, *Phaedo*, 64D–E.
7. Curtin, p. 5.
8. Wolf, p. 419.
9. Singer, p. 586.
10. Wolf, p. 419.
11. Wolf, p. 422.
12. Dinesen, p. 3.
13. Dinesen, p. 27.
14. Kortsmeyer, pp. 209–10.
15. Dinesen, p. 30.
16. Wolf, p. 421.

Bibliography

Aristotle, *Nicomachean Ethics*, Martin Ostwald trans. (Upper Saddle River, NJ: Prentice Hall, 1999).

Berry, Wendell, 'The Pleasures of Eating,' in *Cooking, Eating, Thinking: Transformative Philosophies of Food*, Deane W. Curtin and Lisa M. Heldke, eds., (Indianapolis: U of Indiana Press, 1992) pp. 374–79.

Curtin, Deane, 'Food/Body/Person,' in *Cooking, Eating, Thinking: Transformative Philosophies of Food*, Deane W. Curtin and Lisa M. Heldke, eds., (Indianapolis: U of Indiana Press, 1992) pp. 3–22.

Dinesen, Isak, 'Babette's Feast,' in *Babette's Feast and Other Anecdotes of Destiny* (New York: Vintage Books, 1988).

Easterbrook, Barry, 'Do I Dare to Eat a Shrimp?' *Gourmet*, v LXVII: 3 (March 2007: pp 81–83).

Hauser, Marc D., *Wild Minds: What Animals Really Think* (New York: Henry Holt, 2000).

Kingsolver, Barbara, *Animal, Vegetable, Miracle: A Year of Food Life* (New York: HarperCollins, 2007).

Kortsmeyer, Carolyn, *Making Sense of Taste: Food and Philosophy* (Ithaca, NY: Cornell University Press, 1999).

Mills, Claudia, 'How Good a Person Do I Have to Be?' in *Business Ethics: People, Profits, and the Planet*, Kevin Gibson, ed. (Boston: McGraw Hill, 2006) pp. 133–37.

Plato, *Phaedo*, R. Hackforth trans. (New York: Bobbs-Merrill, 1955).

Plato, *Republic*, G.M.A. Grube and C.D.C. Reeve trans. (Indianapolis: Hackett, 1995).

Pollan, Michael, *The Omnivore's Dilemma: A Natural History of Four Meals* (New York: Penguin Press, 2006).

Sapontzis, Steve, ed., *Food For Thought: The Debate over Eating Meat* (Amherst, NY: Prometheus, 2004).

Schlosser, Eric, *Fast Food Nation: The Dark Side of the All-American Meal* (Boston: Houghton Mifflin, 2001).

Shue, Henry, *Basic Rights: Subsistence, Affluence, and U.S. Foreign Policy* (Princeton: Princeton UP, 1980)

Singer, Peter, 'Famine, Affluence, and Morality,' reprinted in *Ethics in Practice*, Hugh Lafollette (Cambridge: Blackwell, 1997) pp. 585–95.

Singer, Peter and Jim Mason, *The Way We Eat: Why Our Food Choices Matter* (New York: Rodale, 2006).

Wolf, Susan, 'Moral Saints,' *The Journal of Philosophy* 79 (1982) pp. 419–39.

153

Refined Cuisine or Plain Cooking?
Morality in the Kitchen

Rachel Laudan

What does cooking have to do with morality? In exploring the connections between food and morality this is a question worth asking because almost everything that counts as food has been cooked in the sense that it has been subjected to multiple processes after harvest or slaughter, including though not limited to treatment with heat.[1]

Cooking is unique to humans and it is something that every human group does. Given how important it has been in human history, it is perhaps not surprising that from the first written records we find that philosophers, physicians and priests debating what cooking was and how it shaped human behavior, including the doing of right and wrong. For much of the history of Eurasia, say from at least 1000 BC to the eighteenth century, the literate elite who engaged the debate simply took it for granted that cooking had much to do with morality. They were, however, divided into two sharply opposed camps about just what the relationship was. One camp held that the more refined the cooking, the more thoroughly processed the food, the more conducive to moral behavior. The other thought that the less cooking and the plainer the food, the better chance of creating an ethical society.

This essay brings together in a preliminary way hints about this long history that I have gleaned from my magpie reading on the history of cooking. I deliberately range widely across space and time because I believe the dichotomy between the two camps to have been widespread, persistent, and important. I ask readers to bear with me as I ignore important differences in theories of health, body, soul or spirit, virtue, and morality in an attempt to uncover the essentials of this profound division about the nature of cooking and its consequences.[2]

The refined cuisine camp

The refined cuisine camp in ancient Greece, Vedic India, and I suspect Zoroastrian Persia, defined cooking as bringing foodstuffs to perfection. This was equivalent to refining them or bringing them to full maturity. Cooking had two parts: mixing foodstuffs in the appropriate way and refining or cooking proper. This definition, representing the mainstream opinion of the literate elite, was widely held in the West until at least the eighteenth century and it persists in many parts of the world. I will deal with cooking and mixing in turn.

Cooking, on this view, was a basic natural process. What went on in the kitchen formed one link in a cosmic culinary cycle driven by the fire of the sun.[3] The sun's rays poured down on the earth, cooking seeds in the soil, grains of wheat or rice in the fields, and fruits on the trees until they matured. In the kitchen the fire in the oven or under the cauldron continued the process, cooking wheat and fruit into dishes fit for humans. In the belly, the process continued yet again, the fire there cooking, concocting or digesting – the three terms were equivalent – food into flesh and blood.

Fire, the chief agent in this cosmic cooking, was not thought of as the mere agitation of molecules. Rather fire was one of the elements, an actual thing as anyone who passed their hand through a flame quickly learned. Like the other culinary agent, water, fire cleansed and purified. Water, however, could purify only the surfaces of things. Fire was more powerful. It separated the pure, essential, and permanent essence of what it touched by combining with it. It left behind the imperfect earthly dross with which the substance was combined in nature. Implicit in the thinking of the refined cooking camp, therefore, was the belief that in their natural state grains, flesh, vegetables, or other foodstuffs were sullied with all kinds of impurities. The only way to get to what they truly were, to their essence, was to cook them.

The refined cooking camp saw parallels between the kinds of food that living beings ate and their position on the biological, social, and moral scale. Beasts that ate only raw red flesh or uncooked green grass were slaves to their instincts. The poor who ate coarse, inadequately cooked food were little better. 'Many people see little difference between this class of men and the animals they use to farm our lands,' explained the author of an article in the French *Encylopédie*.[4] The famous eighteenth-century English doctor, George Cheyne was equally dismissive. 'Ideots, peasants, and mechanics,' he said, 'have scarce any passions at all, or any lively sensations, and are incapable of lasting impressions.'[5] The barbarians, whom the settled peoples from Rome to China described as 'eaters of flesh, drinkers of milk' were incapable of civilized moral behavior, thanks to their raw diet.[6] Only civilized peoples who ate foods such as white rice, white bread, meat stewed with tempering spices, and yogurt or butter, all of them highly refined, could reach their full moral potential. At the very top of the scale, the immortals dined on yet-more refined foods such as ambrosia, nectar, ghee, sugar, or most ethereal of all, the smoke from the sacrificial fire

The most processed, the most thoroughly cooked, and the most refined foods seemed to escape corruption. Treated with fire, perishable milk turned into incorruptible ghee; perishable cane juices became incorruptible sugar. Both were golden, the color of the fiery sun itself. Eating ghee and sugar nourished the soul or spirit as well as the body. Right behavior included, for those who were fortunate enough to be able to afford it, choosing these refined foods that did not weigh down the body and soul with coarse, worldly dross.[7]

Refined foods became the symbols of many of the world's great religions: sugar and ghee for Buddhists and Hindus, bread and wine for Christians.

In this scheme, it was only natural that cooking became a metaphor for the purifi-

155

cation of the individual. Perfected by cooking, humans escaped the fate of being 'half baked.' Fifth-century Buddhists described progress toward enlightenment as being like the refining of sugar. Later Indian bodhisattvas in the Mahayana Buddhist tradition had the ability by their appearance, their utterances, their touch, and even their taste to 'cook living beings' bringing them closer to perfection.[8] As a way of summing up his moral and spiritual progress, Rumi, the thirteenth-century Persian poet and philosopher said 'I was raw, I roasted, and I burnt.'[3] Nuns in colonial Mexico used the progress of produce from its arrival at the gate, through the storehouses, processing, and finally cooking into exquisite sweets and sauces as a metaphor for their own spiritual progress from 'raw' novices to holy women.[9]

Refined foods, indeed, even offered the promise of immortality. In an early Vedic text, the protagonist contemplates the bloody carcass of an animal that had been sacrificed to the gods. He says to himself: 'Surely, if I add this (matter) such as it is to my own being, I shall become a mortal carcass, not liberated from evil. Well then, I will cook it with fire.' The narrator continues. 'He cooked it with fire. He made it into the food of immortality. The sacrificial food which is cooked with fire is indeed immortal (or ambrosia).'[10]

Mixing was the second component of refined cuisine. Only by mixing could the ingredients be balanced so that they tempered the bodily humors. These humors, usually three or four, circulated through the body. What was cooked or digested affected the balance of these fluids. That in turn determined the temperament of the individual. By providing the right mix of ingredients the cook could shift a diner's temperament. Any sign of weakness in a king sent Greek and Indian cooks scurrying to prepare meaty broths to enhance his courage, one of the indispensable kingly virtues. A desire for a life of contemplation made Buddhist monks seek out a diet with little meat or alcohol but lots of rice, ghee and sugar.

In Aristotelian theory, at least, virtues, whether moral or intellectual, had to be constantly practiced to be strengthened. One way to do this was by adhering to the right kind of diet, food mixed and cooked in the appropriate way.[11] The cook thus shaded into physician. Both worked to enhance moral as well as physical health. Chinese cooks prepared elaborate dishes that cured as they nourished.[12] The right meals could align the body with seasons and places and hence with transformations of Heaven and Earth. Islamic cooks put together divine medicines, cordials of rose water, pomegranates, egg yolk, saffron, juices of meat, wine, and spices that wafted their aroma, and hence their spirit, for years.[13] European physicians such as Rudolf Glauber pointed to the parallel making dishes and making medicines: 'Vegetables, Animals, and Minerals with the help of any burning Spirit…may be most highly purified, and reduced to the Highest Medicines.'[14]

To be a good cook obviously meant being technically proficient. For much of history, though, to be a good cook meant more than that. It meant rising to the challenge of producing refined cuisine, of giving diners the essence of foods usually concealed by base nature, and of thus facilitating a virtuous life. Their task was simultaneously ethical, aesthetic, and medical. Culinary finesse demonstrated virtue.

Like their confrères the alchemists, cooks shouldered a large moral burden. Cooks in Japanese temples had constantly to be of a 'moral spirit.'[15] Indian Brahmins of the Vedic period had a duty 'to cook the world.'[16] If cooks succeeded in their calling, they could obtain high office and great respect. In Rumi's order of Sufis, the cook could rise to the second highest position. He was responsible for training new initiates who in turn spent the last part of their 1,001 days of community service in the kitchen. Rumi's own cook, Ates baz-i Veli, on his death in 1285 was buried in a mausoleum of red stone that remains a shrine to this day.

In late eighteenth-century Europe, the medical and philosophical foundations of the refined-cooking theory crumbled. Physicians abandoned the humoral theory for modern physiology and nutrition, disciplines that demoted food and digestion to a relatively minor role and said nothing about the behavioral, as opposed to the physical effects of different diets. Chemists and physicists described fire as the movement of molecules not as an element. Philosophers talked about morality as a matter of following moral rules or acting to ensure the greatest good of the greatest number rather than as the practice of virtue.

Eating well ceased to be part of a moral, scientific, economic, and political worldview. It is tempting to see the debates about gastronomy, and about whether there could be a science of taste, that took place at this time as the search for a new justification of refined cuisine now that it could no longer be seen as contributing to the moral standing of the diner. It was now merely an aesthetic matter, food for food's sake.

157

The plain cooking camp

For the plain cooking camp, cooking had nothing to do with perfecting. On the contrary, cooking corrupted and falsified the foodstuffs created pure and perfect by God or nature. Phrases such as 'cooking the books' and proverbs such as 'God sends the meat; the devil sends cooks' echo this suspicion that cooking is a bad thing.[17] In the Western tradition, the first exponents of this minority opinion about cooking were Socrates, the Spartans, and the Stoics. Outside the Western tradition, I suspect the minority view may have been posed about the same time by, for example, Taoists, and later by Zen Buddhists though I have yet to explore this.

Socrates set the tone in the *Republic*. He wanted the citizens of his Republic to dine on simply cooked foods: wheat bread, barley cakes, salt, olives, cheese, boiled vegetables, followed by figs, chickpeas and beans, parched myrtle berries and acorns, not sauces and sweets. When criticized for this he detailed what happened when citizens demanded extravagant dining. The taste for luxury led to avarice. Avarice drained the state coffers (it was widely believed that the amount of wealth in the world was fixed). Empty coffers prompted states to go to war. War bred despots. In short, extravagant dining led to a 'a city with inflammation,' war, and despotism.[18] Like other Greeks, when talking about elaborate feasting Socrates had in mind the Persians, the Greeks' arch enemies. Their emperors were famous for their extravagant feasts that features huge roast joints, sauces, sweets, and undiluted wines, they also served then and for centuries later as the archetype of despots ready to go to war to enrich their coffers. If at first sight, this seems an over-reaction to refined food, it is worth remembering that food was both a scarce resource and the single most important item of consumption.

The Stoic philosophers teased out the individual consequences of a refined diet that paralleled the social consequences Socrates had described. Refined cuisine put humans at the mercy of their passions, or, as we might say, their emotions. Its delicious tastes and aromas, rich sauces and sweets, created an unnatural appetite. Unlike natural appetite that indicated that the body was ready to receive nutritious food, unnatural appetite stimulated the diner to continue eating long after his true needs were satiated.[19] Roman gluttons who indulged themselves in a similar way became stock examples of individuals who had let their passions get the better of them. Down the centuries, authors referred with disdain or mockery to Lucullus, a Roman consul who used his war booty to underwrite his extravagant dining or to Vitellius, a Roman emperor, who stuffed himself at four banquets daily and indulging himself in pike liver, pheasant brain and flamingo tongue. Just as extravagant public feasting caused an 'inflamed' state, so refined cuisine caused a diseased body. 'Are you astounded at the innumerable diseases?' asked the Stoic, Seneca. 'Count the cooks.'[20] It was to be a theme that recurred through the twentieth century. Gandhi argued that 'To be rid of disease it is necessary to do away with fire in the preparation of foods. We must eat everything in its vital state even as animals do.'[21] And Hitler is reported to have said that 'All the sicknesses of civilization are caused by man cooking food.'[22]

To return to the past, the Christian fathers adapted Stoic culinary philosophy to the needs of their faith, initiating a link between Christianity and Stoicism that would be regularly renewed over the centuries. Clement of Alexandria, for example, who wrote a guide to the Christian life in the first century AD, said that the good Christian should eat 'roots, olives, all sorts of green vegetables, milk, cheese, fruits and cooked vegetables of all sorts – but without sauces.' And the meat, he suggested, should be boiled or roasted. A Christian should be 'master and lord not slave of food.'[23] By the Middle Ages, gluttony, the inability to control the appetite was firmly established as one of the seven deadly sins.

Seventeenth- and eighteenth-century Protestants looked to the story of Adam and Eve as justification for a plain diet. In the Garden of Eden, humans lived on fruits and vegetables, God's perfect creations. Cooking became necessary only after the Fall and thus was a consequence of sin. The famous scientist Isaac Newton believed that returning to eating raw foods would be a return to the Golden Age. Live on fruit, he suggested, and 'you will be as innocuous as the [herbivorous] sheep.'[24] John Evelyn,

158

another scientist and contemporary of Newton, sought to simulate the Garden of Eden on the large scale in his vegetable garden and on the small scale on his vegetable plate.

The republican movement in the eighteenth and nineteenth centuries favored Stoic philosophy with its virtues of wisdom, courage, justice and temperance. The Dutch believed that French cuisine would spell death to their political experiment. The French *philosophes* avoided the intimate dinners of the French court and aristocratic houses where cooks embellished food to create unnatural appetites. Instead they haunted the salons whose hosts and hostesses conspicuously did not serve refined cuisine.[25] Similarly many Americans, including Patrick Henry, thought Thomas Jefferson's enthusiasm for French cuisine to be singularly inappropriate. For them the ragouts (rich sauces), fricassees, and mousses of French High cuisine were the contemporary version of Vitellius's pike liver, pheasant brain, and flamingo tongue. Many people believed that Count Brühl, a Saxon nobleman and state bureaucrat, who served up to a hundred dishes, including ragouts, fricassees, and mousses, on the most expensive dinner service ever made to guest lists of as many as three hundred, drained the coffers of the Saxon state.[26] This opened its way to conquest by Frederick the Great of Prussia, a man who knew how to curb his appetite and build a strong state.

The British, in the nineteenth century, thought that children, particularly the children of the well-to-do, needed to be sent to schools and fed in a way that would strengthen Spartan and Stoic values. To fuss with foods seemed an indulgence unworthy of those who were being trained to lead.[27] They received support from nineteenth-century nutritionists who preached that appetite-inflaming stimulants such as spices and vinegar were to be avoided, especially by children. Ideal foods included whole grains boiled as porridge or pudding, or baked as bread, roast or boiled meat, simply boiled vegetables, and fruits. Similarly, to return to mixing as a part of cooking, these same experts argued that mixing foods together was bad for the digestion. It was better to serve meat, starch and vegetables separately on the plate.

It is worth noting that the distinction between refined cuisine and plain cooking did not map on to the distinction between vegetarian and non-vegetarian. There were, and are, many who avoided meat yet dined on the most refined of cuisines. Hindu temple cuisine is an example. When Gandhi experimented with a diet of sprouted wheat, he was abandoning the tradition in which he had grown up for the plain cooking tradition he encountered in England.

Nor does the dichotomy between refined cuisine and plain cooking reflect a dichotomy between delicious food and coarse food. The proponents of refined cuisine have over the centuries relished the tastes of rich sauces and elaborate desserts. But those who favor plain cooking are equally enthusiastic about the taste and texture of whole wheat breads, crisp, fresh apples, and sweet corn rushed straight from the garden for a quick dip in the pot.

What the distinction between refined cuisine and plain cooking does parallel are two different attitudes to the relation between cooking and morality. Those who argued for refined cuisine thought that the manner of cooking itself could actually produce foods that made diners more or less moral. Those who argued for plain food saw virtue as being strengthened by controlling desire for food.

Conclusion

In light of this brief survey, it seems likely that the distinction between refined cuisine and plain cooking explains much about the attitude of entire societies to what we call 'gastronomy.' When the elite in an empire or state believed that refined cuisine enhanced the virtues then gastronomy flourished, as in, say, the Ottoman, Mughal or Safavid empires, or in pre-revolutionary France. When the elite chose plain food in the interests of strengthening self-control, then plain food ruled as in nineteenth-century England and America. On this account the long lament over the (supposed) poor quality of English cooking fails to take into account that this was not simply philistinism.

There were good reasons why many found refined cuisine objectionable. Lurking behind the decision about whether or not to adopt refined cuisine were deeply held beliefs about the distribution of resources in a society and about the relation between food, individual morality and the ideal state. And, I suggest, many contemporary debates about food and morality draw, perhaps unconsciously, on these long-standing themes and arguments about what we do when we cook.

160

Notes

1. For a similar broad definition of cooking, see Symons, Michael, *The Pudding that Took a Thousand Cooks* (Ringwood, Australia: Penguin Books, 1998), ch. 5.
2. For body, soul and spirit in the Mediterranean see Brown, Peter, *The Body and Society*. New York: Columbia University Press, 1988.
3. For the European belief, see Laudan, Rachel, 'Birth of the Modern Diet,' *Scientific American* 238 (2000), pp. 62–67.
4. Quoted by Eugen Weber, *Peasants into Frenchmen: The Modernization of Rural France, 1870–1914* (Stanford: Stanford University Press, 1976), 5-6.
5. Cheyne, George, Essay on Health and Long Life (London, 1725), p. 135.
6. Herodotus, *Skythika* III, 99 quoted in Shaw, B.D., 'Eaters of flesh, drinkers of milk: the ancient Mediterranean ideology of the pastoral nomad' *Ancient Society* 13–14 (1982/3) 5–32, 5.
7. Sabban, Françoise, 'Un Savoir-Faire Oublié: Le Travail du Lait en Chine Ancienne,' Reprinted for private circulation from *Zinbun: Memoirs of the Research Institute for Humanistic Studies*, Kyoto University, 21 (1986), p. 53; Buddhagosa, *The Path of Purification* (California: Shambhala, 1976).
8. Mrozik, Susanne, 'Cooking Living Beings: The Transformative Effects of Encounters with Bodhisattva Bodies,' *Journal of Religious Ethics* (2004), pp. 175–194.
9. Loreto López, Rosalva and Benítez Muro, Ana, *Un Bocado Para Los Ángeles: La Cocina en Los Conventos*. México: Clío, 2000.
10. In the Satapatha Brahmana, a prose how-to text for Vedic religious services probably dating from no later than the eighth century BC and possibly much earlier. I have combined translations from Malamoud, Charles, *Cooking the World: Ritual and Thought in Ancient India* trans. David White

(Delhi: Oxford University Press, 1996), p. 23, and *The Satapatha Brahmana, Part III Sacred Books of the East*, Vol. 41 translated by Julius Eggeling (London, 1894), 6.2.1.9.

11. Sorabji, Richard, *Animal Minds and Human Morals*. Ithaca, NY: Cornell University Press, 1992.

12. Lo, Vivian and Barrett, Penelope, 'Cooking up Fine Remedies: On the Culinary Aesthetic in a Sixteenth-Century Chinese *Materia Medica*,' *Medical History* 49 (2005), pp. 395–422. Roel Sterckx, 'Food and philosophy in early China', in *Of tripod and palate: food, politics and religion in traditional China* ed. Roel Sterckx (London, Palgrave Macmillan, 2005).

13. Peterson, T. Sarah, *Acquired Taste: The French Origins of Modern Cooking* (Ithaca and London: Cornell University Press, 1994), p. 18.

14. Glauber, Rudolf, *A Treatise concerning the Purifying Fire*. Trans. Christopher Packe (London, 1689), p. 1.

15. Yoneda, Soei, *Good Food from a Japanese Temple*. Tokyo: Kodansha International, 1982.

16. Malamoud, Charles, *Cooking the World: Ritual and Thought in Ancient India* trans. David White (Delhi: Oxford University Press, 1996), pp. 23–53.

17. Symons, *Pudding* (1998), p. 98.

18. Quoted by John Wilkins, 'Introduction, Part One,' in John Wilkins, David Harvey and Mike Dobson, eds. *Food in Antiquity* (Exeter, UK: University of Exeter Press, 1995), p. 7.

19. Grimm, Veronika E., *From Feasting to Fasting, The Evolution of a Sin* (London: Routledge, 1996), ch. 2; Albala, Ken, *Eating Right in the Renaissance* (Berkeley and Los Angeles: University of California Press, 2002), pp. 54–56.

20. Seneca, *Ad Lucilium: Epistulae morales*, vol. 3 (London: William Heinemann), 67.

21. Quoted by Stuart, Tristram, *The Bloodless Revolution* (New York: W. W. Norton, 2007), p. 377.

22. Stuart, *Bloodless Revolution* (2007), pp. 47, 439.

23. Grimm, *Feasting to Fasting*, pp. 103–4.

24. Stuart, *Bloodless Revolution* (2007), p. 81.

25. See articles by Jaucourt in Diderot, *Encyclopédie* (Paris, 1751–).

26. Young, Carolin, *Apples of Gold in Settings of Silver* (New York: Simon and Schuster, 2002), ch. 7.

27. Mauriello, Tani, '"Feed Their Vile Bodies . . . Starve Their Immortal Souls": Food as Moral Instructor in Nineteenth-Century Homes and Schools,' this volume.

161

Morality and Servants of Empire: A Look at the Colonial Kitchen and the Role of Servants in India, Malaysia, and Singapore, 1858–1963

Cecilia Leong-Salobir

Foodways is one way of looking at the discourses of race and domesticity in the context of colonialism.[1] It examines the most personal and intimate of colonial relationships, that of the physical nurturing of colonizers by the colonized. Specifically, cookbooks of the Victorian and Anglo-Indian era portrayed colonial attitudes towards servants. These publications perpetuated the myth that native servants were unworthy and sought to teach colonists how to behave toward servants in order to uphold the ideals of Empire. Armies of domestic servants procured, cooked, and served colonizers in the colonial household and in the recreational facilities of the hill stations, clubs, and hotels. And yet for all their efforts, domestic servants in colonial India, Malaysia, and Singapore were seen as dirty and untrustworthy.

While nineteenth- and early-twentieth-century cookbooks and household management manuals for the colonies provided practical help in housekeeping they also reminded British women to maintain appropriate behaviour, as befitting empire builders. Among the recipes and household hints were deliberate attempts at positioning native servants as 'other,' through race and class. The manuals recommended treating native servants as childlike, unworthy, and needing discipline.

Scholars Kenneth Ballhatchet and Simon Dagut attribute this to the notion of 'social distance' in the context of domestic service in the colonial household when servants were engaged in the personal chores of food preparation and other household tasks;[2] colonizers attempted to put physical distance between them and the colonized. Ballhatchet states that the official elite in India regarded themselves as the upper crust. As they were mainly recruited from a middle class that emulated the lifestyle of the landed aristocracy in England they saw themselves being in the highest rank of Indian society and social distance was essential to their authority.[3]

F.A. Steel and G. Gardiner's comprehensive manual on housekeeping in India recommended delegating as much work as possible to the servants so that memsahibs had ample leisure time.[4] They advocated a strictly supervisory role for the memsahibs. Local servants, inept and untrustworthy as they were seen, were to be trained and strictly monitored in their duties and tasks. The cookbooks and manuals also advised guarding against the filthy and dishonest ways of servants. Mrs John Gilpin in her memsahib's guide to cookery in India wrote that when servants were 'unspeakably filthy in their habits' it usually was because the memsahibs had not trained them properly.[5] R. Riddell's nineteenth-century household manual and cookbook for India stated that native servants' faults – laziness and dishonesty – were attributable to the way they were brought up. He however conceded that native servants as well as their European counterparts stole tea, sugar, bread, milk. and paper.[6] 'Eleanor,' author of a cookbook that also promised to be 'a ready help to every wife in India' declared that native servants of all classes often cheated and pilfered their employers' rice, sugar, coffee, and oil. She complained that that the mistress of a house needed to constantly supervise 'the most trifling details' otherwise more quantities of oil, wood, or eggs would be needed.[7]

Swapna M. Banerjee asserts that the British description of native servants perpetuated the European notion of Indians as the 'distant' and 'other' – the latter being primitive, dirty, lazy, physically and mentally inferior.[8] E.M. Collingham holds the view that Britons saw Indians as potential carriers of disease and states that there was anxiety about 'Indian dirt' being 'particularized onto individual servants as potential carriers of deadly germs into the household on their bodies.'[9] She explains that this fear of infection, particularly with the bubonic plague in Bombay in 1896, had encouraged the building of servants' quarters away from the bungalow.

This paper suggests that although the British in colonial India, Malaysia, and Singapore required the services of their domestic servants they were ambivalent toward them. Cookbooks and household manuals of the era reinforce the thinking of the time that native servants were lazy, lying, thieving, and filthy individuals. This thinking directly contradicted the essential services that servants provided in preparing, cooking, and serving food to the colonizers. To diminish the importance of these servies, the servants were held at a 'social distance,' as discussed by Dagut and Ballhatchet.[10] The rapidly growing number of cookbooks and household manuals attempted to promote the values and representations of Empire. These prescriptive publications advocated the supervisory and authoritative role of the memsahibs and attempted to instill notions of how to discipline servants. Effectively the overriding message was that the security of the colonial home was of great importance and its integrity must be guarded zealously. Nevertheless, for all their shortcomings, domestic servants played a crucial role in smooth running of the household and not least for the feeding of the colonizers.

Notes

1. Stoler, pp. 36–37.
2. See Ballhatchet; Dagut, 1997; Dagut, 2000.
3. Ballhatchet, p. 164.
4. F.A. Steel and G. Gardiner, pp. 5–8.
5. Gilpin, p. 2.
6. R. Riddell, p. 6.
7. Eleanor, p. 10.
8. Banerjee.
9. E.M. Collingham, p. 171.
10. Ballhatchet and Dagut.

Bibliography

Ballhatchet, K., *Race, Sex, and Class under the Raj: Imperial Attitudes and Policies and Their Critics, 1793–1905,* London: Weidenfeld and Nicolson, 1980.

Banerjee, S. M., *Men, Women, and Domestics Articulating Middle-Class Identity in Colonial Bengal,* New Delhi: Oxford University Press, 2004.

Collingham, E. M., *Imperial Bodies: The Physical Experience of the Raj, c.1800–1947,* Cambridge: Polity, 2001.

Dagut, S., 'Gender, Colonial 'Women's History' and the Construction of Social Distance: Middle-Class British Women in Late Nineteenth-Century South Africa,' *Journal of Southern African Studies,* vol. 26, no. 3, 2000, pp. 555–572.

Dagut, S., 'Paternalism and Social Distance: British Settlers' Racial Attitudes, 1850s–1890s,' *South African Historical Journal,* vol. 37, 1997, pp. 3–20.

Eleanor, *Gems from the Culinary Art and a Ready Help to Every Wife in India,* Madras: Printed by Hoe and Co. at the 'Premier Press,' 1916.

Gilpin, J. M., *Memsahib's Guide to Cookery in India,* Bombay: A.J. Combridge & Co., 1914.

Riddell, R., *Indian Domestic Economy and Receipt Book; Comprising Numerous Directions for Plain Wholesome Cookery, Both Oriental and English; with Much Miscellaneous Matter Answering for All General Purposes of Reference Connected with Household Affairs, Likely to Be Immediately Required by Families, Messes, and Private Individuals, Residing at the Presidencies or Outstations Bombay.* Printed at the 'Gentleman's Gazette Press', no publisher name given, 1849.

Steel, F. A., and Gardiner, G., *The Complete Indian Housekeeper and Cook: Giving the Duties of Mistress and Servants the General Management of the House and Practical Recipes for Cooking in All Its Branches,* London: William Heinemann, 1898.

Stoler, A., 'Making Empire Respectable: The Politics of Race and Sexual Morality in 20th-Century Colonial Cultures,' in Jan Breman (ed.), *Imperial Monkey Business: Racial Supremacy in Social Darwinist Theory and Colonial Practice,* Amsterdam: VU University Press, 1990.

The Morality of Anti-Picnics

Walter Levy

Picnics and anti-picnics

It's taken for granted that picnics are intrinsically pleasurable and meant for sharing food. Some picnics are not. I call these anti-picnics because they turn expectations topsy-turvy, often for the purpose of arguing or illustrating a moral precept. These anti-picnics are usually constructs of writers, poets, and dramatists who have used the picnic setting as a context for transgressive behaviors such as disobedience, lust, hate, war, murder, and death. If you have ever thought of anti-picnicking, and chances are that you have not, please bear with me while I explain.

The earliest definition of picnic, *piquenique*, that I've found is 1692. The word denotes that picnickers each bring a share of the meal. There's no mention of pleasure, but I presume that this is implicit.

Jean-Jacques Rousseau recalls, in his *Confessions*, that he dined in his rooms *en piquenique* with the Abbé Condillac, *circa* 1747, and that they enjoyed discussing their writing projects on friendly terms. Is there moral edification here? Perhaps? More likely it was helpful to share the cost of a meal when you're hard-up. Rousseau's other picnic adventures take place out-of-doors, and it is here, as romantic moralist, that he claimed that the simplicity of the natural world was a restorative for the ravages of civilization.

When he picnicked *en plein air*, Rousseau fondly recalled that these were moments of beauty, love, and innocence that were indelible to him. He scarcely mentions food, and when he does, it's coffee and cherries. The coffee, he remembered, was made for Madame Françoise-Louise de Warens, his mentor and lover, at a campfire. Rousseau boiled the water, and he was twenty-four years old and pleased to serve. The moment in 1745 was vivid, and he remembered it into his old age: 'Everything seemed to conspire to the day's happiness. There was no dust, the streams were full. A little fresh wind shook the leaves. The air was clear and the horizon free of clouds. Serenity prevailed in the heavens, as it prevailed in our hearts.' (232) According to Rousseau the power of nature is translated into love, healthy-mindedness, and good moral character.

Another picnic occurred when Rousseau, about sixteen years old, helped two young women in trouble along a mountain road, and they asked him to accompany them on a picnic. After eating, the three played games and flirted. Rousseau climbed a cherry tree and with great amusement harvested the ripe fruits for dessert: 'Once Mlle. Galley presented such a mark with her apron held out and her head back and I aimed so well, that I dropped a bunch into her bosom. How we laughed!' (135)

Decorum prevailed and the day passed in the 'utmost decency,' though seething sexuality remained below the surface. The ripe cherries express high moral sensibility and good behavior, though the sexual allusion is potent: Why are not my lips cherries? 'I said to myself. How gladly would I throw them there, for both of them, if they were!' (135)

Looking over these examples, and taking Rousseau at his word, picnics are pleasurable and conducive to good moral behavior. In fact, it's a good bet that you have tucked away fond memories of a picnic, and that this has bolstered your sense of self and character for the better. I know that this is the case for me. But this is not always so. For anti-picnics are illustrative of immorality: Think disobedience, lust, hate, gluttony, murder, death, and heartbreak.

Anti-picnicking

Who among us thinks of picnic immorality? I confess that I do, and I've got examples. To begin, there is Barbara Kingsolver's anti-picnic in *The Poisonwood Bible* (1998). It's the story chronicling the mis-adventures of the Price family who leave Bethlehem, Georgia, to spend a tumultuous year in the soon to be independent Belgian Congo in 1959. They are emotionally, spiritually, and financially unprepared. The father, Nathan, a Baptist minister, is slow in adapting to local culture and the alien environment. For the great glory of Christ, he attempts converting the locals but fails in the process, even losing his family – Orleanna Price, and their five daughters.

Here are the incongruities of Kingsolver's anti-picnic: Reverend Price's picnic occurs on July 4th, but he celebrates the day as Easter Sunday. With unthinking racial arrogance, Price decides that since no one will ever know or care about real time in the Congo, July is as good a time to celebrate Easter as March or April. The day is typically hot, hazy, and a monstrously humid. The picnic, really a church supper, is held on the banks of Kwilu River that smells of mud and dead fish. A community baptism is proposed, but there are crocodiles in the river and the villagers will not enter the water. The shared food is Southern fried chicken which Orleanna makes from scratch, a gesture that seriously depletes the family's store of food. The locals enjoy the pleasures of the flesh, but do not come forward for spiritual redemption. Nathan is disappointed, ignores the family's sacrifice, and offers no thanks to Orleanna. As his daughter Rachel says, 'The picnic was festive, but not at all what he'd had in mind. It was nothing in terms of redemption' (49). Missionary zeal prevents him from knowing that his mission is failing.

In short, Kingsolver's picnic is really an anti-picnic. Deftly she demonizes the picnic mystique: pleasure is subsumed by missionary earnestness, zeal overpowers common sense, and understanding is undercut by racial colonial antagonism. What good can come of this? The father is lost, one child is dead of snake bite, and Orleanna leads her four daughters out of the jungle for home and a vague promise of restoring harmony. As they leave, the jungle obliterates their trail and erases their presence. Kingsolver's allusion to Darwinian Theory is unavoidable When Reverend Price shouts '*Tata is bangala!*', he means 'The word of Christ is beloved!' Locals, however, know that *bangala* means jungle poison ivy, and what they hear is '*Tata* Jesus is poisonwood!' (70) The moral is that life in the jungle is no picnic.

Disobedience

My reading of Genesis suggests that picnicking began on the Sixth Day, and that it was good. How long the picnic lasted is uncertain, but it did come to a crashing halt. The primal pair was expelled through the gates of Eden onto the plains below. Though Genesis is not explicit on the subject, John Milton is sure that Eve and Adam picnicked, though he does not use the word, and dined:

> Under a tuft of shade that on a green
> Stood whispering soft, by a fresh fountain side
> They sat them down, and after no more toil
> Of thir sweet Gardning labour then suffic'd
> To recommend coole Zephyr, and make ease
> More easie, wholsom thirst and appitite
> More grateful, to thir Supper Fruits they fell,
> Nectarine Fruits which compliant boughes
> Yeilded them, side-long as they sat recline
> On the soft downie Bank damasket with flours. (IV, 325–334)

167

Alas, the picnic turned bad when Eve wandered off for some forbidden fruit. You've heard the story, I know, but probably not considered the picnic aspect and the moral consequences of rash acts. It was disobedience that ended in the picnic in Eden.

Lust

Lust is no stranger at anti-picnics, and is the main event at William Inge's *Picnic*, (1953) a play about the sexual awakening of Madge Owens. *Picnic*, later revised as *Summer Brave* (1962), is the story of what leads up to the last holiday of summer, a Labor Day picnic in a small Kansas town. It focuses on Madge Owens, who at eighteen years old is beautiful, innocent, and aware of her unfulfilled sexuality. The climax of the play is a seduction scene in which Hal Carter, a young man of dubious character and great sexual power makes his move to make love to Madge. The moment comes when Madge arrives to drive Hal to the community picnic; he suggests otherwise, and drawing her near takes her in his arms and kisses her passionately. Madge is equally aroused, and the picnic be dammed, she returns his passion. If there is a moral issue here, it is not evident. Madge is ready, willing, and able. As the curtain falls signaling the end of Act Two, the picnic and the fired chicken that was to be the picnic meal remains in the car, uneaten. The picnic is a non-event, and when Act Three begins the next day Madge is a new woman, pleased with herself and ready to take on the world. She packs a suitcase and leaves relative safety of Kansas for a more difficult life elsewhere.

The Hollywood film version of *Picnic* (1955) directed by Joshua Logan and with a screenplay by Daniel Taradash, makes the picnic episode obligatory. There is social conviviality and food that slowly leads the action to the seduction episode, which is played out step-by-passionate-step as Madge (Kim Novak) and Hal (William Holden) dance by the light of holiday lanterns. It's a steamy dance that is offered as a metaphor for love-making. The darling 1950's moral attitude toward sex prevails, but we all know what happens when picnics turn libidinous and passionate behavior rules.

The choice of September for a picnic echoes the picnic episode at Kittiwar Island in Dubose Heyward's novel *Porgy* (1925). Though the novel is neglected, the picnic scene is most remembered as the central scene (2,ii) in the opera *Porgy and Bess* (1935), almost always associated with George Gershwin. *Porgy*, the novel, is skimpy on food but not steamy sexuality. Bess, a gaunt, drug-addicted woman, lusts for Crown, even though he is brutal and on the run from being arrested for murder.

Heyward's plan for Porgy is that it is a spring/fall romance between irreconcilable lovers. The September picnic at Kittiwar Island (Part IV, 111–129) contrasts Porgy's innocent nature with Bess's passionate sexuality and promiscuity. The excuse for the picnic is the annual church outing by Charleston's African-American community, including all the denizens of Catfish Row. They march to the wharf parading joyously and carrying a banner that proclaims them all 'The Sons and Daughters of Repent Ye Saith the Lord.' (111) You can't get more morally uplifting than this.

Upon reaching Kittiwar Island, a picnic committee prepares lunch, while picnickers wade in the 'cool thunder of the sea and the unremitting hum of sand, as tireless winds scooped it from the dunes and sent it in low, flat-blown layers across the hard floor of the beach.' Porgy, at a disadvantage on the beach, patiently sits caring for the small children who are sleeping beneath the palms. He hums softly to quiet them. Meanwhile, Bess wanders off to find palmetto leaves for a picnic cloth and suddenly is accosted by Crown, who has been hiding on the island. At once, she is conflicted by her resolve to live a new life with Porgy. She is afraid of Crown and attracted to him at the same time. Heyward's prose is florid, but it's still a good scene: 'His body was naked to the waist, and the blue cotton pants that he had worn on the night of the killing had frayed away to is knees. He bent slightly forward. The great muscles of his torso flickered and ran like the flank of a horse. His mall wicked eyes burned, and he moistened his heavy lips.... "I seen yuh land," he said, "an' I been waitin' fuh yuh…"' (119) Bess tries to fight her passion but she cannot. 'I know yuh ain't change,' he said, 'Wid yuh an' me it always goin' tuh be de same. See?' (121) With that, he snatches her body, Bess inhales deeply 'and sent out a wild laugh out against the walls of the clearing.' (121) Bess does not return to the picnic until it is evening, just before the boat leaves to return to Charleston. On the trip home Porgy asks if Bess has seen Crown. After some hesitation, she answers truthfully and tells Porgy that Crown will come for her in October when the cotton comes to town. What the picnic at Kittiwar suggests is Porgy's loss of innocence. Bess's life is tawdry and the picnic undermines whatever shreds of good intentions she has. Bess may love Porgy, but she lusts for Crown. In the opera, Heyward and Gershwin keep Porgy in Catfish Row to await his doom. Bess goes to the picnic with the church crowd. Porgy hunkers down at home. In any event, the picnic is a disaster for Porgy, and he never recovers.

John O'Hara takes picnic sharing to an extreme of sorts by serving-up his protagonist as picnic fare. No it's not cannibalism. Instead, 'A Few Trips and Some Poetry' is a story about a picnic in which the pleasure of sharing is sexual. O'Hara's picnic-sex episode provides a memory that lasts a lifetime. O'Hara's sardonic sense of humor has it that Jim, the narrator, and Isabel Barley, his sporadic lover, make love on a picnic table. Long-time friends who share passion without compassion, pleasure but not love, Isabel Barley turns off the main road and drives along a dirt road to a picnic ground furnished with rough tables and benches, a small bandstand. Without discussion, Isabel prepares for making love: 'I don't want to lose you entirely,' she says matter-of-factly. Not caring for spontaneity, Isabel says 'When we're really ready I'll lie on a picnic table.' (119) Jim asks if this is wise but Isabel has it figured out, and she gets out of the car and spreads herself on the table. Taking Rousseau at his word, she sardonically says, 'Back to nature.' (120) No food is required: none is served.

169

Hate

Sylvia Plath's idea of trashing her father, Otto Plath, is to picnic amidst the ruins of his memory. 'The Colossus' (1967), a precursor to the better-known poem 'Daddy,' reveals Plath's hate for her dead father by staging a metaphorical picnic in her mind. The site is anti-picnic – a fragmented landscape, filled with chunks of a fallen statue, which gives the poem its name. The ruins suggest Plath's turmoil and inability to deal with her hatred of her father who she felt abandoned her when he committed suicide years before. As a result, the picnic is hateful and horrific. The ruins are antithetical to a picnic on the grass; the mood is black, and the imagery unpleasant. Even the air is suffused with the smell of Lysol disinfectant, Plath's attempt to convey the sense that memories of her father need to cleansed and expunged. What Plath needed in real life was a joyful picnic, but all she could muster was an unpleasant picnic in the unrestful cemetery of her mind.

Murder and death

On Tuesday, July 6, Clyde Griffiths takes Roberta Alden to Grass Lake for a day picnicking and rowing. Roberta, who is pregnant, wants to marry Clyde, but he is determined to murder Roberta, so that he can freely court Sondra Finchley, a rich young woman who has taken him up. The couple is operating at cross purposes: as

Clyde looks for a secluded place to drown Roberta, who cannot swim, she looks for a perfect picnic landing. When they do find a picnic spot, they share sandwiches spread on newspaper, but what they eat is not disclosed or necessary to know. What is important is the impending murder, and Dreiser's interest is to disclose Clyde's increasing moral quandary of guilt and premeditated murder. Clyde's angst is partially mitigated, for as luck has it, he accidentally capsizes the boat and Roberta drowns. But Clyde's picnic ends badly, for he arrested, charged and comes to a bad end facing an unsympathetic jury of his peers. Dreiser's title *The American Dream* (1925) is scathing satire of American penchants for bettering themselves and rising in the world. It's a send-up of Horatio Alger Jr.'s life-is-a-picnic heroes, young men who work hard, think good thoughts, do good, believe in Providence, and get a lucky break. Dreiser's picnic on Grass Lake purposely contravenes assumptions that picnicking is good and joyful. Clyde Griffiths' mind is a conflict mass ablaze with the pros and cons of murder. This is not standard picnic fare and a topsy-turvy enactment of cold-hearted selfishness.

Joyce Carol Oates' *Black Water* (1992) is a picnic mix of gluttony, alcoholism, seduction and death which transpires at a July 4th picnic. *Black Water* is historical fiction based on the accidental drowning of MaryJo Kopeckne in a car driven off of a bridge at Chappaquiddick Island by Senator Edward Kennedy in 1968. The July picnic is used as the antithesis of the national holiday, and among the novel's themes is how degraded American national holidays have become. The plot deftly reveals the *carpe diem* of picnics as we watch the sexual selfishness of the politically powerful US Senator and his seduction of Kelly, a woman young enough to be his daughter. The holiday is described sardonically: 'It was the Fourth of July. A meaningless holiday now but one Americans all celebrate, or almost all Americans celebrate. Rocket red glare, bombs bursting in air. Which is how you know, isn't it – the flag is still there.' (136)

Though they share a kiss, the Senator and Kelly never get to make love, though there is adultery in their hearts. As with Clyde Griffiths, the moral issue of the picnic hinges on death, in this case an alcohol-induced accident that causes the Senator's car to speed off a bridge into the black water from which the novel takes its name. Alas, the Senator saves himself and makes no attempt to save Kelly. It's selfish, and for Oates the moral equivalent of murder. As metaphor, the black water is America, and like Lizzie Borden, Oates has taken an axe to the July 4th picnic psyche. The backyard barbeque food suggests affluence and gluttony: 'slabs of marinated tuna, chicken pieces swabbed with Tex-Mex sauce, raw red patties of ground sirloin the size of pancakes. Corn on the cob, buckets of potato salad and coleslaw and bean salad and curried rice, quarts of Haagen-Dazs passed around with spoons.' (138) It's also unappetizing, when you realize that it is all described in a flashback while Kelly is cramped and pinned in a small rented car filling with black water waiting for a rescue that never happens. Thus ends the anti-picnic. Though Oates is not a moralist, it seems implicit that when one seizes the day, there is a price to pay.

Heartbreak

Tennessee Williams thrived on bizarre behavior, and *A Clear Day for Creve Coeur* (1979) is so anti-picnic that it ends the action before the picnic begins. The action concerns Bodey Bodenhaven's attempt to match her brother, a beer-drinking, overweight, no-neck monster (of the kind Williams satirized in *Cat on a Hot Tin Roof*), with her roommate, Dorothea Gallaway, called Dotty, a name that puns on her character. Bodey is set to sacrifice Dotty to her brother's crudity at a picnic in an amusement park where she will supply such staple picnic foods as fried chicken and deviled eggs. As Bodey explains to Dotty, 'I've wrapped up the picnic. It's nice and cool at Creve Coeur Lake and the ride on the open-air streetcar is lickety-split through green country and there's flowers you can pull of the bushes you pass. It's a fine excursion. We'll say out till it's close to dark and (55) and the fireflies – fly. I will slip away and Buddy will be alone with her on the lake shore. He will smoke no smelly cigar. He will just respectfully hold her hand and say – "I love you, Dotty. Please be mine," not meanin' a girl in a car parked up on Art Hill – for the long run of life' (56). It's all a garish pastiche of floundering character locked in a world of frenzy and bad taste. The picnic promises to be a moment of despair for Dotty, but Williams' sardonic humor keeps us from it, though there is no doubt of its outcome. The play's title is a pun on the French *crève-coeur* which means heartbreak.

War

Fernando Arrabal's Absurdist play *Picnic on the Battlefield* (1967) is meant to dispel the cliché that life is a picnic. Working against the grain, Arrabal trashes picnics because they represent good, friendship, love, parental affection, and sharing food. When Monsieur and Madame Tépan, the well-meaning bumbling parents of Zapo, a soldier at the front, arrive with a basket of food, the battle is in progress. Zapo is alone and crawling on his stomach, an allusion to the adage that an army travels on its stomach. After the perfunctory greetings, Zapo says to them: 'I'm sorry, but you really must go. You can't come into a war unless you're a soldier.' Mom and Dad are insistent and M. Tépan snaps back 'I don't give a damn, we came here to have a picnic with you in the country and to enjoy our Sunday....' Mom chimes in, 'I've prepared an excellent meal, too. Sausage, hard-boiled eggs – you know, how you like them! – ham sandwiches, red wine, salad, cakes.' Giving in to this innocent but dotty plan, Zapo says, 'All right, let's have it your way. But if the Captain comes he'll be absolutely furious. Because, he isn't at all keen on us having visits when we're at the front. He never stops telling us: "discipline and hand-grenades are what's wanted in a war, not visits."' (all 113)

So there is a picnic, and when an enemy appears, the battle stops, goodwill prevails and the Tépans share their food. For the moment, life is a picnic, and the four dance to the music of a gramophone – until abruptly, they are all shot dead by machine gun fire. Their bodies add to the litter of the picnic and advertise the stupidity of war, which in Arrabal's scheme suggests that the play itself is an anti-picnic basket.

I began with Jean-Jacques Rousseau's wonderful description of picnics which he confessed to carry with him in memory, never forgetting the sharing, pleasure, and goodness of the events. But as I've explained others substituted the positive picnic elements for the negative elements, making what I called the anti-picnic. In the works of Kingsolver, Milton, Inge, Heyward, O'Hara, Plath, Dreiser, Oates, Williams, and Arrabal, the joyous picnic is subverted and turned inside out. Instead of good there is evil, instead of love there is hate, instead of peace there is war, heartbreak, murder, gluttony. The anti-picnic is a counterpoint to what is expected – and food for thought.

Works cited

Arrabal, Fernando, 'Picnic on the Battlefield.' Trans. Barbara Wright, *Guernica and Other Plays* (New York: Grove Press, 1967).

Baring, Muarice, 'Caligula's Picnic', *Diminutive Dramas* (London: Constable and Compay, Ltd., 1911).

Dreiser, Theodore, *An American Tragedy* (New York: The Library of America, (1925), 2003).

Gardner, Alexander, 'A Pic-Nic Party at Antietam [Bridge], Virginia, 22 September, 1862', *Photographic Incidents of the War: Gardner's Gallery* (Washington, D.C.: Gardner's Gallery, 1862–1865).

Heyward, DuBose, *Porgy* (New York: George H. Doran Company, 1925).

Inge, William, 'Picnic', *Four Plays* (New York: Grove Press, 1958).

Kingsolver, Barbara, *The Poisonwood Bible: A Novel* (New York: HarperCollins, 1998).

Milton, John, *Paradise Lost*, ed. Roy Flannagan (Boston: Houghton Mifflin, 1998).

O'Hara, John, 'A Few Trips and Some Poetry' in *And Other Stories* (New York: Random House, 1968).

Oates, Joyce Carol, *Black Water* (New York: Dutton, 1992).

Plath, Sylvia, 'The Colossus', *The Colossus* (New York: Alfred A. Knopf, 1967).

Rousseau, Jean-Jacques, *The Confessions*, trans. J.M. Cohen (New York: Penguin Books, 1954).

Rousseau, Jean-Jacques, 'Livre Quatrième [Picking Cherries with Mlles. Graffenried and Galley]', *Les Confessions*, illus. Maurice Leloir (Paris: H. Launette & Cie, 1889).

Williams, Tennessee, *A Lovely Sunday for Creve Coeur* (New York: New Directions, 1980).

How the Judged became the Judge: the Glutton, the Voluptuary, and the Epicure in Early Gastronomic Literature

Llio Teleri Lloyd-Jones

Connected to the fundamental emotions of desire and guilt, the glutton stands as one of the most flawed and human of characters. Rooted in the bodily process and proximal senses, he is physical rather than cerebral. The eighteenth century may be viewed as a period that created the foundations for our modern culinary world: the development of printed receipt books, the ascendancy of French cuisine, and the birth of the restaurant. This paper looks at the relationship between the glutton and the epicure, citing the birth of gastronomic literature within the matrix of these players.

One of the most obvious sources of moral judgement attached to culinary consumption must be religion – specifically Christianity – as gluttony is one of the deadly sins, the reason for man's fall from the Garden of Eden. Eve's moral lapse was through culinary temptation, a sensory experience that initiated bodily awareness. The moral compass is portrayed in opposition to the desires of the physical body. The Gospel of Luke tells of the rich glutton who 'fared sumptuously every Day' and 'a certain beggar named Lazarus' who was 'desiring to be fed with the crumbs which fell from the rich man's table.' When the rich man found himself 'tormented in this Flame,' 'he cried and said Father Abraham, have mercy on me, and send Lazarus, that he may dip the tip of his Finger in Water, and cool my Tongue.'[1] Abraham replied 'remember that thou in thy Life receivedst thy Good Things, and likewise Lazarus comforted, and thou are tormented.'[2] This biblical parable demonstrates how incompatible overindulgence is with moral virtue; the glutton is denied access to heaven.

While religions may regulate eating through fasting and feasting, the true reality of the prohibition is problematic.[3] Stewart Lee Allen has highlighted the paradox of gluttony as 'the evil lies not in overindulging during dinner but in focusing on earthly pleasures instead of the will of God.'[4] Gluttony, as a sin therefore, is not simply a case of excessive eating but the loss of focus as the body is given over to sensory pleasure.

This fine line of distinction is echoed within the realm of sexual pleasure; simultaneously integral to the human race but socially and religiously moderated through mores that castigate voracity and insatiability. The similarity between gluttony and lust are considered by Henry Fielding's sensuous slave Tom Jones:

That what is commonly called Love, namely, the desire of satisfying a voracious Appetite with a certain Quantity of delicate white human flesh, is by no means that Passion for which I here contend. This is indeed more properly called Hunger; and as no Glutton is ashamed to apply the Word Love to his Appetite, and to say he LOVES such and such Dishes; so may the lover of this kind, with equal Propriety say, he HUNGERS after such and such Women.[5]

The moral quality of these activities is dependent upon the inner psychology of the perpetrator. The distinction between virtuous eating and gluttony are therefore vague and changeable, and the eighteenth century displayed confusion between the terms such as glutton, epicure, voluptuary, and gourmand. Defined by subtle differences within a fluid morality of consumption and judgement these terms express the contradictory opinions toward culinary culture. This paper hopes to shed light on these terms and suggest the reasons for the distinctions; where does immoral behaviour end and gastronomy begin?

Grimod de la Reynière is often viewed as the father of culinary criticism in the sense that he initiated intense consideration and critical analysis of both produce and restaurants in Paris.[6] Through publications like *Manuel des Amphitryons, Journals des belles et des gourmands*, and *L'Almanache des Gourmands,* spanning the years from 1803 to 1812, Grimod de la Reynière pioneered a new type of journal that was dedicated to guiding the public in culinary matters.[7] Interestingly, this guidance was solely focused upon consumption and commercial enterprises within the Parisian culinary world avoiding the physical production of the kitchen that already existed in receipt books. Reynière considered his position toward a cook as that between a theoretician and a practitioner, highly distinct and yet symbiotic.[8] He instigated the *Jury Dégustateur,* at which:

174

> The legitimations are tasted in a large mechanism [*appareil*] and with rigourous fairness; opinions are gathered according to appetites: the whole trial is recorded; and it is when the results are in that the contestants [*prétandans*] get honourable mention in l'Almanach des Gourmands.[9]

His approach was part science, part art, and part diplomacy as group opinions were formed around the dining table. Within this process involved the translation of personal taste to an objective qualitative judgement as though platonic ideals of such dishes could be found. British journals followed Reynière's example, if tentatively, and *The Epicure's Almanack* was published in 1815.[10] Meant as a 'Compendium of Epicurean Topography' *The Epicure's Almanack* was a simplified version of Reynière's publication, choosing to review restaurants, chop-houses, and ordinaries 'with a small section on provisions at the end of the book.'[11]

Writers such as Thomas Walker and Launcelot Sturgeon wrote culinary essays, the former in epistolary journal form and the latter in a published book of essays.[12] To consider why such publications appeared in celebration and discussion of the gourmand's life at the beginning of the nineteenth century is an interesting question. The rise of culinary literature must be put in context of the moral notions of culinary consumption to understand where these authors stand upon the matrix of the glutton and gastronome.

Firstly, it is important to consider the relevance of corpulence within the character of the glutton. Although modern minds would instantaneously connect an overweight body to culinary overindulgence and subsequent illness, eighteenth century minds did not.[13] Stoutness, according to Roy Porter, was 'esteemed as the mark of the wealthy: there was no honour in poverty, but amplitude was appreciated.'[14] Porter considers the portrayal of John Bull, the English patriot in print, as an example of the national prejudice for fat over thin.[15] Corpulence was a symbol of health, success, social standing and the sign of one's capacity for leisure. Contemporary writers sometimes considered the glutton as physically malnourished; the body was under siege from such large amounts of food. The glutton's system was overloaded and the excess food extinguished the heat that aided digestion.[16] Therefore the glutton was not in a healthy state, however, the physical mass of the person did not necessarily betray their indulgences.

The following poem 'The Glutton,' published in 1772, gives a portrayal of such a sinner:

> Tom Guzzle, an ignorant, impudent sinner,
> Having forc'd himself into Sir John's for dinner
> On seeing a buttock of beef, on the table,
> Fell like a swine, and gorg'd what he was able.
> 'Here's cut and come again, Sir' Said the impudent knave;
> When the good-natur'd Knight, with a countenance grave,
> Cry'd 'Cut on if you please, you son of a whore,
> 'But I'm d——d if you come again here anymore.'[17]

175

'Tom Guzzle,' introduced as an all-round sinner and lacking any social graces, barged his way onto the table of 'Sir John.' The glutton in this narrative is one who takes what he does not deserve, what does not belong to him. The glutton here eats others' food, a misanthropic act considering the early modern attitude to resources as finite within the world.[18] Any overeater is in fact stealing from the communal concept of food stores. The character of 'Tom Guzzle' lives for the moment, following sensory gratification. In the first edition of his dictionary, Samuel Johnson defines the glutton as 'one who indulges himself too much in eating' but also secondarily 'one eager of anything to excess.'[19] The glutton is indiscriminate in terms of the pleasures that he chooses. George Eliot considered herself 'in the same predicament with books as a glutton with his feast, hurrying through one course that I may be in time for the next and so not relishing or digesting either; not a very elegant illustration.'[20] For Eliot, the glutton's desire to consume all diminishes the level of satisfaction; in line with her culinary counterpart, she is compelled to consume.

In *The Revolutions of modesty*, the author wrote how 'the Glutton crammed, and out of Breath before his first Service is over, knows no farther Desire.'[21] In comparison, 'the Voluptuary tastes of every Dish, takes indeed but a little of each; Thus by saving himself in particulars, he profits of the whole.'[22] The 'voluptuary' practices discrimination and taste upon the surface of the dining table therefore being defined against the ignorance of the glutton. Within the shadow of the Enlightenment, the voluptuary could be viewed as the enlightened glutton; *The Revolutions of modesty* goes on to state that the 'rational Voluptuary is always attentive to the secret Voice of his expanding Senses. That on one Hand he may better distinguish the Summons of genuine Pleasure: and on the other, that the Senses may be the better prepared to receive it.'[23] Within this characterisation, the voluptuary has an education or a considered method for the best practice.[24] Whereas a glutton is slave to his senses, the voluptuary is 'always attentive to the secret Voice of his expanding Senses.'[25] However this difference does not rescue the voluptuary from the pejorative. The wonderfully named, Vicesimus Knox, wrote that the voluptuary 'endeavours to render the whole of his existence one uninterrupted state of sensual indulgence.'[26] The voluptuary is characterised as a pleasure-seeker, whether culinary or not, he searches for sensory stimulation. Knox, considered the voluptuary one of 'the greatest foes to pleasure: for their eagerness to grasp, they strangle and destroy it' mirroring the physical haste of the glutton.[27] Similar to the narrative of Tom Guzzle, the voluptuary can be sociopathic, destroying pleasure for all. However, the voluptuary offends Knox on a more theological level:

> To be lovers of pleasure more than lovers of God, the giver of every comfort, argues a disposition either foolishly thoughtless, or basely ungrateful. It prevents all consideration of the causes for which, it is reasonably to be concluded such a creature as man was placed in society.[28]

Whereas gluttony was described as 'a mere effort of the appetite,' epicurism was defined against it as 'a refined and discriminating taste.'[29] Similar to the discrimination practiced by the voluptuary, however, the epicure seems focused upon pleasures of the palate. According to Launcelot Sturgeon, the epicure 'possesses a profound acquaintance with the rules of art in all the most approved schools of cookery; and an enlightened judgment on their several merits, matured by long and sedulous experience.'[30] William Kitchiner, of the successful *Cook's Oracle* and a contemporary of Sturgeon, wrote:

> In the liberal acceptation of the term epicure, and as I use it, it means only the person who relished his food cooked according to scientific principles, so

prepared that the palate is delighted, rendered of easy solution in the stomach, and ultimately contributing to health; exciting him, as an animal, to the vigorous enjoyment of those recreations and duties, physical and intellectual, which constitute the happiness and dignity of his nature. [31]

It is interesting to note the use of phrases such as 'scientific principles,' 'physical and intellectual,' and 'dignity' that would never accompany the character of the glutton. Kitchiner's appreciation of 'scientific principles' stems from an understanding of the production of food that then legitimises his considerable pleasure in its consumption. Considered and informed, the epicure – like 'the rational voluptuary' – is in control of his senses, focusing and regulating them for the occasion.

As *The Wit's Magazine* recorded in *The New Anatomy*:

A glutton's brains fly to his nose before dinner, drop into the palate of his mouth at dinner-time, and afterwards descend to his belly, where they sleep for several hours, till the fumes of the kitchen again call them up to their first station.[32]

The glutton's body and brain is centred upon culinary pleasure; his brain, subservient to the senses, follows the parts of the body that are stimulated. The glutton's reactions are involuntary, he does not seem in control of his experiences. Although this is a humorous article it clearly depicts the glutton as physiologically different from the ordinary person, a theme that re-occurs whether glutton, epicure, or voluptuary. Sturgeon wrote that the epicure 'is not only endowed with a capacious stomach and an insatiate appetite, but with a delicate susceptibility in the organs of degustation.'[33] From the gluttonous to the epicurean, to be a culinary character means to have a specific physiology, the body has to be built for such sensory stimulation. The culinary character is therefore predestined; although training and education create the epicure, the physical configuration of the body must correspond. This point was highlighted in detail in Jean-Anthelme Brillat-Savarin's *Physiology of Taste* first published in 1825:

There are individuals who have evidently come into the world destined to see badly, to walk badly, or to hear badly, because they are born short-sighted, lame, or deaf, so why should there not be others who are predisposed to any unusually acute perception of certain sensations?[34]

The definition of such terms as voluptuary and epicure is problematic for a modern reader but there is evidence to show that contemporaries found difficulty also. Grimod de la Reynière, father of gastronomic literature, wrote:

If the *Dictionary of the Academy* is to be believed, *gourmand* is a synonym for glutton or greedy, as *gourmandise* is gluttony. In our opinion this definition is inexact; the words gluttony and greed should be reserved for the characteriza-tion of intemperance and insatiability, while the word gourmand has, in polite society, a much less unfavourable interpretation, one might even say a nobler one altogether.[35]

In England a decade after Brillat-Savarin, Lancelot Sturgeon, highlighted his 'solemn protest against the indiscriminate application of the terms *Epicurism* and *Gluttony*; which are but too commonly applied synonymously.'[36] William Kitchiner wrote that 'the term gourmand, or epicure, has been strangely perverted; it has been conceived synonimous [sic] with a gluttony.'[37] Reynière, Kitchiner, and Sturgeon are culinary authors and therefore careful to define their interests against that of the glut-ton; however, the appearance, development, and subsequent success of their work, as well as that of Thomas Walker and *The Epicure's Almanack* suggests that they were not the only people in search of such a distinction. In comparison to the gastronomic authors who are concerned with self-definition, a letter to *The Connoisseur* addresses the issue from outside of the nascent discipline:

> Indeed, as the politeness of the *French* language has distinguished every glut-ton by the title of *Bon Vivant*, and the courtesy of our own has honoured their beastly gluttony by the name of *Good Living*, the epicure thinks to eat and drink himself into your good opinion, and recommend himself to your esteem by an exquisite bill of fare.[38]

This elitism of French vocabulary is interpreted as a smokescreen behind which the glutton hides. Such nomenclature carried with it the cultural capital of the estab-lished French *haute cuisine* and the more general fashionability of French culture.[39] Yet, although noting the staunchly negative reaction of the writer above, the quota-tion suggests that the question of definitions within the matrix of virtuous eating and gluttony was of public interest.

The existence of this variety of nouns suggests that parts of society accepted the notion of a culinary character. Geraldine Endsor Jewsbury wrote in her diary that 'The dinner was handsomely achieved, and an old gourmand who was here to dinner declared the sauces were excellent.'[40] The gourmand was an expert to whom others looked for guidance. Geraldine Jewsbury felt the need to include the specific reac-tion of the 'old gourmand' as though her experience is legitimised by his regard. So on a personal level, the culinary character could be a respected member at the dining table.

If the culinary expert was respected in certain domestic spaces, when did he appear in print? Although publications such as *The Gentleman's Magazine* included articles describing pleasure gardens and various eating establishments, they rarely discussed or judged the food and drink that was served.[41] A letter to the editor of *The Connoisseur*, first published in 1754, complained that when the magazine wrote of *White's* 'I was in hopes, that you would not have confined yourself merely to the gaming-table, but have given us an account of the entertainment at their ordinaries.' [42] Comically signed 'T. Savoury' of 'Pye-Corner,' this letter expresses the inadequacies of contemporary journals. The letter suggests that 'a bill of fare from thence would have been full as diverting to your readers as the laws of the game, or a list of their bets. These gentlemen, we are told, are no less adept in the science of eating than of gaming.'[43] *White's* was a well-known coffee-house with a reputable and distinguished clients. Mr T. Savoury continues to suggest that 'as the humours of the body arise from the food we take in, the dispositions of the mind seem to bear an equal resemblance to our places of refreshment.'[44] Prophetic of Brillat-Savarin's aphorism 'tell me what you eat: I will tell you what you are,' the writer considers the link between consumption and personality:

> A friend of mine always judges of a man of taste and fashion, by asking, who is his peruke-maker or his taylor? Upon the same principles, when I would form a just opinion of any man's temper and inclinations, I always enquire, where does he dine?[45]

The Connoisseur also includes a letter that complains about an acquaintance, by the name of Mr Cranwell, that was one of 'a sort of men whose chief pride is good taste (as they call it) and a great stomach: and the whole business of their lives is included in their breakfast, dinner and supper.'[46] In this instance, the glutton/epicure is treated with little respect and instead is mocked 'as ranked among the sons of Folly.'[47] Continuing in a similar derogatory vein, the writer considers 'there are many vices and follies, which men endeavour to hide from the rest of the world: but this, above all others, they take pride in proclaiming.'[48] The complainant is worried by the public nature of his acquaintance's culinary habits; 'as the fox-hunter take delight in relating the incidents of the chase, and kills the fox again over a bowl of punch at night, so the *Bon Vivant* enjoys giving an account of a delicious dinner, and chews the cud of reflection on his exquisite entertainment.'[49] The culinary interest shown is only objectionable because it is given voice and space to perform; processes that are intensely personal are publicised and opened for discussion. These two instances taken from the same journal suggest the contradictory opinions towards culinary culture in eighteenth century Britain; on the one hand is a reader *asking* for culinary reviews and literature, and yet, there is another gentleman desperately trying to escape such discussions.

Returning to the letter about 'Mr Cranwell,' the gentleman writes 'as it was said to *Longinus*, that he was a Walking Library, in the same manner I consider this gentleman as a Walking Larder.'[50] He 'even makes use of his stomach as an artificial memory; and recollects every place he has been at, and every person he has seen, by some circumstances relating to the entertainment he met with.'[51] The man in question seems to be characterised within his body, just as the 'glutton's brains fly to his nose before dinner' similarly his body holds a certain cognitive capacity.'[52]

The letter closes with an anecdote of the writer finding his friend 'with his legs wrapped up in a flannel… he was *taking physick*'.[53] Having enquired what the 'man of pleasure' was reading, he replied:

> Oh, says he, nobody can do me so much good as Mrs Hannah Glasse. I am here going through a course of her *Art of Cookery*, in hopes to get a stomach: for indeed, my dear friend (added he, with tears in his eyes) my appetite is quite gone; and I am sure I shall die, if I do not find something in this book, which I think I can eat.[54]

This quotation highlights one of the emerging facets of British culinary landscape in this period, namely the printed receipt book.[55] As the publication and sales of printed receipt books expanded throughout the eighteenth century, the *public* realm of culinary knowledge grew. Prior to printing, receipts tended to be written by hand and communicated across social networks. The printed receipt book allowed unprecedented dissemination of technical and culinary information. Such books not only presented numerous receipts but also included prefaces that could constitute small culinary manifestos. Prefaces by writers such as Hannah Glasse, William Verral, Ann Cook, and later William Kitchiner would propose certain attitudes toward cooking and eating.[56] Printed receipt books introduced and legitimised culinary discussion. These texts could be viewed as the basis on which the later culinary discourses of restaurants and dining were built. Printed receipt books also promoted both definition and the proliferation of choice. Each book outlining its dish nomenclature, positioning each receipt against the other in a culinary matrix makes each publication an individual dictionary of names and ingredients.

As one of the contributors to *The Connoisseur* had highlighted, the eighteenth century saw a rise in range of eating establishments within the metropolis but lacked anyone to guide the hungry.[57] The restaurant, different from its predecessors by the appearance of 'bills of fare' and practice of choice for the diner, requires that culinary nomenclature is understood by its patrons in order to fulfil their dining desires.[58] The restaurant catered for the *individual* dismissing *table d'hôte* in favour of choice. The culinary landscape of Britain in the late eighteenth century was growing in both language and choice and I would argue that these conditions were integral to the birth of gastronomic reviews and essays.

The development of both the printed receipt book and the restaurant legitimised the language of food. The printed word became the realm of cuisine just as the names of dishes forced themselves onto the public dining tables. The culinary character was no longer just a glutton but also a translator and guide within the world of food and subsequently gastronomic literature began. Ironically the works of Grimod de la Reynière, Walker, Sturgeon, and Kitchiner depended upon the nascent specialist vocabulary and discourse and yet their position within society – as glutton or expert – remained arguably undefined.

Bibliography

Allen, Stewart Lee, *In the Devil's Garden* (Edinburgh: Canongate, 2003).

Appelbaum, Robert, *Aguecheek's beef, Belch's hiccup, and other gastronomic interjections* (Chicago: University of Chicago, 2006).

Brillat-Savarin, Jean-Anthelme, *The Physiology of Taste*, trans. Anne Drayton, (London: Penguin, 1970).

Burke, Victoria E. and Gibson, Jonathan, eds., *Early Modern Women's Manuscript Writing* (Aldershot: Ashgate, 2004).

Burnby, John, *Summer Amusement; or, miscellaneous poems* (London: Printed for J. Dodsley, 1772).

Carden-Coyne, Ana and Forth, Christopher E., eds., *Cultures of the Abdomen* (Basingstoke: Palgrave Macmillan, 2005).

Classen, Constance, *The Color of Angels: Cosmology, Gender and the Aesthetics Imagination* (London: Routledge, 1998).

Coleman, George, *The connoisseur, By Mr Town*, 4 vols. (London: printed for J. Parsons, 1757).

Cook, Ann, *Professed Cookery* (Newcastle upon Tyne: J. White, 1774).

Eliot, George, *The George Eliot Letters*, ed. Gordon S. Haight, 9 vols. (New Haven: Yale University Press, 1954).

Fielding, Henry, *The history of Tom Jones, a foundling*, 6 vols. (London: A. Millar, 1749).

A Lady (Hannah Glasse), *The Art of Cookery made Plain & Easy* (London: 1747).

Jewsbury, Geraldine Endsor, *Selections from the letters of Geraldine Jewsbury to Jane Welsh Carlyle*, ed. A. Ireland (London: Longmans, 1892).

Johnson, Samuel, *A Dictionary of the English Language* (London: 1755).

Kitchiner, William, *Apicius Redivivus; or, the Cook's Oracle* (London: Samuel Bagster, 1817).

Knox, Vicesimus, *Winter Evenings; or lucubrations on life and letters* (London: Printed for Charles Dilly, 1788).

Lehmann, Gilly, *The British Housewife: Cookery Books, Cooking and Society in 18th Century England* (Totnes: Prospect Books, 2003).

MacDonogh, Giles, *A Palate in Revolution* (London: Robin Clark, 1987).

Mennell, Stephen, *All Manners of Food: Eating and Taste in England and France from the Middle Ages to the Present* (Urbana: University of Illinois Press, 1996).

Miller, William Ian, 'Gluttony', *Representations*, 60 (Autumn, 1997), pp. 92–112.

Porter, Roy, *Flesh in the Age of Reason* (London: Allen Lane, 2003).

Reynière, Grimod de la, *Manuel des Amphitryons* (Paris: 1808).

Reynière, Grimod de la, *Journals des belles et des gourmands* (Paris: 1806).

Reynière, Grimod de la, *L'Almanache des Gourmands* (Paris: 1803–1812).

Spang, Rebecca L., *The Invention of the Restaurant: Paris and Modern Gastronomic Culture* (Cambridge, MA: Harvard University Press, 2001).

Sturgeon, Launcelot, *Essays, moral philosophical, and stomachical on the important science of Good-Living* (London: 1822).

Verral, William, *A Complete System of Cookery* (London: 1759).

Walker, Thomas, *The Original* (London: Henry Renshaw, 1835).

Weiss, Allen S. and Schehr, Lawrence R., eds., *French Food: On the table, on the page and in French Culture* (New York: Routledge, 2001).

The Epicure's Almanack; Or, Calendar of good living (London: Longman's & Co., 1815).

The Wit's Magazine; or Library of Momus, 2 vols. (London: Harrion & Co., 1784).

The Revolutions of modesty (London: printed for M. Cooper, 1757).

Notes

1. Luke 16:19–21.
2. Luke 16:25.
3. Mennell, pp. 27–30.
4. Allen, p. 51.
5. Fielding, Book VI p. 225.
6. Weiss in Allen S. Weiss, and Lawrence R. Schehr, eds., p. 66.
7. Grimod de la Reynière, *Manuel des Amphitryons* (Paris: 1808) Reynière, *Journals des belles et des gourmands* (Paris: 1806) Grimod de la Reynière, *L'Almanache des Gourmands* (Paris: 1803–1812).
8. Weiss, p. 55.
9. Grimod de la Reynière quoted in ibid., p. 56.
10. *The Epicure's Almanack*, 1815: 'The manual here offered to the Public, is formed on the Model of a Work published annually in Paris, under the title of *Almanach des Gourmands*', preface.
11. Ibid., preface.
12. See Sturgeon, 1822; and Walker, 1835.
13. As William Ian Miller writes, 'Gluttony for us is the sin of ugliness and ill health, but chiefly ugliness.' 'Gluttony,' *Representations*, 60 (Autumn, 1997), p. 93.
14. Porter, p. 234.
15. Ibid., p. 234.
16. Ken Albala, 'Weight Loss in the Age of Reason', in Forth and Ana Carden-Coyne, and Christopher E. Forth, eds. *Cultures of the Abdomen* (Basingstoke: Palgrave Macmillan, 2005), p. 170.
17. John Burnby, *Summer Amusement; or, miscellaneous poems* (London: Printed for J. Dodsley, 1772), p. 90.
18. Thanks to Robert Appelbaum for highlighting this point.
19. Johnson, *Dictionary*, s.v. 'glutton.'
20. Letter from George Eliot to Maria Lewis, November, 6th 1838, in Eliot, *Letters*, vol. 1, p. 378.
21. '*The Revolutions of modesty, To which is added, the reign of pleasure...*,' p. 149.
22. Ibid., p. 149.
23. Ibid., p. 152.
24. See Miller's discussion of Hume's attitude to gluttony William Ian Miller, 'Gluttony,' *Representations*, 60 (Autumn, 1997), p. 105.
25. Ibid., p. 152.
26. Vicesimus Knox, vol. 3, p. 50.
27. Ibid.
28. Ibid.
29. Launcelot Sturgeon, p. 3.
30. Ibid., p. 4.
31. Kitchiner, preface.
32. *The Wit's Magazine, or, Library of Momus*, vol. 1, p. 97.
33. Sturgeon, p. 4.
34. Brillat-Savarin, p. 142.
35. Grimod de la Reynière quoted in Giles MacDonogh, *A Palate in Revolution* (London: Robin Clark,

1987), p. 187.

36. Sturgeon, p. 2 This is demonstrated by various contemporary dictionaries that cite only 'glutton,' 'epicure,' and 'voluptuary' without the other, more respectful, French terms such as 'gourmand' or 'gastronome.'

37. Kitchiner, preface.

38. Coleman, vol. 3, pp. 119–120.

39. See Mennell, chapter 5, pp. 103–133.

40. Geraldine Endsor Jewsbury, p. 42 (letter dated 1842).

41. See *The Gentleman's Magazine*.

42. Coleman, vol. 1, p. 146.

43. Ibid., p. 146.

44. Brillat-Savarin, p. 13 and Coleman, vol. 1, p. 146.

45. Coleman, ut sup.

46. Coleman, vol. 3, p. 119.

47. Ibid.

48. Ibid.

49. Ibid.

50. Ibid.

51. Coleman, vol. 3, pp. 119–120.

52. *The Wit's Magazine*, vol 1, p. 97.

53. Coleman, vol. 3, p. 124.

54. Ibid.

55. See Gilly Lehmann; Sara Pennell, 'Perfecting practice? Women, manuscript recipes and knowledge in early Modern England', in *Early Modern Women's Manuscript Writing*. Victoria E. Burke and Jonathan Gibson, eds. Aldershot: Ashgate, 2004; and Robert Appelbaum.

56. See A Lady (Hannah Glasse); William Verral; Ann Cook; and Kitchiner.

57. Coleman, vol. 1, p. 146.

58. Spang, pp. 64–87.

183

Moral Fiber: Bread in Nineteenth-Century America

Mark McWilliams

From Sarah Josepha Hale, who claimed, 'the more perfect the bread, the more perfect the lady' to Sylvester Graham, who insisted, 'the wife, the mother only' has the 'moral sensibility' required to bake good bread for her family, bread often became a gendered moral marker in nineteenth-century American culture.[1] Of course, what Hale and Graham considered 'good' bread differed dramatically, and exactly what constituted 'good' bread was much contested. Amidst technological change that made white flour more widely available and home cooking more predictable, bread, described in increasingly explicit moral terms, became the leading symbol of a housewife's care for her family.

Americans were hardly the first to ascribe moral meaning to their daily bread. As Bernard Dupaigne writes, 'since time immemorial [bread] has attended the great events of various human communities: monsoon or grape harvest bread, the blessed bread of Catholics or the unleavened bread of Passover, or the fasting-break bread of Ramadan. There is no bread that does not, somewhere in the world, celebrate an agricultural or religious holiday, enrich a family event, or commemorate the dead.'[2] With such varied symbolic resonance, bread seems easily filled with new meanings.

In America (as later in France),[3] bread became a revolutionary symbol. To the early English colonists' dismay, European wheat did not adapt well to the North American climate; the shift to corn as the primary grain was perhaps the most important dietary adaptation made by the colonists. Wheat remained too expensive for common consumption well into the nineteenth century. (By the time wheat became widely available, American tastes had grown accustomed to corn, and it continued to be an important grain, especially in the south, even as the use of wheat surged.) But corn could be used for bread in a wide variety of forms.

This reliance on cornbread was a potential embarrassment for the colonist always afraid of seeming provincial. But during the revolution, provincial fears turned into republican pride. Native foods – particularly corn and molasses – became celebrated as symbols of republican simplicity in virtuous contrast to the more refined foods associated with the debauched luxuries of the Old World. As early as 1750, the records of the Ancient and Honorable Tuesday Club of Annapolis defended corn as 'very well adapted for nourishment' against 'the monstrous and hellish compositions of modern Cookery.'[4] Glynis Ridley cites several instances of British 'loathing' for corn and American defensiveness on the same subject, including Benjamin Franklin's 'bristling response to an English correspondent in the *London Gazeteer* in 1766: "Pray, let me, an American, inform the gentleman, who seems ignorant of the matter, that

Indian corn, take it for all in all, is one of the most agreeable and wholesome grains in the world and that johny cake or hoe cake, hot from the fire is better than a Yorkshire muffin." [5] Once hostilities began, such local fare became essential to surviving the British blockade. As John Adams put it, American substitutes for otherwise imported foods became 'essential ingredient[s] in American independence.'[6]

By the end of the Revolution, then, bread was already charged with moral meaning in the young United States. In the nineteenth century, this meaning shifted in response to agricultural improvements that made wheat more widely available, technological change that made bread easier to make consistently, and, perhaps most important, social change that made good bread the primary symbol of a housewife's care for her family. In effect, bread suffered a kind of identity crisis that paralleled the national identity crisis of Jacksonian America. As Americans thought seriously about who they were in this new nation, about how they should act and even how they should eat, bread's symbolic meaning – and bread itself – changed.

American agricultural production exploded, although the proportion of the population working on farms declined. James Trager notes that even before the McCormick reaper first sold in large numbers as farmers struggled to replace workers leaving for the 1849 Gold Rush, the average time required to produce a bushel of wheat declined 22 per cent from 1831 to 1840.[7] Dramatic improvements in efficiency led to larger yields; for example, wheat production more than doubled between 1840 and 1860. Such increases in wheat production, combined with better milling procedures, made white flour finally available in quantities sufficient for white bread to become more than a luxury good.[8]

185

Even as wheat became easier to find for many Americans, bread remained notoriously difficult to make, or at least to make well. Lydia Maria Child, a baker's daughter who became one of America's leading writers, emphasizes what must have been the intensely frustrating difficulty of learning to cook in the era before predictable heat sources, standardized measurements, and consistent ingredients.[9] With bread, despite her focus on practical advice in *The American Frugal Housewife,* Child can recommend no better solution than experience:

> It is more difficult to give rules for making bread than for anything else; it depends so much on judgment and experience. In summer, bread should be mixed with cold water; during a chilly, damp spell, the water should be slightly warm; in severe cold weather, it should be mixed quite warm, and set in a warm place during the night. If your yeast is new and lively, a small quantity will make the dough rise; if it be old and heavy, it will take more.[10]

As if changes in the weather are not enough to deal with, the recipes themselves vary according to taste and need. Most recipes in Child's book are for some variation of brown bread – even those for 'flour bread' rarely call for just wheat flour: 'Some people like one third Indian in their flour [bread]. Others like one third rye; and some think the nicest of all bread is one third Indian, one third rye, and one third flour, made according to the directions for flour bread' (78). ('When Indian is used,' Child points out, 'it should be salted, and scalded, before the other meal is put in. A mixture of other grains is economical when flour is high' (78).)

Even with Child's help, in other words, American cooks had much to learn, as William Alcott recognizes in *The Young Wife, or Duties of a Woman in the Marriage Relation* (1838): 'It requires as much skill to make a good loaf of bread as to prepare any dish with which I am acquainted; and there are few, so far as my observation of the matter extends, who understand, thoroughly and scientifically, this invaluable art.'[11] And yet, despite this difficulty, Alcott disdains those who devote too much attention to the table: 'She cannot be the best of domestic economists, who spends half her time, while awake, in mere cookery. That cookery has an important place among her duties, there can be no doubt. As little can it be doubted that great skill is required' (170). Alcott's clear implication is that the skill must be mastered young; the good housewife seems required to produce 'a good loaf of bread' without much effort or complaint.

Alcott's prescriptions fit neatly into the well-noted shift in the language of domestic rhetoric as the nineteenth century progressed. Cookbooks of the period reveal increased emphasis on the moral value of domestic labor, a change seen most clearly in the changing descriptions of baking bread. Unlike Child's relentless practicality, later writers like Catharine Beecher and Sarah Josepha Hale insist on explaining the importance of good bread in addition to providing guidance for its preparation. For example, Beecher claims in her *Domestic Receipt Book*, 'Few housekeepers are aware of their responsibility in reference to the *bread* furnished for their family,' and Hale makes this same point in strikingly explicit terms in *Receipts for the Millions*: 'To make good bread or to understand the process of making it is the duty of every woman; indeed an art that should never be neglected in the education of a lady. The lady derives her title from 'dividing or distributing bread'; the more perfect the bread, the more perfect the lady.'[12] While Child encourages home baking on economic grounds – 'Make your own bread and cake. Some people think it is just as cheap to buy of the baker and confectioner; but it is not half as cheap. True, it is more convenient, and therefore the rich are justifiable in employing them, but those who are under the necessity of being economical, should make convenience a secondary object' (9) – Beecher strongly recommends home baking because of the unreliable quality of bakery products; bakery bread is simply not good enough for the American family table.

In the tremendously popular *The American Woman's Home*, Beecher and Stowe continue to equate good bread and high morality by linking the failure to bake proper bread to the 'savage':

186

[Bread] should be light, sweet and tender. This matter of lightness is the distinctive difference between savage and civilized bread. The savage mixes simple flour and water into balls of paste, which he throws into boiling water, and which comes out solid, glutinous masses, of which his common saying is, 'Man eat dis, he no die,' which a facetious traveler who was obliged to subsist on it interpreted to mean, 'Dis no kill you, nothing will.' In short, it requires the stomach of a wild animal or of a savage to digest this primitive form of bread, and of course more or less attention in all civilized modes of bread-making is given to producing lightness.[13]

Unlike Hale, who implies that learning to bake better can be a kind of self-improvement, this passage works more as dire warning to those not yet making the proper daily bread. Though bread becomes the main distinction between the civilized and the savage, Beecher turns quickly, and reassuringly, to the science of her day: 'By lightness is meant simply that in order to facilitate digestion the particles are to be separated from each other by little holes or air-cells; and all the different methods of making light bread are neither more nor less than the formation of bread with these air cells' (170). She then carefully describes how to produce the desired lightness in bread, instructions which must have been welcome to the young housewife now fully convinced of her bread's moral importance.

The path for Beecher, Hale, and others had been prepared by Sylvester Graham, although he is little mentioned in their work.[14] In his campaign to improve bread, Graham's rhetoric 'romanticized the life of the traditional household' in ways that 'unknowingly helped prepare women to find a new role as guardians of domestic virtue,' as Stephen Nissenbaum notes.[15] Bread was only one aspect of Graham's program to educate Americans on what he called 'the Science of Human Life.' Believing on the one hand, unlike many at the time, that overstimulation caused debility and, on the other, that industrialization and commercialization were debasing modern life, Graham proposed a lifestyle based around a strict controls on diet and sexuality.[16] While Graham promoted a range of activities from vegetarianism to temperance, his emphasis on good bread was most influential.

Graham's definition of 'good' bread grew out of his belief that 'food in its natural state would be the best' for human health. Ideally, food should be processed as little as possible; indeed, Graham claimed that uncooked food was not only best for dental and digestive health but also closest to the divine plan. It follows, then, that Graham found:

the coarse unleavened bread of early times, when of proper age, was one of the least removes from the natural state of food – one of the simplest and most wholesome forms of artificial preparations, and best adapted to fulfill the laws of constitution and relation; and therefore best adapted to sustain the most vigorous and healthy state of the alimentary organs, and the highest and best condition of the whole nature of man, as a general and permanent fact.

Graham's task, then, was to define the method by which 'loaf or raised bread can be made so nearly in accordance with the vital laws and interests of our bodies, as scarcely to militate against them in any perceptible or appreciable degree.'

And yet modern conditions make such bread difficult to produce. Each stage of the process is corrupted, according to Graham. Rather than grow wheat in 'a pure virgin soil' required for the best grain, farmers employ fields 'exhausted by tillage, and debauched by the means which man uses to enrich and stimulate it.' As Nissenbaum notes, the 'conscious sexual connotations' of Graham's language here is typical of his larger system, but the language also begins to point to the moral dimensions of good bread (6).

Similarly loaded language marks Graham's condemnation of bakery bread. Graham echoed the common complaints about adulteration by commercial bakers. But he added a unique twist: even the best bakery bread was doubly flawed. The flour itself was inferior because it was over-processed, according to Graham: the 'superfine flour' required for white bread 'is always far less wholesome, in any and every situation of life, than that which is made of wheaten meal which contains all the natural properties of the grain.' The fine flour results when 'human ingenuity tortures the flour of wheat' rather than leaving it in its natural state. Despite such language, the bread Graham recommended was neither revolutionary nor reactionary. As Nissenbaum points out, 'what soon came to be called 'Graham bread' was in fact nothing more than traditional homegrown and homemade whole wheat bread with a few added twists in preparation and an aggressively ideological rationale' (7).

Some of Graham's prescriptions were restrictive, to say the least. He disapproved of fertilizer: 'the flour of wheat, raised on a cultivated soil recently dressed with crude, stable manure, may readily be distinguished by its odor, from the flour of wheat raised on a new and undepraved soil.' And he insisted on hand-grinding flour shortly before baking:

> every family might easily be furnished with a modern patent hand-mill, con-structed after the plan of a coffee mill, with which they could at all times, with great ease, grind their wheat, and rice, and corn, as they want it, for bread and other purposes. With these mills they can grind their stuff as finely or coarsely as they wish, for bread or hominy, and always have it very fresh and sweet.

Such control of ingredients by the cook seemed crucial to Graham.

The biggest problem with commercial bread, however, came not from processes or ingredients but from morality. Here Graham is worth quoting at length:

Correct rules are certainly very valuable; but they can only serve as general way-marks, in the art of bread-making. Uniform success can only be secured by the exercise of that mature judgment which is always able to dictate those extemporaneous measures which every exigency and circumstance may require; and such a judgment can only result from a care and attention and experience which are the offspring of that moral sensibility which duly appreciates the importance of the quality of bread, in relation to the happiness and welfare of those that consume it.

But are we to look for such a sensibility in public bakers? Can we expect that they will feel so lively and so strong an interest for our enjoyment and for our physical and intellectual and moral well-being, that they will exercise all that care and attention and patience, and watch with that untiring vigilance and solicitude in all the progress of their operations, which are indispensably necessary in order to secure us the best of bread?

Or can we reasonably expect to find these qualifications in domestics – in those who serve us for hire? Many a female domestic, it is true, can make much better bread than her mistress can. Many a female domestic has an honest and sincere desire to do her duty faithfully; but can she be actuated by those sensibilities and affections which alone can secure that careful attention, that soundness of judgment, that accuracy of operation, without which the best of bread cannot uniformly, if ever, be produced?

No; – it is the wife, the mother only – she who loves her husband and her children as woman ought to love, and who rightly perceives the relations between the dietetic habits and physical and moral condition of her loved ones, and justly appreciates the importance of good bread to their physical and moral welfare – she alone it is, who will be ever inspired by that cordial and unremitting affection and solicitude which will excite the vigilance, secure the attention, and prompt the action requisite to success, and essential to the attainment of that maturity of judgment and skilfulness of operation, which are the indispensable attributes of a perfect bread-maker.

189

So, if 'the bakers' bread is very rarely a wholesome article of diet,' it is precisely because it was made by a commercial enterprise rather than by a loving mother.

Indeed, Graham seemed to value homemade bread precisely because of the extra labor required. This may well be, as Nissenbaum suggests, a reaction to the increasing industrialization of Jacksonian America, but the resulting emphasis on the mother as breadmaker is unavoidable. In one nostalgic section of the *Treatise on Bread and Breadmaking,* Graham reflects:

Who that can look back thirty or forty years to those blessed days of New England's prosperity and happiness, when our good mothers used to make the family bread, but can well remember how long and how patiently those excellent matrons stood over their bread troughs, kneading and moulding their dough? and who with such recollections cannot also well remember the delicious bread that these mothers used invariably to set before them? There was a natural sweetness and richness in it which made it always desirable; and which we cannot now vividly recollect, without feeling a strong desire to partake again of such bread as our mothers made for us in the days of our childhood.

As Nissenbaum argues, pointing to this passage, Graham's claims invoke 'the vision of a domestic idyll, of a mother nursing her family with bread and affection' (8). Such a vision clearly anticipates the emphasis on cookery as measure of a woman's social worth in the domestic rhetoric that came so to characterize the mid-nineteenth century.

Such language increasingly linking cookery with morality emphasized the virtue not of the food itself but rather of the cooks preparing it. This linkage reached readers not only through the explosion of cookbooks and domestic manuals but also through the growing numbers of sentimental novels. Indeed, this linkage provided a tremendously useful trope for authors seeking a shorthand to define their fictional characters. And that trope, in turn, helped expand the popularity of interpreting cookery in moral terms. For example, in Fanny Fern's *Ruth Hall*, Ruth's mother-in-law, concerned lest any but she prove capable of caring for her son, grills Ruth on her housekeeping abilities soon after the marriage:

> 'Can you make bread? When I say *bread* I *mean* bread – old-fashioned, yeast riz bread; none of your sal-soda, salæratus, sal-volatile poisonous mixtures, that must be eaten as quick as baked, lest it should dry up; *yeast* bread – do you know how to make it?'
>
> 'No,' said Ruth, with a growing sense of her utter good-for-nothingness; 'people in the city always buy baker's bread.'[17]

Such emphasis on bread as the primary measure of a cook's skill quickly becomes a measure of a cook's character, as in this exchange from Louisa May Alcott's novel *Work*:

> 'I see what you mean, Kitty; but I never thought on't before. You be better riz than me; though, let me tell you, too much emptins makes bread poor stuff, like baker's trash; and too much workin' up makes it hard and dry. Now fly 'round, for the big oven is most het, and this cake takes a sight of time in the mixin'.'[18]

Such comparisons between characters, where one is 'better riz' than the other, clearly both draw on and reinforce the link between bread and virtue in mid-century domestic rhetoric.[19]

And yet, by the end of the century, such links between bread and virtue became less common. In a way, this change testifies to the success of domestic reformers like Beecher and Hale. Their push to make cooking both better and more efficient threatened to marginalize those, like Graham, who romanticized kitchen labor. Indeed, Graham's fate is illustrative here. While he helped create this emphasis on the moral value of good bread, his own work soon fell out of fashion. In 1883, for example, Mary Lincoln's widely influential *Boston Cook Book* was flatly dismissive of Graham's claims about bread. Consider these two passages:

> Cheap inferior Graham flour, made of poor flour mixed with bran, is worse than no food at all. Any flour containing much of the indigestible bran causes irritation of the digestive organs; all the food is hurried through the alimentary canal before digestion is complete or all the nutriment can be absorbed, and thus is neither economical nor healthful. Fine flour containing the most gluten is the most nutritious, because it is all digested, and the loss of albuminous material can be supplied from other sources. (42)

and:

191

> The *bran* should be discarded as utterly useless for human food; but it is often mixed with an inferior quality of fine flour, and sold as Graham flour. It was at one time considered valuable as a food for those suffering from constipation, chiefly on account of its coarseness; but science has shown us recently that minute points of glass (and bran is nothing else) are not Nature's best agents in removing effete matters from the system. All of the so-called Graham flour made by this process should be sifted before using. (39–40)

While Lincoln still includes recipes made popular by Graham, they are not only completely divorced from his larger 'Science of Human Life' but presented in a context that explicitly refutes his claims.

While Graham's fate – he's now remembered almost entirely, if at all, in Graham crackers – was more extreme, the emphasis on good bread as a measure of a housewife's care for her family also faded as more and more households turned to commercially prepared bread. One indication of this change in social standards comes from Mark Twain's popular novel *The Adventures of Huckleberry Finn,* written at about the same time as *Mrs. Lincoln's Boston Cook Book.* On Jackson's Island after running away from home, Huck gets a good meal from the riverboat searching for his own dead body. He knows 'they always put quicksilver in loaves of bread and float them off, because they always go right to the drownded carcass and stop there,' so he positions himself where the current will push the bread close to shore, catches a loaf, and prepares to dine: 'I took out the plug and shook out the little dab of quicksilver, and set my teeth in. It was "baker's bread" – what the quality eat; none of your low-down corn-pone.'[20]

Huck was hardly alone in seeking out 'what the quality eat.' After the Civil War, domestic rhetoric evolved away from its roots in the wholesome foods of the nation's past toward the ever-more refined cuisine of the Gilded Age. Graham's refusal to evolve in this direction – his system was based entirely in a nostalgic struggle against modernity, against refinement – may well be a large part of why his work was quickly left behind even by those for whom it had paved the way.

Notes

This essay serves as a companion – and perhaps corrective – to my 'Good Women Bake Good Biscuits: Cookery and Identity in Antebellum American Fiction' (*Food, Culture and Society* 10.3 (November 2007), pp. 388–406). I would like to thank Warren Belasco and the article's anonymous reviewer for encouraging me to consider the work of Sylvester Graham more carefully.

1. Hale, qtd. James Trager, *The Food Chronology: A Food Lover's Compendium of Events and Anecdotes, from Prehistory to the Present* (New York: Henry Holt, 1995): pp. 256–257; Graham, *Treatise on Bread and Breadmaking* (Boston: Light & Stearns, 1837; facsim. ed. Lee Foundation; online at www.soil-andhealth.org/02/0203CAT/020321.graham.bread.htm). All subsequent quotations from Graham's work come from this non-paginated source.

2. Dupaigne, *The History of Bread*, trans. Antonio and Sylvie Roder, New York: Harry N. Abrams, 1999, p. 122.

3. See H.E. Jacobs's *Six Thousand Years of Bread: Its Holy and Unholy History*, New York: Lyons and Burford, 1997, pp. 238–254.

4. Alexander Hamilton, *The History of the Ancient and Honorable Tuesday Club*, ed. Robert Micklus, Chapel Hill, NC: University of North Carolina Press, 1990, vol. I, pp. 206, 207.

5. Glynis Ridley, 'The First American Cookbook,' *Eighteenth-Century Life* 23.2 (1999), p. 118.

6. Qtd. Anne Willan, *Great Cooks and Their Recipes from Taillevant to Escoffier*, London: Pavilion, 1992, p. 138. For more on the use of foods like molasses and cornbread in building American national identity during the Revolution and the early national period, see my 'Distant Tables: Food and the Novel in Early America,' *Early American Literature* 38.3 (Winter 2003), pp. 365–393, and Rafia Zafar's 'The Proof of the Pudding: Of Haggis, Hasty Pudding, and Transatlantic Influence,' *Early American Literature* 31.2 (Autumn 1996), pp. 133–149.

7. Trager, pp. 242, 229.

8. For detailed discussion of milling changes, see H.E. Jacobs's *Six Thousand Years of Bread*.

9. Carolyn Karcher estimates, 'At the height of *The Frugal Housewife*'s popularity in the 1830s, the readers Child addressed probably constituted a majority of the nation's adult female population', *The First Woman in the Republic: A Cultural Biography of Lydia Maria Child* (Durham, NC: Duke UP, 1994), p. 131.

10. Child, *The Frugal Housewife Dedicated to Those who are not Ashamed of Economy*, 1829, 6th ed., Boston: Carter, Hendee and Babcock, 1831, p. 76. Subsequent references are cited parenthetically.

11. Alcott, *The Young Wife*, Boston: George W. Light, 1838, p. 170. Subsequent references are cited parenthetically.

12. Beecher, *Miss Beecher's Domestic Receipt Book*, 3rd ed., New York: Harper Brothers, 1852, p. 227; Hale qtd. Trager, pp. 256–257.

13. Beecher and Stowe, *The American Woman's Home: or, Principles of Domestic Science,* 1869, reprinted New York, Arno Press, 1971, p. 170. Subsequent references are cited parenthetically.

14. While many of these cookbooks include recipes that call for Graham flour, few reference Graham's health claims or the other elements of his system (though Beecher and Stowe's *The American Woman's Home* does include a dismissive note about Graham's promotion of vegetarianism (122).) Indeed, later in the century, some cookbooks become frankly critical of Graham's claims; see, for example, *Mrs. Lincoln's Boston Cook Book,* Boston: Roberts Brothers, 1883, pp. 39–42. Subsequent references to Lincoln's work are cited parenthetically in the text.

15. Nissenbaum, *Sex, Diet, and Debility in Jacksonian America: Sylvester Graham and Health Reform,* Westport, CT: Greenwood, 1980, p. 18. Subsequent references are cited parenthetically.

16. See Nissenbaum, esp. pp. 3–38.

17. Fanny Fern [Sarah Payson Willis], *Ruth Hall* (1855), in *Ruth Hall and Other Writings,* ed. Joyce W. Warren, New Brunswick, NJ: Rutgers University Press, 1986, p. 20.

18. Alcott, *Work* (1873), ed. Joy S. Kasson, New York: Penguin, 1994, p. 6.

19. A larger version of this argument appears in my 'Good Women Bake Good Biscuits.'

20. Twain, *The Adventures of Huckleberry Finn,* New York: Bantam, 1981, p. 37.

193

'Feed their vile bodies…starve their immortal souls': Food as Moral Instructor in Nineteenth-century Homes and Schools

Tani A. Mauriello

Madame…you are aware that my plan on bringing up these girls is, not to accustom them to habits of luxury and indulgence, but to render them hardy, patient, self-denying…Oh, Madame, when you put bread and cheese instead of burnt porridge into these children's mouths, you may feed their vile bodies, but little think how you starve their immortal souls!

Mr Brocklehurst in *Jane Eyre*[1]

What constitutes an appropriate diet for children, at home and in school, remains a major issue in the twenty-first century. Current debates about childhood diet revolve around, for the most part, issues of nutrition, diabetes, and obesity. In the 1800s, children's diet was considered not only in terms of health, but also for its moral quality. Over the course of the nineteenth century, feeding was seen as a method of molding the moral character of middle-class Victorian children. The suitability of certain foods for children, as well as the deprivation of food, played an important role in nineteenth-century child-rearing strategies. This paper considers the influence of three factors on nineteenth-century domestic and institutional childhood diets: the influence of the traditional humoral system of medicine and the subsequent belief in the moral value of 'plain food'; a change in the understanding of childhood through the emergence of two opposing child-rearing philosophies (Rousseauian and Wesleyan) in the late eighteenth century; and finally a burgeoning middle class identity and the efforts of the bourgeoisie to define itself against the stereotypes of the aristocracy and labouring classes.

As illustrated in the above quotation from *Jane Eyre*, Charlotte Brontë's Mr Brocklehurst is bombastic and pontificating; a character who, as the novel progresses, imposes such Spartan conditions on his students that many are ultimately carried off by typhus before he reconsiders his methods. In the novel, the above passage is delivered to the headmistress as his well-fed and bejeweled daughters sit in attendance. Twenty-first century readers often find him cruel and hypocritical; while Victorian readers may have empathised with Jane and considered the disastrous results of Brocklehurst's unfounded self-assurance to be a moral lesson, they would have likely been familiar, if not comfortable, with Brocklehurst's duplicitous beliefs regarding diet and class, and the practice of denying food as a legitimate method of childrearing.

This quotation reveals nineteenth-century attitudes concerning childhood diet and a strategy of food-denial to mold the moral character of children in a school setting, something with which Victorian readers would have been familiar. It suggests the influence of Christianity on food deprivation as a moral instructor, and it shows a class bias in the manner food-denial was applied, and its use as a tool for the middle-class, not only to educate its own children, but poor children as well.

In *The Rise of Respectable Society*, F.M.L. Thompson writes, 'The image of the loving Victorian parent, disciplining her child, feeding only at fixed times with no nibbling between meals,…is far removed from the image of the late twentieth-century parent, for whom indulgence and a minimum of rules and restrictions have become signs of love.'[2] Thompson writes extensively on the middle-class reaction to working-class feeding practices, and the use of strict childrearing methods to create parental dominance and child submission, but he does not explore the origins and extent of this view of nineteenth-century parenting, nor the extent to which food, and how it was fed, was considered an integral part of raising a proper, middle-class Victorian child. This paper shall attempt to address these issues, and to create a more detailed picture of the use of food as a central player in the moral instruction of Victorian children, in both domestic and institutional settings.

Humors and the moral value of food

Moral associations with food and feeding have a long history in British cultural tradition. Early medical, as well as popular, beliefs about diet were largely based on the theories of Galen of Pergamum, whose teachings were laid out in the *Regimen Sanitatis*, a text compiled and brought to England around 1100. Centuries before the reign of Victoria, these beliefs were responsible for initiating a perceived link between the consumption of specific foods and one's resulting character and temperament. Strict adherence to Galenic doctrine persisted into the seventeenth century. Galen's writings elaborated on the humoral philosophy of medicine, which was very nutrition-oriented, and based on balancing the body's temperature and moistness by manipulating the 'humours' (blood, phlegm, black and yellow bile). According to this philosophy, illness was the result of an insufficient or excessive amount of one or more humours. The ideal 'balance' was maintained through the removal of excess blood, phlegm or bile (through bloodletting or the application of leeches) or through diet. Foods according to the humoral doctrine, were related to one of the four elements, and were hot and moist (which would encourage blood), hot and dry (for yellow bile), cold and moist (for phlegm) or cold and dry (for black bile), and could heal specific diseases by redressing the balance between the humours inside the body. The guidelines that Galen established for food influenced cultural beliefs about food and nutrition for centuries after the medical philosophy itself was abandoned.[3]

According to Galen, milk, considered cold and moist, was only suitable for infants and the very old (but its phlegmatic qualities had to be tempered with bread lest it over-stimulate already phlegmatic children), and it was considered entirely unsuitable for invalids. 'Grosse' (red – although not all red) meats were not allowed until a young man was fifteen, along with salads of leafy vegetables, both being considered 'cold,' to temper the hot humors of adolescence.[4] Hence, the qualities of particular foods had the potential to affect the character of the consumer by altering humors and thus upsetting the temperament. In the *Regimen*, Galen explicitly links food consumed by infants with their moral development. Well into the sixteenth century, physicians implored parents to take care in choosing a wet nurse of good moral character.[5] Food historians, Drummond and Wilbraham write, 'Great care was taken in the choice of a wet nurse, in view of the widespread belief that the moral and spiritual character of the child would be influenced by the milk it imbibed. If the nurse was a dolt or a drunkard, the child would certainly take after her; if there was a trace of blood in her milk the child might grow up to be a murderer.'[6]

By the nineteenth century, the belief that a wet nurse could transmit her character to her charge through her milk was no longer prevalent, nor were fears that temperaments could be altered due to the humoral qualities of individual foods. However, many parents still gave credence to Galenic principles regarding the health values of food. Fruit was still considered dangerous due to Galenic teaching. Still thought to be the cause of fevers and infant diarrhea as a result of their laxative properties, some nineteenth century authors of prescriptive literature felt it necessary to reassure parents that eating fruit was not dangerous and to encourage its consumption by children.[7] In addition to a lingering adherence to Galenic views on food and illness and its effect on the health of children, a new preoccupation with the influence of foods and feeding methods on the resulting *moral character* of children was emerging. Opposing philosophies about childhood and the rising power and concern with class identity of the bourgeoisie all further contributed to childrearing practices which revolved around feeding schedules, food choice and food deprivation in nineteenth-century nurseries and schools. This combination of factors made moral instruction through food a distinctly Victorian development.

The new importance of childhood and the crucial childhood diet

While the humoral doctrine had made preoccupation with diet a staple of English life for centuries, the concern with childhood diet increased during the nineteenth century when childrearing began to reflect more closely the modern ideas of childhood. The emergence of childhood as a life stage with special needs could be seen in the increase in toys and change in children's clothing. Slowly, children were no longer expected to act and dress as miniature adults.[8] At the close of the eighteenth century, the French Revolution prompted international reflection on the freedoms of the individual, and the impact of the writings of Rousseau and the Romantic poets began to convince wealthy British parents that freedom of choice and independence, as well as a respect for the rights of children, was necessary for healthy development. 'It was perhaps

196

above all Rousseau's educational ideals, best remembered and expressed in *Émile*, which most influenced educated parents,' writes James Walvin, childhood historian.[9] In *Émile*, originally published in 1762 and widely disseminated throughout Western Europe, Rousseau advocates radical deviations from traditional forms of childrearing, describing childhood as a natural state of perfection in which children, left to their own devices, will make the correct choices for their well-being. On the subject of diet, Rousseau wrote:

> However you bring up children, provided you accustom them to a simple diet, you can leave them to eat, run and play as they please, and can be sure that they will never eat too much and suffer from indigestion. But if you keep them hungry half the time and they can find ways of escaping from your vigilance, they will make up for it by eating gluttonously till they can eat no more. Appetite is only immoderate because we try to impose on it other rules than those of nature among peasants. The bread bin and the fruit closet are always open, and neither children nor adults ever have indigestion.[10]

Rousseau's philosophy of childrearing, while highly influential among certain members of the intelligentsia, was drastically at odds with the childrearing beliefs promoted by John Wesley during the emergence of Methodism at the turn of the nineteenth century and the subsequent Evangelical Christian movement of the Victorian era. Wesley, believer in original sin and coiner of the phrase 'spare the rod and spoil the child,' thought Rousseau an imbecile.[11] In his sermons, Wesley expounded on the absolute necessity of a regimented and Spartan childhood, free of play and indulgence, in which children were held accountable for their actions. Regarding food, its role in shaping the moral character of a child and the methods of its use, Wesley explained:

> [Parents] cherish the 'desire of the flesh'…Yea, they entice them [children], long before nature requires it, to take wine or strong drink; and provide them with comfits, gingerbread, raisins, and whatever fruit they have a mind to…In direct opposition to all this, a truly wise parent will take the utmost care not to cherish in her children the desire of the flesh, their natural propensity to seek happiness in gratifying the outward senses. With this view she will…accustom them to the most simple food, chiefly of vegetables. She may inure them to taste only one kind of food beside bread, at dinner, and constantly to breakfast and sup on milk, either cold or heated, but not boiled.[12]

Earlier in this text, Wesley warns against giving children anything for which they cry, or rewards in the form of food such as gingerbread. He advises mothers to insist that neither grandparents nor household servants offer the children treats, lest it destroy their character. While Rousseau's childrearing philosophy was not as readily accepted as Wesley's, it established a new respect for childhood as a critical period of development, and this was the one point upon which he and Wesley agreed. Both men contended that childhood was the time during which the permanent character of an individual was formed. According to their writings, it was in the tiny details of upbringing that a respectable, healthy adult was created or lost. To a moral Victorian middle class, this belief created a great deal of anxiety. Victorian parents had a brief period in which to instill the mores of their era and they wanted to know the best strategies for doing this and how to avoid reinforcing or creating bad habits out of ignorance. Thus the need for the child-rearing expert was created, and suddenly the use of food took on immense importance as a tool or potential source of failure in raising a child.

Whether middle-class parents felt strongly that childhood was the happy, idealistic state Rousseau proposed or not, fear of raising a greedy, ill-tempered child by a slight ignorance, and a strong tradition of Christianity kept parents fearful of teaching indulgence through food, and so, contemporary advice pamphlets offer much advice on this topic. For example *The Practical Housewife* of 1855 advises:

> One rule, however, will apply to all – never give a child food to amuse and keep it quiet when it is not hungry, or to reward it for being good…There is a great danger, that an infant under three years of age, will be over-fed, if it be left to the discretion of the nurse…they give it something to eat, often that which is very injurious, to tempt the appetite, if it will only eat and stop crying, they do not care for the future inconvenience which this habit of indulgence may bring on the child and its mother.[13]

Advice such as this does not merely suggest the strict disciplinarian tactic of breaking a child's will, but a warning against a lifelong habit that can form while the child is 'under three years of age.' With this, such advice acknowledges Rousseau's beliefs that character is formed during childhood, but recognizes the Wesleyan fear of promoting indulgence with pleasurable food.

Some prescriptive literature offers diet suggestions for the purpose of moral instruction without offering any explanation as to why certain foods are prohibited. According to eminent pediatrician Emmet Holt, author of *The Care and Feeding of Children*, first published in 1895, children under the age of seven should not partake of: ham, sausages, pork, cabbage, stewed potatoes, cakes, hot bread, bananas, and 'all nuts, candies, dried fruits; pies, tarts and pastries of every description.' The only indulgence Holt allows is that children should be permitted plain custard after their third year, but only if 'the quantity given should be very moderate.'[14]

Did Victorian parents follow such advice? Victorian art critic, John Ruskin, born in 1819, reveals in his autobiography, *Praeterita*, a childhood so dietarily regimented that his parents might as well have followed Holt to the letter (had his book not been written nearly eighty years after Ruskin's birth). Ruskin declares:

> I was never allowed to come down to dessert, until much later in life – when I was able to crack nuts neatly. I was then permitted to come down and crack other people's nuts for them…but never to have any myself; nor anything else of dainty kind, either then or at other times. Once at Hunter Street, I recollect my mother giving me three raisins…and I remember perfectly the first time I tasted custard, in our lodgings in Norfolk Street…my father was dining in the front room, and did not finish his custard; and my mother brought me the bottom of it into the back room.[15]

Ruskin's parents were quite religious and had hopes that he would become a minister. Similarly Edmund Gosse, author of *Father and Son* and born in 1849, writes of his strictly religious upbringing having the opposite effect of that intended. Gosse's father was a minister of a fundamentalist Protestant sect, the Plymouth Brethren. Gosse grew up to be, like Ruskin, an art critic and poet. Gosse's recollections of childhood include receiving nursery food, specifically a 'loathly bowl' of milk-sop at every meal, well into his tenth year. This is unusual and may be attributed to continual ill health as he was growing up. However, one incident included in Gosse's memoirs is a perfect example of the moral value that could be placed on food. On Christmas Day of 1857, Edmund's puritanical father, Philip Gosse, had declared that 'no difference whatever was to be made in our meals on that day; dinner was to be neither more copious than usual, nor less so.'[16] But after the household servants secretly made a Christmas pudding and fed some to Edmund, his guilt overcame him:

> At length I could bear my spiritual anguish no longer, and bursting into the study I called out: 'Oh! Papa, Papa, I have eaten of flesh offered to idols!' It took some time, between my sobs, to explain what had happened…He took me by the hand, and ran with me into the midst of the startled servants, seized what remained of the pudding…ran till we reached the dustheap, when he flung the idolatrous confectionery on to the middle of the ashes…The sudden-ness, the violence, the velocity of this extraordinary act made an impression on my memory which nothing will ever efface.[17]

199

The use of food to reinforce class values

It would be difficult to dispute the assertion that middle-class Victorians attributed moral values to foods and feeding practices in the light of their well-documented efforts to reform, throughout the century, what the working classes ate and how they ate it. Like current popular efforts at nutritional reform (i.e. Chef Jamie Oliver's school meals and his well-publicized damnation of 'turkey twizzlers' in the UK in 2005), the declared motive was nutritional concern: to increase the dietary health and economy of the nation's workers and poor. However, the subtext was (and some could argue, still is) one of moral disapproval. Based on the evidence below, I would argue that the true motivation for reform was one of fear that the use of convenience foods encouraged and perpetuated slovenly habits, and that the frequent consumption of sweets and the lack of formal meals, and therefore the dearth of opportunities to instill and practice manners, created children lacking self-discipline and restraint.

During his rides through Surrey, Sussex, and Hampshire in 1823, politician and agricultural reformer William Cobbett praises the agricultural labourers he meets for not growing potatoes, which he refers to as 'Ireland's Lazy Root.'[18] According to seminal food historian John Burnett, Cobbett objected to the potato on the grounds that its ease of cultivation and cooking led to 'slovenly and beastly habits among the labouring poor.'[19] Cobbett also objected to the purchase rather than the home baking of bread, the decline of which was lamented by cookery book authoress Eliza Acton in 1857, despite the fact that baking one's own bread was very rapidly becoming a false economy. Later, at the turn of the century, the dominance of bread in the working-class diet concerned those interviewed by the Inter-departmental Committee on Physical Deterioration in 1904. Middle-class critics considered the use of purchased bread and the manner in which it was served by working-class mothers to be a shirking of their housewifely duties which would engender laziness in their children.[20]

Miss Deverell, junior inspector of schools to the Board of Education, considered the children she inspected to have a 'plentiful, but unsuitable diet, taken at irregular intervals.' Of the class-based criticisms levied in the Report, Elizabeth Petty writes, 'it was claimed that the remedy for poor feeding entailed not only a change in food habits but also the adoption of middle-class behaviour…'[21] In 'The Newer Knowledge of Nutrition,' Petty writes: 'Mrs Deverell deplored the fact that 'anything like a sit down meal' was unknown in many districts (CPD Q7985). According to this view there was a need to teach the working classes not only what to eat and how to cook it, but how to organize the ritual of eating as well.'[22] Of course, this model of eating three meals a day in the morning, noon, and evening, evolved in response to the middle-class work schedule. Meals at which every member of the family was present would have been impossible for many families where children and fathers worked in certain occupations, such as mining, which did not allow for a man to return home for his dinner, and factory and agricultural work, which often required breakfast to be eaten (if permitted at all) at the place of work.

This was the case in Matthew Henry Sheffield's family. Sheffield, a miner born in Coalville, Leicestershire in 1901, was one of 15 children. In the course of an oral history interview, he asserts that during his childhood, there were at most fourteen living in the house at once. When asked by the interviewer how his mother had managed to feed so many people, he responded:

Oh that's a miracle that'll never be known cause… there was daughters, me sisters, all coming from the factory half-past twelve to one. She had to get a meal for them, and some of the miners were on the night work – they used to have their dinner at that time… Then there was us coming from school about four o'clock… we used to stay at school for dinner… so she used to have to cook again for four o'clock time. So how she did it, well, I don't know how she did all that work.[23]

Other families did manage to have all members present at mealtimes, but this in itself often posed a problem for families with limited space and resources. The practice of standing around a table in working-class homes persisted well into the nineteenth century, due to space constraints and chairs being a rare commodity. Matthew Henry Sheffield informed his interviewer: 'Well…what I remember for a start was that there was two sitting downs at the table, we had to sit back, the young ones, while the other older ones had the first course, the first meal, and then we had our meal.'[24] In 1963, Mrs A. H. Stratton, born near Cambridge in the 1890s, wrote about her father for an Age Concern essay competition: 'He was one of eight children of a farm worker, who earned 10/- a week, and they lived in a cottage so small that the younger children had to eat their meals under the table.'[25]

Despite the insistence of middle-class reformers that the working-class ape their meal rituals, and for all of the sermonizing that the labouring classes should bake and eat their own bread because it was morally beneficial *to them*, the middling classes certainly did not seek to better themselves by eating bread they had baked with their own hands. In fact, food-related moral instruction for middle-class children was largely based on defining them against the eating customs of working-class children. Subscribing to popular beliefs regarding anatomy, the revered Mrs Beeton, domestic goddess of her time, advised her readers in 1861 not to let bread enter the undeveloped stomach of an infant.[26] She writes, 'Bread, though the universal regime of the labouring poor, where the infant's stomach and digestive powers are a reflex, in miniature, of the father's, should never be given to an infant under three months…'[27] In the middle of the century, the 'labouring poor' were considered so fundamentally different from the middle classes that they were biologically dissimilar enough to consume food that their middle- and upper-class counterparts would not be able to, quite literally, stomach. This statement exposes the double standard possessed by the woman who set the standard for domestic management, and illustrates that while the moral values that middle-class parents and reformers hoped food would impart were generally similar (obedience, industriousness, etc.), the food itself and the methods of imparting these values differed according to station. This prevailing attitude explains why a man such as Brocklehurst would have been comfortable feeling that he could morally educate his plump and plumed daughters without having to force-feed them burnt porridge, while it was the *only* appropriate method for molding his students who were destined for lives as vicars wives and governesses.

Just as Mrs Beeton, the fictitious Brocklehurst, and like-minded Victorians felt that to morally educate working-class children was to deny them the dietary luxuries of their superiors, they considered it necessary to instill the desired qualities in their own children by denying them the luxuries of their inferiors. While 'three meals a day' may have resulted from the middle-class male's work schedule, the often reiterated 'no snacks between meals' element of Victorian dining and feeding was largely an attempt on the part of the middle class to differentiate its children from those of the labouring poor. Regarding the social consensus on the behaviour of less respectable working-class children, Anna Davin writes, 'Rough children… could go anywhere, including in and out of each other's houses…they could come in to eat at any time, or feed themselves from a fried-fish or pie shop or shellfish stall; it did not matter if they went barefoot or got dirty, and their language might be coarse.'[28] The rougher the child, the more independence he possessed regarding his choice of food and when he could satisfy his hunger. The rough child's hunger pangs were dictated by insufficient funds, but not by the imposed structure of adult discipline. According to food historian Valerie Mars:

> Eating, for the middle-class and upper-class Victorian child, took place only in the nursery, and only at prescribed times. The food of such a child was eaten within the constraining structure of an ordered meal, at the table; promiscuous eating, in the rare instances where it was allowed, gave the child some autonomy, and emphasised his individuality – all the more since sweets were often bought with his or her personal pocket money. Casual snacking, on the other hand, was associated with children who spent time on the streets where they could buy food from the many stalls and walking vendors. The denial of this latter form of autonomy to nursery children effectively emphasised their class exclusivity… Social division was thereby reinforced through the enforcement of structured eating habits: nursery children had to be separated from promiscuous outdoor eaters.[29,]

Just as feeding practices were used to distance middle-class children from labourers, some foods were so closely associated with the poor or the working class that they were avoided by both wealthy citizens and those of the working class attempting to raise their social standing. For instance, Daniel Pool writes that, although the wealthier classes consumed various cuts of pork, 'Its lower-class connotations kept bacon away from upper-class menus.'[30] Similarly, butter and vegetables were avoided by the wealthy for centuries because of its associations with farm labourers.[31]

Interestingly, just as many middle-class dining traditions developed as a reaction to how the bourgeoisie believed the poor behaved, much of middle-class child-feeding behaviour was a response to the supposed gluttony of the aristocracy.

202

The middle-class fear of excess and the admonishment of gluttony were, to a large extent, a reaction against the perceived over-indulgence of the English aristocracy and a result of middle-class desire to seize the moral high ground of the class hierarchy. The use of food and eating practices by different groups to define themselves as separate social entities is a common sociological phenomenon. Often cultural rules about excess that set one civilization apart from its neighbours are turned inwards by society to draw class distinctions. Jack Goody offers an example of this in his work *Cooking, Cuisine and Class* when he describes the 'post-Restoration search for an English (i.e. Anglo-Saxon) cuisine, revealing an ambiguous attitude to the culinary influences of "the continent," a word that in itself invokes the ascetic purity of the island race surrounded by water, in contrast to the excess and indulgence of its neighbours.' Goody claims that 'widely applied to what other nations or religions eat, the concept of excess defines xenophobic attitudes…' and that this food-based 'moral criticism may extend to the nature of society itself.'[32] Strict rules governing the rituals of food consumption allowed the Victorian middle class to simultaneously define themselves and assert their moral superiority over the working and upper classes.

Educating middle-class children through diet

Like nursery diets, and those diets of economy, restriction and regimentation to which middle-class critics would have liked the working classes to adhere, school diets unfortunately bore a strong resemblance to the diet at Jane Eyre's Cowan Bridge School: often monotonous, restrictive in both calories and content, and served strictly at prescribed mealtimes. To the chagrin of schoolmasters, mothers frequently sent hampers and parcels of treats, and if given the opportunity for escape, tuck shops were raided by students – Drummond and Wilbraham refer to tuck shops as the 'schoolboy's salvation' claiming it was likely the only way he managed to obtain sufficient calories during term time.[33]

203

Little thought was given to school food, especially public school food, until the reforms of Dr Thomas Arnold, headmaster of Rugby, in the 1830s. Before this, Charles Lamb's description of the fare he received at Christ's Hospital was an accurate representation of early Victorian school food:

> We were battening upon our quarter of a penny loaf – our *crug* [bread] – moistened with attenuated small beer, in wooden piggins, smacking of the pitched, leathren jack it was poured from. Our Monday's milk porritch, blue and tasteless, and the pease soup of Saturday, coarse and choking…Wednesday's mess of millet (we had three banyan [meatless days] to four meat days a week)…boiled beef on Thursdays (strong as *caro equine* [horsemeat])…scanty mutton crags on Friday – and rather more savory, grudging portions of the same flesh, rotten-roasted or rare on the Tuesdays.[34]

Outbreaks of scurvy occurred at Christ's Hospital at the end of the eighteenth and beginning of the nineteenth century, and Drummond and Wilbraham write:

> The description of the conditions prevailing in many private schools during the nineteenth century make terrible reading. The children were often quite literally half-starved. This was not entirely due to ignorance of the fact that growing children need far more food than their size would suggest; there was a general indifference to their welfare which strikes us to-day as appalling. Moreover, matters were all too often made worse by the widely held view that the short commons and hard-fare were good discipline for rebellious youth.[35]

The end of this quotation highlights one of the great contradictions of the use of food as a moral educator during the nineteenth century: that 'short commons and hard-fare were good discipline for rebellious youth.' Although at first it appears that public and charity schools were following an extreme version of the middle-class nursery diet laid out in childrearing manuals, and that the ill-health resulting from school diets was merely the result of ignorance, it is more likely that schoolmasters were unconcerned with pupils' ill-health because their objectives were different from those of domestic obedience and self-restraint. In middle-class domestic settings and schools for the working class where food was used for moral education, the universal goal for children of all classes was submission and dependence, but the methods and standards of deprivation varied according to class (enforcing mealtimes, and denying potatoes and baker's bread to working-class children versus denying bourgeois children custard and feeding endless bowls of milksop to instill the same moral values). Conversely, in public schools and other private institutions that catered to the superior classes, the methods used were the same as in domestic settings – dietary privation and severe regimentation – but the goal was to harden the students, to make them independent and capable of holding a superior position in society's hierarchy.

The ideal middle-class man of the nineteenth century, especially in the mid-to-late eighteen hundreds, was a capitalist and imperialist. Many of the boys who went to Eton, Rugby, Winchester, etc., were future members of Parliament, soldiers, lawyers, college masters and scholars. Prime Minister William Gladstone was sent to Eton by his Scottish merchant father in order to secure a respectable social position for his son. Schools did not aim to create namby-pamby art-critic Gosses and Ruskins, mamas' boys reared on boiled milk. They wished to train them to be tough, ambitious politicians and industrialists. The food was bland, monotonous and insufficient to raise men, not educate boys; hence the diet was made for character development, not for satisfying a growing student.

In their efforts to create ideal middle-class men and women, parents and educators used food as a means to first create humbleness, obedience, dependence and piety, but then later, ambition, a sense of social superiority, independence, and self-reliance.

These were the intended traits of the well-brought-up, religious, dutiful, middle-class adult. To attain these contradictory qualities, food was used as a tool for moral instruction, and children had to suffer the worst of contradictions – to go hungry in their childhood domestic and educational realms of plenty.

Bibliography

Beeton, Isabella, *The Book of Household Management* (London: S. O. Beeton, 1861).

Brontë, Charlotte, *Jane Eyre* (New York: Penguin, 1997).

Burnett, John, *Plenty and Want; A Social History of Diet in England from 1815 to the Present Day* (London: Scolar Press, 1979).

Davin, Anna, *Growing up Poor: Home, School and Street in London 1870–1914* (London: Rivers Oram Press, 1996).

Drummond, J. C. and Anne Wilbraham, *The Englishman's Food: A History of Five Centuries of English Diet* (London: J. Cape, 1939).

Goody, Jack, *Cooking, Cuisine and Class* (Cambridge: Cambridge University Press,1982).

Gosse, Edmund, *Father and Son* (London: Penguin, 1989).

Gratzer, Walter, *Terrors of the Table: A Curious History of Nutrition* (Oxford: Oxford University Press, 2005).

Holt, Emmett L., *The Care and Feeding of Children* (New York; London: D. Appleton, 1903).

Lamb, Charles, 'Christ's Hospital Five and Thirty Years Ago,' in *The Oxford Anthology of English Literature: Romantic Poetry and Prose* (London: Oxford University Press: 1973), pp. 659–699.

Mars, Valerie, 'Parsimony and Plenty,' *Food, Culture and History*, vol. 1, 1993.

Petty, Elizabeth Celia, *The Impact of the Newer Knowledge of Nutrition: Nutrition Science and Nutrition Policy 1900–1936*. PhD: London University School of Hygiene and Tropical Medicine, 1987.

Philip, R. K., *The Practical Housewife* (London: Ward, Locke and Co., 1855).

Pool, Daniel, *What Jane Austen Ate and Charles Dickens Knew: Fascinating Facts of Daily Life in the Nineteenth Century* (London: Robinson, 1998).

Ross, Ellen, *Love and Toil; Motherhood in Outcast London, 1870–1918* (Oxford: Oxford University Press, 1993).

Rousseau, Jean Jacques, *The Émile of Jean Jacques Rousseau* (1762) trans. William Boyd (New York: Teachers College Press, 1956).

Ruskin, John, *Praeterita* (1885) (Oxford: Oxford University Press, 1983).

Thompson, F.M.L., *The Rise of Respectable Society; A Social History of Victorian Britain* (Cambridge, MA: Harvard University Press, 1993).

Walvin, James, *A Child's World; A Social History of English Childhood 1800–1914* (Harmondsworth: Penguin, 1982).

Wesley, John, *On the Education of Children* (1777) text from the 1872 edition.

Notes

1. Brontë, p. 63.
2. Thompson, pp. 125–6.
3. Drummond and Wilbraham, pp. 65–69.
4. Gratzer, p. 40; Drummond and Wilbraham, p. 66.
5. Gratzer, p. 43.
6. Drummond and Wilbraham, p. 67.
7. For example, in 1855 R.K. Philip, author of *The Practical Housewife*, wrote: 'That fruits are naturally healthy in their season, if rightly taken, no one, who believes that the Creator is a kind and

beneficient being, can doubt. And yet the use of summer fruits appears often to cause most fatal diseases, especially in children. Why is this? Because we do not conform to the natural laws in using this kind of diet. These laws are very simple and easy to understand. Let the fruit be ripe when you eat it, and eat when you require *food*' (p. 50).

8. Walvin, p. 98.
9. Walvin, p. 46.
10. Rousseau, p. 64.
11. Cleverly and Philips, pp. 28–31.
12. Wesley, p. 4.
13. Philip, p. 49.
14. Holt, pp. 106–7.
15. Ruskin, p. 17.
16. Gosse, p. 111.
17. Gosse, pp. 111–12.
18. Cobbett, 1832, http://www.visionofbritain.org.uk/text/chap_page.jsp;jsessionid=70CFDBB2F0A13 2448B299B4EBED06F27?t_id=Cobbett&c_id=12. William Cobbett, a selection from *Rural Rides*, (Letchworth, 1932) 'A Vision of Britain Through Time' http://www.visionofbritain.org.uk/text/contents_page.jsp?t_id=Cobbett.
19. Cobbett, as quoted by Burnett, p. 37.
20. Ross, p. 49.
21. Petty, p. 37.
22. Petty, p. 39.
23. Interview with Matthew Sheffield, Record Office for Leicestershire, Leicester and Rutland, Mantle Oral History Project, audio cassette, MA200/032/032.
24. Ibid.
25. Mrs A. H. Stratton, Essex Record Office, Age Concern Essays, T/Z 25/499.
26. As different from a developing stomach. Nineteenth-century popular medicine believed that children's bodies were not merely growing in size, but were still forming and not yet fully functional, similar to the state of a foetus in the womb. See Pool, p. 205.
27. Beeton, p. 1042.
28. Davin, p. 71–2.
29. Mars, pp. 155–6.
30. Pool, p. 204.
31. Drummond and Wilbraham, p. 129.
32. Goody, pp. 145–6.
33. Drummond and Wilbraham, p. 342.
34. Lamb, p. 660.
35. Drummond and Wilbraham, pp. 403–4.

The Ethics of Food and Environmental Challenges

Brian Melican and Edward Maxwell

Arguments about whether our planet is under threat from human activity have ceased; the argument is now about whether the threat is already beyond control. In theory, most people are also in agreement that since the threat is manmade, and that since it is very grave indeed, man must take action to alleviate it.

Yet, despite the argument having moved to acceptance of man's responsibility for possibly catastrophic climate change, this last step of man's taking action seems to be still[1] in its infancy. Many people reading this paper will have driven here today. All of them will know that cars cause large amounts of carbon emissions. All – unless they belong to an increasingly marginalised, dubious section of the scientific community – will know that carbon emissions are a major cause of global warming. Yet none will have abandoned their cars.

Similarly, extensive media coverage of eating habits in relation to the environment yields a general, if not unproblematic, consensus: our food is produced in a more carbon-intensive way, and travels for longer on carbon-fueled transport, than ever before; industrial farming and production methods mean food is often of reduced nutritional quality and priced in a manner which belies its true environmental impact. Never has food been in such abundance and so cheap, and yet never before have people been so worried about it both in terms of their own health and that of the planet. Yet many of these same people still refuse to take action.

This paper will not examine in detail the problems with our food, for it seems beyond doubt that problems there are; an average week's clippings from national media sources will yield a plethora of worrying articles about both the environmental and public health impact of modern eating habits.[1] Interesting syntheses of different sets of food issues have been offered already, too.[2,3]

Rather this paper will concentrate on the following problem: if we know that flying in a mango from a third world country releases dangerous amounts of greenhouse gasses entirely disproportionate to its size and importance as a foodstuff (and we do);[4,5] and if we know not only that we are at liberty to chose other food produced closer to home, but that we are, in buying the mango, contributing to climate change that may render its grower's land unusable, not to mention our own (and we do);[6] why do we buy the damned mango at all?

As ever in life, the answer will not be single-fold. Why do people buy mangoes? Primarily, because mangoes are available and because people like them, of course. Yet why do they still buy them in the full knowledge that they represent a damaging example of actions that might lead to ecological catastrophe?

Perhaps some do not have this knowledge, although the profile of the issue in the national media suggests that such people are part of a shrinking minority, especially when the average consumer of exotic fruits belongs to the more privileged and better-educated members of society.

Some might have this knowledge, but be suspicious of it, although such 'suspicions' can now be grounded on nothing more than a vague and erroneous conception that climate change is a hoax cooked up by anti-consumerist killjoys.

Some, and I suspect this is the greatest number, will have this knowledge, and be relatively sure, perhaps even convinced to the point of worry, that it is true. They will, however, not act in a way that would seem consistent with this knowledge (e.g. not buying the mango) for various reasons:

1. They believe that global warming is already happening, that it is too late to stop it and that we must simply learn to adapt, as humans have always done, to its consequences (which might, fortuitously, include the ability to grow mangoes in the U.K. before long).
2. They believe that their own personal contribution to cutting emissions in not buying air-miles products is so small as to be not worth making (especially since they really like mangoes).
3. They believe that it is the responsibility of the supermarket, the grower, the government, indeed anyone but themselves to make sure that such ecologically dangerous products are not available (especially since they are unable to resist mangoes, damn it).
4. They believe that not buying air-freighted products will put the third-world farmer who produced it at an economic disadvantage (they are also fond of mangoes).
5. They believe that, since the product is already here, it is wrong *not* to buy it since it will spoil and the emissions will have been released for nothing (indeed, this particular mango here seems deliciously, juicily, temptingly overripe...)

These reasons, for people who enounce them, frequently overlap and support each other; it is rare for a mango-purchaser to stick doggedly to just one. It is not hard to see, however, that they are inconsistent with one another if used in combination. Anyone espousing response number 1, for example, is logically unable to have recourse to any other proposition. Number 2, for example, undermines the blasé attitude of its immediate predecessor by admitting that there is a crisis and that human action might be able to avert it. Number 3 shares this same inconsistency. Number 5 also implies that releasing emissions is morally wrong, something that number 1 seems to contradict in its cheerful relativism .Number 4 is in the most direct contradiction with number 1 not only will global warming, geographically, have a greater effect in third world countries,[7] but these countries are poorer and less able to adapt to it (moreover, growing mangoes in the U.K. would threaten farmers in the tropics yet further).

There is of course an underlying background reason for all of these justifications, and it was the first one given: people really like mangoes. Even the most rudimentary analysis of the facts of modern consumer society shows that ethical concerns form at best a secondary overlay to primary desires; this is so because the logical and moral course of action for everyone to follow under a well-grounded fear of the magnitude of global warming is: to not take the risk of buying anything unnecessary for immediate survival that may contribute to it.

Now, since the effects of global warming stand to be most catastrophic for the poorest people on the planet, and since we insist on contributing to it due to our personal desires, the following observation might at this stage be usefully formulated: we value our own *preferences* above the *needs* of other people.

Morally, this is utterly condemnable; and yet we have just seen that it is the case. Of course, no one caught buying a mango would phrase his or her consumer choice this way. He or she would never say that they value their right to exchange money for a superior alimentary experience above the right of a Bangladeshi family to not have to flee their ancestral home due to rising sea water. Most would simply refuse to see a connection. Yet according to scientific consensus, there is a very, strong connection. In the West, we live ever more above our ecological means,[8] and food production, packaging, and transport forms a large part of this.[9,10]

What do we mean when we say that people value their preferences above those of others? In *What good are the arts?*, John Carey tackles an analogous problem: people who promote 'high art' as superior to 'low art' are essentially labouring under the delusion that the great pleasure and deep intellectual nourishment they gain from, say, opera, outweigh the clearly shallow and meaningless gratification to be gained from fodder for the masses such as soap operas.

Yet, of course, 'how other people feel and think is (…) not precisely knowable'.[11] Carey makes reference to Jonathan Glover to illustrate this: this latter postulates 'internal adequacy'[12] as a way of elaborating on the idea that, although to an educated, active person the life of another, mentally handicapped person in a wheelchair may appear not worth living, this life may in fact please them or pain them to the same extent as the lives of others please or pain those who live them.

Silently, unthinkingly, people contributing to global warming in unnecessary ways are running on the assumption that the emotional ranges of people in the third world are less meaningful. How else to explain buying a mango over an apple? They estimate the pleasure differential gained from the taste of mango as against the taste of apple to be greater than the pleasure differential that might be gained by a third world farmer who discovers that he can stay on land his family have occupied for generations.

Of course, Carey points us towards the mental blockage that gives rise to this:

> to have the same feelings you would have to inhabit the same body, share the
> same unconscious, to have undergone the same education, to have been shaped

by the same emotional experiences – in short, to *be* the other person, which is impossible, even for lovers in bed together, let alone for two humans from different cultures.[13]

This point is surely rather simplistic? So we will never know how a third-world farmer feels without being one. Furthermore, isn't this an admission that, since we cannot know them, the feelings of others must remain a low priority?

Yet Carey is not denying the possibility of valuing other people's inner lives; indeed, he is pointing out that it 'indicates a strange lack of imagination'[14] to think that you can judge your own inner life to be richer and more intense than anyone else's. In fact, if we use our imagination, we might be entitled to think that our preference for one fruit over another is of relatively minor importance compared to that of someone else for a home and a liveable environment.

What we are talking about here, then, is intersubjectivity, empathy, and solidarity. The quotation from John Carey points us toward one central issue with solidarity in the context of the global food debate: 'let alone... two humans from different cultures.' Few people radically underestimate the importance of the inner lives of their friends and family, and so few people would continue to buy mangoes if they had a visibly adverse effect on those around them. Yet it is all too easy to forget the enormity of humanity with which we never come into personal contact.[15]

This is, in fact, a historically recent problem, and may explain why we as a society are still so bad at tackling it. In *A Short History of Progress*, Ronald Wright points out that none of the previous ecological catastrophes that man has caused (and they have been manifold) affected the entire planet: now, however, we are dealing with 'the great experiment,'[16] with the survival of humanity itself. Or, as ecologically committed comedian Robert Newman puts it, 'there is no "planet B".'[17] There is now a central solidarity between us as consumers and the third world as producers: namely, we all stand to feel pain if climate change gets out of control.

So rather than acting to help just those whom we see, we are being asked to act to help not only everyone in this country but everyone in the world: all by not buying a mango, a simple and effective choice that is admittedly difficult to visualise in the context of saving humanity.

After all, even if flown-in fresh produce consumes several times its own weight in carbon dioxide emissions, the average mango doesn't weigh much: yet in a society based on democratic consumer choice, personal responsibility for all emissions must remain undiminished, however small; and the cumulative effect of several mangos per month flown in over the course of several years, and then the example set by purchasing such products, may be collectively very damaging indeed.

This is a nexus of moral responsibility tackled in the ethics of Jean-Paul Sartre. The central tenet of Sartre's philosophy is freedom and it rests on choice.

> *La liberté humaine [ne fait] qu'un avec l'être du Pour-soi : la réalité humaine est libre dans l'exacte mesure où elle a à être son propre néant.*[18]
>
> [Human freedom (forms) but a single entity with the for-itself; freedom is a human reality inasmuch as this latter must negate itself.]

Man's life is choice: he must continually choose between several options because his consciousness ('the for-itself') is always made aware by its ability to imagine, project and plan that reality could always be otherwise (i.e. negates itself). Everything is contingent: there is no one path pre-defined for the human subject ('*Chaque homme doit inventer son chemin*'[19]), and so he must always choose; and if he refuses to choose, then he has made a choice not to choose. Since all humans have this ability, and therefore necessity, to choose, all humans are in this respect equally free, and thus every choice we make is a blueprint for humanity

> *Lorsque sur le plan d'authenticité totale, j'ai reconnu que l'homme est un être chez qui l'essence est précédé par l'existence (…) j'ai reconnu en même temps que je ne peux vouloir que la liberté des autres.*[20]
>
> [Once I've taken authenticity to its completion, recognised that man is a being whose essence is preceded by his existence …, I've also recognised that I can want nothing but the freedom of other people.]

211

Choice and freedom bring responsibility. If we make a choice to oppress people, we are endorsing oppression, since other people could also make this choice.

Of course, the example of oppression brings us to the central Sartrean dialectic. Oppressed people, for example, cannot choose by the very fact that they are oppressed. The earlier Sartre found this fact difficult to integrate into his philosophy, since he firmly believed that everyone was always free to choose. Yet this view unmodified would have led him to inculpate slaves in their own oppression in a way that would be often unrealistic.[21] In wider human terms, it would have denied that people were affected by their upbringing and the society around them. It risked blaming people for not being able to discern choices they had not been educated to be able to see.[22]

So, by *Critique de la raison dialectique*, Sartre had clearly distinguished between ontological and practical freedom. Ontological freedom is the internal freedom of our minds: we are always free to stop imagining something[23] and free to stop absorbing media.[24] Similarly, we are always free to assert our right to choose, our independence, even as slaves, within our minds. We are, in fact, 'condemned to be free' because knowledge of our ability to choose often makes us painfully aware of our limits (*angoisse*), or, even worse, aware when we are committing damaging acts that are in fact avoidable.

L'homme est condamné à être libre ; condamné parce qu'il ne s'est pas lui créé lui-même, et par ailleurs cependant libre parce qu'une fois jeté dans le monde, il est responsable de tout ce qu'il fait.[25]

[Man is condemned to be free; condemned because he did not create himself, and yet again free because, once he has been thrown into the world, he is responsible for everything he does.]

Practical freedom, however, is limited by our situation. A slave may know that he is a human being like all others, yet in practice, he is unable to assert this. People with a poor education have less practical choice since they are unable to evaluate choices in the light of the same knowledge as better educated people; this then further limits their practical freedom by necessitating them to earn their living working longer hours for less money, placing caps on their practical choices.

This has clear implications for the debate around ecologically friendly eating. In the inner cities, fast food and supermarkets are not only cheap, but ubiquitous to the exclusion of everything else. Because we are a democratic society that has enshrined liberty, freedom of choice, inhabitants are theoretically, ontologically free to choose to reject bad food; but practically, they may lack the money, time, and education necessary to do so. Interestingly, studies have shown that farmers' markets are not only more popular and environmentally friendlier but usually better value than supermarkets,[26,27] yet if there is no farmers' market, or if people cannot handle products sold there, their actual liberty to shop there is limited.

Yet mango-buyers are not generally impoverished inner-city dwellers. In fact, they are frequently people who benefit from the best-ever match-up of ontological and practical freedom in human history, from all the ingredients necessary to understanding our choices and their effects on those around us, and then acting in accordance with our moral judgement on them.

In conversation recently, two academic friends in Oxford, aware of my ecological convictions and therefore eager to please with their earnest concern for the environment, started to bemoan the fact that orange juice using oranges from Florida is cheaper and more easily available than its variant using Spanish fruit. How were people supposed to be encouraged to buy products from closer to home if the price wasn't right? My answer that if they were really concerned about this environmental damage, strictly speaking, they shouldn't really be drinking orange juice at all was greeted by a very matter-of-fact response: 'It's a must-have for us.'

We all have a 'must-have' list and stopping the destruction of the planet, as important as it is, cannot be allowed to destroy everyday life.[28] Yet the real response to such an answer should really be 'Why?' A necessity is, philosophically, defined as something that must be so in all imaginable worlds, and is thus limited to mathematical and scientific rules. The fact that people drink orange juice at all is, rather, a contingency, something that is a product of this world and that is not immutable.

We have isolated here a prime example of an avoidable incidence of ecologically damaging behaviour perpetrated by people who really should, and theoretically do, know better. There are, in many other cases, no choices for the private consumer looking to reduce his ecological impact and maintain a basic standard of living, but not here. We are, after all, not asking people to abstain from fresh fruit or vitamin C: what is wrong with apple juice? We are not asking people to be unhealthier and die sooner, and we should note the flourishing of medical science and the general improvement of working conditions as major factors in increasing health and life-expectancy.[29,30]

So food is one area where choice to the greater good is most easily exercised (as opposed to larger issues mostly beyond the control of the individual, such as energy generation), yet one where people seem to be frequently unwilling to change. To rephrase this example in Sartrean terms, we are dealing with people who have not only an ontological liberty fully enhanced by high quality education, but a practical liberty unparalleled in human history to match. Yet they are denying both these freedoms to themselves (with words like <u>must</u>-have), and are thus people living in *mauvaise foi*, or bad faith.

Have we reached the limits of democracy, then? If the country's most highly educated people cannot be relied upon to keep abreast of current affairs and then apply their knowledge to their own everyday actions in an ethical manner, must they not be forced to do so? If man is '*condamné à être libre*,' then people with the time and education to read and understand press reports must be condemned to be freer than most, more obliged to act in accordance with their consciences, and more subject to existential '*angoisse*' that follows from the obligation to make ethical choices.

And if we cannot rely on the country's intellectual elite, surely everyone else, with less time to occupy themselves with such matters, must be made to behave in certain ways? After all, the possible destruction of the planet would seem a worthy enough concern to justify imposing some relatively harsh limits relatively soon, would it not? To preserve the freedom of everyone on the planet to survive, the most basic of freedoms, must we not take away the freedom of people in the West to drive cars and eat mangoes?

Yet here we have stumbled across Isaiah Berlin's concept of 'positive liberty,' where society is organised to renounce some freedoms to achieve a greater one. Berlin shows how this leads inevitably to totalitarianism, and how totalitarianism never achieves its stated aims.[31,32] Climate activists must not be midwives to a dictatorship, however attractive its potential to curb climate change may seem. We must put up with the frustrations of 'negative liberty', whereby people are guaranteed the freedom to reject all systems of thought and all requests (including exhortations to clean up their environmental act). The alternative is too prone to the exercise of cruelty to contemplate.

Richard Rorty's seminal work on the topic, *Contingency, Irony and Solidarity*, provides us with a way of sustaining this dialectic between moral imperatives and the freedom of everyone to act as they see fit, even in contravention of these moral imperatives. Rorty is, however, not sketching out 'the philosophical foundations of democracy,'[33] since he sees that this can never be satisfactorily achieved. Arguments *for* democracy are, like all arguments, free to be undermined, and indeed democracy must-needs submit itself to such critique in order to be democracy: arguments should instead be concentrated *against* undemocratic practice.

On his library ceiling Montaigne had inscribed: 'to every argument, an equal argument is opposed'; Rorty welcomes this continuous debate, arguing that democracy is good precisely because it functions on

> free and open encounter. (Debate) should be fostered for its own sake. *A liberal society is one which is content to call 'true' whatever the upshot of such encounters turns out to be.* That is why a liberal society is badly served by an attempt to supply it with 'philosophical foundations.' For the attempt to supply such foundations presupposes a natural order of topics and arguments which is prior to, and overrides the results of, encounters between new and old vocabularies.[34]

We as people who are engaged in minting a new vocabulary to describe and promote our environmental beliefs must simply hope that this new vocabulary wins out rather than seek to enshrine it. There are grounds for optimism: this essay uses *air-miles*, *climate change*, and *ecologically sound*, terms unavailable until recently.

Furthermore, we must at no point slip into radicalism or exclusion. Whilse I may voice logically legitimate exasperation at the *mauvaise foi*, at the inauthentic nature of many people's ethical choices, I must

> *Privatise* the Nietzschean-Sartrean-Foucauldian attempt at authenticity and purity, in order to prevent (myself) from slipping into a political attitude which will lead (me) to think that there is some social goal more important than avoiding cruelty.[35]

We can content ourselves knowing that trying to spread ecologically sound and equitable eating habits will contribute to avoiding cruelty (of the climate-change kind), without deluding ourselves that any form of undemocratic action can make a bigger contribution to this task without ending in other types of cruelty (of the Orwellian kind). We must therefore commit to advocating, advertising our ideas within the bounds of democratic discourse.[36]

So how best, then, to advocate our ideas? Democratic governments find themselves in an odd position, namely trying to coax their populations to avoid certain types of behaviour while trying to remain elected by them. Such work can only be relatively long-term. The effect of public health campaigns, for example, is unquantifiable but indisputable. The key to fighting smoking has been to make a problem before attempting to ban it, to change public opinion before daring to change the law. F.S.C. Northrop talks of 'positive' versus 'living' law, where the latter is essentially social mores. These are always the primary force in any society, especially a free one.[37]

While it thus seems indisputable that *'le gouvernement... qui conduit les hommes de la manière qui convient le plus... à leur inclination est le plus parfait,'*[38] it is also true that governments can and must change inclinations ('living laws') by subtle and effective actions. The devil is in the detail: how can governments legitimately protecting their populations from themselves be distinguished from dangerous autocracies? Firstly, it may serve us to invert the question: how can governments who adopt so laissez-faire an attitude as to allow their populations to kill themselves be justified?

Secondly, we must examine how government action can stay within the bounds of what is acceptable in a democratic society. Aside from legislation, there are two primary methods: incentives and information. The former works economically by incentivising or *dis*incentivising certain conducts, usually through taxation. The latter often takes the form of public information campaigns. Yet here of course, only information, and never *dis*information, is acceptable.

Research conducted into the nature of public information campaigns shows that, even when all the information presented is free from distortion, all such government-run initiatives have the potential to damage democratic discourse by creating a circularity:

215

> public information campaigns may threaten democratic processes by circularity of democratic control (...) by government agencies. The circularity problem is that government agencies use campaigns to shape public attitudes and values, which in turn shape the public's expectations and demands on government.[39]

Weiss & Tschirhart go on to illustrate ways to avoid this issue, and conclude that one of the surest ways to achieve good outcomes is by using 'mediating organisations' (or 'third-sector organisations'[40]) for 'the multiplicity of voices reduces the dangers of manipulation.' As far as they are concerned, 'the policy objective is to stimulate public discourse, criticism, and exploration of issues, rather then to influence behaviour.'[41]

Are we not back where we started, though? If the concerted efforts of the media have convinced most educated people of the reality of man's effect on the planet, they have singularly failed to alter behaviour. Will government information be any more effective?[42] Our key trope is frustration: for even though ample information has not led to massive changes in behaviour, overweening didacticism is even less likely to effect change: as Diderot wrote of writers, *'si l'on remarque son but, il le manque... il cesse de dialoguer, il prêche'*.[43] Research into propaganda, that most didactic of textual forms, has found it impossible to prove its effectiveness even in the most closed of societies.[44]

We must, both for this cynical reason of effectiveness, as well as out of respect for democracy and people's own decision-making capacities, make available information about the ecological effects of our eating habits, how to change them for the better and wait for 'positive law' to change. Twenty years ago it was not taboo to drink and drive: this has become socially unacceptable. Might this happen with mangoes?

Yet attempting to create taboos is an unrewarding occupation. If information promoting environmentally friendly eating habits is to triumph in a democratic society with plurivocal media, it must conform to the driving forces in that society. We live in a discourse where one of the commonest questions asked is 'what are you offering?' or 'what do I get?' and we must offer people something accordingly.[45,46]

Indeed, this tendency is not to be roundly condemned. As Barbara Ehrenreich, author of *Dancing in the Streets: A History of Collective Joy*, says:

> If we're going to survive as a species on this planet, we're obviously going to have to change how we live, in ways that involve, for many of us, giving things up. So we can't all have our cars and so on. But you can't exactly have a programme that's based on giving things up. We're going to have to be talking about a much greater pleasure that we're going to find. It's not just dancing in the streets, it's all kinds of creativity.[47]

Food is one of mankind's eldest focuses of creativity. It is also one of man's most frequent areas of daily activity. As such, it can offer huge pleasure gains, and has the potential to effect a daily, and cumulatively exponential, reduction of carbon emissions, not to mention other undesirable chemical and industrial processes.

This pairing of sheer pleasure and ecological virtue is embodied in Carlo Petrini's saying 'a gastronome who is not an environmentalist is stupid. And to me, an environmentalist who is not a gastronome is boring.'[48] The organisation he founded, Slow Food, of which we are members, aims to 'restore the connection between plate and planet,' and to do this, proposes that, primarily, food be *enjoyed*. This leads Petrini to an entire philosophy of life in the finest of the considered hedonistic-epicurean traditions, advocating a general 'slowing down' to savour what is important.

Slow Food proposes a 'living law' that is not a series of commandments, but a series of offers. Rather than railing against the consumption of mangoes and fast food, Slow Food valorises the connections to local producers that make it easy to resist, indeed positively hard to fall for the temptations of environmentally unsound eating habits. Instead of fighting industrialised food on its own terms, allowing ourselves to be depicted as abstainers, environmentalist-gastronomes must simply start and develop a new discourse, a discourse that shows the way we live at its best and forces vested interests promoting opposing lifestyles to try and let *themselves* off the charge of abstinence.

So my strategy will be to try to make the vocabulary in which these objections are phrased look bad, thereby changing the subject, rather than granting the objector his choice of weapons and terrain by meeting his criticisms head-on.[49]

Indeed, why waste any more time talking about mangoes when apples are just as delicious and far easier to consume?

Bibliography

Berlin, Isaiah, *Two concepts of liberty: an inaugural lecture delivered before the University of Oxford on 31 October 1958*. Oxford: Clarendon Press, 1958.

Carey, John, *What good are the arts?* London: Faber and Faber, 2005.

Diderot, *De la poésie dramatique* in *Œuvres Complètes de Diderot*, ed. J. Assézat. Paris: Garnier, 1939.

Klapper, Joseph T., *The Effects of Mass Communication*. Glencoe, Ill: Free Press, 1960.

Montesquieu, *Lettres Persanes*, ed. Jacques Roger. Paris: Gallimard, 1964.

Rorty, Richard, *Contingency, Irony and Solidarity*. Cambridge: Cambridge University Press, 1989.

Sartre, Jean-Paul, *L'imaginaire*. Paris: Gallimard, 1940.

Sartre, Jean-Paul, *L'être et le néant*. Paris: Gallimard, 1943.

Sartre, Jean-Paul, *'Huis clos' suivi de 'Les mouches'*. Paris: Gallimard, 1947.

Sartre, Jean-Paul, *Qu'est-ce que la literature?* Paris: Gallimard, 1948.

Sartre, Jean-Paul, *L'existentialisme est un humanisme*. Paris: Gallimard, 1966.

Wilkinson, Fenton; Van Seers, David, *Adding value to our food system: an economic analysis of sustainable community food systems*. Everson WA, Utah State University, 1997.

Wright, Ronald, *A short history of progress*. Edinburgh: Canongate, 2005.

Notes

1. *The Guardian* is an interesting case study with a rubric 'What's wrong with our food' on its website from 2002 until now, having replaced it with 'Food.'
2. See, for example, *So Shall We Reap: What's Gone Wrong With the World's Food – and How to Fix It*, Colin Tudge, 2004.
3. http://lifeandhealth.guardian.co.uk/food/story/0,,2102601,00.html as accessed 14/06/07.
4. Sustain analysed a sample basket of 26 imported organic items, it found they had travelled a distance equivalent to six times round the equator (150,000 miles). Such a journey releases as much polluting carbon dioxide into the atmosphere as a four-bedroom household cooking meals for eight months. (http://lifeandhealth.guardian.co.uk/food/story/0,,1614359,00.html, as accessed 06/06/07).
5. According to the Department for Environment, Food and Rural Affairs food transported by air – mainly fresh fruit and vegetables – accounts for 0.1% of total food miles, but generates 13% of total food transport CO_2 emissions. (http://business.guardian.co.uk/story/0,,1994170,00.html, as accessed 07/06/07).
6. Central American indigenous people are among the first to suffer from climate change but least equipped to adapt.(http://environment.guardian.co.uk/climatechange/story/0,,2090053,00.html, as accessed 06/06/07).
7. See reports by Intergovernmental Panel on Climate Change, such as the 2007 version available at http://www.ipcc.ch/SPM6avr07.pdf.
8. '…because of high levels of consumption in affluent nations, even a slow rate of population growth in these nations is at least as great a threat to the environment as is a rapid rate of population growth in less developed nations. After all, the footprint of the typical American is nearly 25 times greater than that of the typical Bangladeshi.' York et al p. 295 [York, Richard; Rosa, Eugene A.; Dietz, Thomas, 'Footprints on the Earth – The Ecological Consequences of Modernity', *American*

Sociological Review, vol 68, no. 2 (April 2003), pp. 279–300].

9. A 2005 Defra study found that 'Our continued penchant for non-indigenous fruits has a significant impact on the environment. Even fruit that can be grown in this country usually isn't – between 1994 and 2004 UK fruit production declined by 24% while imports grew by 38%.' (http://environment.guardian.co.uk/ethicalliving/story/0,,2097258,00.html as accessed 07/06/07).

10. For a case study of the part food plays in the growing carbon footprint of a UK city (in this instance, Cardiff), see Tukker et al p. 10 [Tukker, Arnold; Collins, Andrea; Hines, Frances; Wells, Peter, 'Reducing the Welsh Footprint – A contribution to the UN's 10 year Framework of Programmes on Sustainable Consumption and Production,' Cardiff University, 2005].

11. Carey, p. 49.

12. Ibid., p. 59.

13. Ibid., p. 91.

14. Ibid., p. 91.

15. York examines this in economic terms through the vector of world systems theory: 'world-system theory argues that core nations have the power to distance themselves from the impacts they generate, and it is, therefore, misleading to focus only on the impacts a society generates within its national borders.' York et al., p. 288.

16. Wright, pp. 29–53.

17. Guardian Unlimited Podcast, recorded 02/04/06.

18. Sartre (1943), p. 529.

19. Sartre (1947), p. 235.

20. Sartre (1946), p. 73.

21. This *Weltanschauung* finds its most nuanced expression in the problem play *Les Mouches*, where Oreste castigates the weak and cowardly people of Argos for not rising up against their oppressors: '*Ils ont besoin d'une plaie. Ils aiment leur mal.*' Yet the 'radically egocentric' (Gore, La Nausée *and* Les Mouches, 1970) nature of Oreste's personality and his privileged upbringing pose questions about just how one-sided Sartre's view of freedom was even at this early stage in his thinking about the subject.

22. Although, as suggested in the preceding footnote, Sartre was by no means as inflexible in his concept of freedom as many inferred from his more radical sound-bites. Directly following his assertion of ontological freedom in the fourth part of *L'être et le néant* (see footnote 15), Sartre is very careful to analyse situations where this ontological freedom has its options limited by factors external to the consciousness in which it is embedded (see for example pp. 531–536).

23. '*L'image involontaire et l'image volontaire représentent deux types de conscience… l'un est produit par une spontanéité sans volonté et l'autre par une spontaneité volontaire,*' Sartre (1940), p. 42.

24. '*A chaque instant je puis m'eveiller et je le sais … La lecture est un rêve libre,*' Sartre (1948). p. 57.

25. Sartre (1966). p. 37.

26. Bullock, Simon, 'The Economic Benefits of Farmers' Markets,' Bath, 2000.

27. Wilkinson et al.

28. Indeed, Peacock cautions us to 'beware of the culture of austerity. It is an almost automatic, unthinking assumption that signs of ecological stress mandate a turn to austerity. But this need not be the case, until we really have exhausted all options and are finally up against an ecological wall…. The lifeboat régime tends …by condoning parasitical authoritarianism, to lock into place the very conditions of austerity which brought it about; and thus ultimately is a great threat not merely to sustainability, but even to the survival of the society or even perhaps the species.' pp. 11–12. [Peacock, Kent A., 'Symbiosis and the Ecological Role of Philosophy,' *Dialogue 38* (1999), pp. 699–717].

29. See Tables 2 and 3, Nixon & Ulmann, *The Relationship between Healthcare Expenditure and Health Outcomes*, Springer 2006 (published online: http://www.springerlink.com/content/y00147rq18r72p77/fulltext.pdf).

30. See also Coale, 'Demographic Effects of Scientific Progress,' *Special Publication of the American*

Philosophical Society no. 44 (1987), pp. 85–95.

31. See Berlin, *Two Concepts of Liberty.*

32. See also Peacock in footnote 28.

33. Rorty, p. 44.

34. Rorty, p. 52.

35. Rorty, p. 65.

36. Moreover, considering ambivalence about the effectiveness of government itself, the ability to critique it in as free a society as possible becomes essential: 'political freedom and civil liberties are expected to lead to environmental reforms because they provide a context in which NSMs, NGOs, and individuals can influence policy and institutional behavior.' York et al., p. 285.

37. Northrop, 'Law, Language and Morals,' *The Yale Law Journal*, vol. 71, no. 6 (1962) pp. 1017–1048.

38. Montesquieu, p. 137.

39. Weiss & Tschirhart, Public Information Campaigns as Policy Instruments, *Journal of Policy Analysis and Management*, vol. 13, no. 1 (1994) pp. 82–119.

40. Kotler & Murray, 'Third Sector Management – The Role of Marketing,' *Public Administration Review*, vol. 53, no. 5 (1975) pp. 467–472.

41. Weiss & Tschirhart.

42. Indeed, York is not convinced of the effectiveness of government in this context: 'Our results do not argue that institutional and technological changes are irrelevant to environmental impacts ... However, the sobering note from this analysis is our failure to detect the ameliorating processes postulated by neoclassical economics and ecological modernization theorists. This suggests we cannot be sanguine about ecological sustainability via emergent institutional change.' York et al., p. 295.

43. Diderot, p. 654.

44. See Klapper, *The Effects of Mass Communication.*

45. '...non-profit organizations are involved in marketing whether or not they are conscious of it. They are involved in various markets and use certain operating principles in dealing with each market. These operating principles define their marketing. The issue is not one of whether nonprofit organizations should get involved in marketing, but rather how thoughtful they should be about it. ...Organizations in a free society depend upon voluntary exchanges to accomplish their objectives ...the designing of proper incentives is a key step in stimulating these exchanges.' Kotler & Murray, p. 469.

46. 'Criticism has a direct *ecological* role, in that it is by far the most effective weapon against parasitical authority. But perhaps it is not too much to ask that we also try to provide some positive visions of what might be possible.... As a proverb says, "Where there is no vision, the people perish" (Prov. 29:18). There can be no green future without a vision of a green future.' Peacock, p. 12.

47. *The Independent on Sunday*, 'ABC,' 06/05/07.

48. Report from the European Conference on Regional and Local Food, Lerum (Sweden), 2005.

49. Rorty, p. 44.

'Morality touched by emotion': Food in the Novels of Dickens

Anne Mendelson

Charles Dickens did not have much use for people who professionally moralize about food. He had, indeed, little use for professional moralizers about most things. His disdain for the tribe did not reflect any want of convictions about good and evil; as a man and as an artist Dickens profoundly embraced Christian moral teaching as he understood it. But he was repelled by much of what he saw being paraded under that banner. He abhorred all kinds of officious special-interest axe-grinding cloaked in airs of moral or intellectual superiority. And as a novelist he was fascinated by how those same hidden or open partisanships privately play themselves out among people in endlessly diverse psychological maneuverings revolving around what he portrays as one of mankind's greatest blessings or curses: food.

Nobody among English novelists ever depicted the act of cooking with a more unerring grasp of detail; the beefsteak-pie scene in *Martin Chuzzlewit*, the dinner cooked by Captain Cuttle for Florence in *Dombey and Son*, and Mr Micawber's rescue of a nearly ruined leg of mutton in *David Copperfield* contain more kitchen sense than a dozen cookbooks.[1] Nobody ever conjured up good food with a solider immediacy. By the same token, nobody ever wrote more devastatingly about dreary, disreputable, or just plain bad food in innumerable guises and surroundings. Among the liveliest exhibits in this gallery are the school breakfast in *Nicholas Nickleby* ('a brown composition which looked like diluted pincushions without the covers, and was called porridge'), the 'Druidical ruin' of assorted tea dregs and bread scraps grudgingly allotted to the Smallweed family's meek little charwoman in *Bleak House*, and the bargain-basement salad – starting with 'either the oldest of lettuces or youngest of cabbages, but at any rate a green vegetable of an expansive nature' – that Betsey Prig in *Martin Chuzzlewit* hauls out of her pocket to grace Sairey Gamp's cold collation of 'two pounds of Newcastle salmon, intensely pickled.'[2] (Henry Mayhew's remarkable contemporary survey *London Labour and the London Poor* relates that over-the-hill 'Newcastle pickled salmon' was regularly palmed off cheap on persons who, like Mrs Gamp and her guest, tended to be chronically pickled themselves.[3])

To see a moral dimension in these marvelous evocations is not far-fetched.

Nearly every portrayal of eating and drinking in Dickens is inseparable from the sense that food *matters* as a mark of how well we do by our fellows, whether or not we recognize them as fellows. The strange intertwinings of different people's destinies that underlie all his plots also underscore a conviction that everybody throughout a vast palace-to-gutter gamut is equally important, because equally human. The mentally retarded unfortunate in *Little Dorrit* whose happiest food memories are of meals in the hospital where she was nursed through a brain fever has as much human dignity as the financial titan who hovers uneasily around his wife's gilded dinner parties in the same book. Food in the novels points to both shared humanity and inhumanities without number. It is a cornerstone of 'morality touched by emotion,' which Matthew Arnold (in *Literature and Dogma*) took to be the meaning of religion.

What Dickens manages to do with this motif often rests on well-judged artistic choices about what *not* to do. He ignores, for instance, impressive gastronomic displays as such, and not because he lacked a discerning palate or an understanding of gastronomy. When he presents the rich and famous at table, he omits all but the broadest, most pantomimic details about what is served, or how. No one could go to *Our Mutual Friend* or *Little Dorrit* hoping to reconstruct typical bills of fare at the glittering feasts that figure in the action. At the other end of the social spectrum, the novels also leave out the horrific particulars that Dickens could well have provided of meals among the very poorest – people like the cigar-end scavengers whom Mayhew saw grubbing 'the smallest scraps and crusts of bread' from dustbins and street refuse in order to boil 'the hard and dirty crusts' with a minuscule amount of oatmeal, for what 'often constitutes all the food [a whole family] taste in the course of the day.'[4] Dickens was neither unaware of such enormities nor disposed to prettify them. Rather, he conveys the horror of extreme want and the offensiveness of ostentation more trenchantly through strategic reticence than he could have with relentless accumulation of detail.

His full powers of description are almost wholly reserved for social levels between these extremes. The characters whose eating, drinking, and cooking Dickens repeatedly and vividly dwells on usually belong to orders that wouldn't have registered on most contemporary cookbook writers' scales of importance and that in turn would have paid no cookbooks: workingmen, under-servants, roustabouts, low-level clerks, street criminals, con artists, tavernkeepers and their clienteles, proprietors of odd marginal businesses, aging eccentrics on the fringes of poverty.

Assorted middle-class families both well and badly off are also among the number. But their food is never portrayed with the comedy-of-manners brushstrokes found in some Victorian novels, like Mrs Gibson's status-chasing reforms of the family table (once in charge, she starts serving French dishes and policing her husband's vulgar penchant for cheese) in Elizabeth Gaskell's *Wives and Daughters*.[5] The absence of such clever nuances is precisely what gives Dickens's food a sense of solid presence and an ability to figure in infinitely varied sorts of moral calculus.

Almost invariably, fare mentioned with any specificity is supremely ordinary grub; 'elemental' or 'primal' might be closer to the mark. It is food that had hardly been touched by fashion – that is, social ambition, sophistication, or 'lifestyle' preference – since Dickens's own childhood or the lifetimes of his parents. Just for that reason, it

221

has a kind of timeless substantiality that can indirectly illuminate the essence of one morally charged situation or another.

The food that people are most regularly shown eating is bread. The food oftenest used to evoke gastronomic pleasure is bread and butter, with each at its best – 'the bread new and crusty, the butter fresh,' as in the pleasant, civilized tea provided (in *Hard Times*) by two hardworking Yorkshire mill-hands to a poor old lady whom they scarcely know.[6] An impromptu three-person feast of cottage-loaves and milk celebrates Bella and John's spur-of-the-moment betrothal in *Our Mutual Friend*.[7] By contrast, the utter deprivation of Jo the London street sweep in *Bleak House* hits home when we glimpse him breakfasting on 'a dirty bit of bread' while sitting 'on the door-step of the Society for the Propagation of the Gospel in Foreign Parts.'[8]

That juxtaposition is a particularly bald piece of editorializing directed at a certain club of English do-gooders. But for every such rude kick in the pants there are a dozen scenes in which plain, familiar food is more obliquely shown to be at the heart of what goes on between people, for good or ill.

It is ordinary people's food that lights up the meaning of cruelty, as in the 'dreary waste of cold potatoes' and 'about two square inches of cold mutton' snarlingly served out by Miss Sally Brass to a malnourished servant girl in *The Old Curiosity Shop*.[9] The meaning of kindness, as in the gravy that Joe Gargery keeps lavishing on the child Pip in attempted atonement for everyone else's enthusiastic Christmas-dinner bullyings in *Great Expectations*.[10] The meaning of hospitality, as in the breakfast of 'vast mounds of toast, new-laid eggs, boiled ham, Yorkshire pie, and other cold substantials,' together with 'about a quarter of a pint of spirits,' that John Browdie, in *Nicholas Nickleby*, thrusts on the old and hungry Nicholas.[11] The meaning of inhospitality, as in the cheap refection – 'two bottles of currant wine, white and red; a dish of sandwiches (very long and very slim); another of apples; another of captain's biscuits (which are always a moist and jovial sort of viand); a plate of oranges cut up small and gritty with powdered [grated] sugar; and a highly geological cake' – that the Pecksniff family sets out in honor of Martin Chuzzlewit's arrival, subsequently arranging the leftovers in 'two chaotic heaps' to see Martin and Tom Pinch through the next several weeks.[12]

Likewise, everyday food and drink can show people at their most naively unaffected, like Sloppy in *Our Mutual Friend* reciting the glorious particulars of the dinners – meat, beer, vegetables, pudding – that he is to enjoy as Mr and Mrs Boffin's new employee.[13] They also are wont to nourish bumper crops of hypocrites, from the dipsomaniac preacher in *The Pickwick Papers* denouncing the sin of drunkenness to Mr Wopsle in *Great Expectations* tearing his attention away from a plate of pork long enough to harangue the small and hapless Pip, 'The gluttony of Swine is put before us as an example to the young.'[14] Where they figure most remarkably, however, is in Dickens's many and virtuosic explorations of family dynamics as a theater of sane or skewed moral priorities.

For perhaps one family in ten, meals are an emblem of family solidarity – or more

222

specifically, parental responsibilities honestly lived up to. That the strong, 'soldierly looking' Mrs Bagnet has her head screwed on right is clear from our first glimpse of the plain but plentiful dinner that she dishes up for her ex-military family and an unexpected guest with 'exact system; allotting to every portion of pork its own portion of pot-liquor, greens, potatoes, and even mustard; and serving it out complete.'[15]

As Dickensians know, however, family dysfunction following on evasion or abuse of parental responsibilities is more of a norm in his fictional universe. Usually it represents not so much wickedness as the loss (or perversion) of moral moorings in a confused and threatening world. Meals are one of the first things to be affected. There are the disjointed, incompetent excuses for family dinner *chez* Jellyby (*Bleak House*) and Pocket (*Great Expectations*), with mothers too invincibly sealed off in their own worlds to notice that they *have* children.[16] There are the horribly numerous cases in which a young child takes on the burdens abdicated by a parent, like Little Dorrit working her fingers to the bone to bring nice dinners to her serenely freeloading father in the debtors' prison; or the painfully crippled Jenny Wren in *Our Mutual Friend*, whose meager earnings maintain not only the 'bad child' who is her father but (when he can get his hands on threepence) his lethal drinking habit.[17] There is the meal as moral blackmail, most keenly typified in the scene in *Little Dorrit* where Arthur Clennam's cold, unmaternal mother, an invalid who has her food prepared and served in precisely compounded portions on a rigid schedule, punishes him for a perceived affront by ostentatiously sending away her usual eleven o'clock oysters untasted – 'placing the act to her credit, no doubt, in her Eternal day-book.'[18]

Nor do literal parent-child relationships exhaust the theme. It extends into all manner of institutional or public spheres where people occupy positions of quasi-parental accountability for anyone else. Those responsible for children regularly make themselves comfortable at their charges' expense, like Mr and Mrs Squeers at Dotheboys Hall in *Nicholas Nickleby* or Mrs Pipchin in *Dombey and Son* regaling herself with mutton chops, 'buttered toast unlimited,' and sweetbreads while the weakly young inmates of her 'infantine Boarding-School' get rations 'chiefly of the vegetable and farinaceous [i.e., cheap] kind.'[19] Others holding power over some class of grownups – for example, Bounderby the mill-owner in *Hard Times* – treat them like greedy children in want of restraining.[20]

The worst parental stand-in of all, however, is government in all shapes and forms from Chancery or the Circumlocution Office to the parish board of workhouse supervisors who, before Oliver Twist's arrival in their clutches, already had arranged to weed out deadbeats by contracting 'with the water-works to lay in an unlimited supply of water; and with a corn-factor to supply periodically small quantities of oatmeal; and issued three meals of thin gruel a day, with an onion twice a week, and half a roll on Sundays.'[21] Possibly even worse than this frank heartlessness is governmental larceny camouflaged in doublespeak, like the smokescreen of pseudo-figures and facts with which two civic busybodies in *The Chimes* take away a harmless old man's bowl of hot tripe – a cheap favorite of the humble classes – while denouncing it as a nutritional outrage tantamount to snatching food 'out of the mouths of widows and orphans.'[22]

For an early-twenty-first-century reader, what is perhaps most striking about the role of food in Dickens is the directness and lack of contrivance with which moral implications leap off the page – the result of a determined concentration on everyday foods that for Dickens and his audience represented universal values. No English or American novelist today could do anything of the kind, the most obvious reason being that we no longer have everyday foods capable of transcending highly segmented values. I think our lack of them is due not simply to the great cultural and ethnic diversity of contemporary Western societies but to certain remarkably parochial brands of modern preachiness. Today no one could invoke even bread, much less bread and butter, without calling down a host of special-interest objections to it as public enemy number something, and it is no easy thing to speak of food as part of our common humanity without being branded as ignorant of anthropology. Even as the chattering classes 'discover' cooking and dining as a subject of academic study or trendy journalism, fewer and fewer writers seem to share one impassioned Victorian's unfailing awareness that food nourishes not only body but spirit, and that we have it in our power to prevent food from becoming a crime against both.

Acknowledgements

My thanks to the Culinary Historians of New York, the Dickens Fellowship of New York, the Cosmopolitan Club or New York, and Ruth Reichl and the editors of *Gourmet* Magazine for the opportunity to present previous versions of this paper.

Notes

All works cited are by Charles Dickens unless otherwise stated. Citations to the novels are by chapter rather than page number, since they are not covered by copyright and now exist in innumerable different editions.

1. *Martin Chuzzlewit*, Chapter 39; *Dombey and Son*, Chapter 49; *David Copperfield*, Chapter 28.
2. *Nicholas Nickleby*, Chapter 8; *Bleak House*, Chapter 21; *Martin Chuzzlewit,* Chapter 49.
3. Mayhew, Henry, *London Labour and the London Poor: A Cyclopaedia of the Condition and Earnings of Those That Will Work, Those That Cannot Work, and Those That Will Not Work* (London, 4 vols., 1861– 62), vol. I, p. 64.
4. Mayhew, *London Labour*, vol. II, pp. 145–146.
5. Gaskell, Elizabeth, *Wives and Daughters: An Every-Day Story*, Chapter 5.
6. *Hard Times*, Book II, Chapter 6.
7. *Our Mutual Friend*, Book III, Chapter 16.
8. *Bleak House*, Chapter 16.
9. *The Old Curiosity Shop*, Chapter 36.
10. *Great Expectations*, Chapter 4.
11. *Nicholas Nickleby*, Chapter 64.
12. *Martin Chuzzlewi*t, Chapter 6.
13. *Our Mutual Friend*, Book II, Chapter 10.
14. *The Pickwick Papers*, Chapter 45; *Great Expectations*, Chapter 4.

15. *Bleak House*, Chapter 27.
16. *Bleak House*, Chapter 4; *Great Expectations*, Chapter 22.
17. *Little Dorrit*, Book I, Chapter 8; *Our Mutual Friend*, Book II, Chapter 2.
18. *Little Dorrit*, Book I, Chapter 5.
19. *Dombey and Son*, Chapter 8.
20. *Hard Times*, Book I, Chapter 11; Book II, Chapter 5.
21. *Oliver Twist*, Chapter 2.
22. *The Chimes*, First Quarter.

¡Prohibidísimo!!!

Alicia Ríos

Setting

Very mysterious. At center stage is a small round restaurant table (a gueridon) with a tablecloth reaching to the floor. The table is set for one. A menu stands on the table.

The customer, Ray Sokolov, is dressed in an elegant modern style, in a colorful shirt and ostentatiously unmatching string tie. It has an eye-catching stripe.

Alicia Ríos. The waitress wears a long vampire outfit and an apron. A mask covers her face. An order pad and a ballpoint pen hang from her belt.

The Action Unfolds

The waitress leads the customer, whose eyes are bandaged, to the empty table. She directs him grandly putting a hand on his shoulder. They proceed in tandem, like a train with two cars, following a curving S-shaped path, with short, tentative mechanical steps appropriate for someone who can't see, and also to emphasize the humor of the situation. She brings him to the table and helps him sit down. Once he's settled, she takes away his bandage. Barely a word passes between them. He indicates to her with a friendly gesture that he feels very comfortable. He moves his head from side to side, trying to orient himself and understand where he is.

The waitress, with a polite look, invites him to take a look at the menu. He puts down his glasses and starts to read it. He glances quizzically at the waitress, as if to say, 'What's this all about?'

The waitress responds with a peremptory gesture intended to force the customer to get on with the inevitable struggle between a diner and a menu. This moment of decision can be frightening and very complicated. Implicit in her manner is a command: 'Obey me. Concentrate, take responsibility for yourself, participate!'

But still the silence has not been broken. The waitress places herself behind the customer. She points to one part of the menu and then another, directing his attention with flamboyant gestures, circling her hand in the air with the pen like someone who is going to practice a grandiose, calligraphic signature before putting it on paper. Then she turns and stands beside him.

The customer looks over the various dishes on the menu. Finally he breaks the silence and asks her for help with this difficult task. He asks her in a loud voice:

RS: Do you think you could possibly help me?

The waitress takes the order pad and the pen and motions him to make a choice. The client pores over the menu once again and finally asks her loudly:

RS: Please help me.

The waitress leans over him and points to various dishes with the pen. Then she turns, and passes him with the sweeping motion of a bullfighter, pirouetting on her right foot, and entering the next stage of the attack, taunting him from the side, as a matador would tease a bull. Looking over the top of the menu, she points to various options and explains:

AR: As you see, there are three menus:
      The Outrageously Dangerous Menu
      The Totally Forbidden Menu
      The Utterly Unnameable Menu.

RS: (*Shaking his head with extraordinary impatience*): Outrageously dangerous? Do you mean it's poisonous?
      He looks her up and down as if to ask: What's with this chick? What's she driving at?

AR: No, it means that if you and I agree on that one, we'll end up in jail.

RS: *begins looking at the dishes in the 'dangerous' menu and cries out*:
      Ragout of fox, hunted by country squires on horseback with the assistance of baying beagles and basset hounds bred out of the Spartan kind: So flewed, so sanded, and their heads are hung with ears that sweep away the morning dew; crook-kneed, and dewlapped like Thessalian bulls; slow in pursuit, but matched in mouth like bells, Each under each.
      He shakes his head and says to the waitress:
      I don't think so. This is not my kidney.
      I've never wanted to taste hunting trophies. What else can you recommend?

AR: Okay, the rack of lynx from the Cotswold Wildlife Park and Gardens is exquisite.

RS: That sounds good but not very filling. And I'm allergic to cats. What about this very expensive dish?

AR: Albino dolphin from the Tigris. I ought to explain that there's only one left.

RS: You mean in the kitchen?

227

AR: No, in Iraq.

RS: *Distressed.*
   No, No. I don't want that. I'm not some kind of crazed foodie. I don't want to eat
   something other folks can't eat.

AR: We also have the tail of a bull that fought to its death in the great bullring in
   Madrid.

RS: But if I don't know the name of the matador, I wouldn't dare eat it. *He returns
   to the menu and begins looking at the 'Forbidden' section.* I don't understand this
   second section. It's cheap and the portions must be huge. But why forbidden?

AR: It's intended for fast days, when you really feel famished.

RS: Sure, but the problem is: today I haven't been fasting. So what about these wines?
   What's special about them?

AR: They're for Muslims. We also have an excellent ham for Jews.

RS: I hardly have the courage to look at the Unnameable dishes.

AR: Shhhh (*puts her finger to her lips*)

RS: (*Shrugs his shoulders*) But what's there?

AR: Shhh. Just read it silently.

RS: *He starts to read , with amazement. Bites his fingernails*

AR: *Horrorstruck.* No. no. Don't do that. The one thing we don't allow here is
   autophagy. You can't eat yourself.

RS: Ok, then. Let's talk about the most expensive stuff, The Unnameable. Can you at
   least say why everything here is so expensive?

AR: Organ transplants just cost a bomb. First, you have to feed the donors until they
   recover from a life of poverty and medical neglect. Then there are the doctors, the
   refrigerated vans, bribes for police. Still, it will be cheaper if you order something
   globalized, say a liver from someone in Calcutta. The beef and kidney pie, with a
   native British kidney is just out of sight.

228

RS: That's too rich for my blood. *He points to the menu.* I'm going to order baby rabbit, the bunny.

AR: OK, big spender. *She shouts into the wings*: One bunny, smothered in onions.

Another Woman's voice is heard, shrieking: Not me. Not me.

A few minutes pass in silence. The Other Woman comes onstage dressed as a Playboy *bunny. She carries a silver serving platter with a domed cover. Raising it on high, she proclaims: Tail of bull slaughtered in the great bullring of Madrid. It was a first rate fight and the matador received both ears and paraded around the ring twice. She passes out chocolates to the audience.*

Applause and laughter.

229

Jainism: The World's Most Ethical Religion

Colleen Taylor Sen

The world's only unconditionally vegetarian religion is Jainism, one of India's eight official religions. Its main figure, Mahavira, was a contemporary of Buddha in the sixth century BCE; both religions were a reaction against the domination of the Brahmins and animal sacrifice. But whereas Buddhism has had little influence in its birthplace in the past millennium, Jainism has been a vital force. Its central idea, *ahimsa*, or nonviolence, was central to the teaching of Mahatma Gandhi, a Hindu who grew up with Jains and had a Jain teacher. Jains were the first group to preach strongly against eating meat and were one of the driving forces behind the spread of vegetarianism in India.

The 2001 Indian census reported 4.2 million Jains in India, 0.4 per cent of the total population. They are concentrated in urban areas in western and southern India, especially Maharashtra, where there are around 1 million Jains; Rajasthan (624,000); Gujarat (468,000); Madhya Pradesh (445,000); Karnataka (300,000); Uttar Pradesh (141,000); Delhi (74,000); and Tamil Nadu (50,000). Not coincidentally, these are the states with the highest proportion of vegetarians. There are also Jain communities in the United States (estimated at between 50,000 and 100,000), the United Kingdom, and East Africa.

Jains are by and large an affluent community. Since their religion prevents them from farming, many are in banking, manufacturing, business, and in the professions. Some of India's wealthiest business families are Jains. Their literacy rate is among the highest in the country – 94.1 per cent – with female literacy rates approaching those of men.

Historical background

Jainism emerged as an organized religion in the Gangetic Basin (extending from modern Pakistan to the state of Bihar) in the sixth century BCE, although it is rooted in a much older tradition. This was a time of great intellectual ferment throughout the civilized world: Gautama Buddha in India, Confucius and Lao Tze in China, Heraclites in Greece, Zoroaster in Persia, and Jeremiah in the Middle East all flourished at this time (a phenomenon that may reflect much more extensive contacts between these centers than we know today.)

Jainism was a reaction against what is sometimes called the Vedic religion or Vedism. Around 2000 BCE pastoral semi-nomads from the region between the Caspian and Black seas, today called Aryans or Indo-Europeans, migrated in small groups into northern India. Moving eastward, they cleared forests, subjugated local inhabitants, established villages and towns, and eventually consolidated into small states. The period between 2000 and 800 BCE is called the Vedic period after the *Vedas,* an enormous collection of prayers, magical incantations, hymns, and poems compiled orally around 1500 BCE and written down a thousand years later.

A unique feature of Vedic society was the caste system. Although there were (and are) thousands of castes (*jati*), based mainly on occupation, they were grouped into four main castes (*varna*): priests (*brahmins*), warriors and rulers (*kshatriyas*), farmers and traders *(vaisyas)*, and some service workers and artisans (*sudras*). The Brahmin priests became extremely powerful, since only they knew the sacred rituals and could perform the animal sacrifices needed to propitiate the gods – forces of nature with parallels in Greek and Roman mythology.

Over time the Vedic religion became infused with more sophisticated ideas, some of which became fundamental doctrines of Hinduism (called by its adherents *dharma*, the sacred law or way), Buddhism, and Jainism. One was reincarnation, the idea that there is an endless cycle of births, deaths, and rebirths that is determined by our actions in this world, or *karma.* Under the law of *karma,* every action has its effects on the future; the sum of our past *karma* determines our present existence and our future lives. The goal of existence was not worldly comforts or wealth but to realize this basic truth and attain release from the endless suffering of rebirths by asceticism, meditation, and yoga.

By the sixth century BCE there were 16 small states and more than 2000 cities in northern India. Trade flourished, merchants became wealthy, and learning flourished at universities such as Nalanda that drew students from as far abroad as China. In this environment, some thinkers began to challenge the existing social order. As the historian Romila Thapar writes:

> The contestation or accommodation between the established orthodoxy and the aspirations of newly rising groups intensified changes in religious belief and practice and in philosophical speculation, resulting in a remarkable richness and vigour in thought, rarely surpassed in the centuries to come.... Rivalries and debates were rife. Audiences gathered around the new philosophers in the ...parks and groves on the outskirts of town. This was a different ambience from that of Vedic thought where teachings and disputations were not held in public. The presence of multiple, competing ideologies was a feature of urban living.[1]

Some of the new ideas were adopted by small groups that initially became sects, and later, as they attracted more followers, orders or assemblies called *sanghas.* Of these *sangha,* two have survived as independent religions: Jainism and Buddhism.

231

The origins of Jainism

The main figure in Jainism and the one who gave the religion its present form is Vardhaman, called by his followers Mahavira (great hero).[2] *Kshatriya* by caste, he was the son of the ruler of a small kingdom in what is today north-east Bihar. Vardhaman married and had children, but, at the age of 30 following the death of his parents, left home to become a naked ascetic in search of enlightenment. For twelve years, he wandered around north-east India and experienced many hardships. In the thirteenth year, after fasting for two and a half days without water and squatting on his haunches in the full glare of the sun, he attained enlightenment (*kevala*). To Jains, this does not mean union with the Absolute, as in Hinduism, or nothingness, as in Buddhism, but rather pure consciousness and absolute omniscience 'which gives direct and simultaneous access to all forms of reality in the universe in every temporal and spatial dimension.'[3]

Mahavira spent the next thirty years traveling around the subcontinent preaching this eternal truth. According to legend, he converted eleven Brahmins who subsequently became the heads of his organization. His followers hailed him as a *jina*, or conqueror. Mahavira was not, however, viewed as the founder of a new religion but as the most recent of twenty-three previous *jinas*, called *tirthankaras*, or ford-makers – omniscient teachers who attained enlightenment and then 'made a ford,' showing others the way to liberation. Some are mythical, others appear to be historical figures, and one is a woman. Although Jain temples have statues of ford-makers, they are not worshipped as gods but rather regarded as perfect beings to venerate and emulate.

One of Mahavira's great accomplishments was to organize his followers into a four-fold order consisting of *sadhus* (wandering male ascetics, sometimes called monks or renouncers), s*adhvi*s (female ascetics/nuns), *shravaks* (laymen) and *shravikas* (laywomen).[4] While both take the same basic vows, the renouncers follow them much more strictly and take additional vows. It is they who embody the ultimate ideal of Jainism. Laypersons can become renouncers if they receive their permission of their families, whereupon they give up their homes, money and possessions, wander around the countryside in single-sex groups, and depend entirely on laypeople for their food and shelter. During the rainy season they stop their wandering and live in villages.

Jains later split into two sects: *digambara* ('sky-clad') and *svetambara* ('white clad'). They agree on the main tenets of Jainism; their major doctrinal difference relates to nudity. Male *digambara* renouncers wander around naked (i.e., clad only in the sky), whereas *svetambaras* wear a white cotton garment. Digambaras believe that a true monk should follow the example of Mahavira by abandoning all possessions, including clothes, as well as feelings such as shame and pride. Another reason for nudity is that clothing might hide tiny creatures that might be crushed. Digambara ascetics cannot own a begging bowl but receive food in their hands cupped together and eat only once a day.

Another difference is that Digambaras do not think women can gain salvation in this life but must be reborn as men, whereas Svetambaras believe women can attain salvation directly. There are also disagreements over which texts should be accepted as scriptures. Today Digambaras are in the minority and live mainly in south-west India. Over time Svetambara and Digambaras split into other sects over such issues as whether or not to build temples and install images of the fordmakers and other deities.

Jain philosophy

Jains do not accept the authority of the Vedas or the Brahmins and are essentially an atheistic religion. The Vedas cannot be not inspired by God since there is no God: The universe has existed from all eternity and its changes are due to the inherent powers of nature, not the intervention of a god. Deities do exist, but they are subject to the same eternal laws as human beings and do not intervene in human affairs. All knowledge is relative and temporary; absolute truth comes only to those enlightened people who appear at certain times in history.

The goal of human existence is to free oneself from attachment and aversion and to purify the soul in order to attain a state of perfect omniscience and ultimate release from the body. We are prevented by doing this by the bondage of *karma*. Unlike Hindus or Buddhists, Jains view *karma* not as a spiritual or intangible element, but as a physical substance – a fine matter not perceptible to the senses that clings to our souls and conforms to mechanical laws of cause and effect. We attract *karma* particles when we do or say something wrong, such as telling a lie, stealing, or killing a living being, however small. These bad actions cause our souls to attract more *karma*, creating a vicious circle.

Jains believe that a person can avoid the accumulation of *karma* and remove it by behaving and thinking correctly and by having the correct mental state, so that even if an action attracts *karma*, it does not stick to the soul. This is done by following three ethical principals, called the Three Jewels – right faith, right perception, and right knowledge – and taking five great vows (*mahavratas*): *ahimsa,* non violence or non-injury; *satya,* truthfulness; *asteya,* not stealing; a*paragriha,* nonacquisitiveness; and *brahmacharya,* chaste living.

Other vows, called the lesser vows (*anuvratas*), entail restricting such activity as unnecessary travel; limiting resources to what one needs; avoiding pointless behavior, such as gossip and self-indulgence; meditation; charity and almsgiving; and prayers (directed not to God but rather to recall the qualities of the *tirthankaras* and receive inspiration from them).

Ahimsa

The heart of Jain ethics is *ahimsa,* a word sometimes translated as nonviolence but more correctly as 'not harming.' It is summed up in the statement 'Do not injure,

233

abuse, oppress, enslave, insult, torment, torture or kill any creature or living being.' Harm is not only physical but mental and verbal. Related to *ahimsa* is the notion of *daya,* a spirit of compassion towards all living beings.

These concepts are rooted in Jains' views of the universe, which is seen as consisting of an infinite number of *jivas,* or living entities, sometimes translated as souls. *Jivas* are made of energy and do not have physical form; after death they can be reborn into different bodies until they are finally liberated. Embodied *jivas* are classified according to their number of senses:

- One sense (touch): clay, sand, rain, ice, fire, wind, trees, bacteria, yeast, flowers, vegetables
- Two senses (touch and taste) worms, leeches, termites
- Three senses (touch, taste, smell): ants, lice, beetles, moths
- Four senses (touch, taste, smell, sight): flies, bees, scorpions
- Five senses (touch, taste, smell, sight, hearing): infernal beings, animals, birds, human beings, and heavenly beings.

A further distinction is made between vegetables with only one *jiva* and those that contain a multitude of living organisms, such as underground roots, bulbs, buds and shoots as well as figs and fruits and vegetables with many seeds.

While in practice it is impossible to survive without killing or injuring some form of being, Jains strive to avoid doing any intentional harm. Thus, they are in theory not allowed to be farmers, because tilling the soil would kill life; perform jobs involving fermentation, digging, selling weapons or pesticides; or trade in meat products, honey, eggs, silk or leather.[5]

Wandering monks wear masks to avoid breathing in small *jiva*s and sweep the ground in front of them with a broom as they walk. During the monsoon season, they stay in indoors as much as possible, because the world is teeming with life at this time. A worshipper cannot enter a Jain temple wearing animal products. Renouncers are enjoined against traveling[6] except on foot. Jains establish animal sanctuaries and hospitals for cows, birds, and other animals. They free the birds when they recover, since they do not believe in confining them; for the same reason, Jains generally do not keep household pets.

Food prohibitions

Nowhere do Jain concerns about *ahimsa* manifest themselves more vigorously than with regard to food. To say that Jains are strictly vegetarian hardly begins to convey either the rigour and severity of the rules which some Jains put themselves under or the centrality of such practices to Jain religious life,' writes James Laidlaw. 'Moreover, it misses the most important fact about Jain rules about food, which is that there is no single set of rules.... Almost everything about food is problematic.'[7]

While all observant Jains avoid certain foods that are absolutely forbidden, there are variations in what they otherwise eat, depending on family customs, sect, age, sex, time of year, personal circumstances, etc. A Jain told me, 'There are no rigid prescriptions; follow the rules to the extent that you want. Willingness is very important; you can't force anyone to eat or avoid certain things.' In general, the old follow more restrictions than the young and women more than men; often people allow themselves greater latitude outside their homes. The practice of *ahimsa* and vegetarianism are on a continuum: as a Jain progresses on his or her spiritual journey, he limits the kind and number of foods he consumes.

From the eleventh century onward, Jain texts contain detailed lists of what can and cannot eaten. Five things are absolutely forbidden for all Jains: meat (including meat products, such as gelatin), fish, eggs, alcohol, and honey. Eating meat is absolutely unthinkable; one renouncer is quoted as saying, 'Meat-eaters have the shape of humans but they are not really human.' In India, many Jains will not frequent stores where meat, fish, or eggs are sold, and on holidays will pay the owners of slaughter houses not to kill animals on that day.

Alcohol is reviled because the process of fermentation and distillation multiplies and destroys living organisms and because it clouds ones' thinking and can lead to violence. Honey is banned because it contains the bodily secretions of bees; if the bees are smoked out ahead of time, it destroys other insects that took their place.

In India, most Jain and Hindu vegetarians are not vegans, perhaps because over millennia the need for the nutrients in milk products became obvious. However, some North American Jains do avoid milk and diary products because of the violence involved in producing milk by machines and the fact that cows are killed when they stop producing.[9]

Other food items are off-limits to renouncers at all times and to laypersons during certain fasts. While not condoned for laypersons, they often form part of their daily fare. These items include:

- Fruits and vegetables with many seeds, including figs, pomegranate, guava, and tomatoes
- 'Empty fruits'; that is, fruits with little nutritional value
- Vegetables that grow underground, including potatoes, turnips, squashes, carrots, radishes, and mushrooms
- Onions and garlic
- Fresh ginger and turmeric
- Foods containing yeast
- Non-vegetarian cheese
- Cauliflower and cabbage
- Buds and sprouts, including sprouted lentils
- Rotting and stale food

Fruits with many seeds are banned because each seed encloses the germ of life[Pulling up root vegetables kills millions of *jivas* in the soil, and the plants themselves contain an infinite number of *jivas* so that even a tiny part will grow if planted. Insects live within the leaves of cauliflowers and cabbages.] Turmeric and ginger are not eaten fresh but may be eaten as dried powdered spices since in this form they cannot grow again.

Ayurvedic theories of medicine and folk beliefs reinforce these selections. Throughout India, onions and garlic are believed to inflame the passions and destroy mental equilibrium and thus are avoided by many orthodox Hindus. Eggplants are reputed to have aphrodisiac qualities. Moreover, the orthodox of any religion are suspicious of what is new and foreign, which may account for the inclusion of tomatoes, potatoes, and guavas on the list of forbidden foods.

[Jains are supposed to avoid eating after sunset, since they may inadvertently destroy unseen live forms,] and to drink only boiled and filtered water in order to minimize the consumption of minute water-borne organisms.[10] Jain writings contain detailed rules about how long foods can be kept before eating. For example, milk must be filtered and boiled within 48 minutes of milking the cow; yogurt should not be more than one day old unless it is mixed with raisins or other sweetening agents; flour is to be kept for only three days in the rainy season and seven days in the winter; and sweets must be consumed within 24 hours.[11] Although these rules may no longer be relevant because of modern refrigeration, they reflect a sophisticated knowledge of hygienic and health issues.

236

The Jain diet

Until recently, most Indian food was produced locally and was highly seasonal. There have always been wide variations in what people on the Subcontinent eat, determined by location, religion, caste, and income, that referring to 'Indian cuisine' is as meaningful as talking about 'European cuisine.' Jain food is also largely regional. Its dietary staples are grains and legumes: wheat (which is rapidly replacing other grains throughout India) and or local crops such as millet, sorghum, and corn. Grains can be ground into flour and made into bread or coarsely ground and boiled to produce *daliya,* a kind of porridge. Wheat can be made into semolina, a common ingredient in sweets, which are very popular among Jains, as they are with all Indians. Rice is also eaten, though not always as a staple.

Legumes are consumed as *dal,* which refers to both the lentils itself and the boiled dish prepared from them. Ghee – clarified butter – is a sign of opulence and health throughout the subcontinent and affluent Jains are known for the amount they use in their cooking. Hing, or asafetida, is a common replacement for garlic. Spices are an essential part of daily cooking, although they may be given up during fasts. Fruits and vegetables are regional. Gujarat and Maharashtra contain lush agricultural regions, so that here corn, mango, papayas, coconut, and green vegetables are part of Jains' daily fare. Much of Rajasthan is a barren desert; here, substitutes for vegetables in stews and curries are made from ground grain or lentils boiled and dried in the sun.

What constitutes a meal also varies by region. In Delhi, the Jains in a community studied by a French researcher eat two main meals: the first at ten in the morning, the second between five and six in the afternoon plus a light afternoon meal.[12] The first meal consists of *phulka*, a puffy wheat bread cooked over a griddle; dal; a vegetable; and sometimes rice. The afternoon meal may be tea with fresh fruits or dried snacks. Dinner consists of a bread lightly sautéed in oil or ghee (*paratha*); two or more vegetable dishes; and sometimes yogurt. *Achar* (pickle) is consumed at both meals. Wedding banquets may consist of three or more vegetable dishes, a rice pilaf, sweet chutney, yogurt with fried lentils; and at least two sweets, such as carrot or mung dal halwa and kulfi, a frozen milk dish. On these occasions, two meals may be served: one for Jains who eat before sunset and the second for those who are less strict.

Jains abroad adapt to local conditions. A young Jain professional in Chicago told me he does his best to avoid harming life 'to the extent possible and practicable.' He never consumes meat, fish, or eggs but he does eat onions, garlic, and root vegetables. Because he does not cook himself, most of his meals are prepared by his mother or eaten in Italian, Thai, and Japanese restaurants. He eats a lot of cheese, but does not insist on vegetarian cheese (i.e. cheese made without using whey, casein, rennet, or other animal products as coagulating agents). In Thai restaurants he requests that the vegetarian dishes be prepared without fish sauce. In Japanese restaurants, he eats vegetarian sushi.

237

Fasting

{An important way of removing *karma* is by fasting, which Jains have elevated to an art.} (Jain fasting served as an inspiration for Mahatma Gandhi, who used it as a political tactic.) The Hindi word for fast, *tapas*, means heat in Sanskrit: A common metaphor is that just as the sun dries up a polluted lake, so fasting purifies the soul by removing negative *karma*. Fasts are considered essential for spiritual growth.

A fast is always preceded by a vow, which means that it is a religious act and done with a predefined intention. There are no hard and fast rules when or how long one should fast or what form this fasting should take, but it is never obligatory, always a matter of free will. It is not enough just to stop eating; one should also lose the desire to eat and not relish food when one does eat. Fasting is not done in isolation but as a family or community event.

Fasts are both an extension and intensification of Jains' regular dietary restrictions. Jain texts classify fasts into many categories and lay down complex rules about what can and cannot be eaten. For example, fasting can mean giving up all food and water for one day, three days, or eight days; every alternative day of the year; twice a year; etc. It can entail drinking only water or *triphala* – the water used to rinse out a pot.

Fasters may eat only one meal a day at a set time, limit the number of items eaten, give up favorite foods, such as sweets (sometimes on a permanent basis), or eliminate salt or spices from their diet. A common form of fasting requires giving up green vegetables, milk, yogurt, oil, fruits, salt, spices, and sugar and eating only dal and rice.

Like some Hindus, Jains fast on certain days of the lunar cycle when the moon changes, especially the eighth and fourteenth days of each fortnight. They fast when the seasons change and during the monsoon, when fasting is thought to also offer protection against illness. Most Jains fast during festivals, especially *Paryushan Maha Pava* which lasts eight to ten days during the rainy season (usually in August-September). Some fast for the entire period, others for shorter times, but fasting on the final day is considered obligatory. In this case, fasting means complete abstinence from any sort of food or drink, but some people take boiled water during the daytime. During this festival people ask forgiveness of those they have offended, visit the temple, and celebrate with a community feast.

Jains may fast at any time, especially if they believe they have committed a sin and need to repent. Women generally fast more than men and the old more than the young; after retirement, some men start to fast on a regular basis. Renouncers may follow the example of Mahavira and fast for months at a time, especially during the rainy season when they practice very strict austerities.

The ultimate fast, called *smadhi maran* or *sallekhna,* involves giving up all food and water and starving oneself to death. This practice is undertaken by people in the final stages of a fatal illness or who are very old and feel they have fulfilled their duties in this life. They must have permission from a senior renouncer. Recently the practice has been challenged in the Indian courts.[13]

A comparison of food attitudes in Jainism and Buddhism

Buddhism and Jainism, which arose almost simultaneously in the sixth century BCE, share many features:[14]princely founders; opposition to Brahmins, the authority of the Vedas and animal sacrifice; rejection of idols, priests, and rituals (although eventually they crept back in); and a distinction between ascetics and lay persons. Women had a position nearly equal to men in the two religions. Both Jainism and Buddhism were fundamentally atheistic and emphasized social ethics rather than caste distinctions. Both aim at helping their followers escape the cycle of rebirths and help others achieve it (although Buddhists regarded *karma* as mental and volitional, not a physical substance).

However, there are important differences, especially regarding food. After undergoing a period of fasting and self-torment, Buddha preached the 'middle way' between the extremes of asceticism and worldliness and based on non-attachment. Insisting on vegetarian food was considered a sign of attachment and excessively austere.[15] Early Buddhism placed no restrictions on the diets of laypersons. Monks were expected to beg for alms and food, and while the monastic order had many rules about what they ate, most were concerned with how food was acquired.

Only a few substances were absolutely forbidden to Buddhists, including alcohol and certain kinds of meat, including human flesh, elephants, horses, dogs, snakes, lions, tigers, etc. Also forbidden was meat from an animal that monks saw, heard, or believed was killed specifically to feed them. However, if a layperson gave meat to a monk, he was expected to eat it, provided that the meat was cooked. Buddhists could also eat an animal that died from natural causes. Unless a monk were ill, he was not to specifically request meat, fish, ghee, oil, honey sugar, milk or yogurt.

Notes

1. Thapar, p. 165.
2. The dates of *Mahvira's* life are uncertain and subject to dispute. Jain texts put his lifetime at 599 to 527 or 510 BCE.
3. Dundas, p. 24.
4. 'Renouncer' is used instead of ascetic since the ascetic often lives in isolation and discards all social obligations, whereas the renouncer only discards social obligations such as family and caste, but enters an alternative society.
5. Jains do, however, serve in the army since religion also prescribes that one follow one's duty.
6. In 1970, when Gurudev Chitrabhanu, a Jain renouncer, decided to come to America, Jains stretched themselves on the ground in front of the plane to prevent his departure. He came anyway, and in 1971 founded the International Meditation Center in New York; see http://www.jainmeditation. org. A compromise was later reach and some Jain scholars as well as ascetics who have not been fully initiated now come to America.
7. Laidlaw, p. 153.
8. Laidlaw, p.167.
9. Jain et al., p. 20.
10. While there is also violence in killing the bacteria by boiling water, it does less harm than killing bacteria that would have kept growing exponentially. Jain, p. 29.
11. Mahais, p. 105.
12. Mahais, pp. 201–203.
13. 'Jains deny rite takes life in vain,' *Chicago Tribune*, October 15, 2006.
14. Ulrich, pp. 239–240.
15. India's population includes eight million Buddhists (0.8 per cent of the total); however, three-fourths of them are descendants of a group of scheduled castes who converted en masse in the 1950s. An intriguing question is why Buddhism declined in importance in its homeland (although it thrived elsewhere in Asia, thanks to Buddhist missionaries) while Jainism, a non-proselytizing religion, survived. Several reasons have been proposed. In the north-east Buddhism became associated with Tantric cults from Tibet, which emphasized ritual over ethics and weakened its ethical appeal. Buddhism broke into a number of sects, many of which were eventually absorbed back into Hinduism. Starting with the reformer Shankacharya in the eighth century, Hinduism underwent a series of movements that reduced the power of the Brahmins and rituals, encouraged individual devotion, incorporated new castes, downgraded the role of ascetics, and encouraged vegetarianism.

Although Buddhism enjoyed a revival in north-east India under the Pala Dynasty (750–1154 AD), from the twelfth century onward Islamic invaders from the north destroyed Buddhist temples and centers of learning in the region. Meanwhile, Jains had moved south and west, where some became wealthy merchants. Because they were also literate, financially astute, and good managers, they often found high office at royal courts, both Hindu and Muslim.

Bibliography

Achaya, K.T., *A Historical Dictionary of Indian Food,* New Delhi: Oxford University Press, 2002.

Dundas, Paul, *The Jains,* London: Routledge, 2002.

Jain, Manoj, Laxmi Jain and Tarla Dalal, *Jain Food: Compassionate and Healthy Eating,* Germantown, TN: Manoj Jain, 2005.

Laidlaw, James, *Riches and Renunciation: Religion, Economy and Society among the Jains,* Oxford: Clarendon Press, 2003.

Mahais, Marie-Claude, *Délivrance et convivialité: Le système culinaire des Jaina,* Paris: Editions de la maison des sciences de l'homme, 1985.

Pruthi, R.J., *Jainism and Indian Civilization,* Delhi: Discovery Publishing House, 2004.

Sen, K.M., *Hinduism,* London: Penguin Books, 2005.

Thapar, Romila, *Early India: From the Origins to AD 1300,* Berkeley: University of California Press, 2002.

Tobias, Michael, *Life Force: The World of Jainism,* Fremont, California: Jain Publishing Co., 1991.

Ulrich, Katherine E., 'Food Fights: Buddhist, Hindu, and Jain Dietary Polemics in South India,' *History of Religions,* V 46(3), 2007, 228–261.

The BBC has an excellent website on Jainism at http://www.bbc.co.uk/religion/religions/jainism/

A good collection of resources, including regional recipes, can be found at the website of the Jain Global Resources Center http://www.jainworld.com.

Mustapha Mond down on the Farm

Alexia Genese Smith and James Gates Ferguson, Jr.

[Mustapha Mond:] 'We could synthesize every morsel of food if we wanted to. But we don't. We prefer to keep a third of the population on the land. For their own sakes – because it takes longer to get food out of the land than out of a factory. Besides we have our stability to think of. We don't want to change. Every change is a menace to stability. That's another reason we're so chary of applying new inventions. Every discovery in pure science is potentially subversive; even science must sometimes be treated as a possible enemy. Yes, even science.'

Aldous Huxley, *Brave New World*, 202

Adulteration began when men started to trade in food. The literature of Greece and Rome contains allusions to the illicit addition of flavouring and colouring matters to wine; Pliny the Elder denounced the bakers who added chalk and cattle feed to bread. The first legal measures to curb such abuses in Europe date from the Middle Ages…but it was the advance of chemistry that created new and varied methods of making inferior products appear more inviting (some of which survive even now).

Walter Gratzer, *Terrors of the Table*, 118–19

We are variously involved in the honors seminar in food and culture (aka Eats 101) at the University of North Carolina at Chapel Hill. Paramount among the charges to our ever bright, overcommitted, and occasionally arrogant undergraduate superstars is to ponder unceasingly the shopworn epistemological query, 'how do we know what we know?' It illumes our opening consideration of medieval piety and fasting just as it does our closing session on evolutionary biology. Last year, Michael Pollan's *Omnivore's Dilemma* became required advance reading for our seminar as it takes this query as a main text – a text that also serves us well for this year's focus on food and morality.

The second author concluded his presentation at the 2005 Oxford meeting with the cautionary but nonalarmist observation that the quest for authenticity had migrated from a preoccupation with concerns contoured by culture, i.e., faithfulness to historical precedent or archetype – read barbecue in the southern United States – to one of safety for the consumer. One set of issues covered in the UNC seminar concerns moral and ethical problems posed by the production of food. Eric Schlosser's cogent and disturbing portrayal of the physical toll of industrial beef production on its workers in *Fast Food Nation*[1] reveals one facet, and Steve Striffler broadens the enquiry through his analysis of the American poultry industry. Contouring the socio-economic topography, he writes, 'the common feature of future poultry-producing regions in the South was poverty, enduring poverty.'[2] The physical and fiscal interface will no doubt be examined by others, but our treatment of this year's topic, however, invites more detailed, and inevitably disquieting, scrutiny of the lingering issue from 2005, the consumer's safety. Indeed, if the current food production/consumption trajectory's upward slope remains unaltered, the global nuclear clock will not be unique in approaching midnight. We may all do ourselves in at the trough. This paper will attempt to explain why and in so doing perhaps illuminate issues for all to ponder. Indeed, to riff a bit on Gratzer's title, our discussion will interweave various 'terrors,' reflecting our shared and distinct interests in the topic of food studies.

By the time we convene this September, let alone when the 2007 Conference Proceedings appear, the quotidian floodtide of alimentary red alerts will have continued unabated. As we complete this draft, the 2 July 2007 *New York Times* features columnist Andrew Martin writing, 'in every American supermarket, labels tell shoppers where their seafood came from. But there are no such labels for meat, produce or nuts.'[3] Martin notes that, although the legislation was passed in 2002, 'the National Cattlemen's Beef Association, which represents both ranchers and meatpackers, opposes origin labeling.'[4] Thus does Mustapha Mond obscure what is grown on the farm, perhaps with good reason if the 'farm' is far from the consumer's table. Nicolas Zamiska and Jane Spencer make this point in discussing the current torrent of publicity surrounding Chinese food exports, 'after decades of industrial pollution, some of the worst contaminants making their way into the country's food come from the soil in which it is grown…residents have been eating such food for years or decades.'[5]

These are simply snippets of what de Certeau et al. call the 'practices of everyday [food] life' – unremarkable activities in the path from soil to mouth. Or are they? Michael Pollan's ingenious and engaging tale of the trajectories of four meals recruits our involvement by inducing us to imagine ourselves in one (or more) of his scenarios as we accompany him on his enquiries. Lying just beneath the surface of the commonplace possibilities of fast food, small- and large-scale organic production and marketing,[6] vegetarian cuisine, and the hunted and foraged meal is a warren of unquestioned assumptions, devious practices, and shadow organizations whose complexity makes the Paris Métro look like a Lego set. It is the murky cross connection among various terrors. Having lived as a vegetarian, slaughtered chickens, and hunted game for his dinner, Pollan can talk the talk of ethical and philosophical issues that separate carnivores and vegetarians. But such discussions almost have the whiff of postprandial brandy and cigars in the salon when juxtaposed with the implications of his analysis of 'industrial corn.' In 2005, Ferguson cited anthropologist Clark Larsen's Native American burial mound data from Saint Catherine's Island revealing the appearance of periostitis and overbites, crooked teeth, and cavities *circa* 1150

AD – about the time they commenced corn cultivation.[7] Pollan fast-forwards to the evolution of WW II munitions and the current unholy alliance of fertilizer, corn, beef, and petroleum. From thence it is a short leap to the grim reaper high fructose corn syrup – one that merits examination as it is drenched in 'morality.'

He dates the onset of the 'corn question' to 1947, 'when the huge munitions plant at Muscle Shoals, Alabama, switched over to making chemical fertilizer…[from] ammonium nitrate, the principal ingredient in the making of explosives.'[8] 'Fertilizer' sounds innocent enough as the traditional handmaid of agriculture, but in this case the sword turned not into a plowshare, but rather a less obvious but potentially more insidious clone. Pollan continues, 'hybrid corn turned out to be the greatest beneficiary of this conversion …[as it] is the greediest of plants, consuming more fertilizer than any other crop.'[9] Greed is not the only 'sin' to taint this transformation. As he notes, the fixing of nitrogen, thus making it available for fertilizer, was the discovery of Nobel Prize winning German chemist Fritz Haber. It was, however, this same discovery that enabled the Nazi war machine to manufacture explosives. Haber's work took an even more sinister turn as 'he…developed Zyklon B, the gas used in Hitler's concentration camps.'[10] For our purpose, another connection has even more global implications – nitrogen-based fertilizer's unalterable dependence on petroleum. This is, per Pollan, a quantum leap, with the 'power to fix nitrogen, the basis of soil fertility shifted from a total reliance on the energy of the sun to a new reliance on fossil fuel…the Haber-Bosch process works by combining nitrogen and hydrogen gases under immense heat and pressure in the presence of a catalyst.'[11] 'Prodigious amounts of electricity' produce the heat and pressure and 'fossil fuels' the hydrogen.[12] Does anyone still credibly contest the connection of such massive resource consumption with climate change? If so, hear Pollan, as he speaks of the steer he had 'adopted' as a calf, 'assuming 534 continues to eat twenty-five pounds of corn a day and reaches a weight of twelve hundred pounds, he will have consumed in his lifetime the equivalent of thirty-five gallons of oil – nearly a barrel.'[13]

But back to corn – from whence it comes, where it goes – and thence to morality astride the twin apocalyptic horsemen of obesity and Type 2 diabetes. The problem with corn is that it can grow most anywhere, and does. There is no scarcity and no financial security in its cultivation. Thus mega processors such as Cargill and Archer Daniels Midland (ADM) can always find someone willing to enter into a Faustian agreement to produce it a bit more cheaply than an obstinate neighbor. But this is but an abstraction – it is time to 'do the numbers.' Among other destinations, our Eats 101 students make a field trip to Peregrine Farm located sixteen miles west of Chapel Hill. Owners Alex and Betsy Hitt show the class where much of the produce for their weekly postclass dinners is grown, and during the tour they explain that, through efficient use of computer software for plot rotation and various labor saving techniques, they derive as much yield and profit from five acres of land as they formerly did from thirteen. During the active planting and cultivation season, an

243

additional three or four interns and full-time staff – generally college students – assist the Hitts with the long and arduous daily labor. It is a model farm in every way. However, UNC colleague and agricultural and economic historian, Peter Coclanis, whose academic specialty is global rice cultivation presents a strikingly different vision to the students. Rice 'fields' in Arkansas tend to be approximately 1,000 acres and are planted and tilled by GPS and laser guided tractors that plant within tolerances of ½ inch of soil depth. Generally irrigation and other maintenance needs are met and controlled by one worker.[14] Presumably this is not the way the Cistercians envisaged the grange in twelfth-century Burgundy.

But rice is a minor crop whereas corn cultivation amounts to 'about 10 billion bushels a year.'[15] The plot thickens, however, as Pollan notes that we *directly* consume very little of this #2 feed corn. Most of what we eat is sweet corn or some other variety. We are implicated in 'consuming' more or less one ton of #2 corn per person annually,[16] but in what form – it seems that steer 534 is a bit player. Archer-Daniels-Midland and Cargill denied Pollan access to their 'wet milling' plants. Analogous to petroleum cracking towers in refineries, these downstream systems convert rivers of processed corn slurry into vast quantities of refined products, chief among them being high fructose corn syrup (HFCS). Pollan maintains it is 'the most valuable food product refined from corn, accounting for 530 million bushels every year.'[17] Flowing from another spigot on the back of the wet milling plant is an 'alcoholic brew' derived from dextrose and destined for ethanol production, which accounts for a 'tenth of the corn crop.'[18] Viewed by many in 'corndom' as the golden parachute from petroleum addiction, ethanol does not merit a star from the morality committee. Per Pollan, one and one half gallons of petroleum are required to produce one gallon of ethanol.[19] As we move inexorably to the 'terror' spawned by corn, we should cast a glance over our shoulder at the lot of George Naylor, the Iowa family farmer with whom Pollan spent a week researching corn production. Despite unceasing labor, impeccable farm management, and thrift, Naylor is – like his colleagues – slowly losing ground by monocropping corn. He is faring better than most – he is not yet bankrupt, but, as he said to Pollan, 'agriculture's always going to be organized by the government; the question is, organized for whose benefit? Now it's for Cargill and Coca-Cola. It's certainly not for the farmer.'[20]

Coca-Cola – surely not the 'Pause That Refreshes?' One might argue that addictive behavior has stalked Dr Pemberton's soda fountain beverage since its Atlanta debut on 8 May 1886, but the current version has global implications that ignore national boundaries. As the 2004 data from Bray et al. make clear, the alarming uptick in obesity is simultaneous with the introduction of HFCS in carbonated beverages such as Coca-Cola and Pepsi Cola in the 1980s (see Figure 1). Of course, we must issue the usual caveat about correlation and causation, but the HFCS obesity connection bears striking similarity to that demonstrated between cancer and smoking. Bray et al. found that 'the consumption of HFCS increased 1000% between 1970 and

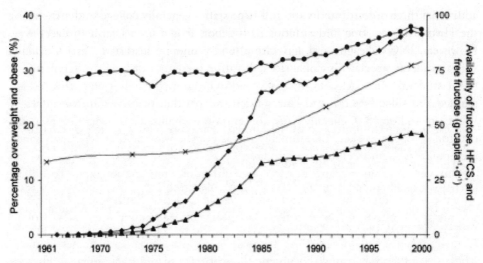

Figure 1. Availability of total fructose (•), high-fructose corn syrup (HFCS ♦), and free fructose (▲) in relation to obesity prevalence (x) in the United States. Data are from references 7 and 35. (Bray et al., Am. J. Clin. Nutr., 2004.)

1990…it's the sole caloric sweetener in soft drinks in the United States. Our most conservative estimate of the consumption of HFCS indicates a daily average of 132 kcal for all Americans aged 2 y[ears] and up, and the top 20% of consumers of caloric sweeteners ingest 316 kcal from FCS [per day].'[21]

But what about plain old sugar from beets and sugar cane – wasn't it good enough? It was and in abundant supply, but it wasn't cheap enough. As Critser writes, 'in what would prove to be one of the single most important change to the nation's food supply, both Coke and Pepsi switched from a fifty-fifty blend of sugar and corn syrup[22] to 100 per cent high-fructose corn syrup…[saving]…20 per cent in sweetener costs, allowing them to *boost portion sizes* [italics ours] and still make substantial profits.'[23] Were it confined to soft drinks, HFCS use might be amenable to reduction via public awareness campaigns. The simple fact is that it is ubiquitous in prepared food and drink – have a look at your Schweppes tonic water label – Commander Whitehead must be turning in his grave. Why must the formerly savory now be touched with sweetness? Why indeed? The answer to this query may be murky, but its implications are sinister and unambiguous – indeed they drive the apocalyptic horsemen at a frenzying gait. Gratzer puts it this way:

> Type 2 diabetes is inextricably linked to obesity, with its attendant evils, for it is in the fat cells that the worst of the mischief brews up. Obesity, even without diabetes, carries a hugely increased risk of high blood pressure, heart disease, hormonal and joint problems, and susceptibility to some cancers, along with

245

a strongly increased tendency to atherosclerosis, gall-stones from the excess cholesterol, and fatty degeneration of the liver. And a large measure of all the ills can be put down, as we have seen, to the huge quantities of sugar in soft drinks, processed foods, and snacks.[24]

But even this is an abstraction – these statistics from the *New York Times* are not:

One in three children born in the United States five years ago are expected to become diabetic in their lifetimes, according to a projection by the [CDC]. The forecast is even bleaker for Latinos: one in every two. New York…has just three people and a $950,000 budget to outwit diabetes, a disease soon expected to afflict more than a million people in the city. Tuberculosis, which infected about 1,000 New Yorkers last year, gets $27 million and a staff of almost 400.[25]

These data, however, simply document the existence of the phenomena – now we must focus on how they come to be within the individuals who make up these anonymous statistics.

Due to its relationship with Type 2 Diabetes, as well as a superfluity of other diseases, including influenza virus infection,[26] obesity has brought about a quest to understand its etiology and, inevitably, its cure. Although the answers lie in a complicated web of biochemical, social, and environmental factors, strands of the web are beginning to unravel, revealing the role of the food industry. Manufactured ingredients, contrived to fill the piggy banks of the executives and their corporate coffers, may be significant contributors to our expanding waistlines and dilapidated hearts. As noted above, Bray et al. advanced the idea of high fructose corn syrup (HFCS) as a direct contributor to obesity.[27] Though highly unlikely a single constituent of food could be to blame for the obesity epidemic, it made us take a step back and really look at how this so-called 'natural' food item affects our overall health.

For centuries fructose has been a part of our diet. Fruit used to be the primary source, contributing approximately 6–20 grams/day of fructose to our diets.[28] The fructose we consume today, however, comes primarily from HFCS, which has infiltrated our food supply due to its low cost and high degree of sweetness. According to Basciano et al., 'Westernization of diets has resulted in significant increases in added fructose, leading to typical daily consumptions amounts to 85–100g of fructose/day.'[29] Consequently, the idea that HFCS contributes to obesity implicates socio-economic factors, taste preferences, and biochemical factors. Because HFCS is less expensive than sugar, it has been argued that it has reduced the cost of sweetened foods, thus indirectly contributing to obesity. HFCS may also contribute to our inflated size by acclimating our palate to a sweeter taste. Fructose, which makes up 55 per cent of HFCS (glucose makes up the other 45 per cent), is sweeter than sugar (which is composed of 50 per cent fructose and 50 per cent glucose). Since

246

the caloric content of foods has not changed with the addition of HFCS, foods may be sweeter than when sugar was main nutritive sweetener. Schiffman et al. proposed that the sustained desire for sweet foods is a learned behavior[30] which suggests that, if early exposure produces tolerance for saturation, we will acclimate to a preference for intense sweetness.

The indirect consequences of HFCS in the food supply are difficult to measure and leave room for arguments on the validity of HFCS as a contributor to the obesity epidemic. However, epidemiological studies have offered support for a relationship between soda consumption and weight gain,[31] although the most convincing evidence comes from analysis of the biochemical pathway fructose follows during its metabolism. Early research demonstrated that fructose has little effect on insulin and glucose levels, and in the 1980s HFCS was even proposed as safe for use by diabetics as a nutritive sweetener, though 'researchers noticed unfavorable influences on obesity and weight gain' with consumption.[32] Although initially praised for its lack of effect on blood glucose and insulin levels, a closer look at the metabolic path fructose takes in the body makes an unequivocal argument for suspecting it as a healthy sugar substitute. The biochemical effects of fructose differ in comparison to glucose and may explain why the Coca-Cola consumed for the last thirty years may be more detrimental to our health than earlier versions. Glucose, best known for its role as a major energy provider and the thorn in the side of any diabetic, is very skilled at inducing numerous metabolic pathways that are advantageous for health. Fructose, on the other hand, follows predominantly one path: fat production. This is because fructose bypasses key regulatory steps that inform the body what to do with the energy it possesses in its carbon skeleton. Instead fructose sets up a system that promotes the production of fatty acids and their storage form triglycerides.[33] Furthermore, fructose alters the production of satiety hormones to favor signals that stimulate the desire to eat.[34] The overall physiological consequence of fructose consumption is the promotion of excessive food intake and fat production – an unlimited prescription for sure, painful, and premature mortality.

Numerous other culinary constituents may be deleterious to our health, but the ubiquity of HFCS in the food supply has made it the center of attention. HFCS has allowed the food industry to sweeten everything from soda to cereal to whole grain bread at a fraction of the cost of traditional sugar. This cost, like energy however, is never really lost, it is just transferred. Americans spend an estimated 78.5 billion dollars in health care costs associated with overweight[35] and obesity, with 50 per cent of those costs paid for by social programs.[36] Children now obtain more than 20 per cent of their calories from sugar, partially explaining the doubled rate of obesity among 2–19 year olds over the last 30 years.[37] Accordingly, the cost of obesity is exclusively monetary no longer, as this generation of obese youngsters may be the first to have a shorter lifespan than their parents.[38] This shocking revelation in 2005 may have paved the way for change.

247

As we walk through the aisles of our local grocery store today, our children's cereal boxes have a different look as nutritional labels provide new information. The tide is starting to turn. Kellogg's has reduced the sugar content of its products targeted at children, McDonald's Happy Meals now offer milk instead of soda, and Disney has limited the number of sugar-laden products it offers in its parks.[39] Has the food industry suddenly become awash with morality? Not exactly. Kellogg's reformulated it products after threats of lawsuits from parents and consumer groups, while Disney may have followed suit to escape a similar fate. Threats of lost profit and bad press appear to be the instructions the food industry follows. Even as recently as 1999 the industry was fighting calls to put 'added sugar' on food labels, as they felt that 'turning labels into encyclopedias and further bombarding consumers with confusing information will do next to nothing in fighting the battle against obesity.'[40] However, a 2005 study demonstrated that when the nutritional content of food was provided to high school students, they made better dietary decisions.[41] And so it seems, in the battle against an industry where money is the bottom line and a person who uses the term morality is not sitting in the corner office, it is our responsibility to cry foul when change is desired.

The goods we put onto our grocer's conveyor belt are now chosen for more than just epicurean delight, and, consequently, we have encouraged the introduction of new marketing practices. The era of weight-loss schemes and functional foods has arrived, as science has provided great marketing tools for the food industry. Now health claims abound. Yogurt promises to reduce inches around the middle while fortified eggs may help prevent heart disease and boost brain function. The *Nutrition Industry Executive*, an industry magazine for dietary supplement and food manufacturers, reported that 'Americans will spend almost $40 billion on functional foods, drinks, and supplements by 2008, a growth of 38 per cent from 2000.'[42] The race to fill our open arms with health-related food items was best exemplified by the vigorous marketing and sales campaigns of Atkins-like dietary regimes. In 2003–2004, at the height of the Atkins frenzy, restaurants like Panera Bread formulated low carbohydrate breads and Carl's Jr. sold bunless hamburgers.[43] Suddenly everything was 'low-carb,' and as a result, good for us. Any concerns over saturated and trans fat was disregarded, as the food industry made a major push to promote low-carbohydrate versions of previously 'unhealthy' items, such as Oreos and ice cream. The idea, 'if some is good, then more is better' resulted in an inundation of food products that generated a potential $30 billion dollar profit windfall despite denunciation of the diet by a majority of the medical community.[44]

If the basis for food creation and sale is simply profit, is it fair for us to expect the food industry to do more than watch its bottom line? Should the best interest and safety of the public be part of the equation? Given the response from the Grocery Manufacturers of America (GMA) when the FDA first proposed adding a footnote to nutrition labels to warn consumers about trans fats, the food industry would

248

likely say no. In a 2003 letter to the FDA, Alison Kretser, the director of scientific and nutrition policy, adamantly argued against the use of a footnote stating, 'GMA strongly opposes the proposed use of a footnote advising consumers to limit their intake of trans fat, saturated fat and/or cholesterol regardless of the wording selected. A footnote represents an unnecessary and inappropriate policy shift in the type of information provided within the Nutrition Facts panel.'[45] If you question the impact of such lobbying, examine the label of any box of crackers or cookies and you will see nothing more listed than the total grams of trans fats.

The topic of trans fat forces consideration of another moral question: When groups such as the National Academy of Sciences and World Health Organization decide that no level of trans fat is safe,[46] and the FDA wanted to put what basically amounts to a warning label on food items containing trans fats, should the food industry still be allowed to use such substances?

Trans fats became a fixture in food in 1911 when Crisco was marketed to the public by Proctor and Gamble. Food manufacturers warmed to the practice of solidifying oils by adding hydrogen because it was less expensive than using animal fat, it extended a product's shelf-life, and it reduced the need for refrigeration. As with HFCS, the insinuation of trans fat into our food system is astonishing. USDA data from 1994–1996 estimated that the average daily intake of trans fats was approximately 2.6 per cent of total energy intake. Although 20 per cent comes from natural sources, 80 per cent of the trans fat consumed is from processed foods and oils.[47] Initially, the use of partially hydrogenated oils was advocated by the Center for Science in the Public Interest[48] since they were thought to be healthier than the saturated fats obtained from animal products. However, by the early 1990s, this same group began its campaign to remove trans fats from the diet after links between trans fats and heart disease began to emerge. Recently, the notion that trans fats have a direct relationship to heart disease has become widely accepted. A review published in the *New England Journal of Medicine* in 2006 nicely reflects the consensus view that, even at very low intake levels, trans fats significantly increase the risk of cardiovascular disease.[49] Figure 2 illustrates some possible mechanisms by which trans fatty acids may potentiate cardiovascular disease.

While on the trans fat journey, a quick diversion must be taken to discover another role in which the food industry shapes our health and Mustapha Mond will be our tour guide.

The sixth edition of *Diet Dietary Guidelines for Americans* was published in 2005. These guidelines, mandated by Congress, are put in place to promote better eating and lifestyle choices. However, the control of such information is not the sole province of the experts. In an article published after the release of the new *Guidelines,* Walter Willet addressed the influence of industry on the published recommendations. He states:

249

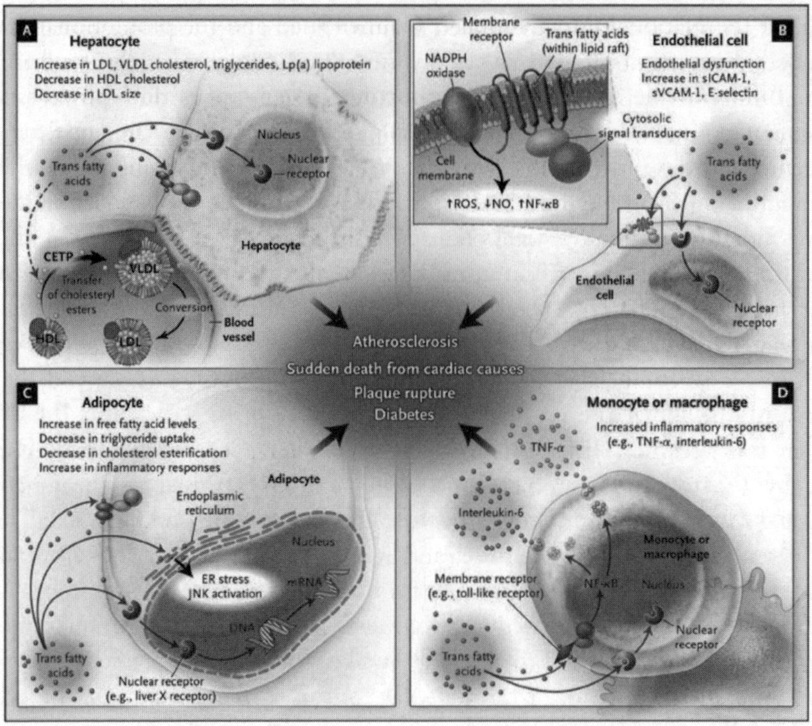

Figure 2. Potential Physiological Effects of Trans Fatty Acids. Mozaffarian D. et al., NEJM, *2006.*

Although there was not a total abandonment of the report of the scientific committee, the published guidelines were written by government staff [instead of the Dietary Guidelines Advisory Committee, who had written the previous five editions] and reflect subtle twists and watering down of some recommendations that suggest heavy industry involvement. For example, instead of the committee's determination that trans-fats should contribute no more than 1 per cent of energy, the report suggests that trans-fats should be 'as low as possible.' The chosen wording is wide open for interpretation and supports the food industry's desire to have wiggle room even though a strict cutoff would be in the public's best interest.[50]

Industry involvement in nutrition policy also contributes to the glut of confusing information. While instructing us to limit intake of saturated fats, the federal government is spending more than $380 million on advertising campaigns that support the saturated fat-laden dairy, pork, and beef industries.[51] This is despite its own efforts to minimize or terminate support of the campaigns. In 2000, when the

Secretary of Agriculture directed the Agricultural Marketing Service to halt its pork campaign, the National Pork Producers Council sued and the promotional program continued. Keeping its fingers in an assortment of cookie jars, the food industry cannot only provide us with vitamin-fortified Diet Cokes and phyto-estrogen-supplemented CocoaVia bars, they can also assure us these items are good for us.

Scientific advancement has led to a seemingly all-encompassing comprehension of biological constituents and processes. Furthermore, it has also allowed us to discover the infinitesimal elements that coalesce to form the foods we eat and how they affect our physiology. Although this knowledge has undeniably boded well for our health, it has also enabled the rise of a powerful industry, the industrial food industry. Science has allowed the food industry to redefine our diet, without moral regard, in the quest for one objective: financial gain. Now, as we stare at the plate before us, we unwittingly see 'terrors' lurking in each prospective bite. The food on our plate is now a composite of many manipulations conceived by the food industry. Fortunately, though, we are beginning to discover what is really in front of us and are slowly arming ourselves in a battle to redefine what is 'good.' Unfortunately, though, it seems a battle of David and Goliath, with the bizarre twist that David is the client on whom Goliath depends for his viability. The question crystallizes as to whether such a vast array of intricately engineered and aggressively marketed products is simply the 'wave of the future' or morally bankrupt.

'A New Theory of Biology,' was the title of the paper which Mustapha Mond *251* had just finished reading. He sat for some time, meditatively frowning, then picked up his pen and wrote across the title-page: 'The author's mathematical treatment of the conception of purpose is novel and highly ingenious, but heretical and, so far as the present social order is concerned, dangerous and potentially subversive. *Not to be published.*' He underlined the words.... It was the sort of idea that might easily decondition the more unsettled minds among the higher castes – make them lose their faith in happiness as the Sovereign Good and take to believing, instead, that the goal was somewhere beyond, somewhere outside the present human sphere, that the purpose of life was not the maintenance of well being, but some intensification and refining of consciousness, some enlargement of knowledge.[52]

Bibliography

Basciano, Heather, et al., 'Fructose, insulin resistance, and metabolic dyslipidemia', *Nutrition and Metabolism*, 2005, 2: p. 5.

Bray, George, et al., 'Consumption of high-fructose corn syrup in beverages may play a role in the epidemic of obesity', *American Journal of Clinical Nutrition*, 2004, 79: pp. 537–43.

Burbank, J., 'Kellogg's is cutting back on sugar and sodium in its products aimed at kids', *Orlando Sentinel*, 15 June 2007.

Centers for Disease Control, 'Overweight and obesity: economic consequences', Retrieved 7/3/07.www. cdc.gov.

Centers for Disease Control, 'Overweight and obesity: childhood overweight', Retrieved 7/3/07. www. cdc.gov.

Cohen, D., 'Low-carb deals seen jumpstarting food industry profits', Forbes.com 1 January 2004. Retrieved 7/10/07.

Conklin, M.T. et al., 'Nutrition Information at Point of Selection Affects Food Chosen by High School Students', *Journal Child Nutrition and Management,* Spring 2005:1.

Critser, Greg, *Fat Land: How Americans Became the Fattest People in the World* (Boston: Houghton Mifflin, 2003).

de Certeau, Michael et al., *The Practice of Everyday Life – Volume 2: Living and Cooking* (Minneapolis: University of Minnesota Press, 1998).

Dunn, J., 'Restaurant Chains, Too, Watch Their Carbs', *New York Times,* 4 January 2004.

Enig, M.G., 'The Tragic Legacy of Center for Science in the Public Interest (CSPI)', *Wise Traditions in Food, Farming and the Healing Arts,* Fall 2003.

Ferguson, James G., Jr. 'Is it the Real Thing™? Lidwina of Schiedam, Chocolate Eclairs, and GM Cornbread', *Authenticity in the Kitchen. Oxford Symposium on Food and Cookery 2005* (Prospect Books, 2006).

Food and Nutrition Board. *Dietary Reference Intakes for Energy, Carbohydrate, Fiber, Fat, Fatty Acids, Cholesterol, Protein, and Amino Acids (Macronutrients)* (Washington, D.C.: National Academies Press, 2005).

Gleason, P. and Suitor, C., 'Food for thought: children's diets in the 1990s', Princeton, NJ, Mathematica Policy Research, Inc. 2001.

Godfrey, J.R., 'Toward Optimal Health: Walter Willet, M.D., Dr. P.H. Discusses Dietary Guidelines', *Journal Women's Health,* 2005, 14: 8.

Gratzer, Walter, *Terrors of the Table* (Oxford: Oxford University Press, 2005).

Grocery Manufacturers Association, Press release, 3 August 1999.

Grocery Manufacturers Association, Press Release, 9 October 2003.

Honors 352 seminar lecture, Université de Bourgogne – Dijon, 9 April 2007.

Huxley, Aldous, *Brave New World* (New York: Harper Perennial, 2005).

Kleinfeld, N.R., 'Diabetes and Its Awful Toll Quietly Emerge as a Crisis', *New York Times,* 9 January 2006.

Malik, V.S. et al., 'Intake of sugar-sweetened beverages and weight gain: a systematic review', *American Journal of Clinical Nutrition,* 2006, 2: 274–88.

Martin, Andrew, 'Labels Lack Food's Origin Despite Law', *New York Times,* 2 July 2007.

Mozaffarian, D. et al., 'Trans Fatty Acids and Cardiovascular Disease', *NEJM,* 2006, 354: 1601–1613.

Olshansky, S.J. et al., 'A Potential Decline in Life Expectancy in the United States in the 21st Century', *NEJM,* 2005, 352: 1138–1145.

Pollan, Michael, *The Omnivore's Dilemma* (New York: Penguin, 2006).

——, Public lecture, UNC Chapel Hill, 12 October 2006.

Schiffman, S.S. et al., 'Elevated and sustained desire for sweet taste in african-americans: a potential factor in the development of obesity', *Nutrition,* 2000, 10: 886–93.

Schlosser, Eric, *Fast Food Nation.* New York: Houghton Mifflin, 2001.

Smith, A.G. et al., 'Diet induced obese mice have increased mortality and altered immune responses when infected with influenza virus', *Journal of Nutrition,* 2007, 137: 1236–1243.

Stevens, A., 'Functional Foods Market: Increasingly, It's a Way of Life', *Nutrition Industry Executive,* July/Aug 2005.

Striffler, Steve, *Chicken: The Dangerous Transformation of America's Favorite Food* (New Haven: Yale University Press, 2005).

Teff, K.L. et al., 'Dietary fructose reduces circulating insulin and leptin, attenuates postprandial suppression of ghrelin, and increases triglycerides in women', *Journal of Clinical Endocrinology & Metabolism*, 2004; 6:2963–72.

United States Department of Agriculture. 'Dietary Guidelines for Americans 2005: Fats', Retrieved 7/8/2007. www.usda.gov

Wilde, P.E., 'Federal Communication about Obesity in the Dietary Guidelines and Checkoff Programs', *Obesity*. 2006; 14:6.

Zamiska, Nicholas and Spencer, Jane, 'China Faces a New Worry: Heavy Metals in the Food', *Wall Street Journal*, 2 July 2007.

Notes

1. Schlosser pp. 169–90.
2. Striffler p. 36.
3. Martin, Andrew, 'Labels Lack Food's Origin Despite Law', *New York Times*, 2 July 2007.
4. Ibid.
5. Zamiska, Nicholas and Spencer, Jane, 'China Faces a New Worry: Heavy Metals in the Food', *Wall Street Journal*, 2 July 2007.
6. Chapel Hill, North Carolina is extraordinarily fortunate to have a robust and thriving Farmers' Market in neighboring Carrboro, a superb Co-op named Weaver Street Market, and a number of restaurants committed to using local, seasonal products. In addition, there are three Whole Foods Markets located in the Research Triangle. In his chapter on organic food, Pollan seems to take issue with the concept of Whole Foods, arguing that it displaces small, local farmers. We rebut this criticism on two counts. As urban concentration continues, 'local' produce becomes tenuous at best, ideal as it might be. Perhaps more important for the present focus on morality and food is the role Whole Foods can play in assuring product integrity. A recent purchase of an 'organic' peanut butter at an 'organic and health' food store in another state from a manufacturer also featured at Whole Foods produced an item containing 'organic sugar and palm oil' whereas the Whole Foods version contained only peanuts and salt.
7. Ferguson, James G., Jr. 'Is it the Real Thing™? Lidwina of Schiedam, Chocolate Eclairs, and GM Cornbread', *Authenticity in the Kitchen. Oxford Symposium on Food and Cookery 2005* (Prospect Books, 2006).
8. Pollan, p. 41.
9. Ibid.
10. Ibid., p. 43.
11. Ibid., p. 44.
12. Ibid.
13. Ibid., p. 84.
14. Honors 352 seminar lecture, Université de Bourgogne – Dijon. 9 April 2007.
15. Pollan, p. 85.
16. Ibid.
17. Ibid., p. 89.
18. Ibid., p. 91.
19. Public lecture, UNC Chapel Hill, 12 October 2006.
20. Pollan, p. 55.
21. Bray et al., 'Consumption of high-fructose corn syrup in beverages may play a role in the epidemic of obesity', *American Journal of Clinical Nutrition*, 2004, 79: 537 – 43.
22. Corn syrup is composed primarily of glucose molecules derived from the degradation of cornstarch. Given that fructose is only a minor component, corn syrup is not as sweet as either sugar or HFCS.
23. Critser, p. 18.
24. Gratzer, p. 230.

25. Kleinfeld, N.R., 'Diabetes and Its Awful Toll Quietly Emerge as a Crisis', *New York Times*, 9 January 2006.

26. Smith et al., 'Diet induced obese mice have increased mortality and altered immune responses when infected with influenza virus', *Journal of Nutrition*, 2007, 137: 1236–1243.

27. Bray et al.

28. Basciano, H., et al. 'Fructose, insulin resistance, and metabolic dyslipidemia', *Nutrition & Metabolism* 2005, 2: 5.

29. Ibid.

30. Schiffman, S.S. et al. 'Elevated and sustained desire for sweet taste in african-americans: a potential factor in the development of obesity', *Nutrition*, 2000, 10: 886–93.

31. Malik, V.S. et al. 'Intake of sugar-sweetened beverages and weight gain: a systematic review', *American Journal of Clinical Nutrition*, 2006, 2: 274–88.

32. Basciano et al.

33. Ibid.

34. Teff, K.L., et al., 'Dietary fructose reduces circulating insulin and leptin, attenuates postprandial suppression of ghrelin, and increases triglycerides in women', *Journal of Clinical Endocrinology & Metabolism*, 2004, 6: 2963–2972.

35. CDC (US) defines 'overweight' as BMI ≤ 30 and 'obese' ≥ 30.

36. Centers for Disease Control, 'Overweight and obesity: economic consequences', Retrieved 7/3/07. www.cdc.gov.

37. Gleason, P., and Suitor, C., 'Food for thought: children's diets in the 1990s', Princeton, NJ, Mathematica Policy Research, Inc. 2001.

38. Olshansky, S.J., et al., 'A Potential Decline in Life Expectancy in the United States in the 21st Century', *New England Journal of Medicine*, 2005, 352: 1138–1145.

39. Burbank, J., 'Kellogg's is cutting back on sugar and sodium in its products aimed at kids', *Orlando Sentinel*, 15 June 2007.

40. Grocery Manufacturers Association, Press release, 3 August 1999.

41. Conklin, M.T., et al., 'Nutrition Information at Point of Selection Affects Food Chosen by High School Students', *Journal of Child Nutrition and Management*, Spring 2005: 1.

42. Stevens, A. 'Functional Foods Market: Increasingly, It's a Way of Life', *Nutrition Industry Executive*, July/Aug 2005.

43. Dunn, J. 'Restaurant Chains, Too, Watch Their Carbs', *New York Times*, 4 January 2004.

44. Cohen, D. 'Low-carb deals seen jumpstarting food industry profits', Forbes.com 1 January 2004. Retrieved 7/10/07.

45. Grocery Manufacturers Association, Press Release, 9 October 2003.

46. Food and Nutrition Board, *Dietary Reference Intakes for Energy, Carbohydrate, Fiber, Fat, Fatty Acids, Cholesterol, Protein, and Amino Acids (Macronutrients)*, National Academies Press, Washington, D.C. 2005, p. 424.

47. United States Department of Agriculture, 'Dietary Guidelines for Americans 2005: Fats'. Retrieved 7/8/2007. www.usda.gov.

48. Enig, M.G., 'The Tragic Legacy of Center for Science in the Public Interest (CSPI)', *Wise Traditions in Food, Farming and the Healing Arts*, Fall 2003.

49. Mozaffarian, D., et al., 'Trans Fatty Acids and Cardiovascular Disease', *New England Journal of Medicine*, 2006, 354: 1601–1613.

50. Godfrey, J.R., 'Toward Optimal Health: Walter Willet, M.D., Dr. P.H. Discusses Dietary Guidelines', *Journal Women's Health*, 2005, 14: 8.

51. Wilde, P.E., 'Federal Communication about Obesity in the Dietary Guidelines and Checkoff Programs', *Obesity*, 2006, 14:6.

52. Huxley, p. 162.

Marketing Junk Food to Children in the United States

Andrew F. Smith

Concern for the lack of nutritional content of many commercial foods had been expressed in the United States since the 1920s, but it was not until the vast post-World War II increase in junk food consumption – fueled by television advertising – that American nutritionists began to raise an alarm. The term *junk food*, heard in the United States since the 1960s, became a buzzword in the following decade when Michael Jacobson, one of the founders of the Center for Science in the Public Interest (CSPI), began using it frequently in his speeches and writings. The term junk food came to mean those foods or beverages with minimal proteins, vitamins, minerals, fiber, or other desirable nutrients, but high in calories, fat, salt, sugar and/or caffeine.

Origins of commercial junk foods

Commercial junk foods fall into roughly four major categories: snack foods, such as potato chips, candy, chocolate, and bakery goods; carbonated and non-carbonated beverages, such as Coca-Cola and Pepsi-Cola, and Kool-Aid; sugary cereals, such as Sugar Pops or Frosted Flakes; and fast foods, such as hamburgers, shakes, hot dogs, and french fries.

255

In their origin, these foods have long histories. Snack foods, for instance, were around long before mass production made them an American obsession. Snacks consumed in the home usually consisted of fruit, unsalted nuts, or bread and cheese. Outside the home, concessionaires and vendors sold salty snacks, such as peanuts and popcorn, on the streets of American cities and at fairs, circuses, carnivals, and sporting events. In the late nineteenth century, commercial salty snacks, such as pretzels and potato chips, hard candies, such as lemon drops and lollipops, and chewy candies, such as caramels and licorice, began to be locally manufactured and sold in grocery stores. In the early 1890s, Cracker-Jacks, a salty-sweet combination of caramel pop-corn and peanuts, became America's first nationally promoted commercial snack food.[1] Milton Hershey's mass produced chocolate bars followed in 1900. Others began manufacturing cookies, such as Oreos and Chips Ahoy, and bakery snacks, such as Twinkies and Sno-balls, and ice cream. By the mid-twentieth century tens of thousands of snack foods were commercially available, sold in grocery stores, vending machines and street kiosks.

Flavored carbonated beverages, such as ginger ale and root beer, originated in drugstores, where druggists concocted mixtures intended to resolve medical prob-lems. Locally bottled sodas were sold in confectionery and general stores by the mid-nineteenth century. The first mass produced soda was root beer, which was promoted in 1876 by Philadelphia drugstore operator Charles E. Hires. Coca-Cola came along in 1886, followed by Pepsi-Cola in 1898. Thousands of other soft drinks were manufactured during the late nineteenth and the twentieth centuries, and most contained sugar and caffeine.[2]

Ironically, ready-to-eat breakfast cereal, which today may be the nutritional equivalent of a bowl of crumbled cookies, was devised by vegetarians looking for a healthy alternative to the traditional bacon and egg breakfast. John Harvey Kellogg, director of the Seventh Day Adventist sanitarium in Battle Creek, Michigan, rolled and dried cooked cornmeal to make Corn Flakes. As a result, hundreds of additional companies began producing breakfast cereals. It wasn't until after World War II that cereal makers focused on sweetened cereals. Kellogg's introduced Sugar Pops in 1950 and Frosted Flakes in 1952. Two years later, General Mills introduced Trix, which contains 46 per cent sugar by weight.[3] Today's Count Chocula, Chocolate Chip Cookie Crisp, and Reese's Peanut Butter Puffs are the descendants of these three kid-friendly cereals. In addition, cereal manufacturers have extended their cereal lines to include confections. Commercial Rice Krispies Treats were first marketed in 1995. Made by Kellogg's, it is packaged in individual servings and is intended as a dessert for lunch boxes. Recently, Snapple and Fruit Loops have co-branded to produce Snapple Candy and Snapplets hard candies, while Kellogg co-branded with Brach's Confections to produce Fruit Loops snacks.

Today's international empires of fast food originated with the fare offered by city lunch wagons in the 1870s and the hotdogs and hamburgers sold by street vendors by the early 1890s. White Castle, the first fast food chain, proved that Americans would line up for a cheap, tasty, quick meal in the form of a hamburger sandwich. This success laid the groundwork for other chains, and by the 1930s, thousands of fast-food outlets dotted the urban landscape and the nation's highways. But not until the 1950s, when McDonald's and Kentucky Fried Chicken (KFC) came to the fore, did fast food emerge as a major component in the American diet.[4]

Advertising junk food to children

When all comestibles were sold in bulk – from a peddler's cart or out of an unlabeled barrel, crock or box at the general store – the companies that manufactured them were little known. With the advent of packaged foods, however, came the need for an appealing brand name, attractive labeling, and a memorable trademark or icon. These features also made possible ad campaigns for these processed foods.

Quaker Oats was the first food company to roll out a national advertising campaign. The trademarked name and the image of a benevolent Quaker were instantly recognizable on the packages of oats, and the company mounted advertising signs on train cars. Quaker Oats also introduced the redeemable premium coupon, which was packed in the box. The National Biscuit Company followed the Quaker model with its national promotion of Uneeda Biscuits in 1898.

Similar tactics would be employed by snack food manufacturers, beginning with Cracker-Jack. The name 'Cracker-Jack' was trademarked early in 1896, and almost immediately the manufacturer launched promotional campaigns in Chicago, New York, and Philadelphia. Ads placed in the local newspapers introduced Cracker-Jack as the '1896 Sensation' – a new confection, not yet six months old, which had 'made the most instantaneous success of anything ever introduced.' The accompanying slogan ran, 'The more you eat the more you want.' Later advertisements touted Cracker-Jack as 'a healthful, nourishing food-confection,' the 'Standard Popcorn Confection' by which all others were judged. By tucking a 'toy surprise' in every box, the Cracker-Jack company assured their product's appeal to children. Cracker-Jack's success inspired the creation of other new confections and snacks, which in turn employed similar advertising methods – ones that are still in use today: trumpeting grandiose slogans, targeting children with toys, and proclaiming the products' healthful qualities.

Since the 1920s, snack foods, cereals, sodas, and fast food have been advertised on radio. From the manufacturer's standpoint, radio's immense power lay in its advertising potential and its relatively low cost. When radio entertainment programs became popular in the 1920s, food companies commissioned on-air personalities to promote their products. Among the earliest food companies to reap the rewards of radio advertising were cereal makers. In 1926, Wheaties was the first advertiser to use a singing radio commercial on radio. In 1933 Wheaties sponsored the popular children's program, 'Jack Armstrong, All-American Boy.' White Castle began advertising on radio by the 1930s.

Television greatly expanded the ability of advertisers to reach children. Children are more vulnerable to commercials, which they view less critically than do adults. Children's programs, especially Saturday morning cartoon shows, neatly deliver the selected age group to the advertiser. By the 1960s, children were identified as a separate market for advertisers, and fast food chains joined snack food, soda and soda companies in targeting children.

McDonald's has been in the forefront of child-centered product promotion. In the early 1960s, a Washington, D.C., franchise began sponsoring a children's show called 'Bozo's Circus,' and this led to the creation of Ronald McDonald, who appeared on local D.C. television commercials beginning in 1963. The following year the national McDonald's Corporation sponsored the broadcast of the Macy's Thanksgiving Day Parade – the first fast food chain to advertise on national television. The holiday commercials produced immediate nationwide results, convincing McDonald's management to expend more funds on ads targeting children. Billions of dollars of corporate funds were expended on child-oriented television advertising. These ads succeeded in making Ronald McDonald identifiable by fully 96 per cent of American children (second only to Santa Claus), and McDonald's became the nation's largest fast-food chain during the 1970s.

In addition to featuring its Ronald McDonald character, McDonald's began offering specially packaged McDonald's Happy Meals in 1978. These offered kid's sized portions along with toys. As these children matured and continued to frequent McDonald's long after they stopped buying Happy Meals, McDonald's learned the importance of gaining brand loyalty from small children. In 2001 McDonald's added 'Mighty Kids Meals' to their menu. It targets children 8 to 10 years old. Happy meals have been criticized for the fat content in the foods in the meal.

McDonald's has scored several major promotional successes based on toys in Happy Meals. In 1997 McDonald's included a 'Teenie Beanie Baby' in Happy Meals. Customers waited in long lines to acquire their Happy Meals with Teenie Beanie Babies inside. This campaign is considered one of the most successful promotions in the history of advertising. Before the promotion, McDonald's sold 10 million Happy Meals per month. During the promotion, Happy Meal sales increased to 100 million per month. In 2006, McDonald's offered characters from the new Walt Disney Pictures/Walden Media film, *The Chronicles of Narnia: The Lion, The Witch and The Wardrobe* in McDonald's Happy Meals and Mighty Kids Meals that came with a free toy, often based on a character from a currently popular movie or TV show. McDonald's also provided 'McDonaldland' playgrounds at many outlets, making a fast-food meal even more inviting to families.

Some chains secured endorsements from sports figures and movie and TV stars; then came movie tie-ins and special arrangements with theme parks such as Disneyland. Many other junk food manufacturers have developed similar promotional activities.In addition to promotion on television, the food industry markets junk foods aggressively in magazines read by children and youth and have placed their products in movies. One of Hershey's greatest advertising successes came in 1981, when Universal Studios approached Mars, Inc., to use M&Ms in its movie, *E. T., The Extra Terrestrial*. Mars turned Universal Studios down, and Universal approached Hershey's, which produced Reese's Pieces. Universal and Hershey's came to an agreement in which Reese's Pieces were used in the movie and Hershey agreed to promote *E. T.* with $1 million worth of promotions. When the movie was released, sales of Reese's Pieces skyrocketed.

Junk food manufacturers promote their products in schools. Channel One, a commercial television network with programming shown in classrooms to eight million middle, junior, and high school students, carried soft drink ads. Soft drink companies have even managed to place ads in prominent locations in schools: on school buses, posters, calendars, book covers, and even mouse pads. In addition to advertising, junk foods are sold directly to youth centered organizations and schools. Coca-Cola, for instance, paid the Boys & Girls Clubs of America $60 million to serve its brand exclusively in more than 2,000 facilities., and junk foods such as soft drinks and snack chips are now advertised and sold in many of the nation's schools. The American School Food Service Association estimates that 30 per cent of public high schools offer branded fast food for sale in their cafeteria or vending machines. It is estimated that 1 million elementary students participate in the 22-year old 'Book It' program, sponsored by Pizza Hut. In this program children who meet targets are offered a free pizza. McDonald's offers coupons as rewards for children who read books and the company advertises on report cards of 27,000 elementary school children.[5]

Coca-Cola, PepsiCo and McDonald's spend million of dollars distributing sophisticated educational programs with videos featuring sports figures who encourage children to be active. Pop Secret uses popcorn kernels in its educational material. Domino's Pizza's 'Encounter Math (Count on Domino's)' materials are highly commercial with activities involving pizza, labeled as Domino's, and the company's logo appears on all materials and its name is mentioned often in the materials. Mars, Inc.'s 'Team Snickers with World Cup Soccer 100% Smart Energy To Go' is considered incomplete, biased, and commercial. The National Potato Board with the Snack Food Association's 'Count Your Chips,' is considered advertisements for potato chips, not math materials. Dunkin's Donuts's program, 'Grade A Donuts: Honoring Homework Stars' offered donuts to those who successfully complete their homework. Encouraging students to complete homework is a good, but critics don't believe that carbohydrate-filled donuts should be the reward.

Some teaching units include nutritional information, but none of it mentions the amount of calories, fat, sugar, salt, or caffeine in junk and fast foods. These materials are intended to promote the image that these companies are interested in health. By omission, it suggests that drinking soda and consuming junk food promote success, wealth and friendship. These materials are promotions for their sponsors. The intent is to deflect attention from obesity and focus it on physical activity; these corporations are interested promoting their products through the materials. By providing the material for free, this also undercuts the distribution of the few non-partisan materials on nutrition provided by medical and governmental groups.

By far the most effective means of promoting junk foods is through television advertising. American food companies annually spend an estimated $5 to $8 billion on advertisements and promotions targeting children. Much of this has been expended on television advertising. Some studies suggest that almost 80 per cent of food commercials aired on Saturday morning kids' TV shows are for products of low nutritional value. Advertisements for high-sugar products form the majority. The average American child sees more than 10,000 televised food ads, most related to snacks, sodas, sugary cereals, and fast foods. High-sugar products are the most heavily advertised. Kristen Harrison's 2005 study of the television's effects on children and adolescents found that 78 per cent of the food advertised during TV programs favored by children ages 6 to 11 is junk food. Harrison found that the most heavily advertised foods included Burger King Kid's Meal Chicken Tenders, Jell-O Pudding Bites, McDonald's Happy Meals, french fries, Post Fruity Pebbles cereal, and Wendy's Kid's Meal crispy chicken nuggets.[6]

259

Hollywood and sports celebrities have appeared on commercials and endorsed fast food and soda companies. The comedian Bill Cosby has been a spokesperson for Jell-O since 1988. Halle Berry, Britney Spears, Barry Bostwick, and Beyoncé Knowles have all advertised Pepsi. Michael Jordan, Kobe Bryant, Donald Trump, Serena Williams, and Venus Williams have all promoted McDonald's. Shaquile O'Neal and B. B. King have advertised Burger King. The actor Jason Alexander has endorsed Kentucky Fried Chicken. Garth Brooks, the country music singer, has promoted Dr Pepper.

Ethical issues

The juvenile mania for junk food can rightfully be credited to relentless advertising campaigns. As a result of their promotional campaigns, approximately one-quarter of the vegetables consumed by children are from potato chips and French fries. This increases to about one-third of the vegetable servings consumed by teenagers. In 1998 the Center for Science in the Public Interest's study, 'Liquid Candy,' reported that soft drink companies had targeted schools for their advertising and sales of their products. It also reported that soft drinks 'provided more than one-third of all refined sugars in the diet.' Soft drinks, according to CSPI, are the single greatest source of refined sugar, providing 9 per cent of calories for boys and 8 per cent for girls. CSPI states that at least 75 per cent of teenage children drink soda every day.[7] Estimates suggest that children and teenagers on average consume more than 64 gallons of soft drinks a year.[8] American teenagers drink twice as much carbonated soda as they do milk, much to the detriment of their growing bones and teeth. Junk food displaces more healthful foods, such as milk, fruit, and vegetables, in the diets of many children, leading to obesity and nutritional deficiencies.

The growing consumption of junk foods is correlated with an increase in heart disease, high blood pressure, certain cancers, and other diseases. Medical professionals believe that diet plays a critical role in these diseases, particularly a diet high in fat, salt, sugar, and the excessive empty calories contained in many junk foods. The national rise in obesity also correlates with increased consumption of junk food, particularly among youth. During the last twenty years, consumption of junk food has ballooned, and the per centage of children and adolescents who are obese has doubled. Today, 25 per cent of American children are classified as overweight.

Rather than accept responsibility for these problems, junk food manufacturers offer a number of counter arguments. They believe that they have the right to make, advertise, and sell their products – all of which contain ingredients approved for use by the United States Food and Drug Agency. It is the responsibility of the individual to decide what they want to eat. No one is forced to buy their products: if consumers did not want junk foods, then companies would not manufacture them and stores could not sell them. Many believe that the main cause of obesity in America's youth is the increasing sedentary life and the lack of exercise. In keeping with this argument, many companies have encouraged and sponsored sports competitions and fitness programs. Finally, in the case of children, parents have the responsibility to monitor the foods their children eat. Manufacturers maintain that they should not be blamed for the failure of parental responsibilities.

The arguments presented by manufacturers have some merit: youth do need more exercise; parents should take more responsibility for the foods consumed by their children. However, argue as you may, junk foods clearly contribute massive amounts of calories to young people, and the result is an increase in overweight and obesity. The vast increase in consumption of junk foods have created health problems that are evident today and will likely continue to generate health problems far into the future, even if the promotional campaigns ended today.

Junk food purveyors bear special responsibility for peddling nutritionally inadequate foods so aggressively to kids, who have yet to develop the skills to understand the persuasive intent of advertising. Children are especially susceptible to their charms of junk foods that are intentionally flavored to appeal to children. While children themselves have little buying power, they do have pester power. Busy parents simply take the easy way out and give in to their children's constant nagging for a candy bar, soda, or cheeseburger.

It is ethically impossible for junk food manufacturers to avoid some responsibility for their promotional efforts targeted at children, who need to be protected from this commercial exploitation. Many groups have attempted to ban the sale and advertising of junk foods in schools and on television programs targeted at children and youth. Others have suggested that junk foods be taxed (dubbed the 'Twinkie Tax') and the profits generated are to be given to the schools to promote nutrition education and offset the income derived from the sale or advertising of junk food.

Recently, due to the effectiveness of advertising targeted at children, several other countries have banned advertisements on television and radio programs targeted at children under the age of 12. In the United States, despite calls for similar controls, advertising on children's television remains unregulated. In October 2006, the United States Federal Communications Commission launched a study to examine the links between television advertising, viewing habits, and childhood obesity.[9] Perhaps their findings will encourage junk food manufacturers to refrain from engaging in massive promotional campaigns targeted at youth; if they do not, governmental regulation will become a necessity.

Notes

1. For the history of salty snacks, see Andrew F. Smith, *Popped Culture: A Social History of Popcorn in America* (Columbia: University of South Carolina Press, 1999), and Andrew F. Smith, *Peanuts: The Illustrious History of the Goober Pea* (Urbana: University of Illinois Press, 2002).

2. For additional information about the history of soft drinks, see Frederick Allen, *Secret Formula: How Brilliant Marketing and Relentless Salesmanship Made Coca-Cola the Best-known Product in the World* (New York: HarperBusiness, 1994); David Greising, *I'd Like the World to Buy a Coke: the life and leadership of Roberto Goizueta* (New York: John Wiley and Sons, 1998); Roger Enrico and Jesse Kornbluth, *The Other Guy Blinked: How Pepsi Won the Cola Wars* (New York: Bantam, 1986); Constance L. Hays, *The Real Thing: Truth and Power at the Coca-Cola Company* (New York: Random House, 2005); E. J. Kahn, Jr., *The Big Drink; The Story of Coca-Cola* (New York: Random House, 1960); J. C. Louis and Harvey Yazijian, *The Cola Wars: The Story of the Global Corporate Battle between the Coca-Cola Company and PepsiCo* (New York: Everest House, 1980); Milward W. Martin, *Twelve Full Ounces* Second edition (New York: Holt, Rinehart and Winston, 1969); Mark Pendergrast, *For God, Country and Coca-Cola* (New York: Scribner's, 1993); John J. Riley, *A History of the American Soft Drink Industry. Bottled Carbonated Beverages 1807–1957* (Washington, D. C.: American Bottlers of Carbonated Beverages, 1958).

3. For additional information about the history of cereal, see Scott Bruce and Bill Crawford, *Cerealizing America; The Unsweetened Story of American Breakfast Cereal* (Boston: Faber and Faber, 1995); Gerald Carson, *Cornflake Crusade* (New York: Rinehart & Company, Inc., 1957); Horace B. Powell, *The Original Has This Signature–W. K. Kellogg* (Englewood Cliffs, New Jersey: Prentice-Hall, Inc., 1956).

4. For additional information about the history of fast food, see Robert L. Emerson, *The New Economics of Fast Food* (New York: Van Nostrand Reinhold, 1990); David Gerard Hogan, *Selling 'em by the Sack: White Castle and the Creation of American Food* (New York: New York University Press, 1997); John A. Jakle and Keith A. Sculle. *Fast Food: Roadside Restaurants in the Automobile Age* (Baltimore: Johns Hopkins University Press, 1999); Philip Langdon, *Orange Roofs, Golden Arches: the Architecture of American Chain Restaurants* (New York: Knopf, 1986); Eric Schlosser, *Fast Food Nation; the Dark Side of the All-American Meal* (New York: Houghton Mifflin Company, 2001); Andrew F. Smith, *Hamburgers* (London: Reaktion Books, forthcoming); Morgan Spurlock, *Don't Eat this Book: Fast Food and the Supersizing of America* (New York: G.P. Putnam's Sons, 2005); Jennifer Parker Talwar, *Fast Food, Fast Track: Immigrants, Big Business, and the American Dream* (Cambridge Massachusetts: Westview Press, 2002).

5. Emily Bryson York, 'McD's Newest Ad Platform: Report Cards; Not Surprisingly, Watchdogs Give Fast-Feeder's Play Failing Marks,' *AdAge*, December 5, 2007.

6. Kristen Harrison and A. L. Marske, 'Nutritional Content of Foods Advertised During the Television Programs Children Watch Most,' *American Journal of Public Health* 95 (2005):1568–1574.

7. 'Liquid Candy: How Soft Drinks are Harming Americans' Health,' Center for Science in the Public Interest report, October 21, 1998.

8. B. S. Gupta and Uma Gupta, eds., *Caffeine and Behavior: Current Views and Research Trends* (Boca Raton, FL: CRC Press, 1999); Bennett Alan Weinberg and Bonnie K. Bealer, *The World of Caffeine: the Science and Culture of the World's Most Popular Drug* (New York: Routledge, 2001); 'Children Increasingly Consuming Caffeine,' *Caffeine* (May–June 1998), at: www.ndsn.org/mayjun98/caffeine.html

9. 'Study: Toddlers Target of Fatty Foods,' *Philadelphia Inquirer*, October 2, 2006.

Piscinae and the Myth of Roman Decadence at Table

Raymond Sokolov

We did not need Federico Fellini to make us aware of the wretched excess of Roman banquets. Long before his *Satyricon*, Petronius, in the original, had already painted as broad a picture of prandial extravagance in Nero's Rome. Other soberer Latin writers of the classical period painted such a lurid picture of groaning boards and vomitoria that no one has ever bothered to doubt that rich Romans of the late Republic and Empire habitually stuffed themselves with pretentious vulgarity and showered sestertia on purveyors of rare, showy foods.

Modern historians of ancient Rome, with Gibbon in the lead, have accepted this vision of tasteless gluttony as it came down to them from ancient writers. Nor is it easy to dismiss contemporaneous Roman witnesses' expressions of shock, anger or bitter mockery at the abuses of gastronomy they alleged to have observed firsthand.

Even when (and this is overwhelmingly the case), ancient sources are literary or generations removed from the meals they describe, their uniform revulsion against flagrant overconsumption and *gourmandisme* are both difficult to ignore and impossible to confute. Even though we are not wrong to assume that Petronius exaggerates the menu and trappings of Trimalchio's dinner – he was, after all, avowedly writing satire – but how should we sort out a residuum of fact from this surreal description:

> On the tray stood a donkey made of Corinthian bronze, bearing panniers containing olives, white in one and black in the other. Two platters flanked the figure, on the margins of which were engraved Trimalchio's name and the weight of the silver in each. Dormice sprinkled with poppy-seed and honey were served on little bridges soldered fast to the platter, and hot sausages on a silver gridiron, underneath which were damson plums and pomegranate seeds.

Or this:

> There was a circular tray around which were displayed the signs of the zodiac, and upon each sign the caterer had placed the food best in keeping with it. Ram's vetches on Aries, a piece of beef on Taurus, kidneys and lamb's fry on Gemini, a crown on Cancer, the womb of an unfarrowed sow on Virgo, an African fig on Leo, on Libra a balance, one pan of which held a tart and the other a cake, a small seafish on Scorpio, a bull's eye on Sagittarius, a sea lobster on Capricornus, a goose on Aquarius and two mullets on Pisces. In the middle lay a piece of cut sod upon which rested a honeycomb with the grass arranged around it. An Egyptian slave passed bread around from a silver oven and in

a most discordant voice twisted out a song in the manner of the mime in the musical farce called Laserpitium. Seeing that we were rather depressed at the prospect of busying ourselves with such vile fare, Trimalchio urged us: 'Let us fall to, gentlemen, I beg of you, this is only the sauce!'

There is no easy solution to this dilemma of assessing Roman accounts of Roman foodways, but we can certainly say that Roman writers almost universally draw censorious attention to conspicuous consumption of food and compare modern decadence unfavorably to the humble provender of early, sturdy Rome.

In *Satire* 5, Juvenal portrays another outlandish banquet, with goose liver, wild boar, and truffles, as an affront to the poor. And when Horace writes 'Persicos odi, puer, apparatus' (*Odes* 1.38.1), his puritanical, proto-Rousseauan, xenophobic attitude is more than a pastoral trope. But do we need to join him in this priggish stance? Does it behoove people living in a society as devoted to culinary refinement and display as ours to scorn Roman opulence?[1]

Alan Davidson largely avoids discussing ancient foodways in *The Oxford Companion to Food* (1999).[2] But in the entry on fish he does show sympathy for the 'Roman enthusiasm' for red mullet while expressing puzzlement over the 'extreme financial greed and morbid practices which sometimes attended its consumption.'

Cicero was less restrained. In letters to his friend Atticus,[3] he sneered at his rich enemies in the Senate, calling them *piscinarii*, fish breeders. The implication is that people who maintained fish ponds (*piscinae* or *vivaria*) at their palaces or their opulent villas around the Bay of Naples were effete valetudinarians who neglected their responsibilities as political leaders. Undoubtedly, this was true of his most flagrant opponents in the immense family of the Claudii Metelli, whose moral infractions went well beyond pisciculture, extending, it was widely rumored, even to incest.

Yet fish ponds were not some newfangled fashion of Cicero's day. They are well recorded in the immense Roman literature of farming The physical remains of some of them date back as far as the fifth century BC and were possibly inspired by ponds in Greek settlements.[4]

Some fish ponds were immense, as large as five-and-a-half acres. Others occupied prominent locations within great houses such as the Tiberian and Flavian palaces on the Palatine Hill in Rome. The archeological record, as catalogued by James Higginbotham in *Piscinae, Artificial Fishponds in Roman Italy* (Chapel Hill: University of North Carolina Press, 1997) now encompasses many dozens of excavations that reveal great sophistication in hydrology and the regulation of salinity. The heyday of construction spans the years of the late Republic and early empire, roughly two centuries during which conquering Romans encountered and assimilated the Greek greed for mullet and eel.[5] On the other hand, most of the earlier sites are in Etruria north of Rome, not in the southern lands of Magna Graecia. So it may well be that Italic fish ponds were an indigenous invention.

Pliny the Elder in his *Natural History* attributes the invention of ponds to one L. Licinius Murena some time prior to 91 BC.[6] Since *murena* means eel, it is tempting to believe Varro's claim[7] that Murena got his cognomen because of his work with eels. Yet Pliny credits C. Hirrius with the adaptation of the fish pond for the propagation of eels.[8]

At any rate, eels were by far the most popular fish among the *piscinarii*. And the craze for them is a major reason for the continuing bad odor that surrounds the Roman banquet table. Higginbotham neatly summarizes imperial muraenomania:

> Widespread cultivation of this fish gave rise to many stories concerning the extravagant and ridiculous use of eels. The orator Quintus Hortensius and the triumvir Marcus Licinius Crassus were said to have kept eels as pets and to have wept when they died.[9] *Murenae* were also adorned with jewelry, earrings and neckbands, and were trained to come at the call of their names. A pet *murena*, kept in the ponds of Hortensius at Baculo, was decorated with jewelry by Antonia, wife of Drusus. The fame of this eel is said to have made people eager to visit Baculo in order to view the spectacle.[10] In a more horrific vein, Vedius Pollio punished the occasional disobedient and clumsy slave by throwing the offender into his *piscinae* where the unfortunate servant was eaten by his *murenae*. The cruelty of this particular fish pond owner is widely reported in the ancient literary record.[11]

The other most notorious *piscinarius* transcends the category. Lucullus is the ancient worlds' most notorious *bec fin*, and his name lives on as a standard epithet for a stupendous (Lucullan) repast. He started out as a successful general, but devolved into ostentation as a kind of revenge against the political enemies who denied him the official triumph he undoubtedly deserved for years of ultimately successful campaigning against Mithridates in the East.

Plutarch, writing much later in Greek, provides the most pungent information. As he tells the story, when Lucullus was asked how he could eat so grandly when dining alone, he replied: 'Because Lucullus is eating with Lucullus.'

In order to ensure a constant supply of sea water for his fish ponds, Lucullus not only constructed a canal from the shore to his vast villa, but also had a mountain built over the channel to conceal it.

Plutarch condemns Lucullus, but he is a mild detractor compared to the anonymous biographer of the Emperor Elagabalus (also known as Heliogabalus) in the *Historia Augusta*. Gibbon, basing his diatribe on this account, rises to an unparalleled height of invective:

> The Sun was worshipped at Emesa, under the name of Elagabalus, and under the form of a black conical stone, which, as it was universally believed, had fallen from heaven on that sacred place. To this protecting deity, Antoninus,

not without some reason, ascribed his elevation to the throne. The display of superstitious gratitude was the only serious business of his reign. The triumph of the God of Emesa over all the religions of the earth, was the great object of his zeal and vanity: and the appellation of Elagabalus (for he presumed as pontiff and favourite to adopt that sacred name) was dearer to him than all the titles of Imperial greatness. In a solemn procession through the streets of Rome, the way was strewed with gold dust; the black stone, set in precious gems, was placed on a chariot drawn by six milk-white horses richly caparisoned. The pious emperor held the reins, and, supported by his ministers, moved slowly backwards, that he might perpetually enjoy the felicity of the divine presence. In a magnificent temple raised on the Palatine Mount, the sacrifices of the god of Elagabalus were celebrated with every circumstance of cost and solemnity. The richest wines, the most extraordinary victims, and the rarest aromatics, were profusely consumed on his altar. Around the altar a chorus of Syrian damsels performed their lascivious dances to the sound of barbarian music, whilst the gravest personages of the state and army, clothed in long Phoenician tunics, officiated in the meanest functions, with affected zeal and secret indignation.

To this temple, as to the common centre of religious worship, the Imperial fanatic attempted to remove the Ancilia, the Palladium, and all the sacred pledges of the faith of Numa. A crowd of inferior deities attended in various stations the majesty of the god of Emesa; but his court was still imperfect, till a female of distinguished rank was admitted to his bed. Pallas had been first chosen for his comfort; but as it was dreaded lest her warlike terrors might affright the soft delicacy of a Syrian deity, the Moon, adored by the Africans under the name of Astarte, was deemed a more suitable companion for the Sun. Her image, with the rich offerings of her temple as a marriage portion, was transported with solemn pomp from Carthage to Rome, and the day of these mystic nuptials was a general festival in the capital and throughout the empire.

A rational voluptuary adheres with invariable respect to the temperate dictates of nature, and improves the gratifications of sense by social intercourse, endearing connections, and the soft colouring of taste and the imagination. But Elagabalus (I speak of the emperor of that name), corrupted by his youth, his country, and his fortune, abandoned himself to the grossest pleasures with ungoverned fury, and soon found disgust and satiety in the midst of his enjoyments. The inflammatory powers of art were summoned to his aid: the confused multitude of women, of wines, and of dishes, and the studied variety of attitudes and sauces, served to revive his languid appetites. New terms and new inventions in these sciences, the only ones cultivated and patronised by the monarch, signalised his reign, and transmitted his infamy to succeeding times. A capricious prodigality supplied the want of taste and

266

elegance; and whilst Elagabalus lavished away the treasures of his people in the wildest extravagance, his own voice and that of his flatterers applauded a spirit and magnificence unknown to the tameness of his predecessors. To confound the order of seasons and climates, to sport with the passions and prejudices of his subjects, and to subvert every law of nature and decency, were in the number of his most delicious amusements. A long train of concubines, and a rapid succession of wives, among whom was a vestal virgin, ravished by force from her sacred asylum, were insufficient to satisfy the impotence of his passions. The master of the Roman world affected to copy the dress and manners of the female sex, preferred the distaff to the sceptre, and dishonoured the principal dignities of the empire by distributing them among his numerous lovers; one of whom was publicly invested with the title and authority of the emperor's, or, as he more properly styled himself, of the empress's husband.

It may seem probable, the vices and follies of Elagabalus have been adorned by fancy, and blackened by prejudice. Yet confining ourselves to the public scenes displayed before the Roman people, and attested by grave and contemporary historians, their inexpressible infamy surpasses that of any age or country. The license of an eastern monarch is secluded from the eye of curiosity by the inaccessible walls of his seraglio. The sentiments of honour and gallantry have introduced a refinement of pleasure, a regard for decency, and a respect for public opinion, into the modern courts of Europe; but the corrupt and opulent nobles of Rome gratified every vice that could be collected from the mighty conflux of nations and manners. Secure of impunity, careless of censure, they lived without restraint in the patient and humble society of their slaves and parasites. The emperor, in his turn, viewing every rank of his subjects with the same contemptuous indifference, asserted without control his sovereign privilege of lust and luxury.

I throw this out as a gaudy example of a great historian clothing the testimony of a third-rate historian in a toothsome rhetoric, which gives respectability, appeal, and influence to a scurrilous legend that invites our belief. But, assuming that the basic facts of the life of Elagabalus as Gibbon received them were correct, should we join this post-Roman tradition of viewing the man with horror?

Even the incest taboo has lost much of its sting in our era. The author Kathryn Harrison has published several books in which her adult love affair with her father was a major theme. She has escaped almost any censure and the prospect of criminal prosecution against her or her dear old Dad has never arisen.

A fortiori, in the twenty-first century since the death of Cicero, can anyone imagine a major public figure denouncing an enemy because he spends a fortune on fish? Or any other food? Only the ingestion of endangered species would nowadays arouse the venom that eel ponds did in ancient Rome.[12]

Does this mean that we have sunk into an Elagabalian depravity? Or that Elagabalus and Metellus Clodius Pulcher have been openly despised for centuries as flagrant targets of a hypocritical Roman ideal of abstemiousness at table that was honored, even then, more in the breach than the observance. In our own defense, we may say that no modern foodie has yet thrown a refractory slave into a pond of pet eels.

Notes

1. Puritanical attitudes toward food do run rampant through our world. But the post-Rousseauian principles of Slowfood do not include a ban on pleasure at table, nor do they attempt to reduce or limit culinary elaboration. Our puritanism rests primarily on a dread of or aversion to obesity as well as on a strong empathy for the sufferings of animals. These were not the concerns of Roman food prigs, the killjoys who wrote and passed sumptuary laws forbidding people to eat dormice.
2. p. 302, column 1, second edition, 2006.
3. 1.19.6, 1.20.4.
4. Varro, *Rust.* 3.17.1–10. Columella, *Rust.*8.16.2. For a full bibliography of ancient references, see C. Daremberg and E. Saglio, *Dictionnaires des antiquités grecques et romaines*, 5 (1919) 959–62, s.v. Vivarium (Georges LaFaye) or A. Pauly and G. Wissowa, *Real Encyclopädie der klassischen Altertumswissenschaft* 20 (1950) 1783–85, s.v. Piscina (K. Schneider).
5. Eels from Lake Copais in Boeotia were especially prized. In Aristophanes *The Acharnians*, Dicaeopolis declares a private peace with Sparta, because he cannot endure being cut off from Copaic eels by the Peloponnesian War.
6. 9.170.
7. *Rust.* 3.3.10.
8. For a detailed discussion of this point, see Higginbotham, *Piscinae*, p. 5.
9. Pliny, *HN*, 9.172; Macrobius Sat. 3.15.4; Plutarch *De Sollertia Animallium* 976A.
10. Pliny, *HN* 9.172.
11. Pliny *HN* 9.77; Seneca De Ira 3.40; *De Clementia* 1.18; Cassius Dio 50; Tacitus, *Annales* 1; Tertullian *De Pallio* 5.
12. This gastronomic sin against the dogma of diversity has already found its *Satyricon*, a film called *The Freshman* (1990) in which a club of tycoons imports rare beasts for its banquets.

Plainness and Virtue in New England Cooking

Keith Stavely and Kathleen Fitzgerald

Stephen Mennell has disputed the idea that Puritanism caused English cookery to become plain instead of complex like French cookery. By the time English culinary preferences began to become conscious of themselves as English, Puritanism was on the wane as a decisive presence in English culture. It may be, however, that a stronger case for Puritan culinary influence can be made for New England, where this more intense form of English Protestantism held sway longer. One prominent American historian has argued as much: 'The Puritans of Massachusetts created one of the more austere food ways in the Western world. For three centuries, New England families gave thanks to their Calvinist God for cold baked beans and stale brown bread, while lobsters abounded in the waters of Massachusetts Bay and succulent gamebirds orbited slowly overhead. Rarely does history supply so strong a proof of the power of faith.'[1]

The writer bases these assertions on John Winthrop's autobiography, written in the 1630s. There the first governor of Massachusetts sketches the spiritual framework within which dietary choices should be made:

> The fleshe is eagerly inclined to pride, and wantonnesse, by which it playes the tirant over the poore soule, makinge it a verye slave; the workes of our callings beinge diligently followed, are a speciall meanes to tame it, and so is temperance in diet, for idlenesse (under which are all suche workes as are doone to fullfill the will of the fleshe rather then of the spirit,) and gluttonie are the 2 maine pillars of the fleshe hir kingdome.

Temperance in diet is the partner of devotion to one's work in the world in living a life in which the 'soule' rather than the 'fleshe' is dominant.[2]

By flesh, Winthrop does not mean the body but rather worldliness – the pursuit of pleasure, wealth, or power as an end in itself. The opposite of temperance in diet, 'gluttonie,' would thus be, as John Cotton, the leading minister of early Massachusetts, stated, to 'chear our bodies' with food in such a way that we 'terminate … in eating and drinking.' To approach eating and drinking as ends in themselves is to turn the taking of nourishment into 'a lust of the flesh' rather than a re-energizing of the soul.[3]

This view of eating was widely accepted in seventeenth-century New England. Suppression of 'the fleshe' in order that 'the soule' might rule one's life constituted the core message of the manuals of popular piety by English Puritan clerics that were 'steady sellers' among books circulating in the region. Roger Williams, while dissenting from the order erected by the likes of Winthrop and Cotton, nevertheless agreed with them about the perils of eating in the fleshly mode. 'What are all the Contentions and Wars of this World about (generally) but for greater Dishes and Bowles of Porridge, of wch (if We believe Gods Spirit in Scripture) Esau and Jacob were types? Esau will part with the heavenly Birthright for his Supping (after his hunting) for God Belly.'[4]

As Williams goes on to say, the biblical episode of Jacob and Esau points to abstention from food altogether as the means to secure the soul in its properly superior position: 'and Jacob will part with his porridge for an Eternal Inheritance.' Certainly fast days in atonement for communal sins were an important New England custom. Nevertheless, the principle of 'temperance in diet' did not necessarily entail culinary austerity. John Cotton described pursuit of one's calling in a manner parallel to the way he described temperance in diet. A person committed to godly endeavor would 'rise early and goe to bed late.' He would 'avoid idleness, …takes all opportunities to be doing something, … go anyway and bestir himselfe for profit, this will he doe most diligently in his calling: And yet bee a man deadhearted to the world.' Nonstop pursuit of profit was praiseworthy, so long as the soul continued to govern one's frame of mind and one thereby remained 'deadhearted to the world.' Correspondingly, temperance in diet might allow one to 'chear' one's body with food and drink of the highest quality, as long as one remained as 'deadhearted to the world' gastronomically as Cotton's pious businessman allegedly remained economically.[5]

270

So Puritan dietary moralizing left seventeenth-century New Englanders living above the subsistence level free to eat anything. Regarding what the early New England upper classes actually ate we know very little. Edward Johnson boasted in the 1650s that beef, pork, mutton, and poultry were 'frequent in many houses,' that there was 'great plenty of wine and sugar,' allowing for the making of diverse fruit tarts, and that 'in their feasts' the colonists had not 'forgotten the English fashion of stirring up their appetites with variety of cooking their food.' That description does not suggest 'one of the more austere food ways in the Western world.' All the cookbooks imported into colonial New England – from Gervase Markham's *The English Hus-wife* in the early seventeenth century to Elizabeth Raffald's *The Experienced English Housekeeper* in the later eighteenth century – contained complex recipes, and there was nothing in Puritan doctrine to inhibit the use of such material.[6]

Nevertheless, the tendency to associate plain New England cuisine with New England moral rectitude has persisted. In 1939, Wilbur Cross linked 'the natural and sane diet' of the region to its 'famous conscience.' Possibly a less direct connection between the two can be illuminated by examining those same English cookbooks that the New England upper classes imported. That the reading of cookbooks became more widespread in the eighteenth century is indicated by the 1742 colonial imprint of E. Smith's *Compleat Housewife*. This bestseller, with its ragouts and bisques, reflects the dominance in England of French forms of culinary elaboration. Yet Smith apologized for this dimension of her work: 'since we have, to our Disgrace, so fondly admired … French Messes, [I] present you now and then with such Receipts of the French Cookery as I think may not be disagreeable to English Palates.' More famously, Hannah Glasse's *Art of Cookery*, a book replete with food of French origin, starts off with a blast at 'French cooks' and the 'French tricks' they invariably played.[7]

The terms of this anti-French moralizing had already been set forth by Joseph Addison in 1709. At the house of a friend who was 'a great admirer of the *French* cookery,' Addison was baffled by what he saw: 'That which stood before me I took to be a roasted Porcupine, however … have since been informed that it was only a larded Turkey… . Among other Dainties I saw something like a Pheasant, and therefore desired to be helped to a Wing of it; but to my great Surprize my Friend told me it was a Rabbit.' Solace finally came when Addison detected 'the agreeable Savour of Roast Beef,' emanating from 'a noble Sirloin upon the Side of the Table smoking in the most delicious Manner.' He 'had Recourse to it more than once.' But his pleasure was mixed with 'some Indignation' at seeing 'that substantial *English* Dish banished in so ignominious a Manner to make way for *French* Kickshaws.' Overly refined, vaguely effeminate, and deceptive French methods of preparing food are pitted against solid, honest English fare.[8]

Throughout the eighteenth century, French cooking and the moral condemnation of it were repeatedly dispensed by the same authors. Did this widespread ambivalence arise in any way from the English Puritan tradition? John Wesley's analysis of the relationship between religion and material prosperity has been claimed to be broadly applicable to the development of early modern English society: 'religion must necessarily produce both industry and frugality; and these cannot but produce riches. But as riches increase, so will pride, anger, and love of the world in all its branches.' In this account, only two outlooks are posited: that of the upright 'Protestant ethic,' and the polar opposite into which it ineluctably falls, that of the worldly 'spirit of capitalism.'[9]

But actual historical experience was doubtless marked by a more nuanced array of responses than unalloyed virtue or sinfulness. As a pious early modern English person grew rich and began to exhibit love of the world, he or she probably experienced conflicting emotions. Perhaps it was such a state of mind that cookbook authors were reflecting, catering on the one hand, with their French-derived recipes, to their middle-class readers' prosperity, while expressing on the other hand, with their anti-French moralizing, these same readers' guilty sense of having lost their bearings in the course of their upward strivings. The conjuration of the virtuous simplicity of 'traditional' English food was, according to this argument, a residually Puritan reaction formation (as Freud might call it), generated from the emergence of middle-class consumer society.

As far as Colonial New England is concerned, it regarded itself as having been created by an early-seventeenth-century 'greatest generation' whose like would not be seen again. Perry Miller described the preachers' jeremiads in which subsequent generations were excoriated for having fallen into love of the world, in lamentable contrast to the founders' pristine piety, industry, and frugality.[10]

Just as in England, these denunciations of emergent New England worldliness did nothing to prevent worldliness from continuing to emerge. A 'consumer revolution' occurred in England and America in the eighteenth century. In New England, people began to live in more carefully-designed houses filled with more highly crafted furniture, began to wear clothes made with imported textiles, and began to eat richer food, most often, no doubt, prepared from the French-derived recipes found in cookbooks imported from England. 'A Gentleman from London would almost think himself at home in Boston,' one genteel visitor wrote in 1720, 'when he observes [the people's] houses, their furniture, their Tables, their dress and conversation.'[11]

But as love of the world was making itself more distinctly present in New England society, so simultaneously was ritual obeisance to the region's supposed originating piety, industry, and frugality. In 1769, an organization called the Old Colony Club observed the founding of Plymouth with the first Forefathers' Day celebration. The menu consisted of indigenous preparations: 'a large baked Indian whortleberry pudding, a dish of sauquetash [succotash], a dish of clams, a dish of oysters and a dish of codfish, … a course of cranberry tarts, and cheese made in the Old Colony,' and other items. In club records, the banquet was described as 'dressed in the plainest manner (all appearances of luxury and extravagance being avoided, in imitation of our worthy ancestors whose memory we shall ever respect).'[12]

At the height of the consumer revolution, the members of the Old Colony Club – people on whose tables were to be found the latest Frenchified dishes drawn from the pages of Hannah Glasse – staged a culinary bonfire of the vanities. In so doing, they altered the New England definition of dietary virtue, locating it no longer in the mind of the cook and the diner, whatever was being eaten and dined upon, but rather in some particular foods and methods of cooking (at the same time excluding it from other particular foods and methods of cooking). Food 'dressed in the plainest manner' was now equated with a vision of piety, industry, and frugality. But since that vision was inseparable from a moment in the past guaranteed to become increasingly remote, there was no danger that New England's participation in the consumer revolution would be challenged. Rather, the plain food of the worthy ancestors would serve to legitimize an order of things in which love of the world would continue to be definitive.

Indeed, three years later, the shape of things to come in this respect was further anticipated in a Forefathers' Day feast that was, according to a newspaper account of it, both 'plain and elegant.' This formula suggests that plainness and the virtue it betokened was to be had without sacrificing the improvements brought in by the consumer revolution.[13]

Of course, revolution of a more explicit kind was also brewing in 1772. At the same time that New England was joining with its colonial neighbors to wage rebellion, it was also competing with them to play the leading role in defining the political and cultural contours of the new nation. New England's leaders relied on the region's reputation for moral rectitude and intellectual rigor, based on its Puritan heritage, to achieve dominance. Secularized Calvinisim provided the language, replete with allusions to a sacred Puritan past, with which to speak to – and for – the new nation. Seen in this light, the Old Colony feast was elegant precisely because it was plain.[14]

Such holidays as Forefathers' Day recast the religious zeal of early New England Puritanism so that it could be made to fit the secular tastes and serve the political aims of late eighteenth-century New England. These occasions helped build the myth of the past as a richer time not in spite of austere conditions but because of them. So, too, the cuisine of the past came to be seen as more satisfying because simpler. The enjoyment of culinary diversity, abundance, and sophistication, which had been permitted by Winthrop and Cotton, was thus disdained by their descendants as un-Puritan. Yet would late-eighteenth-century New Englanders really abjure the plentiful banquet table in favor of the pinched diet presumed to be the preference of their ancestors? Asserting allegiance to the ancestors' way of life might seem to necessitate gustatory austerity, but culinary sleight of hand quickly restored dining pleasure.

To see how this trick was accomplished, let us turn to one of the foods on the Old Colony Club's 1769 board – the baked Indian whortleberry pudding. First, would the early settlers of Plymouth have baked rather than boiled their puddings? They were acquainted with bake ovens; by the seventeenth century, bake ovens were in general use in Staffordshire, a region from which many of the Plymouth settlers originated. But in the frontier conditions of settlement, ovens were a luxury. Well into the eighteenth century, one might be shared among several families, or an arrangement might be worked out to use the local tavern's. Even when the bake oven became a common household accoutrement, the labor required to use it meant that most housewives baked only once or twice a week, usually at mid-week and on Saturday. The Saturday baking fit nicely with 'the Puritan custom of saving Sunday-work,' as the nineteenth-century memoirist Lucy Larcom put it, and so a connection was formed in the popular consciousness between baking and Puritan dietary norms. By extension, the most commonly baked foods – beans, brown bread, puddings, pies – also came to be identified, erroneously in their baked form, with the first generations of settlers to New England.[15]

To illustrate the ways in which nineteenth-century New England identified itself with an imaginary Puritan dietary past, we can turn to no better promoter of the New England mystique than Harriet Beecher Stowe. In her 1859 novel, *The Minister's Wooing*, set in Revolutionary-era Newport, Rhode Island, Stowe lovingly describes a traditional New England home's 'motherly old oven.' But like many best-selling writers, she was merely reflecting popular attitudes when she asserted a venerable Puritan pedigree for the bake oven. In an ironic twist, despite the widespread nostalgia for bake ovens, mass-produced cast iron stoves were by that time replacing them in most homes. The new invention may not have had the cultural resonance of the bake oven, but it was cheaper to operate. The old oven, sanctified in fiction and in the popular consciousness, was nevertheless summarily boarded up in most kitchens.[16]

So the corn-based puddings eaten as daily fare by the first settlers were not baked but boiled. The question remains, were the settlers particularly fond of them? The answer, again, is probably not. The necessity of surviving on such New World foods as corn, also the stuff of Indian subsistence, was regarded by the colonists with an attitude more resembling resignation than celebration. Edward Johnson expressed the view when he looked back from the 1650s to the first years of settlement a few decades earlier: 'and assuredly when the Lord created [Indian] Corne, hee had a speciall eye to supply these his peoples wants with it.' Grateful as the first generations may have been for these food gifts of the Almighty, received through the Indians, few at the time would have equated the necessity of consuming them every day with pleasure.[17]

Johnson mentioned corn in the first place mainly to draw a contrast between the penury of the Indians, who, he said, were forced to live on 'parch't Indian corn,' and the English, among whom 'now good white and wheaten bread is no dainty.' Had Johnson returned to the Plymouth of 1769, he would have been surprised to find the grain which had fed 'the poore servants of Christ, in their low beginnings' valorized by their descendants. Only within an expanded market that included an array of food choices could such lowly indigenous products become symbols of regional pride. When they constituted the basis of the New English diet, they were less warmly received.[18]

The whortleberry and its relative the huckleberry, both indigenous American species, were subjected to much the same treatment as corn. Mark Twain was perhaps alluding to the boosting of native products when he named his most beloved character, now the quintessential emblem of rustic American boyhood, Huckleberry Finn.

So, the Old Colony Club's whortleberry pudding, baked in supposed imitation of the practice of the founders and 'dressed in the plainest manner,' perfectly illustrates the metamorphosis of simplicity into elegance. But the question still remains, how could foods such as the pudding and other of New England's plain fare be made gustatorily worthy of the canonical weight they were being asked to bear? Put another way, how could the foods as they were actually eaten by the founding generation be enriched without noticeable alteration so as to be made acceptable to the palates of the grandees of the Old Colony Club? Although the account avoids any explicit mention of it, the ingredient that permitted this subtle transformation was sugar. The proof of the pudding, it turns out, was not in the eating but in the sweetening.

Why was it desirable to downplay the presence of sugar, along with its poor relation molasses, while maximizing its use in New England cooking of the later eighteenth century on through the nineteenth century? The answer lies in the history of this potent and, for both producers and consumers, often dangerous food.

In his late nineteenth-century history of New England, William Weeden makes this sideways approach to the topic: 'Cider and vinegar corrected the West Indian sugar and molasses always coming in; that is, when the molasses did not evolve itself into the fiery rum. Rum was beginning to be the important commercial factor which it came to be later in the [eighteenth] century.' Several of the strategies by which New England blamelessly associated itself with slave-produced sugar and molasses, also the main ingredient in New England rum, are touched upon here: first, West Indian sugar and molasses are 'corrected' by mixing them with cider and vinegar, products of the fruit trees of New England; then, molasses 'evolves itself' into rum, apparently without human agency; and finally, the commercial importance of rum seems to inoculate it from moral opprobrium. The Puritan abhorrence of idleness, shorn of the qualifications and nuances attached to it by John Winthrop, absolves New Englanders of responsibility for engaging in virtually any trade, even one that starts in slavery and ends in drunkenness.[19]

But sugar was a complicated topic well before it became identified with the slave fields and rum distilleries of the New World. In early modern Europe, sugar's whiteness had been taken as evidence of its 'fineness and purity.' It was used in everything from medicines to the 'follies' that decorated aristocratic tables. In Galenic terms, it was considered an almost perfect food, 'warm in the first degree and moist in the first degree-identical, therefore, to the temperament of the human being.' As one historian has said, 'It is clear that in the course of the fifteenth century every householder who could afford to do so began to include this delicious and marvellously beneficial foodstuff in many of the dishes that up until then had been prepared quite successfully without it.' Precisely the same could be said of New England households three centuries later.[20]

In the process of cooling into crystallized form, sugar leaves behind a liquid residue that cannot easily be crystallized further and which resembles honey in both color and texture. According to another historian, this honey-mimicking substance, known as treacle, which because of its cheapness and abundance gradually replaced the more ancient and indigenous sweetener for everyday use, 'even carried off some of the poetic imagery formerly associated with honey.' The English reception of treacle was reproduced in New England, where it was called molasses. The dishes to which it was added seemed to acquire both sweetness and a more antique color and flavor – authenticity in a jug. As the desire to assert a connection with the values and ways of their Puritan past grew among the Puritans' descendants, molasses seemed to end up in almost everything they cooked – from puddings and pies to baked beans and brown bread. These 'antiqued' foods were further coated with a patina of evocative regional names, such as 'Boston Baked Beans' and 'Yankee Pumpkin Pie.'[21]

275

White sugar predominated in eighteenth-century New England recipes, for instance in the gingerbreads in the first American cookbook, Amelia Simmons's *American Cookery*, published in 1796. But for the sophisticated and wealthy white Protestant ascendancy of the later nineteenth century, caught up in 'dreams of Arcadian romance,' only the most strident rusticity could adequately reflect their heritage. Now, only molasses would do.[22]

Visitors to New England may still partake of the 'old-fashioned' baked beans and brown breads on offer in the tourist districts, but to get a taste of regional foods that are more than colonial revival period pieces one must approach the Thanksgiving table. In contrast to Edward Johnson, who noted as a sign of New England's prosperity in the 1650s that most families were again able to eat 'apples, pears, and quince tarts instead of their former Pumpkin Pies,' *Godey's Lady's Book and Magazine*, in the 1880s and '90s, offered its affluent readership no fewer than five pumpkin pie recipes. Sarah Josepha Hale, longtime *Godey's* editor and one of her century's most influential arbiters of American taste, called her own recipe for pumpkin pie, 'this real yankee pie,' which, she added, was 'prepared in perfection' only in rural districts. It is her fantasy of a simple yet delectable culinary past rather than Johnson's desire to reproduce the refined English palate that ultimately caught the American imagination.[23]

In a presumably unconscious replication of Winthrop's identification of idleness and gluttony as the twin pillars of 'the fleshe hir kingdome,' Hale ends her 1839 domestic manual, *The Good Housekeeper*, with two short disquisitions, one on hiring a cook (or rather, *against* hiring a cook and *for* encouraging industry and frugality) and the other on temperance in diet. But where Winthrop's diligence is aimed at taming worldliness, Hale's 'early rising and active employment' are meant only as 'promoters of good health and cheerfulness.' Finally, in 'The Good Dinner,' Hale warns of the dangers of gluttony, which she describes in physiological rather than spiritual terms. 'The oppression of his stomach seemed like the weight of an incubus,' she says of the intemperate eater. But the devil with which the man wages battle is only indigestion. The worldly comforts which John Wesley warned would inevitably follow the diligent deployment of industry and frugality are much in evidence here; so are the evasions and confusions to which New England Puritanism succumbed, as the celebrant of the perfections of 'real yankee' pumpkin pie, packed with molasses, spices, milk, and butter to enhance the taste of the pumpkin, ends her cookbook with a warning against 'eating those things which *taste good*.'[24]

Bibliography

Anderson, Jay Allan, '"A Solid Sufficiency": An Ethnography of Yeoman Foodways in Stuart England,' Ph. D. diss., University of Pennsylvania, 1971.

Bowles, Ella Shannon, and Dorothy S. Towle, *Secrets of New England Cooking*, New York: M. Barrows, 1947.

Brewer, Priscilla J., *From Fireplace to Cookstove: Technology and the Domestic Ideal in America*, Syracuse, NY: Syracuse University Press, 2000.

Carson, Cary, 'The Consumer Revolution in Colonial British America: Why Demand?' in *Of Consuming Interests: The Style of Life in the Eighteenth Century*, edited by Cary Carson, Ronald Hoffman, and Peter J. Albert, pp. 483–697, Charlottesville and London: University Press of Virginia, 1994.

Conforti, Joseph A., *Imagining New England: Explorations of Regional Identity from the Pilgrims to the Mid-Twentieth Century*, Chapel Hill: University of North Carolina Press, 2001.

Crowley, J. E., *This Sheba, Self: The Conceptualization of Economic Life in Eighteenth-Century America*, Baltimore: Johns Hopkins University Press, 1974.

Fischer, David Hackett, *Albion's Seed: Four British Folkways in America*, New York: Oxford University Press, 1989.

Foster, Stephen, *Their Solitary Way: The Puritan Social Ethic in the First Century of Settlement in New England*, New Haven: Yale University Press, 1971.

Glasse, Hannah, *The Art of Cookery Made Plain and Easy*. London, 1747. Reprint, with introductory essays by Jennifer Stead and Priscilla Bain, glossary by Alan Davidson, *'First Catch Your Hare ...': The Art of Cookery Made Plain and Easy*, Totnes, UK: Prospect, 1995.

Godey's Lady's Book and Magazine, February 1880–December 1891.

Gould, Mary Earle, *The Early American House: Household Life in America, 1620-1850*, rev. ed. Rutland, Vt.: Charles E. Tuttle, 1965.

Hale, Sarah Josepha, *The Good Housekeeper*, 6th ed., Boston, 1841. Reprint, with an introduction by Janice Bluestein Longone, Mineola, N.Y.: Dover, 1996.

Hall, David D., *Worlds of Wonder, Days of Judgment: Popular Religious Belief in Early New England*, New York: Knopf, 1989.

Johnson, Edward, *Johnson's Wonder-Working Providence, 1628–1651 (1654)*, edited by J. Franklin Jameson, New York: Scribner's, 1910. Reprint, New York: Barnes and Noble, 1959.

Larcom, Lucy, *A New England Girlhood: Outlined from Memory*, Boston and New York: Houghton Mifflin, 1889.

Lehmann, Gilly, *The British Housewife: Cookery Books, Cooking, and Society in Eighteenth-Century Britain*, Totnes, UK: Prospect, 2003.

Mennell, Stephen, *All Manners of Food: Eating and Taste in England and France from the Middle Ages to the Present*, 2nd ed. Urbana: University of Illinois Press, 1996.

Miller, Perry, *The New England Mind: From Colony to Province*, Cambridge, Mass.: Harvard University Press, 1953.

Mintz, Sidney W., *Sweetness and Power: The Place of Sugar in Modern History*, New York: Viking, 1985.

Morgan, Edmund S., *The Puritan Family: Religion and Domestic Relations in Seventeenth-Century New England*, New York: Harper Torchbooks, 1966.

Neustadt, Kathy, *Clambake: A History and Celebration of an American Tradition*, Amherst: University of Massachusetts Press, 1992.

Scully, Terence, *The Art of Cookery in the Middle Ages*, Woodbridge: Boydell Press, 1995.

Simmons, Amelia, *American Cookery*, 1st ed. Hartford, Conn., 1796. Reprint, with an introduction by Mary Tolford Wilson, New York: Dover, 1984.

Smith, E., *The Compleat Housewife: Or, Accomplish'd Gentlewoman's Companion*, 15th ed. London, 1753. Reprint, London: Literary Services and Production, 1968.

Stavely, Keith, and Kathleen Fitzgerald, *America's Founding Food: The Story of New England Cooking*, Chapel Hill: University of North Carolina Press, 2004.

Stowe, Harriet Beecher, *The Minister's Wooing* (1859), edited by Susan K. Harris, New York: Penguin, 1999.
——, *Oldtown Folks* (1869), edited by Dorothy Berkson, New Brunswick, NJ: Rutgers University Press, 1987.
Tyerman, Luke, *The Life and Times of the Rev. John Wesley, M. A., Founder of the Methodists,* New York: Harper, 1872.
Ulrich, Laurel Thatcher, *A Midwife's Tale: The Life of Martha Ballard, Based on Her Diary, 1785–1812,* New York: Vintage, 1991.
Weeden, William B., *Economic and Social History of New England, 1620-1789,* 2 vols., Boston and New York: Houghton Mifflin, 1891.
Williams, Roger, *The Correspondence of Roger Williams,* edited by Glenn W. LaFantasie, 2 vols., Hanover, NH: University Press of New England, 1988.
Winthrop Papers, 5 vols., Boston: Massachusetts Historical Society, 1929–1947.
Wolcott, Imogene, *The New England Yankee Cook Book,* preface by Wilbur L. Cross. New York: Coward-McCann, 1939.

Notes

1. Mennell, *All Manners of Food,* 103–108; Fischer, *Albion's Seed,* 135–36.
2. *Winthrop Papers,* 1: 193–94.
3. Morgan, *Puritan Family,* 16.
4. Crowley, *This Sheba, Self,* 3, 17–18, 50; Hall, *Worlds of Wonder,* 51–52; Williams, *Correspondence,* 2: 615.
5. Ibid.; Foster, *Their Solitary Way,* 121.
6. Johnson, *Johnson's Wonder-Working Providence,* 210.
7. Wolcott, *New England Yankee Cook Book,* xiii–xiv; Smith, *Compleat Housewife,* 38, 43–44, 61, 63, 29, 80, sig. A3; Glasse, *Art of Cookery,* ii.
8. Lehmann, *British Housewife,* 355–56.
9. Ibid., 113–14, 118, 119; Tyerman, *Life and Times of the Rev. John Wesley,* 520.
10. Miller, *New England Mind,* 36–38, 40.
11. Carson, 'Consumer Revolution in Colonial British America,' 620, 624, 587–605, 635 and note.
12. Neustadt, *Clambake,* 32.
13. Ibid.
14. Conforti, *Imagining New England,* 79–122.
15. Anderson, 'Solid Sufficiency,' 159–160; Gould, *Early American House,* 52, 49; Ulrich, *Midwife's Tale,* 85; Brewer, *From Fireplace to Cookstove,* 80; Larcom, *New England Girlhood,* 51–52; Bowles and Towle, *Secrets of New England Cooking,* 68.
16. Stowe, *Minister's Wooing,* 156.
17. Johnson, *Johnson's Wonder-Working Providence,* 114.
18. Ibid., 210, 85.
19. Weeden, *Economic and Social History of New England, 1620–1789,* 1: 416.
20. Mintz, *Sweetness and Power,* 22; Scully, *Art of Cookery in the Middle Ages,* 189–190.
21. Mintz, *Sweetness and Power,* 22–23; Stavely and Fitzgerald, *America's Founding Food,* 57–58, 61–65, 28–29, 69–70.
22. Simmons, *American Cookery,* 36; Stowe, *Minister's Wooing,* 157; Stavely and Fitzgerald, *America's Founding Food,* 250–52.
23. Johnson, *Johnson's Wonder-Working Providence,* 210; *Godey's,* October 1882, 377; January 1883, 185; November 1887, 413; November 1890, 426; December 1891, 537; Hale, *Good Housekeeper,* 84.
24. Hale, *Good Housekeeper,* 141–144.

The Poppy: Potent yet Frail

Aylin Öney Tan

Every spring graceful poppy flowers carpet the Anatolian plateau. Poppy fields constitute the symbolic feature of the Inner Aegean and Central Anatolian landscapes of Turkey. The pale purple, lilac, and white fields are as characteristic to this region and the city of Afyon as lavender fields are to Provence. The flowers dotting these fields have been flourishing here for almost 4,000 years. Frail as they may seem, these flowers possess incredible power.

The notorious narcotic aspect of opium made this crop controversial in the last century. Following two centuries of increased production to meet international demand, in 1933 Turkey limited the number of provinces where the opium poppy could be grown. In 1971, under pressure from President Nixon, poppy cultivation was banned throughout Turkey. The 'poppy controversy' between the US and Turkey continued throughout the '70s, with the movie 'Midnight Express' being its most infamous by-product.[1] Internal political conflicts in both countries as well as the fluctuating course of American-Turkish relations, had the overall impact of disrupting the age-old agricultural and gastronomic practices of the local population. In this paper, I want to draw attention to the vital economic and cultural significance of opium poppy as a staple agricultural crop providing a sustainable livelihood for the rural communities of the region for millennia. Shifting the emphasis from opium production to the role of poppy in local gastronomic and culinary practices, I would like to explore the possibility of defending its cultivation against a number of global pressures.

My interest in poppy cultivation and its culinary aspect began when I was a member of the International Slow Food Jury in 2001. I nominated a poppy growing village in Afyon for the Slow Food Award.[2] The group of farmers I nominated actually won the award, drawing me further into their story. The more I investigated, the more I became aware of the fact that international interference in local agriculture invariably compromises fairness. More than three decades after the international ban and five years after the Slow Food award, revisiting the case revealed yet another dilemma: corn syrup versus beet sugar. Sugar beet was the major crop introduced as an alternative to poppy. Sugar beet cultivation itself has become a controversial issue in the recent past. It was the signature crop of Turkish economic independence in the early years of the Republic. Yet over the years, in the hands of corrupt politicians and farmers perennially seeking state guaranteed prices and purchases, sugar beet production has been promoted into environmentally unsuitable regions. Leaving aside debates regarding its environmental effects and economic feasibility, local farmers face yet another struggle as genetically modified corn makes inroads into Turkish agriculture. Powerful global corporations, together with their local partners, press heavily for an increase in the corn syrup quota against a radical decrease in beet sugar. It seems that once the socially and culturally fixed productive relation between the farmer and the soil is severed, the farmer is left as frail as the poppy flower against the changing winds of global market forces.

A pinch of history

While there is an ensuing debate among archaebotanists as to where poppy plant was first domesticated,[3] almost all historical references state that the first mention of the opium poppy is found in Sumerian texts from Mesopotamia dating as far back as 4,000 BC. It is believed that the poppy's sedative powers were recognized early – the Sumerians called it *hul gil* – *hul* meaning joy and *gil* meaning plant. Various sources also mention that its cultivation in Asia Minor dates back to the Hittite period, 2,000 BC.

As an investigative food journalist with considerable background in Anatolian history, I plunged myself into reading almost everything I could find on the subject. As I read about Hittite culture, I became confused. I was not able to access the crucial source on Hittite food culture in libraries and archaeological institutes. I decided to consult Prof. Muhibbe Darga, one of the leading Hittitologists in Turkey. Well known for her meticulous studies and high spirits, she still, in her late 80s, has the energy and enthusiasm of a young scholar. Reading cuneiform texts with great ease and speed, she went through many reference books and concluded that the term *gis-haššikka* indeed referred to poppy. A study of Anatolian flora during the Hittite period, based on the findings of the Boğazköy excavation, the capital city of the Hittites, lists the plant.[4] The author, Hayri Ertem concludes that *haššikka* is most likely to be the word for poppy. The Turkish name for opium poppy is *haşhaş* or *haşgeş* in the local dialect, most probably originating from the Hittite word. Actually the epicentre of poppy cultivation has always been the city of Afyon throughout its history, and the name of the city means opium in Turkish. The origin of Afyon dates back to the Hittite period, as clearly demonstrated by Hittite artefacts excavated in various mounds and sites in the region, including a bronze statue displayed in the Afyon museum. Situated at the junction between the Hittite settlements of Karkiša (Kula, Uşak), Pitašša (Afyon, Isparta, Burdur) and Arzawa (İzmir), the Hittite name for the city has yet to be identified.[5]

The word *haššikka* is said to mean to sleep or to calm down. Ertem links the word to the verb *haššik,* meaning to dose off from excess drinking or eating. Darga, adds that *haš* means to give birth and *šeš* means to sleep. *Haš* also means opening something by breaking.

Resemblance of the dialect *haşgeş* to Hittite roots *haš* and *šeš* makes me think that the word may also mean 'giving birth to sleep' or sleep producing. The hard capsule of the plant which can only be opened by breaking may have roots in the verb *haš*.

It has to be noted that the plant has always been referred to as a symbol of fertility in Anatolian folklore. Needless to say, the countless seeds contained in the poppy pod make it an ideal symbol of birth.

Further reading in the path of history brought me to the Greek and Roman periods. The poppy is also referred to in Homer's works the *Iliad* and the *Odyssey* (850 BC). Hippocrates (460–357 BC) prescribed drinking the juice of the white poppy mixed with the seed of nettle. Representations of the Greek and Roman gods of sleep, Hypnos and Somnos, both show them wearing or carrying poppies. In 330 BC, Alexander the Great introduced opium to the peoples of Persia and India.

The term *opium* for the concentrated milky sap obtained from unripe capsules or poppy heads has been used since Greco-Roman times and is related to Greek *opos* 'sap, juice of plants.' The Latin word *Papaver somniferum*, the species name, derives from Latin *somnus* 'sleep' and *ferre* 'bring', referring to the sedative properties of opium. The most popular local variety *Körhaşhaş* is classified as *Papaver somniferum anatolicum*, indicating that the plant is native to Anatolia. As mentioned before the Turkish word *afyon* meaning 'opium' derives from the Greek *opion*, which gradually became *afion* in the local dialect.[6] One significant piece of evidence indicating the existence of poppy cultivation in the region comes from the ancient Greek city of Synnada (contemporary Şuhut), 29 km. south-east of Afyon. The museum of Afyon exhibits the Synnada city coin, dated to the second century BC, depicting an opium pod.

Depictions of the poppy plant continued to turn up in Anatolian cultures. For the Seljukid period I fortunately had direct access to one of the most trusted sources, Prof. Gönül Öney, the art historian who happens to be my mother. I vividly remember from my childhood the Kubad Abad tiles, excavated at the site of a Seljukid palace where my mother toiled during the summer months. Kubad Abad, the summer residence of the Seljuk Sultan Alaeddin Keykubad (1220–1236), located on the southwestern shore of Lake Beyşehir in central Turkey, revealed many depictions of the poppy.

Poppy depictions can easily be mistaken for pomegranates. Both being symbols of fertility, they often appear in depictions of the tree of life. The Sivas Gökmedrese (1276) stone carving is an example, where long stalks and leaves are reminiscent of the poppy while the seeded fruits remind one of the pomegranate. Given the nature of the representations, it could be argued that some of these fruit are neither distinctly pomegranates nor poppies, but actually an amalgam of both into a symbolic fertility fruit. There are even some tombstones from the same period depicting the poppy plant.

During the Seljuk period the city of Afyon was called Karahisar – the Black Fortress, referring to the dark basaltic rocky hill on which the castle nestles. In 1428, Afyon became a part of the Ottoman Empire. Later in the seventeenth century the word *afion* was prefixed to Karahisar in reference to the region's chief agricultural produce. Since then, poppy depictions have appeared in regional carpets and kilims and in folk art as talismans.

The later mentions of poppy in the Ottoman period provide insights to the culinary uses of the poppy. A rough survey of sources reveals a colourful display of poppy use in Ottoman kitchen. One main source is the Bursa Edict of Trading Standards. Issued by Sultan Bayezıd II in 1502 for the municipality of Bursa, it is the world's first standard of trade in the modern sense. Poppy seeds are also mentioned in numerous cases, particularly in baking.[7] The renowned Ottoman traveller, Evliya Çelebi, speaks of poppy seeds being used on the disk-shaped bread loaves baked during the month of Ramadan.[8]

Hans Dernschwam, a traveller accompanying the envoy Busbecq, wrote of Ottoman life in more detail than anyone else in his time. In his account of his visit to İstanbul in 1553 he mentions poppy seeds: 'They sprinkle white poppy seeds on different kinds of baked goods … they normally press a square sign on loaves on which they also sprinkle black seeds. On other loaves, they sprinkle sesame seeds; they sprinkle the thin sheets, called schirdigan jach, with the same kind of oil.'[9]

In the second half of the nineteenth century, Lady Fanny Janet Blunt ate a meal in Afyon in which the dishes had been cooked with poppy oil. Since poppy seed oil contains no opium, the description of her sensation of light-headedness following the meal was either a flight of fancy or the real effect of eating a heavy Anatolian meal and following it with a strong cigarette of Turkish tobacco, to which she was unaccustomed:

282

> During a flying visit I paid to Kara Hissar, in Asia Minor, I took up my quarters at the house of an opium-growing grandee. The dinner offered to me was good, and even refined, but for a slight but peculiar flavour to which I was unaccustomed; I partook of it heartily, and afterwards in order to please my hostess, accepted a cigarette.
>
> Presently I felt a strange languor creeping over me, my head whirled, my ears began to tingle, my eyesight dimmed, and my eyelids heavily closing, I soon found myself in the fool's paradise of opium-eaters…The meal of which I had part taken had been cooked in poppy-oil always used for the purpose in that part of the country, and said not to have any effect on the inhabitants, who are accustomed to it from childhood.
>
> The cigarette, it appeared, was also strongly impregnated with the same narcotic. Let my experience be a warning to travellers in the opium-growing country.[10]

The potent potion, *Nevruzziye,* is prepared for welcoming the spring on the day of Nevruz, the start of the new year according to the old Turkish calendar. Among its ingredients are cinnamon bark, cloves, ginger, galangal, coriander, nutmeg, and such perfumed substances as ambergris, sandalwood, musk, and rose petals. Sugar and poppy seeds are two essential ingredients.[11]

A peek into the kitchen

Poppy is a crop used in its entirety. From seed to pod, leaves to stalk, it provides a year round sustenance for rural communities. The crop's various uses have been so vital that opium gum, from which heroin is processed, seems but an added bonus to the many benefits of the poppy.

To most contemporary Turks, the city of Afyon is famous not for its opium, but for the highest quality clotted cream produced in the country. So much so that the local white Afyon marble is also called *'afyon kaymağı,'* that is, the 'cream of Afyon.' The pure white flawless satin like surface of the marble is reminiscent of the delicious clotted cream. Few people outside Afyon, however, realise the close connection between the praised clotted cream and the poppy seed. Actually, the poppy *küspe,* which is the seed pulp remaining from oil pressing is the main fodder for livestock. It is especially important in the diet of buffalos. The consequent effect is reflected in the quality of dairy products obtained from buffalo milk. The same applies for meat products. Afyon is also famous for its *sucuk* or cured sausage. The list goes on: yogurt, butter, cheese, and *pastırma,* the spice-coated cured meat. Thus the special taste of Afyon's dairy and meat products is the direct result of the animals' diet, and hence of poppy cultivation.

The use of poppy products appears in both savory and sweet dishes. Poppy oil (*haşhaş yağı*), poppy seed (*haşhaş tohumu),* and poppy paste (*haşhaş ezmesi* or *sürtülmüş haşhaş,* made from crushed poppy seeds) are the main culinary products. All poppy products are used both in savoury and sweet dishes. Uncrushed seeds are mainly used as a topping in bread and as filling or coating for confectionery. In fact, Turkish delight and sweet confections are another well-known product of Afyon cuisine. Turkish delight (poppy *lokum*) is a specialty of the city as well as clotted cream candies. Poppy halwa (*haşhaş helvası*) is prepared on special occasions and religious days. Breaking the pod and nibbling a handful of seeds is a favourite snack for children. Sometimes they are added to skewered meatballs *(şiş köfte)* or to bulgur pilaf (*bulgur pilavı)* to add crunch. Poppy paste is the dominant taste of all pies, breads, and such local specialties as *börek, pide, katmer, açma, bükme, lokul.* Often the paste is just sweetened with sugar, honey or *pekmez* – grape molasses – to spread on bread or wrap in *yufka ekmeği* – unleavened flat bread. One interesting use of the plant is Afyon salad, prepared with young leaves, a culinary delight that marks the coming of spring. The shoots collected during the thinning out of the fields make their way to local tables in the form of *börek* fillings, stir fries etc. It is a favourite meal for farmers working in the field, just wrapped in flat bread with some cheese.

Both the paste and oil give their unique taste to almost all baked products. The nutty flavour of poppy seed oil is much favoured by locals and until recently it was used abundantly in all dishes. Along with flax oil, poppy was the only source of seed oil in the region until very recently. The seed oil is favoured not only because of its unique flavour but also for its high nutritional value. The use of poppy oil is not

283

restricted to the kitchen. Its drying qualities makes poppy oil an essential medium for artists. It is also used in the paint industry.

There used to be many oil presses in the villages and in the city centre of Afyon but unfortunately there were only three remaining in the city when I visited in 2001.

Another feature of the region is also very telling. The chief utensil in every household in the region used to be the stone grinding slab (*haşgeş taşı*) used to prepare fresh poppy paste daily. Neolithic-looking, the basaltic stone slab is a reminder of how little had changed in the lives of peasants since Hittite times. That such an ancient practice came to the brink of extinction in the space of a mere thirty-five years is quite shocking.

The decline

Today poppy farmers in Turkey are faced by numerous legal restrictions designed to prevent the production of opium. The cultivation of opium poppies is under the total control of the state and is permitted only for pharmaceutical purposes.

In December 1914, the United States Congress passed the Harrison Narcotic Act, which called for control of each phase of the preparation and distribution of medical opium, morphine, heroin, cocaine, and any new derivative that could be shown to have similar properties. It made illegal the possession of these controlled substances. The restrictions in the Harrison Act were redefined by the Federal Controlled Substances Act of 1970. The act lists all parts of *P. somniferum* plant except the seed as controlled substances. In order to combat illegal trafficking of heroin, the US Government forced the Turkish government to ban all poppy cultivation. In the fall of 1971, poppy cultivation was banned in the cities of Denizli, Uşak, and Konya and in the fall 1972, cultivation was banned in Burdur, Isparta, and Kütahya (Decision no: 7/2654, Date 24/6/1971). Turkey tried to resist banning cultivation for 150,000 families who depended on the crop, but under intense political pressure and offers of compensation for the villagers by the US government, the decision was finally taken to impose the ban.

In 1974, Turkey decided to resume cultivation of the poppy on the condition that the pods would not be incised by farmers. With the efforts of then Prime Minister Bülent Ecevit, poppy cultivation was permitted only for pharmaceutical purposes under the strict control of the government (Law no: 1470, Decision no: 7/8522, Date 1/7/1974). Henceforth, the lancing of the opium pod in the field to collect opium was prohibited even for local medicinal use and preparations began to adopt the straw method, which entails gathering mature pods to extract the pharmaceutically significant alkaloids such as morphine. The seeds are then returned to the farmers and this method eliminated the possibility of opium gum smuggling from the field. In 1980, the alkaloid factory in Bolvadin, Afyon was opened.

284

Bitter-sweet dilemma

The introduction of sugar beet in Anatolia as a major agricultural product began just after the War of Independence. Following ten years of incessant warfare, the newly declared republic was deprived of its most productive regions and population. For the founders, the lesson to be learned from the experience of the last decades of the Ottoman Empire was clear and they declared it openly at the Economy Congress convened in İzmir in 1925: Political independence had to be backed by economic independence and Turkey had to start producing its own basic necessities. The establishment of a sugar factory was a manifestation of much desired economic independence. A group of farmers initiated a campaign to raise funds to establish a factory in Uşak, the town to the west of Afyon. There were emotionally moving scenes. Some could only bring a basketful of eggs or offer their labour, while the better off competed with each other to give more and more. Lâtife Hanım, the first First Lady of the Republic, wife of Atatürk, bought twenty-five shares in the company for a significant sum.[12] As the daughter of a wealthy merchant and from a family originating from Uşak, her contribution was far more than symbolic.

As an early example of a community-driven initiative, sugar factories proved to be a success. Wherever they were founded, they spearheaded progress, bringing schools, farmer training, and social activities such as movie theatres. One retired employee called this spirit *şeker terbiyesi*. This expression is a play on words as it can be translated both as marinated in sugar and as sweet manners. Following an era of private initiative, especially in the aftermath of the Great Depression of the 1930s, the sugar factories came to be owned mostly by the state as a national industry protecting the farmers from falling international prices for their agricultural produce. The farmers opted for sugar beet, which the state guaranteed to buy, sometimes draining wetlands to create new agricultural fields. The farmers in the Afyon region did not show any interest in beets even though the succssful example of Uşak was right next door. Following the ban in 1971, attractive subsidies were promised in return for switching to sugar beet cultivation. The farmers were still reluctant to let go of a crop that had become a way of life for them. An article in *The New York Times* by reporter Steven V. Roberts bluntly showed that empathy was simply not there:

285

> American experts interviewed in Ankara, noting that farmers all over the world complain about their lot, said that opium poppies were never a profitable crop here. The real reason to lifting the ban, they contend, is not economic but political: the desire to stand up to United States.[13]

Villagers did try to compensate for their loss by attempting to cultivate alternatives like sugar beet. Unlike poppy, sugar beets had poor tolerance of the arid conditions of the region and demanded an excessive use of water resources. In some cases, beets became a suspect crop on the black list of environmentalists. In the last few years, the introduction of drop irrigation methods, modernisation of factories, utilisation of waste management facilities, and finally diversification of by-products such as ethanol, began to eliminate the environmental objections and opened a fresh era of hope for beet farmers. Yet the farmers are now encountering another challenge to protect their position, as global corporations press for increased quotas of a totally new crop: genetically modified corn. Besides the currently unknown risks it poses to human health and the environment, such a switch would make the farmer dependent on market forces for seed, the very heart of his productive activity.

Hence, the poppy, once seen as the symbol of potency due to its multitude of seeds and the effects of its juice, no longer seems as formidable. Agricultural technology has mastered the mystery of the seed, giving humans the chance to manipulate its contents and deprive it of its innate power to regenerate anew. The market forces too seem more powerful than the wind in spreading technological products to faraway places. However, neither technology nor the market can claim to produce the taste that the poppy plant gives to the dairy, baked, and meat products of Afyon. Acknowledging the value of this taste might be the only means of keeping those flowers blossoming in the future.

Notes

1. Dündar, Can, 'Kimin Ekspresi?' [Who's Express?], *Milliyet Newspaper*, 18 June 2007.
2. Scaffidi, Cinzia, 'The Poppy Growers of Ismailkoy', *The International Herald of Taste*, Issue No. 25, January 2002. editore.slowfood.com/editore/riviste/slowark/EN/25/papavero.html; www.slowfood-foundation.com/sf_premio/PREMIO/vincitori2001/pagine_en/Turchia.html.
3. The prevailing conception of poppy domestication and of its subsequent gradual dispersal supposes that the plant was domesticated in the Neolithic era, somewhere in Western Europe, where its earliest and most numerous finds come from. In a recent article, archeologist Pavol Hnila argues that this conception is based upon the skeptical opinions of some archaeobotanists who deny knowledge of the opium poppy in the culturally prominent areas. In his view, 'iconographic and archeological sources... indirectly question(s) the justfication of the[ir] resolute statements regarding the lack of acquaintance with the poppy in Ancient Anatolia.' Hnila, pp. 315–328.
4. Ertem, pp. 16–19.
5. Garstang, p. 92.
6. Tournefort: 'We observed in the Fields about this City of very fine Species of Poppy, which the Turks and Armenians call Aphion, as they do the Common Opium: yet they do not extract Opium from the Kind we now speak of; but by way of delicacy they eat the Heads of it when they are green, tho' very acrid, and of a hot Taste.'
7. Akgündüz, pp. 191–212, p. 192.
8. Evliya Çelebi, p. 233.
9. Dernschwam, p. 128.
10. Blunt, pp. 44–46.
11. Nalbandoğlu, pp. 367–8.
12. Çalışlar, p. 295.
13. Roberts, Steven V., 'Turkish Farmers Insist the Opium Poppy is Still the Staff of Life,' *The New York Times*, May 11, 1974.

Bibliography

Afyon Karahisar Mutfağı [Cuisine of Afyon Karahisar], ed. by Afyon Kocatepe Üniversitesi, (Afyon: Eğitim, Sağlık ve Bilimsel Araştırmalar Vakfı, Yayın No: 10, 2001).

Akgündüz, Ahmet, *Kanunname-i İhtisab-ı Bursa – Osmanlı Kanunnameleri* [Ottoman Code of Laws – Bursa Code of Edicts, Vol. 2] (İstanbul: Fey Eğitim Y. Vakfı, 1990).

Blunt, Lady Fanny Janet, *The People of Turkey, Twenty Years Residence among Bulgarians, Greeks, Albanians, Turks and Armenians, by a Consul's Daughter and Wife*, ed. Stanley Lane Poole (London: 1878).

Çalışlar İpek, *Latife Hanım* (İstanbul: Doğan Kitap, 2006).

Dernschwam, Hans, *Hans Dernschwam's Tagebuch Einer Reise Nach Konstantinopel und Kleinasien (1553/55)*, ed. Franz Babinger (München und Lepzig verlag von Duncker & Humblot, 1923), trans. by Önen Yaşar with the title *Istanbul ve Anadolu'ya Seyahat Günlüğü* (Ankara: Kültür ve Turizm Bakanlığı Yayınları, 1987).

Ertem, Hayri, *Boğazköy Metinlerine Göre Hititler Devri Anadolu'sunun Florası* [Flora of Hittite Period Anatolia According to Bogazkoy Texts] (Ankara: Türk Tarih Kurumu Basımevi, 1974).

Evliya Çelebi, *Evliya Çelebi Seyahatnamesi 1. Cilt* [Travelogue of Evliya Celebi, Vol.1] ed. Orhan Şaik Gökyay (İstanbul: Yapı Kredi Yayınları, 1996).

Garstang, John, & Gurney, O. R., *The Geography of the Hittite Empire* (Ankara: The British Institute of Archaeology at Ankara, 1959).

Hnila, Pavol, 'Some Remarks on the Opium Poppy in Ancient Anatolia', in *Mauer Schau. Festschrift für Manfred Korfmann*, ed. R. Arslan (Remshalden: BAG Verlag, 2002).

Hoffner, Harry A., *Alimenta Hethaeorum; Food production in Hittite Asia Minor* (New Haven: American Oriental Society, 1974).

Nalbandoğlu, A., *Tarih Hazinesi*, ed. Konyalı, İbrahim Hakkı (Sayı 1–17, Istanbul: 15 Kasım 1950).

Tournefort, Joseph Pitton de, *A Voyage into the Levant* (London: 1741).

Ünal, Ahmet, *Anadolu'nun En Eski Yemekleri: Hititler ve Çağdaşı Toplumlarda Mutfak Kültürü* [The Early Food of Anatolia: The Cuisine of Hittites and Contemporaries] (İstanbul: Homer, 2007).

'Quality food, honestly priced': Traders and Tricksters in Ben Jonson's *Bartholomew Fair*

Tracy Thong

This essay will evaluate how Jonson's *Bartholomew Fair* uses food as a metaphor to explore the ethical boundaries between eating for sustenance and the early modern cultural implications of eating for pleasure. Central to his presentation of these considerations is a proctor, Littlewit, who persuades his wife Win to 'long to eat of a pig … i' the Fair.'[1] To Jonson's purpose, the play emphasises, on one hand, that the Bartholomew pig that Win craves is for a commodity that is highly sought after. On the other, a pig booth is situated right at the heart of *Bartholomew Fair*, which is run by Ursla, a formidable proprietor with loose morals. Jonson portrays the reciprocal interaction between traders and their clientele through Win and her family's patronage of Ursla's pig booth. Based on this relationship, the extent to which victuallers' profiteering presented itself as a target for satirists like Jonson will be assessed in the second part of this examination.

The issues pertaining to Win's being permitted to eat Bartholomew pig are informed by the following factors. The first is, because Win's longing is associated with pregnancy, whether the satiation of a person's appetite with what they crave can be justified as healthful for someone of a delicate constitution. Moreover, Jonson depicts the couple's family background as one that is staunchly informed by their Puritan beliefs. It is Win's protestation against being permitted to see Littlewit's puppet play because her 'mother will never consent to such a profane motion'(1.5.153–54) that leads to Littlewit's plan, and his conviction that 'Your mother will do anything, Win, to satisfy your longing, you know' (1.5.160–61). Therefore, even if authoritative sources on a woman's diet during pregnancy advise the healthfulness of eating pork, the added consideration of whether religious authorities will condone the eating of such a rich and sought-after meat, adds to the complexity of this matter.

The healthfulness of Win's consumption of pork involves the consideration of whether allowing an expectant mother to venture out to the Fair to satisfy her craving conforms to prevailing social mores governing the care of pregnant women. Win manifests symptoms that suggest, according to Daniel Sennert's account of the signs of conception in *Practical Physick* (1664), that she is in the early stages of pregnancy, and hence that advice governing the confinement of women would not yet apply.

Win's mother and the zealous Busy vehemently object to her longing for pig. Ken Albala's *Eating Right in the Renaissance* offers a useful explanation for the Puritan taboo against eating pork; he asserts that the dietary taboos are inextricably linked to religious teaching, and reasons simply that 'the dietaries promote guilt, because without knowledge of sin, there can be no sin.'

Within the context of Win's strict upbringing and staunchly Puritan family background, her mother regards the desire to eat pig as a monstrosity:

> *Purecraft*: Look up, sweet Win-the-fight, and suffer not the enemy to enter you at this door! Remember that your education has been with the purest. What polluted one was it that named first the unclean beast, pig, to you, child? … Oh, resist it, Win-the-fight! It is the Tempter, the wicked Tempter. You may know it by the fleshly motion of pig. Be strong against it and its foul temptations in these assaults, whereby it broacheth flesh and blood, as it were, on the weaker side, and pray against its carnal provocations. Good child, sweet child, pray! (1.6.5–20)

When Dame Purecraft's religious faith proves to be an impediment against Win's longing, it is significant that Littlewit tries to overcome this taboo by appealing to his mother-in-law's moral conscience and pleading with her to consider the well-being of his unborn child and her grandchild:

> Good mother, I pray you that she may eat some pig, and her belly full, too; and do not you cast away your own child, and perhaps one of mine, with your tale of the Tempter. (1.6.21–24)

289

Unfortunately, early modern dietaries were inclined to advise against the eating of pork, and also overeating, thus rendering Littlewit's entreaty fruitless. In *The Midwives Book* (1671), Jane Sharp also provides strong advice against Littlewit's request that Win may eat her 'belly full.' She writes about 'Gluttony and surfeiting, that choke the Infant,' as causes 'that some Children dye in the womb.'[2] Meanwhile, Henry Buttes makes the following concession in *Dyets Drie Dinner*:

> In olde time they detested Swines flesh, accounting it over moyst; especially sucking pigges; or yong shotes [i.e. shoots?]: and surely they were wiser then we: our appetite, captivates our reason in this matter.[3]

He also advises that while eating of pork is most likely to 'Hurt … those that live delicately or at ease,' this may be corrected if 'the leane of a yong fat Hog [is] eaten moderately: with spices and such hot things.'[4] Win is categorised amongst those who live delicately on account of her feigned pregnancy. However, Buttes's corrective method would also have been a source of anxiety among the patriarchal and dogmatic elders in a community. Based on Sennert's notes on the 'Frenzie of the Womb,'[5] Elaine Hobby summarises how women's 'more general propensity to lasciviousness' could be aggravated by their diet, and therefore encourage sinful behaviour:

Although this 'immoderate desire of Venery' had an 'immediate Cause' (p. 115) in an excess of seed in the womb, it could also be sparked off by women's indulging themselves in unsuitable pleasures, such as 'hot meat spiced, strong Wine, and the like, that heat the Privities.'

The recommended sustenance for a woman in labour is certainly modest, as her condition becomes even more delicate. Hobby emphasises that Sharp, in *The Midwives Book*, is most concerned that the midwife looks to the mother's proper nourishment:

> Midwives therefore must ask how long it was since the woman did eat, and what and how much, that upon occasion she may give her something to strengthen her in her labour if need be, as warm broth, or a potched egg; and if her delivery be long in doing, give her an ounce of Cinnamon water to comfort her, or else a dram of *Confectio Alkermes* at twice in two spoonfuls of Claret wine, but give her but one of these three things, for you may soon cast her into a feaver by too much hot administrations, and that may stop her purgations, and breed many mischiefs. (*MB*, pp. 161–162)[6]

With dietitians firmly voicing their disapproval of pork's sustaining properties, Purecraft's authority – as matriarch of the household – to approve of Win's longing is undermined. Furthermore, because the implication that women's inherently weak constitutions and sinful natures is a further deterrent against their consumption of pork, the gender specificity of the advice destabilises Dame Purecraft's status of being 'a most elect hypocrite and has maintained us [Win and Littlewit] all this seven year with it like gentlefolks' (1.5.167–69). Even with her carefully maintained reputation for being pious and upstanding, she is disempowered from endorsing Win's craving. Thus, when Win's family seek religious permission on her behalf, the aptly named Zeal-of-the-Land Busy, a male and superior hypocrite, is summoned.

Through Busy's justification of Win's longing to eat pig, the play explores how far moral strictures are to blame for the guilt surrounding eating for pleasure, such that eating needs to be proven as a necessity, and for the purpose of sustenance, before it can be justified. While Busy may be referred to as 'our zealous brother,' a 'reverend elder,' 'Rabbi' and 'prophet' (1.4.114–15), it is his zealous hypocrisy that the others seek in his 'help here to edify and raise us [them] up in a scruple' (1.6.41–42). His justification of, and the family's acquiescence to, Win's longing conforms to Moffett's claim before the play was first performed that 'Pigs' flesh by long and a bad custom is so generally desired and commended, that it is credibly (though falsely) esteemed for a nourishing and excellent good meat.'[7] This is certainly the basis of Busy's justification that Win should be permitted to eat it:

Verily, for the disease of longing, it is a disease, a carnal disease, or appetite, incident to women; and as it is carnal, and incident, it is natural, very natural. Now pig, it is a meat, and a meat that is nourishing, and may be longed for, and so consequently eaten; it may be eaten, very exceedingly well eaten. (1.6.50–55)

Therefore, in line with Moffett's observation that the demand for pig's flesh has led to a general belief that it is a valuable source of nourishment, Busy validates its consumption through the convoluted rhetoric that since Win's longing is a carnal and therefore natural one, it is also necessary and sustaining; pig may be 'very exceedingly well eaten' because her body clearly requires the nourishment specifically to be derived from pork.

As for the specificity of Win's craving to eat Bartholomew pig in the heart of the Fair, Busy is persuaded to 'think to make it as lawful as [he] can' (1.6.63–64). This he achieves, once more through his manipulative rhetoric that asserts that so long as the person who eats pork maintains a pious disposition, the deed is of little detriment to their faith, and may even advance the reputation of their religious sect.

He further addresses Purecraft's earlier dilemma that Win's eating of Bartholomew pig would jeopardise her reputation by offering to support their cause. He asserts that it may be sanctified even more strongly if he also eats pork, thus publicly demonstrating that the satisfaction of Win's longing is religiously condoned on account of her frail constitution:

291

In the way of comfort to the weak, I will go, and eat. I will eat exceedingly, and prophesy. There may be a good use made of it, too, now I think on't: by the public eating of swine's flesh, to profess the hate and loathing of Judaism, whereof the brethren stand taxed. I will therefore eat, yea, I will eat exceedingly. (1.6.95–100)

Jonson's satirical presentation of this justification for Win's longing ridicules those who presumed to advise others on the ethics of food and eating. Busy's character encapsulates the range of authors who arbitrarily professed to be authorities on the subject of food and diet. Albala writes that 'The authors of these books may have been physicians, philosophers, poets, or even politicians.' As an ex-baker turned Rabbi, whose 'cakes he made were served to bride-ales, maypoles, morrises, and such profane feasts and meeting' (1.4.121–23), he now purports to moderate the diets of his followers within the limits of religious prudence. Given that Busy's verdict contradicts much of the prevailing advice on diet and midwifery, Jonson seems to have been addressing that section of his audience who were aware of the rules but 'had probably already learned to ignore and ridicule dietary dogma.'[8] He asserts that consumers should be in a position to assess the consequences of the food they eat to their health and public image, and bear those consequences. Certainly, there is no need to consult one who fancies himself an authority on the subject, as Jonson asserts: 'Ha' not to do with him, for he is a fellow of a most arrogant and invincible dullness, I assure you' (1.4.145–46).

In the second half of this essay, a consideration of early modern principles of hospitality will be included to assess whether victuallers' profits in the play are fair, as well as to develop the argument that individuals should be morally responsible for what they eat and regulating trading activities to ensure that food is ethical. Jonson poses this question to his audience by juxtaposing the extremes of Ursla's 'fatness of the Fair' (2.2.119) against the puritanical self-deprivation imposed on Littlewit's household and Busy's moral justification of eating. Early modern principles of hospitality were written in a similar vein to George Wheler's, in *The Protestant Monastery* (1698): 'a Liberal Entertainment of all sorts of Men, at ones House, whether Neighbours or Strangers, with kindness, especially with Meat, Drink and Lodgings.'9 While this acknowledges the necessity of eating for sustenance, its endorsement of convivial dining is more surprising. This possibly supports political propaganda, because it implies that provisions of food and drink are shared among people of all conditions to promote charity and social cohesion.

Ursla's brand of hospitable service subverts Wheler's ideology entirely; it involves serving customers with as much as, preferably more than, they can physically eat or drink so that she profits well from the reckoning. Being an advocate of indulgence in one's appetite to a degree that transcends gluttony, she also epitomises sinful eating in her embodiment of physical excess. When she thinks no one is within earshot, Ursla instructs Mooncalf in her well-developed system for profiteering. Her malpractice includes adulterating her food and drink with cheap fillers to bulk out the measures in which they are served and reckoning customers' bills to her advantage. She also practises price discrimination in her charges for roasted pork: 'Five shillings a pig is my price, at least; if it be a sow-pig, sixpence more. If she be a great-bellied wife and long for 't, sixpence more for that' (2.2.111–13). This scene depicts the notoriety of Ursla's unethical trading practices to raise the questions of how quality of food, and ethics of its production and sale, were assessed. Unfortunately for her customers, Ursla monopolises trade in Bartholomew pig, with the result that the eradication of her amoral practices raises issues over trade regulation.

As Busy is characterised as a religious advocate, and this section is partly concerned with how eating and profits made from food sold in the Fair should be regulated, Busy's attitude towards food and morality will be discussed here in the light of Wheler's assertion that hospitality should be charitable. Before his first appearance on stage, Littlewit reports: 'I found him fast by the teeth i' the cold turkey pie, i' the cupboard, with a great white loaf on his left hand and a glass of malmsey on his right' (1.6.36–38). Not only is Busy's kill-joy attitude antithetical to the pleasures associated with convivial eating, his raiding of, and illicit feast in, his hosts' cupboard

292

constitute a kind of inhospitality. He takes it upon himself to distribute the food and drink in the Littlewit household, which involves withholding it from even the hosts themselves, and exploits his authority by selecting the best of it for his own secret indulgence. Not only does he forbid them against the sinfulness of eating for personal enjoyment, his violation of their resources prevents them from being able to keep an open house and take morally justified pleasure in convivial eating and liberal hospitality. In spite of Busy's assumption of religious authority and enforcement of his extremist views on others, he is presented as failing to uphold the principles advanced by religious advocates like Wheler, that hospitality should be liberal in its inclusion of all men, and be performed with kindness. This evidence supports the reading that according to Busy's attitude towards the morality of eating, it is perfectly ethical to take pleasure in food so long as this is done covertly, with preventive measures taken against public discovery.

In contrast to Busy, Ursla's generosity transcends the liberal entertainment promoted by Wheler. Hence, when Knockem leads the family of Puritans into her tent, she expresses her displeasure that he has invited in 'sippers o' the City; they look as they would not drink off two penn'orth of bottle-ale amongst 'em' (3.3.111–13). However, Knockem uses biblical discourse to present his justification for entertaining Littlewit's company in a manner that addresses and subverts Wheler's charitable ideal. He criticises Ursla's impious resistance against serving Puritans on the basis that they wear 'small printed ruffs' (3.3.114) by calling her a 'fool' (3.3.115) and overturns the meanings of 'hypocrites' and 'innocents' (3.3.117–19) in a similar fashion; the group are 'hypocrites' and 'innocents' simultaneously because their religious hypocrisy makes them innocent in the face of Ursla's prognosis that they are restrained sippers rather than 'good gluttons' (3.3.117). In the true spirit of hospitality – and of the pig vendors' mercenary intentions – Knockem puts an end to the dispute by ordering Ursla and Mooncalf to present their guests with liberal servings of food and drink: 'In, and set a couple o' pigs o' the board and half a dozen of the biggest bottles afore 'em, and call Whit' (3.3.117–19). Hence, in contrast to the pleasure that Busy takes in eating, it is Ursla's liberality with her food and drink that manipulates the principle of open hospitality from its charitable and religious origins to one that suits her exploitative intentions.

Ursla's immoral trade in food extends also to her involvement in the Fair's criminal underworld. Profits are further inflated by tempting respectable women like Win into prostitution to provide proverbial 'meat' for male customers and frisking the men – sluggish from overeating and inebriated – of their valuables. Once Knockem has enticed Win and her chaperones to the pig booth, a bawd is summoned to inspect her. Whit approaches, and riddles his pretence at offering them gourmet food and professional service with sexual innuendo:

293

Whit: A delicate show-pig, little mistress, with shweet sauce, and crackling, like de bay leaf i' de fire, la! Thou shalt ha' de clean side o' de tableclot and dy glass vashed with phatersh of Dame Annessh Cleare.
Littlewit: This 's fine, verily, here be the best pigs: and she does roast 'em as well as ever she did; the pig's head says. (3.2.63–68)

There is ambiguity as to whether Whit is addressing Win or referring to her as a 'delicate show-pig' (3.2.63); the affirmation of 'little mistress' (3.2.63) and other references that follow suggest that Whit is leaning lecherously close to examine her. His allusion to 'shweet sauce' makes perfectly clear that Win is a suitably nubile female specimen. Similarly, the reference to 'crackling like de bay leaf i' de fire' (3.2.63–64) plays on words which are associated with the female orgasm.[10] This scene contains a further reference to 'rosemary branches' (3.2.70), which enable Ursla to 'roast [the pigs] as well as ever she did' (3.2.68). Williams comments that rosemary, one of the plants also 'mentioned by Ophelia in her madness (*Ham* IV.v.175) were recommended by herbalists to induce menstruation or abortion.'[11] Hence this reference, and the association of Win's meal with 'a woman named Annis Clare… reputed to have drowned herself,' draws a parallel between Win's craving and female infamy.[12] Hence, Purecraft's admonition to Littlewit against 'the vanity of the eye' (3.2.72) has reasonable basis, because laid before them is an image pregnant with metaphors for the female body being made ready for sex.[13] The necessary antidotes are even ready to remove any evidence and attempt to restore the body to its pre-coital state, that is, in the event of conception and by inducing menstrual discharge. The staging of this scene would immediately call the legitimacy of Win's pregnancy into question. Whit's 'A delicate show-pig, little mistress' (3.2.63) is ambiguous because his touting of roasted pork is laden with the implication that the 'little mistress' is the pig for sale.

In a final consideration of how trading activities in the Fair are regulated, particular emphasis will be placed on Justice Overdo's role in detecting enormities. The other characters who arguably represent the regulatory bodies within the play have already been proven to be unreliable, and sometimes working cooperatively with the traders. These include Busy, whose religious advice is influenced by dubious moral standards, and Ursla, who controls much of the Fair's trade because of her monopoly in Bartholomew pig and her influence over the proceedings of its criminal underworld. Accompanying his presentation of these two extremes is Jonson's suggestion that Overdo comes somewhere in between. This assertion is mimicked in the plot structure: Justice Overdo's farcical appearance in the second act immediately follows Busy's justification of eating pork, but precedes Ursla's entrance, in 2.2. He enters disguised as a fool and explains: 'Well, in justice's name, and the King's, and for the commonwealth!' (2.1.1–2). Overdo defines himself as a 'detective of enormities' and further explains his purpose :

Many are the yearly enormities of this Fair, in whose courts of Pie-powders I have had the honour during the three days sometimes to sit as judge. But this is the special day for detection of those foresaid enormities. Here is my black book for the purpose, this [*pointing to his disguise*] the cloud that hides me. Under this cover I shall see and not be seen. ... And as I began, so I'll end: in justice's name, and the King's, and for the commonwealth! (2.1.41–50)

This speech establishes that Overdo is situated in a position whereby the regulation of the Fair's activities, or rather, its illicit activities fall within his responsibility.

Critics assert that Overdo's disguise as a fool 'is in fact the proper robe for this pretentious and myopic reformer.'[14] Indeed, Overdo's determination to ensure that food and drink are sold unadulterated and in standard measures would support this notion entirely. His lauding of the virtues of a magistrate who would go 'into *every* alehouse and down into *every* cellar; measure the length of puddings; *take the gauge* of black pots and cans, ay, and custards, with a *stick*, and their circumference with a *thread*; weigh the loaves of bread on his *middle finger* [my emphasis]'(2.1.18–22) is evidence of a character who not so much upholds the 'Justice' of his title, but whose pernickety methods 'Overdo' to the point of subverting the course of justice. However, this speech also suggests quite sinister motives for his determination to detect enormities. He divulges his intentions by saying that having measured the various commodities to ensure they meet weight regulations, and invariably discovering according to his petty intransigence that the goods are unfit for sale, 'Then would he send for 'em, *home*' (2.1.23). Although he claims to 'give the puddings to the poor, the bread to the hungry' (2.1.23–24), one nevertheless wonders if he merely pays lip service to his official duties and perhaps classes his own causes under those categories, for he'll also give 'the custards to *his children*' (2.1.24–25) and declares his determination to 'break the pots and burn the cans, *himself*' (2.1.25), thus granting himself the license to take the offending objects into personal custody. 'He would not trust his corrupt officers; he would do't *himself*' (2.1.26–27) with a double entendre that indicates that he is guilty of the same practices as his 'corrupt officers'. He is, after all, Adam (2.1.40) Overdo, named after the perpetrator of original sin.[15]

At the end of the play, Jonson attempts to resolve the question of how ethical standards in the food trade should be regulated, and goes some way towards achieving this when Quarlous, the play's detached and cynical observer, undermines Overdo's authority by exposing his folly. He also pressures the Justice to redeem his reputation by providing hospitality:

... remember you are but Adam, flesh and blood. You have your frailty; forget your other name of Overdo and invite us all to supper. (5.6.100–3)

Quarlous's religious allusions to original sin, the last supper and man's redemption from sin through the crucifixion are evoked here as a reminder of the Christian origins of hospitality. These associations are used as a means of grounding Overdo's highfalutin aspirations and the moral basis to his deluded claim that he acts 'in justice's name, and the King's, and for the commonwealth!' (2.1.1–2). However, the impact of Jonson's satire is tempered by the political correctness of restoring Overdo's authority.

> I invite you home with me to my house to supper. I will have none fear to go along, for my intents are *ad correctionem, non ad destructionem; ad aedificandum, non ad diruendum*. So, lead on. (5.6.114–17)

Overdo tells the others to 'lead on,' while he follows behind to ensure everyone's compliance. Hence, while Overdo makes all appearances of extending an open and generous invitation to dine, he is really imposing the confinements of his household on all the characters as a means of restoring public order and bringing the Fair to an official close.

With Quarlous in *Bartholomew Fair*, Jonson seems also to take the stance of satirical commentator, and uses his character's independence of any religious, political, or personal agenda as an assertion of his own objectivity. He also presents the licentious indulgence in eating and other physical pleasures supported by the Fair as being similarly distanced from everyday life. Overdo acknowledges this himself, albeit unconsciously perhaps, that 'this is the special day' (2.1.44–45) to detect enormities. The historical precedent of Jonson's fair is 'the cloth fair that for centuries had occurred annually on 24 August in the courtyard of the church of St Bartholomew the Great, in London's Smithfield.'[16] Although 'the religious associations embodied in the Fair's name remained alive,' the fair 'was increasingly a site of entertainment as well as commerce,' This pattern indicates the departure that modes of hospitality took from religious ideals like Wheler's, with the fair's existence for centuries – barring closures during the plague and other troubled times – denoting that this was usually tolerated by religious and political authorities. Laroque writes that 'Festivity had always been an outlet for popular energies; under Elizabeth and James I, it became an instrument of government as much as a means of amusement.'[17] Even Overdo's 'King' would have indulged in licentious pleasures during royal entertainments. Hence, just as such festive occasions were alloted a specific time and place, so too was Bartholomew Fair. Jonson's distinct segregation of his *Fair* from the play's depiction of its characters' everyday life clearly shows his acknowledgement of this dichotomy, and asserts with equal clarity that the pleasures indulged in for the duration of the Fair are removed both from the ethical standards that govern how food is sourced, prepared and served, and the moral tensions between eating for sustenance and eating for pleasure.

Bibliography

Primary Sources

Buttes, Henry, *Dyets Drie Dinner,* London, 1599.

Jonson, Ben, *Bartholomew Fair*, ed. Suzanne Gossett, Revels Student Editions, Manchester and New York: Manchester University Press, 2000.

Moffett, Thomas, *Healths Improvement,* London, 1655.

Sennert, Daniel, *Practical Physick,* London, 1664.

Sharp, Jane, *The Midwives Book,* London, 1671.

Secondary Sources

Albala, Ken, *Eating Right in the Renaissance*, California studies in food and culture, 2, Berkeley and London: University of California Press, 2002.

Heal, Felicity, *Hospitality in Early Modern England,* Oxford: Clarendon Press, 1990.

Hobby, Elaine, ' "Secrets of the Female sex": Jane Sharp, the reproductive female body, and early modern midwifery manuals,' *Women's Writing*, 8 (2001), 201–212.

Laroque, François, *Shakespeare's Festive World: Elizabethan Seasonal Entertainment and the Professional Stage*, trans. by Janet Lloyd, Cambridge: Cambridge University Press, 1993.

Robinson, James E., '*Bartholomew Fair*: Comedy of Vapors', *Studies in English Literature, 1500–1900*, 1 (1961), 65–80.

Williams, Gordon, *A Glossary of Shakespeare's Sexual Language*, London and Atlantic Highlands: Athlone, 1997.

Notes

1. Ben Jonson, *Bartholomew Fair*, edited by Suzanne Gossett 1.5.158. All subsequent references are to this edition and will be given in parentheses immediately following the quotation.
2. Sharp, p. 190.
3. Buttes, 'Porcus'.
4. Buttes, 'Swines Flesh'.
5. Sennert, p. 115.
6. Hobby, p. 203; p. 207.
7. Moffett, p. 66.
8. Albala, p. 1; p. 3.
9. Heal p. 3.
10. *OED* gives this definition of 'crack' as 'A woman of broken reputation; a wench, a prostitute. *Obs*' from 1676; it also 'indicates damaged reputation (with anatomical overtone)', Williams p. 84.
11. Williams, p. 263.
12. Gossett, p. 100n.
13. 'Eye' is another euphemism for the vagina, Williams, p. 118.
14. Robinson, p. 69.
15. The emphases in quotes from the text are all mine.
16. Gossett, p. 1.
17. Laroque, p. 9.

Food on Trial

Elizabeth M. Williams

A foreword in the spirit of full disclosure

Because I live in a land of plenty, I am able to eat what I want. I have generally disregarded the wild swings in the pendulum of recommendations of right-eating, i.e., nutritional right-eating. Instead, I have chosen which food to eat out my cultural upbringing and out of my personal taste. Rather than heed the call, for example, to eschew butter for margarine, because margarine was said to be healthier, I chose to continue to eat butter, and not to substitute for it. I did not do this because I was prescient regarding the current trans fat scare. I simply liked the taste of butter better than the taste of margarine.

I do not take nutritional proclamations with a grain of salt because I think that I know more than scientists who study nutrition. It is that I think that scientists just don't know enough. The watchdogs' warnings are too often extreme and premature. Don't eat sugar. Don't eat fat. Don't eat eggs. Don't eat red meat. Just wait a while. We may learn that we can eat previously suspect food after all, because science has learned more. This is not to demonize nutritionists. I wholeheartedly believe in the study of nutrition. But I do not think that nutritional advice should rule our lives, making the components of food more important than the food itself.

I agree with Julia Child's embrace of moderation. I view both the attempts of well-meaning consumer groups to force us to eat healthy foods and the attempts of the food industry to manipulate us into eating more and more of their highly-processed ersatz food with the same degree of skepticism. I would like to see us want to choose healthy foods, because we have learned that they taste good.

I am tired of the authoritarianism of each of the two parties trying to force us into an adversarial role with food. Eating should be natural and a pleasure. I want there to be a public debate over legislation regulating food. I would like to see people treated as intelligent enough to make good choices, given the facts as we currently understand them. I would like to see people given the freedom to make bad choices without being treated like bad children.

To advocate for the rights of the consumer to make food choices, including bad food choices, I have written this paper. It examines the constitutional rights of the consumer in the United States to eat what the consumer chooses. By analogy it may be relevant to legal arguments in other jurisdictions.

A history of food restrictions

For millennia there have been cultural restrictions and proscriptions about food. These are rules that control the most basic human need and thereby control life. The early rationale for these restrictions may have been religious law, as in prohibitions against eating bottom feeding fish in the Jewish law[1] or class-based restrictions against hunting and eating certain game, based on scarcity and privilege in England.[2] If those who were barred from particular foods were unhappy about their deprivation, they probably were not in a position to do anything to change the law. If they wished to eat proscribed foods they either risked the wrath of the gods or the retribution of the sovereign.

Humans have continued to regulate food. Some of these restrictions have become adopted by federal, state, or local legislation. Five justifications for these regulations have evolved, the two original justifications and three additional ones:

- Religion – Restrictions on sale and manufacture of certain foods because of religious beliefs
- Consumer protection – Legally imposed limitations put on what may be included in food sold to consumers and the requirement for certain product labeling
- Health – Legally imposed limitations of what may be claimed by food product manufacturers, limitations regarding manufacturing and handling of food to avoid tainted and spoiled food, and limitations in the use of certain 'unhealthy' ingredients
- Power and class – Limits on who may have access to food
- Animal rights – Limits on food production methods that are considered cruel and unnecessary to the animals to be eaten.

299

Any of these justifications may form the basis for legislation or regulation that controls accessibility to or restriction from particular foods or beverages. However, whatever the motivation for government action may be, not all justifications are morally or constitutionally supportable. In order to assess the constitutionality of legally imposed regulation, it is necessary to rigorously balance rights and dangers to distinguish the bitter pill of power and control from benign and benevolent protection.

It is the role of the United States Constitution to limit government interference with our basic freedoms, the freedom to eat what we choose being inherent in life, liberty, and the pursuit of happiness. Any limitation on the rights of citizens is an inherently serious and important topic. And because everyone eats, these restrictions affect everyone. Restrictions on constitutional rights for whatever reason are serious and should be justified for only the most important reasons. Knowing the justification tells us something about the society and its values. That justification can be either so important that it overrides the protected freedom to eat what we please, or the justification is unconstitutional.

The methodology

In determining the constitutionality of a legally mandated restriction a court will first identify the constitutionally protected right. The personal right will be viewed in the light of precedent, i.e., has this right been previously restricted and by what justification. It will be examined in light of other rights, both constitutional and legislative, and a priority of rights will be established. And the public good to be obtained by the restriction will be balanced against the harm that the restriction causes to personal and public rights. This assessment is very similar to the assessment of personal rights espoused by John Stuart Mill in his treatise, *On Liberty*. This assessment includes the right to make a harmful decision for oneself, as long it does not harm others.

In applying this analysis, a court, ultimately the United States Supreme Court – the ultimate arbiter of constitutionality – is figuratively determining where to place a phantom fulcrum on a balance. Deciding which rights to protect and how to protect them is a process in constant flux. And today reasonable people can differ as to the need to protect the public from its own actions and the need to protect the right of the public to make personal choices. As I have previously stated, I tend to place the fulcrum closer to personal choice than to legal proscription.

In determining which justifications provide a moral or constitutional basis for the restriction of the consumer's access to foodstuffs, we should examine each of these justifications separately. As is usual in life, they do not fall neatly into categories, but overlap messily. This paper attempts to present these examinations of morality and constitutionality in as orderly a fashion as the messy subject allows.

Religious belief and right-eating

Today's progressive society and principles of separation of church and state or some other form of secularism require us to tolerate the religious beliefs of others and refrain from legally imposing our beliefs on them. Thus if a person desires not to consume alcohol or caffeine for religious reasons, that person is free to abstain. At the same time those substances are available to others. In the United States the religiously observant may refrain from drinking or eating products that contain caffeine, some may refrain from drinking alcohol, and yet others may not eat pork or shellfish at all. But all of these products are generally available. The religious proscriptions are not secular legal proscriptions, because of the constitutional principle of the separation of church and state established in the First Amendment to the United States Constitution.

While actual religious beliefs have not caused restrictions, sometimes it is the fervor manifested by food zealots that has become a threat to the pleasures of the table, cultural foodways, and the constitutional rights of non-believers. Beliefs about right-eating can rise to the level of pious cult, complete with the need to proselytize and convert others, and to impose beliefs on others by force. The cultists justify the use of force – here the force of law – because of their belief that they are morally right and that they are protecting heathens from their own ignorance.

In the recent past we have been subjected to the cult of the bowel by Kellogg[3] and his followers. Fannie Farmer and her followers tried to impose a form of right-eating on the United States.[4] The failed temperance movement is an excellent example of the wholesale failure of legally imposed prohibition of an entire product – alcohol – for spurious moral and health reasons. Little regard was given to the fact that alcohol had been drunk by humans for thousands of years and even forms the basis for some religious rituals.

Religion as a basis for food restriction is not a constitutionally protected justification. The freedom to practice one's own religion or one's own lack of religion is a highly protected constitutional right, and the legal imposition of the religious beliefs of others on a society is an immoral and unconstitutional use of government power.

Consumer protection

Protecting the consumer from adulterated food has a long history. People trying to take advantage of others is not a modern phenomenon, neither is the need to protect the consumer. Old guild laws protected the honest craftsman as well as the unwary consumer. As food is processed outside of the sight of the consumer, it gives rise to the need for laws to protect the consumer from the unscrupulous. The more elaborate the processing, transforming the food into a different product, the more important consumer protection laws are. The safety and condition of processed food is not transparent, thus defects are not observable by simple inspection.

In some instances consumer protection protects the health of the consumer, for example, by prohibiting the addition of or substitution of unwholesome products. The recent recall of dog food containing adulterants is an example of the problem[5] caused by unseen additives. But protection against unseen adulterants is not the only type of consumer protection law. Some consumer protection laws protect the quality of the product – for example, real maple syrup[6] sold in a bottle labeled maple syrup, instead of maple-flavored syrup. The purpose of the consumer law is to ensure that the consumer gets what is promised.

In other words consumer protection law is a use of law to keep the consumer safe from the deceptive and immoral acts of others. After constitutional debate balancing issues of freedom of speech and the notion of caveat emptor, consumer protection laws were accepted as constitutional limitations on freedom of speech and freedom of contract.[7] It has been established that buyers can be protected within constitutional bounds, even though the legislation that protects consumers causes some restriction of the unfettered rights of sellers and manufacturers. Subsets of the consumer protection law are the labeling laws, informing the consumer of nutritional information about processed products. The more information about products, the more informed the consumers' choices can be. The two basic controversies over labeling are what information should be disclosed and who should disclose.

Health

Closely related to consumer protection, regulations to protect our health are generally considered to be acceptable limitations on freedom.[8] As with consumer protection arguments, the more processed a food is, the more we need to rely on the government to protect us. As we learn that a particular cookie may contain peanut oil and a child is allergic to it, reading the label that discloses ingredients is a proper use of the law and regulation to protect our health. However, banning peanut oil, because some people are allergic to it, is overreaching.

Public health is protected in other ways, limiting the number of rodent hairs, for example, present in our food. But the sense of balance – what is the health risk versus what is the cost of restriction to freedom – is the key to a constitutional justification for restriction. Here the science of food and nutrition becomes central to finding this balance. In assessing the health risk, we must rely on scientific study. I am skeptical about the finality of scientific study at any given time. The scientific community cannot always agree on methodology, the number of tests to run, the number of subjects that are representative, and the proper algorithm to use to extrapolate its findings to fit the general population. Without scientific consensus government restrictions may be ill-founded, premature, and extreme.

As a lawyer, I know that when I advocate a position, I will tout the study that proves the point that I am trying to make. I can make my position even stronger when many studies prove my point and that the studies from the most prestigious laboratories and the most respected scientists also support my position. My opponent will similarly advocate its position with selected studies and respected experts. I also know that studies can be used to support political agendas, support hypotheses that zealots believe to be true and right, as well as to justify unscrupulous corporate positions and cover fraud. So my experience has made me skeptical of the authority of science.

Casuistry, science, religion, and politics fueled the Temperance Movement in the United States. It took a constitutional amendment to ban the sale of alcohol.[9] And even that did not ban the consumption of the product on a private level. That amendment was required because the banning of the sale of alcohol infringed upon the freedom to contract, infringed upon the commerce clause,[10] and was not based upon protecting public health.

On the other hand, with the support of the government of the United States, hydrogenated vegetable oil was developed to substitute for animal fats used in cooking.[11] It was touted as a healthful alternative to lard and butter, and it had a long shelf-life. This was better living through science. Ad campaigns made people feel righteous for choosing to eschew lard and butter in cooking, and substitute hydrogenated oil instead. As a result, at least one generation, if not more, has grown up without knowing the taste of animal fat in food, and thus preferring the taste of hydrogenated oil.

Enter science again. Now scientific tests have suggested that trans fat,[12] formed by the use of hydrogenated oil can be harmful to our health. The scientifically manipulated, once 'healthful' food, is now demonized. There have been attempts to ban foods containing trans fat. The City of New York has imposed such a ban.[13] Of course, we can live without hydrogenated oils. But using the law to protect our health, government must take the least restrictive path, and the restriction should be based on well-established science. Although I am not sure that this threshold has been met, the limitations put on food manufacturers is small and there are alternatives that will not be noticeable to the consumer.

While I would not fight to maintain trans fats in food, I think that requiring the labeling of food as containing trans fat may allow the market place to eliminate foods that consumers reject because of labeling. If enough people decide that they do not wish to eat trans fat-laden food, the market will dictate the failure of those products. Consumer protection laws requiring labeling, rather than banning the product for health reasons, may be the less severe path to accomplish the same ends. And although the scientific studies may be sure enough for some people to make a choice not to eat trans fat, they may not yet be sufficient to justify a legal ban.

Banning through the courts

Besides bans created by legislation, a trend in the United States has been to use the courts as a means to enforce a ban. A lawsuit against McDonald's[14] claiming that it caused a person to become fat, a lawsuit against Kentucky Fried Chicken[15] because its product contained trans fat, and a threatened lawsuit against Kellogg's because it markets sugary cereal to children[16] are examples of the use of the courts to advance the agenda of right-eaters. While these cases do often involve constitutional issues such as freedom of corporate speech, they are not the subject of this paper. The existence of these lawsuits, however, shows the degree of fervor of belief held by the health advocates, as well as the interesting position of the corporations re-inventing themselves in the court of public opinion.

Power and class

Being able to have this discussion about freedom and choices is a lesson in the continued distinction between those who are well-off and educated and those who are not. The moral issues that are raised by those who can afford the healthiest food – let us call this the food that is organic, grown using sustainable methods, untainted by hormones and antibiotics – and those who eat the mass-produced food that is less expensive, are myriad. But these are not necessarily constitutional issues. The societal issue is that all have access to food that is wholesome and sustains life.

Too often it is the poor person who does not understand nutrition, who chooses to eat and to allow his children to eat, the least expensive, fat-laden and sugar-laden foods. In trying to arbitrate these food choices, it may be precisely because they are fat- and sugar-laden that they are affordable. By changing the standard of acceptability, we may be making people unable to afford to eat. As Starbuck's scrambles to eliminate trans fat from its muffins, people who never set foot in a Starbuck's because the latte there costs more than an entire meal, may not receive any benefits. The efforts to manipulate our food, however well-meaning, may be creating a further divide by class and power and economics.

Animal rights

The most recent entrants onto the right-eating scene have been animal rights advocates. These are people who wish to advance their agenda of protecting animals by banning the sale of certain animal products. Their most recent, visible achievement is the banning of the sale of foie gras, in particular in the city of Chicago.[17]

From a political standpoint this ban is quite clever. Foie gras is a luxury item unnecessary for survival. Fighting for the availability of foie gras, then, makes the advocates seem elitist and selfish. In addition, the number of producers of foie gras is small, and they are not an organized lobby. This makes them an ineffective group when lobbying for themselves. Being successful against them gives the animal rights advocates a victory. The irony of the victory is that it is a blow to the small farms movement, since most foie gras producers are small independent farmers, not large corporate producers. Their vulnerability to animal rights activists merely parallels their overall vulnerability in an ever encroaching corporate farm atmosphere.[18]

In my opinion the banning of the sale of foie gras is absolutely unconstitutional. The test of constitutionality is to first identify the constitutional right, here the freedom to contract protected by the commerce clause. The producer, the restaurant, and the consumer have a right to produce, sell, and buy this product. The next part of the test is to examine the underlying justification for the restriction. In this case the justification is that the production of foie gras is not conducted in a humane manner. The next part of the test is to balance the infringement against the justification. This is where the justification lacks the strength to overcome the constitutional protection of the commerce clause, which protects interstate commerce.

The right of people to commercial freedom is higher than the rights of ducks and geese, especially when the methods of animal husbandry in other industries are examined. Whether looking at the production of beef, pork, veal, or chicken, the standards of practice in those industries are not higher, and are arguably less humane than the practices employed in the production of foie gras. Thus just claiming the practices to be inhumane is insufficient to deem it so. And further, if the practices are inhumane, then a less drastic form of infringement would be to remedy the practice by changing the production requirements rather than the wholesale banning of the sale of the product.

In Chicago, the city ordinance has the additional constitutional weakness of merely banning the sale of foie gras in restaurants. It can still be purchased by consumers for home use or be given away in restaurants. This means only restaurants have been targeted for the curtailment of the right to contract. Such discrimination has no justification. The statute, read even in its most favorable light, is discriminatory on its face, and thus is unconstitutional.

Unfortunately the way through the courts is not a speedy one and those who have been caught in the net of this ordinance have not been able to afford the constitutional battle that a proper defense would entail. The health department citing of Doug Sohn, owner of Hot Doug's, a sausage store, is an example. On March 29, 2007 he pled guilty to violating the ban on the sale of foie gras and was fined $250.00.[19] He has certainly received more than $250.00 worth of publicity for his trouble, but he no longer sells foie gras-laced sausages. A lawsuit brought by the Illinois Restaurant Association (IRA) challenging the right of the city of Chicago to enact the ban on foie gras was dismissed on June 12, 2007 on the grounds that the ordinance was within the police powers of Chicago.[20] As of this writing the IRA was deciding whether to appeal the ruling.[21]

It remains to be seen whether other industries will also be attacked in the same way or whether practices will be required to be improved rather than the product itself banned.

So what does this mean?

On one hand, today we are again facing the prospect of well-meaning souls who wish to impose right-eating on us all by operation of law. We learn that as a society we eat too much fat, sugar, protein, salt, refined carbohydrates, and overly processed foods. We also are told that we eat too much of everything, even the right things. We eat engineered food – like low-fat cheese-food, soy cheese, fat-free mayonnaise, and textured soy protein. We don't eat enough vegetables.

On the other hand we are bombarded by the marketing of manufacturers of products that have a shelf life of generations. Legislators are succumbing to lobbyists, thus we continue corporate subsidies that distort the market and create the lowest food safety threshold instead of aiming higher. We are too weak to resist supersizing, because we want the most value for our food dollar, even when we wear that extra value around our waists. We read the foodie press praising the flirtation of haute cuisine with highly processed food. The magic of Ferran Adrià and others gives us mixed messages. Why is his use of xanthan gum good and its use in cheap ice cream bad? We are a bundle of contradictions.

I am mindful of the role of the large multi-national corporations that invest huge amounts of money to convince us to eat their products. I even agree that some of these products are of dubious health value, being full of salt, fat, preservatives, and refined sugar. The right-eaters would have us prohibited from eating some of these products because of health objections. By going directly to the government to enforce their beliefs upon everyone, the right-eaters are choosing the path of least resistance, the path that appears to be most direct. That path may be direct, but it is also vulnerable to constitutional challenge. I believe that the market place has shown itself to respond to information presented in a way that confronts the marketing of the corporate food industry head on. If the threat is not immediate, i.e., a person won't die from eating one cookie or muffin, then the fact that marketing and information can change decisions in the market, makes the need for direct banning less necessary and thus less constitutionally protected.

The trans fat transformation is a recent example. As the threat of a trans fat ban loomed, and as information about the negative impact of trans fat on health proliferated, industry immediately began to label prominently products without trans fat and tout them with celebrity endorsements. In a short time products were reformulated without trans fat and once again advertised for their healthfulness.[22] Producers know that if a fad takes hold, the marketplace reflects it. The very recent low carbohydrate fad had a strong negative impact on the bread and pasta industries. There was fear of a similar reaction to products containing trans fat.

An excellent example of marketing the way to change is The Center for Science in the Public Interest. CSPI was able to influence movie theaters across the United States to stop using palm oil and to switch to other oils in making popcorn.[23] The question is not whether in fact the alternate oil was healthier. The point is that consumers will demand what they are educated to demand, whether it is a right-eating choice like no trans fats or a non-healthy choice like supersizing. The tendency to resort to being the food police banning a choice, as opposed to health advocate, makes the right-eaters seem as one dimensional as the corporate shills.

Those who wish to legislate our food choices by creating bans on foods or components of food that they consider unhealthy are limiting freedom in the cause of being healthier. Even assuming that their science is correct and that the degree of health benefit is great, the restriction of the freedom of choice and the abdication of self-direction is not worth the health benefit. This is especially true in light of the success that consumer health advocates have had in promoting large-scale changes in food production through marketing and consumer education. The resort to legislation should be a last and drastic resort, when other techniques have failed.

Conclusion

This paper explores the various justifications for the legal proscription of certain foods and food components. It finds that there is no constitutional protection for religion-based banning of foods. Further it discusses the constitutionality of consumer protection and health as a constitutional justification for limiting certain foods and food components. These two categories require a delicate balancing of constitutional rights and the need for public protection. It is the area in which the most room for difference of perception and difference in philosophy exists. This is where the well-meaning can justify the short path of legal proscription, by-passing the less drastic, but more time-consuming path of marketing and public education to make healthy choices.

The justification of animal rights is one fraught with the changing perception of the rights of animals and the power of large industry to control the legislative process. And the issues of power and class hold the most interesting potential for a development of constitutional rights as yet unrecognized.

There is a difference between morality and law, and the rule of law should be interpreted in favor of freedom. The law should endeavor to encompass as broad a spectrum of positions as is reasonable. When the huckstering of products is legal, but immoral, it is not the role of law to silence the immoral voice. That is the best role of the consumer advocate – educating the consumer and countering the huckstering. I would like to see people make nutritionally sound food choices. But it is about choice first, and the right choice second. I would sacrifice the right choice, in favor of freedom. Reverting to unconstitutional control of consumer choices, however well meant, is a step down the slippery slope away from freedom. It is also a step away from creating a self-reliant and enlightened citizenry, a fundamental goal of democracy.

Notes

1. Grunfeld, Isidore, *The Jewish Dietary Laws* (New York: The Soncino Press, 1972), p. 5.
2. Montanari, Massimo, 'Peasants, Warriors, Priests' in *Food: A Culinary History* edited by Jean-Louis Flandrin and Massimo Montanari, English edition by Albert Sonnenfeld (Penguin Books, 1999), p. 181.
3. See Kellogg, John Harvey, *Plain Facts for Old and Young* (Burlington: I.F. Segner, 1886).
4. Shapiro, Laura, *Perfection Salad* (New York: Farrar, Straus and Giroux, 1986), pp. 100–119.
5. See the various listings on the recall site of the Food and Drug Administration, http://www.fda.gov.
6. Vermont Statutes Annotated, Title 6, Chapter 32, Sections 481 et seq.
7. Hutt, Peter Barton and Richard A. Merrill, *Food and Drug Law* (Westbury: The Foundation Press, Inc., 2d ed. 1991), pp. 1–4. (The freedom to contract is a constitutionally protected freedom.)
8. Ibid.
9. Amendment 18, U.S. Constitution (1918).
10. Article I, Section 8, Clause 3, U.S. Constitution (1787), which protects interstate commerce.
11. Critser, Greg, *Fat Land* (New York: Houghton Mifflin, 2001), p. 15.
12. Mozaffarian, Dariush, , Martijn B. Katan, Alberto Ascherio, Meir J. Stampfer, and Walter C. Willett 'Trans Fatty Acids and Cardiovascular Disease,' *New England Journal of Medicine*, Vol. 354 (April 2006), pp. 1601–1613.
13. Title 24, Rules of the City of New York, Article 81 (NY City Health Code), section 81.08, voted December 5, 2006.
14. *Pelman v McDonald's Corp.* 396 F. 3rd 508, 2005 U.S. App. LEXIS 1229 (2d Cir. NY, 2005).
15. CSPI press release, June 12, 2006, http://www.cspinet.org/new/200606121.html.
16. Kellogg's press release, June 14, 2007, http://www.kelloggcompany.com/uploadedFiles/KelloggCompany/Home/Press%20Release%20–%20U%20S.pdf and CSPI press release, June 14, 2007, http://www.cspinet.org/new/200706141.html.
17. Ruethling, Gretchen, 'Chicago Prohibits Foie Gras,' *New York Times*, April 27, 2006. http://travel2.nytimes.com/2006/04/27/us/27foiegras.html.
18. Pollan, Michael, *Omnivore's Dilemma* (New York: The Penguin Press, 2006), pp. 145–45, 149, 150–151.
19. Sander, Libby, 'Hot Dog Menu Draws a $250 Foie Gras Fine,' *New York Times*, March 30, 2007, http://travel.nytimes.com/2007/03/30/us/30foiegras.html.
20. Spielman, Fran and Leonard N. Fleming, 'Judge says foie gras ban ducky', in *Chicago Sun-Times*, May 13, 2007 at http://suntimes.com/new/metro/425138,CST-NWS-foie13.article.
21. Ibid.
22. See press release of Kraft Foods dated December 20, 2005 re trans fat labeling and reformulation of products.
23. Heath, Chip and Dan Heath, *Made to Stick* (New York: Random House, 2007), p. 5.

Cacao in Brazil or the History of a Crime

Marcia Zoladz

On September 26, 2005 Luiz Henrique Franco Timóteo presented himself at a notary's office in the city of Itabuna, in the cacao region of southern Bahia state and registered a confession. He said that he had been part of a conspiracy, with three others, to destroy the great cacao plantations in the region and thereby put an end to local economic and political power based on ancient alliances. His confession described how, between 1987 and 1992, he and his companions had brought from the Amazon region cacao shrubs infected with a fungus known as witches' broom (*Crinipellis perniciosa*) to spread the disease to the healthy trees of Bahia.

The reasons for these modern-day revolutionaries introducing and disseminating witches' broom in southern Bahia's cacao belt were, among others: 'That they were not cacao cultivators and that they depended on employment and on revolutionary politics in the region' and 'that the only way to take power in the cacao region was to economically weaken the cacao producers.'[1]

They called the operation 'Cruzeiro do Sul' (Southern Cross) after the constellation visible in the night sky south of the Equator. The name derived from the method chosen to spread the disease: to the naked eye, the Southern Cross contains four big stars in the same positions as the cardinal points. With their orientation, they were able to spread the disease to the whole cacao region.

This confession shows how piracy and bacteriological warfare aimed at eliminating competitors or even subverting local power, is not so different from the practices of pirates and corsairs of a bygone age. In 1734, Francisco Palheta, an employee of the Portuguese crown, in a letter to the king of Portugal sought the privilege of exploiting as slaves one hundred couples from the indigenous villages surrounding his lands, since he already had one thousand coffee trees and three thousand of cacao duly acclimatized and productive. In the letter, Palheta also reminds the king that he had suffered for the crown in his expedition to Cayenne, in French Guiana, from where he had secretly brought to Brazil over one thousand coffee seeds and that he had, as he had been contracted to, disseminated them throughout the region, bringing great profit to the king. Coffee had been introduced to the French Caribbean colonies shortly before, from seeds traded between Holland and France.

A pirate's life was not easy, and in his complaint to the king, Palheta recounts how his ship was swamped three times on his way to Guiana,[2] that he had lost all his belongings, and, as the Portuguese were not welcome in those parts, ran great risk to his life. This is not so different from what happened to the self-proclaimed modern-day revolutionaries: on one of their trips to the Amazon, being short of money, they

Figure 1. Workers isolating the sick twigs from the cocoa trees. Ihéus, Bahia, December 1996. (Photo Eduardo Simões/ IMS Archive.)

310

had transported the infected plants by bus, and one of them reappeared years later, saying that he too had suffered losses in his personal life.

Pirating seeds and the illegal transportation of plants between countries competing for primacy in the world market is only one of the aspects of the colonial expansion initiated in the fifteenth century, with sugar cane in the New World. The great powers at the time created a colonial agricultural policy with botanical gardens whose function was to acclimatize plants for their subsequent large-scale commercialization both as cash-crops for food and also for medicine, as occurred with the cinchona plant (*Cinchona officinalis*),[3] the bark of which provided quinine, used to fight malaria, and which, originally from the Andes, was also susceptible to smuggling, being taken by the Dutch to Java and by the English to India.

The equatorial region of South America – colonized at the time by the French, English and Dutch in the Guianas, and by the Portuguese in Pará in the north of Brazil served as places for the acclimatization and perfecting of plants brought from all over the world.

Cacao in Brazil

Cacao was already grown in the Amazon in 1711, and in 1746 was introduced to Bahia. It was not, however, considered economically viable and for over a century went through a series of experiments to adapt it climactically for monoculture, aimed at possible exportation. In contrast to Mexico, cacao did not have a tradition of consumption in Brazil. Production therefore only grew slowly in response to stimulus from the external market.

To set up a cacao plantation, initial investment was needed, and the original indigenous population had to be removed. At the beginning of the Portuguese colonization of Brazil, the government established a policy of grouping the Indians together in villages called missions or reductions.[4] The remnants of the indigenous peoples of a particular region would agree, after many conflicts and burdensome negotiation, to live in a village controlled by the military, with the support of the Catholic Church, which was responsible for their conversion, education and health.

After less than a hundred years, this Indian protection policy was abandoned. In 1850, a new territorial legislation[5] allowed the government to appropriate indigenous lands, the missions and all their possessions for subsequent re-distribution or sale. The law separated the owners of the land, the natives, from those who worked the land, who were those same natives. The land no longer belonged to them. The aim was the official appropriation of the land.

For a just state – a theocracy

During the whole colonial period in the Americas, the nature of their original inhabitants was widely and exhaustively discussed. These debates included the question of servitude as well as indignant reports concerning their extermination, whether in warfare or from disease, principally smallpox, which wiped out entire peoples. The Church, with priests such as the Jesuit Manoel da Nóbrega in Brazil and the Dominican friar Bartolome De Las Casas, questioned at the time the methods used during the conquest of the Americas by the Portuguese and the Spaniards.

From the beginning of South America's colonization in the sixteenth century up to their expulsion from Brazil at the beginning of the eighteenth century, the Jesuits had set up and maintained missions on the frontier between Brazil, Paraguay and Argentina. In a unique way, these village missions had become, in the eyes of the Jesuit fathers, a vision of paradise on earth, the maximum expression of a theocratic state.

At the time there were huge theoretical discussions in the Jesuit and Franciscan orders about the indigenous population in Brazil, the significance and methodology of their catechism. As they were trying to justify the forced conversion and the enslavement of the native population, they allowed the establishment of African slaves in Brazil. There are registers of their deportation from African ports to Brazil as early as 1505.

Generally, the missions were well-governed farming estates, inhabited by the natives. The big difference between the Jesuit missions and the others was that they believed in the segregation of the indigenous peoples as a way of preserving them, while the others were also frontier operations, with military governors and garrisons,

*Figure 2. Cocoa beens drying in the sun. Ilhéus, Bahia, December 1996.
(Photo Eduardo Simões/ IMS Archive.)*

312

with the churchmen looking after their education, and the conversion of all the inhabitants. Both were much focused in producing tobacco, cacao, cotton, sugar and medicinal plants, either in the name of God or the Crown.

Gilberto Freyre, in his book *The Masters and the Slaves*, reminds us that the Jesuits saw the native population in a very crude way: 'From the mouth of one of them, the most pious and saintly, José de Anchieta, we recollect his very hard words: "the best way to preach is holding a sword and an iron pole".'[6]

As soon as cacao production increased, and it became obvious that Britain would not allow the transportation of any more slaves from Africa, the Brazilian Imperial government initiated a policy of gathering foreigners into villages, called Colonies, this time with the aim of bringing small-scale farmers as free labour, principally from Switzerland, to the region. In 1865, after the Civil War in the United States, people from the defeated South were also encouraged to settle in Brazil.

Where does cacao come from?

The tree is originally from the Amazon rain forest, today in the region of the frontier between Brazil and Venezuela, and can still be found in its natural state. Biologists return to this area when they need to renew the plant's genetic chain. From there it spread to all of Central America and southern Mexico.

Several times over the last five hundred years Brazil has been described as the best place in the world. Many etchings were produced over the period with an imaginative view of what could be found there. With such creatures as the armadillo and entire tribes of naked men and women, it was hard not to have one's imagination stimulated. The area where cacao originated on Brazil's borders with Venezuela was considered to be the mythical El Dorado, a place where the streets were paved with gold, and gigantic women known as Amazons might appear at any moment. The myth was revealed to be just that when French explorer La Condamine, set out in 1742 from the bay of Tumbez on the Pacific coast and, following the 30th parallel eastwards across South America, reached Belém, in northern Brazil.[7]

Cacao as an individual experience of pleasure

Chocolate and coffee came to be used as beverages during the Renaissance, a time that coincided with European westward expansion to the Americas. Partaking of chocolate in Europe during the sixteenth and seventeenth centuries therefore had a much greater meaning and social impact than we can imagine today. And, what's more, its success continues to this day.

Cacao was certainly an important meeting ground between Europeans and the New World. Firstly, because contrary to most of the new foods that would later be refined for consumption, such as the tomato, for example, a method of preparing chocolate, with its ceremonial consumption, was already well known. Nothing could have been more spectacular. According to the report of Bernal Díaz Castillo, who was part of the conquering expedition of Hernán Cortés to Mexico in 1519, in his chronicle *Historia verdadera de la conquista de la Nueva Espana (True History of the Conquest of New Spain)*, published in 1632, more than two thousand cups of foamy chocolate were served to the troops at Emperor Moctezuma's court every day.

313

Coffee, to give another example of a drink that became popular during the same period, was introduced to Europe from the Orient, and also became quickly available in the seventeenth century, and continues to be highly appreciated, but only chocolate is considered to be a luxurious experience for the palate. Both are obtained by similar means – the seeds of the fruit are fermented, toasted and then ground into powder.

The first impression caused by chocolate when presented to the European courts of the sixteenth century was of total rapture. The Aztecs consumed it cold, seasoned with pepper and sometimes lightly thickened with corn flour. They appreciated the foamy topping, which they achieved by pouring the chocolate from one pot to another from a height of about one metre. The Spanish soon added sugar to the drink. In an anecdote from the second half of the seventeenth century, Francesco Redi, by profession an observer of the courts of Europe employed by the Medici family, noted that despite all the refinement with which the Spanish served chocolate, in Tuscany, mixed with jasmine, cinnamon, orange or lemon peel, vanilla, amber and musk, the beverage reached its maximum point of perfection. Of course he was referring to the way in which his patron, Cosimo di Medici consumed the beverage.[8]

Chocolate, prepared with water, pepper, a little vanilla and honey, without doubt a feast for the palate was also a great novelty, a non-alcoholic drink that was at the same time a stimulant. Cacao has in its chemical composition theobromine, a stimulant similar to caffeine, which brings a sense of well being. Chocolate achieved its great popular success when, at the beginning of the eighteenth century, the English royal doctor Sir Hans Sloane recommended it be taken with milk.[9]

A tasty, healthy drink recommended by doctors and having as its principal ingredient a fruit from the Americas fitted perfectly into the eighteenth century, the great century of disguises – Marie Antoinette, queen of France, in a slight delirium of Arcadia, fantasized that she was a shepherdess and built a small rural village in the grounds of the royal palace. In England, small themed pavilions were fashionable, appropriately called follies, which can be construed in delightful ways, either as a 'fantasy,' a 'small madness,' but always as an extravagance to please the senses.

In the nineteenth century, Karl Marx with an extraordinary understanding of the real and symbolic value of seeds, observed that their value was greater than gold because they could not be kept buried under the earth for long, as their seeds would germinate!

The high specific value of precious metals, their durability, relative indestructibility, the fact that they do not oxidise when exposed to the air and that gold in particular is insoluble in acids other than aqua regia – all these physical properties make precious metals the natural material for hoarding. Peter Martyr, who was apparently a great lover of chocolate, remarks, therefore, of the sacks of cocoa that in Mexico served as a sort of money. 'Blessed money which furnishes mankind with a sweet and nutritious beverage and protects its innocent possessors from the infernal disease of avarice, since it cannot be long hoarded, nor hidden underground!'[10]

Difficulties of yesterday and those of today

The cacao tree needs about eight years to fully produce, and during the eighteenth and nineteenth centuries, crops were abandoned due to the bankruptcies of their owners, to disease and to difficulties in getting the produce to the markets. During the nineteenth century, cacao production was consolidated in Brazil. The cycle at a plantation began with the small-scale cultivator clearing areas under the canopy of the Atlantic rain forest and planting cacao trees. Since they were unable to maintain them, the property was bought by medium-size ranchers who, in turn, sold them to the big landowners with links to exporting companies.

The country always had difficulty in introducing policies to modernize infrastructure with private capital. At the same time as they found difficulties in settling populations in the cacao region of southern Bahia, an inability to build roads ever since colonial times meant that in 1920 cacao was still transported by canoe, as Arthur W. Knapp showed in his *Book of Cocoa and Chocolate*.

Until the end of the twentieth century, the domestic market for chocolate in Brazil was small and undeveloped. Large companies manufacturing chocolate from cacao have been in Brazil for over one hundred years. Nevertheless, in looking for recipes for cakes and biscuits containing chocolate to see how the product was used from the end of the nineteenth century in Brazil, I have never found significant references in their oldest recipes. In one well-known nineteenth-century Brazilian book, *O Cozinheiro Imperial* (The Imperial Chef), there are no recipes for sweets containing chocolate. The recipe books consulted, many written after World War II usually refer to a cake, a soufflé and a pudding. The amounts of chocolate used in the recipes are less than what we use today.

At the start of the witches' broom infestation, in 1986, Brazil was the world's second largest cacao exporter. But the country never had a local consumer market with a variety of chocolate products, just chocolate powder, chocolate and milk beverages like Ovaltine and Nesquik, and some kinds of chocolate candy, famous and much appreciated, with romantic names like Sonho de Valsa (Dream Waltz) or Serenata de Amor (Serenade of Love), but with only a small amount of chocolate in their composition. I grew up with little choice in terms of chocolate bars, and even then they were bad, dessicated and likely to crumble. They were made from the leftovers of cacao paste, which tasted like rancid butter.

Chocolate was always produced for export and with little interest on the domestic market, it was never incorporated into the Brazilian diet like coffee or sugar or the banana, originally from India but nevertheless completely integrated into the national diet. We have no records of cacao's systematic use among the indigenous population of the Amazon forest. The German naturalist Karl Von Martius observed in 1820 that Indians of the Munducurus people ate the fruit of cacao shredded and sieved to accompany other foods.[11] We have no myths associated with cacao among indigenous peoples such as that of manioc. There is no dish in Brazilian cuisine prepared with its pulp, nor are its ground seeds used to make chocolate as practiced by the Aztecs.

The plot to infect cacao plantations with fungus was not so different to what occurred in the seventeenth and eighteenth centuries with botanical control. The transportation of plants was controlled to ensure the hegemony on the market of a particular product. In the instance referred to, control was sidestepped through the dissemination of a disease, aimed at reducing the political power of a particular group.

Why is cacao and chocolate so important that first the crime was confessed to in a notary's office and then published in the press?

What happened in Brazil?
Production in Brazil only managed to increase in the twentieth century, mainly after World War I, and especially after 1925, when cacao began to be traded on the stock

exchange in the United States. However, conditions of hygiene on the plantations were always a problem. In 1911, Bahia already had problems in controlling disease.[12]

The cacao region in Brazil was unable to settle a population and promote local development as did regions cultivating coffee, oranges, and now, in the state of São Paulo, with the sugar cane being grown principally for ethanol fuel. The landowners and the traders lived in Bahia's state capital Salvador, or in Rio de Janeiro, and the problem of absentee landlords continues to this day. Political and economic influences are exercised with greater interest in obtaining loans and tax exemptions, in getting government investment, than in regional socio-economic development. The workers did not, and still do not have any reason for settling in and contributing to the local economy.

When cacao as a commercially viable crop took off in Brazil, the country had officially abolished slavery, so instead an extremely perverse system was created that even today has to be systematically contained. The farm hand, the agricultural worker, the fruit picker hired as temporary labour are eternally indebted to the boss, and part of their wages are always retained to pay for the implements, food and medicine sold at the stores on the plantation itself.

So, in 2006 the guilty parties appeared

A disease of the magnitude that crippled cacao production could not have been propagated by the work of one man alone or even a small group of men transporting tree branches in a truck. 'I'm in no doubt that the introduction was criminal, but this story, in the way it was told, is highly improbable,' said Gonçalo Pereira, researcher at the Universidade Estadual de Campinas – State University of Campinas (Unicamp) and coordinator of the Witches' Broom Genome Project, to the weekly magazine *Veja*. His argument is based on the results of a genetic study concluded last year.[13]

In the Amazon, the trees are not close to each other, so that when the witches' broom releases its spores, the fungus will land on some species that aren't susceptible to the disease as well as on wild cacao trees, but with varying genetic characteristics so they will not necessarily develop the disease, a kind of cancer that consumes the trees' energy. Because the disease is one of the cacao tree's natural predators, any plants brought from the northern region are quarantined in Bahia, where thousands of trees grow very close to each other, even when planted beneath larger trees of other species to provide shade.

How the fungus arrived is still questioned. What is important is that after a disease has been found covering a large area, the whole area must be sprayed with fungicide. However, because of the combination of poorly educated local workers, poor sanitary conditions and lack of investment on one of the plantations, infected trees were cut down and thrown into a river. The witches' broom decimated a large part of the plantations, and today Brazil produces just 4.75% of world production.[14]

The author of the confession had to leave the region where he lived, and the others continued their lives as technicians, agronomists or politicians. Like Palheta, upon realizing that he was not part of a circle of winners, he complained publicly. In an interview, upon being asked if he knew what he was doing, he excused himself from guilt, 'No, I thought it would just give them a scare. I thought that Ceplac (the government body responsible for cacao) would control the fungus and then act as the hero.' (Interview to the *Estado de São Paulo* newspaper, September 10, 2006.) And he also complains about the amount of money he was given: 'US$ 20,000, but this was to make myself scarce from the region.'

Faults in the system of cultivation ended up facilitating the disease's spread, and providing a political opportunity for assuming responsibility for the crime. Neither cacao nor chocolate has ever, to steal a figure of speech from the language of psychoanalysis, been internalized into the Brazilian national diet.

The political opportunity occurred precisely because the disease is extremely damaging to trees planted close to each other, as in Bahia. In the Amazon, within the forest, the mixture of species and the distance separating trees of the same species means that they do not get sick at the same time.

And the most interesting thing is how the question reappeared in 2006. The crime, which apparently had a revolutionary motive, in practice resulted in the inclusion of the political party to which the possible disseminators of the disease belonged, and still belong, into local power. It accelerated the region's urbanization. As the engineer Sérgio Nobre de Andrade said in 1995 in an article in the newspaper *Folha de S. Paulo*, the disease was already highly predictable when the producers abandoned a plantation system integrated with the Atlantic rain forest – the cacao trees should have been planted in the shade of the taller trees of an original forest that was only thinned, as opposed to cut down; investment in technology was negligible and the local population that could have acted as a specialized labour force was untrained.

In addition, the maintenance of an antiquated production system kept the cacao in a feudal plantation social system, isolated from the country's modernization, semi-hidden, with production handed over to multinational exporters, however not openly globalized and far from the pioneering production of premium seeds. The witches' broom infection was therefore the last straw in the collapse of production. And, after all, if the favourite chocolate cake is called a brownie, in English, in a country that speaks Portuguese, what difference does it make where the cacao comes from?

Cacao and the region today

Some solutions have begun to appear, after so many years of devastation. These preserve the original forest cover; propose the restoration of planting in the shade of large trees, which at the same time enables the reforesting of the Atlantic rain forest. Further, the more professionally run the property, the greater the opportunities for commercial reciprocity with exporters and manufacturers.

What is important is that these forms of cultivation, even though from the viewpoint of an international planter, and in fact in the same way as in the sixteenth century, are a long-term investment, and offer an opportunity to regenerate cacao in Brazil, enabling the formation of a genetic databank. As with people, the plants sometimes forget who they are and stop giving their best fruit.

Cacao is recovering, with many new discoveries and with the partial sequencing of the witches' broom's genetic code.

Notes

1. Luiz Henrique Franco Timóteo, deposition at the notary's Office in Itabuna, Bahia, 26 September 2005.
2. Letter from Francisco Palheta to the King of Portugal in 1734.
3. Schiebinger (2004), p. 38.
4. Freyre (2002), p. 211.
5. Freitas p. 73.
6. Freyre (2002), p. 214.
7. Cunha, p. 529.
8. Camporesi, p. 108.
9. Schiebinger (2004), p. 7.
10. Marx, Karl, Chapter 4, 'The precious metals', par. 3.
11. Cascudo, p. 635.
12. Freitas, p. 103.
13. Veja.
14. Ceplac – 1.2 Produção Brasileira.

Recipe Notebooks
Mrs Marieta Marinho de Azevedo, 1906.
Mrs Francisca de Escobar, 1917.
A private notebook, circa 1880 – s.d.

Bibliography

Andrade, Sérgio Nobre de, 'A saga e a ilusão' (Saga and illusion), *Folha de S. Paulo*, section Dinheiro (Money), p.2, 23 September 1995. < http://www1.uol.com.br/cgi-bin/bibliot/arquivo.cgi?html=fsp 1995&banner=bannersarqfolha> [accessed 8 July 2007].

Arpide, José Luis, *El cacao y los aztecas* <http://www.afuegolento.com> [accessed November 2006].

——, *El cacao y los mayas* <http://www.afuegolento.com> [accessed November 2006].

Breteuil, Julio, *Novo cozinheiro universal, contendo as melhores receitas das cozinhas francezas e estrangeiras e numerosas receitas brasileiras* (Rio de Janeiro: H. Garnier, 1901).

Bright, Chris. 'Mata Atlântica: bioma ameaçado. O chocolate pode resgatar a floresta', *WWI – World Watch Institute/UMA*. <http://www.wwiuma.org.br/ww_mat_choc1.htm> [accessed 7 July 2007].

Caramel, Blanche, *Le nouveau livre de cuisine* (Paris: Editions Gautier-Languereaux, 1927).

Camporesi, Piero, *The exotic brew*, trans. Christopher Woodall (Cambridge:Polity Press, 1998).

Cascudo, *Luis da Câmara, História da Alimentação no Brasil* (São Paulo: Global Editora, 2004).

Coe, Sophie and Coe, Michael D., *The True History of Chocolate* (London: Thames & Hudson, 1996).

'Cometi crime biológico'. Interview with Luiz Franco Timóteo, *Estado de S. Paulo*, section Economia e Negócios (Economics and Business), 10 de setembro de 2006.

Costa, Maria Thereza A., *Noções de arte culinária* (São Paulo: Augusto Siqueira e Comp, 1921).

Cunha, Euclydes, Fronteira sul do Amazonas, *À margem da geografia*, *Obra completa*. Ed.org. Afrânio Coutinho. (Rio de Janeiro: Nova Aguilar, 1995). < http://www.euclides.site.com > [accessed: 7 July 2007].

Darnton, Robert, *George Washington's False Teeth, An unconventional guide to the eighteenth century* (New York: W.W. Norton & Company, 2003).

Escobar, Herton, 'Praga que devastou o cacau veio mesmo de ação humana, *O Estado de São Paulo*, 21 June 2006.

Flandrin, Jean-Louis and Montanari, Massimo, English ed. Albert Sonnenfeld, *A Culinary History of Food* (New York: Penguin Books, 2000).

Francisco de Mello Palheta, Carta régia de 16 de fevereiro de 1734, Wikipedia Portugal<http://pt.wikipedia.org/wiki/Francisco_de_Melo_Palheta> [accessed November 2006].

Freitas, Antônio Fernando G. de and Paraíso, Maria Hilda Baqueiro, *Caminhos ao encontro do mundo*. Ilhéus 1534-1940 (Ilhéus:Editus, 2001).

Freyre, Gilberto, *Assucar* (Rio de Janeiro: José Olympio, 1939).

Freyre, Gilberto, *Casa Grande & senzala* (The masters and the slaves) (Rio de Janeiro: Record, 2002).

Gay, Peter, *The Education of the Senses. The Bourgeois Experience: Victoria to Freud* (W.W. Norton: New York, 1984).

Íntegra da denúncia registrada por Luiz Henrique Franco Timóteo (Integral text of the original confession), *Jornal A Região*,Depoimento ao cartório de Itabuna,26 de setembro de 2005.<http://www2.uol.com.br/aregiao/serv/denuncia-timoteo.html> [accessed 7 July 2007].

Knapp, Arthur W., *Cocoa and Chocolate. Their history from plantation to consumer* (London: Chapman and Hall Ltd., 1920) in The Project Gutenberg <EBook #19073>.

Horta, Nina, *Não é sopa. Crônicas e receitas de comida* (São Paulo: Companhia das Letras, 1995).

Hearn, Lafcadio, *La cuisine creole, A collection of culinary recipes from Leading chefs and noted creole housewifes, who have made New Orleans famous for its cuisine* (New Orleans: F.F.Hansel &Bro., 1885). <http://www.archive.org/details/lacuisinecreoleoohearrich > [accessed 07 July 2007].

Lorenzi, Harri e Abreu Matos, F.J., *Plantas medicinais no Brasil* (Nova Odessa: Instituto Plantarum da Flora Ltda, 2002).

Marx, Karl, *A contribution to the critique of political economy*, Chapter 4 – The precious metals. (Moscow: Progress Publishers, 1859). Marx and Engels Internet Archiv, <http://www.marxists.org/archive/marx/> [accessed 7 July 2007].

'Mercado de cacau', 1.2 Produção Brasileira. Ceplac – Comissão Executiva do Plano da Lavoura Cacaueira, <http://www.ceplac.gov.br/radar/mercado_cacau.htm> [accessed 7 July 2007].

Maria, Rosa, *A arte de comer bem* (Rio de Janeiro: Livraria São José, 1961).

Mintz, Sidney W., *Sweetness and Power, the Place of Sugar in Modern History* (London: Penguin, 1986)

'Panorama da economia mundial do cacau'. Ceplac – Comissão Executiva do Plano da Lavoura Cacaueira, <http://www.ceplac.gov.br/Sinopse_Cacau/Panorama/paranorama1.5.htm> [accessed 7 July 2007].

Poivre D'Arvoir, Olivier and Poivre D'Arvoir, Patrick, *Pirates & Corsaires* (Paris: Mengès, 2004).

Policarpo Junior, 'Terrorismo biológico do PT', *Revista Veja*, 21 June 2006, <http://veja.abril.com.br/210606/p_060.html> [accessed 2 July 2007].

'Praga foi Sabotagem', *O Estado de São Paulo*, 28 June 2006. <http://txt.estado.com.br/editoriais/2006/06/18/ger-1.93.7.20060618.17.1.xml> [accessed 7 July 2007].

R.C.M, *O cozinheiro imperial*, facsimile of the 2nd edition of 1843 (São Paulo: Editora Nova Cultural, 1996).

Rozin, Elisabeth, *Blue corn and chocolate* (New York: Alfred A. Knopf, 1994).

Schiebinger, Londa, *Plants and empire, colonial bioprospecting in the Atlantic world* (Cambridge: Harvard University Press, 2004).

Schiebinger, Londa and Swan, Claudia, eds., *Colonial botany. Science, commerce and politics in the early modern world* (Philadelphia: University of Pennsylvania Press, 2005).

Todorov, Tzvetan, *La conquête de l'Amérique* (Paris: Éditions du Seuil, 1982).

Ukers, William H., *All about coffee* (New York: The tea & coffee trade journal, 1935).

Ventura, Roberto, *Casa-grande e senzala*, coleção Folha Explica (São Paulo: Publifolha, 2000).

Alison Stuart was born in Thurrock. She trained as
a legal secretary and worked in London, where she
dreamed of being a writer and indulging her passion
for historical drama. She lived in London in the early
years of her marriage and became fascinated by the
social history of its people. Her first novel, under a
different name, was published in 1987. As a dedicated
author she is meticulous in her research and enjoys
revisiting the settings of her scenes. She now writes
full time, and lives with her husband in Sussex. She
has two children and is now a grandmother.

Alison Stuart's previous novels, COUNT YOUR
BLESSINGS, SIN NO MORE, LOYALTY DE-
FILED, FATEFUL SHADOWS and INNOCENCE
BETRAYED, are also available from Headline.

Barefoot Angel

Alison Stuart

HEADLINE

First published in 1997 by
HEADLINE BOOK PUBLISHING

First published in paperback in 1998
by HEADLINE BOOK PUBLISHING

10 9 8 7 6 5 4 3 2 1

ISBN 0 7472 5557 1

Typeset by Palimpsest Book Production Limited,
Polmont, Stirlingshire
Printed and bound in Great Britain by
Mackays of Chatham plc, Chatham, Kent

HEADLINE BOOK PUBLISHING
A division of Hodder Headline PLC
338 Euston Road
London NW1 3BH

As with so many of my novels this is dedicated to the memory of my father John Frost who died when I was eight. My deepest regret is never truly knowing him. He was renowned for his easy-going manner and refusal to say a harsh word or pass critical judgement upon anyone. I doubt he was a saint – few mortals are – but his capacity for tolerance and understanding has been my most abiding memory of him.

Also to Chris – simply the best.

Not forgetting my children Alison and Stuart. I'm proud of them both and of their achievements. Who would I be without you?

A special thank you to Andi Blackwell at Headline for being there when I need her and for creating calm out of chaos.

PART ONE

1940

For Mercy has a human heart,
Pity a human face,
And Love, the human form divine,
And Peace, the human dress.
William Blake

Prologue

'We've got to get away. It's too dangerous to stay. I know too much.' Grace's father's voice was sharp with fear as he accelerated the car through the countryside.

Grace was curled on the back seat, her hands over her ears. At nine she didn't understand why her loving father had suddenly become so angry in the last week. Her parents never used to quarrel, now it was incessant.

'I'm not leaving England,' her mother snapped. 'And where would we go? The Germans have overrun Europe. Ships are sunk every day in the Atlantic by U-boats.'

'I've got forged passports. We'll have a new identity. A new start.'

'Why should I leave all my friends? You should have realised what was happening sooner and got out. Go on your own. I'm not leaving London. I gave up everything for you. I'm sick of the secrecy. I don't want a life built on lies.'

'I won't leave without you and Grace. The Big Man can get at me through you.'

'Take the child then. I don't want to be stuck bringing her up alone. What have I got to fear from the Big Man? He's never made a secret of the fact he fancies me.'

'That won't save your life if he thinks you know what I've found out.' He tapped the brown leather notebook in his jacket pocket. 'It's all here. Dates. Payments. Enough information to put him inside for his treachery. Except that if he goes down so do I as an accomplice. Even though I didn't know what he was up to until now. He's had people done away with for knowing less about him than I do.'

'Then you shouldn't have threatened to expose him.'

The voices droned on. Grace couldn't bear to listen any more. Their words didn't make sense, but they frightened her.

Her father stared ahead, his mind in torment. Why was Amy being so difficult, couldn't she see the danger? Or was it that she no longer loved him? She had been his mistress for twelve years. He would have married her had it not been for her brutish husband who refused a divorce. Yet when he had died six months ago from a heroin overdose, Amy had refused to marry him.

The thought of losing Amy filled him with as much fear as the Big Man's thugs being after him. Amy was more in love with the exciting life he had given her than with him. She had never been a true mother to Grace, never wanted a child and ignored the girl's existence. Now he had to accept that he was losing Amy, but he would never give up Grace. Never.

Still he tried to reason with Amy. He couldn't cope with a young girl in a new life on his own. Amy was adamant. She wanted out of his life and he was welcome to Grace. Their daughter was his responsibility not hers.

Grace clutched her white shaggy teddy bear closer and shut her eyes, a tear trickling down her cheek. Mummy was being mean again. Mummy didn't want her. Mummy could go. It was Daddy she adored. As long as she still had her daddy everything would be all right.

The swaying of the car lulled her into a light doze. The arguing voices dimmed. They rose once briefly as her father shouted, 'He's out to kill us, Amy! Our only chance is to forget the past. Forget it.'

Grace cried out, starting awake. 'Who wants to kill us, Daddy?'

He turned to her. 'I didn't mean to frighten you, kitten.

4

Go back to sleep. You're going to have a new name. You'll have to forget you were Grace, then we can be together.'

'That car is still following us.' Her mother's voice was no longer angry. It was now shaky with terror.

The car swerved violently off the road and bumped on to a farm track. Even Grace knew they were going too fast. Her heart raced and she began to cry. Then she was pitched forward. The car shuddered to a halt with a sickening crunch of steel. Pain shot through her skull as Grace was thrown on to the floor.

Chapter One

'Our marriage is a failure because we don't have children,' Lily Carrington accused, her voice rising with hysteria. 'That's why you play around with other women, isn't it, Ted? You're never in of an evening.'

'Chance would be a fine thing with this gammy leg,' Ted attempted to joke but saw to his dismay that Lil's mouth was tight with anger. He changed down a gear to take a bend in the road and his voice was weary when he answered, 'Children have nothing to do with what's wrong with our marriage.'

He kept his tone level and his eyes riveted on the winding road which was shrouded in a thickening mist. Because of the blackout they'd planned to be home before dark. But this looked like becoming a real peasouper and the falling leaves made the road treacherous as they drove through the outskirts of Epping Forest. This Sunday was supposed to be a day of celebration. They were driving home to Forest Gate from Chingford after visiting Lil's sister, Annie, to celebrate her birthday.

Ted had a headache from the pints he'd drunk at lunchtime and was in no mood for one of Lil's arguments. The wounds in his thigh and lower back where the German bullets had nearly killed him at Dunkirk were giving him hell.

Without warning Lily's handbag clouted him across the side of the head.

'For crying out loud, woman!' He swerved dangerously close to a ditch and hauled on the steering wheel of the old

7

works van to get back on the country lane. 'Now what's got into you? You'll kill us both.'

He pulled over to the side of the road and turned to face his wife. 'That's just what's wrong with our marriage. You're a bloody maniac when you've been drinking!'

Even in the gloom he could see the wildness in Lily's eyes. Her wavy blonde hair was dishevelled and her peaked hat askew. Ted shook his head and sighed. Lily's beauty always moved him. She was tall for a woman at five foot eight and she still had a trim figure with curves in all the right places. Once that wildness had captivated him, but recently there was a bitterness to her which saddened him. He tipped back his cap from its usual rakish angle. 'How many times do I have to tell you there's no one else? There never has been.'

'All day you've been flirting with our Annie.' Lily struck his shoulder with her bag, her lovely eyes bright with tears. 'You fancy her, don't you? I saw you kiss her. I bet you wished you'd married her and not me. Annie's had three kids. She ain't barren.'

She began to hit out at him and he caught her wrists. He smelt the booze on her breath as he pushed her against the back of the van seat. Lil had always been jealous if he paid attention to another woman. She was getting worse. 'Lil, don't do this to yourself,' he reasoned. 'Don't do this to us.'

'Annie fancies you. She always has.'

'Don't be daft, woman. She dotes on Charlie.'

'Ay, but Charlie's at the front fighting, ain't he? And Annie is a randy little cow. Always has been. She were four months gone when Charlie wed her.'

Lil continued to struggle but Ted held her wrists firmly whilst trying not to bruise her. Ted was of medium height and build but he was afraid of his own strength. He'd been a typical street-urchin brought up in the Stepney slums where brawling was as natural as thieving. He'd never held with harming a woman.

8

He controlled his sliding temper. It was Lil's ill-founded jealousy that was driving them apart. He was a placid man. The horrors of Dunkirk where the British army were pinned down on the beach still invaded his sleep. And Lil gave him little peace during the evenings with her moods and rages. He'd only been out of hospital two months. The army had declared him unfit to fight and he'd returned to his old job as Works Manager at an engineering company which was now manufacturing munitions for the war. He hadn't liked being invalided out of the army while his mates were still serving, but at least he helped the war effort as best he could. Tonight was a rare night off from his ARP duties. From the way Lil talked you'd think he was down the pub every evening instead of picking bodies from the rubble after bombing raids.

'Give it a rest, Lil.' His exasperation got the better of him. It was another half-hour's drive to Forest Gate and he couldn't see more than ten yards in front of the car. Today's outing was possible because he'd had to pick up some machine parts in Essex. With petrol rationing all trips had to be accounted for. The works delivery van was a godsend and he'd done some business of his own in Chingford which had earned a pretty profit.

'Lil, you're the only woman for me.' He forced her hands down between them and, knowing the best way to subdue her, began to kiss her passionately. When they were both breathless, he murmured, 'Besides, a man can only cope with one firebrand at a time.'

Little traffic was on the road and they were isolated by the fog. Lily continued to struggle. 'You're too free with your kisses. Does Annie get excited when you kiss her?'

'What do I have to do to prove I don't play around?' His kisses became passionate, his words of love soft and coercing against her ear. 'I love you, Lil. There ain't no woman like you.'

At hearing her soft moan of capitulation, his hand slid

under her dress and over her stockings to the soft flesh of her thighs. Her response was immediate. Her fingers became frantic upon his trousers as she opened her legs. 'Make love to me, Ted. Prove I'm your woman.'

The gear stick got in the way and Ted cursed. 'Let's wait till we get home, sweetheart.'

The accusation returned to her voice as she glared up at him. 'You never used to wait, Ted. You took me enough times in this van before we were wed. Show me you still love me. Oh Ted, I can't wait till we get home.'

Ted chuckled. Then two loud bangs made him sit up with a start. 'What was that? It sounded like gunfire.'

'Don't be so daft. You've been watching too many Cagney films. It's probably a car backfiring.'

'It was gunshots. I should know.'

Lily sighed. 'Then it's a farmer out shooting pheasants.' She drew his hand back to her breast. 'Make love to me, Ted.'

He grinned. This was more like his old Lil, the exciting, passionate woman he'd married. He'd rather make love to her than fight any day. His kisses deepened, the windows rapidly steaming up as their passion mounted. When a screech of brakes and revving engine warned Ted of a car taking the corner ahead too fast, he tensed. His passion ebbed. A glance out of the window made him swear. The bloody idiot would ram them. The van rocked violently as a car sped past missing them by a hairsbreadth.

Lily screamed and, disengaging herself, sat up. Ted shook his fist at the rear mirror as he saw the car swerve round the bend, its tyres screeching. There had been four men inside. 'Bloody idiots! Dozy toffs with more money than brains,' he growled. 'They make me sick. They think they own the road.'

'Put me right off, that has.' Lily pulled her dress down over her knees. She turned to Ted but there was still an over-bright glitter in her eyes. 'I get so mad when you flirt with Annie. I'm

10

sorry for acting up. If you ever left me, Ted, I don't know what I'd do.'

Ted sighed. He didn't like it when Lil spoke that way. It had only started since her last miscarriage which had been the third in five years. It had broken his heart to lose another baby, but her obsession for a child was destroying the sweet woman he'd fallen in love with. 'Ain't we wed for better or worse? I ain't gonna leave you.' He kissed her lips and switched on the van engine. 'You only get like this when you've been drinking.'

'Every day I pray for a child.' Lily began to sob. 'A baby will make everything right. You'd never leave me then.' Her voice was no longer slurred with drink but impassioned. 'I'll lay off the booze. But it makes me forget me troubles.'

Ted hid his misgivings. Not having a kid was destroying Lily. 'We ain't got no troubles, Lil. A baby will come along in time. And I wouldn't want a kid coming into the world while London is being bombed. The doctor says there ain't no reason why we won't have one when the war ends. I've got a good job and we get the use of the van whenever we need it. Ain't I done up the house we rent real nice? And despite clothes rationing you ain't gone short of a new frock or two. Come the end of the war I reckon I'll have saved enough for a deposit to buy a place of our own.'

'Just as long as you don't get caught flogging that dodgy stuff on the black market.' She covered her face with her hands and groaned. 'I want a baby so bad.'

'We could adopt. There's enough kids been orphaned in the bombing.'

'It ain't the same as one of our own,' Lily said, her tone and expression fierce. 'Our baby will be a special part of you and me, Ted.'

He didn't comment. He was worried about Lily. She was always hanging round the kids' playground and often insisted that they took Annie's children out for the day on a Sunday. What worried him most was she'd recently got this bee in her bonnet about him being interested in other women. Her jealousy was unfounded and getting beyond a joke.

His hands tightened on the wheel. He couldn't fathom Lily out these days. They'd been married for seven years and he'd been in love with her since they began courting when they were both seventeen. They married a year later. Ted adored her. She was the first person in his life he could truly love and who loved him in return.

He never knew his father and suspected that his mother was never married. She abandoned him when he was four to carry on with a wealthy, married businessman who took her abroad. She died of typhus a few years later in a back street of Naples. Ted had been raised by his grandparents who were bitter about the shame brought upon the family by their daughter. They grudgingly brought up an illegitimate child and never showed him love or gave him a kind word. They were both dead by the time Ted was fifteen. Before his gran died she insisted he learn a trade and he had been apprenticed to an engineering company. The pay was abysmal and wasn't enough to rent a room let alone feed and clothe him. To make ends meet he got in with a gang of villains and acted as their look-out which enabled him to live in a small degree of comfort. By the time he met Lil, he had been taught to drive by the company and began using the van for a bit of ducking and diving on his own. He never saw this as dishonest. It was a way of supplementing his meagre wage packet. And once he fell for Lil, nothing but the best was good enough for her.

On his first meeting with Lily Dawkins, he'd fallen for her. She was the most stunning woman he'd ever seen, with looks and figure like a filmstar. Her dad ran a clothes stall in Hoe Street market and Lil worked as a machinist in the shirt factory. But Lily had style. Not for her cheap clothes from her dad's stall. She bought the best she could afford from exclusive shops in the high street or the West End. In their courting days even her fiery temper had captivated him.

It was part of her passionate nature and love of life. That was before the miscarriages and the drinking began.

He glanced at her face which was still beautiful although the lovely features were blurring with drink. He loved her, but he couldn't take much more of this. Lily needed help. She was destroying their marriage by her jealousy. He'd never looked at another woman since he'd met her. The birthday kiss he'd given Annie was innocent. But Lily had been drinking heavily since they arrived and Annie had announced that she was pregnant again. Always sensitive to Lil's moods he had been aware of her pain at the news.

Deep in thought as he drove, Ted caught only a glimpse of something white by the edge of the road. Dimly, he assumed it was a newspaper blown into the hedgerow.

'Stop!' Lily yelled. 'There's a child out there.'

'Don't be daft, luv, there ain't no houses round here for another mile.'

Lily grabbed his arm. 'It was a kid. A young girl in a white dress. Stop. Turn round and go back.'

'You've had too much to drink. You'll be telling me it was a ghost next.'

'It were a kid. Turn round,' she demanded. Winding down the window, she peered back along the road. 'She's sitting by the side of the road. Something's up for her to be out here all alone. She needs help.'

Reluctantly Ted reversed and Lil called out, 'Hey, sweetie, what you doing out here alone? Are you lost?'

Ted was concentrating on reversing and didn't hear a reply. When he turned to the front again he saw a girl of about eight sitting on the grass by the hedgerow. She had silvery-blonde Shirley Temple curls and was wearing a white full-skirted party dress which was streaked with dirt. Her eyes were wide and staring fixedly ahead of her. What disturbed him was that she gave no sign of having seen or heard them.

Lil jumped out of the van and ran to the girl and gathered

13

her into her arms. The slight body was cold and tremors shook her form. The white dress was of expensive white satin overlaid with heavy lace. 'What's happened, luv? Tell us where you live and we'll take you home,' Lily said, gently rubbing some warmth back into the girl's chilled arms. It was then she saw that her legs and feet were bare. The girl's legs were mottled with cold and also scratched and bleeding as if from walking through the undergrowth. Something dreadful must have happened for the girl to be alone and in such a state.

'Poor luv, what happened to you?' Lily's heart pumped with pity for the traumatised child. The girl had still shown no sign of acknowledging their presence.

'Where's your mummy or daddy?'

Large blue eyes were turned towards her. Then with unexpected strength, the girl pushed Lily away and ran back up the road. Several yards ahead she disappeared through the hedgerow and headed towards the nearest trees.

'Go after her, Ted!' Lily yelled. She began to follow and cursed her high heels which impeded her running. The girl had disappeared into the fog. 'Stop! Wait for us!'

Ted hobbled after her. 'Hang on, kid. I've got a gammy leg. Where are you?'

Within yards of leaving the road Lily was ensnared in the milky blankness of the fog. Sounds were muffled but she could hear Ted ahead of her. Lily followed blindly. Twice she stumbled and wrenched her foot. A bramble coiled around her ankle ripping her stockings. 'Blast it! That's my last pair.' She hated having to draw pencil lines up the back of her bare legs.

'Ted, where are you?' She strained to hear any sound of her husband's movements. At each step her heels sank deep into damp earth. The cold air had sobered her. The countryside gave her the creeps. And certain that something terrible had happened to the girl, her heart pounded wildly. Why else was the angelic youngster in such a state of shock and wandering alone?

14

'Stay where you are, Lil,' Ted shouted. 'There's been some kind of an accident.'

Lily had come this far and wasn't about to turn back. She felt safer knowing that Ted was close by. She moved in the direction of his voice and gasped as she saw a large expensive car crashed into a tree. Ted had the driver's door open and was peering inside.

'Keep an eye on the kid,' he said in a choked voice. 'Looks like her mother's a gonner. Nasty head wound. Pulse is very weak and she's lost so much blood. She's trapped somehow. I can't get her out. There's no sign of the driver.'

'Perhaps they've gone for help,' Lily suggested, moving towards the girl who was now sitting on the ground with her back pressed against a tree. Her eyes were wide and tears streaked her cheeks. Although her shoulders heaved she wasn't making a sound.

'Do you reckon she's dumb, she ain't said nothing?' Lily asked.

'Probably the shock.' Ted frowned at the girl. She was beautiful with an angelic face and looked bright enough.

'Why did the driver go off and leave her?' Lily persisted. She put her arm around the girl and drew her stiff body away from the sight of the crashed car. 'It's going to be all right, luv. You'll be safe with us. Ted will report this to the police and get an ambulance out here for your mum. It is your mum, isn't it?'

The girl did not answer but buried her head against Lily's chest.

'What's your name, love?' she said gently.

Again silence. Lily peered over Ted's shoulder and saw blood on the woman's head and coat. Her stomach rebelled and she almost gagged on her rising nausea. She conquered it for the sake of the girl. They had to find out who she was and where she lived.

'Everything will be all right,' she comforted. 'You have to

speak to us so we can help you. Can you tell us where you live?' Lily insisted. 'Was your daddy driving the car? He'll be worried about you. We should get you home.'

Again silence and all Lily's maternal instincts rose to comfort her.

The mist was beginning to thin. Ted pointed to a hedge to their right. 'That's where the car went off the road. That looks like a farm track. The engine is still warm so it didn't happen long back. Nasty business.' His voice was gruff as he guided Lily and the girl away from the grisly contents of the car. 'God knows what happened here. This weren't no ordinary accident. Police will have to be informed. Lucky I got rid of that last lot of stuff at Charlie's this afternoon, or I'd have some awkward questions to answer about that bedding nicked from the warehouse.'

'You take too many chances, Ted,' Lily scolded as she stroked the girl's hair but her attention was on the crashed car. 'They look so well off.'

'Appearances can be deceptive,' Ted replied. 'Some of the biggest rogues in the East End are rolling in it. No one said crime don't pay. Who knows what happened here. Even toffs get into debt and fall foul of moneylenders. That's for the police to sort out.'

With a fierce protectiveness Lily clasped the girl. 'What if we hadn't stopped when we did? Anything could have happened to her.'

Ted crouched next to the girl so that his head was on a level with hers. 'Did you see who did this to your mum?'

The girl turned her head away from him, her shudders more violent.

'Leave off, Ted,' Lily snapped. 'She's in no state to answer questions. Poor blighter's half frozen. Are her things in the car?'

Ted wrenched open the back door of the vehicle and found a coat, shoes, socks and a white scruffy teddy bear. Lily took the coat. It was deep red with a real fur collar. The black patent shoes were also expensive. She quickly dressed the girl. 'You'll feel better once we get you warm. Let's get back to the van, Ted, or she'll get a chill.'

Ted held out the bear to the girl. 'Here, kid. This looks like an old friend. And I reckon you can do with a friend or two at the moment. You're gonna be all right with us, kid. We'll look after you until we find your daddy.'

Tentatively the girl took the bear and hugged it close to her chest. With her other hand she held tightly on to Lily's coat. The girl's eyes remained large and staring as she pressed the side of her face against Lily's body. Ted touched her bubble curls and shook his head sadly as he met Lily's troubled stare. 'Poor little sod. We'd better get her to a doctor. And this will have to be reported and an ambulance sent for. There might be a chance the woman's alive. Doubt it though.'

He picked the girl up and strode back to the car. His heart went out to her and he closed his eyes feeling her pain as he held her tight. She made no attempt to struggle although violent shudders continued to shake her body. No wonder. He hadn't told Lily but the woman in the car had been shot.

Chapter Two

The last tentacles of mist were dispersing as they reached the van. Lily climbed in and Ted put the girl on her lap. She stared anxiously at her husband. 'Where's the closest police station to report the accident?'

'I'll stop at a pub. They're bound to have a phone. If that woman is alive she needs help fast.'

Lily spoke softly and reassuringly to the child as they drove a mile before they found a public house at a crossroads with only four small cottages around it. It was closed until seven in the evening. Ted got out of the van and banged on the door while Lily rocked the girl in her arms. Throughout the journey the girl had not responded to any questions. Lily's heart ached at the thought of the trauma and fear the young girl had experienced. Whoever had run the car off the road had chosen a remote spot.

Ted got no immediate response to his knocking and he began to shout, 'There's been an accident along the road. A woman's been hurt. I need to phone the police and ambulance.'

Eventually bolts were shot back and a grey-haired man in a waistcoat, his sleeves rolled up to show several tattoos, glared out at him. Ted repeated what they'd seen.

'Phone is in the passage. Best get your wife and kid in here out of the cold. Police will want statements I reckon.'

Lily kept her arm around the girl as she sat in the landlord's parlour. It was dominated by a large table covered by a green baize cover. One half was piled high with newspapers and magazines and a collection of jam jars were scattered amongst the dirty dishes from the last meal. There was the smell of blackberry jam cooking. The room was as cluttered as the table with cheap knick-knacks on a scuffed sideboard and an assortment of odd armchairs. Several cobwebs garlanded the ceiling and it hadn't been dusted in weeks.

Lily suppressed a shudder and resisted the urge to scratch her arms. Four cats were curled up on the chairs. She didn't like animals in a house, their hairs got everywhere and they made a mess. She was loath to sit down, convinced that the heavy-horsehair chairs were alive with bugs and fleas. She remained by the door where she could hear Ted on the phone. His voice was urgent as he gave the name of the pub.

'The car is about a mile further on,' he explained. 'Get the ambulance there fast. But I think the woman's dead.'

The landlord returned with Ted. 'I'm Wilf Addison and that's Doris, me wife.' He smiled at the small woman who came into the room.

Doris was a plump homely woman in a red twinset and tweed skirt. The cream cross-over apron was splattered with blackberry juice and other indeterminate grime. She took off her pinny, tossing it on to the table, and patted her tight, frizzy grey curls. Pushing a tortoiseshell cat from the sofa, she gestured for Lily to sit. 'Lawd, an accident, you say. Just you make yourselves comfy. I'll make some tea.'

'Pity I ain't got nothing stronger.' Wilf pulled a face. 'We ain't had no spirits to sell for a couple of weeks. You're welcome to a pint though, Mr Carrington.'

'Thanks, mate, and I reckon me wife would prefer a beer to a tea. Nasty the accident was.'

Doris fired excited questions at Lily when the landlord went for the drinks. Lily, who had reluctantly sat down on the sofa, put her hand to her head and held the girl tighter.

The image of the bloodied woman was carved in her mind. After a bombing raid she had seen some gruesome sights but there was something sinister about this accident which upset her. She evaded Doris's questions. It would be bad enough having to go through it all with the police. She couldn't face it twice.

Ted sat opposite Lily on a wooden dining chair. He looked haggard and his hands shook as he lit up a Woodbine. 'The police are on their way. They'll want statements. They're contacting the ambulance service and a doctor to check over the kid.'

He took the beer glass from the landlord and downed half of it. 'I needed that.'

Giving up on Lily, Doris began to question Ted about what they'd seen. Ted shook his head and nodded towards the girl. 'No disrespect, missus, you've been good to us. But the girl's in shock. That don't mean to say she don't hear. Might make things worse, especially as the police will be asking her questions.'

Doris pouted, clearly put out at not getting the facts of the accident. An uneasy silence settled over the parlour which was finally broken by the sound of two police car bells clanging. Ted and Wilf went outside. Wilf came back with a thick-set, pinch-faced man. 'Mrs Carrington, your husband has gone in the Inspector's car to show them where the incident happened. This is Detective Sergeant Crawford. He wants to ask you some questions.'

Lily told them what they had found. Several times as she spoke the girl flinched or shivered and Lily paused to hold her close and reassure her. When the policeman addressed the girl, she gave no sign of having heard him.

Dr West, a thin, asthmatic man in his sixties, arrived. After examining the girl, he declared, 'Severe shock. Nothing else seems to be wrong with her. Not surprising after what you tell me. I'll get her admitted to Whipps Cross hospital. Then depending on what happens regarding her parents, she'll be discharged or sent to a home.'

Lily's maternal instincts rebelled at the prospect of the girl thrust into the care of strangers. 'There's nothing wrong with her, is there? Clearly her mother is in no state to care for her. Couldn't she come home with us? She needs love. A sense of security. The child won't get that in a home.'

The girl snuggled deeper in Lily's arms and trustingly laid her head in her lap, the teddy bear clutched to her chest.

Dr West rubbed his chin. 'It's most irregular, but she seems to have taken to you. Yet there could be relatives.'

'How long will they take to trace, unless the driver of the car or her mother can tell us?' Lily's eyes pleaded with the doctor to be compassionate. 'The child hasn't spoken since we found her. It's getting late and she needs a place to stay tonight. Somewhere she feels safe.'

'It's not that simple, Mrs Carrington,' Dr West hedged. 'There are regulations on these matters. You'd have to pass a board of approval as being suitable.'

Lily's patience ran out. 'Without us the poor mite would still be roaming round the countryside in this state. I'm a respectable married woman with a decent home to take her to. You've seen how she trusts me. Isn't that what's important?'

'I'm sorry. Rules can't be disregarded.' Dr West reached to take the girl from Lily's arms.

The child stiffened and clung tighter. When he tried to pull her away she began to scream.

'Stop it!' Lily ordered. 'You're frightening her. She's been through enough.'

'Mrs Carrington is right,' the landlady intervened. 'You can see this lady isn't going to do anything to hurt the child. She should stay with them.'

The screams filled the room and Lily held the girl close, rocking her gently and whispering words of reassurance. 'They ain't gonna take you, sweetheart. Hush, love. It will be all right. You're safe. I'll look after you.'

Gradually the screams abated. Lily looked at the policeman. 'Please, don't take her to be with strangers.'

Detective Crawford looked at the doctor. The doctor shrugged and answered, 'I suppose in the circumstances a night or two won't harm her until her relatives are traced.'

'It doesn't seem right to upset the girl further,' Detective Crawford agreed. 'We'll be checking the owner of the car from the number plates. But the Inspector will know more of the situation when he returns.' He made to pat the child on the head but she flinched away from him and clung tighter to Lily.

The doctor left and Lily gathered the girl close with a fierce possessiveness. 'No one will harm you. You're safe with us.'

Ted directed the police driver to the crashed car. As they drove he told Inspector Harris all he'd seen. The Inspector was of average build, middle-aged with a balding head and his remaining hair clipped close to his skull. His manner was abrupt, caustic and cynical, which Ted disliked.

'Did you see anything suspicious, before you saw the girl?' Harris grunted.

'I couldn't see much at all. It was thick fog. We only passed a couple of cars on the road,' Ted answered. 'But the wife and I were having a bit of a set-to so I pulled over as she was getting upset. Then some bloody maniac came haring round the bend towards us and nearly took us off the road. Must have missed us by an inch. The van shook as it passed.'

'What time was this?'

'About half five.'

'You said that was when you saw the girl?'

Ted rubbed his brow with his fingers. 'The incidents were no more than ten minutes apart. I'd forgotten the car after seeing the girl and then what followed.'

'Did you see the car, or who was in it?' Inspector Harris fired out so brutally that Ted felt that he was the one under suspicion of some crime.

'It was a big car, possibly a Bentley.' He paused and tried to picture the car as it sped past. 'There were four men inside. I didn't see their faces.'

A short distance from where Ted had first seen the girl, he saw a farm track. 'That's where the car must have turned off. It was in a field and it hadn't spun off this road.'

The police car bumped along the track and came to a break in the hedgerow. In the field beyond Ted recognised the tree the car had crashed into.

'That's where the car left the road. It hit that tree.'

Inspector Harris got out of the car. 'There's no car.'

'There must be.' Ted leapt out and stared incredulously at the field. It was empty. 'The bonnet was all smashed in. It didn't look driveable.'

The Inspector looked dour as he walked across the field. Although the fog had gone it was overcast and gloomy. 'Those tyre marks prove there was a car here. We didn't pass a vehicle with a smashed bonnet on the way to the pub. The driver must have returned and driven off in the opposite direction.'

'And abandoned the child? What sort of a person does that?' Ted scoffed. 'And why wasn't the driver around when we called out and got no answer?'

'We'll check with the hospitals for a woman with gunshot wounds being admitted and also local doctors. If she was unconscious the driver would be worried about her. She'd need immediate attention.'

Inspector Harris turned to the two policemen with him. 'See if you can find anything.'

Ted scratched his head. 'It doesn't make sense that they'd leave the girl.'

One of the policemen gave a shout. 'There's part of a chrome bumper over here.'

'Not much we can do here for now.' Inspector Harris strode back to the car and gestured for Ted to get in. 'Clearly the car was driveable. We'll take you back to the pub, Mr Carrington. The girl will be reported missing and we'll reunite her with her parents.'

Ted wasn't so confident. People didn't get shot for no reason. Were the couple running away from something or someone? Could they afford to contact the police? He was uneasy. Nothing about this was cut and dried. But it wasn't his concern. He'd done his bit and was beginning to feel uncomfortable in the Inspector's presence. He didn't want too many questions probing into his life. Police were bloody busy-bodies sticking their noses where they weren't wanted. Though he hoped they discovered the kid's parents.

The image of the girl – so lovely and so obviously in deep shock – harrowed him. The poor mite. How could they have left her? And where was the driver when they returned to the car? It was all very odd and disturbing.

In the pub Detective Crawford was pacing the parlour having finished his questions and taken details of Lily and Ted's address. Doris talked non-stop about the tragedy as she fussed over Lily and the girl. Her manner irritated Lily, the constant chatter jangling her own frayed nerves. What had the police found at the overturned car? Was the woman alive or dead? She wished Ted would return and tell her what they'd found. She wanted to get the girl home and into bed.

She stared down at the angelic face lying in her lap. The girl had curled her legs up on the sofa and fallen asleep. The doctor had given her a sedative before he left. Lily's heart went out to her. She was so lovely, her face sweet and innocent. Yet she had clearly been disturbed by the detective's presence. Why? What was her background? Only kids whose parents had something to hide were nervous of the law. Not that nowadays Lily welcomed any policeman turning up on her doorstep.

There were too many gifts that Ted acquired for her which did not bear too close investigation as to their origin.

Not that Ted did anything that bad, she justified his dishonesty. She would never hear a word said against her husband. He was just looking after his own, as any man would given the opportunity. The works van came in handy to help a mate move any stuff that had fallen off the back of the lorry, so to speak. Her dad had benefited on several occasions with dresses and coats being sold on his stall; the labels picked out by Lily and sold as second-hand. Clothing coupons never stretched far enough for any family. No one got hurt. No one suffered or so Ted justified his involvement. The clothes warehouses done over were insured.

Lily saw no wrong in what Ted was doing. But she worried that Ted could get caught. Her husband got paid good money for the use of the van and her dad made a nice profit even though he sold the clothes at a fraction of their value. When they first married she'd been able to furnish their home with good quality furniture where no questions were asked of the seller. She touched a heavy gold chain at her neck. She had a box full of gold jewellery of which she was proud. Ted could never have afforded to buy such expensive presents for her on the legitimate market.

A few vicious tongues would condemn Ted for making money on the black market. But hadn't he done his bit for his country? He'd been wounded at Dunkirk and he was never free of pain. Not that he complained. Ted was a good man. He treated her right. She knew that he didn't play around as she accused him. Loving him so much could make her crazy with jealousy. Ted was the best. That was why she was so scared of losing him. He was careful with his money. He didn't blow it all on booze down the pub every night like most of the men where they lived. He'd put a good bit by and soon they'd be buying a place of their own. That was Lily's dream: to own her own house and fill it with children.

Lily blinked aside the hot sting of threatening tears. Why had she failed Ted? There was no apparent reason she couldn't have kids. God knows they tried hard enough. She couldn't wish for a more passionate man. Hardly a night went by when Ted didn't make love to her. Even his wounds hadn't stopped him when he came out of hospital. He was a randy devil and she loved him for it. From the moment she had set eyes on him, she'd fallen for him. And so had every other young woman in the East End it seemed. But Lily knew what made a man like Ted Carrington tick. They liked to be seen with a beautiful, classy woman on their arm. And she fitted the part. She'd had dozens of boyfriends since the age of thirteen, when she'd lost her virginity to a fairground gypsy over Victoria Park one Whitsun. Ted hadn't stood a chance once she decided that he was the man for her.

After her miscarriages she lost her confidence in herself as a woman. That's when she began to doubt him. Too many women gave Ted the eye. He drew them like a magnet.

She bit her lip as she stroked the silvery-blonde curls spilling on to her lap. Every now and then the girl twitched or a shudder passed through her frail body. The sight tore at her heart. This was the girl she'd always dreamed that she and Ted would have. The earlier need to help and protect the child swelled in her breast. Her mind raced ahead. What if the girl had no relatives?

Excitement pounded through her veins. Shona – that was how she was beginning to think of the girl. It was the name she had picked out for her first daughter. Shona would be safe with them and be cared for. She and Ted would be a proper family with Shona living with them. It wasn't like adopting. It was fate. What else but fate had made her and Ted stop on the road at that precise spot and time? Shona had been given to them tonight.

She closed her eyes, picturing how it could be. Her obsession for a child, which would make everything right within her marriage, blocked rational thought. Ted wouldn't look at other women. Ted would never leave her if they had a daughter he loved.

Chapter Three

When the engine had failed to restart after the crash Grace's father felt his panic swell. He cursed the day he'd ever got involved with the Big Man.

There were only minutes to get away before they were found. He'd given his pursuers the slip, but it wouldn't take them long to realise he'd taken the farm track.

He hadn't been hurt in the crash, just shaken. Grace had been asleep on the back seat and the impact had thrown her on to the floor and she was crying. When he glanced at Amy he saw she was unconscious. There was blood streaming from a wound in her head where she had banged it on the side of the door when they hit the tree.

In the distance he could hear a car drawing closer. He tried the engine again. It spluttered and failed. There was no time to inspect the damage. They had to get away. The fog would cloak them.

Sweating with fear, he lifted Grace out of the car. 'Hush, kitten. It's all right. Don't be frightened. Daddy's here. You mustn't make a sound.'

She stopped crying but her expression was dazed from the shock of the impact. He led her to another tree placing her out of sight of both the track and the road. 'Stay there. I've got to get Mummy out of the car. She's hurt. Then I want us to hide in the trees.'

He ran back to help Amy. Her door was jammed against the tree and the side of the car was pushed in. The sight of the blood welling from her head wound was alarming. When he tried to pull her free he discovered her legs were trapped between the door and the overnight case on the floor. He couldn't move her. Then he heard the harsh revving of a car. His pursuers had turned back. He panicked. They were after him, not Amy. They'd kill him for what he'd found out.

Fear pumped through him. The screech of tyres told him his pursuers had turned into the farm track. Amy moaned softly. He had no time to help her. If he was caught, they'd kill him. He knew too much.

He backed away from the car. They wouldn't hurt Amy. She knew nothing. She'd be safe. He'd get away and phone for an ambulance. Thank God for the shielding fog!

When the car on the track screeched to a halt, he hurried away. He couldn't stay. He must hide. Dear God, don't let them harm Amy. At least Grace was safe.

He spun round and went to grab his daughter to run with her to safety. His heart plummeted. She wasn't by the tree. His desperate gaze searched the grey enshrouded landscape. He could see nothing. There were angry shouts from the farm track. Any second now he would be spotted. He fled further into the concealing fog.

As he crossed the field, his thoughts matched the wild pounding of his heartbeat. It wouldn't be the first time those henchmen had killed to hush up the scandal which could bring a corrupt politician down. The other had been a tuppenny ha'penny pimp who had tried to blackmail the Big Man after one of his girls got roughed up at a wild party.

He prayed that Grace would be all right and stay hidden until the Big Man and his thugs left. If only it wasn't so foggy. His little girl would be frightened. Once the men had gone he'd find her and after getting Amy out of the car they'd all go somewhere safe. How could he have been so greedy and ambitious to put his loved ones in danger?

He ran his long fingers through his pale gold hair and cursed himself for a fool. When he'd first been elected to Parliament he'd had such grand ideals. When had he lost sight of them?

Gunshots from the direction of the car brought him to his knees as though the bullets had entered his own body. Agony engulfed his heart. The bastards had shot Amy!

'That's a lesson to you, old chap.' The Big Man's cultured voice rasped with menace. 'We know you're out there. And this is just for starters. We'll get you. You can't escape us. You're a dead man.'

'Kill me and my solicitor will be handing over some very condemning facts to the Prime Minister,' he shouted back. 'It doesn't have to be like this. We're friends, aren't we?'

The Big Man laughed. 'You're bluffing. I don't like threats.'

'It's no bluff. You can't take any risks. It will be the end of your career. Do you think I'm going to jeopardise all I've worked for?'

He moved stealthily away from the sound of searching. Over the hammering of his heart, he prayed for Grace to be spared. Dear God, she's innocent. Don't let them find Grace. His mind raced to find a solution. No one had got the better of him yet.

He took his handsome looks for granted. He was tall and well built and his self-confidence was limitless. His prowess at rugby and cricket had made him the most popular boy at school. With little effort he sailed through his exams with top marks. Both his parents were dead by the time he was twenty and he was shocked to find that there was no money. The family home had to be sold to pay death duties and debts. He was a born chancer; his popularity meant he was offered the spare room in wealthy friends' flats and enjoyed their hospitality to the full. Older married women were generous and grateful for his attentions: Savile Row suits and cars were his rewards.

Then he met Amy and fell in love with her. She was a ballet dancer and married to a musician who was a heroin addict.

When she injured her back and could no longer dance her husband began to beat her. That's when they took a house and Amy moved in, ostensibly as his housekeeper to avoid gossip. Amy's husband refused to divorce her and resorted to blackmail to stop their affair appearing in the papers.

He had been flattered when the Big Man had taken an interest in him after his maiden speech in the House of Commons. Within months he was a member of this politician's inner circle and in the following two years they became close friends. The Big Man trusted him and put a few lucrative deals and investments his way. But the Big Man did nothing out of kindness. He had lured him into his web and then he expected the price to be paid for past favours done. He had been up to his eyes in corruption and taking backhanders before he realised how deeply he'd become involved. It had been impossible to extricate himself unless he gave up his career in politics. He wasn't prepared to do that.

Finally the sounds of the search faded. The Big Man's voice rose harsh and threatening. 'We'll get you. Wherever you go, we'll get you.'

He heard the car reverse down the track and roar off into the distance. Shakily, he got to his feet. They hadn't found Grace. Where was she? Now he cursed the fog which made it impossible to see more than a few yards. He shouted her name several times but she didn't appear. He was in torment. His fear was growing at what had happened to Amy. Were the shots bluffs or had they killed her?

He stumbled towards the car still calling out his daughter's name. He had to know what had happened to Amy. As he retraced his steps to the car, he heard another vehicle on the road. From the voices drifting through the fog he realised that a man and a woman had found Grace. Then before he could call out he could hear them running across the field towards him. If they found the car with Amy inside complicated questions would arise. He daren't face the police.

Fear iced his body as he stayed hidden but he was able to hear the couple's conversation. They were going to get help for Amy and seemed unsure whether she was dead or alive.

He heard the couple taking Grace back to their vehicle. He was torn by love for his daughter, his worry for Amy and the need to keep his identity secret. If this hit the papers all hell would break loose and there would be no way he could salvage his career. In the meantime if Grace was with him she could still be in danger from the Big Man. He edged forwards and saw that they were in a van. He could just make out the name of an engineering company on the side. He could track the couple down through the company. Grace wasn't lost to him. He'd find her again.

The van engine started up and the couple drove off. Guilt and love made him stagger forwards. That was his daughter in there. He couldn't let her go. Yet he couldn't call out. He needed to know that she was safe, then he could plan his action against the Big Man. The sound of the van faded. Fate had dealt its hand. He must take it.

He ran back to check on Amy. He had to know whether she was alive or dead. He braced himself to expect the worst when he returned to the car. Blood was everywhere. It ran from her head and it spread in a pool over her coat. She had been shot through the heart.

He sat back on his heels and sank his head into his hands. If Amy's body was found in the car it would have serious repercussions for himself as well as the Big Man. If he was to survive with his reputation intact the police had to be kept out of it. Amy deserved a decent burial. He knew a doctor and undertaker who, for a price, would sign the death certificate and bury her without informing the police. There would be a quiet service in a country church. At least there'd be no awkward questions from her dead husband.

He got out the starting handle and cranked the car engine. This time it started. The buckled front wing was rubbing on the wheel. He took a wrench from the tool box in the boot and knocked it away from the wheel and drove away. He needed to be far away before the police, summoned by the couple, arrived on the scene.

Grief racked him. He had loved Amy so much. She deserved better from him than a secret funeral but what choice did he have? He stared in the direction the couple had driven off with his daughter and made an impassioned vow. 'I know I've let you down, kitten. I'm sorry. Your daddy will always love you. One day I hope you can forgive me. And I will come back. I promise, one day I'll find you again.'

PART TWO

1947

There's a divinity which shapes our ends,
Rough-hew them how we will.

Shakespeare

Chapter Four

The March evening in the rush hour was bitterly cold and Shona pushed her hands deeper into her coat pocket. It had been a freezing winter, culminating in heavy snowstorms in February and fuel shortages which resulted in extensive power cuts.

When a police car, with its bell ringing in high-pitched warning, sped down Walthamstow High Street, Shona jumped back on to the kerb.

'Someone's in a hurry for their tea-break,' she said with a grin.

'So is his mate,' observed Marion Lockyer. A second police car screamed past with its bell jangling. 'Regular cops' tea-party by the looks of it. There's no need to deafen us though.' She rubbed her ears and shook her short chestnut curls. 'So what are we doing Saturday to celebrate getting our first wage packet as secretaries? Have you persuaded your dad to let you go to the dance at Stratford Town Hall?'

'Mum wants me to babysit the twins so she can go down the pub with Dad.'

'That's not fair,' Marion groaned. 'Can't someone else babysit? We're sixteen and bringing in a wage now. Can't your grandad do it?'

'His darts team are playing a Tottenham pub. He likes to get back to Tottenham and see his old mates. He misses them since Gran died and he moved here to stay with us.'

Marion pouted. 'Lily puts too much on you. She's down the pub most nights and only lets you out twice a week.'

Shona felt guilty that Marion would have to suffer because of Lily's selfishness. Since the family moved to Walthamstow five years ago Marion had become her best friend. They lived next door to each other and had both decided to train at secretarial college, although Shona's ambition was to use her shorthand and typing skills to become a journalist. There had been no openings in journalism when she left college. As a temporary measure she had taken a job in the same typing pool as Marion for an insurance brokers near the Bank of England in Threadneedle Street.

'I'm sorry, Marion. I hate to spoil your fun. But you can go with the other girls.'

'It's not the same if you're not there.'

Shona didn't answer. She didn't want to be disloyal to Lily but she hated letting her friend down. There was no way Lily would give up her Saturday night down the pub. Ted would be down there with his mates and their wives and she would insist on accompanying him. Or rather watching over him. Lily's false airs and graces hadn't endeared her to their new neighbours since they had bought the Victorian terraced house.

Why did Lily have to make life so difficult for everyone? She was so possessive, although since giving birth to identical twins three years ago she was no longer obsessive with Shona. Quite the opposite nowadays. Lily seemed to loathe her presence. She regarded Shona as an intruder now that she had children of her own.

Lily had no friends. Even Marion's mother, who was a warm-hearted woman, had little time for Lily who had a vicious tongue when it came to gossip. Ted, however, was liked by everyone. Shona experienced that special glow which any thoughts of her adoptive father always aroused. She adored him. Ted was always ready with a joke to make people smile, generous to a fault and would do anyone a favour. Most of those favours involved getting anything they needed on the black market. And with rationing still on food and clothing, he was the most popular man in the district.

In recent years Lily had become jealous of Ted going out alone. She was insecure and again obsessive in their relationship. Even her love for the twins paled against her fear of losing Ted. It was absurd. Lily was convinced that any attractive woman was after Ted. He wasn't interested in other women, he idolised his wife. Yet if Ted went down the pub Lily insisted on accompanying him. She watched the women like a hawk and God help any who tried to flirt with her husband. They would feel the rough edge of her tongue and so would Ted for the rest of the week. Jealousy turned her into a shrew.

'Shona, can't you get round your dad?' Marion cut through her thoughts. 'He worships you. He let you go out the other Saturday.'

'And Mum didn't let him hear the last of it. They had an awful row and he stormed off to see his mates. He wasn't at the local pub when Lily went looking for him. When he came back she wouldn't speak to him all week. It was horrible. Dad was so miserable. He loves Mum.'

'Why does she have to spoil everyone's fun?'

'You know what the twins are like. They can be devils. They play any babysitter up if it's not me.'

Marion kicked a stone against the wall. 'Your mum is using you. I don't know why you put up with her. She's getting a reputation for being a right madam. We all know she grew up in the back streets of Tottenham and her dad's a market trader.'

'There's nothing wrong in Grandad running a market stall,' Shona defended. 'I enjoy helping him out on a Saturday. And I'm proud of the way Mum and Dad have bettered themselves and managed to buy their own home. It's not like you to be such a snob, Marion.'

'I'm not a snob.' Marion was indignant. 'Don't forget it was my gran's house the Carringtons bought when she died. My own dad's only a bus driver. It's Lily's manner which gets my goat. She thinks she's better than everyone else now. And she doesn't treat you right. She isn't even your mum. She can't keep you in if you want to go out.'

'She is my mum! The only mum I remember anyway. They went through a court battle with the authorities which lasted two years so they could adopt me.' She was fierce in her protest. If Ted and Lily hadn't adopted her she would have ended up in a children's home. No one had come forward with information about her past when the press ran her story after she was found. It had been gruelling to accept that her parents had abandoned her. Ted and Lily's love had eased the pain of rejection.

She frowned. Even so it wasn't easy to accept that she could remember nothing of her past. Even her name wasn't her own but one given to her by Lily. She wasn't even certain of her age though she had said she was nine when Lily found her and the tests she had done at school and with psychiatrists had confirmed that nine was likely her age. She could remember her age and all her schooling, but not where she had lived or anyone she had known. The doctors had said loss of memory induced by shock could often be selective. It somehow made it all the more disturbing.

'Even so, she's no right to be such a slave-driver.' Marion saw Shona's jaw clench and knew if she said any more about Lily they would end up quarrelling. Privately, Marion thought her friend's loyalty was misplaced. Lily was a lazy slut. Also, Marion reckoned that Lily was jealous of Shona.

She studied her friend as they walked and couldn't help a stab of envy herself. Shona was vivacious, sensitive and caring. There was also a rod of iron within her make-up which gave her resilience and courage. She would never abandon a friend, fail in her duty, or stand by and allow anyone to suffer if she could help them.

Marion wished she had half of Shona's poise and personality. Her shoulder-length silvery-blonde hair was unusual and drew men's attention. She wore it swept over to one side in the style of Veronica Lake and to Marion's mind, Shona rivalled the Hollywood filmstar for looks. Though not in the way of a superficial beauty. There was nothing shallow or doll-like about her friend. She was down-to-earth and practical. It was an inner beauty that shone forth and made her so attractive. It radiated from the curves of her high cheekbones and large almond-shaped eyes, in a way far more memorable than beauty alone could ever achieve. It was her eyes which captivated people. When Shona looked at you she encompassed you in her lively, intelligent gaze. She gave you her whole attention and made you feel cherished and special.

The unfair way Shona was treated by Lily upset Marion. Shona never said a word against her mother, yet it couldn't be easy having to put up with Lily's moods and tantrums. Despite being best friends Marion still found Shona a mystery. It was odd being friends with someone who had no memory of her first nine years. Shona's unknown past intrigued Marion.

'Isn't it weird not being able to remember anything about your life before the Carringtons found you?' her curiosity made her ask for the umpteenth time. 'Have you remembered anything yet?'

Shona frowned and shook her head. The doctors had said that her memory could return at any time, or it may never return. She'd stopped trying to make herself remember. All it produced was crippling headaches. Even the first months with the Carringtons were a blur. The shadows in her eyes deepened. At times she felt cast adrift without roots. Her last plea most nights before sleeping was for her memory to return. Sometimes during sleep the veil was less opaque:

shadows appeared of a man and a woman. From the man she felt an encompassing warmth and love. A faint echo called through a blanketing mist. '*Where are you, kitten? It's all right. Don't be frightened. Daddy loves you.*' That sustained her. Her father had not deliberately abandoned her. Something had stopped him coming to find her. It still stopped him. She didn't believe that he was dead. A different feeling came from the woman. There was no warmth – no love. The woman remained ethereal, remote, spectre-like. It was her daddy Shona craved to be reunited with. Intuition told her that her mother had not loved her. Then Shona would feel nausea, her body drenched in an icy sweat. She would begin to shake. Fear suffocated her. Her head would throb with a violence that blotted everything but the pain from her mind.

The familiar nausea now churned her stomach. Ruthlessly she blocked her memories and drew a shaky breath to combat the sensation of panic. Ted had told her that he believed her mother had been shot, but the police had discovered nothing and a body was never found. It had been a month after the accident before she spoke. The doctor said it was love and being made to feel safe and secure which brought a return of speech. Love she had been given in abundance by Ted and Lily. From Ted it was an instant bonding. Lily could be suffocating in her affection, smothering her with kisses, proudly parading her before their friends. Ted had not changed with the arrival of the twins. Shona knew she had a special place in his heart: she would always be his Barefoot Angel, as he often called her.

Her eyes darkened to sapphire as she stared into the distance, unaware of the press of people around them in the High Street. 'I shall never forget their kindness when I was found. Lily was different then. She used to shower me with presents and was always cuddling me. We did everything together. She wouldn't let me out of her sight. Sometimes I dream of a dark-haired woman and a blond man, but their figures are shadowy. If I try to recall them when I'm awake I get an overwhelming sense of panic. It scares me.'

'It's eerie.' Marion shuddered. 'I don't think I'd like not knowing what my real name is, or who I really was.'

An assured light blazed in Shona's eyes. 'I know who I am. I'm me. And I know where I'm going in life. I know it's frowned on if a woman wants a career. But I'm going to make it to the top as a journalist. I'm lucky to have Ted Carrington as my dad. He couldn't love me more if I had been his own daughter. I adore him. And I'm proud to be Shona Carrington. A name isn't who you are. You are how you think and behave and treat others.'

'Gawd, you've lost me on that one.' Marion often wondered where Shona got such an insight into life. She was always so perceptive. 'But I can see what you're getting at. Even so, your real name is part of you. It's your heritage. You could be the daughter of a prince and not know it.'

'That's for fairy stories.' Shona voiced her scorn and watched two young girls playing hopscotch on the pavement. Her voice was strained when she continued, 'They were more likely up to no good. Why else did they abandon me? Sometimes I want to remember so much . . . at others I feel so cold and frightened I think it's best not to know. Dad is convinced that someone tried to murder my parents that day.'

Marion stared at her friend, her expression incredulous. 'You never told me that before. Wow, you could be the daughter of a famous gangster or something.'

'Thanks, Marion.'

'Some of them are heroes in the East End.'

'Forget the Robin Hood image. Ducking and diving is a way of life for many. My dad included. I know he would never hurt anyone, but, according to Grandad, too many go on to hard crime and think nothing of ruling by terror and violence.'

Marion remained persistent. 'Surely you have some idea

43

who your parents could be. Didn't Ted tell you they drove a flash car? They must have had money.'

Shona pressed a hand to her stomach which had started to feel queasy. 'If Dad is right about the attempted murder of my parents, then I want to know what happened. I want to see justice done and their assailants brought to trial.'

'Is that why you want to become a reporter?'

Shona shrugged. 'Not knowing my past makes me fascinated by other people's and also why they act as they do. Eventually I'd like to be an investigative journalist.'

'And there's you always complaining that Mrs Brown at number forty-six is such a nosy-parker peering out the window from behind her curtains.'

Shona laughed and struck her friend playfully on the arm as they turned into their avenue. 'It's not the same thing at all.' Her attention was caught by the sight of the two police cars parked halfway down their road. A stab of unease pierced her.

'Blimey, aren't the cops outside our houses?' Marion said. 'Don't say some kids have broken in to steal the money from the gas meter. That will be the third break-in down our street this month.'

Shona didn't answer. Her heart was pounding in alarm at seeing the two black police cars outside her house. She offered up a hasty prayer, 'Don't let them be for Dad.'

She knew all about his late nights using the works van. Two days ago he'd come back with a wad of white fivers in his pocket and tossed gold bracelets into both hers and Lily's lap. Lily had seized on hers laughing with pleasure. Shona had forced a smile as she kissed Ted's cheek.

'Don't you like it, angel?' Ted said looking crestfallen. 'I got them off Terry. Not bad for three quid and a carton of tinned ham.'

'It's beautiful, Dad. But I wish you wouldn't get involved

44

with stolen stuff. What if you get caught? They'd put you in prison. I don't want you shut away, Dad. I don't want to lose you.'

'No one is going to put Ted in prison,' Lily answered and put her arms possessively around her husband. 'He's too clever for any copper.'

Ted disengaged himself from Lily's grasp and kissed Shona's cheek. 'You ain't never going to lose me, angel. Your old dad won't get caught.'

She wasn't so confident and it made her hold him tight. 'I still wish you wouldn't do it. You've a good job. We can live without the extras.'

'Speak for yourself,' Lily snorted. She scowled at Shona. 'Ain't the life we've given you good enough? The little extras paid for you to go to your fancy secretarial college. I told Ted there weren't nothing wrong with you working in the shirt factory same as I did. But he wouldn't hear of it. So don't you go sneering at what your dad does for you.'

Shona kissed Ted's cheek, her stare brimming with love as she gazed up at his face. 'I'm not sneering. I can't help worrying about him. His freedom is more precious to me than any trinket, no matter how valuable it is.'

Ted laughed and wrapped his arms around Shona. 'You're a good kid. You're something special. Real special.'

From behind Ted's back Lily glared at Shona with unconcealed loathing. Shona hid her pain. Why was Lily so jealous of the love Ted gave her? Wasn't it Lily who had been so insistent that they adopt her?

'Shona, I can hear Johnnie crying,' Lily snapped. 'Go and calm him down.'

Shona went upstairs to the double room the twins shared. This had once been her room, but as soon as the twins were old enough for a room of their own, Lily had moved Shona's things into the cramped box room. It hadn't bothered Shona, for it made sense that the boisterous boys needed more space.

Yet Lily's gloating when she informed her proved that she had done it out of spite.

Shona took the small dark-haired twin, who was so like his father, into her arms and quietened his tears. She had the impression that Lily's coldness as a mother towards her was an echo of her forgotten past. There was something about the atmosphere when Lily watched Ted fuss over Shona which permeated the edges of her memory. It wasn't recollection but more of a certainty that her mother had been indifferent and that it was her father who had loved her. But he had gone out of her life. Whether dead or alive he had left her. She couldn't bear for the same thing to happen with Ted. Her greatest dread was that Ted would one day go to prison.

Now as she neared her house with the police cars outside, her alarm increased. Their front door was open and several neighbours were twitching at their curtains or standing by their gates. The raised voice of Lily shouting abuse fuelled Shona's fears.

'Bastards, you can't come in here ransacking my home. We ain't got nothing hidden. My Ted is innocent.'

'See you later, Marion,' Shona said as she hurried into her house. A policewoman was in the hallway and a policeman was holding Lily's arms to stop her hurling herself at a sergeant.

Lily was screaming, her face red and twisted with rage. 'We ain't done nothing wrong. You won't find nothing here. That's private stuff in that bureau. You've no right poking through it.' She let out a wail. 'Look at the mess you're making. You're wrecking my lovely home.'

Shona could hear heavy footsteps upstairs and the sound of furniture being moved. Surely Dad hadn't been so foolish as to bring any stolen goods into the house. Her heart clenched with fear. He didn't need to store stuff here. The police only had to look in Lily's jewel box. There was also the fur stole in her wardrobe which Ted had given her for her birthday last month. That must have been stolen, for it was too expensive for him to afford to buy.

The policewoman, who was tall and heavily built, turned at the sound of her approach.

Shona demanded, 'What's happening here?'

'We've a warrant to search the place for stolen goods, miss.' Her voice was gruff and unemotional. 'You'd save us all a lot of time if you told us where anything is hidden.'

'We're not thieves,' Shona answered with cool dignity. She had to stay calm. Lily's hysterics were only antagonising the police. In the kitchen Shona heard the twins crying. Someone had to soothe them and it clearly wouldn't be Lily.

As she passed her mother, she said softly, 'Mum, you're upsetting the boys with your screaming.'

'It's these bastards doing the upsetting, coming into an innocent man's home and wrecking the place.'

'Calm down, Mum.'

'Calm down?' Lily yelled. 'They've arrested your dad. Say there were black market goods in the works van. Someone must have put them there without Ted knowing. Ted's straight as a die. Never stole a thing in his life.'

The police sergeant emerged from the front room and paused to look Shona up and down before turning to Lily. He looked at them as though they were scum. Shona's cheeks burned with embarrassment. Lily was making it worse by her attitude. She was overdoing the outraged innocence. The arrogance in the sergeant's manner made Shona's anger flare but she strove to master it. For Ted's sake they must be calm.

'My mother is upset, sergeant. It must be the shock of learning her husband is suspected of some crime.'

'Don't get smart with me, miss.' He rounded on Shona.

'That was not my intent, sergeant. My father is Works Manager. Are you sure there has been no mistake?'

His thin lips compressed with censure. 'We've had our eye

on Carrington for some time. And others like him. There's road blocks all over London to put an end to this black marketeering. He'll be one of many going down for some considerable time. Decent folks abide by the rationing. Men like your father are scum profiting . . .'

'My father is a decent man,' Shona defended heatedly. 'Ask anyone. Everyone likes him.'

Fear turned her insides to a searing, bubbling cauldron. The twins' cries were getting louder and Lily made no move to soothe them. She couldn't think with them screaming and Lily continuing to shout Ted's innocence. At the kitchen door another policeman barred her way. 'You can't go in there, miss, until it has been searched.'

Shona glared at him. 'I'm going to quieten the twins. They're frightened. That's not your job is it, frightening three-year-olds? You can watch me. I'll take the boys into the garden so they can play with their cars.'

The constable glanced at the sergeant who nodded. 'Anything to shut the brats up. They're giving me a headache.'

Lily sprang at him, her hands raised to strike him. 'Don't you touch my kids.'

Her hand was caught and as the sleeve of her cardigan slid back, the sergeant grinned in satisfaction. 'That bracelet is one of several stolen from a jewellers last week.'

Lily snapped her hand over the bracelet. 'This weren't stolen. I've had it years. My father bought it for me when I was twenty-one.'

Shona silently willed her mother to shut up. She'd have the coppers going over Grandad's stall next and she knew that last Saturday he'd had over a dozen dresses and coats which Ted had got for him.

A policeman thudded down the stairs holding the fur stole and the open jewellery box. The sergeant barked out in triumph, 'Twenty of those stoles were taken from a shop in Golders Green. Bring it and the jewellery to the station for evidence.' He spun on his heel and marched out the door, the constables following him. 'Looks like we've cracked that case as well. Scum, that's what these black marketeers are. Lining their pockets whilst decent folk go without.'

'Dad didn't steal the furs. He bought it off a mate.' Shona paled. She knew that was true as she'd heard Ted telling Lily. But it was still receiving stolen goods and a punishable offence. The policeman sounded as if he wanted Ted locked up for good. He made her dad sound evil. He didn't steal. He just had contacts in the docks who could get their hands on tinned ham, or other necessities hit by the rationing. He hadn't made a fortune, not like the real spivs.

Shona didn't dispute that the fur stole was stolen. In the East End someone always knew someone who had a bargain to sell and no questions asked.

She put out a hand to the policeman who had been standing by the kitchen door. 'What will happen to Dad now?'

'He'll be charged and held in custody to await his trial unless you can raise the bail money.'

'Grandad will help us out.' She wished he was here now but it would be another hour before he packed up his stall for the night and came home. Since Gran had been killed by a direct hit from a doodlebug on their home, whilst her husband was working the market, Grandad had lived with them.

Lily burst into tears and sat on the foot of the stairs. It was unlike her to so neglect her sons, she must be really worried about Ted. The twins had now worked themselves up into a screaming fit after being left for so long unattended. Shona ran into the kitchen to calm them. They were hungry having missed their tea when the police arrived. As Shona prepared their food she heard Lily sobbing loudly from her bedroom. She shook her head, her own heart heavy. Tears were self-indulgent. They wouldn't help Dad. And it was obvious that Dad needed all the support his family could give him.

At sight of Shona the twins ran to her and wrapped their arms around her legs. Irrepressible as naughty kittens, they had managed to wreck the kitchen. They had pulled the tablecloth on to the floor breaking the dishes placed on the table for their tea. Johnnie's face was smeared with the last precious rations of butter and James had cut his hand.

She sat down on a chair with a twin on each knee and cuddled them until their cries stopped. Pacified, they squirmed to be free and play outside in the garden.

'First I must get Jamie's hand cleaned and then I'll tackle the kitchen. I can't let Mum see this mess. You keep quiet, or you'll upset her with your noise.'

Not that Lily would blame the twins. It would be Shona she raved at if they got out of control. 'Let's get you two sorted and this mess cleaned up. Hopefully there's something in the larder for your tea apart from dry bread and pullit.'

She waved a finger at the two dark-haired boys. They yelled excitedly and ran outside to play with their toy cars. Sticky fingermarks were wiped from the otherwise immaculate cupboards and the floor washed. Shona found some dripping to scrape on the bread for the boys' tea and they were called to the table with a warning not to make a mess. She took a cup of tea up to her mother who had finally fallen quiet.

Lily was sprawled across the bed, snoring. She hadn't even removed the blue silk, ruched eiderdown which was always carefully folded and laid aside before she went to bed. There was a half-empty sherry bottle on the bedside table which had been unopened in the sideboard last night. Lily was drunk.

The twins were shouting and fighting over a toy in the kitchen when there was a knock on the front door. Shona opened it and stiffened at seeing the plump figure of Mrs Brown on the doorstep. There were two metal kirby grips in the front of her brassy hair, the rest of which was hidden under a green and orange paisley scarf tied on top of her head. A lighted cigarette was dangling from her lips which she didn't bother to remove when she spoke.

'Just called to see if everything was all right, dearie.' Mrs Brown craned her head to see into the house. 'Dad home is he? Must have given you all a nasty turn having the police turn up like that? Lily took quite a turn didn't she?'

Mrs Brown wasn't interested in their welfare. She was itching to know what the police had wanted. Shona regarded her coldly. She knew that soon enough the whole street would know that Ted had been arrested, but she wasn't letting this gossipmonger have any information.

She plastered on a smile. 'Dad never gets home before six thirty. Mum got upset that so many police turned up just to investigate the gas meter being broken into. It's the third down this street recently. They messed up her polished lino.'

'I heard her screaming her Ted was innocent.' Mrs Brown's fleshy face was intense, her puffy eyes through the smoke of her cigarette as merciless as a vulture gleaning a carcass. 'We all know that father of yours gets up to no good.'

'You didn't complain when he got you a sack of coal when your Freddie was sick with influenza last winter and fuel was scarce.' A wail from Jamie gave her the excuse she needed to get away. 'That's Jamie hurt himself. Goodbye, Mrs Brown.'

She shut the door firmly in the woman's face before she lost her temper with her. Jamie had banged his head and needed consoling. Then Johnnie, feeling left out, began to grizzle to get attention. Shona's nerves were frayed when ten minutes later there was another knock on the door.

To her relief it was Marion. 'I saw Battle-axe Brown leaving. Sticking her nose where it wasn't wanted, was she?'

Shona nodded. 'I dare say everyone's talking about it.'

'I'm sorry, Shona. We could hear every word Lily was screaming at the coppers. Have they arrested your dad?'

She told Marion what had happened, knowing that even if she told her mother, Mrs Lockyer wouldn't repeat it.

'I'm sorry, kiddo. That's rough. It don't look good for Ted, does it?'

'It wouldn't be so bad if he hadn't got that jewellery and fur stole for Mum. They'll do him for receiving stolen goods as well as selling food on the black market.'

'Yeah, but he was never into that in a big way, not like some. It was just eggs and poultry he got from that farmer in Wanstead.'

'He used to get things from his mates in the docks and sell them on. It could be serious, Marion. We're not talking about an odd pound of bacon or half a dozen eggs. The van was often full of tinned stuff. He could go to prison for a long time.'

Chapter Five

Bad news travels fast. Twenty minutes after the police drove away from the Carrington house Percy Dawkins learned of his son-in-law's arrest. Shona would be out of her mind with worry and his daughter Lil would very likely be hysterical. He'd had a nagging feeling since lunchtime that something like this might happen. He'd heard whilst having his lunchtime pint that Dickie Bird and his brother Harry had been nicked over Barking way with a vanload of spirits and fags. It was rumoured that there were police roadblocks round the outskirts of London in an attempt to put a stop to the sale of goods on the black market. There'd also been a check on all the market stalls by a dozen or more coppers that morning. Thankfully he'd sold the last of his dodgy dresses and coats yesterday.

He packed up his stall early, piling the garments on his handcart to wheel it back home. He left the cart in the hall and walked in the kitchen to find a twin sitting on the draining board while Shona washed his legs. He could never tell which was which. One look at Shona's strained face confirmed his fears.

'I heard Ted has been arrested, is that right?'

To his consternation Shona burst into tears.

Percy hovered awkwardly. He loved Shona, but he wasn't a man who could handle a woman's tears and was embarrassed by any show of emotion. He had to tilt his head to look up at her now as she was several inches taller than his short stature.

He coughed and pulled some boiled sweets out of his pocket and gave them to the boys to keep them quiet. 'Let's get the nippers to bed. Then we'll talk. Where's Lil?'

'Upstairs asleep.'

'Drunk I suppose. Or she'd be screaming the house down with hysterics. Gets her tantrums from her nan who worked the music halls. Filthy temper my old ma had and like Lil drank more than was good for her. It killed her in the end.'

Percy picked up the twins and carried them upstairs. 'I'll see to these. You look done in.'

Shona didn't want to stop and think. She was worried how Ted was coping in a police cell. She hated to think of him shut away. To stave off her bleak thoughts she peeled some carrots and potatoes to go in the remains of the rabbit stew they'd had yesterday.

Unable to eat a mouthful herself, she related all she knew to Percy while he ate. His ruddy, weather-wrinkled face had lost its healthy hue since he'd come back from his stall. He was a short, stout man with white hair and a close-cropped beard. When she first met him he had reminded her of Santa Claus. He had the same merry disposition which had disappeared now as anger darkened his eyes while he ate. He was a man of few words and Shona knew he was considering all the implications of Ted's arrest before speaking.

'It don't look good, I'm afraid. Lil was always too fond of flashing her jewellery.' He ran his calloused hand through his thatch of white hair. 'Silly bitch. I've told her time and again not to be so greedy. She's always on at Ted to get her something special. Like a fool he can't deny her nothing. Looks like he's done for now.'

'Don't say that, Grandad.' Shona wiped tears from her cheeks. 'I can't bear the thought of him going to prison. I know he did wrong. But he never hurt anyone. Dad wouldn't harm a fly. The policeman said something about bail so he won't have to remain in custody until the trial. Has Dad got any savings Mum can draw out?'

'I'll get it sorted. I've got a bit put by for a rainy day. Yer dad will be home tonight, don't you worry.'

'How? The banks are shut.'

'I don't trust no bank. My old mattress is the only bank I need.'

The large blue eyes studying Percy across the table were misty with pain. 'He'll go to prison though, won't he?'

There was no point lying to Shona, she was too astute for that. He sighed and nodded. 'Your dad was caught red-handed with the stuff. And we know he's guilty, don't we? Ted took his chances as I've taken mine. Happen I won't have no more dodgy stuff on the stall. I'm too old to go inside.'

'How long will he get?'

'Depends what he had in the van. And it's the first time he's been caught. They may go easy on him. I don't reckon he'll get more than eighteen months. With remission for good behaviour, he'll be out in less than a year.'

At her stricken expression, he patted her hand. 'Don't think bad of him. Ted's a good bloke.'

'I could never think ill of Dad,' she said with passion.

Percy nodded. 'You're a good kid. Lil will take it hard. Losing Ted for months will be bad enough, but she'll have her stuck-up nose put out of joint when it hits the papers.'

'Just let me hear anyone putting him down.' Shona's eyes flashed with ire. 'There's a few down this road who've been grateful for what Dad could get them.'

'That's it,' Percy encouraged. 'Keep your chin up and to hell with the gossipmongers.' He smiled but his eyes remained sombre. 'If Ted does time, Lil's gonna need you. Ted is her life. She won't be able to cope without him.'

Shona dropped her head into her hands. Lily had shown today how easily she could go to pieces. Shona knew she mustn't give in to despair, although her life again felt it had fragmented into pieces. She would be strong for Ted's peace of mind.

To stop herself worrying about Ted and how his arrest would affect their future, Shona kept herself busy. Lily had briefly woken after Grandad left for the police station and stumbled downstairs to use the outside toilet. She reeled drunkenly, forced to cling to the wall for support, and now there was vomit down the front of her dress. Shona put out a hand to steady her which was roughly shaken off.

'Get away from me! I can manage. I don't want your bloody help. Bloody cuckoo in our nest, you are.' She staggered through the back door and Shona heard her being sick again.

Lily's words had stung her. They voiced the resentment Lily had been showing towards her recently. Yet she had done nothing to earn her hatred. She was happy to help in the house and babysit the twins. It showed her gratitude for all the Carringtons had done for her by giving her a loving home. Only it wasn't so loving any more as far as Lily was concerned.

It hadn't always been like that. The first years she had lived with Ted and Lily, Lily had doted on her, dressing her in expensive frilly dresses which were impractical and Shona hated. Her hair was wound every night in rags so that during the day flaxen ringlets fell to her waist. Most of the children had been evacuated in the blitz. Lily had taken Shona to Wales. There Lily had missed Ted and, refusing to be parted from Shona, had brought her back to London.

Throughout the war in a London repeatedly bombed and lacking most of its children, Lily had employed a retired chorus-girl to teach Shona to dance. Then whenever they had company, Shona had to put on her tap or ballet shoes and perform. She had hated it. She also hated her silly girly hair and dresses, but out of love for Lily she did everything she could to please her. The dancing lessons had stopped when Lily became pregnant with the twins. Shona's hair had been cut off to a manageable shoulder length and never touched by Lily again. By the time the twins were born, Lily rarely had a kind word to say to her adopted daughter. All her obsessive love was now turned on her own children.

Ted however had never faltered in his love for her and Shona couldn't love him more if he was her own father.

She was jerked from her reflections upon entering the passage leading to the front room. The rancid stench of vomit coming from upstairs made her gag. If Ted returned tonight as Grandad had promised, it would be a poor welcome to find that in his bedroom. Fetching a bowl of hot water, a towel and disinfectant, Shona went upstairs to clear it up. There was vomit on the silk eiderdown and on the brown linoleum and pink and beige carpet.

Her own stomach heaved as she worked. There was a crash from the kitchen and throwing the towel into the bowel Shona carried it downstairs. Lily was slumped on the floor where she must have tripped over the kitchen step. Shona helped her to a chair and Lily's head flopped down on to the table.

'Oh, my poor Ted. What am I gonna do without him?'

'Mum, Dad's coming back tonight.' Shona tried to comfort her. 'Grandad has gone to pay his bail. I've cleared up in your bedroom. Why don't I bring in the bath so you can freshen yourself up for when Dad returns?'

Lily scowled up at her. 'I don't want you fussing round me. They're gonna lock my Ted up. I can't go on without him.' She burst into tears.

Shona hid her irritation at her mother's self-pity. 'Then at least change your dress. You don't want Dad seeing you like this. It will be some weeks before he goes to trial. Don't you think it's going to be hard on him as well?'

Lily pushed herself up from the table, her voice slurred.

'Who do you think you are, Miss bloody Goody Twoshoes, telling me what to do?' She ran her hands over her dress front and frowned at the stickiness she encountered. 'I'm going up to change. Get that towel washed and the toilet cleaned.'

Behind Lily's back Shona did a German salute, saying under her breath, 'Heil, Mütter!' She was sick of Lily treating her like a skivvy but this wasn't the time to confront her.

Lily weaved to the kitchen door and Shona heard her trip twice on the stairs. Despite her annoyance Shona was concerned for Lily. Her world revolved around her husband. She could be the life and soul of a party or a raging termagant in her jealousy, but she was also self-centred, and given to drinking too much if she didn't get her own way. Yet Lily's plight was slight compared to what Ted may have to face in the coming year.

Why couldn't Lily be more supportive? Her greed had got Dad into this mess. Whatever Dad did was never enough for her. She always insisted on the best clothes and furniture in her need to outdo everyone else in the street. She had even started complaining that they had no transport except the works van. It had been the start of several arguments that had come to a head last Sunday lunchtime.

'I want a car,' Lily had demanded as she put Ted's lunch of roast lamb in front of him. 'I want to drive down the road and hold my head up. It's so common being in a works van.'

Ted picked up the gravy jug and tipped some over his dinner without answering.

'Did you hear me, Ted?' Lily shrilled.

Shona came in with the twins' plates. Johnnie and Jamie, who had been pinching each other and mock fighting, stopped at the sound of their mother's angry voice. They shifted uneasily in their chairs and exchanged covert glances. They were frightened of Lily's angry outbursts.

Shona returned to the kitchen to bring in her own plate and her mother's. Lily was standing by her chair with her hands

58

on her hips and her scarlet lips compressed with anger. She knew that stance. It meant Lily was determined in having her own way. Shona glanced at Ted. He sipped at his half pint of pale ale.

'Lil, I've told you we can't afford a car this year. I've just bought you a washing machine because you didn't like the old copper. There's the bathroom to have built on as you hate having to bathe in a tin tub. That will cost me a packet. Not forgetting the week's holiday in the summer at Butlins in Bognor Regis you're insisting on this year. I ain't made of money.'

Lily pouted, her expression sour as sloes. 'You're just being mean, Ted Carrington. You could get the money for a car if you put your mind to it.'

'Whatever I do is never enough for you, is it, Lil?' Ted spoke sharply. He pushed aside his plate and stood up. 'I'm going down the pub to get some peace.'

'Don't you walk away from my dinner table!' Lily screamed. She picked up his lunch to hurl the plate after her husband. It hit Ted's shoulder and splattered on the floor. He swung round and glared at his wife and then down at his dinner. 'Get that cleaned up.' His voice was threaded with steel.

'Go to hell, I'm not your slave,' Lily returned. 'You're off down the pub because you fancy that bloody tart Daisy, the barmaid. I've seen how she gives you the come on. I'll show her what happens to any woman who tries to steal my man.'

'I go to the pub to get some peace. There's little of it here lately.'

Shona stooped to pick up the broken plate and pick the meat and vegetables from the carpet square.

'Leave it, Shona,' Ted rapped out. 'Lil will pick it up. She threw it.'

Lily lashed out at her husband. Ted caught her wrist and

his eyes were narrowed as he pushed her down so that she was kneeling on the floor. In a low scathing voice he warned, 'I'm weary of your tantrums and ingratitude. Be satisfied with what you've got.'

All at once the fight went out of Lily. She scrambled to pick up the pieces of broken crockery and congealing dinner. When she finished and had wiped up the carpet with a cloth, Ted nodded, then turned on his heel and walked out of the house.

Lily burst into tears and ran up to her bedroom to sob loudly. The tone of the Carringtons' quarrels had changed over the years. When Shona first came to live with them, Ted always pacified Lily. Gradually her tantrums became more violent and her accusations that he was unfaithful more absurd. That was when he had changed his tactics. He never raised a hand to her: that wasn't Dad's way, but he wouldn't give in to her rages. He walked out and spent the evening down the pub. Then during the next week or so he'd bring home whatever Lily had been demanding. Shona knew that Ted still adored his wife, but her jealousy was destroying them both.

On that Sunday Shona forced herself to eat her dinner and encouraged the twins to do the same. She had cleared the table, washed up and decided to take the boys over to the park. Lily would be in a foul mood all the time Ted was out of the house.

She returned to the living room and was surprised to see Lily standing in front of the mirror over the fireplace and applying her lipstick. She'd changed into her newest dress which flattened her plump figure and had redone her hair. In three-inch heels her legs were as shapely as a young woman's and there was no sign of any ravages to her lovely face caused by her tears. When she dolled herself up Lily could still look like a filmstar.

'Keep an eye on the boys,' she ordered. 'I'm off to the

pub. And God help your dad if that tart Daisy is playing up to him.'

'Mum, is that wise? You know Dad has never looked at another woman. He adores you.'

'That bitch Daisy is a marriage-breaker. She's a right tramp. She's got tits like bloody melons and she knows how to flaunt them. I'm not going to cause a scene.' Lily twisted her head from side to side studying her reflection in the mirror, then smoothed her hands over her plump hips. 'Your dad likes his women with a bit of meat on them. But a woman's a fool who lets her man go drinking after a quarrel. Especially with man-mad tramps like Daisy around who's only too ready to flatter his pride.'

She picked up a fox-fur stole and there was a determined set to her chin as she left the house.

Lily and Ted did not return until closing time and they were kissing and cuddling in the hallway. Shona had looked after the twins. After putting them to bed she asked Marion in for the evening and they had pored over Lily's fashion magazines and played Glenn Miller records.

Marion had giggled at hearing Ted and Lily. 'Right couple of love-birds your mum and dad. It's almost indecent at their age. Who'd have thought it after the way we heard them going at it hammer and tongs at lunchtime.'

Shona shook her head at the memory. Three times in the following week Ted was out at night in the works van. He was trying to get the money to buy Lily the car she wanted for the family. That's why he must have taken the risk today. He'd picked up some goods from the docks on his way to the suppliers.

The sound of a key in the lock took her into the hallway. Ted stood outlined by the street lamp, his shoulders slumped and his dark head bowed. His limp from the war was more pronounced as he came inside. Grandad was behind Ted, his expression grave.

'Want a cup of tea, Dad?'

His head shot up and his shoulders straightened. 'I thought you'd be in bed. I'd love a cup of tea. Where's Lil?'

'She's upstairs changing her frock.' Shona's voice fractured. 'I've been so worried about you, Dad.'

'You're a good kid. The best. Come here and give yer old dad a hug.'

Grandad moved past them. 'I'll put the kettle on.'

Shona was enfolded in Ted's arms. 'Why did you do it, Dad? Was it to get Mum the car she's been insisting on? We don't need a car.'

'I can't refuse Lily nothing,' he said with a sigh. 'I know I should be more firm, but when I see a way of getting her what she wants . . .' He shrugged fatalistically and looked up the stairs. His face broke into a smile as Lily hurried down to throw herself into his arms.

'Ted, I've been out of my mind with worry! What's going to happen to us?'

His shoulders drooped. 'It's a mess, Lil. I'll do time for this. If I plead guilty they reckon I'll get a lighter sentence. Even so, it could be a couple of years.'

'No!' Lily wailed. 'I'll go crazy without you.'

'You'll get by. You've got Percy and Shona's working now. We won't lose the house or any of you go hungry.'

Lily burst into weeping and Ted's eyes were bleak as he held her close against him.

Shona's heart ached. She could see the torment in Ted's face and was angry at Lily for making it so much harder for him. She forced a smile. 'I'll visit you every week, Dad.'

He shook his head. 'I don't want you to do that. Prison ain't no place for someone as sweet as you. I don't want you queuing up with those women. Some of them are real mean. And the blokes can be like animals if they see someone as pretty as you. I don't want you subjected to their lewd comments.'

'I'd put up with them,' she protested. 'Words can't hurt me. I want to know that you're going to be all right.'

A stark penetrating stare held her anxious gaze. 'Promise me, you won't come to the prison. I don't want you seeing me like that.'

'But Dad . . .'

'Promise me, angel,' he insisted. 'You know I couldn't love you more if you were me own flesh and blood. Let your old dad keep his pride. I don't want you seeing me as a gaolbird.'

She wanted to put her arms round him, but Lily held him fast, sobbing uncontrollably and refusing to relinquish her possession. Shona wiped a tear from her cheek. 'You're my dad. I know what you did, you did for us. It will be hard not seeing you for so long, but if that's what you want.'

He nodded, his eyes brightening with relief. 'Just make sure you'll write to me?'

'Twice a week, I promise.'

'I'll be there, darling,' Lily vowed. 'I won't abandon you.'

He disengaged her hold and took the cup of tea from Percy. Shona could smell it was laced with whisky. Ted nodded his appreciation to his father-in-law. Percy sat at the kitchen table and sipped his own drink before speaking. 'The trial won't be for some weeks. What's happening about your job?'

Ted rubbed his hand across his jaw, his voice heavy. 'They sacked me on the spot. I've got a bit put by but not enough to see us through the year.'

'Don't worry about us, Dad.' Shona's body was tense with determination. 'You taught me the Carringtons are fighters. We don't let anything pull us down.'

Chapter Six

Throughout the spring and early summer Ted showed a brave face to his family. He did what jobs came his way from his many friends: a week down the market here, a fortnight labouring there. When Princess Elizabeth's engagement to Lieutenant Philip Mountbatten was announced in July, he insisted that Shona take a day's holiday from work. Unfortunately it was raining but the family were cheerful at this rare outing. They took a bus up to Buckingham Palace and stood huddled under two umbrellas with hundreds of other well-wishers to wait for the Princess and her fiancé to come out on the balcony.

The cheers were deafening when they appeared. Even at the distance they were standing happiness radiated from the couple.

'Best wish them well now,' Ted said as they turned away to walk back along Pall Mall. 'I'll miss a great booze up the day they marry.'

Lily began to sob. 'How will I manage when you're doing time? I can't face life without you, Ted.'

'You'll bear up, love. You got through the war when I was away. Don't get upset.'

Shona wished yet again that Lily would be more supportive. She was making it harder for Ted. The anguish he was suffering at knowing that his family would find life hard while he was in prison had robbed him of his jauntiness and carefree manner. He would force a joke and good humour, but his eyes were haunted with remorse.

The twins were grizzling that they were cold, putting a further dampener on the afternoon.

'I'll tell you what will cheer us up. A cake and cuppa at Lyons Corner House and then on the way home we'll stop off at the flicks. I saw one was showing *Pinocchio*. The boys will love that. How about you, Shona?'

'Sounds good enough for me.'

Lily was pouting. 'Bloody *Pinocchio*. I thought we were going out tomorrow night to see the John Wayne film. We can't afford both.'

'Yes we can. Just this once. C'mon, Lil, cheer up. You'll get wrinkles pulling a long face like that.' He pinched her bottom to make her squeal and when she opened her mouth to protest planted a resounding kiss on her lips.

Shona blushed at their antics in such a public place, but it was good to see Lily's scowl replaced by a laugh.

It was the last happy day the family were to share for a long time. The following week Ted's trial was scheduled. Lily spent the week weeping until to get some peace Ted took off down the pub with Percy. The evening before the trial Lily had come back from the pub too drunk to stand and after Ted had put her to bed he came into the living room. His face was strained as he studied Shona. To stem her own tears she had been doing a complicated jigsaw puzzle, many pieces of which were suspiciously damp. Percy was lost in his own heavy thoughts, sipping a brown ale and smoking his pipe.

'Lily is taking it hard,' Ted announced. 'Thank God, she's got you two to help her through it.'

'Lily is thinking of herself as usual,' Percy snorted.

'Oh, Dad.' Shona couldn't control her fear any longer. She ran into his arms and hugged him tight. 'I love you. I hate to think of you being shut away.'

'I'm going to miss you so much, my Barefoot Angel.' He kissed her hair. 'You'll always be that to me. I remember so clearly the day we found you. You've brought such joy into our lives. Lily will need your strength in the months ahead.' His voice shook as he spoke of the problems they would face whilst he was in prison.

Percy banged out his pipe. 'Everything will be looked after, Ted. Don't worry about us. Shona's got a fine head on her shoulders, she'll be a great support to Lil.'

Ted sleeked his hands over his Brylcreemed hair and smiled at Shona. 'Your mum's been hitting the bottle hard lately. Keep an eye on her. I've failed her. And you and the boys.'

'You haven't failed us, Dad,' Shona assured him.

'I'm pleading guilty tomorrow. My lawyer said it will go better for me and I'll get a lighter sentence. I *am* guilty, Shona. I've done things I ain't always been proud of.'

She hated to see him tormenting himself this way. 'You wanted us to have a better life. What you did was dishonest, but it wasn't wicked. You did it with the best intention.'

He patted her hand. 'You're amazing. You've got a strange logic. Whoever your real parents were they must have been remarkable. I reckon your father was a diplomat the way you always smooth things over.'

She laughed at Ted's teasing, then frowned. Something about the idea seemed familiar. Had her father been a civil servant or in public service of some kind? The question hovered in her mind, the answer elusive as were all the answers about her past. Now was not the time to dwell on the unobtainable, there were more pressing problems.

'It's gonna be hard for you all,' Ted warned. 'Especially Lil. She'll find it difficult having to go without things she takes for granted. My savings will pay the mortgage for the next nine months. If I'm not out by then I've left papers with my solicitor which allow the house to be sold with my consent.'

'There'll be no selling the house,' Percy declared. 'This is my home as well. Besides, renting will cost as much as the mortgage. With Shona helping out on the stall on a

Saturday we always do well. Her sunny smile draws the crowds.'

'If the worst comes to the worst we'll turn the living room into a bedroom and take in a lodger,' Shona suggested.

Ted gave a dry laugh. 'I can't see Lil doing that.' He squeezed Shona's hand. 'And I don't want you overdoing things. You put in a full week at the office and more than pay your whack. I know Lil can be demanding at times. Be firm with her. You're not a slave – you're our daughter.'

She didn't answer. She may be Ted's daughter in his eyes, but since Ted's arrest Lily's antagonism had grown towards her. Shona was an intruder in this family as far as Lily was concerned and an unpaid skivvy to boot.

Shona had been upset at the change in Lily. She had thought Lily loved her before the twins were born. As she grew older she realised the affection Lily had shown her had been a sham. Lily hated the way Ted was so proud and affectionate towards Shona and it had won her jealousy. Lily would never share her husband with another woman – even an adopted daughter.

Ted made up for all the love Lily denied her. Shona had accepted that her new home was not the ideal it had at first appeared. When Johnnie and Jamie were born, when she was thirteen, they had been such adorable boys, she had been proud to have them as her brothers. She even accepted that Lily would naturally put the children she had given birth to before one she had adopted.

Shona was a fatalist. Lily saw her as competition just as she saw all women as competition. But Shona never forgot that it was Lily who had given her a home and been the one to insist that they adopt her. Whatever Lily's motives at the time, they had saved Shona from the orphanage. Shona would never forget the debt she owed Lily Carrington.

It was three in the morning before they stopped talking. When Shona was in bed there was a tap on her bedroom door. She switched on her bedside lamp to see Ted hovering in the doorway.

'I just wanted to say goodnight. If you were a little girl I'd tuck you in.'

'Tuck me in anyway, Dad.'

He sat on the edge of her bed. He still hadn't undressed and she sensed he was reluctant to close his eyes and lose these last hours with his family. He picked up the worn teddy bear he'd taken from the crashed car all those years ago and looked down at it. 'Do you ever think of your parents?'

Shona drew her hand from under the coverlet and clasped his. 'You're my dad. The best dad in the world. I still can't remember them.'

There were tears in Ted's eyes as he stroked a flaxen tress of hair away from her tear-streaked cheeks. 'Don't cry. My Barefoot Angel was always so brave. Promise me that no matter how difficult Lil becomes, you'll always be there for her. She needs you more than she admits.'

'I'll always be there for Mum and the kids, you know that. And stop acting as though you'll be away for years. It's your first offence. Grandad reckons you'll be out by next Christmas with remission.'

The lantern-jawed judge peered over the top of his horn-rimmed spectacles at the accused. 'You have resorted to crime out of greed not necessity. Decent families bear the brunt of rationing with dignity. Men such as you threaten the very economy of the country and it will not be tolerated. You had a responsible, well-paid job which many men today would be grateful for. An example must be made. I thereby sentence you to five years' imprisonment.'

Shona combated a wave of dizziness at the shock. Her father's lawyer had warned her when the case started that the judge was a hard man. But the sentence was harsh for a first conviction. She stared at Ted who looked pale and shaken. When he was led away between two warders he looked up at Lily who was weeping hysterically. His handsome face was lined with pain.

'I love you, Dad,' she shouted to hearten him.

His gaze turned to her and he forced a bleak smile and blew her a kiss. The anguish in his eyes smote her. 'Take care of your mum.'

She nodded. Her stare was riveted upon his broad back as he was led out of sight. She could be twenty-one before she next saw him. Again she was cast adrift without a father. But this time she had memories to cling to and sustain her.

'Five years!' Lily wailed as she sat in the courtroom. 'What am I going to do? I can't live without Ted for five years.'

Her sister Annie put her arms round her. 'You'll cope. Ted will be out in three years with remission, just you see. At least he's coming back to you. Unlike my Charlie who I ain't never gonna see again thanks to the bloody war.'

Lily wouldn't be consoled. She couldn't walk she was so distraught. Shona saw Annie's patience was wearing thin. Aunt Annie had lost weight in the five years since Uncle Charlie was killed fighting in Africa. With four children to support she'd had to give up her large rented house in Chingford and was squashed into sharing a prefab in Stepney with Charlie's parents. The buxom Annie whom Shona had first met seven years ago was now gaunt, her hair dyed copper to cover its premature grey.

'You don't know when you're well off, Lil,' Annie snapped. 'You've got Dad and Shona bringing in wages. What I earn serving in Woolies barely feeds us. Charlie's parents may have given us a roof over our heads but they've blown all their money down the pub come Monday. If me eldest, Tommy, didn't skip school to go out on Old Stumpy's rag and bone cart for a few bob a week, I don't know what we'd do.'

'I can't live without my Ted,' Lily persisted. 'I'll go out of my mind.'

Annie sighed. 'Pull yourself together. You've just got to make the best of it.' Annie looked at Percy. 'Got ten bob to spare, Dad? Lil could do with a drink to steady her nerves.'

Percy handed it over. Then he pressed a creased white five-pound note into her hands. There was no warmth in his eyes as he regarded his elder daughter. 'Just mind you spend that on food for you and the kids and not booze. I offered you a home with me when Charlie died. You made your choice, Annie.'

''Cos I was sick of your lectures on how I led my life.'

'You mean I wouldn't stand for your whoring. You played fast and loose with the Yanks when your Charlie was away fighting. You might have convinced him that young Sally was his, but she's got the look of that Texan you were seeing before Charlie's last leave.'

Annie glared at him. The skirt of her red costume was too tight and too short and her frilly chiffon blouse had a low neckline revealing an indecent amount of cleavage. 'If it weren't for the kids I wouldn't take a penny of your rotten money, old man.'

'If it weren't for the kids I'd have disowned you years ago.'

Shona intervened. Percy and Annie were always at loggerheads. 'Stop it please. This is hardly the day for family squabbles; we should be united.'

'Little Miss Do-Good,' Annie sneered, taking her tone from Lily's constant ridiculing of her.

Shona bristled. 'Bickering won't bring Dad home. And Mum shouldn't go drinking. The twins will be missing her.'

Annie scowled and Lily leaned more heavily upon her. Percy glared at his daughters. 'Don't start on Shona. She's worth more than the pair of you put together. She understands about family loyalty.' Percy spun on his heel and with his hands

71

thrust into his trouser pockets strode away. 'You coming with me, Shona?'

Annie and Lily ignored her. Annie had linked her arm through Lily's and was taking her across the road to the nearest pub. 'Don't you worry about us,' Annie shouted back sarcastically. 'I'll see Lil gets home all right.'

Shona glanced anxiously at Percy who had halted at the corner for her to catch him up. She was torn, guessing Lily would drink too much and stagger home on her own. But it was obvious Lily didn't want her company. Then there was Mrs Lockyer to rescue from the twins. They were screaming blue-murder when they were taken next door this morning.

She hurried to join Percy. 'Mum needs someone to talk to. She don't get to see much of Annie lately with her sister working all hours.'

Percy snorted disparagingly. 'Don't defend her. Her greed got Ted in this mess, but she won't see it. Fine pair I got landed with for daughters.'

He looked pale and she had earlier noticed him rubbing his chest during the trial. Last winter he'd taken a funny turn with his heart and Shona was worried about him. She slid her arm through his. Ever since she could remember Grandad and Annie hadn't got on. Lily had said that Annie had broken his heart when she had to get married to Charlie. She'd only been seeing him for a month when she got pregnant.

'Don't get upset, Grandad. Annie and you are too alike – too independent and won't say what you really feel. You don't really hate her, do you?'

'She was always wilful. And flighty. I may be old fashioned but I don't hold with the way she carried on. She ain't changed either. She dresses like the tart she is.'

The rare outburst of emotion showed how disturbed Percy was by the day's events. Usually he wouldn't be drawn why he had no time for Annie. Shona had long suspected that Annie was free with her favours, which explained the long line of

72

boyfriends she talked of so animatedly to Lily. She was always boasting of the presents they gave her.

'She dotes on her children. They've never gone without.'

Percy shot her a stern look under his white bushy brows. 'You'd find something good to say about the devil himself. Annie's a bad influence on Lil.'

He lapsed into silence for the rest of the journey home and Shona's own mind was whirling from the shock of Ted's punishment. His imprisonment would affect everyone in the family. Each of them would be counting the days until he returned to them.

The next months were hard. The country was buzzing with expectation over the wedding of Princess Elizabeth in November. It was a poignant reminder to Shona of the last outing they had been on as a family to see the couple on the balcony at Buckingham Palace. She missed Ted dreadfully. A gloom had settled over the house since his trial and even the twins were more subdued.

Lily meanwhile became more belligerent with each day. Shona bore it stoically. Percy interceded when Lily was being especially spiteful. Annie dragged her kids over to them every Sunday, knowing that Percy would provide a decent lunch for them all. Then Annie and Lily sat in the front room drinking sherry while Shona and Percy took the children over to the park.

When they returned home, Lily was usually drunk and asleep in her chair. Annie raided the larder stuffing their precious food into her copious bag, leaving Shona to clear up the mess made by six boisterous kids.

Each week Shona became more restless. The office job at the insurance company bored her. Mostly she was typing policies or accounts all day. The supervisor in charge of the typing pool was a dragon who forbade any talking. She would berate a typist over the smallest misdemeanour or error, often reducing them to tears. Shona hated her and hated the work. She stuck it without complaint because they needed the money. Every week she searched the papers for a job in journalism but her young age went against her.

With the twins to look after, Lily couldn't work and wouldn't hear of taking in a lodger.

'I'm not having strangers in my home. Percy will have to help us out more if we can't manage.' Her looks had deteriorated since Ted was convicted. Her hair was lank, the permanent wave long grown out so that it frizzed around her jaw. There was also an inch of darker roots showing where she no longer troubled to bleach it regularly.

'That's not fair on Grandad. That's his life savings. It should only be used in an emergency.'

Lily took a cigarette from a packet and lit it. There was also a new bottle of sherry on the sideboard.

'We'd manage better if you gave up smoking and drinking.' Shona's exasperation at Lily's selfishness overspilled.

'Don't you give me any of your lip!' Lily slapped her across the mouth.

Shona reeled back. It wasn't the first time Lily had hit her. Her hand itched to retaliate but she harnessed her anger. The strain of Ted being in prison was affecting them all. By retaliating she would only make matters worse. 'Mum, we can't afford for you to smoke. You never used to before Aunt Annie started coming round.'

'It's my nerves. I have to smoke to stay calm. And would you begrudge me a glass of sherry of an evening? I never go out now. Drudge, drudge, drudge, that's all my life is. What pleasures do I have?'

'There's a notice in the window of the Crown advertising for a barmaid. You could work a couple of evenings. That way you'd be getting out and earning your fag money.'

Lily scowled. 'I ain't working in any pub.'

'It won't be all work. It's a lively pub.' When Lily continued

74

to look appalled at the notion, Shona persisted. 'I'm sorry, Mum, but I'm not handing over any more of my money to you to waste on cigarettes and drink. I'll buy the food and pay the bills. And I don't think Aunt Annie should come over every week. Her kids eat all our rations.'

'Don't you tell me I can't see me own sister. What other pleasures do I get? Annie has been a real friend since Ted was put inside.'

Shona lost her patience. 'Some friend! Annie is bleeding us dry with her kids scoffing our food. She didn't come here when Dad was around because she knew he wouldn't tolerate her sponging off us. Annie uses people. And what about the porcelain figure which went missing from the glass cabinet after her visit last week? That's the second expensive piece to disappear.'

'Don't you blame Annie,' Lily screamed. 'You've broken them and hid the pieces. Annie wouldn't steal from me. You can cough up the money for those breakages out of your wages.'

'I didn't break them and I won't pay for them.' Shona stood her ground. 'And I won't pay for your fags and drink.'

Lily's eyes narrowed but she didn't pursue the matter. She knew Annie had taken them but wouldn't admit it. Her face flushed. 'You'll hand your pay packet over every Friday as normal, young lady. Don't I give you three and six back for yourself? You're an ungrateful brat. All the money Ted and I lavished on you over the years, and this is how you repay us, by denying us small comforts.'

'I've never asked for anything. I was grateful for the home and love you gave me. I didn't need fancy clothes and dancing lessons.'

Lily raised her hand to hit Shona again and this time Shona countered by grabbing her wrist. 'I do right by you and the twins,' she answered firmly. 'I haven't been out with Marion for weeks. I won't put up with you hitting me. I'm not a child and I won't be bullied. If you can't manage the housekeeping properly then I'll buy what's needed for us. If you want luxuries then you'll have to work for them. I'll babysit the twins so you can work.'

'How dare you talk to me like that!' Lily's face screwed up with rage. 'You little bastard. You'd have mouldered in an orphanage but for us.'

The emotional blackmail had been used too often to have its desired effect on Shona. She had to be strong with Lily. It was the only way she could cope. 'And I shall always love and respect you for what you did for me. But I won't be used.'

Shona was shaking. Not because she was frightened of Lily, but because she felt guilty at having to act so meanly. But things couldn't go on as they were.

A crafty expression entered Lily's eyes. 'I just might take you up on that job. I'm bored staying in every night. The Crown gets a good crowd and has a regular sing-song.'

She disappeared upstairs and when she came down she was wearing her best frock under her brown fur jacket. Lily had also hidden her hair under a fetching half-veiled hat and put on some make-up. 'I'm off to the Crown.'

An hour later she returned, her expression triumphant. 'I'm working six nights a week,' she gloated at Shona. 'So that's put paid to you gallivanting with your mates. Tuesday is my day off, you can go out then. You can't expect Grandad to cope with the twins at his age.'

'That's fine by me.' Shona knew Marion wouldn't be pleased but it couldn't be helped. The extra money would be useful and Lily might be more cheerful working in a lively pub. It was only until Dad came home. Percy had said that with good behaviour Ted could be out in three years. Three years wasn't an eternity. It was a small price to pay back all that Ted and Lily had showered on her in the past. More importantly Ted was relying on her. She would never let him down.

Chapter Seven

'Best bargains in town! Dinky cars or dolls, you won't get them cheaper!'

'Get your Christmas trees here! Cheapest in the market.'

'Stocking fillers for a tanner!'

The hubbub of the market traders rang out above the Christmas carols blaring from the nearby music shop. Shona stamped her feet and rubbed her hands in her fingerless mittens. She was half-frozen and had been working with Percy for ten hours since eight that morning. She served another customer, wrapping the garment in brown paper and fumbling in her money apron for the right change.

'Merry Christmas,' she nodded to the customer.

'Here, get this down you.' Percy Dawkins thrust a steaming cup of tea into her hands.

Shona sipped it and coughed. Her grandfather grinned. 'Splash of whisky in there to warm your cockles. Drink it and don't pull faces.'

He pointed to a large bundle wrapped in newspaper. 'That's the goose for Christmas and I got Harry the Veg to fill up your bag and put in some nuts and oranges.'

'Grandad, you shouldn't. You pay more than enough to us as it is. We can manage now Mum's working at the Crown.'

'It's my pleasure. Besides, I'm partial to a bit of goose.' He glossed over his generosity and drew out a half dozen ten-shilling notes from his money apron and pushed them into her coat pocket. 'Now you get yourself off and get your presents bought. That's a Christmas bonus for you for all the hours you've put in over the last months. I'll bring the goose and stuff home on me barrow tonight.'

She knew it was pointless to argue and hugged him tight. With Ted in prison, Shona wasn't in the frame of mind to celebrate Christmas but for Johnnie and Jamie's sakes they had to make the most of it. For weeks the boys had spoken of nothing else but what Santa Claus would bring them.

'Thanks, Grandad. Now I can get a tree on Christmas Eve for the boys to decorate. The market is still busy, are you sure you don't need my help?'

'Get your presents sorted. I can manage.' He tipped some more whisky into his tea from a pewter hip-flask. 'And I want you out enjoying yourself tonight. It's time you had a night out with your friends.'

'But you've got your darts match, haven't you?'

He waved his hand dismissively. 'The Saturday before Christmas is a time for you young 'uns to have fun, not an old codger like me.'

'Thanks, Grandad, I'd really like that. Marion's been badgering me to go to a dance with her.'

Percy nodded. 'I should have given me Saturday darts night up weeks ago. It's too much after a freezing day in the market. Once the twins are abed they don't wake up. I want you to get out more. You should be having fun with a nice young fella.'

'I have fun with Marion when I see her. And as for a boyfriend, I've enough on my plate without any added complications. Besides, I don't mind looking after the boys,' Shona reassured him. She'd been worried about Percy this winter. He often complained about the cold and pains in his chest but wouldn't go to a doctor. 'It gives me the time I need to do some research for my articles. I've started interviewing some of the older people of Walthamstow. So many have led interesting lives. I'm going to write their stories and send them to the local paper. I wish I could get a job on the paper. I'm bored with the typing pool. I want something more.'

'Don't be so impatient,' Percy cautioned. 'Besides, I don't reckon being a reporter is right for a woman. People can get nasty if you go poking your nose into their affairs.'

Shona shook her head. 'I've no intention of printing anything nasty. These people's memories are fascinating. So many things have changed since the war. Even the streets don't look the same with the rebuilding. We need records of what life was like growing up in the Victorian or Edwardian age. How they coped with the cholera and typhoid epidemics. Their lives should be recorded for posterity.'

'Then why haven't you come to your old grandad?' Percy looked affronted. 'I could tell you a thing or two about life in the East End when I was a nipper.'

She lifted a brow in mock astonishment. 'I lost count of the times I asked you about the old days. You always said the past is the past and best forgotten. I reckoned you had a few family secrets you didn't want me finding out about,' she teased. 'You were a bit of a Jack the lad when you were younger according to some of the costers.'

'They know nothing, my girl,' Percy said rubbing the side of his nose. 'Happen I might have a story or two for you. But it's about time you made some memories of your own. You're only young once.'

Shona stared down the double line of stalls in the twilight. Many were now lit by naphtha lamps. If she was going to get her shopping and get ready for the dance tonight she had better shift herself.

She was buying some stockings for the dance when she noticed a tramp huddled in a doorway opposite Percy's stall. His grey hair was long and matted and a thick bushy beard hid most of his features. The frayed army greatcoat was tied about his waist with string and had holes in the elbows. He had first appeared around the market about four years ago.

The doorway was a favourite place of his and on a cold day such as this Shona often brought him a cup of tea. It was taken with wary acceptance and no word of thanks. His name was Bill Miles and he was a loner. All too frequently he was moved on by the police. Some of the stallholders cursed him – his presence wasn't good for business. Yet Bill was almost self-effacing, never openly begging or accosting people as some of the other tramps did. Shona frequently saw him in the nearby park or rooting at the end of the day for scraps of food left by the stallholders. Often he was drunk.

Today he sat with his knees drawn up to his chin and was shivering. It was cold enough to snow and the sight of his bare hands and open-necked shirt aroused her pity. She removed the red scarf she had knitted herself to match her favourite red beret. He started as she wound it around his neck.

'What you doing?' he accused. He peered up at her in the gloom, his blue eyes narrowed with suspicion.

'You look as if you need this more than I do.'

'I don't want your charity.'

'It's a gift,' she improvised. 'A Christmas present. Your name's Bill, isn't it?'

He didn't answer. His stare was shuttered of emotion but as piercing as knives. It made her uncomfortable. 'Don't bother to thank me,' she retorted, refusing to be intimidated by his manner. 'Merry Christmas.'

She turned to walk away.

'You're the Carrington kid? Shona? What sort of fancy name is that?'

His cultured voice halted her and made her retrace her steps. It was the first time he had spoken to her.

'It's just a name.' Her flippant reply was a form of protection against her unease at not knowing who she was.

'You sound like it doesn't matter.' His gaze held hers briefly then he looked away and wound the scarf tighter around his neck.

Unaccountably she was stung to retaliate. 'It matters if you can't remember the name you were born with.'

He stared straight ahead, his voice gruff when he answered. 'Some memories are best forgotten.'

'Is that why you took to the road, Bill?'

He looked at her for so long without speaking she thought he had ignored her question. Pain flickered in his eyes. 'I lost everything in the war. Wife. Family. Home. Who needs responsibilities?'

His stare sharpened, a fierce imperious stare defying her to pity him. Then he turned his back on her and settled down to sleep. Clearly he had no intention of talking more about his past. His voice was that of an educated man. His story was tragic, but surely he couldn't want to live the way he did.

Percy lifted a brow at her when she returned to the stall. 'What you doing giving him your scarf? He's a waste of space, Shona. He's a drunkard.'

'He's a man who's had a lot of tragedy in his life.'

'Likely he's spinning a yarn to get your sympathy. You're a soft touch for a cuppa.'

'I don't think he was. He seemed embarrassed when I gave him the scarf.'

'Steer clear of him, Shona. That sort ain't nothing but trouble. Save your pity for those who deserve it.' He scowled in the direction of the tramp who was now curled up asleep. 'Get yourself off home, girl. The twins will need their tea before you go out. I don't suppose Lil has bothered to cook.'

Shona glanced at her watch and pulled a face. She'd have to put her skates on to be ready in time.

The dance was great fun. Shona, Marion and three other friends had attended. They didn't stop dancing all evening.

'See what you've been missing,' Marion chided in a moment between dances. Both of them were glowing with perspiration after an energetic jitterbug. 'You should come every week,'

Marion added. 'Derek Simpson has asked to take me home. I've fancied him for months. And Derek said his mate Nick wants to take you home.'

Shona had danced with Nick Blake twice. He was dashingly handsome with thick dark hair brushed back from his brow and grey eyes ringed by thick lashes. He wasn't much above medium height but he had a worldly, commanding air about him which was as disturbing as it was exciting.

While they danced he had paid her compliments. The way he gazed deep into her eyes had made her feel that she was the only one in the room for him. He had also danced with several other partners so she had taken his flattery with a pinch of salt. But too often for her comfort she had found her gaze scanning the ballroom to alight upon Nick as he danced with another partner. Several times he had glanced her way and given her a wink when he saw her watching him. It had made her resolve not to look in his direction again.

'Nick seems to have taken a shine to you.' Marion nudged her in the ribs. 'He keeps looking this way.'

'Hardly, I've seen him with six different partners.'

'So you *are* interested in him?' Marion teased.

'Nick seems very popular.'

'That's putting it mildly. He's got a reputation for living and playing hard. Likes the ladies too. Never takes the same woman home twice.'

'Then I'm not interested in him,' Shona replied, yet she felt a stab of disappointment. While they danced Nick had made her forget the dreariness of her life in recent weeks. He had made her laugh.

She realised how seldom she now laughed at home. She could tease the twins and they made her giggle but it wasn't the laughter of happiness. Lily usually ignored her presence and any comments she made were derogatory. She was always finding fault with anything Shona did. Since Ted's imprisonment Lily frequently lost her temper with the boisterous twins. She no longer took pride in the house and dust and cobwebs were left for Shona to tackle. Often when she got home from the office, the twins hadn't been fed and were whining with hunger. Nor had a meal been prepared for Grandad or herself.

Shona pushed her grim thoughts aside, refusing to allow them to spoil this evening. It would be nice to have a young man as handsome as Nick to take her home.

When she accepted his offer, he grinned. 'Might as well leave now. More time for me to get to know you better. You're Ted Carrington's daughter, ain't you? I heard about Ted. He was a good bloke. He didn't deserve a stretch like that for what he did.'

'Did you know my dad well?' Shona warmed to him. She suspected that Nick was something of a rough diamond. His speech was rough, though no more than most of the men in the East End, but he dressed smartly. It was a pity that with his handsome looks he rather fancied himself with the ladies. Men like that were best kept at arm's length.

'Well enough. We did some work together so to speak.'

She bit her lip and digested this. Was Nick also a black marketeer? It made her cautious. She was usually a good judge of character on a first meeting. Nick seemed a decent bloke. Then so was Ted Carrington despite his wheeling and dealing on the side. Yet Nick was a natural charmer and more complex than most men, so was it wise to encourage him?

'This is my first time out in weeks. I'd rather not leave the dance yet. Can't we get to know each other while we're dancing?'

Marion giggled. 'Don't be such a wet blanket. We can have more fun on our own than on a crowded dance floor.'

Still Shona hesitated. Marion had been nagging her for weeks to come dancing with her and now she wanted to go home. Her friend was clinging to Derek's arm like ivy. Marion had changed in recent months. While Shona was stuck at home babysitting the twins, Marion had been out with several boys. Until now Shona had only had one boy-friend, a lad called Neil. He had been shy and had seen her three times before he plucked up courage to give her an inexperienced kiss. They had broken up after two months as his only conversation revolved around football and his heroes playing for West Ham.

Nick was studying Shona; she felt she was being pressured into a situation she didn't care for. The band began to play a waltz and with a beguiling smile Nick slid his arm around her waist and led her back on to the dance floor.

'There's nothing like a waltz to bring out the romantic in a man,' he whispered against her ear. 'But it's noisy and crowded in here.'

The warmth of his breath against her cheek sent delicious shivers through her body. She looked up into his grey eyes and felt her heart give a traitorous flutter. She didn't want to feel such a building attraction to this man. All her senses warned her that he was dangerous to know. Dangerous but also exciting. And excitement was sadly lacking in her life at the moment, therefore Nick Blake was irresistible.

'My place is round the back of Stratford station. The four of us could go back there for a drink.'

Warning bells clanged. She stiffened in his arms. 'And would your mother be there for me to meet? I think you've mistaken me for the wrong kind of woman.'

He looked at her nonplussed. Then seeing the glitter in her eyes, he smiled. 'I live alone. And that wasn't meant as it sounds.'

Shona wasn't convinced but she was prepared to let it pass. The seductive rhythm of the waltz was playing havoc with her senses. Nick was a wonderful dancer and their figures moved in harmony. Aware of the ease with which their bodies blended together, Nick executed a few intricate turns which Shona followed as fluently as a shadow.

Several slow numbers followed the waltz and the ballroom lights had dimmed. 'You move like a goddess,' he praised, his heavy-lidded gaze caressing her.

He grinned and drew her closer so that she could feel the heat of his body through the thinness of her sapphire satin gown. The neckline of her dress was scooped below her shoulderblades at the back and his hand moved so that the tips of his fingers were on her cool flesh. Their touch seared her and he moved so that her breasts grazed his chest. It sent a tingling through her body and she drew back with an embarrassed gasp. Nick laughed softly as they turned in the dance. His cheek rested against hers and she felt the light touch of his lips brush her skin.

'You're really something, Shona.'

Her body's reaction perturbed Shona. Every nerve end was suddenly aware of his masculinity and sexuality. It threatened her composure, drying her throat and making her heart pound. It also made her feel out of control of her senses and that put her on her guard.

'I think it's time Marion and I left.' She pulled away from him, unable to meet his admiring stare.

'Derek and I will take you home.' Nick led her back to Marion and Derek standing at the back of the ballroom.

Shona knew she should refuse. Nick was too worldly for her peace of mind. His reputation made him a man best avoided. Yet the excited fluttering in her stomach was like the wings of a moth, compelled and drawn inexorably to the flame. He nodded to Derek who guided Marion towards the cloakroom. Nick's hand was again possessive upon her waist as they followed them.

'What time do you have to be home?' he asked as they left the dance hall. 'Not too early I hope?'

'There's a bus in ten minutes. I told Grandad I'd be back

by eleven. He won't go to bed until I get in and he's had a long day at the market.'

'Your grandad won't make a fuss if you're a bit late,' Marion said, gazing adoringly up at Derek. 'And Lily don't get back from the pub until much later.'

'Grandad will worry. I never break my word to him.'

'Not even for exceptions?' Nick said, slipping her arm through his.

'When I give my word I keep it.'

Derek gave a derisive snort. 'Regular saint, ain't you? You're gonna have your work cut out with that one, Nick. Got yourself a bit of a madam.'

'Leave it out, Del,' Nick snapped, his breath forming a cloud in the cold air.

'Bloody brass monkeys weather,' Derek grumbled. 'It's only just gone ten, ain't we going back to your place, Nick?'

Shona paused in pulling on her gloves and regarded him warily. Nick feigned shock. 'What you on about, Del? These are decent women. We're taking them home.'

'You losing your touch then?' Derek growled.

Nick ignored him and turned to Shona. 'This one is special, Del.'

She had thrust her hands in her coat pockets and was staring at the frost which had glazed the paving stones in the road. She didn't like the undercurrent to the conversation between the two men. His flattery made her heart skip but it was just that – flattery. Her suspicions about Nick made her edgy. She meant what she had told Percy this afternoon, that she didn't want the complication of a boyfriend in her life. Neither did she relish the thought of being one of Nick's conquests: charmed, courted and discarded within a week. Perhaps it would be better if she refused to let him take her home. With his reputation their relationship wasn't going to go anywhere.

Before she could speak her thoughts, Nick tenderly pulled up the deep collar of her coat so that it settled snugly around her ears. When she looked up at him he was smiling. He put his arms around her and drew her close.

She stiffened. 'Someone will see us. It isn't done to cuddle in the street.'

'We've got to keep warm. Would you rather freeze?'

Shona moved out of his embrace and looked away from him. Under his admiring gaze it was difficult to refuse him. 'I have my reputation to consider. And I don't want you getting the wrong idea. Perhaps you'd be better off not taking me home. It's out of your way.'

'Is this a brush off?' He sounded amused.

She forced herself to hold his teasing stare. Then taking a sustaining breath, she answered, 'I don't think I'm the usual type of girl you take home of a Saturday night.'

The laughter died in his eyes and they flashed with anger. His voice was low and accusing. 'What kind of a bloke do you think I am?'

'You're a charming man and I enjoy your company. But you have a reputation.'

'Which you think I'm bound to live up to?'

His forthrightness disconcerted her. 'I suppose so.'

'That's bloody charming, that is. I'm condemned unheard.'

'I'm not judging you, Nick.' She faltered at realising that she had prejudged him.

To her relief the bus drew up. 'Goodnight, Nick. Perhaps you should take someone else home. The dance isn't over for another half hour.'

She leapt on to the bus and ran up the stairs. Marion would be furious, but she knew she had done the right thing. Nick Blake would only complicate her life and bring her heartache. She heard Marion on the steps behind her and went along to the front of the top deck and stared out at the shops lit up with Christmas lights and decorations.

'Gawd, Shona, you're a case you are,' Marion groaned. She didn't sit beside her but in the seat behind.

When Shona turned to explain to her friend she saw Nick sitting on the seat opposite. His handsome face was sombre as he studied her. He lounged against the window with one arm along the back of the seat. Derek was next to Marion.

Shona didn't know whether to be irritated or secretly pleased at Nick's persistence. To retain her composure she stared straight ahead as the bus pulled away. To her consternation she was stingingly aware that Nick was watching her from across the aisle.

The conductor approached for their fares and as Shona was fishing in her purse for the right change, Nick paid for them all. He tossed the tickets into her lap and moved into the seat beside her. 'Mind if I join you?'

'Free country.' She had wanted to sound nonchalant and instead felt gauche. She wasn't going to let him see that she was bothered where he sat.

He sighed theatrically. 'I suppose that's it then. Our first lovers' tiff. Can we cut the apologies and get on with the kissing and making up?' He pecked her on the cheek and when she turned her head to remonstrate with him, planted another kiss on her lips.

'Nick!' she groaned with mortification. 'Stop that. You're embarrassing me.'

He was grinning. 'So do you forgive me?'

'I forgive you for stealing kisses you aren't entitled to. But don't do it again. I don't like being made to look cheap in public.'

'So you agree to me kissing you in private?'

She glared at him, then seeing the twinkle in his eyes, shook her head and laughed. 'You're incorrigible!'

'If you say so, sweetheart. I'll be anything you want.'

That made her laugh and he kept her laughing all the way to Walthamstow. Soon she forgot her reservations about him and found she enjoyed his company. When the bus halted outside the Crown pub, Shona glanced into the brightly lit bar. It was crowded and a sing-song was being belted out by the customers. Some of the women had linked arms and were spinning each other round.

'That lot are having fun,' Nick observed. 'Fancy going in for a drink?'

'I couldn't,' Shona replied. 'That's the pub my mother works of an evening. She'd skin me if she caught me drinking.'

'There's Lily now.' Marion tapped Shona on the shoulder and pointed into the bar.

Shona's expression froze as she saw Lily climb on to two tables which had been pushed together. Her mother lifted her skirt above her knees and began doing the knees-up. With each kick her skirt rose higher. Shona looked away, blushing at the sight of Lily showing the tops of her stockings and a bare expanse of thigh.

She could feel Nick watching her as the bus pulled away and was grateful he didn't say anything. When they drew up at their bus stop, Shona hurried down the steps, her cheeks still burning with embarrassment.

'Why the rush to get home?' Nick said. He took her arm and drew her to a standstill. 'There's twenty minutes before it's eleven. Your friend and Derek have got the right idea.'

Shona swung round to see the back of Derek in a darkened shop doorway with Marion's arms wrapped around his neck. With an expertise which caught Shona unawares, Nick drew her into the embrasure of a haberdasher's shop. His arms went round her. 'I've come all this way. Don't I get a kiss?'

'Someone will see us,' she evaded, nervously.

He laughed softly and his hand cupped her chin, tilting her face up to his. 'You're quite something. I knew the moment I set eyes on you that you were special.' His head lowered and his gaze was riveted upon hers. She could feel the pressure of his thigh against her hip and his other hand tenderly stroked the hair from her cheek.

She reached up to remove his hand and found her own clasped in his. 'Ted was always talking about you,' he said, unexpectedly. 'I can understand why.'

The mention of her father brought tears to her eyes and she blinked them rapidly aside. 'I miss Dad so much. He won't let me visit him.'

'He wants you to remember him as he was: proud, self-assured and in control.'

'You sound like you know him well.'

'Yeah, well enough.'

Nick's nearness was bedevilling her senses. She didn't want to get involved with someone who could end up inside like Ted. It was crazy. She'd only known him a couple of hours; it should be easy to say goodbye and go home, yet she was loath to part from him. The magnetism of his presence and the warmth of his breath on her cheek undermined her resolve.

Somehow she found the strength to erect a gossamer barrier between them. She eased back. 'I don't approve of dishonesty but I never condemned Dad for what he did. But nothing was worth him losing his freedom and us being deprived of him. Nick, if you're into wheeling and dealing that's on the wrong side of the law . . .'

'There you go, blackening my name again.'

'No, I'm not, it's . . .' She couldn't explain.

'Don't you think we've done enough talking?'

Before she could protest his lips skimmed hers in a tender and sensual caress. His supple mouth moved expertly until her senses began to swirl. Like ripples on a pond the sensation spread through her body, until she swayed, her arms linking around his neck. A soft moan escaping from her throat startled her. The sound deepened Nick's kiss. His tongue tasted the seam of her lips and gently eased them apart. The light flicker of his tongue on hers caused tiny explosions of pleasure to spiral through her.

When his hand slid inside her coat to close over her breast, she jolted her head back and angrily pushed his hand away. 'What do you think you're doing?'

'C'mon, sweetheart, you ain't so innocent. Not with a mum who flashes her drawers in a crummy pub.'

Humiliation inflamed her anger. She shoved him aside. She was burning with shame. 'Get away from me!' She looked over to where Marion was still locked in an ardent embrace in the next shop doorway. 'Marion, I'm going home. Now!'

Her friend's pale face appeared round the shoulder of Derek. 'Don't be so daft. We ain't got to be home for quarter of an hour.'

'I'm going. Do what you like.'

Nick put his hand on her arm. 'I'm sorry. Don't go. Most girls like . . .'

'Don't compare me with most girls.' Her eyes flashed with anger. 'I'm not like Lily. And I don't allow myself to be mauled by any bloke.'

She wrenched her arm from his hold and began to walk away. That would be the last she saw of Nick Blake. Decent girls were no use to men like him.

Before she'd taken a dozen steps he'd overtaken her and was barring her way. 'Don't run off. I shouldn't have tried it on. Can I walk you to your house?'

'Why?'

'Gawd, woman, give us a break! I want to that's why. Besides it ain't safe for a pretty woman to be alone on the streets at night.'

'It isn't safe in certain company, it would seem.'

'I apologised, didn't I?' He spread his arms in mute appeal.

She moved round him but didn't object when he kept pace with her. They walked in silence and he made no attempt to touch her as they halted by her garden gate.

'Can I see you again, Shona?'

She looked up at him, his handsome face clearly visible in the nearby gaslamp. It was madness. It would never work

91

and only lead to heartache, but as she stared at him she was tempted. 'With Mum working every evening I don't get much chance to get out. I have to look after my twin brothers. They're nearly four.'

'I'll pay for someone to babysit.'

'That's generous but not the issue. They're little terrors and won't settle if I'm out. Grandad lives with us but they're too much for him other than once a week. Mum's day off is Tuesday.'

'I'd really like to see you again, Shona.' He moved closer and put his arms around her waist.

There was a huskiness in his voice and his lips again claimed hers, this time with a thoroughness and passion which set her blood pounding through her veins. He broke away and she had to put a hand on the gatepost to support herself.

'That's so you don't forget me.'

Then with a jaunty whistle he strode off down the street.

Shona watched him for several seconds still stunned by her response to his kiss. She shook her head and laughed. 'You're incorrigible all right, Nicholas Blake. I suppose that was to teach me a lesson for rejecting your advances earlier. I won't hold my breath expecting you to come courting at my door.'

Chapter Eight

Shona was determined that the twins enjoyed their Christmas. Each night after a tiring day at the office she was baking, improvising on the meagre rations where necessary to make a cake and mince pies. Two days before Christmas she boiled up a pig's head to make brawn which had always been Ted's favourite. She put this into two bowls to set. The smaller one together with a small Christmas cake and a dozen mince pies Percy was taking to the prison for Ted. Ted still refused to let Shona visit him. Lily had twice become hysterical during her visits and now no longer went to the prison.

'Why doesn't Mum go any more?' Shona asked Percy as she washed up the baking dishes. He sat at the kitchen table reading the *Sporting Life*. 'Dad must miss her dreadfully. She's not helping him get through his imprisonment.'

'I think he prefers it. All she does is complain at how hard things are for us, which isn't true. Then she gets upset and makes a scene which is the last thing Ted needs.'

'She's changed since starting work at the Crown. She's drinking heavily. And Aunt Annie's a bad influence on her. I heard her trying to set Mum up with a date.'

'Lil is many things but she wouldn't betray Ted. Not that she weren't as wild as Annie before she met him. She loves Ted. There'll never be anyone else for her.'

Shona hoped Percy was right, but Lily had a funny way of showing her love. It was becoming wrapped up in bitterness and reproach. Ted deserved more support from his wife.

Cooking his favourite dishes was all Shona could do to try and alleviate his unhappiness at being away from his family at Christmas. Keeping herself busy and ensuring that Christmas was not spoilt for the twins eased her sadness that Ted would not be with them.

Tonight the twins had finished making paper chains out of coloured paper cut into strips then glued together. She was standing on a chair drawing-pinning the last around the sitting room when Lily came home.

Lily propped herself against the doorframe. Her eyes were glazed and her voice slurred. 'I don't want no bloody decorations up. You can take the tree down as well. What's the point without Ted here?' She burst into tears.

Shona climbed from the chair and put her arm around Lily. It was shrugged off. 'Don't touch me. You're a bloody cuckoo taking over my home. Always interfering. What the hell have we got to celebrate? You can take that lot down. There'll be no celebrating while my Ted's shut in a miserable prison.'

Shona recoiled at the violence of loathing Lily directed at her. Lily's lipstick was smeared and her lips swollen from what had obviously been a passionate kiss, making hypocrisy of her words.

'It's for Johnnie and Jamie. They miss their dad and don't understand what's happening. Ted wouldn't want the boys to miss out on Christmas. He always made it so special. They've spent hours making these chains and doing the tree. Can't we keep them up for their sakes?'

Lily scowled and tottered to the sideboard to pour herself a sherry. She tossed it back before replying.

'You kids are all ungrateful. Ted's inside because he wanted the best for you. Go on, be selfish and make merry while your father is shut away. I won't have nothing to do with it.'

'You don't mind enjoying yourself at the pub though, do you? I saw you dancing on the tables on Saturday night.'

'Why you . . .' Lily made a grab for Shona's hair.

94

She sidestepped and Lily overbalanced and fell down in an armchair. She was too drunk to get up.

Shona hated to see Lily like this. Despite all the insults in recent years she still loved Lily. She just didn't like her any more. 'Mum, I don't condemn you for trying to enjoy yourself. You work hard and deserve a bit of fun. But don't impose one rule for yourself and another for us. The boys don't understand why Dad's not here. You're not being fair on them.'

The family who had taken her in and showered her with love had changed, but Shona was idealistic enough to want to see a return to those happy days. 'It's hard for us all, Mum,' she accused. 'For Dad's sake we must hold our heads up with pride. Dad deserves our respect. Getting drunk every night brings the family into further disrepute.'

Lily glared at her. 'I ain't drunk. And any more of your lip, my girl, and you're out on your ear. I'm sick of your airs and graces. Ain't we good enough for you now? You were abandoned by your la-di-da bloody parents with their flash clothes and car. We were mugs to take you in. You're an ungrateful wretch. Go on, bugger off. We don't want you.'

Tears stung Shona's eyes and she battled to contain them. Lily's hatred stabbed deep into her heart. 'You need my money or you will lose the house. I won't desert you. I promised Dad, I'd help you and the kids.'

'I don't want you here. I saw how you used to suck up to Ted so he would buy you pretty things. You want to steal his love from me. I hate you.'

Shona faced her and the colour drained from her cheeks. She'd had enough of Lily's tantrums but she couldn't abandon her duty to Ted. 'I won't leave while you need my money. But don't worry, as soon as Dad's out of prison and working, I'll be off.'

'That's enough, Lil.' Percy stood by the door. 'Why do you keep picking on the girl? She works her fingers to the bone to help out.'

'Go on, take her side.' Lily's mouth curled with malice. 'You're just like Ted. You don't see her sly side, only her pretty face.' She erupted into noisy tears.

'Shona is one of the best. I know it's not easy for you, Lil, but don't take it out on her.'

Lily scowled at her father. 'She's a bloody cuckoo. She's always trying to steal Ted's and your love from me. Now she's after making the twins love her more than me.'

'I'm not trying to steal anything from you, Mum.' Shona clenched her fists at her side, fighting against the pain Lily's words had inflicted. 'I love the twins. They're my brothers.'

Lily lifted her tear-streaked face, her reddened eyes puffy and full of loathing. 'No they sodding ain't. They ain't nothing to you.'

Shona's eyes blazed. She didn't have to stand for this. Nothing Shona did was right in Lily's eyes. It was obvious that Lily hated her and regretted the day she had adopted her. 'I'll take the day off work and get myself a place tomorrow,' she declared and marched to the door.

Percy put out his arm to stop her. 'Calm down, both of you. Shona ain't going nowhere. This is her home.' Percy glared at his daughter with disgust. 'Shona, don't pay any heed to Lil. It's the drink talking.'

Shona wished she could believe that. She knew otherwise. Lily meant every cruel word she spoke. She smiled sadly at him. 'No it isn't, Grandad.'

Lily glowered at her. 'Still here, are you?'

Percy took Shona's shoulders and stopped her leaving. 'I won't hear another word about this. This is Shona's home. And it will break Ted's heart if she leaves. Ain't he got enough to put up with, Lil? And you'll lose this house without Shona's money. You should be grateful she tolerates your bloodymindedness.'

Lily flopped down in a chair. 'She can stay.' The words were grudging.

Shona accepted them. She owed it to Ted to help his family. It would only be until he was released from prison.

When Shona left the room Percy sighed and continued to regard his daughter. 'Why do you act so crazy? Shona's a good kid. And you shouldn't drink so much.'

Lily ploughed her fingers through her hair and groaned. 'I can't bear Ted being locked up. I miss him so much. It's my fault. I kept on at him to get us nice things. I wanted a home he could be proud of. I know the drink makes me mean but I need it to dull the pain. Shona's so bloody perfect no wonder Ted adores her.'

'You're his wife and he loves you dearly.' Percy sounded weary. 'You always want too much. You were the same as a kid. You always had to have the best.'

Lily hankered for a drink. Drink made her forget her misery. It dampened her loss and feelings of inadequacy. She hated being second best. Percy had doted on Annie as his favourite until she got pregnant. Her childhood had been consumed with jealousy. Now there was Shona to compete with. She was young, beautiful and vivacious. Everything Lily had once been. The pride in Ted's eyes when he looked at their adopted daughter poisoned the love she herself had for Shona. When she married Ted, she wanted to look nice and have a lovely home so that people would envy her. It never worked out how she wanted. Some neighbour always got something better than them, or a woman would look at Ted with a glitter of enticement in her eye. Jealousy would rear up and consume and drive her to act as she did.

As Shona undressed she could hear Lily and Percy talking downstairs. When she got into bed her thoughts were on Ted. 'I'm doing all I can for Lily, Dad, but she won't listen to me.' She stared up at the cracks in her ceiling, fighting against her anger at Lily's attitude. 'I miss you, Dad. Nothing is the same without you.'

97

As her mind slipped into a soporific haze just before sleep claimed it, she felt a presence as though Ted was in the room with her. He was telling her to be strong. The image of Ted distorted, becoming taller, and she was on a swing hanging from a wide branch of an oak tree. She looked up into the oak canopy, the momentum of the swing and its familiarity lulling her. As the swing went back she saw a Georgian town house and a tall, blond man seated in a wooden garden chair was waving to her. Then the scene changed. The house was full of people and the blond man was in a doorway greeting people. Laughter and music filled her dreams. But she wasn't part of the crowd of grown-ups. She was watching them through the banisters of the stairs. The man was smiling and, seeing her spying on them, winked at her.

Suddenly Shona was fully awake. That was her home. She was certain of it. The man was her real father. His image had been clearer this time. A handsome face with high cheekbones, full lips and teasing, merry eyes. She clung to the image, striving to imprint it on her memory. She mustn't let it escape her again.

She realised she was perspiring and her breathing had become erratic. She now knew what her real father looked like and that the house was not in the East End of London but the suburbs. But where? It would be like looking for a needle in a haystack. She struggled to remember more. It was hopeless. But the image of the man stayed in her mind. It was a start. In time other layers would peel back and her past life would be revealed.

By nine o'clock on the evening of Christmas Eve Shona was exhausted. The twins were overexcited and wouldn't go to sleep as they wanted to see Father Christmas when he filled the rainbow-coloured stockings Shona had knitted for them. Lily was working and Percy had gone out to another pub.

Although he was very partial to his beer, he rarely came home the worse for drink, unlike Lily.

'Father Christmas won't come while you're awake,' she warned the twins for the hundredth time. 'So quieten down and go to sleep.'

Eventually they slept and Shona sank into a chair to regard the lighted tree. Her heart ached as she remembered past Christmas Eves with Ted joking as he wrapped the presents. Then he would set off to the pub and come back at closing time with a crowd of friends for an impromptu party.

Another image, hazy and indistinct, hovered at the edges of her mind. A man, too tall to be Ted and with pale blond hair, was standing over her bed holding out a large doll. The shadowy form of a woman was at his side.

Shona concentrated on the image. Were they her parents? The moment the thought formed the image faded. When she tried to reconjure it, it slipped away, elusive and intangible. She pressed her fingers to her head forcing herself to remember. A dull pain formed behind her eyes, its intensity building and with it the suffocating sensation of panic. It was always the same when she tried to recall the past.

Standing up she paced the sitting room floor. Her hands were trembling. She switched on the wireless, seeking to shake off the feeling of oppression. A play would take her mind from her troubles. A carol service was being broadcast but the sermon irritated her and she switched it off. The house was silent and in darkness except for the tree lights. Outside the voices of revellers were boisterous with merriment. More carol singers were progressing along the street and she took some coppers from her purse to give them when they knocked on the door.

All at once she felt lonely, something she had never experienced before. Marion had gone to a dance with Derek and Percy had offered to babysit while Shona went out. But Percy was looking drained after a busy week on the stall. He needed to relax with his friends, not cope with two boisterous, overexcited boys. Besides, all her girlfriends were spending the evening with their boyfriends and, though they had suggested that she join them, she didn't fancy being the only woman without a partner.

'Nick will be at the dance. He'll be disappointed if you don't show up,' Marion had suggested.

'I doubt it. If he wanted to take me, he'd have invited me. I doubt Nick will be alone either. A new girl every week, isn't that what you told me?'

'Derek reckons Nick fancies you. Nick's been busy all week, that's why you've not heard from him.'

No amount of persuasion from Marion had changed her resolve. Today was Wednesday and while Marion had seen Derek on the Sunday and Monday nights following the dance, she'd had no word from Nick.

A knock on the door broke through her reverie and picking up the coins for the carol singers she went to answer it.

Nick stood on the doorstep holding a spray of mistletoe over his head. The brim of his trilby was shading his eyes but his teeth flashed white as he grinned at her. 'I've come to get my Christmas kiss from my favourite girl.'

He looked very debonair in a dark suit and overcoat speckled with the large snowflakes which were beginning to fall. So great was her surprise she stared at him, speechless.

'Ain't you gonna ask me in? It's freezing out here.'

'I'm not sure Mum would approve of me having a man in the house when only the twins are here.'

His grin became wolfish. 'Derek said you were alone. That's a crime for a beautiful woman on Christmas Eve.' He shivered dramatically and his grey eyes were soulful and pleading. 'Don't I even get a cup of tea after coming all the way from Stratford to see you?'

When she still hesitated, he put his hand over his heart.

100

'I promise I ain't gonna try nothing on, if that's what you fear. Except for a Christmas kiss.' He removed his trilby and his mesmerising eyes bored into her in a way which made her heart pound wildly. His voice dropped to a husky promise. 'Trust me. I've been thinking about you a lot. You're the girl I want to celebrate Christmas Eve with.'

'I can't go out, Nick. The twins . . .'

'It's the company that's important, not the place.'

Temptation overrode judgement. There was laughter from revellers at the end of the street and music coming from several houses. Everyone else was having fun.

'Do you promise to behave yourself?'

He pulled a rueful face. 'OK.'

'Just for half an hour,' she cautioned as she stepped back for him to enter. 'Go into the sitting room, the fire's alight in there.'

He whistled in appreciation when he saw the tree lit up and the room bathed in a cosy orange glow. When Shona went to put on the light, he stopped her. 'This is far nicer. I ain't got a tree at my place.'

'You don't live with your family, do you?'

'I moved out when I was sixteen. There were seven kids in our family cramped into three bedrooms. I like the freedom having a place of me own gives me.'

'Do you still see your family?'

He shrugged. 'The old man and me don't see eye to eye. I call in to see that Mum and the kids are all right every fortnight or so.'

It was clear from his tone that he didn't want to talk about his family. She remembered her manners. 'Do you want some tea? I've got some mince pies as well.'

He pulled a half-bottle of whisky and a bottle of port out of his overcoat pockets. 'I'll give the tea a miss. You're gonna have a drink. Me mum says it wouldn't be Christmas without a drop of port to merry things along.'

'Just one. I'm not much of a drinker.' Having seen how it affected Lily, Shona usually avoided alcohol.

Nick grinned. 'What's Christmas Eve without a drink?'

She got two glasses from the sideboard. Nick removed his hat and coat and filled both glasses to the brim. He raised his. 'Merry Christmas, Shona.'

'Merry Christmas, Nick.'

The sprig of mistletoe was held over her head, his grey eyes alight with promise. 'A kiss for good luck.'

'The curtains are open. People can see in.'

'Close the curtains,' his voice coerced. 'It's cosier.'

'But if anyone saw you come in, they'd think we're up to no good. I don't want unnecessary gossip getting back to Dad.'

'You're a worrier. No one saw me come in.'

'But if we have nothing to hide, why shut ourselves away? My reputation is very precious to me.'

He put his head on one side and regarded her for a long moment in silence. Then he pulled one curtain as far across the window as the tree. 'That suit you? Discreet but not secretive.'

The room was charged with intimacy. Again she was aware of the potent pull of his masculinity. Had she been foolish to ask him in? Her heart began to pound in anticipation. In the days since the dance when she had heard no word from him, she had told herself that Nick had forgotten her. But her dreams had been filled with his image and the sensations his kiss had evoked.

He looked from her to the mistletoe and lifted a dark brow. Self-consciously she moved towards him, the tenderness in his gaze making the breath snatch in her throat. When his mouth took hers, her senses reeled. She didn't protest when he led her to the sofa and they sank down upon it. His kisses became more passionate and she answered their frenzy. Then the touch of his hand closing over her breast caused her to stiffen. She could feel her nipple swell and a glorious tingling sensation spread to the pit of her stomach. It took all her willpower to push his hand away.

'No, Nick. You promised.'

His hands moved to her face and he drew back to gaze down into her eyes. 'Do you know you're driving me crazy with wanting you?'

His lips blazed a trail of kisses along her jaw and down her throat. They were no longer sitting but reclining, moulded chest to thigh, the hardness pressing against her hip a warning she must end this madness. She broke away from his tantalising kisses and pushed against his chest. 'That's enough, Nick.' Her voice was husky and breathless.

He silenced her protest with another kiss. His passion was unrestrained. Spurred by the hunger of desire, he feasted on her, crushing her against him. Spirals of exquisite sensations encased her. His kisses wove a seductive magic, turning her blood to fire and her flesh aflame. Innocence was shed as age-old intuition made her hips undulate against him. Nick with masterly precision insinuated closer, deft hands unfastening her bra to caress her breasts.

There was a loud rap on the doorknocker and several voices burst into: '*Once in royal David's city stood a lowly cattle shed.*'

Shona heaved Nick from her and stood up. With hands that shook, she straightened her clothing and smoothed her hair. 'You said you wouldn't try anything,' she accused as she picked up the coins for the carol singers.

'I weren't doing nothing you weren't enjoying.'

Shame burned her cheeks. 'I think you'd better leave.'

She left the room to pay the singers. Their chorus of Merry Christmases followed her back into the sitting room. Nick was sitting up but had made no move to go. Shona leaned against the doorway. 'Please leave, Nick. You shouldn't have come here tonight knowing that I was alone.'

He stood up. 'I want to see you again.'

'Tonight proved that I can't trust you.'

'And if I say I've learned my lesson?' He touched her cheek in a featherlight caress. 'I didn't force you, Shona. I've got too much respect for you for that.'

She hung her head. If she looked at him and saw the coercion in his eyes, she would waver. 'It's best if we don't see each other, Nick. You want more from me than I am prepared to give.'

'We could be good together. Surely your grandad will babysit on New Year's Eve? If you prefer safety in numbers we'll go out with Derek and Marion. I'll be round for you at eight thirty and we'll paint the town red.'

He shrugged into his coat and holding his hat between his hands gave her a smile which melted her resistance. He wouldn't take no for an answer and deep in her traitorous heart she was glad. No matter that she knew he was a scallywag and it was all bound to end in heartache for her, the thought of not seeing him again devastated her. His farewell kiss was almost brotherly in its brevity, leaving her even more confused at the emotions he aroused in her.

Chapter Nine

'Let's all make a wish as Mummy cuts the Christmas cake,' Shona encouraged. Her eyes pleaded with her mother. Lily had not touched her lunch or pudding and was steadily knocking back the sherry.

A silence fell on the room. It was obvious there was only one wish wanted by the family. Johnnie suddenly burst into tears. 'I want my daddy.'

Jamie joined him.

'Stop that wailing,' Lily fumed. She pushed herself up from her chair and staggered to the door. 'Your daddy ain't bloody here. I'm going to bed.'

Shona consoled the twins. 'Dad can't be with us this year. It's not that he doesn't love you. Look at the lovely toy fire-engines he asked Father Christmas to bring you.'

Percy coughed and surreptitiously wiped a tear from his eye. 'There's some chocolate money on the tree waiting for someone to eat it.' He winked at Shona and led the distracted twins out.

All day Shona and Percy had tried to keep the twins' spirits up while the dark shadow of Lily's brooding destroyed the festive mood. Shona spent the next hour clearing the table and washing up. From Marion's house next door could be heard the sound of riotous laughter. They had been invited to join them at tea-time but Lily had insisted they participated in no celebrations.

She fingered a silver bracelet. Percy had given it to her saying it was what Ted had asked him to buy her. Lily had been given a gold and amethyst brooch.

'I don't want a bloody brooch. I want my Ted,' Lily wailed.

'Then you should have thought of that before you kept demanding more and more from the man,' Percy raged.

Lily threw a full ash-tray at him and had run weeping from the room.

Shona's own heart was heavy. It would have been easy to give in to tears but melancholy solved nothing. In the next room the boys were now playing noisily and Shona felt isolated. Without Ted this house no longer felt like her home. There had been no present from Lily and Lily hadn't bothered to open the perfume Shona had bought for her. A lump rose to her throat, she missed Ted so much.

Her eyes misted and she stood at the kitchen sink staring out of the window to the darkened garden. A large hand rested on her shoulder and when she glanced round, Percy's expression was grave.

'This ain't no Christmas for you. Why don't you go next door for an hour or so with your friends? And make some plans to go out New Year's Eve. That's a time for the young. Another year passing just reminds me I'm another year older.'

She wrapped her arms around him. 'I have been asked out New Year's Eve. Are you sure you don't mind babysitting?'

'What would make me happy is to see you enjoying yourself.' His eyes sparkled with a teasing light. 'And is it a man who's asked you out?'

She blushed. 'I met him at a dance before Christmas.'

'Who is this chap you've kept so quiet about? And why hasn't he been round?'

'He stopped by briefly on Christmas Eve to ask me out. His name's Nick Blake.'

Percy frowned. 'Not Roy Blake's son from over Limehouse, is he? Roy is a nasty piece of work. You don't want nothing to do with any of that lot.'

'Nick lives in Stratford. His family come from Hackney and he knows Dad.'

Percy shook his head. 'In the circumstances that don't hearten me. He don't work at the engineering factory, does he?'

'He works in the docks.' Her own misgivings about some of Nick's activities resurfaced but her attraction to him made her want to believe that he was a good man. She supposed that in many ways he was like Ted and that made her forgive the rogue in him.

'I know you wouldn't have nothing to do with a wrong 'un. All the same I wouldn't like to see you get hurt.'

'You'll like him, Grandad.' There was confidence in her voice which overlaid her twinge of uncertainty. 'You'll meet him when he calls for me on New Year's Eve.'

She dressed with care for her date with Nick. Her excitement had been building all week and she couldn't put him out of her mind. Lily left for the pub at six thirty and with typical naughtiness the boys would not settle and insisted Shona read them a story. She was still trying to quieten them when there was a knock at the door at a quarter to eight.

She rushed to the top of the stairs and saw Percy open the door and after an exchange of words invite Nick in.

A rush of nervousness made her descend the stairs slowly. Nick lifted his gaze to her and at encountering the admiration in his eyes, a heady excitement heated her skin.

The moment was broken by Johnnie running to the top of the stairs. 'Who's at the door? Is that my daddy?'

The question had begun a week before Christmas. Each time it was spoken it made Shona's heart wrench. Johnnie wouldn't accept his daddy wasn't coming home soon.

'I told you Daddy won't be home for a while. Now get back into bed and I'll tuck you in.'

'I'll see to them, Shona,' Percy insisted. 'You go out and

enjoy yourself. Mind you're back by one o'clock, or there'll be hell to pay from Lily.'

Marion wasn't ready, for they could see through the front-room window that Derek was talking to Mr Lockyer.

'Let's wait out here,' Nick said drawing Shona behind the high privet hedge of the Lockyers' front garden. He took her into his arms and kissed her with restrained passion. When he eased back his voice was throaty. 'You're ruining me social life. I've been thinking of you all week.'

She smiled up at him. 'I hope that means you intend to behave yourself tonight?'

'If that's what it takes to see you again, looks like I'm gonna have to.'

Marion's door opened and her friend giggled at seeing them standing behind the hedge. 'You two don't waste time. Pity me mum will have her nose to the window or we'd have a kiss and cuddle ourselves before we hit the town. So where we going?'

'Only one place to go on New Year's Eve,' Nick declared. 'Up West to join the revellers in Trafalgar Square at midnight.'

'But it's freezing,' Shona observed.

'We've got each other to keep us warm,' Nick countered by putting his arm around her shoulders and drawing her close.

The West End was crowded. Shona had never been there at night before and when they came out of the tube at Piccadilly Circus she was startled at the press of people on the pavement. The statue of Eros was silhouetted against bright electric lights and women of dubious repute were parading the steps of the fountain and the surrounding pavements. Nick guided Shona expertly through the crowd.

'There's a jazz club round here which is sensational and we can dance.'

'Aren't jazz clubs rather seedy and disreputable?' Shona queried. 'And this is Soho, isn't it? Mum warned me to stay clear of it. It's a bad place, Nick. Aunt Annie often comes up here and Grandad says it's an evil place. Let's go somewhere else.'

'Your grandad is old fashioned. Would I bring you somewhere dangerous? Some of the clubs should be avoided but not the one I'm taking you to. It's classy.'

They turned down a side street and Shona felt her skin prickle with unease. It was poorly lit and when a drunk lurched out of a doorway almost colliding with her, she barely managed to smother a scream.

'Watch where you're going, mate,' Nick said, drawing Shona away from the drunk. 'Sorry about that, sweetheart. Here's the club. It's respectable and popular with the toffs.'

The well-lit entrance dispelled some of Shona's doubts. A jazz combo was playing a lively number. When they were taken to a table with a pristine white cloth with a small art-nouveau table lamp and posy of pale yellow chrysanthemums, she relaxed. Nearly all the tables were full. Several men were in dinner suits and the women wore satin and sequinned dance dresses. Flashes of gemstones were added proof of their wealth. In the centre of the floor was a small area for dancing.

'Does it meet with your approval?' Nick asked as he helped her out of her coat and the waiter took it to the cloakroom.

'I've never been anywhere like this. It's lovely. I'm sorry I doubted your choice.'

Nick looked extremely handsome in a dark suit with a tie. Shona had on the same sapphire dress she wore when she met Nick at the dance at Stratford but she had sewn two sprays of cream silk rosebuds over the shoulderstraps to make it more elegant for a special occasion.

Nick stood behind her chair as she sat at the table and leaned over her shoulder to whisper, 'You look sensational.'

The table was small and when they were seated his thigh and shoulder constantly brushed hers. Each touch ignited a tingling flame in her flesh. Nick took her hand and raised it to his lips. The romantic gesture and his unexpected good manners impressed Shona.

'Champagne,' he ordered from a passing waiter.

'Nick, you mustn't! That's too expensive,' Shona protested.

'Only the best for you, sweetheart.'

They were words so often spoken by Ted. Nick was so like Ted, whom she adored. It both attracted her and made her cautious.

Marion giggled at overhearing his words and winked at Shona. She was snuggling up to Derek, unable to keep her eyes or hands off him. Marion was clearly smitten. Shona was naturally more restrained. Nick was lavish in his compliments, their glibness making her suspect that they rolled easily off his tongue to any woman he wanted to charm.

'You make me sound something I'm not,' she remonstrated, gently. 'And you're embarrassing me.'

He laughed and raised his champagne flute to her. 'You're something else, Shona.'

She sipped her drink and wrinkled her nose at the rising bubbles. 'This is nice.'

'There'll always be champagne for you,' Nick said. 'Nothing but the best *for* the best.'

The combo began to play a slow number and Nick drew her on to the dance floor. Again they moved in harmony. The evening became magical. The upsets of the past week were forgotten.

The evening passed quickly and Shona was disappointed to leave the romantic atmosphere of the club when Derek insisted that they make their way to Trafalgar Square in time to hear Big Ben strike midnight. The cold air after the warmth of the jazz club made Shona sway.

'Oh dear, I shouldn't have had that last glass of champagne. I feel rather dizzy.'

'Hold tight to me.' Nick put his arm around her. 'I don't want us separated in the crowd.'

They reached Trafalgar Square with ten minutes to spare. People were climbing on the base of Nelson's column and clambering to sit on the bronze lions. Some young men holding drink bottles were prancing about in the fountains. Buskers played popular tunes and people sang and danced with an air of frivolity. The traffic honked as it wove its way around the square towards Westminster or Charing Cross.

The atmosphere was electric. Rough cockney voices mixed with aristocratic nasal twangs. Drunkenness made some revellers maudlin and others boisterous. A group of young men were jostling a chestnut seller and throwing the hot nuts into the crowd.

A cry went up that it was nearly midnight and gradually the hubbub subsided to a hush of expectancy. Nick put his arm around Shona's waist and drew her against him as the crowd jostled and sought to be reunited with friends.

Then the first chimes from Westminster reached them and as the famous bell began to strike twelve the Square erupted with cheers. Several hats were thrown into the air and a raucous cheering all but deafened Shona.

Nick had drawn Shona tight into his arms and kissed her long and passionately until she thought her lungs would burst. Lightheaded from his kiss and the champagne, she clung to him and laughed as they were buffeted by the revellers. He pulled her into a deserted doorway and kissed her again. When he finally broke away he cupped her face into his hands.

'I want you to be my girl, Shona.'

'You hardly know me, Nick.' Her words of reason belied the frantic and ecstatic pounding of her heart.

'I know what I want and I want you. I'm twenty-two next month. I've got big plans for this year. A new year means a new beginning. With you at my side I'm gonna go places.'

'You don't need me to make something of your life, Nick.'

'But I do. You give me a vision of a better future. I'll go and speak with your dad if you want his permission for us to

111

see more of each other. I'm serious, Shona. I'll call round tomorrow and talk with your mum.'

The euphoria which had been building in Shona drained away. How could any relationship between Nick and herself work? He had a reputation for always having a woman on his arm and she was so rarely free to go out. 'I'm not sure how Mum will react to me having a boyfriend who is older than me. I'm not seventeen until March.'

His grin was self-assured. 'Don't you worry, sweetheart, I'll get round your mum. She's a woman, isn't she?'

His confidence heightened her fears that her attraction to him was ill-fated. She tried to explain. 'Things are difficult with Mum at the moment. She can be unpredictable with her moods.'

Nick smiled with bold assurance. 'I want you, Shona. Leave your mum to me.'

Why did that smile have the power to persuade her everything would be fine? She viewed Lily more objectively. 'I don't see why Mum should object. She was courting Ted at seventeen and was married a year later.'

Nick's expression became wary. 'Hey, let's not jump the gun. I'm talking about you being my girl so we can get to know each other better. I ain't ready to settle down for some years yet.'

The warning was as chilling as it was uncalled for. She wasn't a woman whose only goal in life was marriage. 'Don't worry, I'm not after stealing your freedom. I've got some living of my own to do before I tie myself to a life of housework and bringing up children.' Colour flared into her cheeks, warming them like a brazier in the chill air. 'Let's forget the whole idea. I don't need complications in my life at the moment. We can be friends and see each other now and then, if that's what you want.'

'That's not what I want,' he replied, clearly rattled. 'I want you to be my girl. I don't want you seeing anyone else.'

'I don't think you know what you want, Nick. You've got a reputation for liking the ladies. I don't run with the pack.' Her own temper was rising dangerously. She didn't want to lose him but she had too much pride to allow herself to be taken for granted. Neither would she join a line of women all pining for him to take them out.

'You've got it wrong. I've had my share of girlfriends but I know when I've struck gold.'

It was tempting to believe him. Common sense made her cautious. To her relief Marion and Derek were approaching.

'I have to get home now. I think it's better if we are just friends. Then we both know where we are with each other.'

She could feel his anger and they spoke little on the journey home. Although he drew her arm through his when they alighted from the bus, the gesture was abstracted and she could feel the tension in the muscles beneath her fingers. When they passed Marion's hedge her friend and Derek ducked behind it to say goodnight. Shona regarded Nick's continued silence as a sign that he was displeased with her. The thought of not seeing him again brought an ache to her heart. She fumbled in her bag for her doorkey.

'Thank you for a lovely evening, Nick.' She was unable to prevent a catch in her voice, convinced that he would not want to see her again.

His hands rested on her shoulders and prevented her from opening the door. 'Will your grandfather have the boys for you tomorrow evening? I meant what I said about you being my girl. Sure I've played the field a bit in the past. I hadn't met you then. I haven't asked anyone else to be my girl. Does that convince you I'm serious about you?'

'Oh, Nick.' She melted into his open arms. 'I'm sure Grandad will agree. I'm not so sure about Mum.'

He kissed her and they were locked in an ardent embrace when the door was flung open and Lily stood glaring at them as they broke apart.

113

'So this is what you get up to, acting like a cheap slut on my doorstep. You were supposed to be home quarter of an hour ago, young lady. Does this man know you're only sixteen? Little more than a child.'

The words were calculated to humiliate Shona. 'I'm sorry we're late, Mum. The buses were held up. The streets are still full of people.'

Nick stepped forward. 'Mrs Carrington, I'm sorry I couldn't get her back by one o'clock as agreed.'

'You wouldn't be carrying on with her like this in the small hours of the morning if her father was here, would you?' Lily's words were slurred with drink. She glared at Shona. 'Get inside, you little tart. What's your dad gonna say about this? What else have you been up to? You've been very secretive about having a boyfriend.'

'There's nothing secretive about me seeing Shona, Mrs Carrington.' There was an edge of righteous anger in Nick's voice. 'I'm a friend of Derek, Marion's boyfriend. I've asked Shona out tomorrow. I was hoping you'd be home from your work tonight to ask your permission.'

'Got an answer to everything,' Lily sneered. 'Regular smart Alec, ain't yer?'

Shona could feel Lily's antagonism. She was drunk and at her most difficult. 'Could Nick come in now for a cup of tea and you'll see there's nothing underhand about him.'

'I was about to go to bed. It's all right for you gadding about. I've been rushed off me feet at the pub.'

'Just for ten minutes, please, Mum.'

Nick stepped forward, the light from the hallway full on his handsome face. 'I wouldn't do anything to harm Shona's reputation. I know your husband quite well. He's a great bloke and didn't deserve such a harsh sentence.'

'You know my Ted?' Lily's voice changed to a softer note. 'Come in, young man.'

Lily steered Nick into the front room. 'Get us a cup of

tea, Shona. I want to hear how this young man knows my Ted.'

Grandad was sitting in the chair by the dying fire in the back room. 'Sorry, luv, she came home early and got into a taking at finding you out.'

'Don't worry. Nick knowing Dad has won her over.'

When Shona returned with the tea, Lily was sitting on the sofa next to Nick with a sherry in her hand and he had a glass of Grandad's whisky. Lily monopolised Nick's conversation for half an hour making him talk about Ted. Then her eyes began to droop and the drink finally overcame her. Head lolling back, she fell asleep.

Nick stood up. 'See you tomorrow, Shona. I told you it would be all right.'

She should have been reassured. Instead as she helped her mother up the stairs and put her to bed, Shona knew that Lily's mellowing towards Nick was because there was so much about him that was like Ted.

Was that why she was so captivated by Nick, because he was a charmer, a lovable rascal, like her father? Adoring Ted as she did, no ordinary man would attract her. Yet by seeing Nick was she also courting heartache, or even danger?

Chapter Ten

Shona had been seeing Nick for two months. He worked in the docks with Derek but, unlike his friend, he had his finger in other pies.

At first Lily had been reluctant for Shona to see him more than once a week although Percy had agreed to give up his Saturday night drink so that she could go out. Nick won Lily round. He never came to the house without some item still on rationing, usually extra eggs or bacon and sometimes luxuries like tinned salmon or even stockings. During the severest of the cold weather he arrived with a friend's van at eleven one night to deliver a sack of coal.

'You're a godsend, Nick,' Lily crooned. 'You couldn't get us some more knitting wool? We could all do with an extra jumper. I've unpicked all my old ones and Shona's knitted them up for the boys. A dab hand with the needles is Shona. She'll do you a couple of those nice cable patterned jumpers, if you want.'

'I'll see what I can do, Mrs Carrington. It's not one of my regular lines but this weather I reckon Percy could sell it under the counter on his stall.'

Shona protested; she hated Lily asking Nick for things. 'Mum, don't be so ungrateful. Nick's done so much for us already.'

'If your dad was here, he'd be doing the same. What with Ted inside we can scarce afford the necessities of life, let alone any extras.'

'It's my pleasure, Mrs Carrington.'

'Lily.' She smiled at him. 'It's time you called me Lily and also time you started coming round of a Sunday for lunch.'

Shona knew the invitation was given as Nick never came empty-handed. When she walked him to the door as he was leaving, she said, 'Much as we appreciate what you do for us, Nick, I wish you wouldn't get involved with stuff on ration. What if you get caught like Dad? It's not worth getting banged up for.'

'Don't worry about me,' he said, echoing the words Ted so often used to reassure her. 'Fainthearts get nowhere in this life. You have to seize your opportunities. I'm saving to get some capital for the future. There's gonna be a boom in building and in manufacturing. I want to get in on that.'

'There's honest trading. Percy will put a word in for you with the market inspector to get a stall.'

He shook his head. 'No disrespect to Percy, but it's a bigger business I'm after. With new houses shooting up to replace the bombsites, people are soon gonna want all the new gadgets that are coming on the market. You should see what I saw in American magazines some of the blokes had got hold of in the navy when I did my National Service. Refrigerators, washing machines and at affordable prices for those with a bit of spare money. Rationing won't go on much longer and every housewife is gonna want those things come another few years.'

'Somehow I can't see you as a shopkeeper, Nick.'

'Wholesaler. If you've got an eye for a future trend you can make a bomb. I've big plans for the future.'

'Just take care. Dad always said he'd never get caught.'

Nick grinned but his self-assurance didn't halt her misgivings. Intuition counselled that she didn't want a man who couldn't make a living honestly, but intuition didn't take account of emotions. Love was too powerful to be governed by caution. And with each meeting Shona was falling more deeply and irrevocably in love with Nick.

In March Shona was delighted when Nick invited her to meet his family the following Sunday for tea, although it brought on an unaccustomed bout of nerves. They were in the pictures and Marion and Derek had gone to buy ice-creams in the interval.

'What if they don't like me?'

'Mum will adore you. But Dad . . .' Nick paused, his eyes glinting. 'He can be awkward. We don't hit it off. And the road . . . The area's rough, not like where you live.'

Shona knew Nick was raised in one of the poorer districts. 'I won't be shocked if that's what you fear. The slum clearance is long overdue and most people are glad of a roof over their heads after so much bomb damage. You've spoken so much about your mum, I'm looking forward to meeting her.'

Despite Shona's reassurance, she was shocked when they turned down the narrow street. It was as though they had stepped back in time to the turn of the century. There were no gardens to the houses which were flat-fronted and featureless. A dozen scruffy children were playing tag in the street. Two elderly women sat on kitchen chairs outside their front doors, their legs spread wide revealing knee-length knickers as they gossiped. The paintwork was flaking on many of the houses. Some had torn nets and filthy windows. Others had immaculate white-stoned doorsteps and although the nets were creamy with age, they were spotless and the windows gleamed. It was to one of these houses that Nick led her. Even the door had a fresh coat of green paint.

Nick chuckled. 'Mum's doing you proud. She would have gone through the house until it sparkles and she's whitewashed the step and painted the door again.'

'That makes me sound rather formidable. What have you been telling her about me?'

'It's Mum's way. She'd be ashamed if I brought someone special home and her doorstep was dirty.' He hesitated before opening the door. 'You're the first girl I've brought home. Mum's invited all the family over.'

The honour Nick had accorded her brought a blush of pleasure to her cheeks. For her to meet his family meant that she was special to Nick, that he treated her differently to previous girlfriends.

When Nick pushed open the front door voices came from the front room and the smells of a cake baking and beeswax welcomed her. The lino each side of the narrow carpet runner shone in the light from the doorway.

'Mum, it's us,' Nick called out, helping Shona out of her coat and hanging it on a peg in the hall. He ushered her into the front room where the conversation had stopped.

Four men and two women stared at her with open curiosity. Two of his brothers with the same dark hair and grey eyes were younger than Nick and regarded her with shy interest. The two older men leered with open appreciation of her trim figure.

'Trust our Nick to get himself a looker,' commented the oldest and shortest. He was thick-set with a narrow moustache and had a shifty way of glancing round the room which Shona distrusted.

The women were more judgemental in their regard and Shona shifted uncomfortably. The older man, obviously Nick's father Bert, had a stern countenance, his face almost skeletal in its gauntness. There were deep furrows in his brow and from his nose to his mouth. After a piercing stare, he took his pipe out of his pocket and proceeded to fill it with tobacco in silence.

'This is Shona,' Nick began. 'Shona, my tall brother, who looks like he's going to eat you for tea, is Ronnie and that's his wife Eileen.'

Shona smiled at them. Ronnie had a broken nose and

heavy features and body. He was staring at her figure in a way she found uncomfortable. Eileen was wearing a dowdy grey dress which stretched tightly over her large bosom and hips. She was holding a grizzling six-month-old baby to her shoulder. She smiled nervously. She was a mousy woman, who looked weary and nervous. He introduced her to the others and another brother sauntered in from the kitchen.

'And I'm Henry.' He was good looking and from the lazy way he studied her knew it, but there was a cruel twist to his mouth. He was a man who used his looks to manipulate people but if that failed he'd resort to brute strength, Shona guessed.

It made her appreciate Nick's easy charm. He could look after himself in a fight but he wasn't driven by meanness, neither did he turn to force to get his own way.

'This is Sheila, my elder sister.' Nick indicated the other woman. Judging by her dark brows the woman in her middle twenties had dyed her hair blonde and it had a brassy tinge. She also wore bright red lipstick and heavy make-up.

'Nice to meet you I'm sure.' Her voice was shrill and unwelcoming as she studied Shona's royal blue dress with its full skirt. 'Nice that. Bet you didn't get it on clothing coupons. From your grandad's stall is it? Reckon he'll see me all right now you and Nick are so pally?'

'Take no notice, Shona.' Nick gave his sister a blistering glare. 'Sheila always wants something for nothing.'

'Pardon me for speaking,' Sheila snapped. 'I was only trying to make your girlfriend feel at home.'

'Let's find Mum.' Nick turned from his family, his expression taut. 'She'll be in the kitchen with my younger sister, Iris.'

The scene in the kitchen couldn't be more different. A short, plump woman hastily whipped off her apron at seeing Shona. Her grey hair was wound in a neat coil at the nape of her neck and her apple-cheeked face broke into a wide smile as she bustled forward to take Shona's

121

hand. 'I've heard so much about you, luv. It's a pleasure to meet you.'

'Thank you, Mrs Blake. Nick talks a lot about you. He thinks the world of you.'

Nick blushed and his mother struck him lightly on the arm with a tea-towel. 'He's a good boy. He's good to his old mum. And call me Queenie, it's more friendly.'

Shona saw that Nick got his cheery manner from his mother. She liked her immediately. Queenie didn't have a mean or malicious bone in her body. Despite her diminutive height there was a strength in her. Her pride showed in the way she kept her house spotless. Poverty would never rob this woman of her dignity. Seeing the scrubbed top of the kitchen table filled with sandwiches and cakes, Shona remarked, 'I hope you haven't gone to a lot of trouble on my behalf, Queenie. It looks lovely.'

'Mum always cooks enough to feed an army on a Sunday if the family come round,' Nick teased.

'And you make sure we have a treat or two.' Her love for her son shone in her eyes. Queenie smiled at Shona. 'It's good to see that Nick's found himself a decent girl at last.'

'Mum, you'll embarrass Shona,' Nick protested.

A slim girl of about thirteen hovered shyly by the back door. Nick strode to her and put his arm around her waist and drew her towards Shona. 'This is Iris, my kid sister.'

The girl had the family dark hair which hung down her back to her waist. Unlike Sheila she took after her mother and Nick with a warm and generous nature. 'Mum let me make the chocolate cake. It's Nick's favourite.'

Nick had often spoken of Iris, whilst he obviously had no time for Sheila. Shona took a twist of brown paper from her handbag and handed it to Iris. 'I thought you might like these. They're very popular at the moment.'

Four pretty mother-of-pearl and tortoiseshell hair-slides

spilled into Iris's hands as she opened the paper. Her face lit up with pleasure. 'They're beautiful.'

She handed another twist of paper to Nick's mother. 'I wondered if this would be of use to you. Grandad's started selling trimmings on his stall.'

Mrs Blake pressed the white lace collar to her ample bosom. 'It's lovely. It will brighten up my old maroon dress a treat. But you shouldn't have.' She kissed Shona's cheek. 'You're generous like my Nick.'

Shona liked Queenie and Iris. While enjoying Queenie's reminiscences of Nick as a child and details of all the naughty escapades he got up to, she also took the trouble to draw Iris out of her shyness.

Shona's distrust and wariness of other members of the family remained. For their own reasons they resented Nick and were more interested in their own concerns than in other people's. They were Nick's family and she was always friendly and polite to them but on other visits it was the growing friendship between herself, Queenie and Iris which was important to her.

It was the same in their own house. Percy accepted Nick but was guarded towards him. 'He's a charming rogue and too like your father for you to see any wrong in him. I'd hate to see you get hurt, Shona,' was his only comment.

Nick's gifts ensured that in Lily's eyes he could do no wrong and eventually she agreed that he could visit on a Thursday evening when Shona was babysitting.

'Just as long as you behave yourselves,' Lily warned. 'I don't want no shame brought to this house, Nick Blake.'

Lily was more virulent when Nick wasn't present. 'A man like Nick don't get us that stuff on the black market and expect nothing in return. If you shame us and get yourself pregnant, then you're out on the street, my girl. Your parents were no good or they'd have wanted you back.'

Shona had an unpleasant feeling that Lily would be delighted if she became pregnant, thereby proving that she was no good and neither were her real parents. It made Shona determined that she would walk down the aisle a virgin.

Nick was proud of her resolution, often saying, 'Too many girls don't value themselves highly enough. I'd never marry a girl who weren't a virgin.'

After a few drinks and a session of kissing when they were alone, desire frequently got the better of him. His passion carried Shona along in its wake. Yet always for her there was a point when she found the strength to pull back.

'No, Nick, that's enough.' She sat up on the sofa and turned away from him, shocked to discover how far she had allowed things to go. She was naked from the waist up. Her breasts were full and aching from his caresses and kisses and her hands shook as she fastened her brassiere and pulled on her blouse. Standing up, she kept her back to him as she fastened the buttons and tucked the blouse into her skirt. When she turned to him his face was dark.

'We can't go on like this, Shona. You're driving me crazy. I want you so much.'

'You know how I feel, Nick. It isn't easy for me.'

'I love you, Shona. It isn't wrong if we love each other.'

He had never told her he loved her before. Her heart pounded with joy. She had known that she loved him for weeks. It made denying him harder than ever.

'If I didn't love you, I wouldn't have permitted you so much. But I am determined to be a virgin when I marry. And I thought that was what you wanted from your bride.'

He dropped his gaze and stared into the flames of the coal fire for several moments. 'Then we'll get married, if that's what you want.'

Sensitive to his moods she caught the antagonism in his tone. It crushed her happiness. 'It has to be what you want, Nick. And because you want to spend the rest of your life with me, not just to get me into bed.'

He slammed his balled fist into his palm as he moved towards the fireplace. 'I do love you, Shona. But the truth is . . . marriage, well, I ain't ready for it yet. Too many of me mates are regretting getting tied down with kids. And I'd end up staying in the docks just to bring in a decent wage each week. I ain't gonna be a docker all me life.'

'Then maybe we shouldn't see each other any more.'

A groan was torn from him. 'That's not what I want. Perhaps I shouldn't come round so often. We'll see each other just at weekends.'

Iron bands seemed to have clamped around her heart and throat. She felt stifled, bereft at his words. The danger was always when they were alone together.

'It would be for the best. There's too much temptation on evenings like this. And even if you were ready to get married, I'm not going down the aisle until I can walk there on Dad's arm. It would break his heart if I denied him that honour.'

Nick nodded in understanding. 'It will all come right for us in the end, sweetheart. There ain't ever gonna be anyone else for me but you, Shona. We'll get hitched when Ted gets out. That ain't gonna be for another eighteen months or so even with remission.'

He kissed her with a tenderness that set her body on fire. Was she foolish to cling to her maidenly ideals? It would be so easy to give Nick what he wanted. But it meant she would surrender more than her virtue. It would mean abandoning her integrity. And something told her that once Nick had possessed her, she would cheapen herself in his eyes. He was a cocky devil and arrogant enough to mean what he said about marrying a virgin.

'I'll miss you terribly, Nick.'

He winked at her. 'I don't deserve you, Shona. You're in my blood. No other woman drives me crazy like you do. You're gonna still be my girl, ain't you? You wouldn't go out with another bloke?'

'You're more than man enough for me.'

He drew back. 'I'd better go. I've got to meet a man at the Bakers Arms. I'll see you on Saturday. I'll pick you up at eight.'

She loved him too much to demand more from him than he was prepared to give.

Chapter Eleven

The spring evenings without Nick made Shona restless but they gave her the chance to review her other goal: to be a reporter. Even her recent promotion out of the typing pool to act as junior secretary to one of the directors had not changed her focus. She was determined to break through the male dominance of male reporters and become established in her own right.

To this end she had already sent in three articles to the local newspaper about people who had led amazing and interesting lives. They had been returned. She picked up the editor's letter and scanned it. The editor commented on her lively style and suggested that as a woman she should concentrate on articles for the women's page such as advice for coping with shortages and other domestic issues. He even suggested she try the women's magazines.

Shona screwed the letter into a ball and flung it into the fire. 'Is that all he thinks a woman is capable of?' she fumed. 'There's enough middle-class women pontificating about utilising this and conserving that. That isn't my style. I want to write about real life and important issues.'

The following Saturday she was helping Percy out at the market in the afternoon when Walter, the one-legged busker, stopped to talk to them. Before he hobbled away Percy pressed half-a-crown into his hand. 'Get yourself a nice pie and mash on me, mate.'

Walter pulled the frayed peak of his cap to him. 'You're a good mate, Perce.'

When he was out of hearing, Percy sighed. 'Poor bugger. Got a month inside for begging and vagrancy. He found his possessions chucked out on the street and anything decent stolen for not paying his rent. No one will employ a cripple and now he ain't got a roof over his head. Poor sod queues up for a bed in the Sally Army's hostel every night. It makes me sick to me gut. He lost his leg fighting on the Somme and that's how his country repays him.'

'Surely he gets some pension from the government?'

'Not according to Walt. He ain't the only one either. And now there's another generation of men facing unemployment because of the wounds they received in the war, and little or no money to keep their families. Ain't nothing they can do about it.'

'Perhaps they can't, but others can.' A fierce light blazed in her eyes. 'Those men deserve better. I'm going to write to our MP and interview these men and stir up public sympathy. If I can get some articles accepted concentrating upon the human interest and injustice of what has happened to men like Walter . . .'

'Hold on now.' Percy scratched his head and stared at her in amazement. 'Blimey, girl, regular firebrand ain't yer? That sounds all very grand but no one is gonna print that stuff.' He glared at her fiercely. ''Ere, you ain't turned commie on us, 'ave yer? I'm a labour man myself, I don't go for this left-wing Bolshie stuff.'

Shona laughed at his vehemence. 'I'm not interested in the politics. I just don't think men like Walter should be forgotten.'

She looked up from serving a customer to see the tramp Bill staring at her from the doorway opposite. He had been listening to their conversation. Even though the days were warmer he still wore the red scarf she'd given him at

Christmas. 'No one will listen to you,' Bill said gruffly. 'The government doesn't want to know.'

His statement surprised her and her curiosity was piqued. An educated man like that could help her with an article on street life. The stall was suddenly busy with three women demanding service and she lost her chance to talk to Bill. But his words stayed with her. What if she could write an article that made the government take notice? Now that would be something. It would prove she could make a good journalist.

Over the weekend Shona couldn't stop thinking about Walter and the injustice he had suffered. On Sunday evening she was all for going down the Salvation Army hostel with Nick and talking to Walter and some of the other homeless men.

'I don't like the thought of you mixing with those winos. 'Cos that's what most of them are.'

'Don't prejudge them, Nick. I only want to talk with a few of the First World War veterans. If you don't want to come with me then I'll go alone.'

'No you won't. I ain't letting my girl loose in a place like that. I think you're mad though.'

Although the hostel didn't open for another hour there were twenty or so men huddled outside its doors. A bitter wind was blowing and some didn't have shoes and their feet were bound with rags.

'Isn't there anywhere they can go out of the cold?' Shona said, appalled by their suffering.

'Down the tube station until they get moved on by the police, that's about all,' Nick replied.

'I can at least buy some hot soup from the corner tea-stall for anyone who will talk to me. I can't see Walter in the queue.'

Nick held her back. 'Stay here. I'll talk to them. Some of them are a bit rough and they can be abusive.'

Shona was dismayed when only one man returned with Nick. He was scratching his head and had a yellow scarf tied over his frayed cap and a mat of tangled hair stuck out over the collar of his holed and torn overcoat. He smelt of rotting fish. Several others were scowling at her. Bill was there but he leaned against the wall with his eyes shut.

'Don't you want a cup of soup, Bill?'

He turned away. She tried again. 'I need to hear as many stories as I can, so that people will understand the injustice many of you have suffered.'

'What do you know about injustice?' Bill spoke without looking at her. 'Leave us alone. We don't want your pity. Some of us prefer the road to society.'

Shona was indignant. 'Pity has nothing to do with it. So maybe you're fine as you are. But what of those who want a home to live in and a job?'

The man with Nick coughed and spat on the pavement. 'I fought for me country and lost an arm.' He waved his stump at Shona. 'I went through hell to give others a better life. Look at me.'

'You never went through hell,' a burly man shouted. 'You spent the war in the nick.'

Shona realised that the tramp was trying to con her. 'You act as though this is all a joke or a free meal ticket. You'd rather lie for a measly cup of soup than tell the truth and see justice done.'

The tramp who had tried to lie to her turned nasty. 'Who's gonna take any notice of anything what a young chit like yourself writes?'

'I'll make them take notice,' she said with quiet confidence.

'Bah, you and whose army.' He shuffled off mumbling to himself.

'Let's go, Shona,' Nick said. 'This lot aren't worth your time. You can't help those who won't help themselves.'

Shona pulled away from him, made stubborn by so much aggression. 'Someone has to speak out for them. I won't stand back and see people suffer.'

'They won't thank you for it.'

Shona was surprised to hear Bill's voice directly behind her. 'I don't need their thanks. I want to do what's right.'

His red-rimmed eyes stared thoughtfully at her. Then he grunted, 'How about a cheese roll as well as the soup and I might be interested in telling you a few things.'

'Don't encourage him,' Nick warned. 'That's Batty Bill Miles. He's off his head and gets fighting drunk most nights. I once heard him declare that he worked with the French Resistance when a copper tried to arrest him for being drunk and disorderly. Batty as hell he is.' He laughed cynically. 'He don't half tell 'em, Shona.'

'Don't say that.' Shona rounded on him. 'I think he has something relevant to say.'

Nick scowled and squared up to Bill. 'I don't want no trouble for the lady. She's my girl.'

There was a nasty glint in Bill's eyes and for a moment Shona thought he was going to take a swing at Nick.

'Would you get Bill the roll and soup, please, Nick?' She attempted to defuse the situation.

When Nick went to the tea-stall she smiled at Bill. 'Don't mind Nick. He doesn't like me doing this.'

Bill scratched his beard. 'Your young man is a bit of a Jack the lad, but he's right to keep an eye on you. Some of these men would rob you as soon as look at you.'

'Did you work with the French Resistance, Bill?'

'What do you think?' The suspicion was back in his voice as he tested her.

'That you're an intelligent and well-educated man. Why should you lie? Do you want to talk about it?'

He turned his head away staring at Nick walking back towards them. He took the roll and soup. Shona waited until he had finished eating before asking, 'What made you take to the road?'

'That's my business.'

She back-tracked, unwilling to antagonise him. 'So what can you tell me?'

His opinions burst from him in a torrent and Shona had difficulty in getting everything down in shorthand, he expounded at such length. There were snatches of profound insight into the deprivation and neglect suffered by many who had spent years in mental institutions following the war and who found on their release that there was no place for them in society. Their descent into vagrancy was often swift and for many there was no alternative. He even had the solution to some of the problems the men faced.

The doors of the hostel opened and breaking off in mid-sentence and without even a goodbye, Bill rejoined the shambling queue.

'I told you he was off his head,' Nick stated. 'Waste of time that was. Did you hear his grand schemes?'

'A lot of them made sense, Nick. Bill is an educated man and must have come from a good family.'

'He's one brick short of a wall, if you ask me. Forget him, Shona.'

'I don't think Bill is off his head. He said some interesting things I'd like to talk to him about another time.'

'It's too dangerous, love. He was sober today. He could turn violent if he's been drinking. It ain't safe.'

Shona wasn't convinced that Bill would turn nasty towards her. She also knew that if she wanted to make a name for herself as a journalist she would have to place herself in dangerous situations to get a good story.

She had put aside her ambitions for too long, taking the easy and safe option of staying as a typist because they needed the money. She had enough evenings free and she was determined to use them to write articles no newspaper editor would ignore.

During the next two months Shona sent in a dozen articles to various newspapers. The subjects covered war veterans, the homeless, orphans, war widows raising young children, and also the courage and resilience of families struggling to survive with few possessions after being bombed out.

Several papers rejected them, saying they were too depressing and that their readers wanted more positive articles, hinting at prosperity to come. Also they insisted on photographs to go with the stories and Ted's old box camera didn't give clear enough pictures. One paper took two articles and sent their own photographer to get pictures of the people. The stories were of Cecil Bowen, a centenarian who still had a newsstand down the market and reminisced about his life as a barrow boy in Victorian times; and of Rachel Bloomfeld, a teenager who had both legs amputated after being trapped in a cellar after a direct hit and had started a support group for similar amputees.

She had one job interview as a junior reporter on a local weekly paper, but the work entailed covering weddings and writing a cookery page with household economy tips. The wages were half what she was getting now. The interview also coincided with a promotion at the insurance company to be assistant secretary to the head of the general accident department with an increase in salary. The house roof had been leaking since the storm last week and the builder had quoted a high fee for repairing it. Reluctantly she chose the promotion.

'That's your second promotion,' Marion said enviously. 'I'm still stuck in the typing pool. But you hate office work.'

They were sitting on the wall at Tower Green looking across at the Tower of London as they ate their lunchtime sandwiches. Shona shrugged. 'I haven't got much choice.'

'I thought you were keen to work on that paper,' Marion persisted.

'I was. Though covering weddings and writing household tips is not my idea of journalism.' Frustration tightened Shona's voice. 'It would have meant getting into the business and showing them I can do better. Unfortunately the pay was lousy. Mum wouldn't hear of me giving her less towards the bills each week.'

'But it was important to you,' Marion sympathised.

Shona threw her crusts on the pavement and watched a score of pigeons scrabbling for crumbs. 'Even Percy said that as money was tight it wasn't practical.' She shrugged fatalistically. 'He's right. I'd have to give up the market on a Saturday to cover the weddings which means Grandad would have to pay someone else, which he can't afford. It will only be until Dad comes out of prison. I can still do some freelance work.'

'Why take on so much? You should be out enjoying yourself in the week when you don't see Nick. I don't stay in pining the nights Derek is with his mates.'

'I can't afford to go out. I'm saving for a camera. I put a deposit on one in the pawn shop but it will take six months to pay for it.'

'Couldn't Nick get you one?'

'I didn't ask him. He gets so much for us already and he wouldn't take any money for it.'

Marion's expression was concerned as she regarded her friend. 'That shouldn't stop you having a bit of fun. I'm going up West tonight with some girls from work. It isn't one of Percy's darts nights. He won't mind staying with the twins. Why don't you come?'

'I'm broke this week.'

'Have you been buying meals for those tramps again?'

'Only Bill, and I had the devil's own job getting him to accept it. He's opening up more now. He worked with the

French Resistance in the war. A man like that and he lives on the street with no family.'

'That's if it's true. He could be feeding you a pack of lies. There's something weird about a person who lives like that. He could be a murderer on the run from the law.' Marion spread her arms in mock despair. 'I give up on you, Shona. And tonight will be my treat. It's been ages since we went out together without Del and Nick. It'll be a laugh.'

'I can't tonight. There's a meeting at the Town Hall I want to go to. An MP is talking about slum clearances in the East End.'

Marion pulled a face. 'Rather you than me. It would be more exciting listening to grass grow.'

'It could be relevant to an article I want to write. We can go up West tomorrow.'

'And I thought having a journalist for a friend would mean I would meet glamorous people. OK, tomorrow night it is.'

Shona agreed but her mind was already on the meeting she would attend and some pertinent questions she wanted answered by the MP.

Shona arrived late at the Town Hall. The twins had been playing up and wouldn't go to bed. The hall was full and the MP, Gerald Long, was already speaking. As she squeezed past several people to an empty seat in the middle of a back row she was struck by his attractively husky voice. She glanced up at the speaker and was disconcerted to find his piercing gaze upon her. For a moment his speech faltered as he stared at her.

Shona was flustered, feeling conspicuous with the politician regarding her so severely. She dropped her gaze and hurried to a seat. Gerald Long quickly recovered the momentum in his speech and was now addressing a row of aldermen and the mayor seated in the front seats. Taking out her shorthand notebook Shona began her notes. Soon she was caught by the command and assurance in his tone. She glanced up to study him. He was tall, well built without being stout, and looked much younger than the late forties which her initial research had revealed was his age. The photographs of him had made her surmise that his thick, pale gold hair had been grey. He was still handsome although his face and figure had fleshed out since the photographs taken during his last campaign for re-election. He spoke with convincing passion and with eloquent assurance. Undoubtedly he had charisma. Even the hecklers he took on good-naturedly and his wit turned upon them, drawing laughter from the gathering.

As she stared at him her heartbeat began to rise. Seeing him in the flesh, his mannerisms and the force of his personality and charm triggered the strangest feeling that she knew him. Her notes forgotten, she continued to study him. With each moment her certainty grew. His words blurred as her eyes rounded. His build, colouring, the way he moved, were all familiar. The musty, drab Town Hall faded. In her mind she saw a glittering hallway and a houseful of guests. The hallway was familiar. She was seeing it from above and knew that she was perched on a stairway looking down. The MP was standing in the doorway of the front room greeting people as they entered. He looked up at her and winked.

Her notepad slid to the floor. He was the image of the man she saw in her hazy dreams. Could Gerald Long be her father?

Stunned, she couldn't take her eyes off him. Twice she saw his stare flicker in her direction, pause, then slide away. Her heart thundered in her breast. Could it be true?

She retrieved her notepad. Her mind was whirling too fast for her to take any notes about the meeting. Instead she was scanning her memory for what she knew about Gerald Long. He was one of the most popular politicians and cabinet ministers of the day. He had been a junior minister in the War Cabinet and had the credentials of most politicians:

old family, public school education, followed by Oxford. Though his family was an old one it had been almost bankrupt. His first marriage to the daughter of a senior minister had launched his career in politics. His wife was also a wealthy heiress in her own right. She had died tragically a few years after their marriage in a car accident, leaving Gerald Long a wealthy man. He had then returned to his playboy existence, escorting starlets and debutantes to parties. It was now rumoured that he was about to remarry, this time to a wealthy young widow.

Hot prickles stung her spine and a shudder passed through her. Her hands were shaking and she pressed them tightly together. She could recall only the recent facts about Gerald Long she had read in the newspapers. Although the image within the house remained, nothing more from her past was reclaimed.

She rubbed her brow. This was crazy. She was imagining things. Throughout her childhood with the Carringtons she had fantasised who her real parents could be. Her mother had not figured much and was always a shadowy figure. Thoughts of her real father dominated with the certainty that he would find her again, unless he had died in the war. A profound conviction told her that her father was alive. Yet the war had been over for years and he had not found her. Did he no longer care? Or was it too dangerous?

Another shiver chilled her although the room was hot and stuffy. The sense of danger persisted. She tried to concentrate on taking notes of the speech which were important for an article. After half a page her mind drifted. Another careful scrutiny of the politician increased her belief that she had known him as a child.

It was unnerving. She struggled to analyse her mounting certainty that this man could be her father. Why had he not come forward when the papers had printed the story of her loss of memory? Gerald Long had served as a politician at

Westminster throughout the war. Had circumstances and his career changed the loving man whose image she had clung to? Perhaps to acknowledge her existence could be an embarrassment to him. Again her eyes bored into Gerald Long. His face was in profile as he answered a question from a man on the opposite side of the room. He was a known playboy with a long line of mistresses behind him. Was she his bastard daughter? A liability that could damage his flourishing career?

With a jolt she realised from the round of applause and some heckling that the questions were ended. Gerald Long was being escorted from the stage. She couldn't let him go without speaking to him. Surely that moment of hesitation when she arrived had been because he recognised her? She stood up as he was approaching the back of the hall. His stare was fixed on the doorway ahead. She cleared her throat.

'Mr Long, when do you intend these new houses to be built to replace the slums?'

A thick-set man at his side was between her and the MP. Gerald Long didn't acknowledge that she had spoken and his step quickened. He was out of the door before she could go after him. Had he recognised her as his daughter, surely he would have given her a final look?

Her mind was still shocked at the revelations she had confronted tonight. On the journey home on the bus, she cursed herself for not going after Long. Then reasoned that such action would have been foolhardy. How could she have asked him if he was her father with reporters and photographers outside the Town Hall? She wrestled with the notion that Gerald Long was no stranger to her. Why couldn't she remember more?

Her head was pounding from the effort. She had gone two stops past her road and had to walk back half a mile. By the time she reached her house her headache was blinding and she went straight to bed. If she had hoped that the veils of the past would lift in her sleep now that she had recognised Gerald Long, she was disappointed.

When she woke in the morning she forced herself to consider that her imagination had been overactive. She concluded that tiredness had played tricks with her mind. She laughed wryly at herself. Fancy believing that a man as important as Gerald Long could be her father. It was just another fantasy.

When she met up with Marion for lunch she made light of the incident. They were in a basement restaurant opposite the office. Marion paused in eating her apple pie and custard.

'You've been quiet all day. You barely spoke on the train this morning. There's more to this than you're saying. Why should you remember Long standing in a house which was familiar to you, if he wasn't your father?'

Shona groaned and stirred her cup of tea. 'But I didn't feel a rush of love. And he ignored me. Though I thought at the time he had recognised me when I walked in. That's stupid, isn't it? I was only nine when Ted and Lily found me.'

'I doubt you've changed that much. And your silvery hair is very distinctive.' Marion's eyes sparkled. 'Wow! Fancy if you are his daughter. He's famous, rich and important.'

'And he wouldn't want a bastard daughter putting a spanner in the works, would he?'

Marion looked surprised at the unusual sarcasm and bitterness in Shona's voice. Her brow wrinkled in concern. 'Hey, don't let it get to you. This is only speculation, isn't it? Perhaps he just looks similar to how you have pictured your father. What else did you remember?'

'Nothing. That's what's so frustrating. The doctors said that anything could trigger my memory. Why didn't everything return last night?' Her fist clenched and her nails dug into her palm. A headache was building. She took two Aspro from her handbag and took them with her tea. 'I hate not knowing.'

'You'll find out one day,' Marion sympathised. 'Meanwhile you've got Ted. He's a lovely man.'

'The best. Perhaps I should be satisfied with what I've got and not hanker after what I've lost. If my father was alive, he would somehow have found me by now.' Shona paused and regarded her friend seriously. 'Don't let on to anyone about what I said. I'd look pretty silly if it was just my imagination. And you know how Lily would go on if she had any inkling.'

'Aren't you even gonna tell Nick?'

'I'm not telling anyone else until I know for sure. I had to talk to you. The experience was so bizarre.'

'Your secret is safe with me. It is a bit far-fetched. But whoever your father is, I reckon he'll be someone special.'

Marion was saying that to cheer her. Yet nestled deep in Shona's heart remained the hope that her father was alive. It was time she began her own search. She would find a way to approach Gerald Long. In the meantime she would read all she could about his life, especially during 1940. If nothing else, it could eliminate him from her investigation. Or confirm the hope that was again beginning to unfurl.

Chapter Twelve

The Lyceum in the Strand was crowded but it didn't feel right to Shona to be dancing with other men when she was courting Nick. Marion had no such compunction.

'Don't be so daft, Shona. It's only a dance. And Nick ain't gonna find out.'

'It's almost ten fifteen and I have to be home by eleven.' She had been unsettled all evening. She missed seeing Nick in the week and the dance emphasised how much she wanted his company. 'One bloke is getting persistent and keeps asking me out. I'd rather go now.'

Marion's eyes were bright with excitement. 'This great bloke, Sid, wants to walk me back to the station.'

'What about Derek?' Shona didn't like Marion two-timing him behind his back.

'Del's all right but lately his only conversation is work and football. I'm thinking of chucking him. You don't mind this Sid bloke coming to the station, do you?'

'As long as you don't expect me to hang round playing gooseberry.'

It was obvious that Marion was keen on Sid as they walked to the Underground station. She clung to his arm and her expression was adoring. In the crowded entrance to the platforms Shona whispered to Marion, 'I'll meet you by the barrier in ten minutes so you can say goodbye to Sid. But no longer, mind, or I'll be late home and Lil will make a song and dance about it.'

Sid pulled Marion behind a kiosk and Shona stood back at the barrier to allow dozens of passengers from the trains to file through. She rested against a wall and glanced across at Marion. Sid was kissing her passionately and Shona looked away, her stare roaming aimlessly over the crowds. This was one of the most popular stations in the West End as it was close to the nightclubs around Soho and the theatres. To her surprise she recognised a man coming up the escalator as Ian, a friend of Nick's. He was with a new girlfriend. Then a couple of people behind him she saw Nick's dark head. Her heart skipped a beat at this unexpected encounter.

With a delighted smile lighting up her face, she raised her hand to attract his attention. Her call froze in her throat. Nick had his arm around a woman as he stepped off the escalator. There was a queue at the ticket barrier and the woman unashamedly drew his head down to kiss her. Nick was grinning as they parted and stooped to whisper in her ear. He was giving the blonde his full attention. The same look of rapt concentration he would give to her, which made Shona feel so special and that she was the only woman in the world for him. The woman was gazing at him with adoration.

Shona reeled as though she had been punched in the stomach. She saw through the shallowness of Nick's charm which had so entranced her. It was an act to ensure his conquest.

Shona snatched back her hand. Unable to drag her gaze from the couple, her eyes were large and dark with shock. The woman was buxom with a mass of frizzed blonde hair and heavy make-up. Her clothes were cheap and flashy. Nick pinched her bottom as they passed through the barrier and she let out a shrill of laughter.

'Yer a naughty man, Nicky luv.' The rough cockney accent grated on Shona's ears and the woman wriggled closer to him. 'That's what I like about yer.'

The woman was so obviously a tart it made Shona's temper

erupt. Her first instinct had been to slink into the shadows to hide her pain, but Shona had never been a coward. It was outrage which drove her to confront him.

'So this is how you double-time me behind my back?' Her voice was low and her eyes flashed dangerously as she stepped in front of him. 'Enjoy your date tonight and don't bother to come near me again. You're nothing but a cheat and a liar.'

Before the tears smarting her eyes betrayed her, Shona pushed past Nick and ran down the escalator. Nick shouted her name but she didn't look back. She was hurt, angry and humiliated. How could he prefer the company of such a common woman to herself?

A train had just pulled out and the platform was almost empty. She loathed scenes and after her outburst now hoped to hide away from Nick in the crowd. Since that was impossible, she ran on.

Nick caught up with her halfway along the platform. He grabbed her arm and spun her round. 'It's not what you think, love. I was just having a bit of a lark.'

His face was a blur through her tears. Angrily, she shook off his arm and stepped back. 'Don't say anything. I know what I saw. That woman was all over you.'

''Ere, Nick, what's bleeding well going on?' The blonde wobbled along the platform in her ridiculously high heels. 'We've got a date, ain't we? What yer doing chasing after that snotty cow? Who the 'ell is she?'

'Go back to your date, Nick.' Shona poured all her contempt into her voice. 'I don't ever want to see you again.'

'You don't mean that.' Nick was distraught, his handsome face white with anguish. 'You've got the wrong idea.'

'Don't add more lies to your cheating on me. It's obvious what she's giving you that I'm not. If that's how you prefer your women, then good riddance to you.' She turned her back and walked away. Although her heart was breaking, she squared her shoulders and held her head high.

Nick ran after her. 'I'm sorry, Shona. Phyllis is nothing to me. A stupid mistake.'

She ignored him, her gaze fixed on an advertisement for Shippams' Pastes.

'Nick, honey, you coming or what?' Phyllis demanded. 'I ain't standing 'ere like a bleeding lemon while you chat some bird up.'

'Shona, you've got to listen to me,' Nick pleaded. 'It's you I love. Please, Shona, let me explain.'

His voice was harsh with torment. She could detect the underlying guilt and hardened her heart.

'I think your girlfriend is saying it all.' She kept her head turned from him, struggling to control her tears and the wobble in her voice. 'How many others like her have there been? At least spare me the indignity of that woman creating a scene. You made your choice of company for tonight.'

Phyllis grabbed Nick's arm, her shrill voice demanding, 'What's going on?'

Shona kept her head turned away. 'Goodbye, Nick.'

Phyllis continued to screech at Nick as a train pulled in. Shona got on it without a backward glance and as she sat down a red-faced, panting Marion leapt into the carriage as the doors were closing.

'You could've waited,' she gasped out. 'Was that Nick getting his ear bent by a brassy blonde? I saw you take off down the escalator and Nick chase you.'

'He's seeing her. I've finished with Nick.'

Marion took her hand. 'No, you haven't. You love him. You'll see this is all some silly mistake.'

'The mistake was mine in trusting him.' Shona was fighting back her tears. She wouldn't break down on the train but she felt wretched.

Marion was persistent in her attempts to reassure her.

'It didn't look like Nick had finished with you. He looked gutted. I think he was close to throttling that blonde tart. He came after you, didn't he?'

Shona was fighting a losing battle against her tears. Aware that several curious glances were turned on her, she rummaged in her handbag for a handkerchief to blow her nose.

'Nick's potty about you,' Marion consoled. 'That tart won't mean nothing to him.'

'She means a great deal to me. She means he's a cheating, lying, no-good bastard.'

'Well, I never said he was perfect.' Marion tried to cheer her. 'But you love him.'

'What if I do?' Shona's eyes glittered with anger. 'That doesn't mean I'll stand by and let him two-time me. A man who treats you like that has no respect for you.'

'Oh Shona,' Marion's voice was sympathetic. 'Happen it's respect which is the cause of the problem. Nick is a ladies' man. He's used to getting what he wants from them. It's because he respects you that he's still seeing you when he isn't having his wicked way with you.'

Shona was white-lipped with suppressed anger. 'So am I supposed to be glad that he has sex with other women and not with me? And how long has this been going on? How many times has he made a fool of me? How can I face his mates when they know he's screwing around? I'm better off without that sort. I just wish it didn't hurt so much.'

Marion squeezed her hand. 'I never liked to say so before, but Del reckons Nick leaves a trail of broken hearts behind him. He ain't the sort to be faithful.'

Shona glared at Marion. 'Did you know he was playing around?'

'I'd have told you if I did,' Marion responded, clearly affronted. 'Del has been Nick's mate too long to spill the beans on him.'

* * *

When she arrived home Shona hoped to escape up to her room without seeing anyone. Lily was just going up to bed and caught her in the hall. 'What's the long face for? Didn't you enjoy yourself?'

'I saw Nick with a woman. I won't be seeing him any more.' She ran past Lily and up the stairs.

'Gawd, how are we gonna manage without the things he brings us?' Lily shouted after her. 'You're so bloody selfish. If you've got any sense you'll make it up with him.'

So much for sympathy, Shona reflected as she crawled into bed. Her heart was breaking over Nick's unfaithfulness and all Lily could think of was missing her tinned salmon and stockings.

During the next two weeks Nick called round three times on evenings when she was babysitting alone. Shona saw his silhouette through the glass of the front door and refused to open the door to him. Her emotions were too raw. She tried to hate him, but the sound of his voice sent a shaft of longing through her. She dare not open the door to him. She couldn't risk lowering her guard for an instant. Not if she wanted to keep her self-respect.

'Go away, Nick. I've told you I don't want to see you. You cheated on me and I'll never forgive you for that.'

'I love you, Shona. You're my girl.'

'And so it appears is any other woman you take a fancy to. Go away, Nick. I have nothing more to say to you.'

'Shona, let me in. I made a mistake and I'm sorry. Give me another chance.'

She was tempted but Nick's reputation stopped her. He was a passionate man and perhaps she had been unreasonable to expect him to be celibate while they were courting. But being a virgin on her wedding day was important to her. She had thought it was important to Nick. Perhaps it was. From the talk in the typing pool it was obvious that few women were virgins when they married. Nick was the type of man who'd be proud of that boast. Yet how many innocent women had he deflowered by his charm and ardent seduction? Shona despised double standards. Her mood was cynical as she reflected that the only thing such a man changes is his clothes or address.

Before her resolve crumbled she turned out the hall light and went into the kitchen closing the door behind her. When he continued to call to her, the twins woke up and started to cry and yell for her.

'Now look what you've done! Go away, Nick,' she fumed as she rushed up the stairs to comfort the boys. There was no such comfort for herself. Pride made a lonely bedfellow in the dark hours of the morning when truth can painfully reveal itself.

On Saturday she came home from the market to find the front room full of flowers and Lily beaming. 'They're from Nick.'

She hoisted the flowers out of the vases and threw them in the dustbin.

Lily scowled. 'Don't be so stubborn. Nick thinks the world of you. He's coming round for dinner on Sunday.'

'Don't interfere, Mum,' Shona retaliated, angry at Lily's scheming. It was hard enough remaining strong; she missed Nick. But she no longer trusted him. Lack of trust would eventually destroy their relationship if she went back with him. 'Then I'll go out with Marion if she's not seeing Derek. Or take some sandwiches over the park. I've finished with Nick. You're only encouraging him for the gifts he brings us.'

Lily curled her lips back and her eyes narrowed with spite. 'You don't know when you're on to a good thing. Nick is going up in the world. He'll make something of himself. Do you want to throw all that away?'

Shona rounded on her. 'I don't need this, Mum. The only place he's going is gaol. He'll end up the same as Dad. I could take that, but not him playing around. The cocky sod thinks he's God's gift to women.'

'You always were an ungrateful bitch,' Lily screamed. 'Nick Blake is welcome here any time he chooses to call.'

All that evening Shona was tormented by memories of Nick. She couldn't stop loving him and part of her wanted him back so badly. Common sense told her it would only lead to further heartache. How could she trust him again?

On Sunday Shona knew the only way she was going to get Nick out of her system was by never seeing him again. His image haunted her dreams at night, his voice seductive, incisive, all persuasive. Her body would crave the warmth and excitement of his kisses and touch and she would wake sweating.

Marion was seeing Derek. She had gone up West for a date with Sid on Thursday and he'd stood her up. Shona realised Nick would be round soon. For the first time in months Lily had prepared the Sunday roast, putting the meat in the oven before she left for the pub, the vegetables peeled and in saucepans on the hob. Shona refused to have anything to do with the meal and was making herself sandwiches to eat at the park. When Lily returned from the pub she was furious.

'Nick will expect you to be here,' she shouted.

'You invited him. You can keep him company,' Shona responded.

'You're a little fool. An ungrateful wretch. Nick's been good to us.'

Percy threw his paper across the room. 'Stop interfering, Lily,' he stormed. 'Nick is a tyke. A charming tyke, I'll give the rascal that. Shona can do better for herself. I'm going down the pub. Put me dinner in a saucepan and I'll have it when I get back.'

Lily rounded on her father, her face flushed with rage. 'Go on, take her side. You always do. Just like Ted. This is my house and what I say goes!'

'You ain't bossing me about like you do Ted,' Percy returned. 'I can get rooms elsewhere and Shona's welcome to live with me. Where would that leave you?'

Lily picked a carrot out of a saucepan and hurled it at him. 'Go, see if I care. Make your grandchildren homeless, it will be on your conscience.'

As Percy lifted his overcoat from the peg behind the door, ignoring Lily's outburst, he rubbed his other hand across his chest.

The one thing Lily could never stand was being ignored. She flew at him, hitting his back with her fists. 'You've never had a good word to say about me. Even as a kid Annie was always your favourite, until she got pregnant. Now it's Shona. Didn't I take you in when Mum died? Ain't I done right by you?'

'You only ever did what was right for you.' There was pain in his eyes as he pushed her from him. 'As a child you were spiteful and always telling tales hoping to get Annie into trouble. Now you're making Shona's life a misery by your spite.'

The unaccustomed anger stopped Lily's tirade. Percy rarely raised his voice. Shona looked at him and saw he was unusually pale and there was a tightness about his mouth. He sighed heavily. 'If you buttoned your lip more, Lily, you'd do everyone a favour.'

Then Percy hunched and let out a groan, his hand rubbing his arm.

'Grandad, what's wrong?' Shona put her arm around him.

He straightened. 'It's nothing; just a twinge. A touch of rheumatism from being on the stall all weathers.'

His step was slower than normal as he walked down the

hall. Shona ran after him. 'You don't look well, Grandad. Why don't you go and lie down? I'll get you a jug of beer from the pub.'

'Don't go fretting about me. I ain't as young as I used to be. I'll get a bit more peace and quiet at the pub.' He put his hand on her shoulder. 'You're a good lass. I'm sorry Lily is making it so difficult for you by encouraging Nick. You're still keen on him, aren't you?'

She nodded. 'It won't work out though.'

'You could be being too hard on him. If he loves you, it could be he's learnt his lesson.'

'I wish I could believe that, Grandad.'

To escape the house before Nick arrived Shona took her sandwiches over to the recreation ground which was bordered by the station and the library in the High Street. It was a mild evening although overcast. She doubted Nick would leave until after dark. He'd been so persistent he was bound to wait until she returned.

Perhaps she had been a fool to run away. She hated such cowardice, but the thought of Lily egging Nick on and taking his side made a painful situation intolerable. She had to go back to the house to babysit as Lily was working tonight and Grandad hadn't said what time he'd be back. To keep in Nick's good graces, Lily was capable of letting him stay on with the twins so that he would be alone with Shona when she returned.

A feeling of entrapment was smothering. She should have faced him when he arrived and told him once and for all it was over between them.

Shona decided to return home in an hour. Then she would insist that she and Nick go for a walk and she'd convince him that it was finished between them. At least that way she would have proved that she would not be manipulated by Nick's and Lily's scheming.

Impatience to get the matter over with made her restless and edgy and she wondered how to occupy herself. Her mind flitted to her other dilemma: how to find out whether Gerald Long was her father. Her plans to read up about his life had been abandoned when she was so upset over Nick's betrayal. When she allowed herself to dwell upon it the usual headache forced her to desist. It began to form now. She had too much on her plate to solve that problem now.

Suddenly she recognised Bill Miles lying asleep on a bench with newspapers over him.

Her anxiety at meeting Nick had robbed her of her appetite. She wandered over to the tramp and softly called his name. When he didn't stir she placed her sandwiches inside Bill's coat. Her touch made him start awake. His fist lashed out catching her on the shoulder. She could smell the stale beer on his breath.

'It's all right, Bill. I put some sandwiches in your coat.'

He stared at her blearily and sat up. 'I don't want your charity. Why do you keep pestering me? I don't want nothing written about me in one of your articles.'

'I gave you my word I wouldn't do that. I won't break it. I thought you might be hungry. You don't have to talk to me if you don't want to.'

He grunted and began to eat the food in silence. Shona paced up and down near him and because she didn't want her mind to picture Nick, now at her home, she struck up a one-sided conversation. 'I've had two of my stories taken by a paper. One was about Cecil Bowen who's a hundred. He's a remarkable man.'

Bill continued to eat in silence and to her surprise when a sparrow hopped towards him he flicked it a crust off his bread. For a man who must be constantly hungry it was a generous gesture.

'You make out you don't care, Bill. But I think you do. I don't know why you took to life on the road but that's your

151

affair. Yet you're an educated man, you could get a job if you wanted one.'

'Why should I work when the whole world is my oyster?' He regarded her sagely.

'This last winter killed scores of vagrants. You don't look more than fifty. Is that how you want to end up, frozen to death on a park bench?'

'Who would care?'

'I care, Bill. Because I know you could make something of your life if you wanted to.'

He stared at her out of red-rimmed eyes. His grey hair and beard were matted and there was a graze on his cheek where he'd either fallen or been in a fight. 'I'm a lost cause,' he said, gruffly.

'Fighting over a bottle of beer is more important to you than fighting to get your life back on track. You say you don't want pity. You don't need it do you? You've enough self-pity to wallow in.'

He reared up and thrust his clenched fist close to her face. Fear pumped the blood through her body in a scalding torrent. He was a large man and easily provoked to violence. She swallowed hard but didn't flinch. Then he gave a rusty hoot of laughter, his eyes mocking her. 'You've got guts. And you're stubborn.' He held his arms wide and turned in a circle. 'Who is going to give a home or a job to an old tramp? Leave an old sot in peace before I forget how kind you've been to me and give you a mouthful of abuse.'

Shona smiled. There was something about Bill which wouldn't let her give up on him. In the past she'd had several abusive mouthfuls from him. They were his defence against the world. She let him get his anger off his chest and then tossed him a half-crown to get something more to eat, saying, 'You're a foul-mouthed, miserable old bugger, but you're not as bad as your bite. Unless you've been drinking.'

The last couple of times she'd come across Bill, he'd been

grudgingly tolerant of her and there was respect in his tone. Undaunted by his mood today she issued a challenge.

'All it takes is a bath, a shave and a second-hand suit to change how you look. Grandad heard there's a job going as nightwatchman at a factory in Blackhorse Road. They want someone who can handle themselves and scare off troublemakers.'

He shuffled away from her mumbling to himself. She called out and ran after him and pressed another three shillings into his grimy hand. 'I'll be here at eight tomorrow morning before I get my train to London. You can either spend that money on beer or go down the baths, get a haircut and shave. Grandad picked up some second-hand suits to sell cheap on his stall. I'll bring you one tomorrow and you can pay me back out of your first pay packet.'

Bill waved her away. 'You've got bats in your head, woman. Leave me alone.'

'Don't be late. I can't miss my train,' she shouted, refusing to be discouraged.

Shona watched him shuffle away, limping in split shoes too small for his feet. 'I'll bring a pair of size ten shoes as well, shall I?'

She didn't get an answer. Buying Bill a pair of second-hand shoes would take all her spending money for the week. But she was convinced that Bill wasn't a hopeless case.

Her stare was thoughtful as she gazed after him. There was a flash of light which startled her and a train whistled as it approached the station. Another flash of light made her spin round with curiosity. A third flash a few feet from her face made her blink and distorted her vision. It had come from a camera.

Another flash made her hold her hand to her eyes and it was some seconds before she realised that Nick was pointing a camera at her.

'Nick, are you crazy?'

He circled her taking another photograph.

'Nick, stop it!'

'Not until you give me one of your gorgeous smiles so I can capture it on film.'

She moved away to avoid him, wishing her heart wouldn't beat so treacherously fast that he had come to find her. The camera flashed, the film rolled on and it flashed again. He ran in front of her and when she sidestepped again blocked her passage. His face was obscured as he peered through the viewfinder but she could see the beguiling twitch of his lips at his confidence to win her attention.

He chuckled. 'Frowning will give you wrinkles, sweetheart. Come on. One smile. Is that too much to ask?'

He lowered the camera to wink at her. When Nick was playing the fool, he was difficult to resist. Damn him for looking so handsome in a dark suit and his hair falling over his brow in the way which always made her heart tug. She wasn't going to humour him.

'Sourpuss,' he taunted. 'Smile. Or I'll be thinking you've been distraught with unhappiness at not seeing me.'

His audacity destroyed her composure. 'I could kill you, Nicholas Blake, not bloody smile at you.'

'So you do still care.' There was no arrogance in his manner and his handsome face was taut with remorse. 'You never swear unless you get riled up over something. So it must be me. Kidding apart, sweetheart, I've missed you. I was a fool. An idiot. A swine. Please, give me another chance.' He held out the camera. 'I got you this as a peace offering. I know how much you wanted one.'

'I can't be bought with gifts, Nick.'

'I want you to have it anyway for the pain I caused you.' He put the camera on the ground at her feet. 'I don't want to lose you, Shona. Phyllis was a stupid fling. She meant nothing to me.'

154

'I can't accept the camera.' His contrition and thought-fulness in choosing a gift which was so important to her was breaking down her defences. But she wasn't like Lily. She couldn't be won over by presents.

'I can't trust you, Nick.'

He moved closer. 'It won't happen again. I've learnt my lesson.' His grey eyes were dark with remorse.

An insidious longing swelled in her breast. She wanted to believe him, but dare she? Her stare searched his. The intensity of his gaze destroyed her composure.

'What about the evenings we don't see each other? Won't they be a temptation to go out with your mates? They'll be picking up women.'

'I love you, Shona. If you won't accept the camera, then perhaps this will convince you.'

He flipped open a small leather-bound box and revealed a solitaire diamond ring. 'Let's get engaged. I know you want to wait until Ted comes out of prison before we marry. But I want the world to know you're truly my girl.'

Her throat clamped with emotion. She still wanted to rant at him for his betrayal, but her heart was doing somersaults. His charm and genuine contrition were undermining her resolve. She found the strength to shake her head but her voice could not form a denial.

To Nick it was a sign of encouragement. 'A long engage-ment will give us time to get some money behind us. I want a place of our own. I don't want my wife living in rented rooms. I'm gonna get an evening job three nights a week so we can save some extra money.'

'I know your evening work. It's not exactly legal is it?'

He looked affronted. 'It's not thieving. It's on the door of Ilford Palais.'

'So you'll be getting paid to pick up women. How con-venient. I've seen those doorman chatting up the girls.'

'Sarcasm doesn't suit you, Shona. I'll forget the Palais

job. It's less money but there's a job as petrol attendant.'

'I can't see you as a petrol attendant, Nick.'

'For you, for our future, I'll do it. Just until Ted comes out and we're married.' He put his hand over his heart. 'I'm serious about us. Trust me.'

A lump of emotion formed in her throat making an answer impossible.

'Don't you like the ring? You can always choose another.'

'It's beautiful, Nick. But . . .'

His hands cupped her face, his stare cherishing and tender. 'I love you. We were meant for each other. There's no one else for me.'

'Oh, Nick.' She was overwhelmed. She had tried so hard to hate him. It was impossible; she loved him too much. Her resistance crumbled.

He kissed her, lifting her into his arms and spinning them round and round until they broke apart breathless and laughing.

'People are watching. Put me down.' She tried to sound stern but couldn't stop her mouth from turning up in a smile.

He took the ring out of the box and, taking her left hand, kissed her fingertip before sliding it on to her third finger. 'Say yes. You won't regret it. I've learnt my lesson.'

The passion in his voice and adoration in his eyes gave her hope that he had changed. 'It could be two years before Dad comes out of prison. I haven't changed my mind about being a virgin when I marry. If you cheat on me again, Nick, that will be it finished between us. No more chances.'

'I ain't gonna risk losing you again.'

She knew then that she would never love anyone as she loved Nick.

'So you two made it up.' Lily beamed at Shona and Nick. 'I

knew you were meant for each other. Shona was just being stubborn.' She wiped a tear from her eye. 'We'll have to have a party to celebrate.'

'No, Mum,' Shona interrupted before Lily got carried away. 'We'll go out for a meal. I couldn't enjoy a party without Dad here to share it. Nick understands how I feel.'

'I'm going to visit your husband next week,' Nick stated. 'It means a lot to Shona for me to ask him properly for his permission. Then we'll put an announcement in the paper.'

'Ted would want Shona to have a party,' Lily persisted. 'Not that I can afford to lash out on one, things being as they are.'

'It wouldn't cost you a penny, Lily,' Nick assured her. 'But it's what Shona wants that's important.'

Shona linked her arm though Nick's. 'I'd rather it was simple, Nick. Perhaps a meal somewhere on Mum's night off.'

Lily pouted and Nick interceded, 'I know my mum will be delighted to do a special spread and have you all over. You could even bring the twins.'

'I can't drag the twins across London at night,' Lily complained. 'They'll be murder to get home on the bus.'

Nick looked triumphant. 'That's another surprise I was going to give Shona. I've got myself a car. A little Morris, nothing grand. I pick it up next week. We can all squeeze into that.'

'Your own car.' Lily puffed herself up with pride. 'My, you are going up in the world. Shona's a lucky woman. My Ted was gonna get one for us, if that last job hadn't gone wrong on him.'

Lily's face folded and she began to weep. 'I miss him so much.'

Nick put his arm around Lily's shoulders. 'Here, this will cheer you up.' He produced a slab of chocolate from his pocket. 'I'd got this for our Iris, but I know you've got a sweet tooth, Lil, and the twins will love it. Now how about my mum doing a spread for us to celebrate our engagement the first Tuesday in June since that's your first night off?'

Lily nodded and broke off a piece of the chocolate. 'I suppose if that's the best you can do. Not that I would have enjoyed a party, my Ted not being with us.'

'Don't you worry, Lily,' Nick assured her. 'When Shona and I are married it will be the grandest wedding this street has ever seen. You'll be proud of her.'

Lily sniffed and dabbed at her eyes, her shoulders heaving in her distress. Her make-up had run. There was a blowsiness about Lily's face and she had put on a great deal of weight since Ted's arrest. She pulled herself together as she nibbled the chocolate and then pouted in a sickening way at Nick, enjoying the attention he was giving her. 'You couldn't get us some of that sherry out the cupboard to go with it could you, Nick dear.'

An hour later when Nick left, Shona helped Lily up the stairs. She was too drunk to make it to the pub for work. Shona had hoped that working until so late of an evening Lily would lay off the booze. It made no difference. She was often tipsy when she came home from the drinks bought for her and then always had a few sherries before retiring.

It was eleven months since Ted Carrington's trial. If Lily didn't ease up on her drinking, Ted would come home to find his wife was a complete drunkard.

Chapter Thirteen

The next morning Shona woke with her mind racing with excitement. She couldn't stop gazing at the solitaire on her finger. She broke into song as she dressed and ate breakfast. She had to leave early to take Bill Miles the clothes she had promised him.

'Shut that bloody row!' Lily glowered at her. From the state of her bloodshot eyes, she was nursing a hangover.

Shona saw Percy's coat still on the hook in the hall. 'Hasn't Grandad left yet? He's late this morning, isn't he?'

'Too much booze last night,' Lily snapped. 'He's still sorting his barrow out.'

Shona went out to the shed and was concerned to see Percy leaning heavily against the doorframe.

'Are you all right, Grandad?'

He straightened and coughed, clearly embarrassed at being observed. His face was unusually pale and his mouth looked pinched. 'I'm fine. Just getting me second wind. I reckon someone slipped a Mickey Finn in me beer last night when we won the darts match. Someone's crackpot idea of a joke.'

'Do you need any help?'

'I ain't so old and feeble I can't get me barrow sorted of a morning. Ain't it time for your train?' He had straightened and gave a sprightly skip to prove he was fine before he wheeled his barrow along the garden path.

Shona knew when she was being dismissed; Percy hated being fussed over. She left for the recreational ground with a suit, shirt, tie, clean underwear and socks wrapped in brown paper. She had just time to pick up a pair of second-hand shoes from Bertie the Boot. She chose a pair of black lace-ups which she hoped would fit Bill.

Shona had been waiting for fifteen minutes and there was no sign of the tramp. Disappointment spiked her. She'd had such hopes that he would come. You could only offer help, you couldn't force someone to take it, she reasoned. Her train left in ten minutes and she couldn't wait much longer. Now she was stuck with carrying the parcel of clothes and shoes round all day.

'Miss Carrington.' She turned with relief at the sound of Bill's voice. She smiled at seeing that he had obviously had a bath and his beard had been neatly trimmed.

'I'm glad you came, Bill.'

He rubbed his short beard, his expression rueful rather than its usual belligerence. 'I don't know what I'm doing here.'

She smiled encouragement. 'Have you still got the money?'

'Less the price of a pint but I borrowed a pair of scissors from the attendant at the hostel to trim my beard, so there's enough for a haircut.' He spread his hands and sighed. 'I must be mad. They ain't gonna employ me. But God knows why, I felt I couldn't have lived with myself if I let you down.'

She thrust the parcel into his hands. On top she put the shoes. 'I've got to run, or I'll miss my train. It's not much of a job. It's a start to get you back on your feet. And if you need lodgings I know of some. Can you meet me here at five thirty?'

'I can't pay for lodgings. They want at least a week's rent in advance.'

She drew a piece of paper from her handbag. 'There's an address on there of a charity. An institution that gives small loans to men like yourself trying to make a new start for themselves. You pay it back so much a week. I'm seeing

160

their secretary next week to do a story on them and follow up on some of their successes.' With a wave she hurried to catch her train.

All day she kept crossing her fingers and willing Bill to get the job. The girls in the office exclaimed over her ring and wanted to go out after work to celebrate. She put it off until Friday.

When Bill didn't turn up to meet her after work her disappointment was acute. If he hadn't got the job he'd probably got drunk. She cut through the recreational ground to go into the library to get a book she needed to research an article. A half-hour later when she came out she wandered down to her grandfather's stall to see if he was ready to pack up for the day and to give him a hand.

The stall was already stripped of its clothing and there was no sign of Percy. It was unlike him to finish so early. Minnie Pitt who ran the hardware stall opposite waved to her.

'Percy went home mid-afternoon. He weren't feeling so good. He'd had a fall earlier – tripped over some rubbish and hurt his side.'

'Thanks, Minnie.' Concern gruffened Shona's voice. 'You and the kids all right?'

'Driving me bonkers, the whole lot of them. Then that's teenagers for you. Always up to something they shouldn't be.'

Shona hurried back home. The house was deserted. Marion, who had gone straight home from the train, knocked on the door. 'Mum says for you to pop in. She's got the twins.'

'Where's Mum and Percy?'

'Your grandad's been taken bad. He's in Whipps Cross hospital.'

'What's wrong with him?' Fear snared her in a frozen web. She prayed he wasn't seriously ill.

Marion looked distraught. 'I'm sorry, Shona. It's his heart.'

'It can't be, Minnie Pitt said he fell over down the market.' Shona refused to believe it could be more serious.

'He had a heart attack putting his barrow away in the shed. Mum heard Lily screaming and went to the station to phone for an ambulance.'

Shona picked up her handbag. 'Thank your mum for having the twins. Can she keep them here until I get back from the hospital? I must find out how he is.'

'Don't worry about the boys. Del and I were going to the pictures tonight. We'll skip it and babysit.'

'Thanks, Marion. You're a good friend.' She ran down the path, her mind focused on Percy lying seriously ill in a hospital bed.

'Shona, hang on!' Marion shouted. 'How you gonna get to Whipps Cross, you haven't got any money. You told me you blew it all on that dumb tramp.'

'Oh hell! I'd forgotten.' She turned a pleading stare on her friend. 'Have you got a couple of bob to lend me until Friday?'

Marion had it in her hand already for her. 'I borrowed this from Mum as I knew you were skint. I hope your grandad is OK.'

The bus ride to Whipps Cross seemed to take for ever. Then she had to find the Men's Ward and was stopped by an imperious-looking ward sister. 'Visting hours don't start for another half hour, miss.'

'It's my grandad. A neighbour said he'd been admitted with a heart attack this afternoon. How is he? His name's Percy Dawkins.'

The ward sister looked less starchy. 'There's a waiting room along the corridor. Wait there. I'll find out for you.'

Lily was sitting in a chair in the corner, her head sunk into her hands. 'Mum, how's Grandad?'

Lily lifted her ravaged face. 'He's unconscious. The doctor is with him now. They're doing all they can.'

Shona knelt at Lily's side and put her arms around her. For once Lily did not pull away and sobbed into Shona's shoulder. 'It will be all right, Mum. Grandad is a tough old workhorse.'

'What will I do if he dies?' Lily wailed. 'I've been so mean to him lately what with everything getting on top of me. But I do love him.'

'Grandad knows that.' She continued to pacify her mother.

Lily wouldn't be consoled. 'He can't die. He's not that old. Only fifty-seven.'

There was the rustle of starched linen and the ward sister came over to them. Shona and Lily stood up and Shona took her mother's hand.

'Mr Dawkins is as well as can be expected. But it was a severe heart attack and it will be touch and go how he fares through the night. Sometimes another attack follows. If he survives the next couple of days he should be over the worst. But he'll need lots of rest in the weeks to come. It would be foolish for him to return to work too quickly.'

Lily flopped down in the chair inconsolable. 'Do you want to go home, Mum, and I'll stay here? The twins can't be left with Mrs Lockyer all night.'

'He's my father. I can't leave him when he's so ill.' Lily shot her a venomous glare. 'You're trying to steal him again. If he dies you want to be the last person he sees.'

The pettiness of her reasoning appalled Shona. 'I was thinking how tired you looked. I'll go back. Though I won't be able to sleep for worrying about Grandad. I'll call in at the Crown and tell them you won't be in.'

Lily nodded. 'You'll have to let Annie know. She'll want to be here.'

'I haven't got enough money for the bus fare. I'll have to ring the corner shop where she lives and ask them to give her the message. Are you going to be all right on your own, Mum?'

'God, I wish Ted was here.' Lily turned her face away as Shona stooped to kiss her. 'Just get the twins settled.'

Her coldness smote Shona. She felt excluded at a time when a mother and daughter should be a comfort to each other.

The twins had led Marion and Del a song and dance and when Shona arrived home, Del was crawling round on his hands and knees giving them rides on his back.

'How's your grandad?' Marion asked.

Shona wiped a tear from her eye. 'If he gets through the next couple of days he has a good chance. Lily is staying over at the hospital. I came home to see to Johnnie and Jamie. I won't get a wink of sleep.'

'I'll stay with you,' Marion offered. 'Or would you rather Del found Nick?'

Del stood up to shouts of protest from the twins. 'Nick's working until midnight. I'll go over to his flat and tell him what's happened.'

'That won't be necessary, but thank you.' Shona turned to Marion. 'And you've got work tomorrow. I'll be fine on my own.'

'No you won't. I'm staying. Now let's get these holy terrors to bed, my head's ringing with their yelling.'

When the twins were finally asleep Shona slumped in a chair opposite Marion and sipped at a mug of Ovaltine. Marion kept up a flow of chatter but Shona's comments were abstracted.

She couldn't shake her sense of guilt. 'Grandad kept

rubbing his chest and arms lately. He said it was rheumatism or a strained muscle from setting up the stall. I should have taken more notice.'

'How were you to know it was his heart? Don't blame yourself. He's a tough old codger. He's going to be fine.'

Shona was sick with worry and felt so helpless.

Marion valiantly tried to distract her. 'This is rotten happening just as everything was going so right for you. I was so thrilled Nick asked you to marry him. Though you could've knocked me down with a feather when you told me this morning.'

Shona stood up to pace the front room. 'I feel so guilty. Grandad was obviously ill this morning, but I was so wrapped up in my engagement and encountering Gerald Long that I hadn't noticed how ill he was. He's my family. He's the one who's been caring for me all these years.'

'Don't go blaming yourself. And Percy isn't the sort to let on he's ill. He's like my old grandad. He don't believe in doctors.'

The conversation faded as Shona continued to torment herself with feelings of guilt. Marion began to doze in the chair. At one o'clock Nick turned up. Marion rubbed her eyes. 'I'll be off to my own bed then. Or do you two need a chaperone?'

'Charming. What kind of a louse do you take me for?' Nick snapped.

Marion paled. 'I meant it as a joke, Nick.'

He ignored her and took Shona into his arms. 'I'm sorry about Percy. I couldn't leave you alone. I know what it was like when my mum was rushed into hospital with a burst appendix. She almost died with peritonitis.'

'Thanks for coming, Nick. But you've got to be in the docks early tomorrow.'

'I'll survive.' He pulled her down on to the settee and

rested her head on his shoulder. 'This isn't a time when you should be alone.'

Finally in the warmth of his chaste embrace Shona fell asleep, awaking to find it was light outside. She had fallen sideways on the settee and Nick had put an eiderdown over her. He was kneeling at her side with a cup of tea in his hand.

'I'm off home to get changed before I go to the docks. Are you going to be all right on your own?'

She nodded and sat up, pushing a hand through her tousled hair. She saw a blanket thrown over two chairs which had been pushed together where Nick had slept the night.

He grinned ruefully. 'It wasn't how I planned to spend the first night I was alone with you.'

Her eyes shone with love. 'Having you here helped. I don't think I could have slept otherwise. Thanks. You'd better get off or you'll be late for work. I've got the twins to see to. They'll keep me occupied until Mum gets home.' Sadness tightened her face. 'I wish I knew how Grandad was.'

'I reckon he's gonna be fine. Lily would've been home by now if he hadn't made it.' Nick kissed her tenderly then made a speedy exit.

An hour later Lily dragged herself wearily into the kitchen where Shona was giving Johnnie and Jamie their breakfast. They were making so much noise Shona hadn't heard her key in the door.

'Mummy, Mummy,' the boys yelled, running round her.

'How's my babies?' Lily kissed them and hugged them both.

They squirmed out of her hold and ran out of the kitchen, arms spread pretending to be aeroplanes.

'How's Grandad?' Shona asked. Lily had ignored her and slumped down on one of the kitchen chairs and lit a cigarette.

'Holding on. He came round in the night. They told me

to come home and get some sleep. I'm going back after lunch.'

'Marion's going to let work know what happened. I'll be here to look after the boys.'

Lily grunted. 'Get us a cuppa, would you?'

'Did they say how long he'll be in hospital for?'

'Couple of weeks if all goes well. It could be longer.' Lily stubbed out her cigarette and dropped her head into her hands. 'God, how will we manage? Dad's money from the stall brings in more than the two of us earn. I'll have to pay someone to have the twins and run the stall myself.'

'That's not practical, Mum. Apart from the cost the twins won't settle with anyone. It would also mean you have to give up working at the Crown. I'll leave the office. I can get another job when Grandad is better. The stall is his life. He'll lose his customers and probably his pitch if no one runs it for him.'

Lily dragged her fingers through her hair and her face was hard as she glared at her. 'I suppose it's the least you can do after all our family has done for you.'

There was no gratitude in her voice at the sacrifice Shona was prepared to make for the people she loved.

She put out a hand wanting to comfort Lily, but she had turned away and was hugging Johnnie who had run back into the kitchen.

Shona wearily closed her eyes. Her senses were heightened by the worry over Percy. She could feel Lily's hatred striking her like arrows. Lily was shutting her out, denying her right to be part of the family. A series of images flicked like snapshots through her mind.

Another woman with dark hair turned away from her outstretched arms. The sense of rejection intensified. The images changed. Her real father was shouting, holding out his arms but the words were indistinct. A feeling of menace encompassed her. He was calling her name but she couldn't hear it. There was a car. Other people and more shouting. Cold terror stippled her spine. There were shots. Blood splattered the image of a woman.

The pain in Shona's head was crippling. All that remained was the smell of gunfire in her nostrils.

Shona reeled back shaken. She put a hand to her head, willing the images to return and with them her memory. Both eluded her.

Chapter Fourteen

It was one thing for Shona to run Percy's stall and deal with suppliers and another to get the heavily laden barrow to and from the market in the mornings and at night.

The first morning she was in the shed trying to sort out how much she could manage on the barrow when Lily came into the garden carrying a bowl of washing to put through the mangle. 'There's a bloke here to see you. Gawd knows where you attract them from. He's not the sort I want coming round here. Get rid of him fast.'

Puzzled, Shona didn't at first recognise the smartly dressed man with neatly cut and slicked-down grey hair who stood in profile. He was on the doorstep and hearing her approach turned towards her.

'Bill, what a transformation! You look terrific.'

He shrugged but from the sparkle in his eyes she could tell he was pleased. 'I wanted to tell you I got the job. I start on Monday. I couldn't meet you last night as I was looking for lodgings. That charity place gave me some addresses and enough money to cover the first month's rent. I was going to leave a message with Percy but his stall wasn't set up this morning.'

The pleasure drained from her face. 'He's been taken bad. It's his heart. He's in hospital. But I'm delighted at your news.'

'I wanted to thank you.' His eyes bored into her. 'I'm not proud of how I was living. I had lost so much – it didn't seem to matter what happened to me. You showed me that self-respect is important.'

'Time is a great healer. It was obviously right for you to put that life behind you.'

'Or end up dying,' he said with harshness. 'I thought I was showing my contempt for the world. As if anyone cared. Last winter was a killer. A dozen homeless that I know didn't make it through the freezing weather. I suddenly realised I didn't want to die.' Embarrassment at expressing his emotions made him turn away to stare along the road as he continued, 'But I couldn't see a way out and was too stubborn to take charity. I'll pay back every penny I owe you. And if there's anything I can do for you . . .'

'There is actually. I'm going to keep Grandad's stall open so he doesn't lose his pitch. And we need the money it brings in. But I can't manage his barrow. Is there anyone at the hostel who'd be willing to earn a few bob by helping me out in the mornings and evenings? He'd have to be trustworthy and turn up every day.'

Bill squared his shoulders and stood taller, no longer the supplicant but taking charge. She glimpsed then the man of authority he had been before the war and during his years in the French Resistance. He was used to taking charge of situations. The futility of war and the destruction it wrought even upon the survivors twisted at her heart.

'I'll give you a hand today and I'll have a word with Alf Marten,' he offered. 'Alf's not from the hostel. He does what odd jobs he can. Can't get regular work. He's lost his sight in one eye and suffers from shell shock. It's hard on his wife and five kids. They live in the ground floor of a house the other side of Hoe Street.'

'I can't pay much.'

'Alf will be grateful. I'll send him along while you're working today and if he can't do tonight I'll come back.'

That was another problem solved. She had already written

a letter of resignation to Miss Shield[...]
work explaining why she couldn't wor[...]
luck Alf Marten would be reliable enoug[...]
stall for an hour or so when she needed to [...]
for goods. At least she'd been several times wi[...]
the years and knew the best places for stock.

When they arrived at the stall Bill stayed to help[...]
it up as customers were already interested in the cloth[...]

With clothing coupons still in use Percy sold a mix of ne[...]
and good quality second-hand clothes. The second-hand
children's clothes were a new line Shona had suggested a
couple of years ago and they had proved very popular. By a
canny part-exchange and bartering system, Percy got round
some of the clothing restriction laws, made a good profit and
ensured a steady supply of second-hand clothes.

Minnie came over as soon as Shona finished serving her
first customer. She gave Bill a wolf-whistle on seeing his
smart appearance. Minnie was the first of many stallholders
to enquire about Percy's health.

'Don't you worry, girl,' said Ray Newcombe who ran the
tool stall. 'We'll square it with the market inspector if he gives
you any trouble.' Ray was a wiry, wizened man with tanned
leathery skin and only four brown teeth which showed when
he laughed – something he did often. A cigarette constantly
dangled from his mauve lips. 'No one's gonna take over
Perce's pitch. Forty years he's worked this market. Blimey,
'is dad 'ad the stall before him. He's practically an institution
down 'ere.'

Being midweek it was quieter than at the weekends but
Shona was still kept busy. Some of the women wanting to
sell clothes in part-exchange tried to trick her to give them
higher prices than Percy would have done. Shona soon proved
she was experienced at bargaining. She enjoyed the haggling
as much as they did and sent them away pleased with their
new purchase.

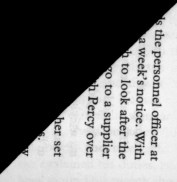

d worked without Percy for
when the stall was quiet, her
tened to overwhelm her.

duced himself. He was over
brown hair cut short under
t face dominated by a large
-patch. The skin on that side
is injury. His other hazel eye
manner eager to please. As
d occasionally twitched. The
the hardship and suffering of
recent years. Although his clothes were worn they were clean and neatly pressed. She liked him instantly.

'I'm sorry I can't offer you more money or longer hours.'

'Every bit helps, Miss Carrington. It fits in well with other jobs I do round here. I often hold the fort while me mate Mick on the record stall has his lunch break.'

'It's only until my grandfather returns to work,' she warned.

'As I said, Miss Carrington, every bit helps.'

'I couldn't manage without you,' she admitted. 'It won't be easy without Grandad. I worry about letting him down.'

There was admiration in his eyes. 'I don't think there's much chance of that. You're getting a name for helping those in need. Percy was a generous man. There's too many people who owe him to allow anyone to do you down. Unfortunately, there's rogues in the market as well as friends. It won't all be plain sailing for you.'

Hiring Alf proved a godsend. Percy was getting over his heart attack when he developed pneumonia and had to spend another two weeks in hospital before starting to recover. Then he was sent to a convalescent home in Eastbourne for a month.

The hours in the market were long and Shona was exhausted when she got home at night. There were no more flashes of memory to help her discover the secrets of her childhood and the identity of her real parents. Whilst coping with the troubles experienced by the Carringtons and with Grandad's health remaining precarious, it seemed callous to start delving into newspaper archives to learn more about Gerald Long.

Because of Percy's heart attack there was no official celebration of Shona's engagement to Nick with the two families meeting. Nick shrugged it off. 'They'll get together soon enough at the wedding. Mum was a bit upset though. She wanted to show her approval.'

As the weeks wore on without the wages she had earned in the office, debts began to mount. Lily refused to economise and each month Shona worried they wouldn't have enough money to meet the mortgage. The twins were growing so fast they were constantly in need of new clothes or shoes. Lily refused to have anything second-hand for them.

The long summer evenings meant the stall stayed open later but it was only on a Friday or a Saturday this made any great difference to sales. Then young women working in shops or offices would come after work and hunt for bargains to wear on a date. But the longer hours took their toll. Shona saw less of Nick. Without Percy she was forced to babysit while Lily worked. Lily was drinking heavily and taking even less interest in her home. Even the twins were becoming neglected. Most nights the twins were up when Shona returned from the market. Shona was left to wash the boys and coax them into bed when they were tired, whining and at their most disruptive. Afterwards she had to tackle the dirty dishes Lily had allowed to accumulate during the day and put away the toys scattered throughout the house.

Shona suspected that Lily was putting the twins to bed of an afternoon to sleep for an hour so that she got a rest. It meant they were more fractious in the evening for Shona to cope with. Apart from seeing so little of Nick her biggest regret was being too tired to concentrate on her articles. She had managed only three and had heard nothing from the local paper she had sent them to.

At the market problems seemed to multiply instead of ease. Alf and Ray were right about the rogues. She'd had suppliers demanding money for goods already paid for and refusing to give her more stock unless she paid up. She refused and had to search for other manufacturers. Fortunately the second-hand clothes were popular enough to ensure a thriving trade, but the larger profits came from new clothes. Twice, garments were offered to her by a spiv. When she declined, suspecting they were stolen, he got nasty, threatening violence. Within seconds she was surrounded by Percy's friends, the men forcefully marching the spiv out of the market.

But that had been three weeks ago and things had begun to settle down. Percy was due to return from Eastbourne at the weekend when Shona and Nick were driving down to collect him. He would still need to take it easy for a time.

When Percy returned he was impatient that he still had to take things easy. On the warmer lunchtimes he would amble down to the market to spend an hour or two on the stall. He tired easily and as soon as Shona saw him looking pale and drawn, she ordered him home.

'Stop fussing,' he protested. 'I'm fine. This is my stall. My responsibility.'

'If you don't go by yourself then Alf will pack up the stall and I'm coming back with you. You're pushing yourself too hard, Grandad. Do you want a relapse? Give yourself another couple of weeks.'

Two weeks later after a busy Saturday's trading Percy had wanted to stay to help her pack up. Shona declined. He had been in the market since midday and apart from having a drink at lunchtime with some friends he had been working all afternoon. For the last hour he had been sitting on a bar stool the landlord had loaned him from the corner pub.

'You won't be helping me if you have a relapse,' Shona

admonished. 'Get off home. Alf and I will finish off here in a couple of hours.'

'It ain't right, your doing so much.' Percy shook his head. 'I ain't in me box yet.'

'And I don't intend that's where you end up,' Shona voiced her fear. 'Please, Grandad.'

He saw the worry on her face and grimaced. 'I hate being a burden. When was the last time you had a day off, or went out with Nick?'

'I'm going to the pictures with Nick tonight. Stop fretting.'

He sat on his stall for another twenty minutes but Shona made sure he didn't do any serving. The crowds were beginning to thin and finally Percy stood up. 'I'll get some fish and chips for our tea later,' he said by way of parting. His step was slow and it tore at Shona's heart for he had been such a sprightly man before his heart attack.

It was gone seven when the stall was finally packed away. The late afternoon trade had picked up and sales had been good. Shona was laughing and joking with Alf as they made their way home. The day's takings ensured they'd have no money worries once the mortgage was paid in the week and the food bought. They also had a bit extra to spend at the warehouse on Monday which would replenish their stocks.

She didn't pay any heed to the four men lounging against the wall of the railway road bridge ahead of them. She gripped the handle of the barrow more firmly as they pushed it up the incline of the bridge. When the men split into two pairs each side of the pavement, Shona felt her first quiver of unease. There were no other people close to them and strangely there was a lull in traffic. On the warm July evening they all wore neckerchiefs and before she could see their faces these were pulled up over their noses.

Their attack was swift. Alf was knocked to the ground.

Two of them kept hitting him and another assailant pushed Shona up against the wall, a knife pressed to her throat.

'Hand over the cash,' the attacker demanded.

It was in the money apron tied around her waist. Shona screamed and struck out at him, bringing her knee up into his groin. He grunted in pain and the knife blade was deflected. Before she could get away his companion grabbed her. As a second scream scratched her throat, a punch to her stomach doubled her over in pain. She heaved, bile rising to her mouth. Forced to her knees, she clutched at the money apron whilst kicking out with her feet. She could hear the thuds of Alf being beaten and his groans of agony. They sounded as though they were killing him. She couldn't let that happen.

'Stop hurting Alf,' she croaked. 'He hasn't got the money.'

Then several shouts came from behind them. 'That's Shona and Alf. Those bastards are robbing them.'

Their hobnail boots pounded along the pavement. Feet scuffled around her. The barrow was overturned, the garments strewn on the dirty pavement and trampled on. Shona hauled herself up and staggered back against a wall. Five men – three who were stallholders and two whom she recognised from her visits to the hostel – were lashing into their attackers. Two of the robbers ran off and one was on the ground begging for mercy. Another was nursing a bloody broken nose and held between two of her rescuers.

The entire incident had taken less than a minute. Shaking with shock Shona went to Alf. His face was swollen and cut and he held his side as one of the stallholders helped him to his feet.

'Are you all right, mate?'

'I'll live. I wasn't much use to you, I'm sorry, Shona.'

'They took us by surprise.' She took several deep breaths to calm her trembling. Her rescuers were kindly picking up the scattered clothing.

'It's all in a bit of a state, luv,' one advised.

Shona grimaced. 'Hopefully they'll wash up and haven't been torn.'

She was breathing heavily as she thanked the men who had saved them. A policeman arrived late on the scene and took charge, arresting the man held by the two costers.

'If you don't mind me saying you're asking for trouble, miss,' the constable said sternly. 'A slip of a woman like yourself is easy pickings to someone who knows you're carrying a day's takings from the market.'

'I'll make sure Miss Carrington gets home safely in future, constable.' Angus, a large auburn-haired Scotsman whom she'd interviewed at the hostel, was speaking. 'She got my mate Bill a job. Changed his life for him. I share his flat and that enabled me to get off the streets and find work in the bus depot cleaning the buses at night. Bill would never forgive me if anything happened to Miss Carrington.'

Shona regarded him in wonder. 'I can't possibly expect you to give us your time every day.'

Angus waved aside her protests. 'I'm in the pub that time of an evening before going into work. It's only a short walk to your house. Indirectly you made it possible for me to regain my self-respect and find work.'

Alf looked shame-faced. 'I guess you won't be needing me to help with the barrow now. I weren't much use to you tonight.'

'I still need you in the mornings.' Shona squeezed his good arm. 'I'll still pay you the same. You're too good a worker for me to lose.'

The appearance of Angus at the house upset Percy. 'Time I stopped lazing around and pulled my weight again. Those bastards could've killed you, Shona.'

Shona was too kind-hearted to point out that if Percy had been set on by the attackers, it would have brought on another heart attack. 'It proves that you've more friends than you think. I wasn't hurt, just shaken.'

Percy's face flushed with angry colour. 'The stall is my responsibility not yours. I've let you do too much. That barrow is heavy even with Alf helping you. I'm back on the stall full time first thing on Monday.'

The determined set of his chin meant he wouldn't listen to arguments. It was also a matter of pride. Shona relented. 'Come and help me set the stall up and get back into the selling, but you can't push that barrow. We can afford to pay Alf. He's been a good friend and he needs the money.'

Even though her grandad was making steady progress, too much exertion would stain his face red and tinge his lips blue, which the doctor had warned was a dangerous sign.

'I wouldn't like to see Alf's family suffer.' He eyed her sternly. 'I appreciate what you've done these last weeks. But you can do better than working in the market. What about those stories you were writing? You're too tired to do much work on them of an evening.'

Shona folded her arms across her chest and squared up to him, her eyes flashing with exasperation at his stubbornness. 'I'm not leaving the market until I know you are stronger. I enjoy the work. It's not for ever.'

He shook his head. 'It's a crime not to use the talent you were given.'

'Grandad, another month or so won't make any difference to my determination.'

'See that it doesn't. Another paper took that story on that charity for the homeless. It's time you concentrated on the career you set your heart on.'

'Once you're strong again I'll take any job that's going on a newspaper. Then heaven help the editor. He'll be inundated with my work. He'll have to print some of it.'

Lily gave a derogatory snort. She was filing her nails and didn't look up as she snapped, 'What does she need a career for? She'll be married to Nick in a couple of years with a baby on the way. He's going places that young man. He won't need his wife to work.'

'Nick accepts that I don't want children straight away. I'll only be nineteen when Dad gets out of prison. I want to feel I've accomplished something with my life before I settle down to start a family. Once I'm established I can do freelance work for the paper at home.'

''Ark at 'er,' Lily scoffed, 'she thinks she's bleeding something with her high and mighty ideas.'

'Stop putting her down, Lil.' Percy turned to Shona and winked at her. 'From the sound of it you've already accomplished a great deal. If you can win the trust of men like Angus and Bill you'll make an ace reporter.' He paused and rubbed his face. His stare was fierce as he studied her. 'I'll take it easy and keep Alf on to help me with the barrow. I want you to begin looking for a job on a paper. If that's what you want, don't settle for anything less this time.'

Lily slammed down the metal nail file on the table, her face twisting with anger. 'And how are we supposed to manage? Junior reporters are poorly paid, which is why she couldn't take the last job.'

Percy rounded on his daughter. 'We ain't paupers. Shona's had little or no social life these last weeks whilst I've been ill. We'd've lost the stall but for her. Where would we have been then? We owe it to her to give her this chance.'

'And doesn't she owe us? Didn't we take her into our home? She'd have no grand idea of being a journalist if she'd spent her childhood in an orphanage.'

'I've done my share,' Shona fumed. 'Dad wouldn't make me sacrifice something so important.'

Percy intervened. 'She's right. How are you going to defend your selfish motives in preventing her taking up a worthwhile career to him?'

Lily's mouth clamped shut and she marched out of the

house slamming the front door. Percy again winked at Shona. 'Lily knows which side her bread is buttered. She won't stop you. Ted would never forgive her.'

Shona had always believed that as one door closes another opens. With Percy so insistent that she concentrate on her career as a journalist, she put aside her resistance to such a drastic change and trusted that everything would work out beneficially to herself and the family.

Within a week a paper in Tottenham took one of her articles and another, the local *Tribune*, expressed interest in her work. They even asked her to visit their offices the following Tuesday for a talk with the editor, Stan Hardcastle.

'How many other ideas like this have you got?' Mr Hardcastle asked, waving her articles on veterans of the First World War who were still languishing forgotten in mental institutions. 'And how did you substantiate your evidence? A paper needs facts or we'll end up in the libel courts.'

Stan Hardcastle was a short, barrel-chested man with small podgy fingers. He wore a red and white polka-dot bow-tie and his greying blond hair had receded in an erratic fashion leaving a tufted island above his brow. His eyes were black, piercing and cold as jet.

Shona reeled off a dozen topics. As she answered, he lowered his unsettling gaze and proceeded to shuffle through the piles of papers on his desk. His rudeness was disconcerting but she refused to be intimidated. 'As to the evidence for that article, I spoke to the sister of an inmate who had been forbidden to visit him and to a retired male orderly.'

'Hearsay isn't good enough,' Mr Hardcastle rapped out with the ferocity of a round of machine-gun bullets. 'You should have questioned those in charge. Have you followed the story up? Or abandoned it as the investigation became too difficult?'

'My attempts to interview the administrator or matron of the institution were met with an unequivocal refusal. I wrote several times to our local MP but received no answer.'

'A pretty woman like yourself would have been served by going to one of his meetings and heckling him for answers. If he liked your face he may have granted you an interview.'

'I couldn't attend any meetings as my grandfather had suffered a heart attack. And I've more integrity than to use my femininity in the vain pursuit of getting such information. Any man wily enough to become a politician is too clever to be careless with words especially if it could damage his reputation.'

Mr Hardcastle pondered her reply, his stare calculating. Shona went on. 'I'd have brought the subject up at the meeting as though drawing it to his attention for the first time and then asked what he intends to do now that he is aware of the suffering of so many war heroes. Put like that his reputation would be endangered by not answering my question.'

The editor formed a steeple with his fingers and continued to study her in the most unnerving manner. 'In what other way would you pursue the investigation, Miss Carrington?' The black eyes appraised her and she felt she was facing the Inquisition instead of a job interview.

'I have some notes from the original interviews which need verifying. They deal with the inhumane conditions within some of these institutions in the present day. Some are still run like Dickensian workhouses with no regard to the dignity of their patients. Drugs such as Lithium are administered indiscriminately for all mental disorders. Many of these men aren't dangerous. They need expert counselling to overcome the mental scars and traumas they suffered in that war.'

'Fine sentiments, Miss Carrington. But the paper needs proof.'

'The retired orderly has given me the name of an associate

who works in the institution and is willing to co-operate and take photographs of the inmates and some of their files. Apparently his own father died in such a place and working there he was appalled at some of the archaic treatments used.'

Mr Hardcastle sat back in his chair, tapping his pen on the desk. 'Surely not all institutions are that way?'

She leaned forward, her passion for the subject animating her. 'To give a balanced view I would like to discover a modern institution with a more enlightened approach which has returned many patients to their families.'

He nodded. 'However, Miss Carrington, you are young. You write with passion about subjects which are emotive. A good journalist should temper that idealist passion. There are too many hacks who exploit the obvious and don't delve deeper into the problem or resolution. Don't be so quick to see everything as good or bad, black and white. Neither be too hasty to discriminate. Use discernment. That comes with maturity and experience.'

Disappointment weighted her heart. He was telling her her articles were too immature and idealistic. She was too young to be taken on. He was looking down at his papers, his brow furrowed in concentration as he ran his pen through several lines. Had she been summarily dismissed?

Her chin tilted. 'You have given me invaluable advice. I will heed it. I'm determined to succeed. I can't help my age and experience comes with dedication, perseverance and the ability to learn. I want to learn, Mr Hardcastle. I know I have to start at the bottom. I don't care. I'll do anything. Cover weddings. Attend the most mundane court appearances. Even, if it's necessary, write obituaries. I cannot get the experience you talk of without being part of a newspaper and learning from the experts.'

He tossed an article she had sent him back at her. 'Rewrite this and have it on my desk by Thursday. Then we'll see about a job. As for the one on institutions, it has merits. I'll set my top reporter on it.' He held out his hand. 'I'll have the names of your contacts.'

Shona stood up, her body tense with indignation. 'It would be a poor journalist who handed over the source of the information for a story they intend to sell. If you don't want it, Mr Hardcastle, there are other papers who will be interested. I'll give it a more balanced approach and have concrete facts to back up the story.'

He gave a harsh laugh. 'That's what I like to hear. Nevertheless most of the time stories like that will be handled by a senior reporter. Though you could be assigned to assist his investigations and get a by-line. There's no better way to get experience.'

He had been testing her mettle. If she had meekly left the office she would have been no good to Stan Hardcastle as a reporter. Her defiance and spirit had earned her the chance to show him that she had the courage to follow up her convictions. She looked down at his hand which remained outstretched.

'Were I an employee of this paper then I would naturally do my best to aid a senior reporter in his research were I assigned as his assistant. The article will be on your desk Thursday morning, Mr Hardcastle.'

The article he had chosen was one about a mother whose child was killed playing on a bombsite when she fell into the cellar of a ruined house. The woman had set up a group who were lobbying their local councillors to clear the bombsite and put up some swings and a slide for the children to play on. There were bombsites all over London which still drew children like magnets and all too often they were injured playing on them. This time she telephoned Whitehall to discover the name of the Minister in charge of such affairs and secured his opinion and support for the scheme.

The article was accepted and ten days later Shona started

work on the *Tribune*. She was assistant to the editor of the women's page and when they learned of her dance training they used her as the theatre critic to review the plays in the local theatres put on by amateur dramatic societies. There was an ironic twist to Stan Hardcastle's lips when he announced she would also do the obituary column.

Her first weeks at the *Tribune* were hard slog and little glamour. Shona, as junior reporter, was expected to make the tea, man the telex machine and run general errands. She took it in her stride and during her lunch hour she would go down to the paper's archives and read about Gerald Long's life. During his short marriage there was no scandal attached to his name. In 1939 when he was a widower, he was often photographed with different beautiful women on his arm. These liaisons were numerous and continued up to a few months ago when he had met Lady Amanda Huntington-Smythe. They had become engaged last month and were to marry later in the year.

Nothing which was written could confirm that Gerald Long was her father. Yet the notion that she knew him remained. Her feeling grew that her parents had not been married. If he had lived a secret life with her mother, then he would have taken pains that the press never learned of it. And there was the car crash and her mother being shot, according to Ted. There was nothing in the papers about that. Only that the car had crashed and Shona was found by the roadside with no memory.

One fact had always troubled her. If her mother had been murdered as Ted suspected, what had happened to her body? Was the lack of it the reason nothing had appeared in the papers? How could the murder have been covered up?

She shuddered and prayed that her mother wasn't buried in some shallow, unmarked grave in a wood somewhere; or worse, thrown into a river to rot. She couldn't believe her father would have allowed that. An important man with influential contacts could possibly arrange a funeral and the facts of the death not be revealed to either the police or press. But then what type of man did that make her father? There were dark aspects in her past which belied the fairytale fantasy of a loving man who adored her.

Shona read the articles about her own discovery and the search for her parents. Nothing jolted her memory and no details of her past had been unearthed. That in itself was a mystery. Unless someone in high places had been able to suppress information that could have damaged a Cabinet minister.

She rubbed her brow in exasperation. It was strange that nothing had been reported about her past, or that no one had recognised her picture. What about schoolfriends or teachers? Or had she been educated at home? She had certainly received a first-class education. The more Shona thought about it, the more it smacked of subterfuge.

A fortnight later when Shona discovered that Gerald Long was to be guest of honour at a concert at the Town Hall in aid of charity, she pestered Stan Hardcastle to allow her to cover the function.

'Sorry, Shona, Davina Short is attending.'

'Can't I go with her? It would be good experience.'

'There are no complimentary tickets. The tickets are pricy and it's strictly dinner dress. Davina loves classical music and bought her own ticket.'

There was no way Shona could afford the price of a ticket. She refused to be beaten. When writing her articles she had made several contacts at the Town Hall. All it took was a phone call to learn who the caterers were for the refreshments served during the concert interval. Then a couple more calls and a two-pound bribe to one of the waitresses and Shona was employed to serve drinks during the interval.

On the evening of the concert, she was nervous. She had to get Gerald Long's attention and also find a way to speak to him privately. It wouldn't be easy. Also she had to be cautious and consider her questions carefully. She had no actual proof that he was her father after all.

People were crowded around him during the interval. Other waitresses were serving that part of the room. Keeping one eye on the minister's group, she saw him drain his champagne glass. No other waitress was nearby and she wove swiftly through the press of people to present her tray to him. He turned a charming smile on her, then a shutter came down over his eyes and he turned and drew a man several paces away from her before she could speak.

Shona knew that he had recognised her. Why had his expression changed? She had to get him alone and challenge him. But how? Once he left, the two bodyguards who followed him everywhere would stop her approaching him.

She waited until she saw him go into the gents which was further along the corridor to the concert room. Putting down her tray of drinks she picked up a programme for the evening which had been laid aside by a guest. She hovered by the door watching for him to return. He approached with another gentleman and taking a deep breath to calm her nerves she hurried forward.

'Mr Long, could I have your autograph? I'm a great admirer of yours.'

His figure stiffened and the man next to him said in a low voice, 'I wouldn't mind giving her more than my autograph. Pretty little thing, isn't she?'

Gerald Long cleared his throat and looked about to pass her by.

'Please, Mr Long. Surely an autograph is not too much to ask?' She thrust the programme in front of him together with a pen she had taken from her uniform pocket.

He smiled graciously and signed it with a flourish. His

companion had moved on and Shona said quickly, 'I have to ask you, sir. Do you know me? I'm Shona Carrington, or that's the name my adoptive parents gave to me.'

'I beg your pardon, miss.' He looked amused but his eyes were cold and he looked over her head warning her that at any moment someone could approach them.

'It sounds a silly question but it isn't,' she said in a rush. 'I lost my memory as a child. I can remember nothing. Just a tall blond man who I think was my father. I saw you a while ago at a political meeting and I thought I knew you – not from the paper but as someone from my past. And I thought when you saw me that you recognised who I was.'

He lifted a brow, his expression mocking. 'You flatter me. I may have recognised that you are an exceedingly attractive young lady. Then many men must do the same. I do not know you, miss.'

'I was found in Epping after a car crash,' she blurted out knowing that time was short.

'How very unfortunate for you.' His tone was clipped with impatience. 'Now please excuse me, the second half of the concert is about to begin.' He walked away.

When Shona turned to follow him she saw that several people were standing in the doorway watching them. She blushed. She had been a fool to confront him in such a public place. But for all his denial she'd swear he'd recognised her. Yet there had been no warmth in his eyes. It left her more confused than before.

Chapter Fifteen

For the next seventeen months Shona performed the mundane tasks set for her by Stan Hardcastle. Her ambition was boundless but within a few weeks of starting at the paper she was aware of the jealousy of Bert Watson who covered current affairs and Davina Short who was sub-editor and ran the women's page. It was an uphill struggle to overcome their prejudices and resentment of her talent and have her work accepted by them. Too often Stan Hardcastle took her idea and then handed it over to Bert Watson. She then did all the research and he got the credit for the story.

'You can't run before you can walk,' Bert often sneered. He was balding, fiftyish, with the brutish face of an ex-boxer. He wheezed as he spoke or walked from smoking sixty cigarettes a day. Davina Short was exceptionally tall for a woman and barge-pole thin. Her narrow face always had a pinched expression as though she had a bad smell under her nose. She resented any suggestions from Shona as her assistant and although she often stole her ideas, she presented them to Mr Hardcastle as her own.

To overcome the obstacles which stopped her advancing her career, Shona spent her evenings thoroughly researching and polishing new articles until Mr Hardcastle could find no fault with them and agreed to print them. She had been at the paper nine months by then but because she was the youngest reporter she was still regarded as the general dogsbody and teamaker for the senior reporters.

She didn't complain. She had faith in her ability and knew she had an apprenticeship to serve. So she laboured over the obituaries, paring them down to fewer than fifty words and hid her resentment when any eminent townsperson died and Bert Watson wrote a full page on their life.

Shona wasn't deterred. Every week she presented Stan Hardcastle with at least one article, many of which he published. For each of these he paid her extra and often in recent months her weekly salary was doubled. Finally he agreed to release her from writing the obituaries and weddings. Instead she was allowed to cover the more important court cases and some of the minor news events which happened in their area. To her delight, once a month he gave her a full-page spread for an article on a local person of interest. It meant that she was now earning good money and there was less onus on Grandad to work long hours.

She continued to collate facts about people who had been reported missing at the time of her parents' disappearance. Intuition told her to centre her research around people living in London. She had no success getting to speak again with Gerald Long. Two letters requesting an interview were ignored. If she attended a meeting or function where the minister was present, his bodyguards prevented her getting close. If he was her father, surely he wouldn't shut her out? But what if he daren't acknowledge her because of her mother's murder? She had no other leads on her father's identity and was loath to abandon Gerald Long as a possibility. Each time she saw him or a photograph she knew that he was the man in her dream standing in the hall doorway.

Problems at home stopped her pursuing the matter too ardently. Any hint of her research and Lily would scream at her that she was stuck up and thought herself too good for the family who had adopted her. She let it ride. Grandad hated their quarrels. Once Ted was out of prison, she would marry Nick. Nothing would make her stay under Lily's roof once her obligation to Ted was over.

Some things had improved. After his heart attack Grandad and Annie had patched up their differences. When Shona began to earn more money he insisted that she should stop working Saturdays in the market and have some free time to herself. Alf still helped him out in the week and now that Annie's children were older he took on Brian her eldest son to replace Shona on a Saturday.

'You should be cutting back yourself, Grandad,' Shona remonstrated. 'You'll make yourself ill again if you keep up these long hours.'

He shook his head. 'The market is me life. Besides, it's more peaceful there than round here with the twins running riot.'

'Then at least cut down your hours when the weather's bad. Please, Grandad.'

He didn't answer. But neither did he refuse. She hoped that he meant he would be more careful. Brian had proved a hard worker which meant Grandad was at last taking things easier now.

Percy had been advised by his doctor to cut down on his drinking and smoking and lose some weight. 'What pleasures are there left in me life without me fags and booze? The doctor's a kill-joy. Now rationing is lifted and we can have a decent meal he wants me to starve meself. Not bloody likely.'

Shona could do nothing about his smoking and drinking but since she cooked the evening and weekend meals she cut down on his favourite fry-ups and spotted-Dick puddings. In the summer he had taken up playing bowls and slowly over the months he had trimmed his figure down and had lost the reddish flush brought on by any exertion.

With her weekends free throughout the summer Shona and Nick could spend more time together. They had fallen into a pattern of taking a picnic and spending a couple of hours driving around the surrounding streets. Nothing was familiar and the circle was widening, spreading into Essex. Because she was found in Epping, Shona assumed she had lived north of the River Thames. It didn't bear thinking about how vast the search would be to take in the south side and suburbs as well. It would take her years. It was like looking for a needle in a haystack. Afterwards they would picnic in a park, by a river or canal and then go on to the cinema or a dance in the evening.

Now that Christmas was approaching Shona wanted to make it special for the twins. Lily as usual wanted nothing to do with Christmas as Ted was still inside. Annie was coming over with her family on Christmas Day and even that had failed to rouse Lily from her lethargy. As usual Shona was the only one doing the cooking and organising everything.

Lily was still working at the pub and on Christmas Eve it was again left to Shona to put up the decorations and do the tree. Johnnie and Jamie had started school in September and Lily was now working lunchtimes at the Crown as well as in the evenings. That's if she managed to keep her job much longer. She was drinking more heavily and was often tipsy when she came home in the afternoon and fell asleep. Too often for Shona's comfort a neighbour brought the twins home with her own children from school as Lily had failed to turn up.

Lily had changed from an attractive woman into a slut. Her hourglass figure was bloated and shapeless, her face puffy and heavily made up to cover the ravages of her drinking. She had also taken to dying her hair but its colour had faded to a brassy sheen.

'Can't you ease up on the drinking, Mum?' Shona tried to encourage her. 'Dad could be out in a few months. You haven't been to the prison to see him for months because you say you hate how you look. Don't you want to look your best for him when he comes out?'

'You saying Ted don't love me?' Her manner was belligerent. 'I'm his wife. I've stood by him through all this. He ain't gonna leave me now. Not if he wants to keep his sons. And he needn't think I'm slaving my fingers to the bone in that pub for the rest of me life.'

This was another change and for the worse. Lily was no longer obsessive about keeping Ted because she loved him. She resented scrimping and saving for two years and having to work to support the children. Her attitude towards her marriage was that Ted owed her for making her suffer the deprivations since his imprisonment. It worried Shona. It wouldn't be easy for Dad to find work now he had a record. If Lily was greedy she'd turn him back to crime as a way of getting money and then he'd end up inside again. When attending the court sessions for the paper Shona had seen the circle too often.

'It isn't going to be easy for Dad when he comes out,' she cautioned.

'And you think it's been easy for me, I suppose.' Lily walked away from Shona. 'What do you care? You'll be married to Nick. He'll take care of you.'

Shona didn't pursue the matter. Lily never listened to her. Lily never listened to anyone unless it served her own selfish interests.

At nine o'clock there was a knock on the door. In the distance Shona could hear carol singers. She had a sense that Christmas Eve had been like this two years ago when Nick had turned up and asked her out. She knew it wasn't Nick knocking on the door. He was going drinking with his mates tonight up the West End. Shona wasn't seeing him until he came over for Christmas lunch. They were taking the twins to a pantomime matinée at the Theatre Royal Stratford on Boxing Day and then they were spending the evening with Nick's family.

Marion was on the doorstep, her face radiant. 'I've done it, girl! Ken asked me to marry him and I've accepted. We're getting married in March. I might even beat you down the aisle if Ted don't get the remission you're hoping for.'

'That's wonderful news! Show me the ring.' Shona dragged her inside into the warm and admired the two diamonds each side of a ruby.

Since Marion had ditched Derek over fifteen months ago she had had a string a boyfriends. She'd also had four changes of job before leaving the city to work in a local solicitor's office. There she'd met Ken Forrester who was an articled clerk. They'd been going out for five months and he had recently qualified as a solicitor.

'Ken's just left after bringing me home from his parents'. His mum was a bit stand-offish. She don't think a secretary's good enough for her only son. Especially now Ken's father is taking him into partnership in his own firm of solicitors.' Marion threw her arms around Shona. 'Just think, I'm going to be married to the son in Forrester, Forrester and Son.'

'Who's the other Forrester?'

'Some doddering old uncle who only comes into the office once a week to deal with the estate of some Ladyship or other.' Marion released Shona to twirl around the room. 'It's so wonderful. We can look for our wedding dresses together and bridesmaids' dresses, since we've always said we'd have each other as chief bridesmaid. We can go up Oxford Street and get a right bobby-dazzler bargain in the January sales.'

'Hang on.' Shona held up her hands and laughed. 'Nick and I haven't set the date yet. I'm not superstitious but it would seem like attracting bad luck to get my dress without the date set.'

'But you won't get another chance until next year to get such a good bargain.'

'I'll come with you. But I won't decide on a gown for myself until I know when Dad is being released.'

*   *   *

When Nick drove Shona home on Boxing Day evening only the landing light was on.

'Looks like Grandad has gone up to bed,' Shona observed as she turned the key in the front door. 'When we dropped the twins off after the pantomime they were bursting with excitement. They probably wore him out.'

'And Lil won't be back from the pub for another hour. Let's have a nightcap.'

They went into the front room with only the tree lights to illuminate it. Nick pulled the curtains and Shona had a sensation of *déjà vu* from that Christmas two years ago. Nick half filled a tumbler of port and filled it up with lemonade and handed it to her.

She sipped it and gulped. 'That's a bit strong.'

'Port's good for you. It's like a tonic.' He poured himself a large whisky from the bottle he had brought round on Christmas Day and pulled Shona down on to the settee. He flicked the large oval locket he bought her for Christmas. 'Got my picture in that yet?'

'Of course and a photo of Dad.'

Nick traced the line of the locket which nestled between her breasts over her sage woollen shirtwaister dress. When his gaze lifted to hold hers, it was dark with passion. 'Sometimes I still can't believe my luck that a scamp like me has won your heart.'

'It's the scamp which makes you different. But don't put yourself down, Nick. You've many good qualities. I wouldn't love you otherwise.'

He closed his eyes and his words came out with a groan. 'I need you so much, Shona. This waiting is torture.'

His kiss had a deeper fervour than ever before. He wasn't just seeking a response but compelling her submission. There was a special magic in his kisses and caresses which heightened Shona's own need. It had been a month since they last had time alone together. Nick worked long hours with his evening work at the garage. He had saved the money towards a deposit on a house and he'd use the rest as capital to start his own business in another six months. It meant they didn't see each other except at weekends and as a precaution against temptation Shona never went to Nick's flat. Consequently with Percy baby-sitting at the weekend they rarely had time alone together in private.

Shona trusted Nick and had no reason to suspect that he played her false as he had before.

His gaze burned into hers as he eased her purposefully down on to the rug in front of the fire. There was an intensity in Nick's gaze which warned her that if she didn't halt him now the consequence would be her capitulation. She had been so strong for so long in restraining his desire. Her own body burned for release from the agony of unfulfilled longing. A part of her wanted to be completely and forever his. When his caresses became bolder she was loath to halt them.

'Let this be our night, Shona my darling. I've waited two years. I love you. I want to make you mine completely. You drive me wild.'

His touch was more persuasive than his words. The long days apart heightened her own desire. She was by nature passionate and each week it became harder to resist the demands of her young, ardent body.

'Nick, we agreed to wait until we were married,' she murmured, knowing that her own will was crumbling under the onslaught of his caresses.

'You were seventeen then. You'll be nineteen in a few weeks. Most women are married by your age. We delayed our marriage because you want Ted to give you away, but why must we wait to express our love for each other? At least let me see you, my darling. I won't go further than you want me to.'

'We can't, Grandad is upstairs.'

Nick got up and pulled the settee across the door. 'Not that Percy will wake up, doesn't he always sleep like a log? It's best not to take chances that he'll walk in on us.'

When Nick was at his most persuasive and charming it was impossible to resist him and tonight Nick was determined upon seduction. When he lowered himself on to the rug beside her and began to unfasten the buttons of her dress she made no protest. She gasped as his knuckles brushed over the peak of her breast sending delicious shivers through her. She closed her eyes, languid and pliant in his arms as he slowly undressed her. Each limb or curve exposed was covered with burning kisses, chasing the chill of the air from her body until it glowed with an iridescent heat.

'Look at me, Shona,' he said, his voice deep and husky.

She opened her eyes and saw her naked limbs bathed in a rosy glow from the fire. Nick's strong muscular body was above hers and when their naked flesh touched it was like the crackle of static electricity between them.

'Oh, Nick, I love you so much. But you'll hate me tomorrow if I give in to you.' She was struggling to retain the last vestige of sanity before passion destroyed coherent reason. Never before had she permitted Nick to see her more than half-naked. They had petted heavily to relieve the tension of their frustration but she had always insisted that he stopped short of possessing her. 'We agreed to wait until our wedding night.'

'I never thought I'd be waiting for two years.' His voice was gruff. 'I need you, Shona. It's driving me crazy wanting you but never having all of you.'

She struggled to summon reason through the sybaritic haze her body seemed to be floating in. The clamour of her heart, the fever of her flesh dictated submission: intuition cautioned. 'You always said your bride would be a virgin on your wedding day. You'll despise me if I give in to you.'

He took her wrists and eased her arms over her head behind

her and moved his leg to lie across her. 'I could never despise you. Hell, Shona, we can't even set a date because you want to wait until Ted is free. You should have been my wife months ago. I'm going crazy with wanting you. I'm crazy with love for you. I'm not going to lose my respect for you. In all but name you're my wife.'

He kissed her, his lips teasing, his tongue leisurely tracing the outline of her trembling mouth. Had he used force or rushed her she would have fought him. Instead she was ensnared in the slow, sensual, seductive web he was weaving. To deny him would be to deny her womanhood and her sense of being. If she was honest it was what she wanted. What she dreamed of and every part of her craved. Yet her conscience allowed her no peace.

'This is madness, Nick! If Grandad did come down I'd die of shame.' She pulled her dress towards her.

He took it from her hands and kissed her fingertips. 'Stop worrying. Can't you hear Percy snoring?'

Seeing the uncertainty in her eyes, he smiled down at her. 'You're so lovely, Shona. Don't deny our love. I've been patient. You're going to be my wife. This isn't wrong. How can it be when we love each other so much?'

He began to kiss her eyelids. His voice became soft and coercing, piercing the now gossamer threads of her resistance. 'You can't doubt my love. That you're the only woman I'd ever want to marry.'

Then his mouth was upon hers, his hands unhindered by clothing roused her body to a fever. When the throbbing heat of him pressed against her, she moved languorously to accommodate him, then she tensed. 'Nick, what if I become pregnant?'

'You don't think I'd be that careless. I'll take precautions.'

'You planned this!' Shock momentarily tempered her desire. His eyes were demon bright reflecting the orange flames of the fire. Had he planned to seduce her tonight? Or was he always so prepared? The memory of the tarty Phyllis fed her suspicion. Had she been right to trust him? There were so many evenings she didn't see him.

'Sweetheart, I've been planning this for months.' His voice was huskier than she had heard it before. It taunted and coerced. 'You don't think I'd be unprepared when you finally agreed.'

For a long time she stared up at him, her fear crowding in. 'Nick, while we've been engaged have there been others?'

'Do you think I'd risk losing you? There's no one but you.' His expression was angry that she should doubt him.

'Two years is a long time for you to be celibate. You had so many willing girlfriends before me.'

'Christ, Shona. What's brought this up?' His fingers curled through hers pinning her beneath him. His face was in the shadow from the fire but his eyes glittered with pinpoints of light and his voice was harsh. 'You're worth a dozen of those women and worth waiting for.'

Wordlessly she stared up at him. The anger in his eyes was replaced by tenderness. 'You're the only woman for me, Shona.'

His lips swooped upon hers, stifling her protests. The subtle persuasion of his kiss made a mockery of her doubts. Relief relaxed her muscles and brought a submissive sigh to her throat. When he lowered himself over the length of her body, every contour and curve tingled with awareness of the heat and hardness of his body. With an expertise which knew every pulse and sensitive part of her body Nick dissipated her inhibitions. His kisses left her breathless and half swooning. A relentless pressure was building within her. Lips and bodies were melded in a cataclysmic fusion. Her passion startled Shona. She had never expected to feel this blossoming, shuddering, all-consuming, driving force. A wave of ecstatic convulsions held her enthralled and she arched up crying out Nick's name in surrender.

Nick groaned, he had held himself back savouring the moment of Shona's abandonment and fulfilment. Then his control was gone, his own primeval need driving him to his own shuddering release.

They lay replete, hearts beating in unison. Nick turned on to his side, gazing down at her in wonder. 'I love you, Shona. I could spring Ted from prison tomorrow just so that we could be married. You've no regrets, have you?'

She smiled. 'Only that we have to wait to make our vows.' Her body was bathed in an incandescent glow from his lovemaking. She was loath to put the barriers of clothing between them, but as the mantel clock struck quarter to the hour she knew she must.

'It's getting late, Nick. Mum won't be long now. You'd better go.'

He put his arms around her as she fastened her dress and lifted the back of her long blonde hair to kiss her neck. 'There ain't never been no one like you, Shona. I wish we could wed tomorrow. Having you once has only made me realise what I've been missing.'

She turned to face him. 'I never realised how wonderful it could be. I wish we could have the whole night together.'

'Tell Lil you've got some research to do for the paper out of town and have to stay overnight. We'll spend it at my flat.'

'You're incorrigible.' She was tempted. Then slowly she shook her head, her smile wistful and provocative. 'Let's keep something special for our wedding night. Having a whole night together before that would spoil it.'

Nick let out a harsh breath against her hair. 'Temptress! Even now you hold back and remain elusive. Looks like I'm gonna have to wait until our wedding before you are truly and wholly mine.'

'Isn't that how it should be?'

Nick shook his head in resignation. 'I'll never understand a woman's reasoning.'

After she closed the front door behind Nick, she leaned against it. She could still feel the tingle and taste Nick on her breath. She hugged her arms close around her, savouring the memories of their lovemaking. She had not wanted it to end. It was harrowing to acknowledge that she could feel such unequivocal passion.

As she made her way upstairs a shadow flickered into the corners of her mind dimming the brightness of her euphoria. He had described her as elusive but often she sensed that Nick was the same. Not in a mysterious way but a withdrawing, a secretive side to his nature which was evasive. Was it the scamp, the rogue in him which made her feel that he kept things from her?

Chapter Sixteen

Any fears Shona may have harboured that Nick would no longer respect her after she had given herself to him were quickly dispelled. He was more attentive to her than ever and on their evenings together they now went back to Nick's flat before he took Shona home.

Marion badgered Shona to go with her when she bought her wedding dress in the January sales. With clothing coupons now a restriction of the past the latest styles could have adorned a fairytale princess. Marion chose a dress of heavy lace which fell in layers over a bustle and train at the back. Shona had fallen in love with a gown she could never have afforded if it hadn't been a third of its original price. As she stared at it wistfully, still feeling it would be unlucky to buy it until a date for her wedding was set, Marion egged her on.

'You'd be a fool not to buy it. Your dad's bound to be back home within six months. You'll regret it if you miss this chance.'

Shona allowed herself to be persuaded. She had fallen in love with the gown because of its simplicity. It was made of watered silk and was medieval in design with a high waist. The V-neck and tight bodice were encrusted with seed pearls. It fitted snugly over her hips. The skirt was cut cleverly on the bias so that it fell into folds to her feet. The sleeves were close-fitting and ended in points over the back of her hands. The dress was now wrapped in layers of tissue paper and inside a large white box on top of her wardrobe.

In February they learned that Ted Carrington would be out of prison in April if nothing happened to block his parole. Nick had booked the church and church hall for the first Saturday in May. In a daze of happiness Shona had bought her head dress and veil and Marion's dress as maid of honour as she would be a bride of six weeks when Shona was married.

By March all the wedding arrangements were made with Nick regularly visiting Ted Carrington to keep him informed. Nick insisted that all the expenses of the wedding would be met by him. Shona received a long and emotional letter from Ted saying that he felt he had let her down by not providing for her wedding. It had taken all Nick's persuasion for her not to visit him. Her own letter in reply was passionate, saying that all she wanted for her wedding day to be perfect was for him to be at her side as she walked down the aisle.

When she entered the church behind Marion on her friend's wedding day tears blurred Shona's eyes. In six short weeks she would be walking down this same aisle to become Mrs Nicholas Blake. When she caught Nick's gaze as she walked back down the aisle after Marion was married, he winked at her and mouthed, 'We're next.' Her heart was singing with joy.

After Marion and Ken left the reception for their honeymoon Nick and Shona drove to Nick's flat. Both were tipsy from the champagne lavishly provided by the Forresters to toast the happiness of the couple.

Nick's flat was small. You entered it by climbing a flight of stairs at the side of the house. They were cuddling and laughing as Nick threw open the front door which led into the main room. Three doors opened off from it, one each to the bedroom, toilet and kitchen. The bath was in the kitchen and was filled by a gas water heater. It was covered by a wooden top which served as a table. There was little furniture in the main room apart from a radiogram, a battered sofa and armchair and a low table.

Nick gave a theatrical groan as he drew Shona into his arms. 'Those six weeks seem like an eternity. I wish that had been us today.' He kissed her neck and began to undo the zip at the back of her apricot satin bridesmaid dress.

'You've got a one-track mind.' She half-heartedly pushed him away with a laugh.

Joining in her laughter he scooped her up into his arms and carried her to the bedroom. There was a deeper urgency to their lovemaking. Marion's wedding had brought their own so much closer. Yet afterwards as Shona lay in Nick's arms with the rising moon bathing them in its silvery glow, she shivered. She pulled the sheet across her naked breasts and snuggled closer to Nick, feeling the hardness and warmth of his body. 'Dad comes home in a fortnight,' she said to dispel the moment of panic that something would go wrong to prevent their marriage. A tear slipped from the corner of her eye.

'Tears, my darling? What are they for?' Nick wiped it away with his finger. He grinned in the self-assured way she loved and tilted his head to one side to regard her with mock severity. 'You're not going to change your mind and jilt me, are you?'

'Don't be silly. I'm just so happy. Today was beautiful. Marion's happiness was wonderful to see. With Dad coming home and our own wedding getting closer I can't believe it's finally going to happen.'

Nick kissed her and pulled her on top of him. 'I'll never have enough of you, Shona.'

Her desire matched his with an ardour that transcended anything which she had experienced before. She sat back on her haunches, her legs straddling him. Her long hair streamed down her spine as she arched gracefully back then shifted to impale herself upon him. Her hands gripped his shoulders and her head came forwards, her hair swinging in a feathering caress across his chest. Passion quickened her heartbeat and set the blood pounding in her ears. It was some seconds before she realised there was someone banging on the front door.

She froze. There was a violence to that hammering which was alarming.

'Who on earth can that be?' she asked.

Nick linked his arms round her, pulling her towards him. 'Forget them. We get little enough time together.'

The insistent banging was now accompanied by a man's shout. 'I know you're in there, Blake. Open up or I'll break this bloody door down.'

'You'd better answer it, Nick.' Shona slid off him and pulled the sheet around her.

Nick swore roundly and reached for his trousers, fastening the fly but leaving the belt undone.

The knocking and shouting continued. 'Blake, you bastard! Open up. You and me got a reckoning.'

'Be careful, Nick.' Shona was frightened by the anger in the man's voice.

Nick pulled the bedroom door to so that whoever was outside would not see Shona and the rumpled bed.

'Blake. Open up!' The shouts were now a guttural snarl. There was the crash of glass as a window pane was shattered.

'What the bleeding hell's going on?' Nick yelled, equally incensed. 'I'm coming.'

'You've got more than a broken window coming to you, Blake,' the threats continued.

Fear channelled through Shona. Stumbling over the end of the sheet she ran to the bedroom door. 'Don't answer the door, Nick!'

He ignored her. Shona felt suddenly vulnerable. She could almost taste the menace emanating from the street.

She snatched up her bridesmaid dress and stepped into it without bothering with her underclothes. Her body was still clammy from their lovemaking and the tight-fitting bodice stuck to her and she found herself wrestling with the zip.

The front door banged open. 'Right, Blake. What have you got to say to this? It's your doing.'

'I ain't responsible.'

There was an edge to Nick's voice which sent a shiver down Shona's spine.

'You're lying,' the man snarled. There was a thwack of knuckles on flesh and then the sound of scuffling. A chair thudded to the floor and several thumps and grunts followed the unmistakable sound of fighting. A woman screamed.

'Stop it,' the woman cried out and then burst into hysterical weeping.

Nausea rose to Shona's throat. She stopped struggling with her zip and flung open the bedroom door. Nick hadn't switched on any lights but the moonlight showed two men wrestling on the floor. Nick was on top of a sailor in uniform. Both men had their hands round each other's throats.

Shona crossed the room to the light switch and turned it on. She blinked at the sudden brightness and saw Nick roll aside and drag the sailor to his feet. Then she saw the dark-haired woman cowering in the corner and sobbing. Her face was bruised, one eye cut and swollen. Most noticeable was the fact that she was heavily pregnant.

The woman's jealous glare which briefly flickered over Shona was like a razor slashing at her heart. It told her that the woman had been Nick's mistress. Was it his child she carried?

Shona backed away, her eyes large with horror. Nick saw her movement and his guilt was stamped on his face.

The sailor let out another growl of rage. 'That another of your whores, Blake? Got them bloody queuing up to get in your bed? She married too? Her old man away, is he?'

He swung his fist which Nick lithely sidestepped. But he was looking at Shona and a second blow caught him in the stomach, doubling him over. The sailor lashed out with his foot, kicking Nick in the ribs.

'That's enough!' Shona demanded. 'Strike him again and I'll report you to the police *and* your commanding officer.' The sailor's cap which had fallen to the floor bore the name of his ship.

'He's got it coming to him.' The sailor's face twisted with fury. His glare was contemptuous as he regarded her. 'You women make me sick.'

Nick had risen to his feet and swung a punch which sent the sailor staggering back against the wall. Nick grabbed the front of his uniform and hauled him to the door. 'Get out of my flat and take her with you.'

'She's carrying your bastard!' the sailor shouted. 'She's your responsibility now. Not mine. It ain't my kid. I've been at sea a year. You can have her. Good riddance to the rotten whore.' He shrugged himself out of Nick's hold and spat on the floor in the direction of his wife. 'You can have your bastard in the gutter where you belong. You won't get another penny from me.'

Shona turned her back on the room. Nausea was threatening to overwhelm her.

'Shona!' Nick entreated.

'What you gonna do about the mess I'm in, Nick,' the other woman wailed.

Tears blurred Shona's eyes as she slammed the bedroom door behind her and began hunting for her coat and shoes. She wanted to get out of this nightmare. Nick opened the door as she pulled on her coat.

'You've got to listen to me, Shona. That kid ain't mine.'

'She thinks it is. You slept with her, didn't you?'

He shrugged. 'It was before we . . . Before Christmas. God, Shona, you wouldn't let me near you for months.

She was a fling. She threw herself at me. I only slept with her a couple of times. It was nothing. She's nothing to me. What's a man supposed to do. I swear there ain't been no one since Christmas.'

'You can't escape your past, Nick, or your responsibilities.'

'That kid could be anyone's. God knows why she picked on me. The woman's the local bike. Everyone's had her. She's a joke.'

'I'm not laughing.' She pulled off her engagement ring and tossed it on the bed.

Nick was pale, his face haggard. 'You can't leave me, Shona. I'll make it up to you. I love you. I swear. I love you. You can't chuck what we had away because of a stupid mistake.'

'I didn't do the chucking away. You did, Nick. It's not the first time you've cheated on me. I told you when I took you back there'd be no more chances. I trusted you. You betrayed that trust. I never want to see you again.'

'You don't mean that.'

She looked him in the eyes. Her tears dried and her voice carried the ring of steel which had wrapped itself around her heart. 'I mean it from the depths of my soul. Stay out of my life, Nick. I never want to see or hear of you again.'

PART THREE

1957

By the time you swear you're his
Shivering and sighing
And he vows his passion is
Infinite, undying
Lady, make a note of this:
One of you is lying.

Dorothy Parker

Chapter Seventeen

Shona pressed her fingers to her temple. The noise of ringing telephones, clacking typewriters and raised voices in the busy Fleet Street newspaper office droned in her ears. Was she becoming paranoid? Recently she couldn't shake the feeling that she was being followed.

It had happened again this morning as she climbed the escalator at St Paul's and walked down Ludgate Hill to Fleet Street. In the press of morning commuters it was impossible to discern any one person constantly watching her.

So why the paranoia? The feeling she was being followed? It had started after the scare she'd had in Fleet Street three weeks ago. Surely it had been an accident when someone on the crowded pavement had shoved her into the road as a bus was passing? If the man beside her hadn't caught her she could have been killed.

On the busy London street accidents like that happened all too easily. But the next night she had heard muffled footsteps behind her as she left Stratford station. It was late and there were still several people hurrying along the Broadway even though it was raining. When she glanced over her shoulder no one appeared to be taking any interest in her.

She drew in a shuddering breath as she remembered the incident. Aware of the dangers of walking the London streets alone at night, her senses were heightened. It seemed that the footsteps kept the same distance away from her even as she crossed the main road. She wished she'd used her car for work that morning, but she had taken it to the garage for a service.

The Two Puddings public house was ahead of her and she could hear the babble of voices and a piano being played. The light from its windows spilled out on to the pavement. She turned as she approached the pub. The footsteps had halted. There was no one in sight. The street was eerily deserted. The passengers from the train had dispersed as they made their way home. A bus rattled past splaying out water from the gutter with its wheels. Shona jumped back to avoid getting wet. Still she couldn't shake the sensation that someone was watching her. There were enough darkened doorways for a figure to hide.

Seeing an empty taxi cab she hailed it although her house was no more than a ten-minute walk. Safe indoors, she thought no more of the incident, putting it down to an over-active imagination. Ever since she had been attacked by the robbers leaving the market with Alf the sound of footsteps behind her made her nervous.

Even so, several times in the next few days she again felt the hairs on her neck prickle and she couldn't shake the feeling that she was being watched.

Shona rubbed her brow where a dull ache was forming. Pull yourself together, she chided. Who'd want to follow you?

She hadn't made any enemies that she knew of, though some of the journalists resented her popularity and successes. She had worked on two other papers since leaving the *Tribune*. Last year she had been employed by the *Globe* in Fleet Street.

Life was rewarding and fulfilling. She had achieved the success in her career which she dreamed of and it kept her busy. Too busy to notice that there was no permanent man in her life. Her circle of friends was wide although she was still closest to Marion who now lived in a grand house in Chigwell and had four children. Shona had travelled extensively on assignments in the last year and felt no regrets at not having married and settled down.

Today she had a difficult story to write and a deadline to meet, but her attention kept returning to a fat file of papers on her desk. She flicked it open and spread a dozen of the old newspaper cuttings in front of her. The face of Gerald Long stared back at her.

She looked at her notes. There were too many questions without answers about Gerald Long's early career. Many of his foreign visits before the war were shielded by the Secrecy Act, the documentation unavailable to the public for twenty-five years.

She flicked through the notes and photographs on her desk. Whether Gerald Long was her father or not, she knew there was a story here, but what? It had prompted her to dig deeper and recently her investigations had linked Long's name with that of a Laurence Shelton in the late 1930s. That name was familiar. She was sure she'd come across it earlier in her research. Unless she was mistaken there was something sinister about Shelton. He'd been involved in some scandal or other. She would have to check the facts.

Again she frowned, her temples throbbing painfully. The name Shelton definitely disturbed her. Her long nail tapped the photo of the two men. Frustratingly, the picture of Laurence Shelton was unclear. His features were shadowed by the brim of his fedora. When she questioned Long's press office about Shelton the man's voice had turned nasty, rapping out, 'No comment.'

It had aroused her suspicion that they were hiding something. And more than that she felt a tingling deep inside. The photo of the two men haunted her as though it was trying to tell her something. Staring at it increased her headache. Gerald Long and Laurence Shelton were standing side by side leaving a political conference together. Her attention was on Shelton. The two men were tall, blond and of a similar build. A pain stabbed behind her eyes. Shelton looked familiar or was it because of his resemblance to Gerald Long? She could not place having met him or even having heard of him before she hunted out the press cuttings. Her increasing headache made thinking impossible. She took out two Aspro to take with her tea.

Tomorrow she would start her investigations into Laurence Shelton. The name ran naturally off her tongue as though he were an old school-teacher or an acquaintance from the market. Yet he was neither of those. She was sure there had been some scandal about the man and that's why his name struck a chord. Perhaps Ted would know when she met him for lunch. She couldn't do any research today as she had another story to get on the editor's desk before she left the paper tonight.

She glanced at her watch and put the press cuttings into a folder. She was meeting Ted in half an hour. They met every week for lunch since she'd left home shortly after his release from prison. He worked as a maintenance engineer over at Walthamstow greyhound stadium. No engineering company would employ him as a foreman, or manager, with a prison record and he had been too proud to take a supervised job on the factory floor. He seemed to thrive on the outdoor life and enjoyed mixing with the punters at the race meetings. On his day off Ted caught the train to Liverpool Street station and met Shona in a small restaurant off London Wall.

At lunchtime the sun was shining in a clear sky which was a joy after so many recent days of fog. Shona decided to walk instead of taking a bus. She had all but completed her copy for tonight's edition and could spare the extra time.

With its tall newspaper buildings Fleet Street always seemed in shadow. As usual it was bustling with people and the road was jammed with traffic, the air heavy with exhaust fumes. Ahead the sun was shining on the dome of St Paul's Cathedral as it rose like a giant crown above the City. It was a sight that always made her heart beat faster. The Tower of London had the same effect on her. Both were famous landmarks which were a part of their heritage. The Tower, a fortress, familiar and yet forbidding. Its history tainted by use as a prison for so many famous people who had displeased a despotic monarch. Wren's famous cathedral had risen from the darkness of the horror and ashes of the Great Fire to shed a light of hope upon the City. Its beauty and symmetry of lines never failed to move her. She spent many lunchtimes in its gardens away from the noise and clamour of London traffic.

A display in a shop window caught her eye and she paused a moment. At the same time the hairs at the nape of her neck began to prickle. The sensation of being watched scalded over her shoulders, making her turn quickly. It was midday and the pavement was packed with office workers. No one looked suspicious or was taking any special notice of her. Her glance alighted on a man in a trenchcoat who had stopped to buy a newspaper from the street vendor.

'Here, darling, catch!' The familiar voice of Toby the fruit seller spun her round. He was swarthy and dark-haired as a gypsy. He was a couple of years older than Shona and had been asking her out since her first day at the *Globe*. He winked and tossed a rosy apple to her. 'Have that one on me, darling.'

Shona caught the apple and blushed. 'Thanks.'

'Any time, sweetheart. And if you're free tonight . . .'

She smiled and shook her head. A middle-aged woman who looked like an office tea lady with her tight permed greying hair and cross-over apron under her opened coat, sniffed her disdain. 'Those apples going free, mate? I'll 'ave one. Or they just for the pretty women? Ain't I a regular customer?'

The coster laughed. 'Here's a couple of lemons for you, Mavis. Go with your sharp tongue.'

The banter reminded her of her days on the market stall

and Shona's step lightened. Percy still worked his stall with Annie's son helping him out.

Shona glanced back to see if the man in the trenchcoat was in sight. He had vanished. There's no one following you, she told herself as she cut through the back turnings to reach London Wall. Even so she couldn't stop herself scanning the pavement behind her each time she crossed a road. There was no man in a trenchcoat. Seeing Ted sitting at the window table of the restaurant, she waved to him.

The restaurant was full. It was a no-nonsense place with red gingham tablecloths and wooden chairs. The food was cheap but delicious.

When Shona kissed Ted's cheek, he gave a cough of embarrassment at her display of affection in public, but his eyes were shining with pleasure as he squeezed her hand before they were seated.

He pushed back his cap which covered his thinning crown and Shona noticed that the grey threads were more prominent in his brown hair around his temples. He carried no spare flesh on his wiry body and although of little more than medium height, to her he always stood out from other men. Despite his permanent limp his walk was always brisk and jaunty, although there was often a sadness around his eyes which he covered by telling countless jokes.

'So how's life treating you, angel?' He studied her intently. 'You look tired. That editor of yours working you too hard?'

'I should be so lucky. The men get all the exacting assignments like the Suez Crisis. Although it was fun being sent to Monaco to cover the marriage of Prince Rainier to Grace Kelly.' It had been hard for Shona to accept the limitations placed on her by her editor. It was the same for all women journalists and one of the reasons she was pursuing her research into Gerald Long's background in her own time.

'You're mixing with the high life now,' Ted said with a grin. 'I was so proud of you rubbing shoulders with all the nobs and royalty in Monaco.'

Shona laughed. 'We were kept firmly in our place. I told you we stayed in a run-down hotel a mile outside Monaco. Anyway that's old news. How's the twins?'

He rolled his eyes. 'They are always in some scrape or other. They both got picked for the school soccer team and they want racing bikes for their birthday. That's all they go on about. I've put a deposit down and the rest on the never never.'

'I'll pay half if it will help you out, Dad?'

He shook his head. 'Lil won't like it. The best present has to come from us. She wouldn't let Percy chip in.'

Shona didn't press the matter. The twins were spoilt. They had to have the best of everything. Shona didn't begrudge them but she wasn't sure it was good for them. They were bright boys and big for their age, but both had failed their eleven plus because they wouldn't do their homework. 'How's Mum?'

Ted's gaze slid from hers to stare out of the window. 'About the same. She says she's eased up on her drinking but I doubt it. The dustbin was full of empties last week. Says she drinks 'cause she's lonely with me working so many evenings and long hours.'

'Doesn't Percy keep an eye on her?'

'They row all the time. Percy's had enough. He wants to get a place of his own. Widow Bishop has got a room going and there's a lockup for his market barrow. She's got two other lodgers. Mind you I think she's taken a shine to Percy. They've been to the pictures a few times.'

'Grandad never said,' Shona chuckled. 'It would be nice if he remarried. Have someone fuss over him a bit. He's only in his mid-sixties.'

'There's plenty of life in the old dog yet, but Lily and Annie will see red if he gets hitched. They don't want some other woman getting her hands on his money. Widow Bishop is twelve years younger than Percy.'

'Then good for him. I'd like to see Percy happy. And Annie is a fine one to talk. Since she got herself that fancy man from Muswell Hill a couple of years ago, she never visits her father.'

'Lil ain't too happy about that either. At least she had Annie to go out with before.'

That was a mixed blessing, Shona reckoned. Annie always had been a bad influence on Lily. Annie had a string of boyfriends who were never short of money. Most of them were low-life, petty villains or con-men. As fast as Annie got money she spent it and usually on herself not her kids. She encouraged Lily to do the same. Lily and her sister were always up Oxford Street and came back laden with shoes and clothes. Ted took on more hours to keep them out of debt. To his credit he had not slipped back into his old ways to make extra money on the side. Lily resented that. His ducking and diving in the past had been profitable. Ted had vowed never to go back inside. He didn't speak of those years but he had a dislike for enclosed spaces and spent any time he could out in the open. He'd even got himself an allotment which he worked on when he wasn't at the stadium.

Shona also suspected that it was an excuse to keep out of Lily's way. In recent years she had become a nagging shrew who was drunk most days when she wasn't out shopping. There appeared to be little love or comfort left in their marriage. Only bitterness and resentment on her part and resignation on his. Yet Ted wouldn't have a word said against his wife. He'd married her for better or worse.

It saddened Shona how much Lily had changed. She never went round there now. Lily wouldn't allow her in the house. She had never forgiven Shona for not marrying Nick, who had done so well for himself and now owned a string of electrical shops. He was involved in several other successful ventures all of which were legal. He'd bought a house for his parents and one for himself.

Lily's jealousy at the affection Ted had for Shona had erupted within a month of Ted's release from prison. Shona knew that if Ted was going to have any kind of peace in his life she had to get a place of her own. There had been tears in Ted's eyes the day he helped her move into a flat in Stratford. Lily's parting words were, 'Good riddance.'

Shona kept in touch with the family. She met Percy one evening a fortnight when they went to the dogs together. Life without the twins causing havoc around her was quieter, but Shona missed them. If she wasn't working on a Saturday afternoon and West Ham was playing at home, she met Ted and the boys over Upton Park to watch the match.

'So what you been up to this week, Shona?' Ted quizzed. 'Still seeing that bloke Danny?'

Shona shook her head. 'He didn't like the unsociable hours I often work. Or me going away to interview someone.'

A waitress appeared and Ted ordered steak and kidney pudding for them both. When the woman left, he regarded Shona seriously. 'It's an unnatural life for a woman. You should be thinking of settling down.'

'One day I'll marry and have children.' Despite her independence, in the future she wanted a family of her own. Her life with the Carringtons was fragmented because of Lily's jealousy. She had come to feel like the cuckoo in the nest as Lily had so often called her. She wanted roots and a loving, solid relationship. Yet it had to be with the right man. A man she could trust.

The scars were still raw from Nick's betrayal. Her own parents had abandoned her and that was something which even now left an unsettled feeling in the pit of her stomach. Lily had professed to love her and discarded her when she had children of her own. Ted and Percy remained steadfast.

They accepted her for what she was, made no judgements, loved her without question.

Ted had tucked into his meal and he paused with his fork halfway to his mouth. 'You're too fussy, my girl. You've got looks and brains. That Danny fellow was daft about you. You'd been seeing him for a year. I thought you'd settle down with him.'

'Danny was a good man. But . . .' She spread her fingers wide. 'I didn't love him enough to emigrate to Australia with him and never see you or Percy again.'

His gaze was searching, probing deep and missing nothing. 'You got your fingers burned by Nick Blake but not all men are like him. He was a fool to play around. And he regretted it. He was at the track again the other night. Asked after you as usual.'

She didn't answer. The succulent steak and kidney pudding turned suddenly sour in her mouth. She swallowed and pushed her plate aside. She didn't want to think of Nick. She'd seen him around on several occasions and each time her heart did a traitorous leap. She left the dance or dived into a shop to avoid a meeting, then cursed herself for being a coward where he was concerned. She hated him for what he had done to her. Yet, curse him, no man she had met since had made her feel so carefree and alive as he had. Nick hadn't married, she knew that much. She had bumped into his mum in Stratford Broadway a couple of years after they had split. Shona had felt a rush of affection for the plump woman who had greeted her warmly.

'Our Nick were a bloody fool for losing you,' Queenie declared in her forthright way. 'That tart who reckoned she were carrying his child was never any good. She'd been on the game for years when her husband was at sea. She fancied Nick. Thought he'd see her all right. When she had the kid it were only black, weren't it.' Queenie shook her head. 'What's done is done, I suppose. I would have liked you as a daughter-in-law. I hope you find happiness. I were right cut up it didn't work out between you and our Nick.'

'It wasn't meant to be, Queenie.'

She shook her head. 'Our Nick's changed. He don't play around no more. Got his head stuck into his business. That's what drives him these days. Shall I send him your regards?' There was hope in her pale eyes.

'If you weren't his mother I'd tell you to send him to the devil.'

'But you wouldn't be meaning it though, would you?'

Shona laughed as the irony struck her. Was she that transparent? She had done everything in her power to forget Nick, but damn him for the scallywag he was, she couldn't entirely banish him from her heart.

Two plates of jam roly-poly and custard were put in front of them and Shona's fingers curled over Ted's as he picked up his spoon. Whatever she felt for Nick was locked safely away, the key thrown aside. She smiled at Ted Carrington, belatedly answering his remark. 'Any man I meet has got a tough act to follow after you, Dad.'

He blushed and her eyes sparkled with mischief as she added, 'I couldn't have had a better father.'

'Nor I a daughter. I couldn't be more proud of you if you were my own.' He paused, his gaze again penetrating. 'You done any more of that other research? You don't still think Long is your father? It don't fit, angel. An important man like that, someone was bound to know he had an illegitimate kid.'

She knew how much the question cost him.

'I suppose not. From touring the streets of London and its outskirts, I'm pretty sure that my childhood was spent in Ilford. Cranbrook Park, the high street and around the station with Bodgers on the corner is familiar. But I can't find anything else. Not my name or address.' She shrugged and rubbed the back of his hand, feeling the need to reassure him. 'You're my dad. Nothing could be more special than what you gave me. Though, as a journalist, the mystery of what happened the day I was found will always haunt me. It's so long ago, it's almost as though it happened to someone else. I've no regrets.'

She remembered the photo which had puzzled her earlier. 'I uncovered something about Gerald Long. It was a photo taken before the war. He was with a man called Laurence Shelton. His press office turned nasty when I mentioned it. Wouldn't comment. Do you remember the name?'

'Shelton.' Ted rubbed his top lip. 'Rings a bell. Weren't he the bloke who defected? Some hoo-ha about state secrets being leaked. It'll be in the papers. I think he was a traitor. Is that the bloke?'

'It must be someone else.' Shona was surprised at her vehemence and denial. Ted looked at her with surprise. Her headache was coming back and she rubbed her brow. 'When was it in the papers?'

Ted shrugged. 'After I was injured. Perhaps the year we found you.'

Shona shuddered as though someone had walked over her grave. 'I'll check out the man's story tomorrow. I know Shelton was involved with Long; I've just got to find out how.'

Ted's eyes became shadowed. 'Take care, Shona. Gerald Long is an influential man. He won't take kindly to anyone investigating his past.'

'If he's innocent what has he got to fear?'

Chapter Eighteen

The rain slashed across the window as Shona drove along Forest Road towards Maryland Point. The windscreen wipers were inadequate. The long straight road ran parallel to the railway line and as a train puffed towards Forest Gate station the steam drifted over the high brick wall separating the railway tracks from the road. She had just passed the hospital. It had been a long day ending up in Barking at a political meeting where Gerald Long was supporting a party candidate in a forthcoming by-election.

Anger and frustration bubbled in Shona and her fist struck the driving wheel. Her head was full of all the research she had been doing on Long and Shelton. She had found the lead she sought within the stark headline: MISSING POLITICIAN DEFECTS. Yet as she read the story she felt no elation, instead a sense of inexplicable injustice consumed her.

The newspaper had condemned Laurence Shelton as a spy during the first years of the war. He had been missing for a month and no trace of him or the woman rumoured to be his mistress was found. Then reports came through that Shelton was in Germany. A photograph of a tall, blond man on the platform of a Nazi rally was printed. The photo was blurred and could have been anyone. It was no proof.

Shona's hands had balled into fists as she read, a swirling cauldron of outraged heat churning her stomach. The date of the story had been ten weeks after she had been found by Ted and Lily.

Was there a link? How could there be? The paper reported that Laurence Shelton had been missing for only six weeks before his defection. Or had there been a cover-up?

The questions ricocheted through her mind. She'd gone to the meeting tonight to confront Long. Heckling wasn't her way. She'd waited until the politician had left the platform and was mixing with the constituents.

'Mr Long, I'm Shona Carrington of the *Globe*. I'd like to ask you a few questions. Is Barking a borough you have particular links with?'

The fleshy lips stretched into a practised smile and he turned to her. His hazel gaze took in her pale gold hair upswept into an elegant chignon, discreet gold studs in her ears and smart navy tailored suit with a pencil-slim skirt. There was nothing in his expression to say that he recognised her.

'Is that the national *Globe* or a local paper of a similar name?'

'The national, Mr Long.' She stood poised with her shorthand notebook and pencil in her hand. 'You are renowned for the work you do in the East End. What are your party's policies about the homeless and crippled war veterans who cannot find work?'

He gave her a practised glib answer and she asked several more questions before firing out, 'You were once associated with Mr Laurence Shelton who disappeared. Do you really believe he defected as was reported at the time?'

His features froze, white lines of anger chiselling his brow and around his mouth. 'You'd do better sticking to the fashion page, Miss Carrington, rather than raking up old muck.' He turned abruptly away.

His attitude angered her and she accused, 'There's been no evidence that Mr Shelton was in Germany. I suspect that Mr Shelton was innocent of the crimes he was accused of in his absence. Doesn't it concern you that someone who once worked closely with you has this slur against their name? To prove his innocence would also be in your interests. Have you any comment on that, Mr Long?'

Her face was flushed, she had been more virulent than she intended in her need to goad him into some kind of a response.

'Shelton was a traitor,' he rapped out, his face suffusing with angry colour. 'I knew nothing of his treachery. It came as a great shock to me. He betrayed a position of trust. I was appalled to discover he was a Nazi-lover.'

She had to walk quickly to keep up with him as he headed towards the door of the hall. 'Yet there has been no news of him in Germany,' she persisted. 'Surely if Laurence Shelton had defected, Hitler would have used it as propaganda.'

'It is old news, Miss Carrington,' he snapped. 'No one is interested. Least of all myself.'

Throughout this conversation he had kept a steely gaze on her face. They say that liars never look you in the eye, but this man was a practised politician used to evading issues and gulling people into believing that his party was the best for this country. She didn't believe him. And she certainly did not want to learn that this arrogant, egotistical man was her father.

He nodded to a muscle-bound hirsute man a few feet away. The Neanderthal placed himself between Shona and the politician. Shona's eyes hardened. What was Gerald Long hiding? You'd have thought he'd want to clear the name of an associate.

Her pencil was snatched from her fingers and the Neanderthal snapped it in two. 'If you value your job, keep your nose out of what don't concern you.'

The threat was unmistakable. A dart of fear lodged in her chest. This bully was capable of breaking every bone in her body. She conquered her fright. Her chin tilted with defiance. 'Justice is something which should concern us all. If no one has seen or heard of Mr Shelton for sixteen years, how do we know he wasn't murdered?'

'You need a body to prove a murder,' he smirked, sarcastically.

Again her body chilled. 'The war was at its height. Scores of bodies remained unidentified in the bombing raids. But if Shelton was alive he could have learned something which could endanger his life.' It was a wild guess but the words repeated hollowly in her mind like an echo from the distant past. She could taste fear.

Unnerved by the experience, she walked to her car. Her body was shaking and rain splattered her face but she refused to hurry. That would allow Long's ape-man to suspect she was frightened.

The Morris saloon started easily. Thank God she didn't have to get out in this weather and use the starter handle.

Now as she drove towards Stratford the downpour had become torrential. She couldn't shake the feeling of panic which had risen in her. The car behind her was driving annoyingly close, its headlights dazzling her as they reflected in her rear-view mirror. She turned the mirror aside and was forced to slow down as the gutters ahead overflowed, flooding the road. The car behind swerved and accelerated past her.

'Stupid fool!' she muttered. Then she had to slam on her brakes as the car in front slewed round, skidding across the road ahead of her. With the high wall one side and the car directly in her path there was no way to avoid a collision. Shona screamed. She felt the wheels slide round. There was a sickening crunch and her head slammed against the windscreen.

The smell of antiseptic tingled Shona's nose. There were muffled voices and footsteps. 'Screens, nurse. Be quick about it.'

Shona's head felt like a steamroller had been across it.

Her body ached and her hands stung. The steel band which seemed to encase her head tightened when she tried to open her eyes. It was easier to lie still and succumb to the blackness which beckoned around the edges of her mind.

'The poor kid. The bastard who did this to her needs stringing up.'

Percy was speaking, his voice gruff with emotion. Who was he talking about? Shona wondered.

'The car was stolen. They left it and scarpered.' Ted's voice sounded choked, overlaid with anger. 'Lucky that nurse was going on duty and came across her. A mercy too the hospital were so close, the amount of blood she lost.'

Shona forced her eyes open. She was puzzled to find herself lying on a bed with Ted and Percy standing over it. 'Where am I?'

'Ssh, don't talk.' Ted patted her hand. There were tears in his eyes. 'You're in Forest Gate hospital. You were in a car crash. You got thrown through the windscreen. You've been unconscious for a couple of hours.'

The rain. The car slewing across the road in front of her all came rushing back. 'I'd been to Barking. Gerald Long was at a meeting.'

Another image flashed into her head. A large car with a blond-haired man and Gerald Long in the back seat. The blond man got out waving to Long as the car drew away. She put her hand to her head and winced. There were bandages on her hand and around her head. She tried to sit up and cried out as pain shot through her arm and side. Ted gently pushed her back on to the pillows. Her other arm was heavy and she stared at the shiny white plaster encasing it.

'Lie still. The doctor wants to see you now you've come round. You had a nasty bump on the forehead that needed a few stitches. There's a cut on your neck which they had to put ten stitches in. Luckily your face wasn't badly cut. The doctor reckons those cuts will heal without scarring. You've also broken your arm and severely bruised your ribs.'

Shona was still bemused. Her head was pounding. She knew Ted was her father but another image was flashing in and out of her mind like a Belisha beacon. She closed her eyes. The veil peeled back.

'Dad. Oh Daddy.'

'I'm here, angel,' Ted answered, stroking her uninjured arm.

She opened her eyes. 'I remember who I am.' Her voice was low. 'I'm Grace Shelton.'

Before she could speak further a short, spindle-thin doctor with a drooping moustache appeared and ushered Ted and Percy away. The screens were pulled around her. He examined Shona, then peered into her eyes and nodded with satisfaction.

'You're a lucky woman. You could have been killed in an accident like that. You'll be up and about again in a couple of days. We'll keep you in hospital for observation. You can't be too careful with concussion. And you'll have to come back in a week to have the stitches out of your forehead and neck.'

'Will that leave a scar?'

He nodded. 'I'm afraid so. It shouldn't be too disfiguring once the swelling and colour fades. The cuts on your face are superficial and shouldn't leave scars.'

Shona was in the hospital for five days. When Ted came to collect her she insisted that he drive her over to Epping.

'Are you sure you're up to it?' Ted regarded her with concern.

They had removed the bandages from her head and the four stitches were hidden under her fringe. She looked as if she'd been done over with a truncheon. Her eyes were swollen and black and the bruising had spread down across her cheek. It was agony to walk, each step jarring her bruised ribs, and her left arm would be in a sling for six weeks.

'I need to see the place where you found me. I've waited for so long for my memory to return I won't let a few bruises stop me starting my search for my father. The doctor said I need four to six weeks off work to recover properly. I intend to use it. I remember where we lived in Ilford. I'd like to go there also, just to see the house. It might have been rented. I know we were there for two Christmases but before that we moved around a lot.'

'I'll take you, but if you start feeling ill, we're going straight back home.' He paused and added hesitantly, 'Do I call you Shona or Grace?'

'Oh, Ted. I'll always be Shona to you, won't I, and that suits me fine. Besides, it sounds odd being called Grace. She was another person with another life.'

Ted parked on the farm track in Epping. 'Does it look familiar?' he asked in a gentle voice.

She couldn't answer. A lump had lodged in her throat clamping against her vocal cords. A millstone seemed to be pressing down on her chest. The sky was overcast and drizzle dampened the air. Shona shivered.

The horrors of that night came back to her. She was curled up on the back seat of the car. Her parents were arguing. They had argued a lot lately. It made her mother bad-tempered and often for some trivial misdemeanour Shona was slapped and shut in her bedroom until her father came home.

Shona shuddered as she remembered the angry quarrelling as they drove through the fog. The argument was more violent than usual. Her mother was tearful, her voice high and hysterical. Her father spoke softly, reasoning. 'I've worked it all out. We'll be safe. Start a new life.'

'I had a good life here. You ruined it. You should have realised what was happening sooner.'

The voices droned on. Young Grace clutched her teddy close to her chest and closed her eyes trying to blot out their angry words. Her father said with unusual force, 'For Chrissakes, Amy. I made a mistake. I should have known not to trust that slippery bastard. We'll be safe. I've got new names, forged passports for us. You've got to forget the past. Forget it.'

'Go on your own. I'm not leaving London,' her mother shrilled. 'I gave up everything for you. This is how you repay me. I'm sick of the secrecy. I don't want a life built on lies.'

'We have no choice. The Big Man won't rest until he destroys me. I know too much.'

Their words had made no sense then to Grace, they didn't now to Shona. But it was obvious that her father was frightened. What was he running away from? And who was the Big Man? Why must she forget her past? Had those last words been the trigger to lock the memories away for seventeen years?

The veil once lifted left her with an overwhelming sense of fear. She had been too young to understand what was happening; nothing was explained to her.

Having fallen asleep on the back seat of the car, her next memory was the crash and being thrown to the floor. Her head hurt. Her father was breathing strangely as he lifted her out of the car. The pain and shock blurred the words he was saying. But she could sense his fear, his need for secrecy.

She was disorientated. Confused. Frightened. The fog was thick and distorted sounds and vision. It pressed in on her, smothering, clawing at her nostrils and throat. The long grass was wet beneath her bare feet. Her memory again was disjointed. She recalled a screech of brakes. Angry shouts. A feeling of terror swamped her. Her daddy was no longer close by. The shouts got closer and she ran away. Ran away into the suffocating cobweb of fog.

Shona pressed her hands to her temples, a ragged sob escaping her lips.

'It's all right, angel,' Ted soothed. 'Nothing can hurt you today.'

Her eyes were round and dark with fearful shadows. Two loud bangs echoed from the past. The shouts were menacing. Violence crackled in the air. Angry words made her flinch. Their threat was unmistakable. She was crouching in the wet grass hidden by the trunk of a tree. The figures were indistinct dark forms walking away. The fog was thinning. Then she saw their car. The bonnet and side was all crumpled. The driver's door was open, Mummy lay at an odd angle and wasn't moving. And there was blood. Blood everywhere. A loud voice continued to threaten: 'We'll get you. Wherever you go, we'll get you.'

A car engine revved and with the wheels spinning and screeching sped away. The sound chilled her mind. They were going to get her. They had already killed her mummy. Had they killed her daddy? Why else was he not here to rescue her?

Fear drenched her body in a stinging sweat and her limbs trembled as the memories painted a macabre tableau. She felt again her bare feet slithering on the wet grass, her lungs bursting as she ran away. She was pursued by avenging monsters. She had to become invisible. Then she would be safe.

She remembered nothing of Ted and Lily finding her. Their kindness and love was a haven and months floated by as she settled into a strange home. Even so there remained an emptiness deep inside. It was easy to trust and then grow to love Ted and Lily, they became her family, her stability. Yet still the fog remained in her mind, cloaking, muffling, keeping her invisible. The young girl Grace Shelton was effaced and reborn as Shona Carrington.

Chapter Nineteen

'I'll never believe my father was a spy,' Shona vowed. She sat in Ted's old car and pulled away from his comforting embrace. 'If it takes my entire lifetime I shall prove him innocent and clear his name.'

She had broken down sobbing uncontrollably as her past was revealed. Ted had held her. His arms were a haven. The solid wall of his chest was a rock which would sustain her.

'I wouldn't expect any less from you. But you must be careful. Your mother's body was never found. She could have survived. But it's obvious from what you say they were fleeing the country. Why hasn't your father tried to clear his name?'

'Perhaps they killed him and put his body where it would never be found or identified.' Shona stared along the road bordered by the trees of Epping Forest. 'What other reason could there be that he never tried to find me? There was enough publicity at the time.'

Ted shrugged and took a packet of Woodbines out of his jacket pocket and lit up. 'They branded him a traitor. If his life was in danger, perhaps he couldn't risk looking for you. Maybe he feared that you would be in danger if he tried. The newspapers didn't run any stories about your father's disappearance until over a month after you were found. That sounds odd to me. He would never have gone back to Westminster after that attempt on his life.'

'So someone was covering up something? That would take a man of influence.'

'Yes. The Big Man is someone important.'

Anger burned through Shona. 'My father said he knew too much. That's the key.'

'So who is the Big Man?' Ted said. 'There's no one in the public eye known by that name.'

'He's someone with a lot to lose. Someone my father was close to. Someone like Gerald Long.'

Ted gave a low whistle. 'Don't jump the gun. He's as cunning as a fox but he's powerful.'

'Nothing corrupts more than power,' she responded with derision. 'Ambition to achieve that power is what drives many public figures. Throughout history ambition has led many powerful men to murder when they fear someone can expose or destroy them.'

Ted pushed back his cap and frowned. 'If that's the case then you're putting yourself in danger. We don't even know who the Big Man is.'

'I'd put my money on Gerald Long. Most nicknames come from a physical attribute or out of a name. Gerald Long is built like a scrum-half, tall and bulky. And he's got big ideas and the name Long can be twisted into tall, therefore Big.'

Ted tossed his finished cigarette into the road. 'You could be trying to make fit the solution you want to be true. That lout of Long's already warned you about sticking your nose into his governor's business.'

Fervour blazed in Shona's eyes. 'And that tells me Long has got something to hide. This could be just the story I need to prove that a woman can be a good investigative journalist. I'm tired of all the prejudices I have to contend with.'

Ted took Shona's unplastered hand in his. 'This scares me, angel. Long ain't a man to tangle with. You're laying yourself open to trouble. He could see to it that you lose not only your job but all credibility as a reporter.'

'He's got nothing on me.' Indignation made her all the more determined to pursue this story.

'Except your old dad here is a gaolbird. Lil is a drunkard. He'll use that to discredit you.'

'You paid your debt to society. You've been straight for seven years. I won't go to print until I have proof.'

'But he'll know you're checking on his past. He has contacts everywhere. He'll destroy you before you can get close to anything.' His expression hardened. 'What if he was behind that accident you were in? Sounds fishy to me the way that car spun round in front of you. You were lucky to escape so lightly. You could have been killed. What if Long *is* the Big Man your father spoke of? Shelton knew the dangers. If your father couldn't fight him, what makes you think you can take him on and win? Forget it.'

'I can't.'

At her adamant tone Ted looked haggard. 'If Long suspects you're Grace Shelton, he could have reason to see you six foot under. If it was possible for your father to expose Long or safely come back to you, don't you think he would have done? Perhaps he was trying to protect you.'

Shona put her head on his shoulder. 'Hold me, Dad.' She was more frightened than she cared to admit. Her head was pounding and her ribs were giving her hell. The pain was demoralising her. She mustn't give in to this moment of weakness. She prided herself on her strength of character.

She hadn't told Ted about being pushed in front of a bus. Neither had she connected the accident to the meeting in Barking, she had been too engrossed with the return of her memory. Yet now she recalled that the car had been following her closely for some time – and why had it suddenly skidded across the road in front of her? There was nothing coming the other way. She had thought it a freak accident. But was it?

'You've been watching too many gangster movies, Dad.'

She attempted to laugh the incident aside and grimaced at the pain attacking her ribs and head.

He studied her for a long moment before starting the car. 'Seems to me that you could do with another bang on the head to knock some sense into your skull.'

Shona smiled to reassure him. 'Don't worry about me. I'm not going to do anything until I have proof. And for that I've got to dig deep. Seventeen years deep. I'll be as discreet as I can so as not to arouse Long's suspicions.'

Ted started the car. 'Where to now?'

'Ilford. I'm sure that's where we lived. Near a park.'

Two hours later they pulled up outside a three-storey house in Ilford. It was a five-minute walk from Cranbrook Park. Shona stared at it and shivered.

'That's the house I saw in my dream. It was here that I saw my father get out of a car with Gerald Long in the back.' As she stared at the amber-bricked building with its sash windows divided by miniature Corinthian columns, other images flooded back. 'We used to have regular parties. Long was often there with different women friends. The parties were rather wild. I remember sitting at the top of the stairs one evening and seeing two women who were drunk start to do a striptease. Daddy came out of the room and saw me. It's the only time I remember him getting cross with me.'

Ted didn't speak and Shona fell silent. Euphoria subsided to be replaced by sadness. 'Where is my father? What happened to him? I've got to find out why he disappeared. And if Gerald Long is responsible, I want him to pay for what he must have suffered.'

'Come on, Chancer's Dream! Come on my beauty!' Percy shouted, his faced flushed with excitement as the greyhounds sped down the straight towards the finishing line. His money was on the favourite. 'Move yourself, Chancer's Dream!'

Shona's own heart was pounding fast as she watched the

greyhound race neck and neck against the black dog Ebony Night she had bet on.

Ebony Night crossed the line a head in front of Chancer's Dream. Shona let out a whoop of joy. It was a month since she had left hospital and the doctor was insisting she had another two weeks off work. The bruising on her face had faded and her scars were hidden under a layer of foundation and powder. The wound on her neck remained reddened but even that was starting to fade. A chiffon scarf hid its disfigurement. The only outward sign of her accident was the plaster still on her arm and if she moved too quickly her ribs ached.

She had spent a week recuperating at home, then, unable to drive because of her broken arm, she had used public transport to visit the British Newspaper Library in north-west London and other public record offices to dig up any information she could on Gerald Long or Laurence Shelton. She also hunted down her birth certificate which was not easy as she did not know her mother's surname. There was no marriage certificate for a Laurence Shelton. Finally she found her birth certificate. She had been born in 1931 to Amy Elliot and Laurence Shelton. She also discovered that when she was a year old her name had been changed to Shelton by deed poll. She now had several files of information about the two men but nothing which pointed to anything illegal involving Long. The reports on her father's disappearance and later his defection were circumstantial. There were no leads as to what had happened to her father or why he had disappeared. Twice Gerald Long had made the comment that her father had defected. A minister, unfortunately now dead, but once close to Long, had leaked the damning photograph of a man looking like her father at the Nazi rally.

She had made a list of people mentioned in the reports who would have known him at the time. So far she had only been able to speak to two of them without revealing that she was Laurence Shelton's daughter. They had nothing new to tell her.

Tonight was the first time she'd come to the dog track since her accident. Percy had called in to see her and, finding her pale and frustrated at getting nowhere in her investigations, had insisted they go out and have some fun.

He wouldn't take no for an answer. 'Ted said he hasn't seen you for a fortnight. He's worried about you.'

'I'm not going to see much of him while he's working tonight. But I'll come.'

Shona was glad she had. She always enjoyed spending time with Percy and over the years had become quite an expert on the dogs. Percy wasn't looking too pleased at her win and threw his betting ticket on the floor in disgust. 'Chancer's Dream should have won on form. How do you do it, Shona? That's the third winner you've picked tonight.'

'I fancied the name. It's just luck.'

'Then you should be putting your winnings on Golden Girl in the next race,' he teased. 'Couldn't have a more apt name to suit you.' He studied the form in the evening paper. 'I'll have a quid on it to win.'

'It's not like you to pick a dog on a whim. You only back the favourites.'

He winked at her. 'This one was named for you. It's got to win.'

'Don't be daft, Grandad. What are you talking about?'

'Have you seen who the owner is?' He thrust his paper at her.

She stared at the owner's name and her stomach clenched. 'It's a common enough name if the dog is golden in colour. So Nick Blake is into dogs now. I thought that was too much of a mug's game for him. It can take a fortune to train a winner.'

'He's got a half-dozen dogs and had a couple of winners recently over at Romford. He's got one in the last race which is a certainty.'

Shona scanned the dogs' names in the last race and felt the hairs on her arms prickle, sending a sensation of heat through her body. Nick's second dog was called Proud Shona.

Her expression was bland as she slapped the newspaper into Percy's hands, using sarcasm to hide the disturbing feelings and memories which were surfacing. 'He'll bankrupt himself if he intends to name a dog after all his former girlfriends.'

Percy shook his head, his eyes sparkling with merriment. 'It's time you learned to take a compliment.'

She turned on her heel. 'I'm going to place my bet for the next race. And it won't be on Golden Girl. My money's going on Free Spirit and then No Regrets in the last race.'

When she placed her bets she almost gave in to the impulse to place another bet on Nick's two dogs. It took all her willpower to resist it.

As she moved away from the betting window she saw Ted talking to Bill Miles. Bill waved to her as she approached.

'Thank you for the flowers you sent to the hospital,' she said after greeting him.

'I should've come myself, but I reckoned you'd have your family fussing round you. Percy told me you weren't in any danger. Nasty business.'

She shrugged off his concern. Bill was looking well. He still kept his beard, which was neatly trimmed, and his grey hair was cropped close to his head. Over the years his face had lost the fleshiness induced by drink and the lines around his eyes were less pronounced. With the return of self-respect he was more upright and his step confident. It was sometimes hard to remember that he was the disgruntled tramp she had known in the late forties. Transformed, Bill was a good-looking man though he kept himself very much to himself. He had prospered in recent years. After six months he'd given up the nightwatchman's job. He bought himself an old car and began working as a sales representative but had changed employers several times.

'I got used to moving freely on the road. Some habits I can't break,' he joked whenever he changed the firm he represented or moved to a new address.

'I haven't seen you around much lately, Bill. Is work going well?'

'I've given up the rep job and have been working on a new project.' He was looking unusually pleased with himself.

When he didn't enlighten them, she prompted: 'Are you going to tell us what it is?'

'I've just had a play accepted by a touring company. It's premier will be at the Connaught Theatre in Worthing, then it'll tour several other theatres throughout the country.'

Shona's eyes widened. 'That's fantastic. You never told me you wrote plays.'

'Well, not everyone succeeds, do they? I've been lucky.'

'That's marvellous news, Bill. Congratulations. Was it your first?'

'Fifth actually. I've been scribbling away unsuccessfully for years.'

'What is it about?'

He looked embarrassed at talking about his success. 'It's a comedy about a man's ambition and how his self-importance was his downfall.'

Impulsively, Shona threw her arms around her friend. 'I'll run a story on you to publicise the play.'

He stiffened in her arms. 'No. I don't want any publicity.'

'It would help get you established. Other players might want to perform your work.'

He shook his head. 'I write because I've got something relevant to say. I don't like a fuss or all that luvvy stuff actors go in for.'

The piercing penetration of his gaze made her glance away. She had never got used to the direct way Bill studied her.

'Ted said you're convinced Gerald Long is up to no good.'

His voice had sharpened. 'Leave well alone, Shona. He's dangerous.'

'I thought you championed fights against injustice.' His warning antagonised her. 'And this investigation is personal.'

His gaze slanted and the lines about his eyes indented. 'How so?'

She looked at Ted before answering, her stare on him when she spoke. 'It isn't exactly a secret that Ted adopted me. I was fortunate. For years I had no memory of my past. I was knocked unconscious in the car accident and my memory returned. I remember the night I was found. My real father was in danger. Men with guns were pursuing us. I've never learned what happened to Laurence Shelton, my father. But now my memory has returned I intend to. I think Gerald Long is behind his disappearance, maybe even his murder.'

'Stay out of it, Shona,' Bill grated out. 'You don't know what you're getting into.'

She rounded on Bill, her eyes flashing with excitement. She could taste a story and knew he had some information she could use. 'What do you know about Long?'

He wouldn't hold her forthright stare. 'He's dangerous. Ruthless. I spent several years sleeping in alleyways invisible in the darkness behind a boxing club or nightclub. Not just round here but up West. I wasn't always drunk. You overhear conversations. Snippets best ignored if you want to live. Keep well away from him, Shona.'

'You've as good as told me there's a story here. I'd be a fool not to follow it up.'

His large hand covered her elbow and his beard grazed her cheek as he spoke gruffly, 'But you'll be alive. Long will get his come-uppance.'

He turned abruptly on his heel and walked away. She made to run after him and was stopped by Ted putting a hand on her shoulder. 'Let him go. Bill's an odd bloke. He's been around and knows a great deal. You'd be wise to heed his warning.'

'I became a journalist to bring public awareness to injustices. I'd be failing in my ideals. And I need to know what happened to my parents.'

His face looked suddenly older and she was instantly contrite. 'This is important to me, but it doesn't change how I feel about you, Dad.'

'I know that, angel. I worry about you. I can't help it. I'll have a word with Bill. If he's got something on Long he might let me know.'

'I doubt it. Even when I met him and he was drunk he was close-lipped. The best I can hope for is that if I get a whiff of a scandal, he may confirm it.'

Percy sauntered over to them, tapping his tote ticket. 'I've backed Golden Girl. I saw Nick talking to his trainer. He's looking affluent.'

To prevent Percy talking about Nick Blake, she teased him about the Widow Bishop as they walked back to the stands to watch the next race. 'So are you going to move in with her?'

'I will be one of her gentlemen lodgers,' he corrected primly.

'Oh, a gentleman lodger. Very grand.'

He looked uncomfortable and she regretted her teasing. He must feel guilty about moving out from Lily and Ted's. 'You've always been a gentleman, Grandad. A real gent in every sense because you treat people right. I hope you'll be happy there.'

'It wasn't an easy decision.'

'You're not responsible for how Lily behaves. Mrs Bishop is a lovely woman. I've often chatted to her in the market. She's got a wonderful sense of humour and looks after her lodgers. She'll make sure you don't overdo things. We don't want you having any more turns.'

He patted his breastbone. 'I'm strong as an ox. I'm looking forward to the move. There's life in the old dog yet. It's you who should be getting settled.'

'Don't you start,' she said with a brittle laugh. 'Dad's been having a go at me.' She deliberately changed the subject. 'Look, your dog doesn't want to go in the trap. You still sure Golden Girl is a winner?'

When Golden Girl came in second and Free Spirit came in fifth, she bore Percy's triumphant twirling her around with amusement. Yet when she watched No Regrets finish third to Proud Shona's win she felt a secret pride that Nick had done so well. Her gaze followed his tall figure as he came forward to receive the winner's trophy. He was wearing a black Crombie overcoat over a charcoal suit. His dark hair was brushed back and he had longish sideburns. The Elvis Presley hairstyle certainly suited him and at a youthful-looking thirty-two Nick carried it off. As he took the trophy he turned unerringly in her direction and raised it high. Heat flamed into her cheeks. He had known exactly where she was in the stands. Had he been watching her during the evening?

Percy had disappeared to collect his winnings and Shona waited for him to return. There was no point in getting caught up in the crowds pushing to leave the stadium. The stand had cleared and still Percy did not reappear. He knew so many of the regulars at the track he was probably chatting to a friend. She resigned herself to finding him. When she turned towards the exit she discovered Nick standing alone and watching her. It was impossible to avoid him.

'Congratulations, Nick. A winner and a second. That's quite something.'

'Adds a bit of spice to coming to the track.' His gaze took in every detail of her appearance. 'You look great, Shona. Did you put a bet on the last race?'

The lopsided grin she had always found irresistible twisted

his lips. She steeled herself against its effect. 'Of course. No Regrets came in third.'

He held her gaze, his grey eyes glittering in the overhead lighting. 'My Shona is top class. A natural winner.'

A suitably glib answer failed her so she ignored the comment. She sidestepped to move around him and his voice was low and husky carrying to her. 'You've done well for yourself. I always knew you'd make it as an ace reporter.'

'I'm far from that. I just do the regular stuff.'

She dismissed his flattery but her heart was strumming uncomfortably fast. He hadn't changed. Easy compliments. Easy charm. His face had matured, his cheekbones still high and refined and his mouth full and sensual. She tore her gaze from his lips aware that they had lingered upon their fullness. Why was it that she could remember the taste and thrill of them? He was still too handsome for her peace of mind.

His smile faded to be replaced by a frown. He was staring at her neck. The cream chiffon scarf she had tucked inside the V of her jacket must have slipped.

'What happened to you? I thought you'd just broken your arm when I saw the sling.'

Self-consciously she put her hand to the reddened flesh. 'A car accident.'

'Ted never said.' He spoke as though he often discussed her with her father.

'Why should he? I was only in hospital a few days. It happened in the rain. A car skidded in front of me. I couldn't avoid it and went through the windscreen.'

'Christ, Shona. You could've been killed!' He lifted his hand to touch her neck but she pulled away and hastily straightened her scarf to hide the scar from him.

She struggled to make her voice sound cool and polite. 'You're looking well. You haven't done so badly yourself.'

246

'I have you to thank for that. You showed me what I was capable of.'

'That's nonsense. You made your own luck. You always did your own thing.' Bitterness surfaced and she looked round searching for Percy. 'I have to go. Goodbye, Nick.'

He sidestepped to block her path. When her eyes flashed in anger, he smiled and held out his hand. 'I was a bastard in the old days. You were right to dump me. I hate to think of us parting as enemies.'

Had he tried to flirt with her she had a scathing set-down ready. Compliments she could ignore as part of his slick charm. But honesty and self-deprecation caught her off guard.

'Yes, you were a bastard, Nick.'

'So you gonna reject the hand of peace? I'm asking for your forgiveness.' His stare bore into her and he turned his cheek towards her. 'Or would you rather slap my face?'

'Don't tempt me.' To her surprise, she laughed. 'I don't know whether to be insulted or flattered you named a prize-winning bitch after me.'

'From the moment I saw her I knew she was special.' The low huskiness of his voice washed over her in a seductive wave.

'Goodbye, Nick.'

'I suppose it's too much to ask for a kiss to show there's no hard feelings, but let's at least shake hands.'

She held out her hand and it was taken in his firm grip. 'You don't change do you?'

'Oh but I have. I learned the hard way what an idiot I'd been.'

When she tried to withdraw her hand it was lifted to his mouth. The kiss on her fingers was pure theatrics but it sent a lightning bolt through her arm. 'See you around, Shona.'

She shoved her hand in her jacket pocket and found herself smiling. He hadn't lost the art of making a memorable exit.

Thank God she was immune to it. Nick Blake belonged strictly in her past.

During the next four days she had two phone calls at home from Nick asking to see her. She refused. The third time he rang, her irritation overflowed. His calls had brought back memories of the good times they had together. It took a conscious effort to remember his womanising and how he had betrayed her.

'Don't call me again, Nick. We have nothing to say.'

'But I thought you were interested in getting the dirt on a certain someone – a politician.' His voice was low, husky and at its most persuasive. 'Meet me for dinner and I'll tell you what I've found out.'

'Tell me now.'

'No chance. Anyone could be listening in. I've found a contact for you.'

'Make it lunch and I'll meet you tomorrow.'

'Forget it. I thought you wanted a lead on the man,' he snapped. 'I was doing you a favour for old times' sake. I owed you that at least.' The phone went dead.

Shona stared at it. Her blood boiled. Damn Nick. He was always so provoking. Now she'd have to wait until he rang back. If he rang again. He'd sounded really brassed off. And who could blame him? She'd been rude to him, not trusting herself to soften, lest the barriers she had so painfully erected proved to be built on quicksand.

A week went by without a call from Nick. Every time the phone rang, her heart pounded erratically. She blotted the disappointment from her voice when it wasn't him. She could always ring him, Percy would know his number, but pride intervened. That put the ball too firmly in his court. She wanted the information he had to offer, not the man himself.

She even went so far as to look up in the sporting pages

if any of Nick's dogs were running at Walthamstow. He had one at Haringey and another two at Romford. Nothing at Walthamstow. So that ruled out meeting him there. Percy never went to the other stadiums.

Not that she wasted any of her spare time while she was off work. In another week the plaster came off and she would return to the paper. She did what research she could on Gerald Long going back before the war. He'd made several trips abroad, especially to Austria and Germany. Ostensibly these visits were to cement peace negotiations with Hitler. He'd been at the Munich Olympics and was photographed with several prominent Nazis.

Seeing his smiling face as he shook hands with men who were later to be renowned for the cruelty and atrocities they ordered brought a rush of bile to her gullet. And he had denounced her father as a traitor and German spy. Shona made extensive notes which were kept in the locked filing cabinet in her study at home. Every scrap of such evidence would help to condemn him.

Twice she took the train to Chigwell to visit Marion for the day. Her friend now lived in a mock-Tudor six-bedroom house to accommodate her children and a live-in nanny. They had always kept in touch but Shona's erratic working schedule meant they rarely saw each other more than once a month. Marion had everything she had dreamed of – a family, wealth, position, a handsome husband. Unfortunately she hadn't banked on the snobbery of their wealthy neighbours who sneered at her East End background. She found it hard to fit in and make friends.

'To hell with them,' Shona encouraged her friend as Marion poured her heart out to her as they sat in her landscaped garden. 'Ken loves you. You're worth a dozen of each one of them.'

'But I don't want Ken to be ashamed of me.'

'Stop putting yourself down. You dress with style and your

house is beautifully decorated with good taste. There's little trace of an East End accent now. Don't let those silly women see that they can hurt you. I bet some of their backgrounds aren't so spotless. It's their own insecurities which make them so stuffy.'

Seeing that Marion didn't look convinced she added, impishly, 'You're the wife of a successful solicitor and as good as any of them. Get yourself on one of their committees. They'll be glad of your secretarial skills then and your power of organisation. They'll be eating out of your hand in six months' time.'

'I've already tried. Mrs Hoity-toity Sarah Middleton turned me down.'

Shona lifted a blonde arched brow. 'Sarah Middleton or, if you prefer her stage name, Serinda was a Windmill girl. She was born in Stepney. Though I expect it's a closely kept secret. I happened to see the wedding photo in a forties' edition of the paper when I was doing research. She married Barty Middleton who was then a boxing promoter, although since he retired he's become an estate agent.'

Marion's eyes glinted with delight. 'Just let that snooty bitch try one over on me again.' Then her eyes rolled with mischief. 'Do you think she'd tell me what it was like to be a Windmill girl? Was she one of the ones who stood there starkers?'

'I'm sure you'll find out for yourself.' Shona winked at her. 'And actually Serinda or Sarah isn't such an old tartar; after her marriage she did a lot of work for the war orphans. Out of her own money she paid for several children who'd lost limbs to have prostheses fitted.'

When Shona got ready to leave Marion wouldn't hear of her taking the train. 'I'll run you back. I've got some stuff to drop off at Mum's.'

As Marion's car swung out of her drive, Shona saw a man in a sports jacket and grey trousers standing on the corner.

She frowned. He'd been in the same carriage as her on the train to Chigwell. Was she being followed again?

She studied his face to ensure she'd recognise him again. Since the car accident she had become more conscious of her vulnerability as a lone woman.

When Shona returned to her house she picked up the midday post from her mat and carried it into the lounge. Before reading it she turned on the gas-fire in the modern low fireplace. The cream wallpaper had a narrow gold stripe and the dark beige leather suite and plain burgundy carpet made it a warm, cosy room.

It was getting dusk and she moved to the window to draw the burgundy curtains. Her hand paused on the velvet. There was a black car diagonally across the road which had been parked in the street several times recently. It did not belong to any of her neighbours. Her unease returned. There was a man sitting in the front seat eating a bag of chips. After finishing them he made no move to get out of the car or drive away. As she watched she saw the man in the sports jacket walking from the direction of the station and get in the car. The two men looked to be exchanging angry words. Again they did not drive away. It couldn't be coincidence. She was being spied on. But why?

Her instincts were to go out there and confront them. But that was hardly wise. Instead she picked up the phone and dialled the police. She informed the desk sergeant that there was a Peeping Tom hanging round their street and hung up without giving her name. Five minutes later a police car pulled up and for fifteen minutes the men in the car were given a grilling. The black car drove off followed by the police car. That would give the man in the sports jacket something to think about. It still didn't explain why anyone would want her followed. Unless they guessed that as a reporter she was on to something? There was only one person who had anything to fear from her. Did Gerald Long suspect that she was investigating his past? She'd have to be more careful.

It unsettled her and remembering her post she scanned through the envelopes to find a note from Percy saying he was moving in to the Widow Bishop's on Thursday and had written down his phone number if she needed to contact him.

She shook her head sadly. Things couldn't be going well between Ted and Lily. She wished there was something she could do to help, but Lily would only see it as interference and make thing worse for Ted. She really was a shrew these days.

There was also a letter addressed in untidy childish print. She opened it and stared at its contents in surprise.

Nicksaidyouneededinformation.Icangiveittoyou.Meetme inthebuffetatFenchurchStreetstationTuesdayat5pm.I'll recognise you.

There was no address and it wasn't signed. So Nick had come up trumps after all and no strings attached? Or was it a hoax? Even if it was, it wasn't one she could afford to ignore.

Chapter Twenty

It was the twins' thirteenth birthday on Sunday and Shona took round their presents. Lily opened the door.

'Oh, it's you.' Lack of enthusiasm was heavy in her voice. She walked away leaving the door open and Shona followed her. It was two months since she'd seen Lily. In recent years drink had thickened her figure. She always took pains with her hair and make-up but there were harsh lines of dissatisfaction around her eyes and mouth.

Shona made the effort to be pleasant. She didn't want another row with Lily on the twins' birthday. 'That's a lovely dress, Mum. Is it new?'

Lily didn't answer. She walked into the living room, sat down and picked up her *Woman's Weekly* to read.

Ted got up from his armchair and gave her a kiss on the cheek. 'Hi, angel. I'll make you a cup of tea.'

There was a yell from the back garden and Johnnie and Jamie charged into the room shouting, 'Shona! Shona! Did you get them? Did you get them?'

She feigned surprise. 'Get what?'

The boys' dark eyes were shining with excitement as they tried to peer into her shopping bag which she held close to her chest. They were almost as tall as her and it was difficult to tell them apart, except that Jamie was more heavily built as he had a sweet tooth and was always eating chocolate. 'Let's see your bikes.' Shona continued to taunt them, delaying the moment she handed over their presents.

'Ah, sis. Give over.' Johnnie tried to grab her bag but she pulled it away. 'What you got us? You can see the bikes after. They're great. Red racers. Drop handlebars – a rack to hold a water bottle – chrome front light – the lot.'

'For Gawd's sake, give them their presents and stop winding the boys up,' Lily snapped. 'They're excited enough.'

The laughter died in Johnnie's eyes and he looked guilty. He was the more sensitive of the two and often gave Shona a piece of pottery or woodwork he had done at school.

She regarded the twins' Brylcreemed Teddy-boy quiffs and their new drainpipe trousers. Sadly she shook her head. 'You're looking so grown up. I think I've got the wrong present. I bet you've got girlfriends now.'

Jamie pulled a face. 'Erh, I got better things to spend me time and money on than a girl.'

Ted laughed. 'You'll change your tune soon enough, son.'

Lily dropped her magazine in her lap and scowled at him. 'Don't you start encouraging them. They're too young to have girlfriends. Just because you had your first girlfriend at thirteen, don't mean to say my darlings have to.'

Shona saw the fierce possessive gleam in her eyes. Any women these two brought home would meet with an icy welcome from Lily. No one would be good enough for her sons. Shona could sense the atmosphere becoming hostile and quickly whipped out the two wrapped parcels and handed them to the boys.

They tore them open, throwing the paper on the floor, and both gave a whoop of delight. 'Fantastic, Shona,' Johnnie said with a grin. 'I knew you'd get them. I've wanted the West Ham strip for ages. Grandad got us a leather football.'

Jamie had pulled his maroon and sky-blue football shirt over his jumper. 'Up the Hammers!' he shouted and ran outside to the garden for the football. He returned pushing his new bike through the hall and holding the shiny leather football. 'C'mon, Johnnie. Let's go over the rec and show these to our mates.'

'Hey, don't I get a thank you?' Shona reminded him.

Jamie flashed her a cheeky grin. 'Ta. You're the best, Shona.'

Johnnie looked at her shyly. 'Thanks, Shona.' He gave her a peck on the cheek, blushed furiously, and dashed out the back to get his bike.

Shona picked up the discarded wrapping paper and took the cup of tea offered to her by Ted. Lily kept her head buried in her magazine but Shona noticed that there was a tremor in her hands and she had dark shadows visible under her foundation and powder.

'You look a bit off colour, Mum. Are you all right?'

'I'm fine. Why shouldn't I be?' she spat out.

Ted raised his eyes to the ceiling and mouthed, 'She's off the drink.'

Lily's head shot up. 'What's that? What you saying to her?'

'Nothing, love,' Ted appeased. 'Just telling Shona how proud I am that you've stopped drinking.'

Lily sniffed. 'I never had a problem, mind. But me stomach's been playing up. Doctor's given me some tablets. Said they'd make me bad if I drank alcohol.'

'It's nothing serious, is it?' Despite the antagonism between them Shona hated to think that Lily could be ill.

'Bit of women's trouble,' Lily mumbled.

Shona detected a thread of fear in her voice. Her compassion overrode the years of dissension. 'Look, if there's anything I can do. If you need to rest and need me to help out.'

'I can manage.'

Shona drank her tea and stood up. Lily didn't want her help, that was obvious. Ted walked with her to the door.

'Thanks for your offer. Don't mind Lil. She's finding it

hard not having a drink. And you know what her temper's like.'

'I meant what I said. I wish Lil and I could put the bad feelings behind us. She did so much for me when I needed her as a child. I'll never forget that. I know she got jealous of the affection you showed me, but she didn't get really mean until she started drinking. She's an alcoholic, Dad. If she doesn't stop, she'll end up drinking herself to death.'

'I know, angel. But I never wanted to accept that it was so bad. I'm gonna see she stays off the booze, even if I have to give up me nights down the pub. Nothing would please me more than if the two of you were friends again.'

Late on Tuesday afternoon Shona joined the flow of people converging on the cobbled forecourt of Fenchurch Street station. She paused by a news stand and glanced over her shoulder to see if anyone had followed her. The black car hadn't been in the road today but something about this meeting told her to be extra careful. She had taken the train to Liverpool Street station and then zigzagged through alleyways and office buildings to lose anyone who might be following her. The forecourt was crowded but as far as she could tell there was no figure who had been behind her when she left Liverpool Street station.

Mentally she upbraided herself and gave an inner giggle at her thoughts. You're getting to act like a drama queen. You're allowing coincidences to colour your judgement. The curse of any writer was an overstimulated imagination.

Even so she felt apprehensive as she entered the station building. The interior was gloomy and a steep flight of steps led up to the platforms. It was a small station for a London terminus and the buffet was crowded. She queued for a cup of tea at the counter and took it over to an empty stool at the corner of the window. A deep shelf along the window served as a table. She sipped the tea watching the commuters running towards the Tilbury and Southend train about to leave from platform two.

A woman sat next to her eating a custard tart with her coffee. She looked at her watch: it was five past five. When the woman got up and walked away a soft voice behind her spoke. 'Miss Carrington? No, don't turn round.'

She was aware that a man was standing against the wall to one side of her.

'It don't pay to be careless,' he cautioned. 'There could be someone watching.'

The words resurrected her recent fears. She stared straight ahead, her face impassive as she sipped her tea.

'I'm Freddie Eastern,' he went on. 'I used to be chauffeur to Long. His bigotry cost me my job. Yet he ain't no innocent.'

The name was familiar. She had come across it in her research. He had no reason to be loyal to his past employer. Eastern had been dismissed after being seen leaving a party with his male lover, who was a pimp for high-class prostitutes. Long instantly dismissed him and had flayed him in the tabloids denouncing his homosexuality as a sin against nature. Eastern had been prosecuted and the trial had caused a furore to repeal the laws against homosexuality. Eastern had retaliated and spoken of the wild parties at Long's house in the country and how many of the guests were prostitutes. Long had virulently denied the accusations. Eastern had been ridiculed by the press and sent to prison.

She pushed her empty cup aside and glanced over her shoulder. Eastern was about five foot six in height with sleeked-back, receding grey hair. His lean face had a hawklike profile, his complexion stretched over high cheekbones was ruddy and further marred by purple threaded veins. He had once been handsome with long eyelashes and cupid-bow lips.

'I can understand why you have no fondness for Long,' she

said quietly. 'But the newspapers found no evidence against him when you made allegations before.'

'Keep looking out the window,' he warned. 'Anyone could be watching. Long had the papers on his side. I was labelled a vindictive queen. There always has been one law for the rich and another for the poor.'

Shona fiddled with her teacup, keeping her back to Eastern. It was all so theatrical, like a bad spy novel, that she bit her lip to control a grin.

'I lost me job and went through hell because of Long. Queers in the nick are either beaten up or raped by the inmates. I could kill Long for what he put me through. No decent firm would employ me when I came out, not even as a cabbie. I ended up driving a dust cart.'

'I'm sorry.' It sounded inadequate but she didn't know what else to say. 'I need proof of Long's exploits before a paper will print anything.'

'I was made the scapegoat to cover up Long's and some other prominent people's homosexual relations. Long liked women and handsome lads. He was at that party where I was photographed together with two ministers, a couple of peers and a bishop who is always condemning prostitution. But it's surprising how information can be suppressed when it's about people in high places. Did you know the photographer who took the picture had a fatal road accident a few days later?'

'I don't write stories about sex scandals,' she said, gathering up her gloves.

'How about Nazi sympathisers and shady munition deals during the war?'

Adrenalin pumped through her. This was better than she had hoped for. 'You have proof?'

'No, but I can give you enough information on dates and meetings for you to get the proof. You're an investigative journalist, ain't you?'

'What sort of dates are we talking about?'

258

'The first two years of the war mostly. Something gave him the wind up and he made sure all his deals were respectable after that.'

She could barely contain her excitement. This could be a bigger story than she had anticipated. She didn't want to believe that Laurence Shelton was also involved in it. That fateful car ride to Epping was blurred in her mind but she recalled her father's fear and him saying that he knew too much. Was it about those shady deals? Was it possible that Long had framed her father, spreading the rumours of his defection? Why hadn't he come back to clear his name? Was he then dead?

She pushed that thought aside. It was too awful to contemplate after just learning who her father was. She hoped that Eastern would have some information which would enable her to clear her father's name.

'I'm interested in your story but clearly we can't talk further here.'

'What's this information worth?' Eastern's voice was cold and businesslike. 'A hundred, I reckon.'

Another obstacle. She couldn't get her hands on that sort of money. She doubted her editor would pay out. He was a staunch Long supporter, having been at university with him. She'd have to present him with the undisputed facts before he'd print anything against Long.

'I haven't got that kind of money.' She had blown all her savings on buying the house in Stratford and furnishing it. She still had three rooms to do and the roof had developed a leak in the last storm.

'You're a resourceful woman. You'll find it.'

She swung round on the stool to face him. 'How do I know I can use what you've got?'

His heavy-lidded eyes creased as he studied her shrewdly. He stood up and looked past her to scan the buffet. When he withdrew a hand from his jacket pocket she felt paper crinkle against her bare palm. 'Nick said you'd want proof. Read that. I'll be in touch in a week as to a safe meeting place.'

He strode away from her and his short figure was swallowed up by the surging office workers. A train whistle blew and Shona, feeling self-conscious and not a little foolish at the theatricality of the meeting, headed into the ladies' waiting room. She didn't read the paper Eastern had given her until the cubicle door was locked behind her.

There was a list of three dates and of consignments supposedly of farm machinery shipped to African countries where guerrilla forces were fighting their governments. Were these arms shipments and not tractor parts?

There were also dates of other armaments despatched to the forces depots against which had been written faulty goods. Again the adrenalin rushed in a scalding wave through her body. If Long had supplied substandard weapons to the forces he had made his fortune at the expense of British lives. But how to prove it? Dirt in the barrel of a rifle could account for it misfiring or blowing up in the face of a soldier. Had Long banked on that to get away with little short of murder and cheating the government?

She let out a long breath. If her father had learned of these facts and was somehow, even innocently, involved with Long's factories, he could be equally to blame. Was that why he knew he had to leave the country and make a new identity for himself?

She came out of the cubicle and ran her hands under the washbasin tap. Had the wealth and comfort of her early childhood been stained with the blood of valiant soldiers? The enormity of what she had discovered was alarming. She would not believe that her father was involved in such treachery and greed until irrefutable proof showed her otherwise.

On her return to Stratford she was still buzzing with excitement. She was indebted to Nick. The least she could do was phone him and thank him. Apprehensively, she dialled the number Percy had given her. She nearly hung up as soon as it began to ring, she was so nervous.

The phone rang on without being answered. She was about to put the receiver down when Nick, sounding breathless, answered.

'I was about to hang up,' Shona said.

'I was in the bath. I had to sprint downstairs to get it.'

The image of Nick at the other end of the line with possibly just a towel round his waist brought a rush of intimate memories she preferred not to dwell upon. She could see the water dripping over his broad shoulders and the tangle of dark hair on his chest.

'I won't keep you then.' She schooled her voice to sound cool. 'You'll get cold. I just wanted to thank you for getting Freddie to contact me. I owe you.'

'So now come to dinner with me.'

'I'm busy all this week,' she evaded. The vision of him on the other end of the phone line still taunted her. 'My plaster comes off tomorrow and my editor phoned for me to cover a story in Sussex.'

'You can't drive all that way with your arm just out of plaster. It will be sore for another couple of weeks.'

'I'm going by train and then a local taxi. I can take notes.'

'The story had better be important. The man hasn't got a heart sending you away like that your first day back at work.'

Shona laughed. 'It's my job and don't mollycoddle me. If it gets too much I'll stay in a hotel overnight. After that I've got some shows to review.'

'We'll dine before we go to the theatre then. That's more fun than you attending on your own.'

'I wasn't inviting you.'

'But you said yourself you owe me. I love the theatre. I've even got meself a penguin suit for such an occasion.'

Temptation whispered in her ear. She did have complimentary tickets and Marion couldn't make it as they were travelling down to Cornwall that day for a week's holiday. 'OK. But remember it's by way of me saying thank you for your help. Don't get any other ideas, Nick. Pick me up at six. My address is . . .'

'I know your address. What are we going to see? The Noël Coward play?'

The assurance in his voice sent a shiver down her spine. Perhaps she had been too hasty. She had tickets for that play but she felt Nick had won too easily. 'No. Molière.'

'Molly who?'

Shona laughed. 'Molière. He was a seventeenth-century French playwright.'

'What you trying to do to me, sweetheart?'

'You invited yourself, remember. You can always back out.'

His chuckle was throaty. 'You won't get rid of me that easily.'

'You'll enjoy it. It's his wittiest and bawdiest play.'

'That sounds more like it. See you at six.'

Shona knew she had to act carefully on the information given to her by Freddie Eastern. It could be designed to trick money out of her and also stir up trouble for Long if it was printed. She had another contact, Elsie Hannigan. Shona had first met her when she was writing about the murder of a young prostitute. Elsie had been the girl's friend and was devastated at her death. She had spoken freely. Now from time to time Elsie gave her useful information which helped her research.

Shona glanced at her watch – it was almost nine. Time enough to track down Elsie in her haunts in Limehouse. Back in the early forties Elsie had been a beautiful singer in a top West End nightclub. Now she had fallen on hard times. Her looks were becoming ravaged by her heroin addiction. She supplied her habit by singing in pubs and being on the game.

Elsie was not on her usual corner but further down the dimly lit street, slouched in a doorway. A couple of men, most likely seamen from their rolling gait, walked by. Elsie sashayed alongside them. Two younger women appoached from ahead.

'Get lost, yer old crone.' One of the seamen pushed Elsie aside. They linked arms with the younger prostitutes, laughing as they headed for the girls' rooms.

Elsie stuck her fingers up at their backs and with her shoulders hunched returned to her doorway. It was several months since Shona had last seen her. Time had not been kind. Her face was illuminated as she lit a cigarette. The eyes ringed with kohl were bleak, the scarlet mouth harsh, her excessively rouged cheeks gaunt. Elsie looked ill. In fact she looked at death's door.

'Fancy some pie and mash, Elsie?' she called. 'You don't look like you've eaten properly in weeks.'

She teetered forward on her high heels, her fake fur coat falling open to reveal a plunging neckline and heaving cleavage.

'That you, Shona?' She peered short-sightedly into the car. Recognising her, she gave a brittle laugh. 'Trade ain't so good. Got ter watch me figure these days.'

'I need to talk. There's a fiver in it for you and a hot meal if you want it.'

Elsie looked up and down the street. 'Ain't much happening here. Might as well spend half an hour in the warm.'

The cheap sickly scent she wore filled the car as she got in. Shona drove past a corner café.

'That will do. I can't spare more than half an hour or me pimp will give me a seeing to.'

The café wasn't one Shona would have chosen. It was dirty

and unwelcoming. As they approached the door the juke box began to play 'Heartbreak Hotel'.

Elsie chuckled. 'That's more like it. What I wouldn't give to have a few punters with Elvis's or Sinatra's sex appeal. Once I could pull the most handsome men in the land. Nowadays . . .' She gave a snort. 'Beggars can't be choosers.'

'You should look after yourself more, Elsie,' Shona said as they entered the café. The net half-curtains at the window were grimy and the wooden tables were cluttered with uncleared plates. Elsie picked a table by the window. Shona wasn't so sure that was a good idea. Some of Eastern's cloak and dagger tactics must have worn off on her. They were on the corner of a busy main road.

'Why don't we take the table in the far corner?' she suggested.

'Best here. If that bastard pimp of mine goes past, he can't begrudge me some nosh.' She began to cough. It sounded painful and rasping. In the harsh lighting of the café, Shona saw splashes of feverish colour spreading out from under Elsie's rouge.

'I'm paying for your time the same as any punter,' Shona corrected. 'And you shouldn't be out on the streets with a cough like that. Have you been to a doctor?'

Elsie shrugged. 'I ain't got no time for quacks. And me money's down these days. Too much young competition.' She coughed again and came to the more secluded table. 'Ashamed to be seen with me, are yer?'

Shona shook her head. 'I'm on to something. The scoop of a lifetime but it isn't without its risks.'

'It ain't about any gang leaders in these parts? I don't know nothing.'

Shona knew she was lying. Elsie got her drugs from the gangsters. 'That's not my story. It's about the early forties when you were the toast of the town.'

A shrill peal of laughter from Elsie drew several glances to them. The laughter ended in another coughing fit and it was some moments before Elsie could speak. 'I had it in them days. I could put any one of them tarts out there to shame.' She waved a hand towards the street. 'When you've got the face and body men will fight over, or pay a fortune to get you into their bed, you think it will last for ever. Then some rich bastard gave me a dose of the clap. By the time I got over it, my health and looks had gone. The rich punters want their women young and fresh.'

'Do you remember Laurence Shelton at that time? He was a young politician.' At Elsie's vague expression Shona took out the press cutting with his photograph.

Her face cleared. 'Ah, Larry. I remember him at some of the parties. He didn't go with the girls though.'

Elsie shifted in her seat. 'You gonna sit there all night? Or do I get the meal you promised me?'

Shona went to the counter and brought back a large pie and mash for Elsie and two teas. In the meantime a slovenly waitress had cleared their table leaving a wet streak of pie crumbs in an arc in front of Shona's chair. She returned to the counter to get a cloth and wiped the table dry before returning it. Elsie was tucking into her meal, clearly ravenous. She was bolting the food down so fast Shona held back from questioning her until she had almost finished.

'Was Shelton a friend of Gerald Long? Or did they just work together?'

She had to wait until Elsie controlled another coughing fit. 'They were often at the same parties. I steered clear of Long. He'd beaten a couple of the girls badly when he'd gone back to their place with them. One poor cow lost her eye. Paid them handsomely. Also he was a bit of a shirt lifter. Though since his second marriage he seems to have steered clear of that.'

Shona didn't want to go into the question of Long's sexual preferences. She lowered her voice and leaned forward. 'Did you ever hear anything about dodgy arms deals connected with Long?'

Elsie's face drained of colour. 'Nothing.' She scooped the last of the potato on to her fork and swallowed it. 'Gotta go.'

Shona took another fiver from her purse and held it folded in her hand. 'Just tell me if it is true? Did Long sell faulty guns to the army? Or ship weapons to Africa crated up as farm machinery? Someone has given me some facts I need to check on.'

'Who?' Her stare on the fiver was hungry but her body was stiff with fear. She looked over her shoulder. 'You could get yourself killed with information like that. I don't know nothing.'

'You're lying, Elsie.'

She snatched the fiver. 'Thanks for the meal. Don't bother to run me back.'

'Elsie!' Shona called after her. The prostitute paused. 'You really should see a doctor about that cough and stay off the streets until it's better. It could be pneumonia.'

'It'll take more than a cough to see off an old boot like me.'

Shona's assignment in Sussex had proved arduous with a great deal of running around to get all the interviews and information needed for the story. It was late by the time she had finished and with a splitting headache she had decided to take a hotel room and return to London tomorrow. The next morning she walked into the village to buy a newspaper. The *Globe*'s headline clenched her stomach: PROSTITUTE BEATEN TO DEATH IN EAST END. TIME TO PURGE LONDON OF VICE.

The woman was named as Elsie Hannigan and her life story, embroiled in vice, was printed. Her naked body was found floating in the Thames at Wapping. Elsie was last seen at 10.30 pm leaving her flat.

Shona's head reeled at the news and she felt sick. She'd only seen Elsie a couple of nights ago.

'You all right, miss?' the plump, homely woman behind the counter said. 'That story upset you. It turns my stomach. Glad I don't live in London. Devil's city. Such goings on. It's disgusting. Those women get what they deserve if you ask me.'

Shona rounded on her. The woman was neat and respectable. Her life was cosy, innocent and protected. How could a woman like her know the misery Elise and others of her kind suffered? Or how every day could be a fight for survival? Her rebuke died in her throat. Instead she said, softly, 'No one deserves to be beaten to death, stripped of their clothes and dignity and left to rot in the cold waters of the Thames.'

She caught the next train back to London. Throughout the journey she couldn't stop thinking of Elsie. Could her death be connected with their talk? She didn't see how it was possible. The research into Gerald Long and his involvement and link with her father was making her paranoid.

She presented her assignment to the editor who looked unimpressed. 'Is that all there was to it? Can't you spice it up?'

'I'm not that sort of reporter and I thought this paper had more integrity.'

The editor scowled and sat back in his chair to rub his stomach through his waistcoat. 'We're down on sales. We need something to get our readership up.'

'Anything on Elsie Hannigan's murder?'

'Williams is on the story.'

There was no point in talking to Williams. He had no time for women reporters and all she'd get was derisory remarks.

The editor regarded her with interest. 'What's your interest in an old pro? If we hadn't decided to go for the "clean up

London's vice rings" campaign, it wouldn't have got more than half a dozen lines. Too many Toms like her end their days in the river for it to be news. Even the police are giving it a low profile.'

'Why? Some perverted maniac beat her up and killed her. He could be turning on innocent women next for his kicks.'

He pointed his pen at her. 'Don't go getting ideas on doing a sob story on London's Toms.'

'I knew Elsie. She'd given me a few insights into the shady lives of the rich and famous past and present. She was a high-class call-girl and singer in the forties. There wasn't much which went on in the East End she didn't hear about. I saw her a couple of nights before she died.'

'Anything fishy going on?' His interest pricked. 'Is it worth a story?'

Shona hesitated. She didn't trust him with anything on Gerald Long unless she had concrete proof. 'No. I saw her in the street. I felt sorry for her. She didn't look well.'

'Not many Toms make old age.' He picked up three typed memos which had been transcribed from the telex machine. 'See if you can get two hundred words out of any of those. I need to fill a column on page five.'

One was a report of a flying saucer seen over Salisbury Plain. The third in six weeks. The other two had been identified as a new type of weather balloon. The second was a train crashing into a station barrier in Devon. The information could be checked by phoning the station for details. The other was a Berkshire farmer who had barricaded a public right of way and was threatening council officials who tried to remove it with a shotgun. The police had been called in. There was no need to go to Berkshire, she could check the facts with the police station and have a chat with a colleague on the local rag. If the incident became more volatile she'd have to go down later. It was routine work and could easily have been done by a more junior reporter. If nothing else came up it looked like she could actually finish early.

The internal phone rang on her desk. It was reception. 'Miss Carrington, there's a detective here who would like a word with you.'

She came out of the lift to see a tall man in a black gaberdine trenchcoat talking to the receptionist. The woman giggled at something he said and seeing Shona approach remarked, 'Here's Miss Carrington for you.'

The flirting manner as he chatted to the pretty blonde receptionist was erased as he turned to face her, his demeanour formal and formidable. Shona found herself staring into startling green eyes. His hair, which was brushed back from a wide brow, was the colour of harvested corn. There was an earthy masculine quality about the entire man. He was handsome in a rugged athletic way and about thirtyish. His stark gaze swept over her. She felt she'd been summed up and pigeonholed. From his severe expression she guessed he didn't suffer fools lightly nor was easily impressed or emotionally moved.

He held out his badge stating he was from the Metropolitan Police. 'I'm Detective Sergeant Jackson.'

'How can I help you?' she said walking towards some leather chairs and a low table along the far wall.

'It's about Elsie Hannigan. I understand you met her a couple of evenings ago.'

She hid her shock that he had learned of her meeting. Who had informed the police? 'An encounter,' she answered with reserve. 'I was driving past and saw her on the street. She didn't look well. On impulse I took her for a meal.'

'Do you usually dine with prostitutes?' The question was ironic but his face showed no emotion. Only his eyes looked alive. They were razor sharp and missed nothing.

'No. But Elsie's story had always fascinated me. She never seemed to let life get her down and usually joked and laughed

269

aside her troubles. I got to know her a few years ago when a prostitute, a friend of Elsie's, was also murdered. I covered the story for a local paper. I wasn't working for the *Globe* then. I liked her.'

He raised a dark brow, his only reaction to this information. 'Was she an informant of yours?'

The question sent a prickle down Shona's spine. 'Please, sit down.' Shona indicated the chairs and sat down herself. She had needed a moment or two to compose herself. It was not uncommon for women like Elsie to be snouts for the police and reporters, especially if they got paid. But because of the nature of their conversation that night concerning Gerald Long, Shona was loath to reveal the truth.

'Depends on what you mean by informant. Elsie knew everything that was going on in her manor. But she knew it was more than her hide was worth to blab. A few times when I needed someone to help me with some specialist background, she'd give me a name I could contact. She knew I could be trusted.'

A sudden chill gripped her. Belatedly, Shona remembered the occasions when she sensed that she was being followed. Had someone followed her that night and seen them together? Could it be linked with Elsie's death? She pushed it aside. Her journalistic mind was contriving a plot where there was none.

'I don't think you're telling me everything, Miss Carrington.' His green eyes regarded her and his mouth tightened with censure – the first reaction she had drawn from him. He gave little away.

'You're very perceptive.' She forced a conciliatory note into her voice. 'Actually I was more disturbed at how you know so much about that meeting. Who informed you?'

'It was an anonymous tip-off phoned in to the station. I would have thought knowing Miss Hannigan so well you would have come forward to offer what information you could.'

That needled Shona. 'I saw her two nights before she died and only read about her death in this morning's papers when I was covering a story in Sussex. I've only been back in the office an hour.'

'She trusted you. Perhaps she was worried about something. Had she fallen foul of her pimp? Or made an enemy?'

'We didn't speak about much at all. She was starving. She had a bad cough and seemed edgy that her pimp would catch her not working. Apparently she wasn't getting many punters lately.'

That cool green stare narrowed. 'So what did you talk about?'

'Nothing relevant, I'm afraid. She didn't stay long. She reminisced about her young days. She was really beautiful once. I wish I could be of more help.'

He stood up, solid and prepossessing as a standing stone. Even when she rose to her feet she had to tilt back her head to hold his stare. Unexpectedly he smiled. It transformed his austere countenance. He was disconcertingly handsome and to her surprise she felt a pull of attraction towards him.

'You've been most helpful, Miss Carrington. Could I have your home address? In case anything comes up and I need to question you further.' His smile broadened and there was an admiring light in his eyes. 'You can contact me at Scotland Yard if you remember anything which could assist us.'

'I hope you find Elsie's killer soon. Whoever did that to her is capable of murdering again.'

Chapter Twenty-one

The final curtain came down on the play and Nick clapped as loudly as the rest of the appreciative audience. His eyes were bright with laughter. 'That was terrific.'

'I said you'd like it.' Shona quickly checked her mascara in her compact mirror. She had laughed so hard that she'd cried.

They walked out of the theatre into the night. A strong wind billowed the full skirt of Shona's black dress and she hastily buttoned her coat.

Nick's car was several streets away. He linked her arm through his as he used to in the old days. 'The night's still young. Let's go on to a nightclub.'

'I'm a working woman.' She gently withdrew her arm. 'I've this review to type tonight when I get home.'

'Then a quick drink. You can't go rushing off. It's only ten thirty. Or how about a bite to eat? I'm starving. There's a great Italian restaurant just up the road here.'

She was hungry. She'd got home late and had only time to grab a slice of toast before Nick called for her. It seemed churlish to refuse and she had enjoyed his company. That was the trouble. The old persuasive charm was still as strong as ever.

'A meal would be nice, but it will have to be quick. I really do have to get this review written.'

The restaurant was small, dimly lit to set a romantic mood and extremely busy. There was soft guitar music playing in the background and the food smelled enticing. The atmosphere was Bohemian with wicker chairs and tables. Empty Chianti bottles hung in clusters from the ceiling and there was a mural of Florence along one wall. Red and white linen place mats were on the table and a Chianti bottle held a burning candle.

Two tables were pushed together in the centre. Around it Shona recognised two recently acclaimed young actors and a well-known middle-aged actress with their friends. They were rowdy and high-spirited.

A waiter escorted them to a table on the far side of the restaurant. They both ordered minestrone soup and lasagne.

Throughout the meal Nick questioned Shona on her career and assignments. She hardly had a chance to answer one question before he asked another.

The main course eaten, Nick insisted that she try the zabaglioni for dessert. At that point she put up her hand. 'Enough about me. I'm sure you know all this already. You see Percy and Ted often enough. What about you, Nick? Apart from the dogs what are you up to? Is it still electrical goods?'

He shrugged. 'That and other things.'

'Same old Nick, ducking and diving. I thought the electrical goods were selling well. Dad said you had a warehouse.'

'Two actually. And I'm strictly legit these days. My latest venture is importing wine. That's going to be another boom product. You'd be surprised at the number of people now who like a bottle of wine on the table for a special occasion. It's no longer just a drink for the toffs. Then there's the motorbike shop. All the young men want one these days. Bit of an indulgence that, as I own a couple of classy bikes myself.'

'You're doing well, Nick. I'm pleased for you.'

He took her hand. 'It's all thanks to you, Shona. You put

me straight. Showed me I could make something of myself. Be somebody.'

She eased her hand away and looked at her watch. 'I have to go now. We've been here over an hour.'

'Let's have a coffee before you go. You haven't told me how things went with Eastern?'

Shona didn't protest when the coffee was ordered together with a brandy for Nick and a Sambucca liqueur for her. 'That will be another treat for you. It tastes of aniseed.'

'I know. I love it. I discovered Sambucca when holidaying in Rome a couple of years ago. But you wanted to know about Eastern. We've spoken enough about me.'

'The subject fascinates me.'

Shona ignored him. 'Freddie Eastern has got some useful information.' She frowned. For a moment she was tempted to confide in Nick all she knew about Long and the background of her father. She resisted. It would take half the night and bring a greater intimacy between them. Instead she was flippant. 'Freddie Eastern is an odd man. He made our meeting all very dramatic.'

She told him about the way Eastern had behaved as though he was some foreign spy.

Nick's eyes creased with concern. 'Shona, I don't think you realise what you could be getting into. Why don't you forget this madness? Long is dangerous. He's got contacts with the underworld.'

'He's the only link I have to my father.' Her defensiveness made her say more than she intended.

'So you know who he is? That's great, Shona. I know how important it was for you. Do you think your father is still alive?'

His interest unnerved her. She sipped the Sambucca to recover her composure. Then to her surprise she found herself telling him everything. Finally she concluded, 'I think Long spread those rumours about my father to ensure he never returned to England. What I believe is that Laurence Shelton discovered what Long was up to. Perhaps he'd been embroiled unwittingly but knew he was implicated by association.'

'I think you're clutching at straws to defend a man you know little about.'

'He's my father. I can't believe that I'm the daughter of someone capable of profiting from the deaths of British soldiers by supplying faulty weapons. I couldn't live with it.'

'You're not responsible for your parents' actions.' He took her hand. 'If you build an image of a perfect, wronged man, you're bound to be disillusioned.'

She nodded. 'From the memories I have of my father, I know he had a strong sense of right and wrong. That was instilled in me from an early age.' She withdrew her hand from his and fidgeted with her napkin before adding in a strained voice, 'What if my father is still alive and can't come back to England because of the charges against him? If I can clear his name, he'd be free to return.'

'Oh, Shona, sweetheart, you're such an idealist.' His voice was tender and his grey eyes troubled. 'It was so many years ago. Long would have destroyed any evidence. You're playing with fire.'

The intensity and worry in his stare disconcerted her. The longer she held it the more frightened she became.

'I know it's crazy.' Her distraught gaze held his and the anguish of years was in her voice. 'How else am I going to find my parents if they are alive? I'm aware of the problems. And that it would be dangerous to reveal my true identity at this stage. Yet I have to do it. Deep in my heart I know my father is alive. Perhaps he's stayed silent all these years to protect me. He wouldn't have abandoned me unless his own life was in danger. I know he loved me.'

'At least let me help you. It will be less dangerous. You're too vulnerable on your own.'

'Nick, it won't work us being back together. You can't go back in time.'

'I've changed, Shona. It's been seven years. I'm still in love with you.'

She shook her head. It would be folly to get involved with him. He had wounded her too deeply and she couldn't trust him. Common sense told her that men like Nick never changed. Eventually he would stray and the pain would be all the greater.

'I'm sorry, Nick. It won't work between us. You need trust for that and you destroyed my faith in you when you betrayed me the second time.'

He drew in a harsh breath and the hollows of his cheeks tautened. 'Because I care, I can't let you face danger and do nothing. OK. I admit I blew it between us. That doesn't make us enemies, or I wouldn't be here with you tonight would I? The car accident. Elsie's death. The belief you're being followed. Don't these prove you need someone with a bit of muscle to look out for you? Let me at least do that. No strings attached.'

His sincerity moved her. 'That's a generous offer and I appreciate it. But the answer is still no. Anyway it will probably come to nothing. Eastern wants a hundred pounds for his information which I haven't got. There's no point in my going to my editor. Long is an old university friend of his.'

'I'll give you the hundred, no problem,' he said with a smile.

'No, Nick. It's a kind offer but I won't be indebted to you. It wouldn't be right.'

Annoyance flickered across his face. 'You can be so stubborn. There's no strings to this money. Take it as a loan if you must and pay me back when you can.'

Again she shook her head. If she took it Nick would again have a hold over her. She couldn't risk that. She had enjoyed herself this evening, but she daren't lower her guard and begin to trust Nick. It would be safer to borrow from Percy, he would happily lend it to her.

'Where are you meeting Eastern?' Nick persisted.

'Nothing has been arranged yet. He said he'd get in touch and tell me where.'

'Promise me you won't see him alone. If Eastern is going to so much trouble to keep a low profile over this, it means he's aware of the danger.'

Her heart kept giving erratic flutters. The old attraction was still there, perilous, waiting to overtake her. She would not let it happen.

'I have to go, Nick. This is getting us nowhere.' She asked the waiter to fetch her coat while Nick paid the bill.

Outside the pavements of the West End were still crowded and would be until the small hours of the morning. Nick again took her arm to steer her safely through the throng of people. When later he stopped his car outside her house, she had to admit to herself that it had been one of the most enjoyable nights out in years.

'Thanks, Nick, it was fun.'

His arm slid along the back of her seat and he moved closer. The tangy, expensive scent of his aftershave enshrouded her. When he lifted his hand to cup her chin, she moved her head.

'Not even a kiss for old times' sake?' he queried.

'Especially not for old times' sake. Don't spoil a lovely evening by reminding me what a rat you have been in the past.'

She opened the door and got out. He was round her side of the car and opened her front gate, stepping back for her to enter.

'How about a nightcap then?'

'No, Nick.' A strong gust of wind swirled the litter in the street.

Nick winced and clutched his eye and fumbled in his pocket for a handkerchief. 'Damnit! I've got something in my eye.'

She was instantly suspicious. Was this a trick to steal a kiss from her?

'Stop larking about, Nick.'

'I'm serious. I can't get it out. Can you see it, Shona?'

She hesitated. She'd left her hall light on and a panel of light streamed on to the step from the fanlight above the door. He was stooped over and rubbing his eye.

'You'll make it worse. Give me the hankie.' She took it and drew him round so that he was facing the light. His eye was tight shut and she had to stand close and on tiptoe. 'I can't do anything unless you open your eye.'

He did and at the same time he clamped both arms around her waist and laughed. His mouth was on hers before she could push him away. Its touch was pure coercion. For a second she succumbed. Then as her blood began to ignite and a bud of yearning unravelled, she pulled back.

She took her doorkey from her handbag. 'Goodnight, Nick.'

'When will I see you again?' His voice was confident.

'At the dog track probably.' She was deliberately offhand, having no intention of encouraging him.

She slipped into the house and shut the door before her resolve crumpled. Her hands were shaking. The kiss had affected her more than she wanted to admit. She should have known he'd trick her. There was only one safe way to keep Nick Blake out of her life and that was to make sure she avoided him.

'Are you sure you did the right thing not letting Nick in on this?' Percy looked around him. It was Saturday evening and the track was packed. Already half the races had been run and there was no sign of Eastern. He had phoned her at work saying he'd meet her here tonight.

Shona was becoming uneasy. The hundred pounds seemed to be branding her flesh as it rested in an envelope in the pocket of her thigh-length jacket. She wanted to be able to slip the money to Eastern easily. That's if he showed up.

Percy observed wryly, 'Bloke over there has been giving you the eye for the last half hour. If he ain't Eastern, he must fancy you.'

Used to Percy's teasing, Shona glanced in the direction he had indicated. Her heart sank. 'It's Detective Jackson. The one who interviewed me after Elsie Hannigan's death. Eastern won't show if he's about.'

'The man's interested in you. Go and bluster it out,' Percy advised.

Shona wasn't going to make any approaches to the detective, but it would be foolish and could even look suspicious if she ignored him. She smiled and sketched a brief wave, then bent towards her grandfather to study the form for the next couple of races.

'I said he was interested,' Percy whispered. 'Here he comes. Ten to one he asks you out.'

Shona looked up to see Detective Jackson a few feet away. 'Good evening, detective. Having a flutter or are you on duty?'

'An evening off. I came with some mates who have gone to get some hot dogs. I hadn't reckoned you to be a greyhound fancier.'

'My dad works at the track. It gives me a chance to see him after a meeting. This is my grandfather, Percy Dawkins.'

She turned to Percy who was squinting up at the tall policeman. 'This is Detective Sergeant Jackson, Grandad.'

The detective held out his hand to Percy. 'Greg Jackson will do when I'm off duty.'

'Had any winners?' Percy asked.

Greg shook his head. 'Best I've managed is third.'

Percy laughed. 'You want to take Shona's advice. She's had two winners so far and I expect she'll have a couple more before the night's out. She's got a nose for it.'

'So what's going to win the next race?' Greg Jackson's attention was now all for Shona.

For the next five minutes they discussed the form. Nick's dog Golden Lady was running in the last race and with its current form it was bound to win.

'It sounds a winner to me,' Greg said and there was no mistaking the admiration in his eyes as he smiled at Shona. 'I'll take your advice on the last three races and do an accumulator on a fiver starting bet.'

'That's a lot of money if it loses.' Shona frowned. 'I'm not always right. I never bet more than five shillings.'

'I feel lucky. If they all win at those odds I'll make a couple of hundred. I'll halve my winnings with you.'

Percy winked at Shona. He'd said little during her conversation with the detective. Shona felt uncomfortable at his offer. 'I couldn't possibly accept that.'

He dismissed her protest with a wave of his hand and a smile. She hated being obligated in any way even though she was beginning to find his company stimulating.

'It's my loss not yours. Besides, you picked the dogs.'

'It still wouldn't be right.'

'We'll argue the toss when they've all won,' he answered with a grin.

Greg was showing no sign of returning to his friends. The presence of the policeman would keep Eastern away. She searched the crowds but couldn't see her informant. Somehow she'd have to give Greg the slip or Eastern would never approach her.

Greg's manner was now relaxed and very different from the formality he had shown when he had interviewed her in the office. He told a couple of jokes and had Percy in stitches with laughter. Shona warmed to him. She liked this side of him and she was aware of the admiring way he was staring at her. At any other time she would have enjoyed his company. Now she was conscious that Freddie Eastern could be hovering close by. He'd probably scarper if he saw her talking to a copper. Yet it would look odd if she was rude to the policeman.

Percy intervened. 'I think that's Nick over there looking for you, love. You did say you had to speak to him tonight.'

She was relieved to see Nick watching her from the back of the stands. His expression was bleak. It would give her an excuse to get away. She smiled at Greg Jackson. 'I have to go. It's been nice meeting you again.'

'What if the dogs all win?'

'I'm not leaving the stadium but I do need to see this friend.'

'I'll catch you later then. That your boyfriend?' His face had adopted his formal policeman's look, unemotional, missing nothing.

'Just old friends, ain't you, Shona?' Percy answered for her.

She smiled apologetically at the detective and hurried towards Nick.

'What the hell are you doing talking to a copper?' His grey eyes were glittering with anger.

'How did you know he was a policeman?'

'I can smell them a mile off, darling,' he sneered. 'You seeing him? You seemed very pally. I'm surprised you gave me a look in.'

'I'm not seeing him. Actually I'm supposed to be meeting Eastern here and I met Jackson by accident. I was glad to see you so I could shake him off.'

'Glad I could be of assistance.' His sarcasm lashed her. 'It looked to me like you were enjoying his company.'

'What if I was?' Her own temper erupted and she controlled

282

it with difficulty. 'I shouldn't have used you as an excuse to get away, but you did say you'd help me. I'm sorry, I didn't mean to intrude.' She turned away and he caught her arm.

'I'm sorry.' He jammed his hands in his trouser pockets. 'Cops make me edgy.'

Pent-up frustrations increased her tension. He'd lied to her. Lied as he had in the old days. He hadn't changed. He would never change. 'And I thought your business was legit these days. Don't you ever stop lying, Nick?'

'I *am* legit. Just convince the cops of that. They're always raiding my warehouse on some pretext or other. Two of my brothers are doing time for a warehouse robbery. They thought I was shifting the stuff for them. Jackson was on the case.'

'Were you?'

'They couldn't prove anything. I learnt my lesson. I don't touch anything dodgy these days. Try telling them that though.'

'That makes him a good cop and you a bad loser.' She glanced round and saw that Greg Jackson was no longer with her grandfather. 'Goodbye, Nick. I've got to find Eastern.'

He swore roundly. 'I wish I'd never mentioned you to him. I didn't realise the danger. If you get hurt . . .'

'Stop it, Nick. I don't need this. I must try and find him.'

'I'll help.' Nick fell into step beside her. 'So how come you know Jackson?' he clipped out, his expression tense.

'He's investigating Elsie Hannigan's murder. He interviewed me as I'd seen her a couple of days before she was murdered. I only met him the once.'

'And made quite an impression on him.' The colour had bleached from Nick's face. 'How come you know a tramp like Elsie Hannigan?'

She resented his attitude. He had no rights over her. How dare he judge her? Then she realised he wasn't judging her, he was concerned and her antagonism mellowed. 'It's a long story and this is not the time for it. I met her through my work. She used to mix in higher circles. Long was at some of the parties she attended in the forties.'

'And now she's dead!'

Shona tensed. 'Don't make it sound as if me seeing her and her death are connected.'

'Like your car accident wasn't connected with you putting the heat on Long?' His expression was fierce. 'You've got to drop this, Shona! It's too dangerous.'

She'd heard enough. He meant well but Nick would never understand what drove her. 'Goodbye, Nick.'

She walked away, ignoring his call to come back and be reasonable. The next race had started and she paid no heed to the track. She was too busy searching the crowd for Freddie Eastern. She couldn't see him anywhere. By the end of the next race she was becoming frantic. Twice she had taken evasive action to avoid both Nick and Greg Jackson. Before the last race began she went into the ladies. Her head was pounding with tension. She splashed her face with cold water. A red-haired woman stood at the next basin and applied her lipstick. A third woman was drying her hands on the towel. When she went out Shona moved across to dry her own hands.

'I thought you'd never come in here.' Freddie Eastern's voice came from the redhead.

Shona stared at him open-mouthed. She had to admit he made a stunning woman. Although he had padded his figure to look well endowed, he had kept the make-up minimal and not tartish. Neither was the calf-length navy skirt and check jacket.

'You got the money?' he said without preamble.

She held out the envelope. He took a half-dozen closely written sheets of paper from a large navy leather handbag and handed them to her. She scanned them, noting the list of dates and information.

'Thanks.'

'Get even with that bastard for me. But be careful. He's got eyes everywhere.' Eastern heaved up his false bosom and patted the wig. 'If anyone wants to know where you got that info you never heard of me.'

Shona nodded. 'I'm grateful for this.' She paused, then, worried that someone would come in and Freddie would walk out pretending he did not know her, she asked quickly, 'Did you meet Laurence Shelton when you drove for Long?'

Freddie started and she could see his colour bleach away under his face powder. 'What do you know of Shelton?'

'Only what was reported in the papers. But it didn't sound right somehow. I had the feeling that he had been set up. He didn't seem the type to become a traitor.'

'Shelton was a lesson to all who knew more than was good for them. He was a decent bloke, generous with his tips, always had a good word for anyone. He was Long's partner in one of the companies. But I don't reckon he knew the half of what was going on. He were no more a traitor than my old granny. If he ain't six foot under in an unmarked grave, he's living somewhere like Rio under a false name and keeping one eye over his shoulder to avoid a knife in his back.'

Shona rode this blow, needing all her fortitude to contain her emotion. Her fears were being confirmed. 'What about his family?'

Eastern shrugged. 'I couldn't say. So what's your interest in Shelton and his family?'

'I don't like mysteries and Shelton was obviously close to Long. Another thing. Was Long ever called the Big Man in his circle of friends?'

'To close friends only. Come to think of it, there were four of them. No use trying to contact them. They're all dead except perhaps Shelton and who knows what happened to him. Poor blighter.'

Two women came in groaning about the money they'd

lost that night on unsuccessful bets. Eastern had moved away from Shona and was pouting in the mirror. When the women entered the cubicles still chatting loudly to each other, he whispered to Shona, 'Give us a couple of minutes before you come out. And don't bother to contact me again. It ain't worth the risk. I'd forgotten about Shelton.'

As he walked out she put her hands on the basin and stared down into the sink. She felt shaky at the news he'd given her about her father.

Her sense of humour was a great stabiliser. She must appear calm when she left here. Recalling Eastern dressed as a woman she mentally gave him a round of applause for the theatrics of the occasion. As she came out of the ladies with the list safely hidden in the zipper compartment of her handbag, she saw Greg Jackson emerge from the gents opposite.

'We meet again,' he said cheerfully. 'Thanks for the tips. We've got two winners. Forty quid is all riding on the last race.'

'So much?' She'd been so distracted she hadn't paid any attention to the last races. She had a flutter on the dogs for a few shillings for fun but the thought of losing so much money – nearly a month's salary – made her uncomfortable.

'Don't look so worried. The original bet was only a fiver. Shall we watch it together?'

'I thought you were with friends.'

'I know whose company I prefer.' He smiled at her.

He was flirting with her. The adrenalin was still racing round her body after the excitement and also fear Eastern's comments had caused. She was also angry at Nick. It made her reckless. And Greg was handsome.

Shona crossed her fingers when the dogs were put in the starting gates. The hare came round the outside of the track and the gates clanged open. Golden Lady was fourth at the first bend. It was too far back.

'Come on, Golden Lady! Come on, Golden Lady!' Her voice was hoarse with shouting. Greg's deeper voice yelled beside her. At the last bend Golden Lady was second. Shona's heart was thundering, the blood rushing through her ears in crashing waves. She jumped up and down shouting her encouragement. The dog was neck and neck ten yards from the line. She held her breath, no longer screaming, her heart and soul willing the dog to win. A bulky man moved in front of her just as the dogs crossed the finishing line. She didn't see who won.

'Get out the way! Oh no. Who won?'

Greg turned to her, his expression downcast. 'Oh no,' she groaned. 'It lost. All that money.'

His lips twitched and he punched a fist in the air. 'Golden Lady won.'

Suddenly she was scooped into a bear hug and swung round. 'We won.' She clung to him, laughing and light-headed from the intoxication of the moment.

He put her down and stepped back. His eyes were shining but he looked apologetic. 'I'm sorry. That wasn't very respectful of me to grab you like that.'

'We won, didn't we? Don't be silly.' She was flushed with excitement. 'It's another win for Nick. He'll be thrilled. His dogs are doing so well.'

'It was Nick Blake you were talking to earlier, wasn't it?' The laughter had gone from his voice. 'Is he your boyfriend? He was acting very possessively towards you.'

Her eyes clouded. This copper was suspicious of Nick's activities. It made her defensive. 'I've known him for years. It's good things are going well for him.'

'You'd do well to steer clear of him. He's trouble.'

'Nick isn't perfect. No one knows that better than I do. But he has many fine qualities. I don't like my friends criticised.' She turned from him, surprised at herself for the way she was defending Nick. 'Keep all the winnings. It was your money.'

She walked away. Moments later Greg was in front of her blocking her path. 'I'm sorry, I was out of line. It comes with the job being suspicious of ex-cons.'

'Nick hasn't been convicted of anything as far as I know.'

Greg looked smug. 'He did six months for receiving a few years back. His brothers are inside again. Blake got off. There was insufficient evidence against him.'

Shona glared at him. 'You mean he was innocent.'

Greg put up his hands in defeat. 'We've got off on the wrong foot. I really would like you to have those winnings and we could go somewhere to celebrate.'

She could tell that apologising did not come easily to him. It made her more forgiving and he had just proved Nick hadn't changed even if she had defended him. 'I don't want your winnings; it's far too much money. Though, if you like, we can celebrate your good fortune. But as you're a copper I think you should know that my dad, Ted Carrington, did time for receiving. He's been straight for seven years. I'm not ashamed of his past. But I'll understand if you feel that you would prefer to forget your invitation.'

'The invitation holds.' He didn't hesitate. 'And I respect your honesty. I've met my share of hostility for being a copper. I'm not ashamed of my work. I shouldn't have spoken about a friend of yours as I did.' There was wry humour in the twist of his lips. 'The truth is that I envied Blake for knowing you so well.'

They regarded each other steadily. She was attracted to him and had enjoyed his company. 'Where were you planning to take me for this celebration?'

'I'm off duty tomorrow. I don't get many weekends. Do you fancy a day out somewhere? The weather is supposed to be good. How about Brighton?'

'That sounds fun.' She found herself looking forward to it.

'I'll pick you up at ten if that's not too early for you. You'd better remind me of your address.'

She gave it to him and directions. She had planned to go over Eastern's notes and perhaps start some research, but what was another day. It had been years since Ted had taken her to Brighton for the day when she was twelve.

'I know Stratford well,' he said. 'My grandparents lived near Maryland Point. I was brought up in Mile End and I now live near the Angel in Islington.'

'See you tomorrow then.' She walked away with a lighter step to join Percy who was nearby. He was talking to Nick who walked away as she neared them.

'Congratulations on your win, Nick,' she called.

He didn't turn to acknowledge her, yet he must have heard her. His back was stiff and he was walking with steady purpose towards the exit. Disappointment pricked her. She knew from his walk that he was angry.

'You've ruffled that young man's feathers,' Percy commented. 'Nick ain't such a bad sort. He's still keen on you.'

'I can't forget how he cheated on me, Grandad. Men like that don't change.'

'Some can. You could've judged him too harshly.'

'He had his chances.' Pain gruffened her voice. 'I'm not going to risk getting hurt again. He betrayed me. How can I ever trust him again?'

'Happen you're right,' Percy nodded. 'Oh, Bill Miles was here. He wanted a word with you.'

'Did he say what about?'

'Just said he'd got some info you'd be interested in. He asked if you could call on him Monday evening. He's moved again. He never seems to stay longer than a few months in one place. He's got a flat not far from you. Here, he wrote it down.'

She was curious. Bill had some interesting contacts. 'He's probably heard of someone who I'd like to interview. He's put some good stories my way in the past. Funny he didn't come over.' She put the address in her pocket.

'You were talking to that copper at the time. He seemed rather edgy to me. I think he's worried about this story you're writing.'

'Not another one.' Shona voiced her irritation. All these warnings were making her more stubborn about finding out the truth.

Chapter Twenty-two

Greg was early calling for Shona on the Sunday. She was sitting out in her back garden with a cup of tea and the morning paper enjoying the warm sunshine. The dining room opened on to a paved area with a wooden bench and table. She loved the luxury of a leisurely breakfast at the weekend after the rush of the week.

The garden always soothed her. It had been neglected when she bought the house and although her money had to go on redecorating and repairs indoors, she had budgeted to buy shrubs and climbing plants to cover the six-foot fence which enclosed it. Any free time on a fine day took her outside to dig, plant or weed and this year all her hard work had paid off. The harsh lines of the fences were gone, the narrow borders expanded so that the lawn formed an oval. Hanging baskets and tubs softened the brickwork around the kitchen. It was a haven, peaceful and secluded amidst the bustle, noise and traffic. White and pink climbing roses bloomed along one fence, delicately scenting the air. A purple and a white clematis entwined one another. In a patch of sunlight on the flagstones, Gemini, her tortoiseshell cat, feigned sleep, one predatory open eye upon a robin singing in the branches of a lilac tree.

On the table in front of her Shona had spread out the sheets of notes given to her by Eastern. They made disturbing reading. She hadn't realised how many factories Gerald Long owned which had all produced either uniforms or munitions during the war. There were also names of a couple of the factory managers and three factory workers, all of whom had died in suspicious factory accidents shortly after a consignment was sent out. The enormity of what could be unearthed astounded her. All these facts had to be checked. It seemed inconceivable that no government office was aware of what was going on. Long must have covered his tracks well.

The arrival of Greg ended her conjecture. As she passed through the dining room she stuffed the papers into her handbag out of sight.

He was dressed casually in jeans and a white T-shirt. The jeans encased his long muscular legs like a second skin and the T-shirt emphasised the broadness of his shoulders and his narrow waist. He was driving a dark green MG open-top sports car. Shona wasn't an expert on cars but it looked something of a classic. The chrome on the radiator and bumpers gleamed, the dashboard was of walnut and the seats were covered in beige leather. An expensive car for a detective.

'I came early as I thought you might want to bring your swimming costume. The weather report was for a hot sunny day. Or don't you swim?'

'With one foot on the bottom I'm afraid. I've always meant to learn. I love the water but we never got to the seaside much.'

'Then I'll teach you, if you like?'

The sun brightened his hair to the colour of pale honey and she felt the deepening pull of attraction. Shona was conscious that her primrose yellow dress with its full skirt and stiff petticoat was impractical for a day on the beach. 'While I fetch my swimsuit, why don't you go through to the garden? I'm also going to change into slacks, they'll be more practical for the beach. Do you want some tea?'

'I'd rather get on the road. Traffic could be heavy on a

day like this. And you look terrific as you are. I know what an age women can take to get ready.'

The authority in his voice almost bordered on a command. Also his faintly condescending tone had rankled. She never spent hours preening in front of a mirror. 'Go through to the garden. I won't be long.'

Ten minutes later as the dining room clock chimed ten she appeared in the garden wearing white slacks and a sleeveless red blouse, her bare feet in flat white sandals. She carried a white blazer and her swimsuit wrapped in a bath towel.

She dropped a tube of sun cream into her handbag. She had already rubbed some into her arms as unfortunately her pale skin burned easily.

'That didn't take so long did it?'

He gave a low wolf-whistle as he turned to regard her. As she locked and bolted the kitchen door, he commented, 'You've got a nice place here.'

'It will be when it's finished. I've done most of the decorating myself. Dad helps. The garden is my pride and joy. I spend more than I should on it as it gives me so much pleasure.'

'It's the most attractive garden I've seen in London. Was it established when you moved in?'

'I think it had been used as a rubbish tip for a junk yard. It was months before I stopped digging up old pots and pans. There was even a brass bedstead buried. It was hard work but worth it.'

'I'm not much of a gardener myself. A second-floor flat suits me. Even the pot plant my sister once bought me died because I forgot to water it.'

When he opened the car door for her she smiled, appreciating his good manners. Again she couldn't help reflecting that off duty Greg was relaxed and fun to be with.

He drove skilfully through the London traffic and they spoke easily of inconsequentials. Greg had a dry humour and often his observations made her laugh. By the time they emerged from the Blackwall Tunnel which ran under the River Thames she was as comfortable with him as with an old friend.

The sun was on her face and a refreshing breeze played through her hair streaking it back over her shoulders as they sped into the countryside.

'This is some car for a policeman.'

'My indulgence. I've got a Ford for work but this is my passion. I've spent years doing it up and spent a fortune on it. My ex-wife will tell you I thought more of the car than I did her.'

'So you are divorced then?'

'Five years ago. We got married too young. There was a kid on the way and it seemed the right thing to do. I was in the army at the time. I wanted to make a career of it after my National Service. Patty hated living in quarters. She wouldn't come with me when I was posted abroad. She's got four sisters and they were pretty close. She was shy and didn't mix much with the other wives.'

'She must have felt isolated, especially when you were away.'

'So she never stopped telling me. She was a great complainer. I got out of the army and joined the police. She didn't like that either because the hours were unsociable.' His voice was harsh and his face had set into stern lines. 'She hated my work. She hated this car. She hated me playing rugby. She hated my friends. I think she hated everything about me by the time we got divorced. She's settled down with an insurance salesman and had another two kids.'

He laughed self-consciously. 'I don't usually rattle on like that.'

Behind his sunglasses she couldn't see the expression in his eyes but there was bitterness in his voice. 'Do you see much of your child? How old is he?'

'Kieran is eight.' His voice was guarded. 'Patty makes it difficult for me to see him. Though I'm supposed to have him to stay once a month when I'm off duty, it's surprising how often that clashes with her arrangements. I was supposed to have him this weekend but they've gone to Devon for the weekend to celebrate her new mother-in-law's birthday and she insisted Kieran went with them. She wants him to accept his stepfather as his dad. She says seeing me just upsets him.'

'But you're his father. She's wrong. He'll always want you in his life. That doesn't mean he won't come to care for his stepfather.' The passion in her voice made him glance at her as he was driving.

'It sounds like you know something about it.'

'I was adopted when I was ten. I'd give anything to meet my father. He disappeared in the forties.'

'Missing in action was he?'

'No.'

'A deserter then.'

The condemnation in his voice instantly antagonised her, making her snap, 'Certainly not!'

She turned away to look out at the countryside as they drove down a twisting road.

'Sorry, I didn't mean to be rude. And it's none of my business, is it?'

She had leaned her elbow on the side of the car and her hand rested across her mouth. Her mind wrestled with the pain of memories which had resurfaced. It was only two months since her memory of her childhood had returned. The events were still raw with too many mysteries and too many questions remained unanswered.

'Hey, I was out of order,' Greg persisted. 'I didn't mean to sound like I was interrogating you. Habit of the job I suppose.'

His apology soothed her and she summoned a smile.

'Don't lose touch with your son. He loves you and needs you.'

He was concentrating on his driving, his face tense. 'There's a pub about a mile ahead. Fancy a shandy or something? They also do nice meals which you can take out into the garden. It will save us looking for a restaurant in Brighton.'

'I'd like that.' She forgave his abrupt manner, realising that he was angry at being thwarted in seeing his son. He remained more reserved as though he regretted revealing so much of his life to her.

The halt for lunch broke the tension between them. He asked her several questions about her life. When his mood was relaxed she found it easy to open up to him, but nevertheless she held back on revealing her true identity.

'How long have you been in the police force?' she asked to deflect further questions about herself.

'Six years.'

'You've done well to make detective so quickly, haven't you?'

'I was called up in the last year of the war when I was still at university studying law and economics and went into the Intelligence Service. I never went back to my studies and stayed on in the army where I transferred to infantry and eventually made sergeant.'

'With that background I'd have thought you'd have worked for the civil service.' There were no rough edges to his voice and she had surmised that his parents were middle-class. She also suspected that he was something of a rebel against his background.

'That's what the old man expected me to do. Or go back into law. But I couldn't stand being stuck behind a desk all day. It was the action I liked in the army. He'll probably accept me back into the fold if I make superintendent. We don't see eye to eye on most things. Luckily my two brothers lived up to expectations. They regard me as the black sheep.'

They drove through Brighton and were dismayed to see how crowded it was. They parked along the promenade by the cliffs. Further away from the two piers the pebble beach was less congested.

Greg took a car rug from the back seat and they found a clear place by a breakwater. Shona put on her large-brimmed sun hat to protect her face. The tide was still coming in and Shona went off to change into her black one-piece swimsuit. When she returned Greg was stretched out on his back on the car rug. He'd hired a canvas wind-break which formed a semicircle protecting them from the cool breeze.

The sea was a deep kingfisher blue, calm and inviting. There wasn't a cloud in the azure sky and afraid of burning Shona rubbed her arms and legs with cream. She couldn't reach her back and Greg took the tube from her. The cream skimmed across her warm flesh with sensuous feather-light strokes.

'Skin as pale and soft as yours must burn easily,' Greg said, tossing the tube on to the rug. 'If the sun is too much for you we'll go into town.'

'I'll be careful.' She glanced enviously at his darker skin which was already tanned. His body was without spare flesh, the muscles attractively firm. Light brown hairs covered his forearms, legs and chest which was potently masculine without making him hirsute.

The sun was at its zenith and within minutes Shona was uncomfortably hot. 'I'm going in for a paddle.'

The stones of the beach were scorching and Shona began to pick her way gingerly across them. Greg came up behind her and with a laugh swooped her into his arms and ran to the water. He waded in up to his thighs then made to throw her into the sea.

'No,' she screamed and threw her arms around his neck. 'It will be freezing.'

'It's lovely.' His laughter was infectious as he again made to throw her and she held his neck tighter.

'If I go, you come with me,' she threatened.

'Is that a promise?' He began to wade purposefully into deeper water.

A wave lapped over her back making her shudder. After the heat of the sun it was like ice. 'You monster, put me down!'

Greg grinned, unrepentant. 'Anything you say, lady.' He sank down into the cool water, holding Shona close so that the waves flowed over her body.

She gasped as the cold water stung her flesh. In her outrage she hit out at his shoulder. 'You're a brute. Let me go.'

'It's not that cold.' He rose up out of the water and released her legs, holding her body steady until she found her footing. His eyes were bright with laughter and crinkled attractively against the sunlight. The water came up to Shona's chest, its gentle swell lapping over her shoulders. Now her body was used to the cooler temperature, it was invigorating.

'It's too deep for me, Greg. Let's go where it's shallower.' She waded towards the beach and once the water was down to her hips turned and began to splash him. They laughed as they played. Shona was determined to get her own back on Greg, following him into the deeper water. She put all her energy into splashing the water over him just as a larger wave swelled in volume and lifted her off her feet. She floundered and gulped in a mouthful of sea water as she sank under the waves. Her feet found the bottom and she staggered upright spluttering and pushing her wet hair back from her face.

Greg's arm was around her waist supporting her. Behind his laughter his eyes showed their concern. 'Are you all right?'

She nodded and took a deep breath to still the rapid beating of her heart. It made her aware of how vulnerable she was in the water by not being able to swim. 'I wish I could swim. It looks such fun.'

'Then I'll teach you. First you should learn to float on your back. Just relax and I'll support you.'

They stayed in the water an hour and to her delight Shona had managed to swim a few yards on her own. She was tired but exhilarated as they walked back to their towels. The warmth of the sun caressed them, the tension of recent weeks had eased from her. It was a long time since she had enjoyed a man's company so much.

'I'm going back in for a quick swim, you don't mind, do you?'

'Go and enjoy yourself. I'm fine.' Shona rubbed the cream on her arms and legs and watched as Greg ran down to the water and dived into the sea. She envied the way he expertly cut through the waves. Her gaze followed him for several minutes and she was surprised to discover that she missed his company. She liked his sense of fun and the way he so often teased her. With a contented sigh she lay down. The day had been unexpectedly pleasurable. Relaxed she turned on her stomach and closed her eyes. The sounds of seaside pastimes drifted over her: children squealing with pleasure, portable radios tuned into a cricket match or the afternoon play, an organ playing on a distant roundabout and the chimes of an ice-cream van.

Inevitably her mind began to focus on Freddie Eastern's notes. Shona cut herself short. Today was for relaxation. The sun was soporific. She smiled to herself as she remembered the touch of Greg's hands on her body as he taught her to swim and the tenderness in his eyes as he encouraged her feeble efforts.

She must have dozed. A shadow had passed over the sun. She opened her eyes and rolled on her side. Greg was standing over her drying himself with his towel. He was so tall and handsome, her body was aware of his physical attraction. Since she'd finished with Nick she had had only one other lover whom she'd gone out with for a year. He worked away and was only in London once every six weeks. When he decided to emigrate to Australia she realised she didn't love him enough to leave her family and her hope of discovering her real father. There had been plenty of other men friends but she had not slept with them. Sometimes she wondered why she held back. She prided herself on her independence and her body often craved a lover. None of them had been special enough. As she gazed up at Greg, she knew that he could be special.

'You need some more cream on your back, it's getting red,' he commented. He picked up the tube and lay on his side. Again his hand slid languorously over her shoulders, the cream cooling but his touch searing. Her body tingled and glowed and a soft moan rose to her throat and she rolled on to her back.

Greg was leaning over her, his expression taut with desire. Then it changed and she saw that he was staring at the scars on her neck and face. The sea water had washed off the make-up she used to conceal them. Self-consciously she covered the side of her face with her hand.

'What happened?' he said softly. 'Those look recent.'

'A car accident. It happened a couple of months ago. I've just had my arm taken out of plaster.' She briefly explained the details and the extent of her injuries.

He took her hand away from her face. 'Maniacs who drive like that should be locked up. Probably a couple of youths who'd been drinking. It's about time they did something to tighten up the law where drunken driving is concerned.' His voice softened. 'Don't cover them up on my account. They don't spoil your looks. I didn't notice them in the water when we were larking around.'

She suspected he was being kind. 'I know they'll fade in time but I can't help being self-conscious about them.'

He kissed the scar on her temple and one on her cheek and when his lips touched the reddened tissue on her neck, she gasped at the tenderness of his touch. Greg was smiling as he drew back to gaze at her. She wanted him to kiss her, to take her in his arms and make her forget the fears of recent weeks. Their gazes held and her throat dried. The touch of his lips was like molten fire. The wind-break and the breakwater gave them privacy and Shona wound her arms around him, revelling in the pleasure of his kisses. She was breathless when he pulled back and brushed a lock of her silvery-blonde hair from her brow. The intensity in his gaze sent a shiver of longing through her. 'I could fall for you, Shona Carrington.'

Wordlessly she pulled his head down, her tongue teasing his. All her senses were pitched into a maelstrom as his kiss deepened. The slow gliding penetration of his tongue wove a potent spell. A purr of pleasure trembled in her throat and her body moved, her breasts crushed against his hard chest. When he pulled abruptly away, she drew a ragged breath. Their gazes again linked, intense and mesmerising.

He rolled on his stomach and took her hand to kiss each finger. 'I'm going to have to go for another swim to cool off,' he said, smiling into her eyes. 'Are you coming back in the water?'

'You have your swim, then perhaps we could go into town. I don't want to overdo the sun.'

He ran down into the water and Shona followed more leisurely. Her body was throbbing with wanting him. She had never felt such desire on so short an acquaintance. It was heady and exciting. She lifted her face up to the sun and realised that she was happier than she had been for a long time.

She stayed where the water was waist-deep and practised her swimming and decided to go to the swimming baths at least once a week to improve her ability.

Again dressed, they left their swimsuits and towels in the car and decided to wander around Brighton's famous

Lanes, the narrow interconnected alleyways renowned for their antique and jewellery shops. Many of the shops were treasure houses with ornaments and objects from all over the globe. Their old-world atmosphere enthralled her. It was so different from the Regency squares with their tall bay-fronted houses in long formal terraces off the sea-front. In the Lanes buskers played on some of the corners and although Greg eyed them balefully as they were breaking the law, Shona stopped to listen to two beatnik skiffle players creating music on a washboard and tea chest.

They found an espresso bar which wasn't full of noisy teenagers and afterwards walked until they came to the Royal Pavilion.

'It looks like something out of the *Arabian Nights* and not what you expect of a royal seaside palace,' Shona said. 'It must have cost a fortune. It's an opulent monument to a dissolute Regent, yet at the time he ruled, thousands of England's poor were starving and living in hovels.'

'You sound angry. Are you an ardent socialist?'

'It was a decadent age, where those with wealth squandered it on their own selfish pleasure. Few people cared about the poor or the misery and suffering they endured. I hate that sort of injustice.'

Greg put his arm around her shoulders and led her to a park bench in the gardens in front of the Royal Pavilion. 'Your views interest me. As you interest me, Shona. What drives you to write the articles you do? They are often controversial and stir up public opinion.'

'Perhaps I'm driven more than most because of my background. I lost my memory as a child and was later adopted. I've spent over half my life with a name that wasn't mine.'

'What happened to your parents? Isn't it odd to be adopted at the age you were?'

'It took time for the courts to allow my adoption. No one knew who I was. It was in all the papers at the time. I couldn't remember my name and Ted and Lily raised me. Eventually, although the legal proceedings were complicated, they were allowed to adopt me.'

She found that she still couldn't speak of what she knew about her father. Greg was a policeman for all she found him fascinating and enjoyed his company. Her secrets had been locked within her for too long to be easily released to a virtual stranger, no matter how attractive and enjoyable his company.

'And what about you?' She turned the conversation. 'Surely to become a policeman it's some kind of a vocation. You want to put murderers and villains behind bars. And the law isn't just broken by the poor. The rich can corrupt it to their own ends.'

'It's something I'm good at,' he answered dismissively. He stood up. 'You ready to eat, it's almost six? There's a good steak house up near the Palace Pier. You're not in any rush to get back are you?'

'Not at all.' In fact that was the last thing on her mind. She was enjoying Greg's company too much to want their day together to end.

After the meal they walked along the Palace Pier and then as the tide had gone out leaving an expanse of wet sand below the pebbles they walked arm in arm along the beach which was almost deserted now, except for a few couples and people exercising their dogs. The sun was beginning to set, a bright crimson ball amongst a scattering of apricot and purple feathery clouds. 'The sunset is glorious.'

Greg halted and drew her close and rubbed his hands over her arms. He kissed her long and lingeringly, even the restraint of his passion had the power to send a pulsating heat radiating through her veins. When he broke away Shona laid her head against his chest, her voice throaty. 'It's been a wonderful day, Greg.'

'For me too. It doesn't have to end yet. How about we

drive up to the cliffs past Roedean school and watch the sunset before we set off back to London.'

'You old romantic,' she teased, loving the idea.

They missed the sunset and the full moon rising. They had found a secluded place to park and as soon as the engine had died Greg took her into his arms. She had been about to comment on the beauty of the sunset on the water, but the words were dispelled by the supple sweetness of his mouth on hers. His hands slid down her spine moulding them closer, then the bridge of his fingers contoured the lower swell of her breasts. When the kiss finally ended, Shona was breathing shallowly, her heart pounding a wild tattoo.

She put a hand up to caress his lean jaw and found her fingers were shaking. For several moments they stared into each other's eyes without speaking. The tenderness shining in Greg's gaze dried her throat and made it difficult for her to swallow.

It was crazy. Madness. She hardly knew him. No man except Nick had affected her this way before. Yet Greg was so different. The opposite from Nick in looks and he was a copper where Nick was a bit of a rogue. It was the differences which increased her attraction.

'Let's walk along the cliff,' Greg suggested and reached over to the back seat to pick up the car rug.

She walked in a dream, her body attuned to Greg's lithe movements, her head against his shoulder. The evening was warm and below them the sound of rolling waves mingled with the call of seagulls and cormorants.

Greg spread the rug and drew Shona down beside him. Desire sparked in the air between them. They were isolated by the night, their figures shielded from the infrequent passing cars by thick gorse bushes.

Yet when he reached for her, she hesitated. 'Greg, I'm not sure. I don't sleep around.'

His breath carried a suppressed groan. 'I'm not going to

rush or force you. Neither have I any wish to return to an empty flat or a pint down the local with a mate. I want to get to know you better. Today has been full of surprises.' He tilted up her chin with his forefinger and kissed the tip of her nose. 'I want to hold you, kiss you, taste the sea and the moonlight on your skin and in your hair.'

'Have you ever thought of becoming a poet?' she taunted, then regretted it at seeing him frown. 'I'm teasing. I hadn't expected you to be such a romantic. But I like it.'

She was enfolded in his arms and gently lowered to the ground. His kisses were at first coercing, then as she responded, they became fiercer, more demanding, expertly arousing. She wasn't aware that he had unbuttoned her blouse until his hand moved to unfasten her bra. She tensed. This was going too fast for her peace of mind.

Her hand closed over his, staying his movement. His answer was to kiss the curve of her breasts, his fingers closing over their fullness. 'That's enough, Greg. It's too soon.'

His fingers were gentle as they moved over her shoulders. 'I adore you, Shona. You're reasoning with your head not your heart. What does your heart say?' His lips skimmed along her throat to nuzzle the sensitive hollow at its base, his warm breath as tantalising as his words. 'Since I saw you again at the dog track I couldn't get you out of my mind. The more I've come to know you the more I want all of you. Not just for a day, a week or a few months. For always.'

She gazed wordlessly into his eyes, at that moment his words echoed her own chaotic feelings. His tongue continued to tantalise her flesh and awake her passion. When his teeth grazed each sensitive peak, she gasped, her head rolling back and her back arching. The heat of him as he lay half across her burned like the blast from a furnace. His arousal was against the nub of her womanhood; the pressure provocative, creating a bitter-sweet torment of yearning. Her hips moved of their own volition and desire swamped her reservations.

With feather-soft caresses his hands moved over her, stroking, freeing clothing, insinuating into the intimate source and softness of her. She forgot everything but the waves of sensuality lapping through her body. She gave herself to him unreservedly, clothes discarded until they were covered only by moonlight.

A wild passion carried Shona along in its frenzy. Greg was a skilled lover. He seemed to want to taste every pore of her flesh and she writhed in abandonment, her cries of pleasure captured in his mouth as he finally possessed her. Even then he remained in control, expertly expanding the pulsing vibrations which gathered momentum. Her nails scored down his spine to his hips. She was bound in a sensual cocoon: ecstasy shimmering and shivering through her body. Even the aftermath was cataclysmic as his rhythm slowed, extending the pleasure until finally both satiated they lay at peace.

Shona stared up at the full moon and the watching eyes of the stars. Greg cradled her in his arms and drew half the car rug over them, trapping the warmth of their bodies. Shona smiled and ran her fingers through his thick hair.

'You've made a wanton of this woman. You should be ashamed of yourself, Detective Sergeant Jackson.' Laughter was in her voice. 'What have you to say in your defence?'

'I'm innocent, m'lud.' He propped himself on his elbows to grin down at her. 'She was a wicked, shameless seductress who bewitched me. And me a young, innocent lad.'

Shona laughed and lightly slapped his shoulder. 'How dare you malign my good name, sir. You have lured me into sin.'

'And I will do so again and again and again,' he chuckled against her ear and rolled her across the grass. A light dew was forming. Feeling its coolness against her hot skin, she squealed and wriggled against him and ended up astride his hips. He reached up to caress her breasts and desire resurged within her. 'You cannot escape your sentence for your wicked ways, sir. I demand justice.' She began to move over him, feeling him harden beneath her. 'I demand satisfaction.'

'Strumpet,' he breathed tenderly against her ear and rolled her over to again possess her.

The moon was far across the sky when they finally left the cliff top. Shona lay back against the seat of the car. Her eyes were closed and her body glowed with contentment. Greg had put up the fabric hood to protect them against the cooling air and they drove in companionable silence. Shona had no regrets about giving herself to Greg. It had been a wonderful, carefree day. Sea, sun and sex were a potent combination.

When they pulled up in front of her house Greg leaned across to kiss her again before he allowed her to leave the car. 'Do I get asked in for a cup of coffee?'

'It's almost midnight. I'm a working girl.'

'You're a terrific woman. Are you free tomorrow evening? There's a new club opened up West where we can dine and dance.'

'That sounds like fun. I'd like that.'

Greg escorted her to the front door. As Shona went to put the key in the lock she saw that the wood was splintered.

'Someone's broken into my house!'

'Don't touch anything.' Greg took charge, his manner brisk and formal. 'I'll go in first. The burglar could still be inside.'

Chapter Twenty-three

Shona followed Greg inside. She halted inside the front room, a sob of anguish squeezing from her throat. She put her hands to her head, her blue eyes wide with shock as she took in the devastation to the room. The house had been ransacked. The front room was a wreck. The books from two bookcases were flung across the floor, many with pages torn where they had been trampled on. The sofa was upside down as were the two armchairs. The roll top of her antique bureau which was always kept locked was smashed and papers were strewn all over the floor. The carpet square was torn up and thrown in a corner which had knocked her record player off the coffee table. Several of her favourite 78s were smashed, though her collection of long players seemed to have survived. Every cupboard and drawer in the sideboard was open, its contents scattered. Two tall porcelain dogs Ted had bought her as a teenager lay broken on the mantelpiece.

'Who could have done this?' She swayed and sickness contracted her stomach. She felt violated. Her home, her special sanctuary, had been desecrated.

'Bastards!' Greg snarled. 'We'll get them, Shona.' His expression was dark with fury. 'Robbery is bad enough. This type of destruction always sickens me.'

Her legs trembled as she walked into the dining room. Here two bow-fronted cabinets had been emptied. A bottle of whisky lay empty on the carpet which had again been thrown aside. The stench of urine rose from a dark stain in the centre of the floorboards.

The kitchen looked as if it had survived a bomb blast. Pots, pans and utensils had been swept from the cupboards. One door was hanging on a broken hinge. Glasses and crockery were smashed on the floor. They'd even emptied the food cupboards – bags of flour and sugar were sprinkled on the lino and eggs had been smashed to form a congealing mess.

She reeled back against the doorframe. Greg took her into his arms. 'Someone was searching for something. From the look of the mess they didn't find it. Do you keep money in the house?'

She shook her head. 'A few pounds, nothing more.'

'What on earth have you got that someone could want that badly?'

'I've got little of value except the bureau and they smashed that.'

'Are you sure?' His voice was harsher. 'This looks like someone has tried to frighten you. Give you a warning. I noticed there wasn't a single footprint in the kitchen. They were no ordinary burglars.'

She had suspected that Long's men could be behind this but had deliberately blanked their sinister motive from her mind. She didn't want to dwell on it now or she would break down. Greg was watching her closely, his face tense, awaiting an explanation. Shona ignored his statement and became coolly efficient. 'I'll look upstairs to see if anything was taken.'

'I'll phone the station and report the break-in. Have you got a phone?' Greg said, curtly.

'In the front room.'

A few minutes later he followed her into the bedroom. 'They're sending someone round to dust for fingerprints. I said I'd deal with this investigation as I was here. I thought it would be less upsetting for you.'

Shona nodded but her mind was dazed by the violence of the destruction around her. It was a nightmare. What sort of animals did this to someone's home?

She had left the bedroom neat and tidy. Now every item of clothing was flung on the floor, her lingerie spread out obscenely across the bed. Whoever had done this had fingered her most intimate garments. That thought made her sick. She buried her head into her hands, unable to stop the violent shudders which suddenly overwhelmed her.

Greg held her close, whispering in her ear. 'It's all right, sweetheart. Thank God, you weren't here when they broke in. We'll get the bastards.'

'Why have they done this? I haven't got anything of value.'

'What about jewellery?'

He kept his arm around her as she checked her jewellery box. 'The gold necklaces and bracelets Ted bought me are gone. And a diamond ring.' It was Nick's ring. He had refused to take it back and had returned it to her on an occasion he had tried to win her round. She had never worn it again, neither had she felt able to sell it or give it away. Her voice was threadbare with shock. 'That wallet on the floor had ten pounds in. I always kept some by for an emergency in case I couldn't get to the bank.'

'Is anything else missing that you can see?'

She gazed despairingly around the room and then walked into the spare bedroom which she used as a study. She had left this room until last, dreading what she would find lest it confirmed her fears.

In the doorway she swayed and put a hand over her mouth. She shivered. Fear writhed like a nest of serpents in her stomach. The drawers of her desk and filing cabinet were open and the floor littered with papers. Every file had been opened and emptied on to the carpet. There was no doubt in her mind now that Long was behind this. Had he somehow learned that Eastern had spoken to her? It made her the more determined to find out the truth. If Long had resorted to these tactics then her suspicions about him must be correct.

She stared at the mess for several moments, anger slowly replacing her initial fear. Damn Long! If he had tried to scare her off, he had failed. She wouldn't be beaten.

'It will take me days to get this lot back in order,' she groaned and despite her resolution to be strong had to fight against a rush of tears. She had been so proud of her little house. From the first moment of seeing it, it had welcomed her, the atmosphere warm and friendly. Now that was tainted, menace had chilled the air, destroying its calm and peace.

Greg put his hand around her shoulders. 'Could they have been searching for something to do with your work? I don't want to frighten you but I sense there's more to this than a mere robbery.'

'Who knows what drives the twisted minds of someone capable of this?' she evaded. She was tempted to confide in Greg about Gerald Long but something still made her hold back. Her memory had returned and with it the echo of her father's insistence to build a new identity for their own safety. She couldn't speak of her suspicions about Long without explaining everything and she wasn't up to that on top of the shock of the robbery. Neither did she want to sound like an irrational or hysterical woman bent upon vengeance. Besides, no one knew better than she that she had no proof against any of the crimes Long might have committed. A quick scan of the room showed her that the two files containing newspaper cuttings about Long and her father were missing. She couldn't see any of the papers amongst the debris on the floor.

'How can I tell what's missing until I clean this lot up?' she groaned. She wanted to get down on her knees and search for any of the cuttings she'd collected about her father in case the thieves had dropped any. They were so precious to her. 'Can't I make a start?'

'I'm sorry, Shona. You could be destroying evidence. I'll talk to the neighbours to find out if they heard anything.'

She turned in his arms, burying her head against his chest. Tremors rippled through her body. 'Hold me, Greg. I feel as if I've been defiled, my privacy invaded and abused.'

He held her tenderly and his lips brushed her hair. His body was stiff with tension. 'You're taking this well. A lot of people become hysterical when they get burgled.'

'Hysterics won't clear up the mess.' She pulled back feeling stronger and more composed. 'Can you leave the neighbours until the morning? This probably happened hours ago. It's midnight now. Mr and Mrs Henshawe next door are both elderly. They go to bed at nine and besides, he's as deaf as a post.'

'There were lights on in a couple of the houses. I'll call on them and leave the rest until tomorrow. Or would you rather I stayed with you? Can I ring your dad to get him to come over?'

She ran a shaking hand through her hair. 'They're not on the phone. I'm all right.' She walked out of the bedroom and ran down the stairs. 'Damn the evidence,' she called back, 'those bastards had better have left me some brandy. I need a drink.'

The brandy was missing but the vermouth and gin bottles were intact and also the tonic. She mixed herself and Greg a large Martini and went out into the garden to sit on the bench. This at least had not been debased. As she tossed back the Martini her shock gave way to anger. In the moonlight and light from the kitchen the garden looked tranquil. She heard a meow and Gemini crept out of the bushes to sit on her lap. She stroked her. 'Thank God, they didn't hurt you.'

She heard Greg calling her. 'I'm in the garden.'

He took the proffered Martini and raised it in a toast to

her. 'To us.' He sipped it and his expression became serious. 'It's not a very propitious start to our relationship, is it?'

'It certainly takes the gilding off the day. But this has nothing to do with us, Greg. I'm grateful you're here.' Although she was putting on a brave face, she was shivery with shock and reaction. She asked, 'Did anyone hear anything?'

'Mr Dyson was walking his dog at about seven this evening and saw two men come out of your house and get in a car. The men were stocky and wearing caps shadowing their faces.'

'That's not much help, is it?' Shona groaned.

'Unfortunately, his evidence is unreliable,' Greg added. 'He reeked of whisky and wasn't too steady on his feet. He had no idea what make the car was either. Though as it drove past him he saw it was black.'

Shona paled and suppressed a shudder, forcing herself to concentrate on what Greg was saying as he continued.

'The young couple next door were out until ten. Hey, what the hell's the matter? You look like death.'

Greg came to the bench and took her in his arms. Gemini meowed in protest and jumped on to the flagstones and ran off.

'That car. I think the men in it have been following me. But there are so many black cars. It's hardly an unusual colour.'

'This could be serious, Shona. Have you written an article on any young men who could bear you a grudge?'

'Nothing that I can think of.'

She felt Greg tense. 'Did the police find out who caused the accident where you broke your arm?'

'No. They sped off. A woman heard the crash and looked out of her window and saw a battered black car drive away. She phoned the police and an ambulance.'

'Have you had a run-in with anyone so they'd want to retaliate?'

He was making her more nervous. 'The car could be a coincidence. There's a lot of beat-up old cars round here.' She closed her eyes to hide their troubled stare. Had they been looking for Eastern's notes which were still in her handbag?

There was a shout from the front of the house and Greg went to let the forensic team in. Shona stayed in the garden. She didn't want to go into the house. Each time she heard movements within the building another tremor ripped through her. Eventually when they left, Greg put his arm around her and led her back inside. 'I've fixed the front-door lock. I don't think you should be alone tonight. Do you want me to stay here? Strictly on the sofa if you prefer. Or you're welcome to come back to my flat.'

'I couldn't sleep. I have to start on this. I won't be going into work for a couple of days either.'

'Then I'll help. I'm due a couple of days' leave.'

She leaned against him. 'You don't want to spend your leave cleaning up this mess. But thanks for the offer.'

He took her face in his palms. His eyes were sparking with angry lights. 'I'd like to get my hands on the scum who did this. Teach them a lesson about respecting other people's property. But my main concern is you. This has been a shock. I don't think you should be alone. Let me help. What if they came back?'

'Why should they?' She studied him with suspicion. He was making a lot of this incident. 'How many burglaries have you dealt with where they come back?'

His brows drew together with annoyance, then he spread his arms wide in submission. 'OK, I'm overreacting. That's because I care for you. But you shouldn't be alone.'

He was being very sweet and considerate. She was too sensitive. Neither did she want him to leave. His presence was reassuring. 'Then make yourself useful and make some strong black coffee. First of all I'm going upstairs to throw out every piece of clothing those fiends touched. I couldn't bear them near my skin again. Then I'll start down here.'

They worked until four in the morning sweeping up broken crockery and glasses. The utensils in the kitchen were piled on the floor and Shona wanted to disinfect the cupboards before they were put back. She felt the need to fumigate the entire house to rid it of contamination. The living and dining rooms were in some semblance of order by the time they both slept fully clothed on Shona's bed.

She woke at six after a fitful two hours' sleep. Greg was sleeping peacefully. She stared down at him for several moments, grateful he had stayed. A perfect day had been ruined by the burglars but it had proved to her that Greg was someone special. Perhaps she had been foolish not to confide in him.

With so much cleaning and tidying still to do, she was too restless to stay in bed. She rolled away from the warmth of Greg's body and had a quick bath which refreshed her before she tackled the kitchen. An hour and a half later she sank wearily on to the kitchen chair. All the cupboards were scrubbed and ready for the contents to be replaced. Her mood was morose. She hated to admit it but she was frightened. There had been a violence behind the vandalism of her home. It *was* a warning. And it made her angry. If Gerald Long was behind the break-in she was more determined than ever to bring him to justice.

At eight she phoned the paper and explained what had happened. She was allowed to take two days' holiday although the editor wasn't pleased as she had so recently returned to work after her sick leave.

She then went down the corner shop to buy bread, bacon and eggs for breakfast. Not that she could face anything herself but Greg deserved a decent meal after all the work he had done last night. She heard Greg moving about upstairs and took him up a cup of coffee. To her surprise he was in her study.

Resentment flared through her at finding him riffling through her papers. He had put the beige file covers in one pile, press cuttings and notes in two others.

'Leave them.' Her voice was crisp. 'I'd rather sort them out myself.'

His smile was conciliatory. 'Just trying to help. What do you want me to do next?'

'I felt like death when I woke up. Why not have a bath to refresh yourself while I cook breakfast?'

'Sounds fine to me.'

The smell of the bacon frying made her realise she was hungry after all. At a loud rapping on the front door, she turned off the gas under the bacon before answering it. Nick stood on the doorstep, his face gaunt with worry. He was wearing black motorbike leathers and his hair was attractively tousled from the wind.

'I phoned you at the paper. They said you'd been burgled and wouldn't be in. I came to see if there was anything I could do.'

A movement behind Shona shot Nick's head up and his eyes narrowed. She knew Greg was behind her. He said, 'Our breakfast is getting cold, love.'

The words were deliberately proprietorial in manner, a man staking his claim on her. When she glanced over her shoulder, Greg's shirt was open and outside his trousers, his hair still wet from washing it in the bath. His words and appearance made their relationship obvious.

At seeing the fury in Nick's eyes, Shona shifted awkwardly. She was moved that Nick had come round and was clearly worried. 'Thanks for your concern, Nick. I'm all right. A bit of jewellery was taken and some cash.'

Nick backed away. 'Since you've turned cop-lover you don't need me.'

His scathing tone lashed her. It made her defensive. Why should she feel guilty? Nick knew the score because he played the field so extensively himself. He marched towards his motorbike and beneath her defiance Shona experienced a stab of remorse. But wasn't it better this way? Nick could still tie her in emotional knots. Yet Greg was all she had wanted in a man – handsome, fun-loving and, more importantly, dependable, reliable and honest. That he was a policeman instead of a villain enhanced his standing in her eyes. Crime had brought pain to her life. First her father and later Ted. If she was ever to settle into a steady relationship, the one thing she demanded more than even fidelity was honesty. Nick had failed her on both counts.

'You said you were old acquaintances with Blake.' Greg sounded distrustful as they returned to the kitchen. 'His interest was more than friendship.'

His sarcasm provoked a rush of anger. 'I used to be engaged to him.'

She pushed past him, unnecessarily riled by the turmoil churning within her. She walked out to the garden where the wreckage from the burglary was tied in three old sheets. To calm her mood she paced among the flowerbeds. Then, aware that Greg was standing by the door watching her, she summoned a smile and returned to the kitchen.

Greg showed no sign of relaxing. 'That meeting upset you more than finding your house wrecked last night.' Condemnation thickened his voice. 'Are you sure Blake is history?'

'Yes.' It was impossible to hold Greg's stare and Shona emptied the percolator into the sink to make more coffee.

When Greg put his hands on her shoulders she could feel his tension. 'Blake's a rogue. You want to steer clear of his sort.'

She was about to retaliate when he lifted the hair from the nape of her neck and kissed the warm flesh. 'Last night rather put the damper on yesterday's fun. You need cheering up.' His hands moved over her breasts, his fingers teasing her nipples to tautness. 'I can't believe I lay all night at your side and kept my hands off you. It wouldn't have been right in the circumstances.'

His touch fired her blood. After the trauma of the last few hours, the release of her anger and frustration through sex was too powerful to resist. When he took her hand and led her back up to the bedroom, her step was light with anticipation and a hunger to find peace from the torment within.

Greg left at midday after he had interviewed the other households. Mr Henshawe had been playing records of brass band marches loudly in the early evening. His wife had heard some noise but had thought Shona had friends in. No one else in the street had noticed anything.

Shona sat on the floor of her study and began the arduous task of sorting the papers into their relevant files. She had been working for twenty minutes when it became obvious that all trace of any information she had accumulated on Gerald Long had been stolen.

With the papers scattered around her she sat on the floor. Her arms hugged her body as she wrestled with her fear. The warning was unmistakable. Long now knew that she was on to him. And since her father's file was also missing had the connection been made between herself and Laurence Shelton?

She dragged her fingers through her long hair and focused her thoughts on what notes and cuttings of her father had been left behind. There were only two, the ones proclaiming him a traitor and defector. She was convinced that the robbers had been here for some time. The missing jewellery and money and vandalised house was simply a ploy to cover up their true intent.

Panic welled, leaving her shaking and gasping for breath.

Next it could be herself that got done over and not her house. She battled to regain control of her breathing and as calm returned she remained resolute. Gerald Long was the link to her father. How could she give up? It was time she confided in Greg. She was seeing him tonight and would tell him everything.

The phone rang, making her jump. Her nerves were jagged.

She hurried down the stairs guessing the caller was Greg. He had been reluctant to leave her and had been so caring and concerned. She would ask him to come back and then tell him everything. With that decision made her relief was immense.

The voice on the line was muffled and distorted. 'That stuff I gave you is lies. Get rid of it.'

It took a moment for her to recognise that Freddie Eastern was speaking. His breathing was laboured as though he was in pain.

'Have they got to you? Are you all right? My place was done over last night. Long's file was stolen and a few bits of jewellery to make it look like an ordinary burglary.'

'Forget it,' Eastern rasped. 'There's no story. I was short of dough. You were an easy target.'

'You're lying now, Freddie. Not earlier.'

'Be grateful I managed to convince them I ain't told you nothing. I was recognised at the dogs. I've dressed as a tart too often to get away with it I suppose. Or they twigged you were on to something and had you followed. They knew we were in the lav at the same time.' Another groan of pain cut off his speech, it was stilted when he grated out, 'You stupid tart. You use that stuff and I'm done for. They've already given me a beating. I'm gonna lie low for a month or so. You should too! If you try and pin that stuff on Long we'll both wind up dead!'

The line was disconnected. Shona dropped the receiver

into its cradle and staggered back against the wall. Shock numbed her. Elsie Hannigan's death so soon after talking to her had been no coincidence. Eastern was terrified he would be next.

Her hand shook as she dialled Greg's number at Scotland Yard. He was out. Shona couldn't stay in the house alone. She had to talk to someone. Then she remembered that Bill Miles had some information for her.

Immediately she felt calmer. Her relationship with Bill over the years was a strange one. He was frequently at the track and sought her out. Often he had given her the lead on a good story he had picked up on his travels. Several times when they had met by chance they went for a meal or a coffee in a café. Yet she knew so little of his past, while at times she had found herself confiding in him. She had come to value his friendship and advice.

But would Bill be in? He worked erratic hours to suit himself but he wasn't expecting her until the evening. When she got into her car and turned right at Stratford Broadway she glanced in her rear-view mirror. A grey A40 and a green Morris were behind her. As she approached Maryland Point the Morris was behind two other cars. The hairs at the nape of her neck prickled. Had Eastern been right and she was being followed? Before the car accident she had been conscious of footsteps behind her when she travelled by tube, but recently she had been going everywhere in her car.

Her knuckles whitened over the steering wheel. If they were Long's men, she couldn't lead them straight to Bill. If they thought he might have information on Long, he might get beaten up. She couldn't risk it. As she passed his turning she saw with relief that his car was outside his lodgings. Relaxing she drove to Forest Gate and parked in a sidestreet. The Morris drove past as she locked her car door. She glanced inside and fear pitchforked into her. The driver was the man who had been with Long at the meeting and threatened her.

Shona walked quickly without looking as though she was running away or frightened. Her only hope of escaping from them was to act as though she was ignorant of their presence. As she turned the corner she saw the thick-set man get out of the Morris now parked a dozen cars in front of her own.

There was a parade of shops opposite. She crossed the road and went into the hairdressers. The shop window was heavily curtained and you couldn't see in from the street.

'How can we help you, madam?' enquired a young woman Shona recognised from school even though her brown hair was now dyed blonder than her own. 'Glynis Barker. What a surprise! I'm Shona from school.'

Glynis picked up her spectacles from the reception desk and laughed. 'So you are. I'm Glynis Gunn now. Got married two years ago. You married?'

'No. And I'm in a fix.' She leaned closer so that the woman with her hair half in rollers, who was taking an avid interest in their conversation, couldn't hear. 'There's a man hanging round outside who's been following me. He keeps asking me out, but he's a creep and won't take no for an answer. He gets a bit nasty and abusive. You know the type. Do you think I could slip out the back to avoid him?'

'Yeah, sure.' Glynis obliged. 'But mind you come back sometime. We only opened three months ago. I'll give you a special rate for a cut and perm.'

'Thanks.'

Shona darted through the shop. Her hair curled naturally and she had no intention of having it cut shorter. Still Glynis had meant well. Shorter styles than her shoulder-length hair were all the rage now, but not for her. There was a back gate to the shop which led into an alley. Picking her way carefully through overloaded dustbins, Shona came out of the alley close to the station. There was no sign of the Morris or the man who had followed her.

She tied a black scarf over her hair to hide its distinctive colour and hurried to the station. The train back to Maryland Point was already in the platform. Her ticket in her hand, she sprinted down the steps and jumped on to it just as it began to move forward.

Chapter Twenty-four

Shona's heart was still hammering wildly when she knocked on Bill's door.

'I hope you don't mind me coming so early, Bill,' she blurted out. 'But I need to talk.'

'It's always a pleasure to see you, Shona.' He guided her into his three-room flat on the ground floor of the Victorian bay-fronted house.

Bill had done well for himself in recent years. His suits were tailor-made and of good quality. Apart from his car and two tea chests of books which accompanied his constant moves he was unmaterialistic.

Since coming off the streets he never drank and he had an easy-going temperament and sometimes a wicked sense of humour which made Shona cry she laughed so hard. He was still very much a loner and didn't encourage friendships. Shona realised in that respect she was privileged.

He showed her into the sparsely furnished living room. Shona went over to the shelves holding part of his book collection; others were stacked on the floor, each pile a relevant subject. The books were mostly on philosophy and the sciences, especially archaeology. In so many ways Bill was still an enigma to her. He often took off for weekends to the country to visit archaeological digs of a Roman villa or Stone Age fort. With his lively, intelligent mind she puzzled that he chose such a mundane job as a salesman.

'My needs are simple,' he had once told her. 'I'm my own boss answerable to no man.'

There were some papers spread across a small dining table and on glancing at these she was surprised to find the pages closely packed with Bill's handwriting. He was working on a new script for a comedy play. The Spartan room and Bill's presence had a calming effect on her. Her curiosity triumphed over her recent fears.

'You're a man of many talents,' she said with fondness. 'Comedy writing and an interest in archaeological sites. You can't get more diverse than that.'

'I studied archaeology at university. There's plenty of melodrama in Roman history and the feuding of early British monarchs. So what do you want to talk to me about?'

His habit of directing conversation away from himself still had the power to disconcert her. Bill remained reticent about talking about himself. Any chance to delve deeper and learn more about him roused her curiosity.

'Not so fast. I want to hear more about your play being put on at Worthing. Even if you don't wish me to review it I want to see it. I phoned them but they said there's no play being produced under your name.'

'I used another name. The play isn't on until September.'

'Why won't you use your own name? You deserve to be acknowledged for your success.'

'All the best people have pseudonyms.' His evasion exasperated her. 'I'll get you some tickets. Besides, what does a name matter?'

'A great deal when you didn't know your real one for several years.' The painful observation slipped out. She was feeling unusually vulnerable after recent events.

'I'm sorry, Shona, that was a tactless statement. And you came here wanting to talk about a problem. You looked scared out of your wits when you came in. What's happened?'

It all poured out about the burglary, Elsie Hannigan's death and Freddie Eastern's frightened phone call.

'You've got to stop this investigation. It's too dangerous.' He took hold of her arms and his blue eyes were dark with anguish and suppressed anger.

'I can't give it up. Gerald Long had some link with my father. What if I could clear his name? I'll never believe my father was capable of all they printed about him.'

His stare intensified and he lifted a grey brow. 'What has this to do with Ted Carrington?'

'I'm talking about my real father, Laurence Shelton.' She had forgotten that she hadn't seen Bill to talk to properly since the car accident. 'After the car crash my memory returned. My father was a member of Parliament. He was close to Gerald Long. I remember Long coming to our house. Laurence Shelton disappeared a month after I was found by Ted and Lily. The papers branded him a traitor. He couldn't be. It's all lies. It must be. Some cover-up. And Gerald Long is behind it.'

Bill turned abruptly away from her to stare out of the window. 'You don't know what you could be getting into. I believe Long is capable of murder. He has the right contacts within the underworld. In the past he's been part of some shady deals which if known would destroy his political career.'

'Like dodgy arms deals? I had some facts and dates from Freddie Eastern on those. Luckily they were in my handbag when the house was burgled.'

Bill remained silent, his stance tense as he stared out of the window.

'I'm not going to give up,' she asserted. 'What information have you got for me? Is it on Long?'

'Shona, I don't want you getting involved. Hand the information over to the police.'

She studied him closely, puzzled by his manner. He

sounded angry. It made her defensive. 'As yet I haven't got the proof I need against him. The police won't act against such an eminent figure on hearsay. And don't forget I could clear my father's name. Perhaps then he could come back to England.'

He turned to face her, his voice gruff. 'He's probably dead, Shona.'

'No, he isn't.' Her anguish was bright in her eyes. 'I'd feel it. We were once so close – more so than I was to my mum. I don't remember her very well at all.'

Bill rubbed his beard, his stare penetrating as he regarded her. 'Have you considered that your father never contacted you because he feared it could place you in danger? I remember Shelton's story. He's a wanted man.' His manner was again guarded. 'Information against Long involving anything which went on during the war could cost you your life.' His restraint broke and with unexpected passion he gripped her arms. 'Just leave it, Shona!'

'So you *do* know something. Do you want a man like that to remain in power?' she accused.

He dropped his hands to his side and she could see him wrestling with his emotion.

Forcefully, she proceeded. 'What if Long became his party leader? He could be Prime Minister. England deserves better than a common crook. Because that's what you're making him sound like. What do you know about him? Have you proof?'

'When did you first realise that you were being followed?'

'A couple of months ago.' She searched her mind to recall exactly when. 'I'd made several calls to Long's press office.' She gave a bitter laugh. 'Do you know that for years I wondered if I was Long's bastard daughter. A photo of him and Shelton together showed that they were of similar colour and build. It tricked my faulty memory. Anyway, I phoned his press office because I'd discovered some press cuttings linking Shelton's name with Gerald Long. And then of course there was the story of Shelton's defection. I was so certain that Shelton was innocent. I wanted to learn more of the mystery. I was driven I suppose. I got nothing from the press office but it was about that time I was aware that someone was following me.'

Bill had been rubbing his beard as she spoke and now gave a derisive laugh. 'You must have scared the hell out of Long by those calls.' His expression sobered. 'But he couldn't afford to act rashly. Long needed to be certain that you had proof. Hence the burglary.'

'So my car crash was no accident.' Shona pieced together other events. 'He must have guessed I was getting close to something when I tackled him at the party meeting.'

Her eyes were over-bright as Shona regarded him, her figure stiff. Bill stared at her for a long time in silence and when he spoke his voice was strained. 'Forget Long. It's a matter for the police.'

Shona glared at him. Her mind was in turmoil, disjointed thoughts chasing one another as she assimilated these facts. She took a deep breath to calm down. Bill had often given her sound advice in the past. He would never try to frighten her off a case if he did not believe she was in danger. Was she being stubborn in persisting? Special Branch, MI5 or whichever department dealt with these matters would bring Gerald Long to justice. Perhaps it was wise to back off. Except it went against the grain. And she still needed proof before any government department would investigate. If Bill had that information she had to try another way of getting him to reveal it to her.

'I'm being stubborn and you're right, Bill,' she finally admitted.

He visibly relaxed. 'Sit down. You're all keyed up. I want to help, but I'll do nothing if it means you could get hurt.

You think a lot of Ted,' he said solemnly. 'So why are you so obsessed with finding out about your father?'

'Because I know he loved me and I adored him.' She broke off. Tears filled her eyes and she blinked them away. 'Forgive me. I'm not usually this emotional. It's been a traumatic day.'

He reached across and patted her hand. 'I'm glad you confided in me.'

She smiled. 'Thanks for being here and listening. I always find it hard to talk to Dad about new information I have about my father. I feel I'm betraying him after all he's done. I'd never hurt him.'

'I'm sure he knows that. He's a lucky man.'

Bill fell silent and Shona was lost in her own thoughts and did not answer. It was some moments before Bill spoke again. 'They say there's no such thing as coincidence. Before I enlisted in the army for the war I worked for a couple of years in Whitehall. I knew of Laurence Shelton. I'd left by the time he disappeared. I didn't believe he was a traitor.'

'How well did you know him?' Shona sat forward on her seat, her heart racing with expectancy.

'I said I knew of him,' he reminded her guardedly. 'I saw him at a few of the functions and around the building. He was ambitious and was often in Gerald Long's company. Long had influential friends even in those days. That was before Long got into politics.'

'Did you like my father?'

'He was a decent enough chap. He liked fast cars. The good life. He thought Long was the rising star to follow. That was probably his downfall.'

She put aside her prejudices against Long at this unexpected chance to learn more of her family. 'I remember there were lots of parties at our house. Did you ever meet my mother? All I remember is that her name was Amy and she was dark-haired.'

'Shelton kept his life outside of Parliament very private. There were always rumours. Your mother was reputedly beautiful.'

She was disappointed that he knew so little. 'My father did know something which endangered his life. That day in the car he spoke of someone called the Big Man. Was that the nickname given to Long by his friends, do you think?'

'I heard Long called that once. What else do you remember?'

She told Bill all she could recall about her parents and past. When she spoke of the day her mother had been shot tears streamed unchecked down her face. 'Daddy was out there in the fog calling to me. I couldn't find him. I was frightened. So very frightened.'

Bill looked distraught. 'You shouldn't speak to anyone of this. If Long thought you knew so much and it was him involved that day—'

He broke away from her, his voice becoming gruff and impatient. 'Something's got to be done. But not by you, Shona. Promise me, you'll drop this story. If you act now you'll be signing Freddie Eastern's death warrant if not your own.'

To avoid a direct promise she wasn't sure she could keep, she evaded by saying, 'Then at least tell me what you know about Long. I deserve that much at least.'

'It could be no more than what you've already discovered by yourself. He married a wealthy woman. Her father died a year before the war and Long's wife inherited the lot. She didn't have much time to enjoy her inheritance. Ten months later she died in a car accident. The brakes failed on a steep hill near their home. The car went over the bridge at the bottom and into the river.'

'That's well documented. The Coroner's verdict was accidental death.'

'The marriage was a turbulent one,' Bill continued. 'Her

death made Long an exceedingly rich man and again free to pursue his playboy lifestyle. The brakes could have been tampered with.'

Shona was more interested in the years when Long knew Shelton. 'I know those factories he inherited from his wife produced armaments during the war. I also suspect that faulty weapons were sold to the forces. The information Eastern gave me points to shipments of illegal arms to guerrilla forces where countries were involved in civil war.'

Bill had got up while she spoke and was pacing the room. 'That's why you have to forget the story, Shona. Long won't risk exposure. I expect there's a lot more in Long's past he wants hidden.'

Her heart began to beat faster. The danger to herself became frighteningly real. 'You've as good as told me that Long was the Big Man. If he'd killed once he wouldn't hesitate to kill again.'

'You've no proof your mother was murdered. It could just have been a warning, an injury severe enough to frighten your father.'

Shona wasn't convinced. 'But they threatened to hunt him down. That they'd get him wherever he went, or however long it took. They're responsible for my father's disappearance and him abandoning me. They are answerable for that.'

Bill slumped in a chair. 'Doesn't that persuade you that your life is now in danger? Those robbers were Long's men. If they've got your files and notes they know you're on to him. Have they got all the proof you'd accumulated against Long?'

'No. I had Eastern's notes in my handbag.'

'Let me have them.'

Shona hesitated. She trusted Bill but they were all she had left against Long.

'Take a copy of them if you want, then at least there will be a duplicate if anything else happens.'

Her eyes widened with fear. Obviously she had uncovered something sinister involving a very dangerous man who had already murdered to prevent this information becoming popular knowledge.

'What will you do with these facts?'

'No one knows I have this information. There's no danger to me,' Bill assured. 'What would you have me do with them?'

She spread her arms in defeat and there were tears in her eyes. 'All I wanted was to discover who my father was and if he was alive to be reunited with him. Now Eastern is fearing for his safety and I could be placing you in danger. Also, if my father *is* alive I could be making it harder for him to come out of hiding. But if I stay silent . . . ?'

Her eyes pleaded with Bill to give her the solution. His expression was full of compassion but he did not speak to reassure her.

Loyalty and justice continued their combat, tearing her apart as her heart made the only decision possible for the good of the people. 'I haven't a choice, have I? If these documents are so important, then a copy should be made but put in a bank for safe keeping. I'll post them when I leave here. I don't want to risk Long's thugs getting this information. That would put Eastern's life in danger.'

'Let me give the information to the authorities. My time at Whitehall will lend it some weight.'

'Who will you take them to?'

Bill looked grave. 'It's best if you don't know the facts. Deny any existence of this information if Long should get hold of you, which I pray he won't. You can't be too careful, Shona.'

'If you've got some paper I'll copy out these dates and facts.' The copy made and placed in Bill's hands she felt wretched. It wasn't just because of the danger. What would her real father think of her for turning against him?

'You've done the right thing, Shona.'

'Have I? I feel I've betrayed my father. I've destroyed any chance of a reunion. If he comes back to England now even though innocent of being a traitor, he could still be imprisoned as Long's accomplice.'

'Your father should have given this information to the authorities when he found out. He wasn't a scoundrel but an honourable man. He could never be sure that Long wouldn't get back at him through you. It sounds like he loved you too much to risk your life to bring Long to justice.'

'I suppose so. There was a lot of publicity over Ted and Lily's right to adopt me when my parents never came forward. My photo was in the papers. Long was often at our house and would have known who I was.'

Bill nodded. 'While you remembered nothing of the car crash or your parents, Long was safe. He'd have kept a discreet watch on you over the years.'

Shona shuddered. 'That makes me feel unclean. I never suspected anything until recently.'

'When you became interested in Shelton, it would have alerted him that perhaps your memory had returned.'

Shona nodded then remembered her reason for coming here apart from wanting his advice. 'Didn't you have some information for me, Bill?'

'It was sort of linked with Long and what we've discussed today. To be on the safe side, don't go back to your house. It's too dangerous for you to be alone. You can stay here if you want. I'll sleep on the sofa. Or you could do worse than letting Nick Blake know what's been happening. He's a man who knows how to look after himself and others.'

Shona shook her head. 'Nick is no longer a part of my life. He wasn't impressed that my new boyfriend was a copper. I'll stay at Greg's flat. Even Long will think twice about causing trouble there. He's a detective.'

Bill didn't look convinced. 'Nick would never let you down

if you needed him. How long have you known this new chap? Can he protect you?'

She didn't take offence at Bill's questions. After her outpourings this afternoon she felt closer to him than ever. Theirs was an odd relationship. A respectful friendship which bordered on something deeper.

'Are you sure you can trust this Greg?'

'He's a detective. What better protection could I have? And although we haven't known each other long, I know he cares for me. I trust him.'

Chapter Twenty-five

Bill insisted on driving Shona to Greg Jackson's flat. As he watched her ring the doorbell he was unsettled. The man who answered looked tall and brawny enough to protect her, but still he remained uneasy. The envelope in his pocket was as weighty as a millstone.

On the drive to Scotland Yard he stopped off at a pub. He had his own fears to wrestle with. He had sought anonymity for too long to relinquish it easily. It was time to face his demons.

First he rang Ted but couldn't get him at the stadium. He then tried Nick at his warehouse. He was given another number where he could be contacted.

'Why are you ringing me?' Nick barked down the phone. 'Shona's made it clear she doesn't want anything to do with me.'

'Shona's never stopped loving you. But you hurt her badly. Do you reckon this new bloke can protect her? Because I believe she's in danger. I trust you. I don't know this new man she's involved with – copper or not – I don't trust him.'

Nick let out a harsh breath. 'Jackson ain't good enough for Shona that's for certain. But he looks like he can handle himself.'

Bill was exasperated at Nick's manner. The man's pride was placing Shona in danger. 'Are you saying you don't care what happens to Shona?'

Nick didn't answer and Bill's tone became urgent. 'Don't

let her down. She does need you. This is serious or I wouldn't be contacting you. We have to speak. I'm on my way to Scotland Yard with information about Long and there could be difficulties. I need you to keep watch on Jackson's flat.'

'OK. Where are you?'

Nick had initially been tempted to tell Bill Miles to go to hell. He had never understood Shona's friendship with the man. Seeing Shona with Greg Jackson had shaken him badly. He'd never stopped loving her. He had bided his time waiting for time to heal her anger and resentment. He admitted he deserved her scorn. He'd been an arrogant, selfish idiot in those days. He thought he could wrap her around his finger and charm her into anything. She had proved otherwise.

When Shona ditched him he had come to his senses with a jolt. He had always been convinced that they'd get back together. He didn't believe that Shona was as indifferent to him as she portrayed. He'd seen the old attraction flare in her eyes in an unguarded moment. The theatre visit and meal had proved that it could work.

Then he had seen Jackson at Shona's house. He had so obviously spent the night with her. Jealousy had knifed him. For the first time he understood what Shona had suffered when he played around. How could he have been such a fool? Remorse humbled him. Shona had proved she did not need him.

Greg looked startled to see Shona. When she blurted out her reasons for coming he clasped her close.

'My darling, you did the right thing coming here. How did you escape being followed?'

'Bill brought me.' Her eyes misted with affection. Bill had been wonderful, so supportive and understanding. She found it easier to talk to him than anyone. When his car pulled up outside Greg's flat, Bill had been tense with worry for her.

338

'You take care of yourself,' he said gruffly.

Shona kissed him on the cheek and his arms went round her. 'Don't feel down about betraying your father. He'd understand.'

'Thanks, Bill. That helps but it doesn't ease the guilt.'

'You're doing the right thing.'

Now in Greg's flat her doubts returned. It was the first time she had been here and it smelt damp and unlived in. It was also cluttered with old newspapers and clothes strewn across every chair. Greg snatched up a jumper and jeans from the settee for her to sit down. The spring twanged as she put her weight on it. The flat was typical of rented accommodation with sagging, scuffed armchairs, a faded bold-patterned carpet square and dingy floral wallpaper.

'It's a bit of a dump. I'm not here that much. It's only temporary until I buy a place of my own.'

Greg seemed edgy. 'So you think the burglary was down to Long?' he cross-examined her.

'Who else would take his file?'

'Did they take everything?'

'Thankfully not. I had the most important facts in my handbag. I've mailed a copy of them to my bank for safe keeping and the originals are being handed to Scotland Yard.'

His face whitened. 'And you didn't trust me enough to do that?'

The vehemence in his voice pricked her conscience. 'You weren't there at the time.'

'Is Bill Miles taking them?' He looked angry and Shona was uncomfortable at his accusing tone.

'Yes.'

'How much does he know about Long?'

'A great deal.'

'So who is he?'

'Why all the questions?' She didn't like this interrogation. 'He's a friend. A good friend.'

339

Greg held up his hands in mock submission. 'Sorry. I don't mean to sound like the heavy-handed policeman. Habit I suppose. But this sounds serious. I can't help you if I don't know all the facts.'

He took her face in his hands, his stare searching. 'Why didn't you tell me? I could help you. What do you think Long has done in the past which is so terrible?'

She pulled away from him. 'Dodgy arms deals during the war. Supplying arms to terrorists. Suspected murder. Attempted murder. Do you want more?'

His expression was taut. 'You did right to come here. Look, I've got nothing in to eat. I'll go and get us some fish and chips down the chippie. Don't answer the phone or open the door to anyone. No one else but this Bill knows you're here, do they?'

She shook her head and his expression relaxed. He picked up his jacket and went out leaving her prey to her doubts. He seemed to be gone for an eternity and her nerves were tattered by the time he returned.

'The chippie was packed and I had to wait for them to cook some more fish.'

He put on an Ella Fitzgerald LP and brought in two plates for the chips. They both sat on the settee. 'Are you all right eating off your lap? I don't have a table. I don't eat in that much.'

'This is fine. I don't think I can eat anyway.'

Greg tucked into his fish while Shona toyed with her food. She couldn't swallow. Greg put his plate down on the floor and took Shona's from her. He moved closer and put his arm around her.

'You're safe with me.'

When he began to kiss her, she responded. After the fears of the day it was good to feel the strength of his arms around her. Yet when his hands became more demanding, sliding along her thigh, she tensed and pulled away. 'I'm sorry, Greg. I guess I'm not in the mood. I'm worried about Bill.'

Greg got up and poured himself a stiff whisky and drank it down. His face was harsh. This was a side to him she had yet to come to terms with: the way he hid his emotions. Even at Brighton when he had been at his most fun-loving and passionate, she had sensed that he was holding back. Yet what did she know of this man? Their encounters were few and clouded by the instant attraction and the flaring of passion between them. He had told her a little of his background, but what were his aspirations or his ideals? He had been quick to laughter on that carefree day but what made him angry? What plight or injustice moved him? What were his interests aside from his classic car? These were the fundamentals of the man. She hadn't pierced through the outer shell.

When he turned to face her the tension had left his features. 'Is this Bill more important to you than me?'

His jealousy startled her and was out of context. 'Perhaps I shouldn't have come here, Greg. I don't expect my boyfriends to question my loyalty to old friends.'

'I was out of order. Forgive me.' He sat beside her and took her hands. 'I'm having trouble coming to terms with all this.'

'So am I. It has all come to a head so quickly. And I hate having placed Bill in this position.'

'He offered to go to the police. You didn't force him.'

She sighed, her heart weighted with guilt. 'There's bound to be awkward questions. Bill has always been a private man. And Long is a respected Member of Parliament.'

'From what you told me you should be worried about your own safety. What put you on to his treachery?'

'It's a complicated story. Sometimes it feels that the wheel has gone full circle. I think Long was responsible for my father's disappearance. My real father.'

It all poured out about her past and her investigations. Greg was silent throughout. She could feel the tension build in him until he sprang from the settee and paced the room.

She added in a low voice, 'The ironic thing is it began because I wanted to track down my father. Now I'm embroiled in all this and have got no closer to finding him.'

'Given time, you will though, won't you?' It was an accusation not a compliment. 'Once you start something you don't give up on it.'

'I suppose not.'

Greg looked strained. 'God, this is a mess, Shona. Long isn't a man to cross.'

'If he's guilty, he deserves whatever he's got coming to him,' she blustered. It was hard to keep up her bravado. She was beginning to suspect that she was in deeper than she could handle. To clarify another point which still worried her, she asked, 'Did you find Elsie Hannigan's murderer? Was her death linked to Long?'

'Why should it be?'

'Because I had been talking to her about her life in the old days when she knew Long. What if we were seen together?'

'Nothing as yet has been linked to Long. It's a line of enquiries we're still pursuing.'

The phone in the kitchen rang and they stared at each other. Greg looked haggard and Shona's heart pounded, her nerves at screaming point by the constant ringing.

'You'd better answer it, Greg. It could be Bill.'

He seemed reluctant and went out and closed the door behind him. Shona sank her head into her hands. She hated sitting here doing nothing. What if Bill got into trouble because of her? The police would want to know how he came by such information. They might want to check his credentials as a reliable informant. What if he had something in his past he didn't want coming to light? That would explain his reticence to speak of his life.

She could hear Greg's raised voice on the phone but his words were indistinct. When he returned his eyes were glittering with a fierce light and his mouth was clamped into a tight line.

'Is something wrong, Greg?'

'I've been called in to the station. Something has come up on a case I was working on. I've said I can't make it for a couple of hours. It won't hurt the villain they've pulled in to sweat it out in a cell until then. I want to get you away from here. To make sure you're safe.'

'I'm not going anywhere until I hear from Bill and find out what Scotland Yard intend to do with the information.'

'Don't be stubborn, Shona. Long will want you silenced. And I can't be here to protect you. If Long has had you trailed, then they'll know I've been seeing you and track down my address.'

Fear widened her eyes and sent icy shivers through her body. 'Long won't make a move if he knows the information has gone to the police. That will only prove his guilt!'

'He'll make sure your death looks like an accident.' His voice was harsh and he knelt at her side. 'We can't take chances. I've just checked outside. There's no strange cars in the road. If we go now we should give them the slip.'

She didn't like going away without any of her family or friends knowing where she was. 'I can't go without telling Dad.'

'It's safer for them if they don't know. It will only be for a couple of days. Until we learn what's happened about Long.'

His words unnerved her. She no longer felt in control. Her instinct was to stay but Greg was a policeman, he would know how a criminal mind worked and the best course of action. She had to trust him. Even so, she questioned, 'But what if the police want to contact me to substantiate Bill's story?'

'You'll be no use to them dead.'

She gave a horrified gasp at the brutality of his statement.

'I don't want to frighten you, Shona, but you've got into something which is extremely dangerous. You know too much. How can Long allow you to live? You have to get away. And I know the very place. It's a cottage my family own on the Thames past Windsor. We can stay there. The longer we delay, the harder it will be to get away.'

'But I'll still be alone at this cottage.'

'Only for a couple of hours. Then I'll be back. Look, I could telephone a mate on the force. He's ex-army, a big bloke. He'll be there.'

Shona's head was whirling. She was frightened enough to clutch at straws. The danger was real. Elsie Hannigan's death proved that.

'I'm not going. Drop me off at Scotland Yard. I'll find out what's happened about Bill's statement and stay there until I know something is being done about it. They can't hurt me at Scotland Yard.'

'The Yard isn't like an ordinary nick. You can't just drop in.'

'Then I'll go to Bow Street or one of the bigger Metropolitan stations.' Her face brightened.

'OK. If that's the way you want it. I'll get my stuff.'

He hustled her out of the flat and into his sports car which had the hood up. Before he got in he said tersely, 'I've got to get something out of the boot.'

'Don't be angry with me, Greg,' she began as he got in the car.

There was a whiff of something strong and sweet. Then he gripped the back of her head and pressed a handkerchief against her face.

'Sorry, Shona. It wasn't meant to happen like this.'

The chloroform filled her nostrils. She fought against its

suffocating sweet fumes, tasting it on her tongue. The anaesthetic quickly robbed her limbs of strength. She was powerless.

Chapter Twenty-six

Shona returned to consciousness when her body was jolted violently. Agony ground through her shoulders and back. Her head ached and her senses were dulled. There was a foul taste in her mouth and a cloying sweet smell lingering in the air.

Her senses remained disorientated. It was dark and the vibrations going through her body coupled with a steady droning sound told her she was in a car. Memory returned. Greg had drugged her – betrayed her.

To her horror she realised that her hands and feet were tied and she was lying supine with a rough blanket over her head. There was also a gag in her mouth.

Her first instinct was to scream or cry out. Fear kept her silent and under the suffocating claustrophobia of the blanket she began to breathe heavily. She concentrated to pull her lethargic senses together and focus her mind. When a bubble of sickness rose from her stomach, she fought to control it. Her dry throat rasped as she swallowed it down. With the gag in her mouth, if the vomit overwhelmed her she could choke to death.

Inhaling deeply several times through her nose, Shona struggled to conquer her fear and become calm. Panic would weaken her. Gradually her breathing slowed and her stomach no longer roiled queasily.

He must be a copper on Long's payroll. Why else would she be abducted in so ruthless a fashion? Again panic and fear swelled and she battled to overcome them. She had to think clearly, her life depended on it.

Shona strained her ears to detect sounds and try and discern her whereabouts. When she first became aware of her surroundings, other cars had passed them in the opposite direction. Within the last minutes Greg had turned off the main road and the sound of traffic had faded. No car had passed them since then. Neither were there sounds of habitation. They must have left London. In the muffled distance she thought she heard a ship's foghorn sound. Were they travelling to the cottage near Windsor or had Greg headed out to the Thames estuary and the remote Essex marsh land where it would be easier to hide a body?

The bonds around her ankles were tight and both her legs were leaden. Shona wriggled her toes to encourage the circulation to return and was speared by cramp. She bit into the gag to control her groans of pain. When the spasm finally faded perspiration spangled her brow and the pain was replaced by the tingling of pins and needles as the blood began to flow. It brought with it another onset of pain and a gasp was forced from her lips.

'You're awake then?' Greg's gruff voice smote her. 'I didn't want it to be like this.'

He slowed the car and reached back to flip the blanket away from her face. 'I'm sorry, Shona. You gave me no choice. This may look drastic but it will be all right. I had to get you to this meeting.'

Did he think she was a child who could be calmed by inane words? He'd abducted her. He wouldn't have bound her if he hadn't feared she'd escape. Adrenalin pumped in scalding waves through her as her anger rose. She had allowed her attraction to this man to cloud her judgement.

Her eyes blazed up at him seeing his pale, taut expression in the driving mirror. Loathing burned in her. How could she have been such a fool? Greg had swept her off her feet, wooing and seducing, tricking her by his false ardour.

He held her stare in the mirror and she saw his face muscles become more rigid.

'Don't look at me like that,' he ground out. 'I had no choice. It will be all right. I swear it. I'll take care of you, Shona. I won't let anything happen to you.'

Disgusted by his two-faced lies, she turned her head away.

His voice rose a pitch. 'I *do* care for you. Hell, I'm in love with you! I didn't intend for it to happen, but it did. Trust me.'

Her eyes blazed as she turned her stare on him and he looked away, his expression tight with shame.

'OK, I deserve your scorn,' he continued. 'I shouldn't have tied you up. I had to be sure you wouldn't run out on me when you came round.' He was silent for several moments, his breathing harsh as he drove down a dark, winding, country road.

She gazed through the car window and saw the greyness of a thickening night mist. Her heart jumped against her breastbone. She had been lying on the back seat of a car with a thickening mist distorting the wayside trees the day her mother had been shot. Was it now her turn? Had the wheel gone full circle?

At this time of year it was often misty at night in the Essex countryside, especially close to a river. She tried to be rational and reasonable, but the mist had been part of her nightmares for years. It had cloaked her memory, masking her search for her identity. It had always been a part of her inner terror and vulnerability.

She pushed herself into a half-sitting position and stared through the roadside trees searching for a familiar landscape. The darkness and stillness of the mist were those of isolation and separation.

A sinister dark shape with widespread iron arms loomed through the mist in an adjoining field. It was a sand or gravel pit. How often had she read of a body or skeleton being discovered in the workings of these numerous pits dotted throughout Essex?

Greg had seen her movement and slowed the car. 'Get down. Do as you're told or I'll have to use the chloroform again.'

'Bastard!' she gritted through her gag but complied with his order. It was not an idle threat. Unconscious she would have no chance to save herself if the need arose.

They drove on and all she could see were the branches of overhanging trees. A dog barked and a train whistle carried to her. Habitation? But where were they? Her teeth rattled as they bounced over a railway crossing without slowing down. The mist was thinner here. Street lamps brightened the night sky and she sensed they were travelling through a village. Within moments it was behind them and the darkness again closed in. They drove a few more miles then Greg swerved on to a rutted track. The car lurched sickeningly and halted. Just visible was a single grey building which was in darkness.

Greg got out of the car, opened Shona's door and dragged her out. When he lifted her bound figure into his arms, she began to struggle, her curses smothered by the gag.

'Don't fight me,' he ordered. 'It won't do any good.'

She knew she was wasting her energy. Her legs were again numb and unless she was untied and the circulation returned she would never be able to get away. She went limp in his hold, her eyes condemning him.

He cursed softly. 'I'm not delivering you trussed up like a Christmas turkey.' He laid her on the ground and untied her legs and wrists. She hunched over in pain as the circulation returned and he kept hold of her arms so she couldn't make a run for it. When the pain subsided and she lifted her hands to remove the gag, he stopped her. 'There's no one near who will respond if you scream but I can't take any chances.'

His hands remained clamped on her arms as he propelled her towards the isolated building. It was an old deserted chapel. At some time there must have been a hamlet here but any sign of habitation had long disappeared.

A tremor went through her and Greg's arms tightened around her. 'I'm sorry, sweetheart,' he whispered, repeating, 'I had no choice but to bring you to this meeting. It's going to be all right. I'm not going to let anyone hurt you.'

'Then you're a fool.' The words were muffled by her gag but she felt him stiffen as he felt her anger and scorn. She wanted to rant at him. Having gone this far Long couldn't let her live. At the very least she could lay charges against him for abduction. If only Greg would remove the gag she could reason with him.

Greg knocked three times on the chapel door and it was opened. Several candles lit the interior, mocking its once hallowed structure. The narrow slit windows were shuttered from the inside allowing no light to escape and give away their presence. Graffiti was daubed across the walls and the atmosphere was chilly. Three men stood where the altar would once have been and a fourth was slumped on the ground. Nausea gripped her. It must be Freddie Eastern. They'd got to him and she was responsible.

'Miss Carrington.' Gerald Long's voice boomed out. 'Or should I say Miss Grace Shelton?'

Shona knew then that she would never leave here alive.

'You can remove the gag, Jackson,' Long clipped out.

The touch of Greg's hands against her hair was now so repellent to her, Shona flinched as he untied the gag. 'I hope you're proud of yourself,' she said just loud enough for him to hear.

Turning away, her attention focused on Gerald Long. He was dressed in a dinner suit and bow tie. 'I'm honoured you have deemed fit to dress for the occasion.' Nerves and battling against her fear made her sarcastic in an attempt at bravado. 'Had I received a formal invitation I would have dressed accordingly. The expression is "dressed to kill", isn't it? Except you never dirty your hands. You have pet henchmen for that purpose.'

'Your father had a wicked way with words. He also didn't know when to keep silent.' His expression was cruel with impatience. 'I've a political reception to attend in an hour. Forgive me, Miss Shelton, if I cut short the pleasantries.'

'How long have you known my identity? What made you suspicious?'

He gave a cold mocking laugh. 'I've always known who you were. I'd forgotten the child when your father escaped us. The news coverage on your loss of memory was extensive. I could have had you killed then. Children often know more than what is good for them and they can be indiscreet.'

He began to pace the small chapel, his head jutted forward from a thick-set body. His figure might have looked ridiculous in its penguin suit but he emanated arrogance, pompous self-purpose and cold-blooded menace. Shona had thought Bill had exaggerated when he said she could have been watched in the hope of trapping her father if he came for her. Her feeling of vulnerability increased and she glanced at Greg who had moved back into the shadows. So much for his protestations of love. He was distancing himself from her, a bought and paid-for traitor.

Gerald Long shot her a withering glare, his voice harsh and echoing like a vengeful fire-and-brimstone preacher's in the acoustics of the vaulted chapel. 'Your lack of memory saved you and also the fierce possessiveness of Lily Carrington, who never let you out of her sight. But I've kept myself informed of your progress over the years. I always believed that Laurence Shelton would return to England. He doted on you. Through you I would have him.'

'It was a fruitless wait.'

'I had thought so until earlier today. I should have known Shelton was devious enough to try and outwit me. He almost succeeded.'

What was the man talking about? Had Greg made up some bizarre story to increase his standing with this creep? Her scorn erupted both for the two men and the humiliating way she was being treated. 'But I've had no contact with my father. In fact I've not got very far with my search to find him. As you will have learned from my files your men stole. You've been misled.'

Long's thin lips curled back into a sneer. 'You should have heeded the break-in as a warning. I had underestimated your stubbornness. Neither after all these years had I expected your father to jeopardise his freedom by going to the police.'

Shona frowned, confused by his words. Fear was making her breathe too shallowly and her head was fuzzy from lack of oxygen. She couldn't have heard him properly. She took a controlled deep breath. If she didn't breathe properly she'd faint and that would be the end of her. To her relief her voice barely quivered although its tone was shrill. 'Are you telling me my father is in England?'

There was a low groan from the man on the floor. She stared at him. His face had been beaten. Both eyes were closed and blackened and blood streaked from his nose, lips and cheeks. He was unrecognisable. Then Shona saw his suit and the splash of colour of his tie.

Her senses reeling with shock she staggered forward. 'That's Bill Miles. What have you done to him? He was only trying to help me.'

Her hands hooked into talons and with a scream of outrage she launched herself at Long. The violence of her attack took him and his men by surprise. She managed to furrow one cheek with her nails before a blow to her jaw spread-eagled her on the ground.

Greg bounded forward and laid into the man who had hit her. 'You don't lay a finger on her, that was the deal.'

Both men now turned on him, one pinning his arms behind him whilst the other thudded three punches into his stomach and doubled him over.

Long nodded for the man to stop hitting Greg but the other still held him tight. Greg's face was twisted in agony as he slowly straightened. Long rapped out, 'I don't pay you to voice your opinions, Jackson. Keep out of this.'

Shona hauled herself to her feet and shook her head to clear her senses. She'd been winded and her jaw ached from the punch she'd received. Long was scowling at her malevolently.

'So you never knew Miles was your father? It was a surprise to me that the once immaculate and proud Shelton had spent years as a down and out – a drunkard. If my men hadn't been keeping an eye on Jackson's flat, in case you turned up there after you gave the others the slip, he would have got to Scotland Yard where he was headed. They followed him and picked him up as soon as they realised he was going to the police.'

'You've got it wrong,' she insisted. 'Bill isn't my father. He's a friend.'

Long gave a derisive snort. 'You can't save him by lying. He fooled me and the law. Shelton was one of England's most wanted criminals.'

'Because you trumped up charges against him. He was never a spy.' Shona was shaking now but not from fear. She was incensed at so much injustice. 'You're the one who betrayed our country selling faulty weapons to our soldiers. How many died needlessly through your greed?'

'Plenty of others made their fortunes in the war. I was no more unscrupulous than them.' He paused to rub his chin. 'What an idealist you are. Just like your father. He should have destroyed this.' He held up a brown leather notebook.

'It states he's Laurence Shelton. I couldn't allow the police to find out what else it contained.'

Shona paled. The notebook looked like one her father had owned. Long put the notebook inside his jacket, his expression sneering. 'Shelton's disappearance condemned him without trial. If he had tried to resist arrest they would have shot him. Unfortunately, it never came to that and I am still left to finish what should have been done in 1940. Except now you will join Shelton in a hidden grave.'

She saw Greg stiffen. 'You said nothing about any killing. You won't get away with it.'

'I leave nothing to chance,' Long rapped out. 'This reckoning is long overdue.'

His threats only dimly registered in Shona's brain. The candles cast giant macabre shadows of their figures up to the ceiling. The coldness and dark of the chapel added to the menace crackling in the air.

Shona stared at Bill who was beginning to stir. Her thoughts raced seeking answers. Was he her father? A tramp's disguise would have given him anonymity. He had often watched her when she worked on Percy's stall. Had he been watching over her throughout her childhood? As others had watched her: Long's men bent upon exposing her father. Had Bill been aware of that? Even after they became friends he had kept his identity a secret. And he had never spoken of his past.

A strange constriction lodged in her heart. Slowly it expanded and swelled. She had always wondered why Bill had responded to her simple acts of kindness and upon her urging made the effort to better himself. In those early years of their acquaintance he had been surly, uncommunicative to others and caring nothing if they despised him. He may have resisted her help at first, but it had taken little persuasion to win him round. At the time she had been surprised by her own tenacity to get him to trust her. He had been an enigma. Or had it been something in her unconscious mind that had driven her – a subconscious recognition – for such a bond to build between them?

For her Bill had shed the anonymity of the tramp, disguised only by his beard and grey hair. It explained his frequent job changes and moves of house. Yet why hadn't she recognised him if he was her father?

Her stare sharpened and her memory surfed through old images and photographs of her past. Maturity had fleshed out the high, angular cheekbones and changed the facial contours of the man she had known in her childhood. Again she was drawn back to recall the ease with which a bond had formed between them. Yet she had never thought of it as incongruous.

As she stared down at his beaten figure she was overwhelmed with the need to hold him in her arms. She took two steps towards him before she was stopped by Long's henchman.

'Please, can't I even see how he is?' Her voice was thready and tears were streaming unheeded down her cheeks. 'How did you know he was going to Scotland Yard?'

When Long didn't answer, she knew the answer. She turned to Greg, fury stinging her cheeks with colour. 'You told them. You betrayed our trust. Pleased with yourself, are you? God, I can't believe how easily I fell for it. And you a bent copper. The most despicable of men. Damn you, Greg Jackson!'

He had the grace to look shame-faced. His tall body was tense and a muscle twitched along his jaw. Disgusted at him and at herself for being duped, she turned away and this time wasn't prevented from kneeling beside Bill's prone figure. She still couldn't take in that he was her father.

Behind her she heard Greg and Long arguing in harsh whispers but she didn't register their words. What had been revealed to her was too important.

Her throat worked painfully as she took in Bill's battered appearance. She guessed they were both going to die tonight and she still knew so little about him.

He was watching her through his swollen lids. 'I messed up, Shona. Like I messed up in 1940. I never forgave myself for leaving you behind.'

The doubts about his identity fled. Bill was her father. She could feel the warmth of a deep abiding affection emanating between them. He smiled, a sad, tragic grimace distorted by his pain; but it was an echo of a thousand such smiles from her childhood.

'This is all my fault, isn't it?' Her voice was husky with anguish. 'You warned me not to pursue my investigations.'

Bill pushed himself into a sitting position and coughed up a globule of blood. He wiped it away with his hands. 'I'm ashamed for you to see me like this. As I was when you tried to help me as a tramp.' His face was grey with pain and he cradled his ribs where they must have kicked him.

'I should have dealt with Long myself years ago. I knew he had a watch kept on you. I feared that if I spoke out the lies Long had spread about me would weaken my case. I was also afraid that he'd take his vengeance out on you. If you were safe that was all that mattered.' He coughed and wiped away another trickle of blood.

Shona's throat worked before she was able to speak. Emotion was threatening to overwhelm her. 'Why didn't you tell me you were my father? Didn't you trust me?'

'It was too dangerous. I couldn't allow us to get too close or see too much of each other. We would have given ourselves away. I'm sorry it had to end like this, kitten.'

The use of his childhood name for her unleashed the dam of her pent-up emotions. 'Oh, Daddy, Daddy.' She flung herself on to his chest and felt his hand gently stroke her hair.

Brutally she was wrenched away from him and held by one of Long's men. The other hauled her father to his feet. He gave a cry of agony and his head fell forward on to his chest.

'Stop it,' Shona demanded. 'He's badly hurt. Hasn't he suffered enough?'

'His suffering is about to end for good,' Long responded. He drew a revolver from the waistband of his dinner suit and pointed it towards her father.

'No!' Shona screamed.

The revolver swung round and Shona found herself looking down its barrel. Long raised his thumb and cocked the weapon. Her gaze was riveted on the finger which was tightening on the trigger. 'Then you will die first so Shelton can witness it.'

'Spare her,' her father pleaded.

'And lose the satisfaction of making you die knowing your life of secrecy was all in vain? No one makes a fool of me. You and the girl have to be made an example of.'

Outside there was the heavy throbbing of a motorbike engine. It drew to a halt in front of the chapel and the engine was cut. Long hesitated.

'Who the hell is that?' He nodded to one of the men to check outside. Shona seized her chance at the momentary distraction and bunched her fist, ramming it upwards with all her strength to contact with her captor's chin. At the same time she kicked out at his shin. He grunted and loosened his hold. She fled to the far side of the chapel.

'That's enough, Long.' The shout came from Greg. He had drawn a gun and was pointing it at the MP.

Then several things happened at once. Her father was thrown to the ground and the man who had been holding him drew a pistol. The air was rent with the sound of shots. Orange flashes filled the small building and the echoes rebounded off the walls making Shona's ears ring. She expected a bullet to smash into her body. There was no pain. Then through eyes wide with horror, she saw her father's figure twitch and lie still. They had shot him.

She screamed. Her expression was feral, as fierce as a cornered vixen. She half crouched, breath rasping in her throat and her lips drawn back into a snarl. Her stunned mind registered everything in slow motion. Gerald Long reeled back against the wall. His eyes were wide and staring and he slowly slid down the surface leaving a trail of blood in his wake.

Fear. Grief. Anger. Hatred. The violent emotions tumbled like boulders in a landslide through Shona, transfixing her in their wake.

There was a blast of cold air as the chapel door burst open and other vehicles skidded to a halt outside. Nick stood in the doorway.

Relief flared to be instantly doused. Not Nick as well. He couldn't sacrifice his life as well. How blindly and stubbornly she had led those she loved into danger.

'Run for it, Nick!' Shona shouted. 'They've got guns.'

'Stay back, Blake,' Greg rapped out. He pointed his gun at the man who had fired at Shona's father. 'Long's dead. There's no need for this to go further.'

The man who had held Shona was edging towards Nick. Nick had come to save her and now it looked as if they would all die. 'Watch out, Nick.'

Nick pivoted round and threw himself at the man. Two punches to his jaw and stomach flattened him on the ground. Eyes blazing, Nick spun round to confront Greg.

'Bastard! You won't get away with this. Let Shona go!' he demanded.

'Nick, be careful,' she pleaded. 'These are Long's men and Greg betrayed me to them. Don't trust him.'

She saw Greg's jaw tighten but a groan from her father made her discard the danger to herself and run to him. This might be her only chance to be with him as a loving daughter. He was lying very still. Frighteningly still.

Dread scoured her. Her shaking fingers sought a pulse at his throat and felt a weak response. She took his hand willing him to live.

'Don't die, Daddy. You can't die now. Not now I've just found you. I love you, Daddy.'

He opened his eyes and his hand weakly clasped hers. 'Forgive me.'

Tears blurred her vision. She was pouring all her concentration and energy into willing him to live and was only dimly aware of noises behind her.

'It's all over,' Greg yelled.

Again she braced herself against the impact of a bullet. She had allowed Greg to use her and betray her. He must have been Long's man all along. He had taken her to Brighton so that her house was empty and could be searched for evidence. And she had fallen for it.

She held her father's hand close to her heart and looked across at Nick who stood with his hands held wide. He carried no weapon. His handsome face was deathly white. Greg waved the gun towards him. The blood drummed in her ears so powerfully that she couldn't make sense of their words. In that moment Nick's eyes were stark with his love for her.

His image blurred as tears spilled from her lashes. Her pain was unbearable. Two men she had loved most dearly were about to die because of her stubbornness and stupidity.

Chapter Twenty-seven

'It's all over,' an unfamiliar voice shouted.

All at once the chapel seemed to be overrun with policemen shouting. A gun clattered to the floor. Shona scarcely noticed. Her father was breathing erratically and his chest rattled ominously. The hand he raised to hers was covered in blood. He had been shot through the lung.

'Forgive me, Grace. You will always be my little Grace to me.' He spoke with such laboured precision that she had to bend over him to hear. 'It was hard to accept that you had no memory of your name or past. Though it was for the best. It saved your life.' His face screwed up with pain.

'Don't talk. Save your strength.'

'I was Long's pawn. I should have realised what he was up to.' His speech was slower, interspersed with gasps. 'I should have stopped it.'

She brushed a tear from his cheek with a trembling hand. 'You must rest. An ambulance will be here soon.'

'Too late . . . I never stopped loving you . . . Needed to know you were safe . . . Not much of a father . . .'

'You were a wonderful father. More than you will ever know.' She forced the words through a cramped throat. 'Just get well, Daddy. There's so much I want to say. But why did you go to the police? You must have known the dangers. If Long had me followed, he was bound to finally make the connection between us.'

Sorrow mingled with pain in his eyes. 'I wanted to end the

secrecy. Wanted your respect . . . Clear my name . . . Ge
Long behind bars . . . before he hurt you. All information
you want . . . in a red book . . . amongst my things.' His
voice trailed off and he struggled for some moments to speak
'You're so like my mother. Knew you straight away . . . first
time I saw you in the market. She died when I was twelve. Her
name was Grace.' A shudder passed through his body. 'Love
you . . .' His hand became a heavy weight in her hand.

'Daddy!' Even as she screamed she saw the light glazing in
his eyes.

An arm slid around her shoulders. Nick's voice was gruff
'Come away, sweetheart.'

She shook him off and flung herself on to her father's chest
sobs wrenching from her.

Greg stood surrounded by the other policemen. He picked
the leather notebook from Long's pocket and handed it to an
inspector . . . 'Looks like this will close the case for us.'

His expression was haggard as he gazed at Shona. When he
made to move towards her, Nick intercepted him. 'Because
of you her father's dead and she nearly lost her life.'

'It would never have come to that.'

'Wouldn't it?' Nick bristled. 'You can take pay-outs from
scum like Long while getting information to trap him. It was
a low trick to involve Shona. Thank God I got to your road as
you were driving off and glimpsed a body shape on the back
seat. I followed at a distance. She'd be dead if I hadn't got
here when I did.'

Greg thrust his angry reddened face close to Nick's and
jabbed a finger within inches of his nose. 'I'd have shot anyone
who tried to kill her. She was in no danger. I'd have died to
save her. I love her.'

'You don't know the meaning of the word,' Nick raged.
'You put your bloody job first. There'll be a promotion in
this for you. You'll make inspector.' Nick raised his fist to
slam it into Jackson's jaw.

'Stop it!' Shona shouted. 'All this is my fault. I'm to blame for my father's death. He knew he was in danger but he took the risk to clear his name and save me.'

Nick glowered at her. After all the creep Jackson had put her through Shona still loved him. He stormed out of the chapel finally accepting that he had lost Shona for good.

Ted was outside Shona's house when the police dropped her off that evening. Her father's body had been taken to the morgue and a post-mortem would have to be carried out to determine which bullet had killed him. His body would be released for a funeral to be held in ten days' time.

She flung her arms around Ted's neck. 'I'm so glad you're here, Dad.'

He held her tight. 'Nick dropped by to let me know what had happened and brought me over. I didn't want you to be alone. Or is your boyfriend staying?'

'I don't want anything to do with Greg. He used me. He should have been honest about what he was doing. The police said he'd spent months trying to get enough incriminating evidence against Long to nail him. He went on Long's payroll pretending to be a bent copper and take bribes to block any investigations into Long's activities. That way he hoped to get closer to him and get enough information to convict him.'

They sat through the night talking. Ted was as surprised as she was that Bill was her father.

'Yet it makes sense. He always did keep an eye on you. You're the only one he allowed himself to get close to. Poor sod. It must have been hard for him feeling unable to say anything.'

Tears tumbled down Shona's face. 'Why did he have to die? Just when I could have really got to know him. I still know nothing about my life, or about my mother.'

She slumped forward in the armchair, dropping her head in her hands and pushing her fingers through her long blonde hair. 'I still don't know the man he truly was.' The tears fell again.

Ted sat on the arm of the chair and pulled her against his chest. 'Cry all you want, angel. You've been through a lot.'

When her tears finally subsided she summoned a weak smile. 'You've always been there for me, Dad. I've been so lucky.'

'I'll always be there for you. And it's time this family put an end to the differences which are breaking us up. Life's too short to carry grudges.'

'I have tried to smooth things with Lily. But I can only take so much of her bitchiness.'

'I know it's not all your fault. It's Lil.' He paused, finding it difficult to criticise the woman he loved. His voice was weary when he continued, 'For all her hard talk she's always been vulnerable and needed constant reassurance that she's special. Annie was always Percy's favourite when she was little and I don't think her mum had much time for her. She was too busy looking after Lil's gran who was a sick, cantankerous old woman. The drinking made Lil worse. When I met her she was such a sweet-natured woman, so eager to please and full of fun.'

'She was certainly different when I was first adopted. She almost smothered me with her love.'

'Lil was desperate for kids. She always wanted a daughter – her little Shona. She'd started drinking before the twins were born. Though it weren't a problem then, it just made her difficult . . .'

'And is she staying off the booze now? She didn't look well the last time I saw her.'

Ted looked brighter. 'She is. It ain't been easy. The doctor put her in touch with Alcoholics Anonymous. They're a support group which started up in 1948. I've gone along to the meetings with her.'

'That's good. Let's hope she beats it.'

A sparkle lit Ted's eyes. 'You wouldn't believe the change in her even in so short a time. She's not so tetchy. She's lost some weight. When I've mentioned my recent worries about you, she didn't bite my head off.'

Shona felt a rush of sadness at the split in her family. She didn't want to lose Ted or seeing the twins. But she had a lot to forgive Lily for and, to be fair, a lot to be grateful to her for.

The next morning Shona was woken by the phone ringing. She had fallen asleep curled up on the settee and Ted had put an eiderdown over her. She groaned at the crick in her neck and rubbed it as she listened to the voice of a solicitor on the other end.

'We saw the murder of our client, Mr Miles, reported in the paper. He left instructions that on his death we were to contact you. You are the sole beneficiary of his estate. Would three o'clock this afternoon be convenient for you to visit our offices?'

Shona agreed. She looked up as Ted came into the room. His hair was dishevelled and his clothes crumpled from sleeping in them. 'That was my father's solicitor. Will you come with me this afternoon to see them?'

'Of course, angel. Do you want me to make the funeral arrangements? Best to get it over and done with.'

'Let's see the solicitor first. He may have stated his wishes in a Will.'

When the Will was read out, Shona found the funeral arrangements had been made and even paid for a couple of years ago. Her father wanted no fuss and to be cremated. She was startled to learn that there were several hundred pounds in a bank deposit account with a simple clause added to the Will:

I would never take away Ted Carrington's right to pay

for your wedding as he had spoken of it and I know how much it means to him. He has raised you well and for that I thank him. Use some of this for a honeymoon. Take a month off and see Europe – Paris, Vienna, Venice and Rhodes. See the places I loved but never had the chance to take you to. Above all, my dear, sweet daughter, have no regrets.

Those words stayed with her as she went with Ted to her father's lodgings. There was little of personal value there – except for the manuscripts of his plays which she was determined she would still try to get produced as a memorial to him. The red book he had spoken of was with his collection of books. It was as large as a ledger and written in a neat copperplate hand. The few personal possessions were bundled up into just three tea chests and Shona decided that his clothes would go to the Salvation Army to benefit the homeless.

She rushed through the flat like a whirlwind to clear it but later, when the pain of her grief was less raw, she wanted to go through his papers thoroughly, finding out all she could about the man behind the façade he had created for himself. A box of army war medals proved he was no defector.

It was late that night when Ted, who still refused to leave her on her own, had gone to bed that she opened the red book and began to read.

At four in the morning the book was clasped to her breast and she was staring wide-awake and hollow-eyed out of the window. Ted came into the room with a mug of Ovaltine for her. She hadn't even heard him come downstairs and make it.

The tenderness and concern in his eyes drew the basic facts of the story from her.

'Daddy saw you and Lily find me and take me away. He knew I would be safe with you.' Her voice was rasping with emotion as she spoke of how Laurence had arranged her mother's funeral. 'She's buried at a remote churchyard near Colchester. I shall find it and visit her grave after Laurence's funeral.'

She sighed and forced herself to go on. She had felt her father's guilt pouring from the pages he had written as he felt that he had failed her. 'My father had sworn to get revenge on Long for killing my mother. But Long wasn't taking any chances. He'd set a dozen men to hunt my father down with orders to kill him. He was in fear of his life. While he was in hiding my story hit the papers. He knew that I was safe and well cared for. Unfortunately Long also read the story and knew who I was. When Laurence tried to see me outside school one afternoon he recognised one of Long's henchmen keeping watch. He knew then that if he acted against Long, Long would retaliate by having me killed. In a moment of panic he fled south and enlisted in the army, taking the name Bill Miles. His grandmother was French and he spoke the language fluently. He ended up working with the French Resistance as a radio operator.'

'That was brave and very dangerous,' Ted observed.

She nodded. 'He kept the name Bill Miles on his return to England. He had planned to give himself up and get his name cleared, trusting that his war record would help his case. First he wanted to learn how I was and from checking old papers and electoral rolls he discovered we were living in Walthamstow. He laid low and watched the house and me going to secretarial college for a few days. Apparently Long was still having me watched.' She broke off, stared at Ted and shuddered. 'I never suspected.'

'Bloody hell, neither did I.' Ted lit up a Woodbine and drew heavily on it. 'I'd have gone out of my mind all the time I was in prison if I thought someone was watching the house. So what happened after that?'

'To his shame Laurence began to hit the bottle hard. He couldn't bear to leave Walthamstow as he wanted to be close to me and know I was safe. Over the next couple of years the drink took its toll and you know the rest.'

'Poor sod. He lost everything after the war. Do you think he was guilty of those dodgy arms deals?'

'He says not. But the law would see him guilty by association. There's a whole load of other stuff about Long which will incriminate him. The police will have to see this book as my father's confession. I hope there's enough in it to clear his name. He deserves that at the very least.'

The next days were difficult. The story of Shona's abduction hit the headlines and her house was surrounded by reporters. Shona handed her father's written account and all the facts she had gathered about him and Long to the police. Greg was still on the case but she refused to speak to him. When she left Scotland Yard with Ted, who refused to leave her on her own, Greg waylaid her.

'Please, Shona, listen to me. I'm so sorry about your father. The police were supposed to be hidden on the outskirts of the chapel before we arrived. They were delayed. Long ordered the meeting. It was our chance to arrest him for intimidation. Other charges would follow.'

'You were gambling with mine and my father's life.'

'I didn't know Bill Miles was your father. And I didn't know Long was going to get hold of him. They caught up with him after he left a meeting in a pub with Nick Blake on his way to Scotland Yard. If he hadn't stopped off they would never have got him. He'd have been held in police custody until it was all over.'

'But you told them that Bill had the information I'd discovered.'

'No, I swear it. Once you gave Long's men the slip, he must have ordered both your house and mine watched in case you turned up. They obviously followed Bill once he dropped you off. It was fortunate that he managed to contact

Blake on his way to Scotland Yard and before they picked him up.'

'He trusted Nick to help me. He knew I was in danger. That didn't seem to bother you.'

Greg looked stricken. 'Of course it did. Whose bullet do you think killed Long when he fired at your father? I knew then he wouldn't let you live. I've got to face a disciplinary hearing because of that. For all his villainy Long was an important man. My superiors wanted him to go on trial. I would never have let anything happen to you. I love you, Shona.'

'You used me. You came to interview me after Elsie's death because Long must have begun to suspect my memory had returned. What better way to get information on how much I knew than by seducing me? Our day in Brighton allowed Long's men to ransack my house.'

'It started out as a job, but what happened in Brighton had nothing to do with work. I took you away that day so I knew you wouldn't get hurt. Long's thugs were waiting for a chance to turn your house over. They'd have broken in and knocked you unconscious to do it. Brighton changed everything about how I felt about you. I didn't lie to you when I said I loved you.'

'But you didn't tell me the truth. You deceived me.' Her eyes flashed with contempt. 'And you're deluding yourself if you think that chloroforming me to comply with Long's orders was to protect me. You put your job first and me second. You wanted a result and you got it. My father gave his life to protect me. He wrote in a diary that he had a brown book with information which would destroy Long. It was about his dealings during the war. Was that found?'

'It was in Long's jacket. That's why he wanted both you and your father killed. He feared you knew as much as your father.'

Anger ground through her and she struck his chest with her fist. 'You knew how ruthless Long was and you still placed me in danger.' He didn't stop her blow. His face was impassive. She shoved him away. 'Get lost, Greg. You make a great copper but your work is your life. I could only be second best.'

'It wouldn't be like that. I've been in torment since it happened.'

Her heart which had so briefly been his was now hardened. She had been infatuated by his looks, strength and charm. A few carefree days of abandonment and laughter were not enough to build a future. She hadn't really loved him and she couldn't believe that he had truly loved her.

'Goodbye, Greg. You didn't plot my father's death and I believe you would have risked your life to save mine. If I truly loved you I would be able to forgive you anything.'

Back at her house she had to battle through reporters and photographers who were avid to get her version of the story. 'I work for the *Globe*,' she reminded them. 'They'll have the exclusive which I am writing myself. Please, respect my grief and leave me alone.'

They remained outside her house. The story was too hot for the most hardened reporters to give up on. The sooner the truth went to the press the better. She insisted that Ted went back to work. He couldn't afford to lose any more wages.

She kissed him before he left. 'You've been wonderful over all of this. It couldn't have been easy. You've stuck by me when I know Lily made it difficult for you to meet me. You'll always be my special dad. I'm glad I know the truth about my parents but nothing changes the love I have for you. I feel very privileged that you chose me to be your daughter.'

Ted sniffed and wiped a hand across his eyes. 'I'm proud to be your dad. Bill was a good man. He did right by you the only way he could.'

Closing the door behind Ted, she heard the reporters clamouring for information.

'Sod off,' he growled as he shoved his way through them. 'You're a pack of bloody vultures. I ain't got nothing to say except I'm proud to have raised such an angel as Grace Shelton.'

Shona was desperate to get away. After Ted left she phoned Marion.

'I've seen it all in the papers,' Marion commiserated. 'I've been trying to get through to you by phone for two hours.'

'I took the phone off the hook first thing this morning to stop being pestered by reporters. The *Globe* has given me a couple of weeks off providing they get the exclusive on the story. I spent the morning writing it. It will be in Sunday's edition. I need to get away, Marion.'

'It must be awful. Who's with you?'

'No one. I insisted Dad and Percy went back to work.'

'Stay at the house. Ken's off today so we'll come up. I'm taking you down to Clacton to the holiday home Ken and I bought last year. I'll stay with you there until the funeral.'

'Thanks, Marion. I'm going crazy being on my own. I need to get away and come to terms with what happened. You're a good friend.'

'Have a case packed and we'll be with you in a couple of hours. Mum will have the kids so we'll have some peace and quiet.'

The break away from the turmoil of city life had restored Shona's strength but the ordeal of the funeral still lay ahead. The crematorium chapel was packed with people from the market and strangers who had known her father both in recent times and in the past. Shona had arranged for a buffet to be put on as a funeral tea after hours at the pub in the market where her father was most known. Ted kept close to her side, fending off any of their friends who were too inquisitive about the past. Lily had appeared very subdued and as the mourners finally began to leave she came up to Shona.

371

'I'm real sorry about what happened. Ted's told me straight what a bitch I've been to you in the last years. He's right. I was jealous of the affection he showed you. The booze didn't help neither. I'm off it now.'

Shona had noticed that Lily was slimmer and had been drinking orange juice.

'Dad said you'd found a support group which helps. Those years couldn't have been easy for you.' For the sake of family unity Shona was prepared to meet her halfway. Ted was right, life was too short to bear grudges where family were concerned. 'You're the only mother I really knew. You saved my life by keeping me so close to you in those early years. I'll never forget that. Let's try and be friends again, Mum. It will mean so much to Dad. And I miss seeing you and the boys.'

Lily let out a sob. 'Can you forgive me?'

'I'd like us to be a family again.'

Lily held out her arms and clasped Shona tight. 'Do I call you Grace or Shona?'

'I was always your Shona. Anything else wouldn't be right.'

Lily nodded and pulled away to dab at her eyes. 'I was a jealous idiot. I always wanted a daughter. I had one that was special and through my stupidity nearly lost her. There's a slap-up lunch waiting for you next Sunday and every Sunday. It's time the Carringtons were a proper family again.'

Ted was smiling with pleasure. 'I know this is a sad day for you, Shona, but this has made my heart glad. I wouldn't have blamed you if you hadn't forgiven Lil.'

'Let's forget the recriminations of the past. I don't want to look back any more. The future is what is important.'

'I always said she was a good kid.' Lily was now magnanimous. 'And since this is a day for patching things up, isn't there someone else who you should be making up with?' She nodded significantly to where Nick stood in a corner talking to Percy.

'It's too late for some things, Mum.'

'He's a changed man. He no longer plays around. And he can't keep his eyes off you. But I think any reconciliation has now to come from you. Nick's always been there for you.'

'You don't have to tell me that. His arrival at the chapel caused a diversion which saved my life.' Shona felt her heart begin its familiar chaotic rhythm whenever Nick was near. She had spent several years trying to obliterate her feelings for him. She had failed abysmally.

Shona stared across at Nick. She had caught him unawares and his love for her was clear in his eyes. So too was his pain. She knew in that moment she loved him enough to forgive his betrayal. She smiled and walked towards him holding her hands out to take his. She had spent too long searching for answers to her past. The present was what was important and the bridges it would build for the future.

The Silent War

Victor Pemberton

Sunday Collins is less than happy with her lot in life in bomb-blasted North London, working in the sweaty, steamy 'bagwash', the laundry round the corner from the stark Holloway council flats where she lives. Although her adopted mother, Madge Collins, who found her abandoned on the steps of the Salvation Army as a baby, is as loving as any mother could be, to Sunday her affection is stifling, and sharing their cramped home with Madge's lazy, bad-tempered sister Louie is far from easy.

Sunday longs for Saturday nights when, with her friend Pearl, she takes full advantage of her Betty Grable looks down at the Athenaeum Dance Hall where her motto is a defiant 'life is for livin'!' But Sunday's recklessly lived life is changed dramatically when, on a warm summer morning in 1944, the bagwash receives a direct hit from one of Hitler's V-1s, and she finds she is suddenly and, she has to accept, permanently, deaf . . .

'A wonderful story' Nerys Hughes

'Never a dull moment in this charming story' *Romford Recorder*

'A vivid story of a community surviving some of the darkest days in our history . . . warm-hearted' *Bolton Evening News*

0 7472 5322 6

HEADLINE

Kitty Rainbow

Wendy Robertson

When the soft-hearted bare-knuckle fighter Ishmael Slaughter rescues an abandoned baby from the swirling River Wear, he knows that if he takes her home his employer will give her short shrift – or worse. So it is to Janine Druce, a draper woman with a dubious reputation but a child of her own, that he takes tiny Kitty Rainbow.

Kitty grows up wild, coping with Janine's bouts of drunkenness and her son's silent strangeness. And she is as fierce in her affections as she is in her hatreds, saving her greatest love for Ishmael, the ageing boxer who provides the only link with her parentage, a scrap of cloth she was wrapped in when he found her. Kitty realises that she cannot live her life wondering who her mother was, and in Ishmael she has father enough. And, when she finds herself pregnant, deprived of the livelihood on which she and the old man depended, she must worry about the future, not the past. But the past has a way of catching the present unawares . . .

'An intense and moving story set against the bitter squalor of the hunger-ridden thirties' *Today*

'A rich fruit cake of well-drawn characters . . .' *Northern Echo*

'Fans of big family stories must read Wendy Robertson' *Peterborough Evening Telegraph*

'A lovely book' *Woman's Realm*

0 7472 5183 5

HEADLINE